Starting Strong II

EARLY CHILDHOOD EDUCATION AND CARE

OECD

ORGANISATION FOR ECONOMIC CO-OPERATION AND DEVELOPMENT

ORGANISATION FOR ECONOMIC CO-OPERATION AND DEVELOPMENT

The OECD is a unique forum where the governments of 30 democracies work together to address the economic, social and environmental challenges of globalisation. The OECD is also at the forefront of efforts to understand and to help governments respond to new developments and concerns, such as corporate governance, the information economy and the challenges of an ageing population. The Organisation provides a setting where governments can compare policy experiences, seek answers to common problems, identify good practice and work to co-ordinate domestic and international policies.

The OECD member countries are: Australia, Austria, Belgium, Canada, the Czech Republic, Denmark, Finland, France, Germany, Greece, Hungary, Iceland, Ireland, Italy, Japan, Korea, Luxembourg, Mexico, the Netherlands, New Zealand, Norway, Poland, Portugal, the Slovak Republic, Spain, Sweden, Switzerland, Turkey, the United Kingdom and the United States. The Commission of the European Communities takes part in the work of the OECD.

OECD Publishing disseminates widely the results of the Organisation's statistics gathering and research on economic, social and environmental issues, as well as the conventions, guidelines and standards agreed by its members.

This work is published on the responsibility of the Secretary-General of the OECD. The opinions expressed and arguments employed herein do not necessarily reflect the official views of the Organisation or of the governments of its member countries.

Also available in French under the title:
Petite enfance, grands défis II
ÉDUCATION ET STRUCTURES D'ACCUEIL

Foreword

Background to the OECD thematic review

The Thematic Review of Early Childhood Education and Care Policy was launched by the OECD Education Committee[1] in March 1998. The impetus for the early childhood project came from the 1996 Education Ministerial meeting on Making Lifelong Learning a Reality for All. In their communiqué, the education ministers assigned a high priority to the goal of improving access to and quality in early childhood education and care (ECEC). From the perspective of the Education Committee, the rationale for the review was to strengthen the foundations of lifelong learning. Not only was the provision of care and education for young children considered as necessary to ensure the access of women to the labour market but increasingly, early development was seen as the foundation stage of human learning and development. When sustained by effective fiscal, social and employment measures in support of parents and communities, early childhood programming would help to provide a fair start in life for all children, and contribute to educational equity and social integration.

At the 1998 meeting, twelve countries – Australia, Belgium, the Czech Republic, Denmark, Finland, Italy, the Netherlands, Norway, Portugal, Sweden, the United Kingdom and the United States – volunteered to launch reviews of their ECEC policies and services. Between 1998 and 2000, OECD review teams conducted visits to the twelve participating countries.[2] The reviews of these countries, combined with careful consultation of the national ECEC policy co-ordinators in the participating countries, formed the basis of a comparative report published by the OECD Secretariat, entitled Starting Strong: Early Childhood Education and Care (OECD, 2001). The publication was released on 13-15 June 2001 at an international conference in Stockholm, hosted by the Swedish Ministry of Education and Science.

In order to enlarge the scope of the review, the OECD Education Committee authorised a second round of reviews in November 2001. Eight more countries joined this round: Austria, Canada, France, Germany, Hungary, Ireland, Korea and Mexico. The second round of reviewing began in Autumn 2002 and ended in Winter 2004. In parallel, a series of four thematic workshops were organised by the Secretariat for the national ECEC co-ordinators on topics important for national policy making, viz. financing, curriculum and pedagogy, data needs, and early education for minority and low-income children. In sum, over the six-year period, 1998-2004, some 20 countries have participated in country reviews, and 24 countries in the workshops organised on ECEC policy issues. These countries provide a diverse range of social, economic and political contexts, as well as varied policy approaches towards the education and care of young children.

Purpose and content of the report

The first comparative report, Starting Strong (OECD, 2001), identified eight key elements of successful ECEC policy that had emerged after examination of the ECEC policies and services of the first twelve countries reviewed. The key elements were:

- A systemic and integrated approach to ECEC policy.
- A strong and equal partnership with the education system.

- A universal approach to access, with particular attention to children in need of special support.
- Substantial public investment in services and the infrastructure.
- A participatory approach to quality improvement and assurance.
- Appropriate training and working conditions for staff in all forms of provision.
- Systematic attention to data collectionandmonitoring.
- A stable framework and long-term agenda for research and evaluation.

These elements are reviewed in the present text from Chapter 2 to Chapter 9 with the purpose of examining the progress made in these areas by the countries participating in the review. The research from the second round strongly endorses the eight elements as a framework for policy in the ECEC field. The new country reviews provide further evidence of the centrality of these elements in policy making, and offer new examples of specific policy initiatives adopted by countries in these areas. In the present volume, several policy areas are explored more deeply: the governance of ECEC systems; the impact of financing approaches on quality; and contrasting pedagogical approaches. As in Starting Strong (OECD, 2001), the present report also outlines some of the contextual factors influencing ECEC policy, in particular, the growing need to safeguard equality of opportunity for women when organising ECEC services (Chapter 1). The concluding Chapter 10 proposes ten policy areas for consideration by governments:

1. To attend to the social context of early childhood development.

2. To place well-being, early development and learning at the core of ECEC work, while respecting the child's agency and natural learning strategies.

3. To create the governance structures necessary for system accountability and quality assurance.

4. To develop with the stakeholders broad guidelines and curricular standards for all ECEC services.

5. To base public funding estimates for ECEC on achieving quality pedagogical goals.

6. To reduce child poverty and exclusion through upstream fiscal, social and labour policies, and to increase resources within universal programmes for children with diverse learning rights.

7. To encourage family and community involvement in early childhood services.

8. To improve the working conditions and professional education of ECEC staff.

9. To provide freedom, funding and support to early childhood services.

10. To aspire to ECEC systems that support broad learning, participation and democracy.

Notes

1. The OECD Education Committee is a forum for the Education Ministries of the OECD countries. The Committee meets at OECD headquarters twice a year to discuss education policy and issues.

2. A more detailed description of the review's objectives, analytical framework, and methodology is provided in OECD, "Early Childhood Education and Care Policy: Proposal for a Thematic Review: Major Issues, Analytical Framework, and Operating Procedures" (1998, Paris). Information on the visits and the reports from the review can be viewed on the project Web site: *www.oecd.org/edu/ earlychildhood*.

Acknowledgements

Within the OECD Secretariat, John Bennett was responsible for the early childhood policy reviews and, with Professor Collette Tayler of Queensland University of Technology, Australia, for the writing of this report. The project was carried out in the Directorate for Education, within the Training and Education Policy Division under the supervision of Abrar Hasan. Administrative and statistical support for the project was provided by Sabrina Leonarduzzi and Tyra Malzy, to whom we are very grateful.

The work would not have been possible without the ongoing support of the OECD Education Committee and of the National ECEC Co-ordinators in the 20 countries reviewed. The Co-ordinators and their National Committees gave unstintingly of their time and knowledge in organising the reviews and in revising the national profiles of this report. The high calibre of the experts involved in the review teams was also a vital element in the study's success. The Secretariat would like to thank also the many government officials and early childhood experts who provided feedback on earlier drafts of this report. While these individuals are not mentioned by name, their assistance has been greatly appreciated; they are in no way accountable for errors or inaccuracies in the text, which are the sole responsibility of the authors. We also wish to acknowledge warmly the work of Michelle Neuman in the first volume of Starting Strong (OECD, 2001), on which this report is modelled.

Table of Contents

Tables

Figures

STARTING STRONG II: EARLY CHILDHOOD EDUCATION AND CARE – ISBN 92-64-03545-1 – © OECD 2006

ISBN 92-64-03545-1
Starting Strong II: Early Childhood Education and Care
© OECD 2006

Executive Summary

Introduction

The provision of quality early childhood education and care (ECEC) has remained firmly on government agendas in recent years. Public awareness of gaps in provision and of insufficient quality in services has moved the issue of child care and after-school care onto electoral agendas in many countries. There is a growing recognition that early access to ECEC provides young children, particularly from low-income and second-language groups, with a good start in life.

Twelve countries volunteered to participate in the first round of the review between 1998 and 2000. Recognising the value of the review and the quality of the recommendations produced in the first report, the OECD Education Committee authorised a second review in which eight countries participated. Both rounds of the review have taken a broad and holistic approach that considers how policies, services, families, and communities can support young children's early development and learning.

Chapter 1 – Why countries invest in ECEC

Among the immediate factors turning governmental attention to ECEC issues are: the wish to increase women's labour market participation; to reconcile work and family responsibilities on a basis more equitable for women; to confront the demographic challenges faced by OECD countries (in particular falling fertility rates and the general ageing of populations); and the need to address issues of child poverty and educational disadvantage. Because economic prosperity depends on maintaining a high employment/ population ratio, the wish to bring more women into the labour market has been a key driver of government interest in expanding ECEC services. European governments, in particular, have put into place family and child care policies to help couples to have children and assist parents to combine work and family responsibilities. Another factor driving government interest in ECEC is immigration. Immigration makes a strong contribution to economies but can also raise challenges in the labour, social and education fields. Immigrant parents may not easily find work, child and family poverty rates may rise (between 1995 and 2001, child poverty rates increased or remained stationary in 17 out of 24 OECD countries for which data are available), and immigrant children can encounter difficulties in education. Comprehensive ECEC services help to integrate families with young children. They provide child health, referral and other services, and contribute greatly to preparing young children for school. Support for the view that early childhood education and care should be seen as *a public good* is growing, and has received a strong impetus from the research of education economists.

*Chapter 2 – A systemic and integrated approach
to ECEC policy*

Chapter 2 examines five challenges in the domain of ECEC policy-making and service co-ordination: ensuring co-ordinated policy development at central level; appointing a lead ministry; the co-ordination of central and decentralised levels; the adoption of a collaborative and participatory approach to reform; and forging links across services, professionals, and parents at local level. Where co-ordination at central level is concerned, the chapter notes the complexity of policy-making in the early childhood field. ECEC policy is concerned not only with providing education and care to young children but it is also linked with issues of women's employment and equality of opportunity; child development and child poverty issues; labour market supply; health, social welfare and later education.

Two co-ordination strategies examined in *Starting Strong II* are the creation of *inter-departmental co-ordination bodies* and/or the appointment of a *lead government ministry or agency*. The study notes that co-ordinating mechanisms can work well when they are established for a specific purpose. ECEC policy-making has become a shared responsibility in many OECD countries between national and local governments. A positive consequence of decentralisation has been the integration of early education and care services at local level, along with greater sensitivity to local needs. Decentralisation can also raise challenges. Experience from the OECD reviews suggests that devolution of powers and responsibilities may widen differences of access and quality between regions. In the devolution process, it seems important to ensure that early childhood services are part of a well-conceptualised national policy, with, on the one hand, devolved powers to local authorities and, on the other, a national approach to goal setting, legislation and regulation, financing, staffing criteria, and programme standards.

*Chapter 3 – A strong and equal partnership
with the education system*

Research suggests that a more unified approach to learning should be adopted in both the early childhood education and the primary school systems, and that attention should be given to transition challenges faced by young children as they enter school. The search for a more unified approach has generated different policy options. France and the English-speaking world have adopted a "readiness for school" approach, which although defined broadly focuses in practice on cognitive development in the early years, and the acquisition of a range of knowledge, skills and dispositions. A disadvantage inherent in this approach is the use of programmes and approaches that are poorly suited to the psychology and natural learning strategies of young children. In countries inheriting a social pedagogy tradition (Nordic and Central European countries), the kindergarten years are seen as a broad preparation for life and the foundation stage of lifelong learning. Facilitating transitions for children is a policy challenge in all systems.[1] Transitions for children are generally a stimulus to growth and development, but if too abrupt and handled without care, they carry – particularly for young children – the risk of regression and failure.

Chapter 4 – A universal approach to access,
with particular attention to children in need
of special support

Universal access does not necessarily entail achieving full coverage, as there are variations in demand for ECEC at different ages and in different family circumstances. Rather, it implies making access available to all children whose parents wish them to participate. A universal approach to access is contrasted with a targeted approach to ECEC, whereby a government provides public funding primarily to programmes for chosen groups of children. Chapter 4 outlines the complexity of the notion of access and provides a rationale for universal *and* appropriate access. The chapter also addresses the field of out-of-school care, and the efforts being made by countries to increase provision. Some of the major tables and figures in the report are provided in this chapter: main institutional forms of ECEC; enrolment rates of 3- to 6-year-olds in ECEC services; entitlements to ECEC provision across OECD countries; percentage of 0- to 3-year-olds using licensed services; maternity, paternity and parental leave policies.

Chapter 5 – Substantial public investment
in services and the infrastructure

Chapter 5 explores the critical issue of public investment in services for young children. A few countries with comparatively low public expenditure on children's services in the past have increased spending significantly over the past years. Yet, according to expert evidence indicating what should be spent per child in a quality programme, OECD countries – with the exception of the Nordic countries – are under-spending on ECEC services.[2] The chapter further examines how countries fund ECEC services, discussing whether the modality of funding used – in particular, direct funding to services versus subsidies to parents – has an impact on overall quality. The evidence suggests that direct public funding of services brings more effective governmental steering of early childhood services, advantages of scale, better national quality, more effective training for educators and a higher degree of equity in access compared with parent subsidy models.

Chapter 6 – A participatory approach to quality
improvement and assurance

Chapter 6 examines both regulation and approaches to quality. In many OECD countries, the level of regulation of services for children under 3 gives rise for concern: much of the child care sector is private and unregulated, with staff training and pedagogical programming being particularly weak. In the early education sector, the basic structural standards, such as adequate premises and space for children; child-staff ratios; curriculum frameworks; adequate professional education and certification of staff, etc., are generally respected, but with variations in practice, in particular in regard to child-staff ratios. Parental involvement is generally organised but at different levels of engagement. The chapter also examines the issue of pedagogical frameworks and curriculum development. Two different approaches to curriculum can be identified: the early education approach and the social pedagogy approach. Features of both approaches are compared with respect to a number of criteria. In summary, the early education tradition generally results in a more centralising and academic approach to curriculum content and methodology, while pedagogical frameworks in the social pedagogy tradition remain more local, child-centred and holistic.

Chapter 7 – Appropriate training and working conditions for ECEC staff

Chapter 7 reviews the situation of staff and levels of training in ECEC across the countries covered, and highlights new thinking about the types of skills that are most appropriate in early childhood education. The picture is mixed, with acceptable professional education standards being recorded in the Nordic countries but only in early education in most other countries. In all countries, considerable gender and diversity imbalances exist within the profession. The report also notes that levels of in-service training vary greatly across countries and between the education and child care sectors. Because of under-funding, many of the private, community or voluntary bodies that are part of mixed market systems are unable to provide regular in-service training and/or non-contact time for staff to improve their pedagogical practice.

Figures from various countries reveal a wide pay gap between child care staff and teachers, with child care staff in most countries being poorly trained and paid around minimum wage levels. Not surprisingly, staff turnover in the child care sector is high. Strategies to recruit a mixed-gender, diverse workforce are discussed. Despite good intentions, most countries fail to recruit either sufficient numbers of men or staff from minority communities into ECEC services. Some excellent inclusive programmes exist in the countries reviewed but programmes tend to remain isolated and seldom go to scale across the system.

Chapter 8 – Systematic attention to data collection and monitoring

For ECEC policy to be well informed and realistic, administrations need to organise data collection and monitoring in the ECEC field more energetically. More rational policy-making can be ensured if core early childhood fields are covered annually, e.g. the demand, supply and utilisation of ECEC places; the volume and allocation of public financing; the socio-economic status of the children in and outside services; the recruitment and training levels of staff; the quality standards in place; and other aspects of service delivery that periodically need analysis. The difficulties of data collection in the ECEC field stem to some extent from the newness of the field. The large scale information systems on population, households, social policy or education that are routinely managed by national statistical bureaus were not initially set up to deliver the kinds of data needed to advance ECEC policy and provision.

Chapter 9 – A stable framework and long-term agenda for research and evaluation

Starting Strong recommended that governments should provide sustained support to research on key policy goals. National research agendas should also be expanded to include disciplines and methods that are currently under-represented. A range of strategies to disseminate research findings to diverse audiences should also be explored. In all these areas, progress has been made. Areas of research are also expanding, and Chapter 9 notes renewed interest in qualitative research, *e.g.* in gender and socio-cultural investigations, diversity studies, gender and post-modernist analyses, participant observation and child research. Chapter 9 also outlines some of the more common types of research undertaken, although the research methodologies and themes can vary greatly from country to country and within each type of research.

Chapter 10 – Concluding policy observations

The final chapter proposes ten policy options areas for consideration by governments and the major ECEC stakeholders:

- *To attend to the social context of early childhood development:* Early childhood policy makers can organise children's services in a manner that serves important social and economic objectives, such as, ensuring labour supply, equality of opportunity for women, family well-being and social inclusion. Well-organised services will support parents in child-rearing, provide opportunity to women to work and help to include low-income and immigrant families in the community and society. The ministry-in-charge should forge a broad but realistic vision of early childhood services to which all relevant ministries, local authorities and parents can subscribe.

- *To place well-being, early development and learning at the core of ECEC work, while respecting the child's agency and natural learning strategies:* Children's well-being and learning are core goals of early childhood services, but services for children under 3 have often been seen as an adjunct to labour market policies, with infants and toddlers assigned to services with weak developmental agendas. In parallel, early education services have often placed children 3 to 6 years old in pre-primary classes, characterised by high child-staff ratios, teachers without early childhood certification, poor learning environments, and the quasi-absence of care personnel. A challenge exists in many countries to focus more on the child, and to show greater understanding of the specific developmental tasks and learning strategies of young children.

- *To create the governance structures necessary for system accountability and quality assurance:* Examples of necessary governance structures are: strong policy units with wide expertise; a data collection and monitoring office; an evaluation agency; a training authority; an inspection or pedagogical advisory corps, etc. Some of these structures tend to be absent in ECEC systems, including, in many countries, a national ECEC research council. Strong investment in research, data collection and monitoring is needed to ensure well-informed policy making, system reform and the development of a comprehensive provision structure.

- *To develop with the stakeholders broad guidelines and curricular standards for all ECEC services:* Guiding frameworks help to promote a more even level of quality across age groups and provision; to guide and support professional staff; and to facilitate communication between staff and parents. Frameworks gain in effectiveness when co-constructed with the main stakeholders. In general, they propose broad pedagogical orientations rather than detailing what should be taught; and identify goals in all areas of development. Two pedagogical approaches seem particularly important for the well-being and learning of children: a focus on the agency of the child, including respect for the child's natural learning strategies; and the extensive use of listening, project work and documentation in work with young children.

● *To base public funding estimates on achieving quality pedagogical goals*: Public investment per child in early education ranges from significantly less to roughly equal the investment per child in primary school, although young children need more staff than older children, and generally spend longer hours in services. According to reliable cost estimates, most countries need to double annual investment per child to ensure acceptable child-staff ratios and highly qualified staff. In well-functioning systems, governments develop clear and consistent strategies for efficiently allocating resources, including investment in long-term planning and quality initiatives. Investment should be directed towards achieving high quality pedagogical goals, rather than the simple creation of places.

● *To reduce child poverty and exclusion through upstream fiscal, social and labour policies, and to increase resources within universal programmes for children with diverse learning rights*: Early childhood services are particularly important for children with diverse learning rights, whether these stem from physical, mental or sensory disabilities or from socio-economic disadvantage. However, programmes for their benefit are often irregular, under-funded and non-inclusive. Research suggests that inclusion in universal programmes may be the most effective approach to these children and their families, and that successful inclusion requires enhanced funding, low child-staff ratios, specialist staff and well-planned pedagogies. Targeted programmes segregate, may stigmatise and generally fail to provide for many of the children eligible for special programmes. International data show that child poverty is growing in several OECD countries. For governments to put much effort and investment into targeted early childhood programming – dedicated to assisting young children from disadvantaged backgrounds – while at the same time, doing little to stem the reproduction of family poverty indicates a failure of integrated policy-making.

● *To encourage family and community involvement in early childhood services*: Families play a central nurturing and educational role in their children's lives, particularly in the early childhood period. They should be assisted by early childhood centres and staff to support their children's development and learning. The continuity of children's experience across environments is greatly enhanced when parents and staff members exchange information regularly and adopt consistent approaches to socialisation, daily routines, child development and learning. Community involvement in the pre-school is important, not only for providing expanded services and referrals where necessary, but also as a space for partnership and the participation of parents.

● *To improve the working conditions and professional education of ECEC staff*: Attention to the level of recruitment of early childhood workers, their professional education and work conditions is key to quality services. In several countries, such attention is also critical for workforce development and the long-term sustainability of recruitment into early childhood services. A number of weaknesses in staff policies emerged from the OECD reviews: low recruitment and pay levels, particularly in child care services; a lack of certification in early childhood pedagogy in pre-primary education systems; the feminisation of the workforce; and the failure of pedagogical teams to reflect the diversity of the neighbourhoods they serve.

● *To provide autonomy, funding and support to early childhood services*: Once goals and programme standards for early childhood services have been decided in the national framework documents, educators and services should have the autonomy to plan, and to choose or create curricula that they find appropriate for the children in their care. An independent budget and freedom to achieve national outcomes allow well-trained staff to take responsibility for the pedagogical choices that appropriately serve the children in their care. Ministry support of participatory approaches to quality development, such as documentation, can raise staff understanding and motivation.

- *To aspire to ECEC systems that support broad learning, participation and democracy:* It is important that wider societal interests are reflected in early childhood systems, including respect for children's rights, diversity and enhanced access for children with special and additional learning needs. At centre level, touchstones of a democratic approach will be to extend the agency of the child and to support the basic right of parents to be involved in the education of their children. In this approach, the early childhood centre becomes a space where the intrinsic value of each person is recognised, where democratic participation is promoted, as well as respect for our shared environment. *Learning to be, learning to do, learning to learn and learning to live together* should be considered as critical elements in the journey of each child toward human and social development.

Notes

1. For a review of approaches to transition in different countries see Petriwskyj, Thorpe and Tayler, 2005, "Trends in the Construction of Transition to School in Three Western Regions, 1990-2004", *International Journal of Early Years Education*, Vol. 13(1), pp. 55-69.

2. Estimates by Kagan and Rigby ("Policy Matters: Setting and Measuring Benchmarks for State Policies. Improving the Readiness of Children for School. A Discussion Paper", Center for the Study of Social Policy, 2003, Washington DC), Head Start, the New York Committee for Economic Development; and evidence from Denmark, Finland, Norway, and Sweden place expenditure per child in a quality programme from about USD 5 000 per child in a half-day, academic year programme, and between USD 10 000 to USD 15 000 per infant/toddler in a full-day, full year (11 months) programme.

ISBN 92-64-03545-1
Starting Strong II: Early Childhood Education and Care
© OECD 2006

Chapter 1

Why Countries Invest in Early Childhood Education and Care

Chapter 1 explores why early childhood education and care (ECEC) has become a central issue for governments in many countries. In recent decades, economic development and rapid social change across the OECD countries have transformed traditional family and child-rearing patterns. Although investments in ECEC services have been influenced by the importance of child development and by seeing young children as citizens with their own rights and needs, broader social and economic factors have generally directed government attention to ECEC issues. Through investing in ECEC, governments have aimed: to increase women's labour market participation; to reconcile work and family responsibilities on a more equitable basis for women; to investigate the growing demographic challenges faced by OECD countries, in particular, in the European and the Asian countries reviewed; and finally, to address issues of child poverty and educational disadvantage. The chapter concludes with a discussion as to why countries should consider ECEC a public good, on a par with public education.

A central issue for OECD governments in relation to early childhood funding is not whether to invest, but how much and at what level. What measure of public funding and support should governments provide to families with young children in their jurisdiction? What are the services outside the home that need to be created? What is the adequate level of public funding, taking into account the present climate of controlled public spending? Can new sources of funding be created to finance early childhood services at a level consistent with quality and social equity? Should governments be involved in regulating and mapping services? These are some of the questions being debated across all the OECD countries, marking a profound change from the orthodoxy prevailing in the immediate post-war period. Societies at that time saw the development and socialisation of the child almost entirely in terms of mother-child attachment, within the context of the male bread-winner family model. Child care was essentially home care by mothers, with some marginal use of informal care through other family members or neighbours (Tizard, 1986). This model of child-rearing has now lost its dominant position in the face of four broad contextual challenges:

- The rise of the service economy and the influx of women into salaried employment.

- The necessary reconciliation of work and family responsibilities in a manner more equitable for women.

- The demographic challenges of falling fertility and increased immigration, particularly in European countries.

- The need to break the cycle of poverty and inequality that begins in early childhood.

1. The rise of the service economy and the influx of women into salaried employment

Women have been entering salaried employment in ever greater numbers since the 1970s. This change in labour patterns has been reinforced by a transformation of the industrial countries into service- and knowledge-based economies that require a high population/employment ratio if growth and prosperity are to be maintained (see Figure 1.1). Today, women are needed in the labour market to respond to this requirement, even more so as their higher educational achievement and their relatively lower pay levels make them key contributors to national economies (see Box 1.1). A recent British appraisal shows, for example, that women's work now accounts for 30% of GDP in the United Kingdom (in Denmark and Sweden around 40%), not including unpaid work in the home (Department for Education and Skills [DfES], 2004). The average female participation rate in the G7 economies in 2003 was 66.4% – an 8% increase since 1993.

In several OECD countries, over 75% of women between the ages of 25-54 are now in the labour market. Such significant employment of women has a major impact on modes of child-rearing. It is widely recognised that when a certain level of female participation in the formal labour market is reached (generally from 50% upwards), private solutions to meeting child care needs become insufficient. Parents or other family members are

Figure 1.1. **Employment/population ratio of 25- to 34-year-old women and men in OECD countries, 1980 and 2004**

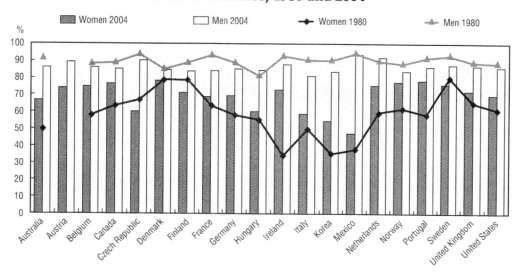

Source: OECD labour force statistics database, 2005.

Box 1.1. **Economic growth in Ireland**

Between 1993 and 2003, Ireland's gross domestic product (GDP) increased by 7.8% annually, the highest rate of growth of any OECD country in this period (OECD, 2004d). In these years, the total number of adults in employment grew by 51% (CSO, 2004). Increases in labour demand were met through falling unemployment levels, labour immigration, and substantial increases in female employment. Between 1997 and 2004, the numbers of women in work increased by 48.5% (from 539 700 to 801 700). Part-time employment amongst women more than doubled in this period (from 124 600 to 251 900) and the number of women in full-time employment, increased by almost a third (from 415 200 to 549 800). Although GDP growth has since slowed to 5% per annum, the dynamism of the economy continues with 87 000 new jobs created in 2005.

The change in female participation in the formal Irish economy is due also to women's increased educational levels and higher individual expectations. Many women gained in economic independence and social status during this period. Nevertheless, all groups have not shared the advance: many women, and consequently children, continue to experience poverty. While improvements in access to education, training and employment opportunities are accepted as primary routes out of social exclusion, there is, in parallel, a growing acknowledgement that public investment in affordable, quality child care is also an essential strategy in facilitating access to work.

Such changes have been complemented by an increased awareness in Irish society around the issues of citizenship and rights. Two important United Nations Conventions were ratified and transposed into Irish law: the Convention on the Elimination of all Forms of Discrimination Against Women (CEDAW) in 1985 and the Convention on the Rights of the Child (CRC) in 1992. There is an acknowledgement that children had been seen traditionally "in terms of their status within families, rather than as individuals in their own right" (CPA, 2005, p. 20). The awareness is leading to a commitment to ensure that policies and provision become appropriate to the needs of children in a rapidly changing society.

Source: National Women's Council of Ireland, 2005.

themselves working, and informal child-minding solutions are unsatisfactory because of quality concerns, shortages and instability (American Business Roundtable, 2003; Dy-Hammer *et al.*, 2001).

Such changes in female employment patterns have been a driving force behind child care policies in many countries. However, approaching ECEC from a female labour market perspective is not without its risks. Firstly, children may be seen as an obstacle to women's work, with child care considered as a necessary evil. For this reason, *Starting Strong* places "education" before "care" in the acronym ECEC – the child's right to development and education being considered a priority in all services organised for young children. A second risk is to reinforce the association between child-rearing and women, as if the rearing of children was unrelated to male patterns of employment or the general organisation of work in our societies. Some of the solutions to child-rearing currently on offer bear witness to traditional gendering, *e.g.* the stimulation of part-time work for women, even of "non-regular" employment devoid of social protection. According to a survey by the European Foundation, the majority of women with young children in Europe would prefer a quality child care solution with a full-time job if they had access to one (European Foundation, 2003). Part-time work also raises an important equality issue. In several countries, part-time employment has become the reserve of women (see Figure 1.2), and if prolonged during the child-rearing years has a significant impact on women's careers, pensions and life-course earnings (Glass and Estes, 1997). In addition, much part-time work for women is "non-regular" or "marginal" (Austria, Korea, the United Kingdom, the United States amongst others), that is, consisting of part-time jobs that are casual and paid on a cash basis. In the service economy, much of this work does not enjoy a contractual status, and is not covered by social security. In sum, if women with young children are to

Figure 1.2. **Female part-time and full-time employment as proportion of total female employment, 2004**[1]

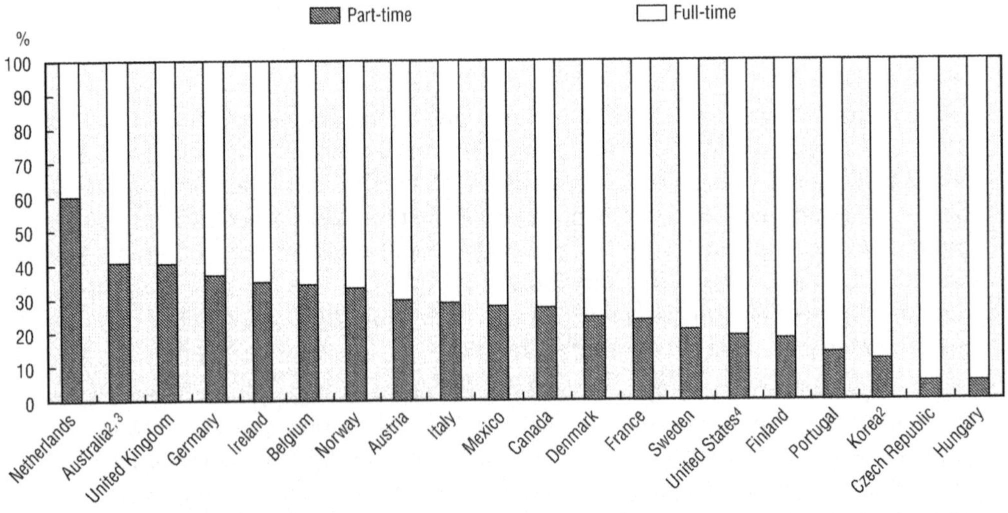

1. Part-time employment refers to persons who usually work less than 30 hours per week in their main job. Data include only persons declaring usual hours. Because of its non-contractual nature, the "marginal" or "non-regular" work mentioned in the text is not covered in these official figures.
2. Data are based on actual hours worked.
3. Part-time employment based on hours worked at all jobs.
4. Data are for wage and salary workers only. Part-time work on a casual is not included.
Source: OECD (2005c).

reconcile satisfactorily family responsibilities and equality of opportunity, public authorities need to examine labour market patterns, while providing or stimulating reliable professional child care services. Further, *equity*[1] between the genders requires that child care or domestic work should not be confined to the responsibility of women alone.

2. Reconciling work and family responsibilities in a manner more equitable for women

In the literature and research on the topic of equal opportunity, three important challenges still exist for women in contemporary societies: the reconciliation of motherhood with a working career; equal opportunity in work; and a more equitable sharing of child-rearing and domestic tasks.

Reconciling motherhood with a working career

According to Esping-Andersen *et al.* (2002), "the compatibility of motherhood and careers is contingent on the nature of institutional support", in particular, on public support for parental leave, the provision of early childhood services and the availability of family-friendly jobs.

Public support for parental leave

Remunerated parental leave has become an important element in family and labour policy in most OECD countries. Leave was initially conceived as maternity leave, important for the health of mothers and infants. Research shows that one-to-one care of babies during the first year of life develops their sense of attachment, and contributes to their emotional and language development (Tanaka, 2005). There is evidence too of the value and importance of male involvement in the care of children (Cabrera *et al.*, 2000; McBride and Rane, 1997). In most European countries,[2] leave includes a maternity leave of at least 15 weeks, followed by a period of parental leave varying in length from 3 months to about a year, on an adequate replacement wage or benefit, with the guarantee of returning to the same or a similar position at work. When the leave period is legally protected and remunerated, a real choice is provided to parents to care for their child at home, without excessive penalty to the family budget or to women's work careers.

Parental leave is a practical solution to a child-rearing challenge that the present organisation of economies and labour markets raises.[3] The policy has both positive and negative aspects. Countries such as Norway and Sweden (joined most recently by Canada and the United Kingdom) have taken the view that remunerated parental leave of about a year is an equitable solution good for the health, well-being and psychological needs of infants and mothers; helpful to parents, who continue to be remunerated during the period, and who preserve at the same time pension rights and attachment to the labour market; and supportive of wider family stability and task-sharing, when men are included progressively into the parental leave field and the care of young children. However, less satisfactory for women is parental leave considered or named as maternity leave (reinforcing the idea that the care of children is a woman's responsibility only); or long parental leaves either unpaid or considered as unemployment benefit. Long leaves from employment tend to break the career patterns of women, leaving them with lower pensions and possible financial difficulties when they have dependent children, *e.g.* in cases of separation or divorce.

How do countries compare with regard to parental leave measures?

Within the European Union, countries are obliged to follow the 1996 European Council directive obliging States to introduce legislation enabling parents to care full-time for their child over a minimum period of three months. However, there are many different approaches in terms of eligibility for leave, leave duration, wage replacement levels and job protection. Table 1.1 provides an overview of the duration of parental leave measures in force in the OECD countries.

Table 1.1. **Provision of statutory leave entitlements in selected OECD countries**

	Maternity leave in months		Paternity leave in months		Parental leave in months			Total post-natal leave	Leave for sick children	
Australia	√ Statutory but unpaid		×		√	12	F	12 (0)	×	
Austria	√√√	3.5	×		√√*	22	F	24 (24*)	√√√	0.5
Belgium	√√√	3.5	√√√	0.5	√√	6	I	9.5 (9.5)	√	0.5
Canada[1]	√√√	3.5	√	<0.5	√√√	8.5	F	12 (11.5)	√	
Denmark	√√√	4	√√√	0.5	√√√	7.5	F	10.5 (10.5)	×	
Finland	√√√	4	√√√	1	√√√	6	F	36 (36)	√	
France	√√√	3.5	√√√	0.5	√√*	33	F	36 (36*)[2]	√	<0.5
Germany	√√√	3.5	×		√√*	34	F	36 (24)[3]	√√√	1
Hungary	√√√	5.5	×		√√√	31.5[4]		36 (36)	√√√[4]	
Ireland	√√	4.5	×		√	6.5	I	12[4]	√√√	<0.5
Italy	√√√	4.5	×		√√	10[5]	I	12.5 (12.5)	√[5]	
Netherlands	√√√	3.5	√√√	<0.5	√	6	I	8.5 (2.5)	√√√	0.5
Norway	√√√	2	√	0.5	√√√	10	F/I	11.5 (11.5)	√√√[6]	
Portugal	√√√	5.5	√√√	1	√	6	I	11.5 (5.5)	√√√	1.5
Sweden			√√√	0.5	√√√	16	F/I		√√√[7]	
United Kingdom	√√	12	√√√	0.5	√	5-6[6]	I	18	√[6]	?
United States	×[8]		×		×			0	×	

Key to reading this figure:

× – no statutory entitlement.

√ – statutory entitlement but unpaid; √√ – statutory entitlement, paid but either at low flat rate or earnings-related at less than 50% of earnings or not universal or for less than the full period of leave; √√√ – statutory entitlement, paid to all parents at more than 50% of earnings (in most cases up to a maximum ceiling). * indicates the payment is made to all parents with a young child whether or not they are taking leave. ? – indicates length of leave unstated.

Unbracketed numbers for each leave column indicate total length of leave in months (to nearest month); bracketed numbers in "total post-natal leave" column indicate length of leave which receives some payment.

Parental leave: F = family entitlement; I = individual entitlement; F/I= some period of family entitlement and some period of individual entitlement.

1. There are differences in length of leave between Provinces and Territories; three Provinces allow 3-5 days of unpaid leave to care for members of immediate family. The federal Budget 2001 increased to two years the time parents can claim maternity and parental benefits when a child is hospitalised for an extended period following birth or adoption; and extends special benefit for maternity for up to 65 weeks in certain cases.
2. Paid to parents with one child for 6 months only after the end of maternity leave.
3. Payment after maternity leave until child is 2 years and means tested.
4. For insured parents, leave is paid at 70% of earnings until child's 2nd birthday, then at flat rate; only mother is entitled to use in child's first year. Leave for sick children varies according to child's age from unlimited (child under 1) to 14 days for a child aged 6 to 12 years.
5. Six months per parent, but total leave per family cannot exceed 10 months. Leave for a sick child is unlimited for a child under 3, 5 days per parent for a child aged 3 to 8 years.
6. Ten days per parent if one child under 12 years; 15 days if 2 or more children. Extended rights to leave if chronically sick child.
7. 480 days of paid leave per family (divided between individual entitlements and family entitlement), 390 days at 90% of earnings and 90 days at a low flat rate; each parent also entitled to 18 months unpaid leave. 60 days leave per year per child to care for a sick child.
8. Parents may take up to 12 weeks unpaid leave for childbirth or the care of a child up to 12 months as part of the federal Family and Medical Leave Act; employers with less than 50 employees are exempt. Five States and Puerto Rico provide some benefit payments to parents missing work at around the time of childbirth.

Source: Deven and Moss (2005).

Figure 1.3 on "effective" parental leave provision is based on work by the Dutch researchers, Plantenga and Siegel (2004). Effective leave is computed by weighing the duration of the legislated parental leave by the level of the replacement wage or benefit offered. Because the level of the replacement wage presumably influences take-up, the table provides an indication of the usefulness of the parental leave package to parents and their probable use of leave. Effective leave ranges from a coefficient of 119 points in Sweden to a low of 11 points in Ireland and the Netherlands. Some countries outside the European Union are included in this figure, but it should be noted that unlike in the EU, parents in these countries generally have no entitlement to leave, nor do they receive substantive public benefits during leave taken. For this reason, the coefficient of 17 allocated to Australia and the United States applies only to "best case" scenarios, as many Australian and American parents do not benefit, in fact, from any parental leave. Korea is not included in the table, as though a legal right to parental leave exists, work culture prevents most women from taking leave, and many mothers simply resign their jobs. Canada with its parental leave entitlement of 35 weeks and replacement monthly stipend of 55% of wages (with an upper limit) is an exception. Canada also provides a Compassionate Care leave benefit that allows for up to 6 weeks of paid leave for employees to care of a gravely ill family member.

Figure 1.3. **Effective parental leave provision**

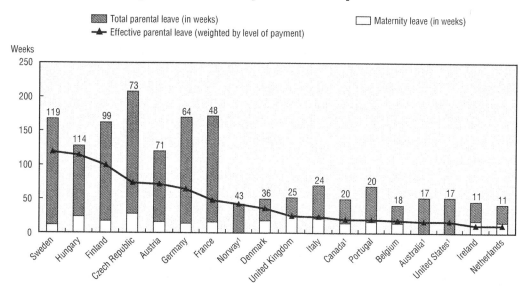

Note: The degree of parental leave effectiveness is calculated by weighing the length of parental leave by the level of payment. Effective parental leave = [(maternity leave in weeks – 14 weeks) * % payment benefit) + (total parental leave in weeks * % payment benefit)].

1. Data taken from Cleveland and Krashinsky (2003).

Source: Deven and Moss (2005); Platenga and Siegel (2004).

The position of the Central European countries in the figure calls for some explanation. Effective parental leave is strong in these countries (at least for employed parents), but the provision of child care services is weak. In Austria and former West Germany, the reaction against care of children outside the home was reinforced by the confrontation of ideologies in post-war Europe. *Maternalism*[4] became the dominant practice in the central European countries allied to the West, with low provision of services for 0- to 3-year-olds, and a long parental leave of two years in Austria (extendable to three years) and of three years in Germany (extendable to six years). In the socialist republics under Soviet influence, child care services were promoted to match high rates of female participation in the labour force. After the transition from communist to democratic regimes in the early 1990s, funding to public sector child care systems was significantly reduced in the Czech Republic and Hungary while parental leave was extended. As a result, child care services in many municipalities simply disappeared, and long parental (maternal) leave, lasting up to three years, has become the rule. As was reported by OECD review teams, the current arrangement has the support of women in these countries and suits the present configuration of the labour market. In the long term, the arrangement may become unsatisfactory in light of negative demographic trends and of future demands on labour supply, which may require improved population/ employment ratios, that is, the recruitment of more women to the labour market.

The position of the Netherlands – with a limited entitlement to a parental leave without pay, for six months for both parents – is also interesting. Rather than invest in parental leave, an attempt was made in the Netherlands during the 90s to provide more flexible work arrangements for parents, allowing them to move towards an equal "two-times, three-quarters" job pattern. In this arrangement, each member of a couple would work, in principle, for three-quarters of the official working period, and so between them, be able to provide parental care for their child(ren) on a half-time weekly basis. The reality has not lived up to expectations, as men have been far less likely to reduce their hours of work. To some extent, this is a rational economic decision, as the opportunity costs are greater for the family budget when the male partner's salary is foregone. Underlying the seeming rationality is an acceptance in our societies that women should be earning less, and a series of decisions made in this sense is likely to reinforce gender inequality even more. Because of the differences between men's and women's salaries, what was expected to be an equitable sharing of child care responsibility has become in practice, a one-and-a-half times (or one-and-a-quarter if calculated on the basis of earnings) job sharing pattern, with again women taking on part-time work and making the sacrifice of salary, career and pensions in order to rear the children. The participation of Dutch women in the labour market at 67% is higher than the EU average, but not on a full-time basis: almost 60% of all women work part-time in the Netherlands, with the part-time rate for women with young children reaching 64%. In fact, of Dutch women with one or two children who are still in employment, 90% work part-time compared to 53% of women without children (*OECD Employment Outlook*, 2002b).

The parental leave policies adopted in Sweden seem most successful in terms of economic and gender equality criteria. Sweden leads in terms of effective leave (calculated in terms of duration and salary compensation allocated to parents), and also in female employment rates, which are among the highest in the world (see Figure 1.3 above). However, as in other countries, parental leave is taken overwhelmingly by women. The Swedish authorities have formulated specific policies to address the imbalance, and 35% of fathers now take their full 6-month entitlement, a far higher rate than in other countries. Research indicates that the period around childbirth is an important moment for the bonding of male partners to their partners and offspring, and a period during which men learn to share caring and household chores (Mezulis *et al.*, 2004; Barclay and Lupton, 1999, Dermott, 2001).

Gender equality: equal access to work and equal opportunity in work

A second challenge for women is equal opportunity in work, which is dependant on a number of conditions:

- *Access to jobs on equal terms:* Working women are still concentrated in lower-skilled professions where atypical hours are more common. They are also, more likely to be in part-time work (see Figure 1.4) that is precarious and poorly paid, *e.g.* in the Netherlands (with relatively good job protection) and Australia. The present reality is that over three times more women than men work part-time in OECD economies (OECD, 2005a). According to the *OECD Employment Outlook* (2002b), the high incidence of part-time work among women (about three times greater than among men) is a contributory factor to the lower professional attainment of women in terms of salary and career position.

Figure 1.4. **Part-time employment as proportion of total employment: men and women, 2004[1]**

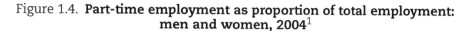

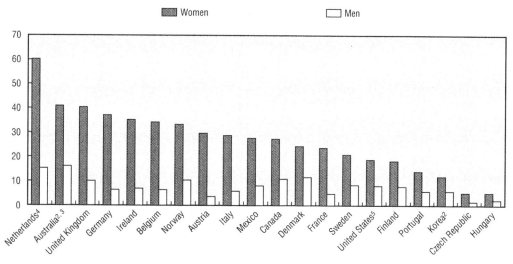

1. Part-time employment refers to persons who usually work less than 30 hours per week in their main job. Data include only persons declaring usual hours. Marginal or non-regular work in which women form a large majority is not included in this figure.
2. Data are based on actual hours worked.
3. Part-time employment based on hours worked at all jobs.
4. Data on population/employment ratios for the Netherlands is for the population aged 15-64, as opposed to the total population.
5. Data are for wage and salaried workers only.
Source: OECD (2005c).

- *Equal wages:* Women still earn less than men in all OECD countries, whatever their level of education. On average, women without upper secondary education obtain 60% of the earnings of men with the same level of education. Women with upper secondary and tertiary qualifications average 65% of equivalent male earnings (OECD, 2004a, *Education at a Glance,* Table A11.1b). In addition, as the country profiles in Annex E show, women take on part-time work far more frequently than their male partners. This weaker attachment of women to the labour market brings in its wake, further inequality with regard to pensions or when divorce with dependent children occurs.

● *Removal of tax penalties on a woman's work linked to her partner's earnings:* Taxation policies differ widely from country to country, but in some instances, the loss of benefits and allowances or a punitive rate of tax removes the financial motivation for a second earner to work.

● *A subsidisation of the costs of child care:* In many countries, the financial incentive for a mother to continue in work may be removed by the excessive costs of child care. This is most likely to happen in situations of government inattention or insufficient supply in countries where providers are allowed to demand the full market price. Among the countries reviewed, Ireland is an example as, on average, Irish parents pay more than 50% of the costs of child care. Without subsidisation or the capping of fees charged by providers, many women in low and moderate income jobs are unable to access child care of an acceptable level of quality.

● *A more equal distribution of domestic and child-rearing tasks:* Many women face the triple challenge of employment, rearing their children and ensuring the greater part of domestic work (on average in EU countries, over 80%). Without a more equal sharing of household chores and child-rearing tasks, women cannot take on full-time work. With the exception of the Nordic countries and the United States, male habits have barely evolved since time surveys began.

● *Parental leave and family-friendly work practices:* During the pre- and post-maternity period, parental leave and flexible work practices can help women to reconcile maternity and work. Family-friendly workplace measures are mostly time-related, *e.g.* breast-feeding periods, child-related emergency leave, school holiday adjusted leave, flexible hours, part-time work, or even teleworking. Measures may also include, as in Austria, access to family counselling services and measures to help re-integration after prolonged parental leave absences. According to OECD studies, "Employers have good reason to provide such measures as they motivate and increase the productivity of the existing workforce, increase workforce flexibility to meet peak-time demand, attract and retain qualified staff" (OECD, 2003a).

Access to jobs on equal terms

Within the workplace, equal opportunity is a question of basic justice and one that in most OECD countries is increasingly subject to legal remedies. For this reason, many advocates for more gender equality plead not for affirmative action in favour of women but simply for gender neutrality (the absence of discrimination) in recruitment and in the allocation of salaries, work and career advancement, welfare and pension outcomes. Finding a better balance in these areas is not simply a women's issue, but one that is important for economic and social progress at societal level and children's well-being at family level. Women's employment has several multiplier effects: on the production side, where women's work adds to the stock of goods and services in modern economies; on the consumption side where the growing contribution of women to household income increases consumption; and on state budgets, where the taxation of women's incomes increase government revenues. At family level, a woman's work may constitute the entire family income, and in all households, contributes significantly to family income and opportunities for children. In addition, in a context of population ageing and increasing longevity in contemporary societies, long-term care and pensions can only be sustained if high employment rates are maintained in the population eligible for work.

To achieve equal opportunity for women in work is a complex challenge (see Figure 1.5). Many discriminatory practices have their source in deep-seated societal views about gender roles and the needs of young children – views that were incorporated into labour and social legislation during the last century. In consequence, although open discrimination against women is considered unacceptable, the world of work still incorporates many systemic inequalities: workplaces that compensate women less for equal work, or define jobs held by women as less valuable, or consider maternity and family leave a nuisance. To improve the situation for women, both the Irish and Korean government have established ministries of gender equality in their countries during the past decade. The Korean ministry, for example, has had to challenge a strong male culture in the labour market, which effectively disallows the use of parental leave (although the statutory right exists) and leads to the employment of a significant proportion of women workers in non-regular jobs that are poorly paid and have no social protection (see Annex E).

Figure 1.5. **Employment/population ratios for men and women (25-54 years), 2004**

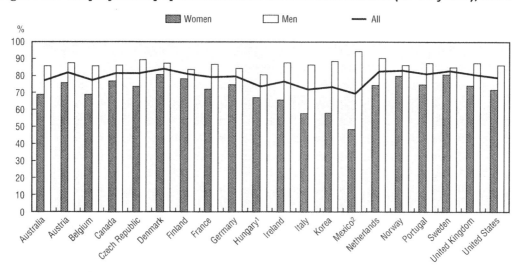

1. The year 1990 refers to 1992.
2. The year 1990 refers to 1991.
Source: OECD (2005c).

Job segregation within the caring professions

Another issue with implications for gender equality is the continued low status and gendering of care work, and of child care work in particular. In the name of keeping public expenditure under control or of creating the conditions to allow commercial providers to enter the child care field, governments can be reluctant to require degree-level qualifications for professionals in charge of young children, and may even see the sector as an appropriate field of activity in which to absorb lowly qualified women into the workforce (OECD Germany Country Note, 2004b, Netherlands Country Note, 1999). From a quality perspective, this approach is short-sighted. Research continues to confirm that the quality of education and care for young is significantly linked to the presence and commitment of well-educated staff (Shonkoff and Philips, 2000). Despite the obvious dedication of many women in the early childhood field, low wages lead inevitably to low recruitment levels, with carers lacking the professional knowledge, interactive skills and the language proficiency necessary for enhanced cognitive and language outcomes in young children. In addition, in high employment service economies, low remuneration also leads to staff dissatisfaction and high turnover – a factor that has negative effects on child attachment and socio-emotional development (AAP/APHA, 2002).

Gender equity – a more equal distribution of domestic and child-rearing tasks

A useful distinction can be drawn between gender equality and gender equity. The former refers to the world of work and constitutes a right that in principle should be enforceable by law: equal treatment in recruitment and access to work; equal remuneration for equal work; equal advancement in work careers based on merit (vs. the "glass ceiling"). Gender equity, on the other hand, refers to an equal sharing of child-rearing and domestic work. Although generally outside the legal field, gender equity issues should not be underestimated: the lack of gender equity within the home prevents many women from achieving gender equality in work. A heavy domestic work schedule can oblige women to engage only in part-time work outside the home, generally in low-paid and feminised fields, such as cleaning, caring, catering, and cashiering (the 4 Cs), and frequently with little reference to their educational levels or qualifications. As the domestic division of labour is considered voluntary and traditional, it is difficult to challenge gender inequity in the home or oppose it through the courts. Time surveys in all countries show clearly that women in full-time employment still devote far more time than men to child-rearing and domestic tasks. Men's work at home in a male bread-winner couple ranges from 13 minutes daily in Japan to about 3 hours daily in Sweden (OECD, 2003a). In consequence, many women face the triple challenge of holding a job, rearing their children and providing the greater part of domestic work (on average in EU countries, women ensure 80% of household and child-rearing tasks). In France, for example, women continue to carry the main responsibility for both domestic and family tasks in the home (Méda, 2001). The French Background Report (OECD, 2003b) noted that mothers with children under 15 years of age devote 1 hour 35 minutes daily to parenting, while fathers devote only 31 minutes. This imbalance in gender roles in the home is reinforced by the lower employment rates of women with young children.

3. Demographic challenges: falling fertility and continuing immigration

Current demographic patterns (see Figure 1.6) are a further reason motivating governments to take more seriously the provision of early childhood services. On the one hand, low fertility rates and population decline touch many countries in the OECD; on the other, many OECD countries cater to large numbers of immigrant and second-language children among their school-entry population, a reality that raises significant educational challenges.

The challenge of low fertility

Current demographic forecasts raise concern about the capacity of some countries to ensure future labour supply and maintain present economic growth, if they are to meet – at present levels – pension and public health obligations for their ageing populations. Outside Mexico and the United States, fertility rates are below replacement levels in all the OECD countries reviewed. One reason for lower fertility rates is that the decision to have children may be contingent on completing education and/or achieving stability in employment

Figure 1.6. **Ageing and immigrant populations in the OECD world**

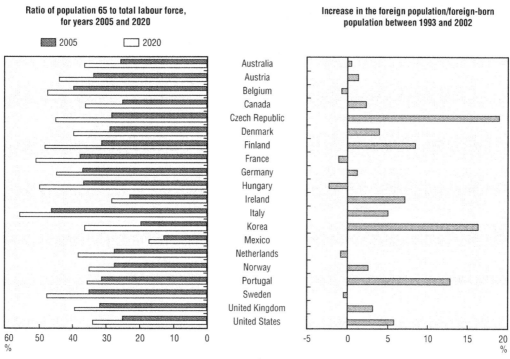

Notes: In the case of Australia, Canada, Mexico, New Zealand and the United States, the data concern the foreign-born population only. Annual average change between 1993 and 2002, except Canada (1991 and 2001), France (1990-1999), Hungary (1994-2002), the Slovak Republic (1995-2002) and the United States (1994-2002).

Source: OECD (2005b, 2005d).

(Becker, 2005). Family formation is thus deferred as more and more men and women pursue and self-fund longer studies at post-secondary and tertiary-level education. In addition, stable employment remains elusive in many economies, particularly for young adults, *e.g.* in France and Germany, or remains precarious, as in Australia, the Netherlands, and the United Kingdom, where high rates of part-time and temporary contracts have become the rule in retail, secretarial and other service sector work occupied by women. In addition, the estimated cost of raising children, both the direct costs of child care as well as its indirect costs, such as opportunity costs relating to the mother's career, have also a dissuasive effect on decisions to have children (Becker, 2005).

In this context of falling birth rates, European governments, in particular, have put into place comprehensive family and child care policies to facilitate couples to have children and to ensure that it is possible for women to combine work and family responsibilities. Several countries provide a continuum of services in support of parents with young children, including child benefits; family-friendly work practices, parental leave policies; child care services and/or subsidies to purchase child care. Some countries, such as Denmark, Finland, the New Federal *Länder* in Germany (former East Germany), Norway (in process), and Sweden have been able to guarantee a child care place once parental leave is over; followed by early education and comprehensive out-of-school provision. This combination of employment, family and child policies brings, according to Walker (1995), a measure of job security to couples and lessens anxieties about child care, thus creating a more reassuring base from which to make decisions about having children. According to Koegel's (2002) analysis of European countries, the opportunity for women to

31

combine child-rearing and paid employment is greatest in the Scandinavian countries and least so in Mediterranean countries.

However, a causal link between early childhood service supply and fertility rates is far from certain. Demographic change is a complex phenomenon, and in the case of fertility decline, many causal factors are at work, *e.g.* the higher educational levels of populations; the pursuit of working careers by women; the length of the working day combined with the absence of family-friendly work practices; the costs of educating children; the costs of first housing and of pursuing higher education, in addition to other social and cultural factors. The American – and Nobel prize-winning – economist, Gary Becker, judges that the public provision of early childhood services and parental leave policies may have some impact on family decisions, but only in "an indirect and inefficient manner" (Becker, 2005). Unlike the United States, total fertility rates in most European countries that promote such policies are still considerably below replacement level. In Becker's reckoning, the best way to encourage births is to provide monthly allowances to families that have an additional child: "an efficient family allowance programme should concentrate subsidies on the marginal fertility decision, that is, on second, third or higher order births that may not happen without subsidies" (Becker and Posner, 2005).

Becker's argument is not always supported by the reality on the ground: for example, despite a large 3rd child bonus, Quebec's fertility rate is not markedly different from the rest of Canada. Again, Austria provides more generous family subsidies than most OECD countries but continues to have a low total fertility rate. In addition, Becker's argument focuses on demographic results and leaves aside the human costs that inadequate parental leave policies and scarcity of early childhood services impose on women. Paid parenting leave offers choice to parents and allows mothers (and fathers if they so wish) to care for infants without forfeiting jobs or income.

Immigration

A second demographic factor pushing countries to invest in early childhood educational services is immigration. In poor urban neighbourhoods in European and American cities, the numbers of children of foreign-born parents in schools and early childhood centres can easily exceed 50%. Such diversity brings many new strengths to societies, but also raises challenges in the social and education fields. In particular, children from immigrant families are prone to being "at-risk" due, on the one hand, to the difficulties experienced by their parents in finding employment and on the other, to a weak knowledge of the host country language and culture. The probability of school failure increases when a number of at-risk factors combine. The factors presented in Table 1.2 are used in the ongoing Effective Provision of Pre-school Education (EPPE) study in the United Kingdom (EPPE, 2004).

Section 4 will discuss how quality early childhood programmes contribute to children's development and success in school, and particularly to the progress of children from economically disadvantaged backgrounds. *A fortiori*, such programmes are needed for young children combining socio-economic disadvantage with immigrant, second-language status who risk arriving at school ill-prepared to avail of education opportunity. In Germany, for example, it is calculated that 25% of immigrant children enter obligatory schooling without the experience of kindergarten (German Background Report, OECD, 2004b). The EPPE (2004) research shows – for the United Kingdom, at least – that where cognitive development is concerned (especially pre-reading skills), most children who

Table 1.2. **At-risk indicators used in the United Kingdom EPPE study, 1997-2007**

Child characteristics	Disadvantage indicators
First language	= English not first language
Family size	= 3 or more siblings
Birth weight	= Premature or below 2 500 grams
Parent characteristics	**Disadvantage indicators**
Mother's highest qualification	= No qualifications
Social class of father's occupation	= Semi-skilled, unskilled, never worked, absent father
Father's employment status	= Not employed
Age of mother	= Age 13 to 17 at birth of EPPE child
Lone parent	= Single parent
Mother's employment status	= Unemployed
Home environment scale	= Bottom quartile

Source: Sylva *et al.* (2003).

attend integrated ECEC centres or nursery school are likely to move out of "at-risk" status, often after only one year. Children's emotional development (co-operative, contented behaviour as opposed to anti-social/worried/upset behaviour), improved in all forms of out-of-home provision and more children moved out of than into "at-risk" status. Again, positive effects were found in terms of cognitive and social development, with integrated centres and nursery schools, in particular, producing superior effects. In parallel, the Preparing for School study in Queensland, Australia found that provision of a universally available, full-time, play-based education programme closed the gap in achievement in social development, numeracy and literacy achievement between socially advantaged and disadvantaged children (Thorpe *et al.*, 2004). Moreover, this study found that absence of group-based experience in the year prior to school was a predictor of poor progress, especially for children from socially disadvantaged backgrounds.

4. Acting against child poverty and educational disadvantage

The fourth factor leading to greater investment in early childhood services is the continued existence of poverty and educational disadvantage among a significant proportion of young children in OECD countries. The presence of child poverty is generally acknowledged when "the income available to a child – assuming a fair distribution of resources within the family and making allowances for family size and composition – is less than half the median available to children growing up in the same society".[5] While one might think that child poverty is a marginal phenomenon within OECD countries, in fact between 1995 and 2005, child poverty rates increased in 17 out of 24 OECD countries for which data are available (UNICEF, 2005). Ten of the twenty countries in the Figure 1.7 below show child poverty rates in excess of 10%, and two, Mexico and the United States, in excess of 20%. Families without the skills sought by employers in the new global economy can easily fall into poverty (Lindert and Williamson, 2001; Minjuin *et al.*, 2002). Given that the effects of poverty are greater and have a longer impact on very young children than on any other age group, a strong social and economic rationale exists for breaking the cycle of child poverty.

Child poverty is determined by a number of factors, including under-employment of parents, income inequalities, insufficient social transfer payments, and in some instances, by lack of affordable child care possibilities. Under-employment of parents includes both unemployment and employment in poorly paid, unprotected (by social security) part-time jobs, which are mostly occupied by women. In order to stay above the poverty line in Europe,[6]

Figure 1.7. **Impacts of social transfers on child poverty**

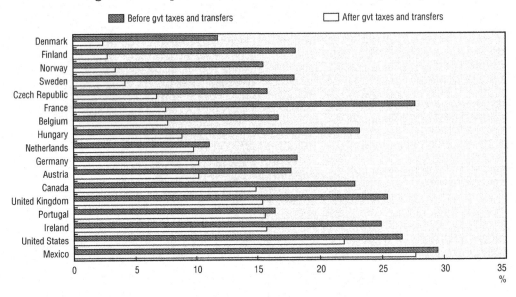

Source: UNICEF (2005).

a couple with children needs one full-time job at the minimum wage and one part-time job, while a single parent needs one full-time job, and allowances (CERC, 2004). This is one reason why child poverty is more likely to be found in immigrant families, who have far greater difficulty than citizens in finding jobs in the formal economy. In addition, many immigrant families may be outside the social security system and the allocation of family benefits. As Figure 1.7 shows, social transfers – income redistribution measures, family allowances, child benefits, and other social expenditures – are critical to preventing child and family poverty.

Family poverty may also be related to the absence of child care. Lone parents (see Figure 1.8) and low-income families are particularly vulnerable when child care is lacking, unaffordable or of poor quality. Lone mothers, in particular, are often obliged to leave the labour market, leading to situations where they and their children barely subsist on welfare benefits. In OECD countries, lone mothers living on welfare benefits are consistently among the poorest groups.

Children at risk of educational failure are the object of a variety of policies and programmes that seek to address the challenge through early education interventions, and increasingly through a comprehensive services approach focusing on the home and community environments (Nair and Radhakrishnan, 2004; Tremblay *et al.*, 2004). Human capital is produced over a lifetime not just by genetic heritage but also by families, schools and work environments. Although the interplay of these four components of human capital is complex, most research confirms the common observation that family environment is critical to producing and reinforcing the child's intellectual capital and well-being. The link is evident not only in dealing with actual families but also across generations. Children from low socio-economic status (SES) families are less likely, statistically, to develop the same level of skills and intellectual capital as children from high SES backgrounds. Feinstein (2003) finds, for example, that a 13% difference in cognitive development exists at 22 months of age between British children from high and low SES backgrounds. By the age of 10 years (118 months), an average gap of 28% in cognitive development is recorded.

Figure 1.8. **Lone parents as a percentage of all families in selected OECD countries**

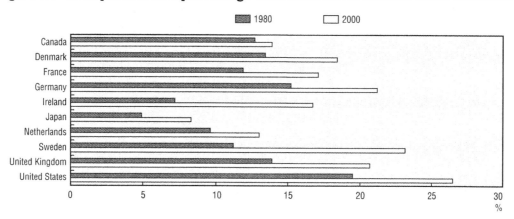

Note: Data from 1981 were used for Canada, Ireland, and the United Kingdom, data from 1985 were used for Sweden, data from 1988 were used for France and the Netherlands and data from 1991 were used for Germany.
Data from 2001 were used for the United States, Denmark, and the United Kingdom, data from 2002 were used for Ireland.

Source: Clearinghouse on International Developments in Child, Youth and Family Policies at Columbia University, 2005.

Family poverty[7] is linked significantly to poor educational outcomes. Evaluations, such as PISA (OECD, 2001, 2004) confirm the correlation between socio-economic status and educational achievement. One reason for the success of children from middle class families is home environment: these children have daily access to the codes, language and cultural resources valued in mainstream education. They perform on average significantly better in all countries than children without such advantages. Another reason is that young children in higher risk categories may not experience successful role models, or acquire in the early childhood period, the fundamental skills and motivations that underlie all learning, such as, adequate concept and language acquisition, self-regulation, and confidence to interact or express themselves. As research shows, the skills acquired in one stage of the life cycle affect both the endowments and the skills of learning at the next stage, or as Carneiro and Heckman (2003) express it: "skill begets skill." In this sense – and with regard also to health and social development – poverty in early childhood has more serious effects than at any other stage in the life cycle, as it can seriously impede fundamental skill acquisition. The link between low SES background and low academic achievement can be further reinforced by the lack of access of children in poor neighbourhoods to adequate primary and secondary education. Even when access to an adequate school is possible, the OECD PISA study demonstrates that within schools, the gap between the children from under-privileged backgrounds and the mainstream is not necessarily reduced but can be further accentuated. However, unequal access and unequal treatment of children in the school system is not a destiny. The school systems in some countries, *e.g.* in Australia, Canada, Finland and Japan, manage to compensate for socio-economic disadvantage, and ensure that children from low-income families do not fall irretrievably behind in academic achievement. Korea, whose national gross domestic product (GDP) is well below the OECD average, also manages to maintain high performance standards across the board for students from all backgrounds, although in this respect the support and ambition of Korean parents for their children should not be underestimated.

International research from a wide range of countries shows that early intervention contributes significantly to putting children from low-income families on the path to development and success in school; see, for example, Thorpe et al., 2004 (Australia); McCain and Mustard, 1999 (Canada); Jarousse et al., 1992 (France); Kellaghan and Greaney, 1993 (Ireland); Kagitcibasi et al., 1991 and 2001 (Turkey); Osborn and Milbank, 1987 (United Kingdom); the longitudinal EPPE project, 1997-2007 (United Kingdom); Berrueta-Clement et al., 1984 (United States); McKey et al., 1985 (United States); and Schweinhart, 2004, Schweinhart et al., 1993 (United States). All concur that well-funded, integrated, socio-educational programmes improve the cognitive and social functioning of children at-risk. If properly linked to labour, health and social services, early childhood services can be expected to deliver additional outcomes, such as enhanced maternal employment, less family poverty, better parenting skills and greater family and community cohesion (see Lynch, 2004 in Annex D). At a presentation to the United States Congress, Professor Brooks-Gunn (2003), focusing on educational returns, confirmed that mainstream research indicates that:[8]

- High quality centre-based programmes enhance the school-related achievement and behaviour of young children.

- These effects are strongest for poor children and for children whose parents have little education.

- Positive benefits continue into late elementary school and high school years, although effects are smaller than they were at the beginning of elementary school.

- Programmes that are continued into primary school, and that offer intensive early intervention, have the most sustained long-term effects.

Despite this evidence, a recent evaluation of the Sure Start Local Programmes in the United Kingdom (NESS, 2005) is not encouraging, although the authors underline that the conclusions of this preliminary research need to be verified by further longitudinal work. The NESS impact study suggests that Sure Start Local Programmes have had only modest effects, either positive or adverse. Most family outcomes appeared to be unaffected and there was little evidence that the programmes achieved their goals of increasing service use or that they enhanced families' impressions of their communities. These findings diverge considerably, however, from a similar American study on the effectiveness of Early Head Start (EHS) – a more rigorously designed programme, with stringent programme standards, for 3-year old children and their parents. EHS was evaluated by Love et al. (2005) through a randomised trial of 3 001 families in 17 programmes. Regression-adjusted impact analyses showed that 3-year-old programme children performed better than did control children in cognitive and language development, displayed higher emotional engagement with their parent and more sustained attention with play objects, and were lower in aggressive behaviour. Compared with controls, Early Head Start parents were more emotionally supportive, provided more language and learning stimulation, read to their children more, and spanked less. However, the uncertain results from "intervention" programmes points to the conclusion that young children have great difficulties in recovering from a poor start. For this reason, the Nordic model of preventing child poverty through upstream fiscal, social and family policies merits more attention.

5. Early childhood education and care as a public good

The theoretical bases of considering early childhood education and care as a public good are outlined by Cleveland and Krashinsky (2003). These Canadian economists suggest that the arguments in favour of treating ECEC as a public good are similar to those used in favour of public education. In sum, early childhood services deliver externalities[9] beyond the benefit of immediate, personal interest or consumption. Early education and care contributes to the public good, *e.g.* to the general health of a nation's children, to future educational achievement, to labour market volume and flexibility, and to social cohesion (see Annex D). Early childhood services are also subject to "market failure", that is, they have characteristics that are difficult for consumers to judge accurately, and purchasing mistakes can have serious consequences on the development of young children. Education is rarely a repeatable process. Unlike buying a product that can be returned or exchanged, to remove a child from an inferior early childhood placement cannot compensate for the previous loss of opportunity, while the continued use of an inferior service may actually harm the development of the child (NICHD, 1997). In addition, early childhood services in market situations are subject to critical shortages and low quality – all of which indicate that government intervention is appropriate. Government involvement is also justified by the fact that the benefits delivered to societies by high quality early childhood services are greater than its costs (see Annex D).

The *de facto* situation in OECD countries confirms these arguments. In most countries, the greater part of early childhood funding is public, and extensive governmental regulation of services is practised. Only in the liberal economies is an important, independent market in early childhood services found, but among these countries, Ireland, the Netherlands and the United Kingdom also provide universal free early education for children from at least four years for some hours every day. In the United States, 46 States have now introduced some form of publicly-funded pre-kindergarten education for 4-year-olds, and three States – Georgia, Oklahoma, and New York (in principle) – have opened these programmes to all children. However, although the notion of early education as a public good is widely accepted, government provision and entitlements to access differ widely across the OECD countries (see Table 1.2).

Some commentators argue that a closer link with public education systems – based on an integrative concept of education that respects the specificity of early childhood services – may be a step towards recognition of ECEC as a public good (Barnett *et al.*, 2004). Once the educational benefits of kindergarten and early education are officially recognised, these services tend to become entitled to regular public financing and, in many instances, have become a mainstream public service.

Learning begets learning

The move towards seeing early childhood services as a public good has received much support in recent years from economists as well from education researchers. Cunha and Heckman, the latter a Nobel prize-winner in economics, suggest that the early childhood period provides an unequalled opportunity for investment in human capital (see Figure 1.9). These authors understand human capital formation as a dynamic process that is ongoing throughout a lifetime (Cunha *et al.*, 2005). A basic principle is that learning in one life stage begets learning in the next. Investment in the foundation stage of early childhood increases the productivity of the next stage and so on (which points also to the importance of sustained investment in learning opportunities throughout the life cycle). The complementarity of stages can be weakened at any moment, *e.g.* by a period of poor lower secondary studies. The early childhood or foundation stage of learning is of major importance. As the authors phrase it: "The rate of return to a dollar of investment made while a person is young is higher than the rate of return for the same dollar made at a later age (p. 19)." In early childhood, positive (or negative) dispositions towards society and

Figure 1.9. **Rates of return to human capital investment initially setting investment to be equal across all ages**

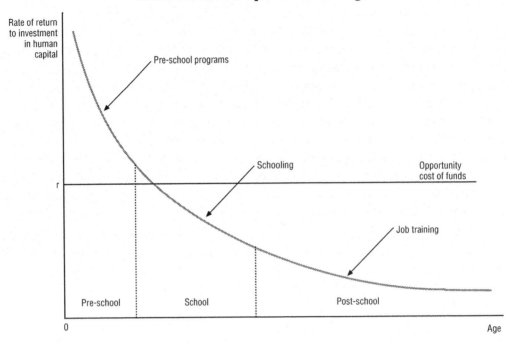

Source: Cunha et al. (2005), *Interpreting the Evidence on Life Cycle Skill Formation.*

learning are absorbed and the basic life skills acquired, such as co-operation with peers and adults, autonomy, meaning-making, creativity, problem-solving and persistence. Additionally, parents are particularly protective of their children at this age, and eager to support early development and learning. Early childhood is then a logical moment to invest in human capital, an investment that reaches not only children but also their families. In comparison, remedial education interventions targeting young school drop-outs or adults with poor basic skills are far more costly and, according to the research, of limited benefit (Alakeson, 2004).

Deeply-rooted traditional attitudes towards child-rearing and early education

The research finding that young children begin to learn very early (even before birth) is interpreted in different fashions by researchers, families and governments. In general, research is reassuring and points to the positive effects of quality child care outside the home, even when it begins early, *e.g.* developmental advantages for young children; economic benefits for women and families; positive socio-economic effects through increased productivity and tax receipts; labour market volume and flexibility; social welfare, social cohesion and community development; and finally, better educational achievement for children if the foundations of learning have been well laid (see Annex D for a summary of this research). Some warnings about the negative effects of prolonged extra-domestic child care have also been issued by researchers such as Belsky (1998, 2001), and McCartney (2003) of the NICHD team. These researchers points to delays in emotional and language development when mothers are absent most of the day and infants are placed in poor quality care. The Nordic countries have been particularly proactive in avoiding such situations through investing in parental leave during the first year of life, while maintaining equal opportunity for women.

In all countries, the attitude of parents to extra-domestic child care has changed radically over the last 30 years. In the OECD countries reviewed, a majority of parents consider child care as an option, particularly if it is local, affordable and of suitable quality. Over half the children aged 0 to 3 years in the United States are placed in some form of child care outside the home. A more traditional attitude also exists, that is, that caring for and educating young children is a family matter, to be organised by parents through maternal care, supported by extended family or other private arrangement. For instance, the 1994 International Social Survey Programme on "Family and Gender Roles" in Europe recorded that 60% of Austrians and 50% of Irish people surveyed felt that mothers with pre-school children should not work outside the home. As the subsequent 2002 Survey showed, public attitudes changed significantly since that time, particularly in Ireland, but the feeling is strong in many societies that exclusive maternal care during the first 3 years is the ideal model for rearing children.

Where governments are concerned, attitudes to ECEC depend much on their particular electorates and on a country's socio-economic tradition. In the liberal economies, although States may help families in their child-rearing tasks, governments generally judge that they have little responsibility to support universal ECEC institutions, except to facilitate the labour market or to prepare young children for schools. As a result, investments in services are still limited, particularly where the youngest children are concerned. However, the argument put forward by Heckman and many other researchers – to see early childhood education and care as an opportunity for public investment in families and future human capital – is gradually making ground. In addition, the evidence from brain research has helped to direct "child care" services to a more developmental approach. The early nurturance of infants and toddlers is seen to be of major importance because of the extraordinary neurological development that occurs in this period. Faced by this evidence, it is more difficult for governments to consider large-scale, extra-domestic child care for children under kindergarten age as having little importance for a country's human capital policies. Electorates and business communities in most countries are calling increasingly for more comprehensive funding and regulation of these services.

Notes

1. As outlined on page 30, a distinction is drawn here between gender equality and gender equity. The former refers to the world of work and constitutes a right that in principle should be enforceable by law: equal treatment in recruitment and access to work; equal remuneration for equal work, equal advancement in work careers based on merit (vs. the "glass ceiling"). Gender equity, on the other hand, refers to an equal sharing of child rearing and domestic work.

2. In Australia, Korea, Mexico and the United States, possibilities of parental leave and family-friendly policies are present in many firms and industries. However, the general lack of paid parental leave and the insufficient supply of affordable child care services mean that many low- and moderate-income parents still struggle to find suitable arrangements for infants and young children (Fuller et al., 2005; Pocock and Masterman-Smith, 2005; OECD, 2004c).

3. Here, parental leave is discussed from the perspective of employment and gender equality. From the perspective of the child, recent National Institute of Child Health and Human Development (NICHD) analyses suggest that from the child's perspective, parental leave of at least 9 months is preferable, even when controlling for child care quality, the quality of the home environment, and maternal sensitivity (Brooks-Gunn et al., 2002).

4. *Maternalism* is defined by (Randall, 2000) as the ideology or strong belief that the young child should be cared for in the family, and in particular by the mother.

5. Definition used by the *Innocenti Report Card: Child Poverty in Rich Countries*, Issue No. 6, UNICEF, 2005.

6. In the European Union, the poverty line is placed at 60% of the median standard of living. The standard of living of a household is defined as its disposable income after direct taxes, divided by it size (the first adult counting as one and all other members at 0.5 each).

7. Poverty is defined in a broad sense to include not just low income but also social exclusion and cultural deprivation.

8. More extensive summaries of the international research on the topic from other countries can be found in OECD (1999 and 2002a) and in Leseman (2002).

9. Externalities is the term used by economists to refer to benefits or costs that accrue to someone other than the individual consumer or producer making the economic decision, *e.g.* to enrol a child in an early education centre brings benefits to the child, but it also generates benefits for the family (mothers are able to work and contribute to the family budget) and for the economy (as the mother's work contributes to economic production, gives rise to extra revenue and taxes, and allows the State to cut back on social welfare assistance).

References

AAP/APHA (2002), (American Academy of Pediatrics/American Public Health Association and the National Resource Center for Health and Safety in Child Care), *National Health and Safety Performance Standards: Guidelines for Out-of-Home Child Care.*

Alakeson, V. (2004), *A 2020 Vision for Early Years: Extending Choice; Improving Life Chances,* Social Market Foundation, London.

American Business Roundtable (2003), *Early Childhood Education: A Call to Action from the Business Community, www.businessroundtable.org/pdf/901.pdf.*

Barclay, L. and D. Lupton (1999), "The Experiences of New Fatherhood: A Socio-cultural Analysis", *Journal of Advanced Nursing,* Vol. 29(4), pp. 1013-1020.

Barnett, W.S., J.T. Hustedt, K.B. Robin and K.L. Schulman (2004), *The State of pre-school: 2004 State pre-school Yearbook.*

Bauer, P.J. (2002), "Long-term Recall Memory: Behavioral and Neuro-developmental Changes in the First Two Years of Life", *Current Directions in Psychological Science,* Vol. 11(4), pp. 137-141.

Becker, G. (2005), *Lloyd Delamar lectures,* American University of Paris, Paris.

Becker, G. and Posner, R. (2005), "Should Governments Subsidise Child Care and Work Leaves?", Becker-Posner Blog, November 2005, *www.becker-posner-blog.com/.*

Belsky, J. (1988), "The 'Effects' of Infant Day Care Reconsidered", *Early Childhood Research Quarterly,* Vol. 3, pp. 235-272.

Belsky, J. (2001), "Developmental Risks (Still) Associated with Early Child Care", *Journal of Child Psychology and Psychiatry,* Vol. 42.

Berrueta-Clement, J.R., L.J. Schweinhart, W.S. Barnett *et al.* (1984), *Changed Lives: The Effects of the Perry pre-school Program on Youths Through Age 19,* High/Scope, Ypsilanti, Michigan.

Brooks-Gunn, J. (2003), "Do you Believe in Magic? What we Can Expect from Early Childhood Intervention Programs", *Social Policy Report,* XVII (1), pp. 3-7.

Brooks-Gunn, J., W. Han and J. Waldfogel (2002), "Maternal Employment and Child Cognitive Outcomes in the First Three Years of Life: The NICHD Study of Early Child Care", *Child Development,* Vol. 73(4), pp. 1052-1072.

Brooks-Gunn, J. and L.B. Markman (2005), "The Contribution of Parenting to Ethnic and Racial Gaps in School Readiness", *Future of Children,* Vol. 15(1), pp. 139-165.

Cabrera, N.J., C.S. Tamis-LeMonda, R.H. Bradley, S. Hofferith and M.E. Lamb (2000), "Fatherhood in the Twenty-First Century", *Child Development,* Vol. 71(1), pp. 127-136.

Carneiro, P. and J. Heckman (2003), "Human Capital Policy", in J. Heckman and A. Krueger, *Inequality in America: What Role for Human Capital Policy?,* MIT Press.

CERC (Conseil de l'emploi, des revenus et de la cohésion sociale) (2004), *Les enfants pauvres en France,* La documentation française, Paris.

Cleveland, G. and M. Krashinsky (2003), *Financing ECEC Services in OECD Countries,* OECD, Paris.

CPA (Combat Poverty Agency) (2005), *Ending Child Poverty*, CPA, Dublin.

CSO (Central Statistics Office) (2004), *Women and Men in Ireland*, Stationery Office, Dublin.

Cunha, F., J. Heckman, L. Lochner and D.V. Masterov (2005), "Interpreting the Evidence of Life-Cycle Skill Formation", IZA Discussion Paper Series, No. 1575, Institute for the Study of Labour, Bonn, Germany, July.

Dermott, E.M. (2001), "New Fatherhood in Practice? Parental Leave in the United Kingdom", *The International Journal of Sociology and Social Policy*, Vol. 21, pp. 4-6.

Deven, F. and P. Moss (eds.) (2005), "Leave Policy and Research: Overviews and Country notes" (CBGS Work document 2005/3), available at *www.cbgs.be/repository/WD_2005_03.pdf*.

DfES (2004), *Choice for Parents: The Best Start for Children. A 10-year Strategy for Children*, HMSO, Norwich.

Dy-Hammer, F.J., C. Ernst, D.M. McCann, W.D. Salter and D.A. Kidd (2001), "How Working Conditions Affect Families: Working Time, Family Health and Gender Equality", Global Economies at Work, Working Paper Series, Harvard Center for Society and Health, Boston.

EPPE project (1997-2007), "The Effective Provision of Pre-School Education (EPPE) Project. A Longitudinal Study Funded by the DfES", *http://k1.ioe.ac.uk/schools/ecpe/eppe/index.htm*.

Esping-Andersen, G., D. Gallie, A. Hemerick and J. Myles (2002), *Why We Need a New Welfare State*, Oxford University Press, Oxford.

European Foundation (2003), *Promoting Gender Equality in the Workplace – Key Findings from 21 Company Structures*, European Foundation, Dublin.

Feinstein, L. (2003), "Inequality in the Early Cognitive Development of British Children in the 1970 cohort", *Economica*, Vol. 70, pp. 73-97.

Fuller, B., S.L. Kagan, G.L. Caspary and C.A. Gauthier (2004), "Welfare Reform and Child Care Options for Low-income Families", *Child and Welfare Reform*, Vol. 12(1), pp. 97-119.

Fuller, B.C., A. Livas and M. Bridges (2005), "How to Expand and Improve Pre-school in California: Ideals, Evidence, and Policy Options", PACE Working Paper 05-1, Policy Analysis for California Education (PACE), Berkeley, California.

Glass, J.L. and S.B. Estes (1997), "The Family Responsive Workplace", *Annual Review of Sociology*, Vol. 23, pp. 289-313.

IRS (Internal Revenue Service) (2000), *Employment Review*, Feb. 2000, Reed/Elsevier, United Kingdom.

Jarousse, J.P., A. Mingat and M. Richard (1992), "La scolarisation maternelle à deux ans : effets pédagogiques et sociaux", *Éducation et Formation*, ministère de l'Éducation nationale et de la Culture, Paris.

Kagitcibasi, C. and S. Bekman (1991), *Cognitive Training Programme*, Finans Vakýf Publications, Istanbul.

Kagitcibasi, C., D. Sunar and S. Bekman (2001), "Long-term Effects of Early Intervention: Turkish Low-income Mothers and Children", *Applied Developmental Psychology*, Vol. 22, pp. 333-361.

Kellaghan, T. and B.J. Greaney (1993), "The Educational Development of Students Following Participation in a Pre-school Programme in a Disadvantaged Area in Ireland", Studies and Evaluation Paper No. 12, Bernard van Leer Foundation, The Hague.

Koegel, T. (2002), "Did the Association between Fertility and Female Employment in OECD Countries Really Change its Sign?", Working Paper No. 2001-034, Max Planck Institute for Demographic Research, Rostock, Germany (available at *www.demogr.mpg.de*).

Leseman, P. (2002), *Early Childhood Education and Care for Children from Low-Income or Minority Backgrounds*, OECD, Paris.

Lindert, P.H. and J.G. Williamson (2001), "Does Globalization Make the World more Unequal?", paper presented at the NBER Globalisation in Historical Perspective Conference, Santa Barbara, California, May 3-6.

Love J.M. *et al.* (2005), "The Effectiveness of Early *Head Start* for 3-Year-Old Children and Their Parents: Lessons for Policy and Programs", *Developmental Psychology*, Vol. 41(6), pp. 885-901.

Lynch, R. (2004), "Exceptional Returns. Economic, Fiscal, and Social Benefits of Investment in early Childhood Development", Economic Policy Institute, Washington DC.

McBride, B.A. and T.R. Rane (1997), "Father/male Involvement in Early Childhood Programs: Issues and Challenges", *Early Childhood Education Journal*, Vol. 25(1), pp. 11-15.

41

McCain, M.M. and J.M. Mustard (1999), *Reversing the Real Brain Drain: Early Years Study Final Report*, Government of Ontario, Toronto.

McCartney, K. (2003), *Child Care and Behaviour: Findings from the NICHD Study of Child Care and Youth Development*, Harvard Graduate School of Education, Boston.

McKey, R.H., L. Condelli, H. Ganson, B.J. Barrett, C. McConkey and M.C. Plantz (1985), *The Impact of Head Start on Children, Families and Communities*, United States Department of Health and Human Services, Washington DC.

Méda, D. (2001), *Le temps des femmes: pour un nouveau partage des rôles*, Champs/Flammarion, Paris.

Mezulis, A.H., J.S. Hyde and R. Clark (2004), "Father Involvement Moderates the Effect of Maternal Depression during a Child's Infancy and on Behaviour Problems in Kindergarten", *Family Psychology*, Vol. 18(4), pp. 575-588.

Minjuin, A., J. Vandemoortele and E. Delamonica (2002), "Economic Growth, Poverty and Children", *Environment and Urbanization*, Vol. 14(2) pp. 23-43.

Nair, M.K. and S.R. Radhakrishnan (2004), "Early Childhood Development in Deprived Urban Settlements", *Iandian Pediatrics*, Vol. 41(3), pp. 227-237.

National Women's Council of Ireland (2005), *An Accessible Childcare Model*, NWCI, Dublin.

NESS (2005), National Evaluation of Sure Start Impact Study, *Early Impacts of Sure Start Local Programmes on Children and Families*, Birbeck, University of London.

Netherlands Country Note (1999), *www.oecd.org/document/3/0,2340,en_2649_201185_27000067_1_1_ 1_1,00.html*.

NICHD (National Institute of Child Health and Human Development) (1997), *Mother-child Interaction and Cognitive Outcomes Associated with Early Child Care: Results of the NICHD Study*, Society for Research in Child Development meeting symposium, NICHD, Washington DC.

OECD (1999), *Education Policy Analysis*, OECD, Paris.

OECD (2001), *Starting Strong: Early Childhood Education and Care*, OECD, Paris.

OECD (2001-2004), OECD Programme for International Student Assessment (PISA), *www.pisa.oecd.org/ pages/0,2966,en_32252351_32235731_1_1_1_1_1,00.html*.

OECD (2002a), *Educational Policy Analysis*, OECD, Paris.

OECD (2002b), *Employment Outlook*, OECD, Paris.

OECD (2003a), *Babies and Bosses: Reconciling Work and Family Life*, Vol. 2, OECD, Paris.

OECD (2003b), Background Report of France, OECD Web site: *www.oecd.org/edu/earlychildhood*.

OECD (2004a), *Education at a Glance: OECD Indicators*, OECD, Paris.

OECD (2004b), Germany Country Note, OECD, Paris, *www.oecd.org/edu/earlychildhood*.

OECD (2004c), Mexico Country Note, OECD, Paris.

OECD (2004d), *OECD in Figures*, OECD, Paris.

OECD (2005a), *OECD in Figures. Statistics on the Member Countries*, OECD Observer 2004/Supplement 1, OECD, Paris.

OECD (2005b), *OECD Factbook*, OECD, Paris.

OECD (2005c), *Employment Outlook*, OECD, Paris.

OECD (2005d), *Society at a Glance*, OECD, Paris.

Osborn, A.F. and J.E. Milbank (1987), *The Effects of Early Education: A Report from the Child Health and Education Study*, Clarendon Press, Oxford.

Plantenga, J. and M. Siegel (2004), "Position Paper – Childcare in a Changing World", prepared for *Child Care in a Changing World*, Conference sponsored by the Dutch Presidency, Groningen, the Netherlands, 21-23 October, available on *www.childcareinachangingworld.nl*.

Pocock, B. and H. Masterman-Smith (2006), "Work-choices and Women Workers", *Journal of Australian Political Economy*, Vol. 56(12), pp. 126-144.

Randall, V. (2000), *The Politics of Child Daycare in Britain*, Oxford University Press, Oxford.

Schweinhart, L. (2004), "The High/Scope Perry pre-school Study through Age 40: Summary, Conclusions, and Frequently Asked Questions", High/Scope Press, Ypsilanti, Michigan, *www.highscope.org/Research/PerryProject/perrymain.htm*.

Schweinhart, L.J., H.V. Barnes and D.P. Weikart (1993), *Significant Benefits: The High/Scope Perry pre-school Study through Age 27*, High/Scope Press, Ypsilanti, Michigan.

Shonkoff, J.P. and D.A. Phillips(eds) (2000), *From Neurons to Neighbourhoods: The science of Early Childhood Development*, National Academy Press, Washington DC.

Sylva, K. *et al.* (2003), *The Effective Provision of Pre-School Education (EPPE) Project: Findings from the Pre-school Period*, Institute of Education, University of London.

Tanaka, S. (2005), "Parental Leave and Child Health across OECD Countries", *Economic Journal*, Vol. 115, No. 501, pp. F7-F27, February.

Thorpe, K., C. Tayler, R. Bridgstock, S. Grieshaber, P. Skoien, S. Danby and A. Petriwskyj (2004), "Preparing for School", Report of the Queensland Preparing for School Trials 2003/4, Department of Education and the Arts, Queensland Government, Australia.

Tizard, B. (1986), *The Care of Young Children: Implications of Recent Research*, University of London, Institute of Education, London.

Tremblay, R.E., D.S. Nagin, J.R. Seguin, P.D. Zocolillo, M. Boivin, D. Perusse and C. Japl (2004), "Physical Aggression during Early Childhood: Trajectories and Predictors", *Pediatrics*, Vol. 114(1), pp. 40-50.

UNICEF (2005), *A League Table of Child Poverty in Rich Nations*, Innocenti Report Card, Florence.

Walker, J.R. (1995), "The Effect of Public Policies on Recent Swedish Fertility Behaviour", *Journal of Population Economics*, Vol. 8(3), pp. 223-251.

ISBN 92-64-03545-1
Starting Strong II: Early Childhood Education and Care
© OECD 2006

Chapter 2

A Systemic and Integrated Approach to Early Childhood Education and Care (ECEC) Policy

Chapter 2 summarises the main findings of the reviews in regard to the Starting Strong (OECD, 2001) recommendation for a systemic and integrated approach to policy. Country developments in this area are mixed. Policy makers in most OECD countries are seeking to improve the continuity of children's early childhood experiences and make the most efficient use of resources. The advantages are considerable. Adopting a more integrated approach to the field allows government ministries to organise agreed policies, and combine resources for early childhood services. Regulatory, funding and staffing regimes, costs to parents, and opening hours can be made more consistent. Variations in access and quality can be lessened, and links at the services level – across age groups and settings – are more easily created. In integrated systems, a common vision of education and care can be forged, with agreed social and pedagogical objectives. These findings raise, however, several policy challenges: ensuring co-ordinated policy-making at central level; appointing a lead ministry; the co-ordination of central and decentralised levels; the adoption of a collaborative and participatory approach to reform; and forging links across services, professionals, and parents at local level.

For historical reasons, policies for the "care" and "education" of young children have developed separately, with different understandings of children and fractured systems of governance. Responsibility for services may be divided among several ministries, based more on traditional divisions of government than on the actual needs of families and young children. In the United States, for example, 69 federal programmes provided or supported education and care for children under 5 years in 1999. Nine different federal agencies and departments administered these programmes, though most were operated by the United States Department of Health and Human Services and the United States Department of Education (United States General Accounting Office, 2000). In Ireland, the picture is similar: in past decades, seven different ministries or agencies have had responsibility for one or other aspect of children's services, although recently, attempts are being made to ensure some co-ordination under the Office of the Minister for Children (Ireland, December 2005). In general, differences of auspices and conceptualisation are translated into a two-tier organisation of services, "child care" for the younger children and "pre-primary education" for the 3- to 6-year-olds. The result can be a lack of coherence for children and families, with a confusing variety of funding streams, operational procedures, regulatory frameworks, staff-training and qualifications.

Child care services, in particular, suffer from this division of auspices. They tend to be less developed in terms of coverage, and in some instances, have become a patchwork of small-scale providers and individual family day carers. Affordability is often an issue, and in many countries, low-income groups are excluded in practice from access to centre-based services. Frequently, staff have low qualifications and remuneration, and may not have employment contracts or insurance. This is particularly true of family day carers, whose only qualification for licensing purposes is often limited to "good character". In contrast, early education services are more available through the school network, and are free to parents. Teachers or pedagogues educated to tertiary level staff services enjoy employment contracts and remuneration roughly equivalent to primary school teachers. However, because of the close connection with primary education, early education services may practice very inappropriate child-staff ratios and be unavailable on a full-day, all-year basis.

Early childhood education and care systems tend to be more fragmented under governments that see early care as a private responsibility for parents, and not a public responsibility. This is often the approach in the liberal market economies (of the countries reviewed: Australia, Canada, Ireland, Korea, the Netherlands, the United Kingdom and the United States). These countries generally acknowledge governmental responsibility for pre-school education from the age of 3 or 4 years (or later, depending on the country), in particular for children from disadvantaged or "at-risk" backgrounds, but less so for children under 3. The younger children are considered to need "child care" rather than early education, and parents may or may not be assisted (depending on income, and/or the need to stimulate the labour market participation of women) to purchase child care in the market place. This policy option lead to far greater fragmentation[1] of an ECEC system than, for example, is experienced in the publicly guided systems of the Nordic countries. It should be noted, however, that different degrees of public involvement exist in the liberal economies, *e.g.* in the United Kingdom, where although the option to encourage private provision and competition has been maintained, the government plans to regulate the private provision as rigorously as the public sector in future years. According to the Department for Education and Skills (DfES, 2004), the same inspectorate, the Office for Standards in Education (OFSTED), will be responsible for standards across the board, a new statutory responsibility will be placed on local authorities to secure adequate, affordable ECEC for all families who need it, and a single qualification and pay structure will be developed for all services.

What did Starting Strong *recommend?*

In order to enhance the integration of early childhood services for 0- to 6-year-olds, *Starting Strong* (OECD, 2001) made the following suggestions:

- To formulate and work with co-ordinated policy frameworks at centralised and decentralised levels.
- To nominate a lead ministry that works in co-operation with other departments and sectors.
- To adopt a collaborative and participatory approach to reform.
- To forge strong links across services, professionals, and parents in each community.

1. Co-ordinated policy frameworks at centralised level

Early childhood policy is a complex field. It is concerned with providing education and care to young children but it is also linked with women's employment and equality of opportunity; child development and child poverty issues; labour market supply; children's health, social welfare and early education. In addition to more programmatic and qualitative issues, ECEC policy makers need to address issues of provision and access, family benefits, parental leaves from work, family-friendly measures, modes of funding, and the status and training of personnel. Countries that aim to create systems that can deliver services to parents and young children in a co-ordinated way feel the need to pull together these various policy strands. A systemic approach entails developing a common policy framework with consistent goals across the system and clearly-defined roles and responsibilities at both central and decentralised levels of governance.

One policy option has been the creation of an inter-departmental and/or inter-governmental co-ordination bodies to generate co-operative policy frameworks. Such bodies are found in Canada, Denmark or the United Kingdom where the government has developed an over-arching strategy for children (including younger children), supported by an administrative unit and a Children's Committee at cabinet level, chaired by the Chancellor of the Exchequer (Minister of Finance). Choi (2003) provides evidence that co-ordinating mechanisms can work well when they are established for a specific purpose, *e.g.* to co-ordinate a particular early childhood task, or to focus on a targeted population.

However, the limitations of co-ordinating bodies and cross-sectoral co-operation can also be seen in countries such as Ireland or Korea, where despite growing understanding of programme objectives for young children, ministerial boundaries remain an issue. In the absence of a lead ministry or agency with a sound knowledge of early childhood policy and a mobilising agenda for young children, government finance departments may treat children's services primarily from a labour market or public expenditure angle (May, 2001). In sum, though the fact of ministries working closely together constitutes real progress, the cultures and aims of different government departments can make it difficult to achieve co-ordinated policies in favour of the development and education of young children. Country experience shows that greater progress is made when a central vision is put at the centre of ECEC policy, and a dedicated ministry nominated to translate this vision into reality. Even then, a lead ministry must be sensitive to past history and embrace the concerns of all sectors, while mobilising their co-operation in particular fields. This requires forging a broad but realistic vision of early childhood services to which all relevant ministries, local authorities and parents can subscribe.

How have countries responded to Starting Strong's call for a more systemic approach?

Alongside the continuation of separate traditional models of care and education, many interesting examples of country progress towards integrating services also exist as outlined in Table 2.1.

Table 2.1. Recent initiatives to achieve a more systemic approach to children's services in selected countries

Australia	In 2004, a draft *National Agenda for Early Childhood* was published by the federal government and is currently being finalised with state and territory governments, to provide an overarching framework for promoting optimal child development. Building a more cohesive early childhood education and care system is recognised in the National Agenda as a key action area, with the inclusion of specific priorities for collaborative action between levels of government for achieving this objective.
Belgium	Although child care and early education services are under different auspices in Belgium, both communities have succeeded in building around the free, statutory school service for young children (from 2.5 years), a cohesive continuum of services for infants and toddlers, covering in Flanders about a third of all children (in the French Community under 20%). Within a context of decentralisation and deregulation, ways are being sought to promote more integrated and effective management of services through regular consultation mechanisms at municipal level.
Finland	In Finland, the ministries (Ministry of Social Affairs and Health, and the Ministry of Education) agency, and the responsible STAKES (The National Research and Development Centre for Welfare and Health) have made strong efforts to involve researchers, municipalities, providers and parents in all aspects of system reform. Leadership, consultation, financial steering, information, and support to providers, parents and staff are characteristic of the approach. A comprehensive database (*http://varttua.stakes.fi/Fl/index.htm*), containing the latest ECEC information on development projects and on studies being currently conducted, has been developed to support ECEC staff across Finland. This portal has also a central role in the implementation of the new curriculum guidelines, again developed after an intensive consultation process involving STAKES, the municipalities, providers, staff and parents.
Norway	Led by the Ministry of Child and Family Affairs, a representative group of researchers, stakeholders in the field and ECEC local participants reported in mid-2004 on revisions needed to the Act of Day Care Institutions and the Framework Plan. A revised curriculum framework enters into force in August, 2006. From that year, all educational services, including the *barnehager* (kindergartens), will have been brought under the auspices of the Ministry of Education and Research.
United Kingdom	The integration of early childhood education and care services under the Sure Start Unit (Department for Education and Skills/Department of Work and Pensions) and the local authorities has been strengthened. Sure Start has the remit to work across government and achieve more integrated services for children and families. To counter the traditional split between child care and early education, plans are underway to generate a new educator profile to cover the whole age group, 1 to 6 years. The Childcare Bill 2005 allows for a single coherent phase of development for all young children, as announced in the ten-year strategy for child care "Choice for parents, the best start for children" (HM Treasury, 2004). The new framework will take an integrated approach to care and education, reflecting the reality of the way child care services operate. A large private sector exists, but the intention is to impose a common inspection process for all regulated services – including schools – that cater for children under 8 years.
United States	In the United States, moves to bring together child care services and early education are also evident at state government level. In May 2004, Georgia created an integrated governmental Department of Early Care and Learning to take in charge more effectively the State's varied early childhood services. Similarly, in April 2005, the State of Massachusetts merged the Department of Education's Office of School Readiness with the Massachusetts' Office of Child Care Services into a consolidated office for early education and care. In 2006, Washington State made a similar move. In addition, several state and local governance structures (*e.g.* governors' cabinets for children, public/private governance boards, inter-agency councils) have emerged to make ECEC policy and oversee implementation (Neuman, 2005).

2. Appointing a lead ministry

Administrative integration, that is, shifting national responsibility for ECEC to one lead ministry, is another means of integrating policy at the national level. Not only the four Nordic countries but also Iceland, New Zealand, Slovenia, Spain and the United Kingdom have integrated their early childhood services under one ministry. It is important in this process that early childhood policy-making should be placed in a ministry that has a strong focus on the development and education of young children. It seems to matter less whether this ministry is education, social welfare, family affairs or gender equality, as each can claim some legitimacy in the early childhood field. Ministries of education seem to have a strong claim as their main focus is children, and many of the subsystems necessary for a quality system – a training authority; an evaluation body; a pedagogical inspection or advisory corps; statistical and monitoring units, etc. – are already in place, staffed by experienced administrators. Countries that have developed systems under a lead ministry at the national level can address the care and education of 0- to 6-year-olds more holistically and coherently. Various analyses, including the OECD reviews, show the advantages that can flow from bringing policy-making under one agency:

- More coherent policy and greater consistency across sectors in terms of regulation, funding and staffing regimes, curriculum and assessment, costs and opening hours, in contrast to high fragmentation of policy and services.

- More effective investment in young children, and higher quality services for them. In a "split" system, younger children are often defined primarily as dependent on parents or simply in need of child care services. As a result, their services have often to make do with insufficient investment, non-accredited child-minding and unqualified staff.

- Enhanced continuity of children's early childhood experiences as variations in access and quality are lessened under one ministry, and links at the services level – across age groups and settings – are more easily created.

- Improved public management of services, leading to better quality and greater access by parents.

How does integration under one ministry occur?

In a study of integration processes in England, Scotland and Sweden, Cohen *et al.* (2004) identify some of the conditions leading to integration of services under one ministry. The authors underline in particular: the cumulative effects of many years of advocacy; political commitment on the part of government to focus on the early childhood field, with leadership being provided by a dedicated minister or government department; no major opposition from other bureaucratic or professional interest groups; and the building of administrative and expert capacity throughout the system.

Building expert capacity under one ministry

Some common patterns of capacity building can be observed in the countries that have integrated early childhood services. These countries have generally:

- *Strengthened ECEC policy units at central level*, through the induction of expert staff trained in the early childhood field. An example is the integration of experienced administrators from the Social Affairs Ministry into the Ministry of Education and National Agency for Education in Sweden in 1996. A critical mass of policy expertise was needed, particularly in the initial phase, to take on the task of creating a systemic approach to early childhood provision, such as common service mapping and needs assessment, common regulatory and funding regimes, and the bringing together of licensing procedures, pre- and in-service training, curriculum development, programme evaluations, and quality assessments. A similar process of consolidation of staff, and integration of ECEC expertise from outside can be seen in the newly integrated early education and care offices in Georgia and Massachusetts in the United States.

● *Devolved management of services to municipal (or county or school district) levels.* A devolution of tasks in the early childhood field is necessary, not only as the concrete acknowledgement of the rights of families and local communities, but also for reasons of practical management. The more numerous providers and fragmented provision patterns in the early childhood field make it difficult for central governments to ensure quality and a rational provision of services in the absence of devolved local management. Issues of democracy, community responsibility for children, parental rights, participation and ownership are also part of this devolution process.

● *Reinforced early childhood expertise in universities, research agencies, associations and unions.* A necessary condition for the development of early childhood systems is to build expert ECEC capacity within the ministry in charge and in the government sponsored agencies. To develop *independent* expertise in universities, research institutes, associations and unions is a linked necessity. This can be difficult to achieve in some countries, *e.g.* in Austria, where pedagogue training takes place at secondary education level, thus preventing most universities from taking an interest in the early childhood field. The situation is a loss for these countries, compared to the involvement of the universities and research agencies in, for example, Australia, Canada, Finland, France, Korea, Norway, Sweden, the United Kingdom and the United States. In these countries, university and agency research currently makes a significant contribution to the volume of policy analysis, data collection and evidence-based research that policy makers have at their disposal.

3. The co-ordination of central and decentralised levels

In education systems, a current tendency in some countries is to bypass local authorities and to give individual schools more autonomy while binding them with regulations, outcome targets and more regular evaluations. For the moment at least, an early childhood system can hardly work satisfactorily in this way given the far greater diversity of providers involved in the early childhood field and the "comprehensive services"[2] character of much early childhood provision. In addition, because parents are legally the first educators of their children, early childhood services must be local in character, combining both the public interest in early education and the wishes of the parents of the children within the service. For this reason, ECEC policy and provision is becoming a shared responsibility in many OECD countries between national governments, local authorities, communities and parents (see Box 2.1). Governments not only devolve the mapping and organisation of services to local authorities, but they also authorise local authorities to regulate, support and evaluate services (*e.g.* in the Federal countries, but also in Belgium, Denmark, Finland, France, Italy, Norway and Sweden). The shift is also motivated by the desire to bring decision-making and delivery closer to the families being served and to adapt services to meet local needs and circumstances.

Box 2.1. **A co-ordinated child development policy at decentralised level in Canada**

Prince Edward Island (PEI), a small maritime province in Canada, has succeeded in establishing a co-ordinated child development policy – the Healthy Child Development Strategy – across five ministries and multiple community stakeholders. The initiative focuses on children from prenatal to the early school years. It integrates the vision, values and goals of the National Children's Agenda and Canada's Early Childhood Development Initiative with the expressed hopes and aspirations of Islanders for their children.

In an open and collaborative process, government and community partners worked together to develop the strategic directions and specific objectives to reach the goals of good health, safety and security, success at learning, and social engagement. PEI's Strategy is grounded in the belief that all Islanders share responsibility for children, and Government's role is to provide leadership in facilitating community action. Guiding principles for the strategy emphasize the need to involve parents, families, business, community, academia and government.

The integrated nature of the Strategy is evident in key focus areas and in the governance structure for implementation. Key areas of action recognise the broad range of influences on child development, including pregnancy, birth and infancy, early childhood education and care, children with exceptional needs, parent support, childhood injury, children's mental health, family literacy, environment, screening and assessment, protecting children, and healthy lifestyles. The Strategy's enabling conditions, *e.g.,* healthy public policy, family income, and community support underline the important influence of social indicators on healthy child development. This type of framework supports the multi-faceted nature of Early Childhood Education and Care, and provides for a rich exchange of ideas and perspectives impacting all aspects of provision of quality programmes.

PEI's Government has established a Children's Secretariat with staff from five different government ministries in order to promote a comprehensive approach to the implementation of this Strategy. The Secretariat represents government as part of the PEI Children's Working Group – a broad inter-sectoral network involving representatives of associations of early childhood educators, community organisations, research, police, federal government, and Acadian and Francophone communities. This "network of networks" ensures that all key areas of action are mutually supportive, and remain focused on the whole child. In addition, Children's Working Group collaborates in preparing an annual Action Plan, which identifies priorities for funding and policy development. Both government and community prepare responses to the Action Plan, resulting in significant partnership based initiatives.

Source: Canada Country Note (OECD, 2004).

A positive consequence of decentralisation has been the integration of early education and care services at local level, leading to a more efficient allocation of resources to children. Less bound by traditional competency boundaries than government departments, many local authorities in Austria, Denmark, Finland, France, Hungary, Germany, Italy, the Netherlands, Norway, Sweden, the United Kingdom, and the United States have brought together children's services and education portfolios to plan more effectively and provide coherence of services for young children and their families. Some local authorities have integrated administration and policy development across age groups and sectors. In Denmark, Italy, Norway, Sweden and the United Kingdom, for example, an increasing number of local authorities have reorganised responsibility for ECEC and schools (and sometimes other children's services) under one administrative department and political committee. Another consequence of local administration has been greater sensitivity to local need. Local authorities can decide, in function of size, occupation and dispersion of populations, the appropriate balance of services to support. Local authorities are also better placed to ensure the involvement of parents, educators, community bodies and other stakeholders in such decisions, creating a more democratic organisation and management of services as well as broad public support for early childhood services. However, as part of the *raison d'être* of these services is to ensure equality of opportunity for children living in circumstances that place them at risk, strong state investment in ECEC services and the national will to conserve social equity and cohesion are also necessary.

Decentralisation can also raise certain challenges. Experience from the OECD reviews suggests that devolution of powers and responsibilities may widen differences of access and quality between States, regions or districts within a country. This has occurred in Sweden (Skolverket, 2004) but the phenomenon is even more evident in federal countries, such as Australia, Canada, Germany and the United States, where unified national policies have been difficult to achieve (OECD Country Notes: United States, 1999; Australia, 2001; Canada and Germany, 2004). In Canada, for example, significant variation exists across the Provinces/Territories on a series of critical variables, such as funding per child, programme standards, teacher certification and school readiness assessment (Doherty *et al.*, 2002). Unless strong equalising mechanisms are in place, decentralised early childhood administrations in poor urban areas can also face difficulties because of low taxation revenues. In such situations, without supplementary funding and management support from the State, families with young children in these neighbourhoods may have access only to low quality services. Country areas are also not exempt from unequal resources, *e.g.* in Canada and Hungary, where decentralisation and well-meaning ethnic policies have led at times to the creation of independent ethnic areas that are too small or too poor to support a high quality health or early childhood service without strong state assistance. Even in situations where funding is available, such as in Australia, a highly dispersed population, separate state auspices (for pre-school education) and aspects of the prevailing market approach to child care can inhibit effective co-ordination.

Such situations raise some key questions: Can a system of decentralised administration guarantee reasonably equal treatment of all children across a country? Is every decentralised administrative structure robust enough to take in charge a range of human services? In small local administrations, is there a critical mass of adequately trained administrators to ensure that national standards are met? In general, central governments have at their disposal powerful steering mechanisms, such as legislation and discretionary funding, to motivate and provide backing to local authorities to deliver agreed outcomes. In some instances, it may also be necessary for central government to assist local administrative divisions so that they can plan, fund and deliver basic services efficiently and effectively (OECD Country Note on Hungary, 2002). An equalising mechanism between rich and poor administrative divisions is also needed to allow all administrations (including those with low taxation bases or with significant population dispersion) to deliver basic services. Consideration can also be given to providing appropriate support to small local authorities to assist them in deciding what services they need and in building up management expertise.

It seems important that in the devolution or federalising process, a role should be retained for the central government ministry in charge. The issue was addressed, for example, during the review of Germany, where the sixteen Länder have full responsibility for early childhood services. This prerogative is jealously guarded, but the advantages of retaining the guiding role and the quality initiatives of the Federal ministry were also acknowledged, even though under the present German constitution the Federal government cannot allocate funds to the *Länder* or municipalities for early childhood or education purposes. By its nature, the early childhood field is subject to local pressures, dispersion and idiosyncratic appreciations of quality. The guidance (and funding) of a central ministry or regional authority can contribute strongly to coherence, to forging common goals, and to promoting empirical, research-based standards across a country. In sum, it seems important to ensure that early childhood services are part of a well-conceptualised national policy, with on the one hand, devolved powers to local authorities and on the other, a national approach to goal setting, regulation, staffing, pedagogy and quality assurance. Clear demarcation of competences, a simplification of funding streams and eligibility criteria, a reduction in the number of special programmes, and the sharing of a common monitoring system are all means of reducing bureaucracy and of lessening confusion among families using services.

4. A collaborative and participatory approach to reform

As shown in Table 2.1 above, many countries show a strong desire for a systemic and participatory approach to the development of their ECEC services. While government should play a large leadership role, regional and local authorities, business representatives, organised civil society, and community groups should be involved in the formulation and implementation of the ECEC policy agenda. This inclusive and participatory approach will help ensure broad public support for ECEC and ensure that multiple perspectives contribute to decision-making. In particular, parents need to be considered as the central partners in policy and programme development in the field. Finland's recent approach to ECEC provides a good example (see Box 2.2).

Counter examples are also found, particularly in federal countries, and in countries in which ministries or different levels of authority fail to co-operate. No doubt, constitutional and other legal texts may provide a right to proceed in this manner, but it seems more reasonable to ensure, through co-operative measures, reasonably equal access and agreed quality for all children and families across a national territory.

5. Links across services, professionals, and parents at local level

Partnerships between different forms of early childhood provision, families and other services for young children (*e.g.,* schools, health, special education) promote coherence for children and parents. Yet, there are challenges to adopting a partnership approach. Service providers can hold different visions of the purposes of early childhood services, as they may come from different training and professional backgrounds, and may prefer to work in isolation from counterparts in other fields. In parallel, different regulatory, funding, workforce and delivery systems may present barriers to integrating services. Thus, while in some countries efforts to co-ordinate early childhood services, professionals and parents of young children are common, in others they are only emerging (*Starting Strong*, OECD, 2001).

Box 2.2. **A participatory approach to ECEC development in Finland**

Although legislation sets out some clear and strong requirements for all parties, the Finnish ECEC system has been strongly decentralised since the early 1990s. A collaborative approach to policy-making in the ECEC field was further strengthened in Finland from the year 2000, based on consultative and participatory mechanisms. The responsible ministry (Ministry of Social Welfare and Health) and the agency STAKES (The National Research and Development Centre for Welfare and Health) have engaged an approach based on consultation, financial steering and information. The system is characterised by trust, dialogue, professional development and effective information flows, and has less need for external inspection or regulation. The approach corresponds to a more contemporary understanding of public management, in which different groups are encouraged to be responsible for quality at their own level.

The government Resolution Concerning National ECEC Policy proposes an action programme for the development of ECEC, including the Project on Quality and Steering in ECEC (2000-2005) aimed at strengthening the local, regional and national systems of steering and assessment. Much support is offered to the municipalities, which, under the regional state offices, are fully responsible for the implementation and steering of services in their own areas. Research on quality continues to expand, with clear cohesive links between several universities, the Ministry and STAKES. A comprehensive database (*http://varttua.stakes.fi*) containing the latest ECEC information on development projects and on studies being currently conducted has been developed to support ECEC staff across Finland. This portal has also a central role in the implementation of the new curriculum guidelines of 2003, again developed after an intensive consultation process involving STAKES, the municipalities, staff and parents. Since 2002, information systems work has been guided by the Social Welfare and Health Care Data and Information Reform Strategy. This strategy is designed to prepare a national social welfare and health care data information system comprising statistics, corporate data and information on regularly repeated studies and separate surveys.

Parents too are given a central role in ensuring the responsiveness of services to child interests and needs. Finland's government Resolution Concerning National ECEC Policy strongly raises the issue of parent involvement. Likewise, parent participation is also an important issue in the curriculum guidelines. National projects such as the Educational Partnership (2003-05) and Early Support (2004-05) seek to respond to parental needs, the former through staff training that enhances capacity to support parents and parenthood, the latter developing the role of parents in early intervention. In day care centres, it is customary to draw up an individual ECEC plan for each child in collaboration with parents. The implementation of the plan is assessed annually. This is a statutory obligation based on the Act on the Status and Rights of Social Welfare Clients (2000).

Source: STAKES, Finland, 2005.

In countries with long-established ECEC traditions (Belgium, Denmark, France, Sweden, etc.), attention to children's transitions has led to the integration of pre-school, school, and out-of-school programmes into a seamless full-day service on the same site. As noted in *Starting Strong* (OECD, 2001):

"*Multi-disciplinary teams of staff have developed new ways of working together to overcome professional boundaries and promote coherence in children's lives. In Denmark, teams of pedagogues and primary teachers plan and organise activities for mixed-aged children from six to nine, bringing together the traditions of both ECEC and school to ease children's transition from one institution to the other. Often the same pedagogues work with children during the school day and in leisure-time activities. This collaborative strategy promotes continuity in children's relationships with adults on a given day and over time, and gives parents more opportunities to communicate with staff."*

For the younger children, co-operation between various types of child care settings is also fruitful. In several countries, groups of family day care providers have been organised into networks, supervised and supported by a local professional centre or specialised agency (Denmark, France, Germany, etc.). A weekly or fortnightly session at the local pedagogical or child care centre brings professional development to family day carers and reduces their isolation in the community. This is an important achievement as so many family day carers withdraw from the occupation owing to lack of support and contact with other professionals (and also because of inadequate work conditions, remuneration and social protection). Linkages across services give family day carers the sense of belonging to a profession, and help to provide service replacements whenever a family day carer is unwell or unavailable for some days.

Co-operation between different services – centre-based services, family day care, school and out-of school – helps to create a continuum of services that is reassuring for parents and can meet the needs of young children. It can also build up a network of dialogue and social relationships that goes beyond the simple provision of services to enhance the participation of parents and other civil society stakeholders. Eventually, co-operation between different services can give birth to a comprehensive services approach that is more sensitive to the full range of children's learning and developmental needs across the day, and to parental need for child care and other opportunities. The new children's centres in England provide an example of an early childhood service, focused on the development and education of young children, but which, at the same time, can provide democratic participation and a range of services, such as employment, job-training, parent groups, and leisure-time activities. As a mechanism of participation and social inclusion, strong linkages between services and communities are of particular importance for immigrant or other socially isolated families and children. Where diversity exists, outreach to parents and communities needs to be maintained, while avoiding a deficit approach – that is, considering children or certain populations to be weak and lacking strengths. An essential aim should be to elaborate appropriate pedagogical approaches for the particular community and its young children, elaborated in consultation with parents.

Notes

1. Defenders of a liberal economy approach to child care prefer to use the word "flexibility" rather than "fragmentation". The issue is discussed in Chapter 5 on public investment in early childhood education and care.

2. A comprehensive services approach to early childhood education and care goes beyond curriculum and activities for children to focus also on wider aspects of development, such as the general health and well-being of children, and on the home and community environments. Typically, a comprehensive services centre works in co-operation with other community services and pays particular attention to parents. The centre will provide when necessary courses and advice on parenting (in particular, how to support child development), employment, job training, and leisure activities.

References

Australia (2004), "Towards the Development of a National Agenda for Early Childhood", Department of Family and Community Services.

Choi, S. (2003), *Cross-sectoral Co-ordination in Early Childhood: Some Lessons to Learn*, Policy Brief No. 9, UNESCO, Paris, France.

Cohen, B, P. Moss, P. Petrie and J. Wallace (2004), *A New Deal for Children? Reforming Education and Care in England, Scotland and Sweden*, Policy Press, England.

Dahlberg, G. and P. Moss (2005), *Ethics and Politics in Early Childhood Education*, Routledge Falmer, London and New York.

Dahlberg, G., P. Moss and A. Pence (1999), *Beyond Quality in Early Childhood Education and Care: Postmodern Perspectives*, Falmer Press, London.

DfES (2004), *Choice for Parents, the Best Start for Children: A Ten Year Strategy for Childcare*, DfES, London.

Doherty, G.F., M. Friendly and B. Forer (2002), "Child Care by Default or Design? An Exploration of Differences Between Non-Profit and For-Profit Canadian Child Care Centres Using the You Bet I Care! Data Sets", Childcare Resource and Research Unit, Centre for Urban and Community Studies, Toronto, Canada, p. 75.

HM Treasury (2004), "Choice for Parents, the Best Start for Children: a Ten Year Strategy for Childcare. Summary of Consultation Responses", *www.hm-treasury.gov.uk*.

Ireland (2000), Background Report of Ireland, Ministry of Education and Science, Dublin.

May, H. (2001), *Politics in the Playground: the World of Early Childhood in New Zealand*, Bridget Williams Books and New Zealand Council for Educational Research, Wellington.

Neuman, M. (2005), "Governance of Early Childhood Education and Care: Recent Developments in OECD Countries", *Early Years*, Vol. 25, No. 2, July, pp. 129-141.

OECD (2001), *Starting Strong: Early Childhood Education and Care*, OECD, Paris.

OECD (2005), *Country Profile: Finland*, OECD, Paris.

Rinaldi, C. (2006), *In dialogue with Reggio Emilia: Listening, Researching and Learning*, Routledge, London and New York.

Skolverket (2004), *pre-school in Transition: A National Evaluation of the Swedish pre-school*, National Agency for Education, Stockholm.

STAKES (2005), Information supplied to the OECD by the STAKES Early Childhood Education and Care Team, Helsinki.

United States General Accounting Office (2000), *Early Education and Care: Overlap Indicates Need to Assess Crosscutting Programs*, No. GAO/HEHS-00-78, Government Printing Office, Washington DC.

ISBN 92-64-03545-1
Starting Strong II: Early Childhood Education and Care
© OECD 2006

Chapter 3

A Strong and Equal Partnership with the Education System

Conscious of the need for continuity in children's education, Starting Strong (OECD, 2001) made a number of recommendations to promote a strong and equal partnership between early childhood education and the primary school. Chapter 3 outlines the progress made by countries in achieving this aim. Support for the view that early education should be seen as a public good is growing, and has received a strong impetus from the research of education economists, including the Nobel prize-winner, James Heckman.

Starting Strong (OECD, 2001) recommended a more unified approach to learning across the two systems. This has generated different policy options. France and the English-speaking world have adopted a "readiness for school" approach, focusing on cognitive development in the early years, and the acquisition of a range of knowledge, skills and dispositions that children should develop as a result of classroom experiences. Contents and pedagogical method in early and primary education have been brought closer together, generally in favour of teacher-centred and academic approaches.

In countries inheriting a social pedagogy tradition (Nordic and Central European countries), the kindergarten is seen as a broad preparation for life and the foundation stage of lifelong learning. The focus is placed on supporting children in their current developmental tasks and interests. The approach to children encompasses care, upbringing and education. Links with the primary school – and free-time services – are maintained through a variety of mechanisms and there is wide acknowledgment that kindergarten pedagogy should influence at least the early years of the primary school.

The chapter deals finally with the issue of transitions for children, and outlines the efforts of countries to ease transitions through building bridges across administrative departments, staff-training, regulations and curricula in both systems.

Historically, programmes for young children and formal education have developed separately, with different systems of governance, funding streams, and training for staff. Primary schooling is the older and stronger institution, and had already been forged into a national system in many countries by the end of the 19th century. Early childhood systems have been slower in their development, as maternal or extended family care was the usual means of rearing young children in OECD countries during most of the 20th century. Today, all OECD countries are attempting to establish early childhood systems for young children. The model adopted in the more mature Nordic systems is to support parental care for the first 10 to 18 months of a child's life, followed then by a stable range of accessible early childhood services.

The co-ordination of early childhood services with education is advanced in most countries, particularly with regard to 3- to 6-year-olds. For these older children, a recognisable subsystem, pre-primary education, is found in most countries, with similar eligibility criteria and system characteristics to those pertaining in the school system (see Table 4.3). For younger children, however, access to a coherent system of early childhood services is more problematic, as provision for infants and toddlers is often characterised by mixed regimes of formal and informal, public and private provision. Compared to early education or to integrated ECEC systems, divergences exist in terms of eligibility, regulation, staffing, aims and programming, even within the same country. Frequently, "care" and "education" operate independently of each other, with insufficient attention to the difficulties faced by children when confronted by different expectations and daily routines.

Conscious of the need to bring the traditions together, Starting Strong (OECD, 2001) proposed a strong and equal partnership between early childhood and the education system. Partnership with the education system would bring together the diverse perspectives and methods of both ECEC and schools, focusing on the strengths of both approaches. It was hoped that co-operation would lead to a more unified approach to learning, smoother transitions for children, and the recognition of early childhood pedagogy as an important part of the education process.

What did Starting Strong recommend?

Starting Strong (OECD, 2001) made a number of recommendations to promote equality of relationship and strong continuity between early childhood provision and the education system:

- Early childhood services should be recognised, like compulsory schooling, as a public good and as an important part of the education process. All children should have a right to access quality ECEC services before starting school.
- A more unified approach to learning should be adopted in both systems, recognising the contribution that the early childhood approach brings to fostering key dispositions and attitudes to learning.

● Attention should be given to transition challenges faced by young children as they enter school, or transit from one type of service to another. There should be a greater focus on building bridges across administrative departments, staff-training, regulations and curricula in both systems.

1. A unified approach to learning

Education systems have recognised for decades that a unified conception of learning in childhood can bring pre-primary education and primary schooling closer together. A wide variety of strategies have been used to link early education to the primary school. In France, for example, a bridging curriculum, focusing on learning areas has been formulated, merging the last year of early education (5 to 6 years) and the first two classes of primary school into a unified cycle. Teachers working in each section are all *professeurs d'école*, and can move freely from one section to another. In addition, the *écoles maternelles* generally share the same building as the primary school. In this close relationship between the two institutions, the question may be asked: Does this constitute "a strong and equal partnership" between ECEC and the formal education system? The response brought to this question is important for the well-being of young children and for an appropriate conceptualisation of early childhood institutions.

OECD countries approach the partnership between early childhood services and the primary school in different ways – all trying to improve co-ordination between the sectors, but starting from different premises. Broadly, one can distinguish two different approaches across countries. France and the English-speaking countries see the question of partnership from the point of view of the school: early education should serve the objectives of public education and provide children with "readiness for school" skills. In contrast, countries inheriting a social pedagogy tradition (the Nordic and Central European countries) see kindergarten as a specific institution turned more to supporting families and the broad developmental needs of young children.

The social pedagogy tradition

A distinctive early childhood approach and pedagogy has been worked out by countries inheriting the social pedagogy tradition (Nordic and Central European countries). A broad concept of *pedagogy* is common to these countries, that is, an approach to children combining care, upbringing and learning, without hierarchy. Rather than "schoolifying" ECEC services, there is a strong belief that early childhood pedagogy should permeate the lower classes of primary school (Martin-Korpi, 2005). This concept and approach is described in the OECD Country Note for Germany (2004) as follows:

> "Originating in 19th century Germany, Sozialpädagogik (social pedagogy) is a theory, practice and profession for working with children (but also often young people and adults). It has become established in many Continental European countries, though varying somewhat in form and role from country to country. The social approach is inherently holistic. The pedagogue sets out to address the whole child, the child with body, mind, emotions, creativity, history and social identity. This is not the child only of emotions – the psycho-therapeutical approach; nor only of the body – the medical or health approach; nor only of the mind – the traditional teaching approach. For the pedagogue, working with the whole child, learning, care and, more generally, upbringing (the elements of the original German concept of pedagogy: Bildung, Erziehung and Betreuung) are closely-related – indeed inseparable activities at the level of daily work. These are not separate fields needing to be joined up, but inter-connected parts of the child's life."[1]

In these countries, kindergarten is seen as a broad preparation for life. Parents are seen as important partners and the early childhood institution is conceived as bridging the public and private spheres, that is, as fully taking into account the rights of parents and the interests of young children. A more holistic approach to learning is practised and greater emphasis is placed on learning to live together and on supporting children in their current developmental tasks and interests. National curriculum frameworks guide the work of the centres and orient, in general terms, the pedagogical work and the content of children's learning. As these curricula are based on previous consultations with the main stakeholders, they are not considered as instruments of normalisation or as curricula in the traditional sense but rather as orientations guiding the life and work of the centres (see Chapter 6). Each centre enjoys much autonomy and is expected to formulate its own curriculum or learning plan guided by the national framework. In turn, pedagogues seek to respect the natural learning strategies of young children, that is, learning through play, interaction, activity, and personal investigation. Co-operative project work is much employed to give children a taste for working together and to build up shared and more complex understandings of chosen themes. The belief is widespread that encouraging the initiatives and meaning-making of children strongly supports cognitive development.

A wide variety of strategies are used to link the early childhood centres to the next stage of learning. In Sweden, in particular, integration of the systems is particularly well advanced, as the Ministry of Education, Research and Culture has responsibility for both early childhood and primary services. A reform of professional education has brought pedagogues and teachers together in shared training modules, but unlike the situation in France or Ireland, early childhood pedagogues must specialise for more than a year in early childhood theory and pedagogy. Continuity is established with the national curriculum for education both through agreement on fundamental values and concepts, and through the identification of general learning areas. The Curriculum for Pre-school (Lpfö, 1998) charges pre-schools to ensure that children:

- Develop their vocabulary and concepts, the ability to play with words, an interest in the written language, and an understanding of symbols as well as their communicative function.

- Develop the ability to discover and use mathematics in meaningful contexts and situations.

- Develop their appreciation of the basic characteristics of the concept of number, measurement and form, as well as the ability to orient themselves in time and space.

- Develop an understanding of their own involvement in the processes of nature and in simple scientific phenomena, such as knowledge of plants and animals.

However, these four aims appear towards the end of the 15 goals set for pre-school, and are prefaced by more personal aims, such as:

- Develop their identity and feel secure in themselves.

- Develop their curiosity and enjoyment at the same time as the ability to play and learn.

In sum, the main objective is that "all children should develop a desire and curiosity for learning, and confidence in their own learning, rather than achieving a pre-specified level of knowledge and proficiency" (Martin-Korpi, 2005).

The practical integration of kindergarten and primary school in Denmark, Finland and Sweden is ensured through the "pre-school class" for children. This class for children 6 to

7 years old serves as a bridge into compulsory primary schooling (which begins at 7 years), and generally takes place within the school. The pedagogy employed in these classes remains active and experiential, and learning is generated not only by adults but through peer relationships, group projects and an active pedagogy. A critique made of the Nordic approach in the past was that pedagogues did not always sufficiently engage themselves in children's play; were not attentive enough to key learning experiences matching the current development of the child; and, whereas the social concept was strong, they did not always work from an adequate cognitive development concept (Weikart, 1992). While this critique may have been true at a certain moment, the reality is that these systems are continually reforming. Classes are conducted in most countries by well-trained educators who plan complex learning projects with children, often inspired by Reggio Emilia project work. In addition, pre-schools and schools, particularly in Sweden, are forging together agreed values and pedagogical approaches, although according to the 2004 evaluation of pre-schools (Skolverket, 2004), pre-school teachers document excessively the children's work and insufficiently their own.

The pre-primary approach to early education

Among the OECD countries reviewed, the pre-primary approach to education is found in many countries, *e.g.* Australia, Canada, France, Ireland, the Netherlands, the United Kingdom and the United States. These countries tend to introduce the contents and methods of primary schooling into early education, or as in the case of the United Kingdom, begin school at the age of 5 years. The current standards-based education model in the United States tends to further reinforce school-like learning approaches and contents across pre-kindergarten, kindergarten and elementary school. Programme standards are formulated, *e.g.* in Head Start or the Arkansas Better Chance Programme (see Box 6.1 in Chapter 6), and recently, most States have introduced child outcome standards for kindergarten and pre-kindergarten. These standards announce a range of knowledge, skills and dispositions that children are expected to develop as a result of classroom experiences, and focus increasingly on knowledge and skills useful for school, *viz.,* literacy, math and scientific thinking. There is a growing consensus among American educators and public policy makers that programme standards are needed in early education, and should include child outcomes – what children should know and be able to do after participating in pre-school programmes.

Common teacher education

In addition to a downward transfer of subject fields, programme standards and pedagogical approaches from the primary school towards kindergarten, common teacher education is also practised in several pre-primary systems. Several countries, for example, Australia, Canada, France, Ireland, and the Netherlands, train their teachers to take up service in either pre-primary or primary school classes. This leads to a unity of goals and methodologies for the two sections, and reinforces pedagogical continuity. For example, in France, common training for teachers (*professeurs des écoles*) exercising in the *école maternelle* and primary schools was adopted in 1993, and takes place at teacher training university institutes, or *Instituts Universitaires de Formation des Maîtres* (IUFM). The government-approved training curricula normally includes: studies in education, philosophy, history of education, sociology, psychology; specialist courses; subject study;[2] preparation for administrative tasks; and optional subjects. (Oberhuemer and Ulich, 1997).

The early childhood component is either given in separate modules, or, more typically, integrated with coursework on older children. Upon successful completion of the initial training, graduates are qualified to teach children aged 2 to 11 years. Concerns are expressed, however, about this option, as primary school methodologies tend to predominate in pre-service training and in the actual practice of the pre-school classes.[3] In contrast, the integrated training courses piloted by Sweden in recent years guarantee a better understanding of the specific needs and learning patterns of the younger children. A common theoretical core is shared by the different teacher profiles (pre-school, primary and leisure-time teachers), followed by an option to take intensive training and *practica* in one of the three branches: pre-school pedagogy, primary teaching or free-time activities (Children in Europe, 2003).

2. Is a "schoolification" of early childhood education and care taking place?

"Schoolification" has connotations of taking over early childhood institutions in a colonising manner. This is not the intention of education ministries, administrators or teachers, who in many countries are strong advocates of learner centred education and active learning methods. In addition, the word "school" has maintained both prestige and diversity in many countries and regions, for example in Reggio Emilia, where the municipal *scuolae* cover education from 0 to 6 years, as well as for older ages. Likewise in Finland, the pre-school class run by the Ministry of Education for children 6 to 7 years old, is characterised by "concrete experimentation, children's own investigation, playful activities, imagination, interaction, drama, active participation, information acquisition, problem solving, and reflection" (Sinko, 2006). In fact, the whole Finnish primary school is marked by a socio-constructivist learning conception in which the active role of children is considered essential, and in which there is no grading or ranking of children.

In contrast, early education was absorbed early on in other countries by a knowledge-transfer, primary education model, and was conceived chiefly as a "junior school". In some countries still, there is no specific unit in education ministries to look after the thousands of children and teachers belonging to the early childhood sector; traditionally, the primary education division has been responsible for the "junior school" and has administered it on primary school lines. In some countries, the school obligation has been brought downwards to enrol 5- and 4-year-olds, or at least, to include them in a common cycle with the primary school. In other countries, young children at the age of 3 or 4 years attend class groups ranging in size from 20 to 30 children, cared for by one teacher without a child assistant. Teachers are trained predominantly in primary education methods and have little or no certification in early childhood pedagogy. Classes are organised – as in primary school – according to year of age, with young children spending much of their time indoors, doing their letters and numbers in preparation for school. While play methodologies are now acknowledged, they are often confined to table-top games, with little of the outdoor discovery play and wide choice of activities that are features of the Nordic pre-school. Teacher instruction is considered essential (see the ISCED Level 0 definition),[4] with a pronounced downward dynamic towards the group class. Less attention is given to horizontal dynamics that encourage peer exchange and children's own discovery and meaning-making. The natural learning strategies of young children – play, exploration of the outdoors and freedom of movement, relations and discussion with other children within the classroom – are not always encouraged. In sum, the historical legacy of the primary school has left in place structures and practices that are critiqued today as being often unsuitable for young children.[5]

To some extent, this "schoolifying" of the early childhood years is reinforced by the current focus on "readiness for school" and learning standards in the United States. Most States have adopted learning standards for pre-kindergarten and kindergarten children, focused often on language/literacy and cognition/general knowledge areas. Reputable bodies such as the National Association for the Education of Young Children (NAEYC), the National Association of Early Childhood Specialists in State Departments of Education (NAECS/SDE) and the National Institute of Early Education Research (NIEER) have issued statements about readiness, appealing in general for a broad interpretation of standards in accordance with the National Education Goals Panel (NEGP) goals of 1997. However, current American policy values a "readiness for school" approach, which the Administration sees as ensuring that all young children acquire basic knowledge and skills, and that continuity is provided between elementary school, kindergartens and pre-kindergarten.

The "readiness for school" model is a powerful one, as it is carried by American (English-language) research to all countries. It holds out the promise to education ministries of children entering primary school already prepared to read and write, and being able to conform to normal classroom procedures. In addition, recent research from the United Kingdom and the United States supports a structured approach to curriculum and learning in pre-school. The American Eager to Learn committee proposes a mixture of self-directed learning and teacher-directed instruction in early education (Bowman *et al.*, 2001). Similarly, the recent Effective Provision of Pre-School Education (EPPE) study in the United Kingdom (EPPE, 2003; Siraj-Blatchford *et al.*, 2003) and the Preparing for School study in Australia (Thorpe *et al.*, 2004) also find that effective pedagogy includes interaction traditionally associated with the term "teaching", the provision of instructive learning environments and "sustained shared thinking" to extend children's learning. A Dutch meta-analysis of different programming types also concludes that the most enduring cognitive results are achieved when both cognitive and socio-emotional outcomes are pursued simultaneously through structured programming (Leseman, 2002). These findings are not incompatible with the pedagogical approach adopted by the social pedagogy tradition, which makes, however, a more determined effort to increase the agency of children and to pursue more holistic aims.

Conclusions to this discussion

Rather than making too sharp a contrast between the two approaches, it may be more accurate to see them as different curricular emphases, one merging into the other as part of the same continuum:

Broad developmental goals   *Focused cognitive goals*

At one end of the continuum, the focus is on broad developmental goals, *e.g.* physical and motor development; socio-emotional development; personal and social skills; artistic and cultural development; and authentic (through lived situations) approaches to literacy, number and science thinking. If one can judge from the Nordic example, the approach seems to give excellent results in terms of readiness for school, and of acquiring the general knowledge that helps children make sense of their experience, including reading and writing. At the other end of the continuum, the emphasis tends to be placed on more focused skills and school-like learning areas, *e.g.* mathematical development, language and literacy skills, with children's life in the centre and the range of experiences offered to them playing a more secondary role. Where the focus falls seems to depend on the tradition of early education in the country, on the age of the child, on current curricular theories and (perhaps above all) on the structural standards in force, *e.g.* the child-staff ratios in practice, the materials and resources available and the training of the educators.[6]

Signs are emerging that better knowledge of young children and their developmental needs are growing in many countries, *e.g.* the influential Experiential Education movement in the Flemish Community in Belgium, with its emphasis on the well-being, involvement and "connectedness" of young children, has changed the focus in many pre-school from programme contents to children. Again, the English curriculum for children 0-3 years, *Birth to Three Matters* (DfES, 2005), stresses four foundation areas that make a break from a former prescriptive approach toward teachers and the division between "child care" and "early education":[7]

- A *strong child* (identity building, being acknowledged and affirmed; developing self-assurance; a sense of belonging).
- A *skilful communicator* (being together, finding a voice, listening and responding, making meaning).
- A *competent learner* (making connections, being imaginative, being creative, representing).
- A *healthy child* (emotional well-being, growing and developing, keeping safe, healthy choices).

The influence of Reggio Emilia, which now has networks in 13 countries, is also growing, particularly in milieus that are open to experimentation, research and reflection on democratic practice in education. The Reggio pre-schools are strongly influenced by their social and historical context (the aftermath of fascism in Italy) and are concerned "to maintain a vision of children who can think and act for themselves" (Dahlberg *et al.*, 1999). Reggio opposes, in the name of young children and their freedom, dominant educational discourses, such as seeing ECEC services as places to produce pre-defined outcomes that have not been discussed with staff and parents or that ignore the interests, experience and choices of young children. Its adoption of a "pedagogy of listening" respects the efforts of children to make meaning of their experience, and contests an increasingly dominant notion of education as transmission and reproduction, or as preparation for school (Rinaldi, 2006).

3. Facilitating transitions for children

Transitions for young children are critical occasions: they can be a stimulus to growth and development, but if too abrupt and handled without care, they carry – particularly for young children – the risk of regression and failure. Some children, for example, may transit on a daily basis between different types of services. Such transitions are often linked to the issue of affordability or to the absence of appropriate full-day services or to the operation of "slot" systems, where parents who work part-time are encouraged to drop off their child at a child-minding service for a few hours daily or weekly. A full-time place may then be occupied by several children on a daily basis, making it difficult for staff to follow the progress of each child, and for the child to make relationships with other children. The situation gives rise for concern as socio-emotional development in young children requires warm and stable relationships with nurturing adults and other children (AAP/APHA, 2002). The risks are even greater in systems in which staff are inexperienced and high turnover is a feature. Within the framework of this chapter (dealing with the relationship between early childhood services and schools), the transition of children from pre-school to school is the central focus, but the relationship between "child care" and "early education" was also a concern of several countries in the review, particularly those with split early years systems. Although the following discussion emphasises governance and centre solutions to transition challenges, it is understood that the main anchor for a child in transitions of whatever type is to have supportive parents (see Chapter 6). The continuity of children's experience across environments is greatly enhanced when parents and staff-members exchange regularly and adopt consistent approaches to socialisation; daily routines, child development and learning. Again, when parents provide information to professional staff concerning their children's development, more accurate assessments of children's strengths and needs can be made, and parent-teacher relationships based on mutual trust and respect are enhanced (Reveco et al., 2004).

From child care to early education programmes: an issue for countries with split systems

In principle, the issue of disturbing transitions from child care to early education does not arise in countries with integrated administration of early childhood services, where a common curriculum across the age range 1-6 years is generally employed, e.g. as in Finland, Norway and Sweden. As discussed in Chapter 2, integration of administration often leads to a unified, single-curriculum approach and the creation of a common educator corps to span the age group, which reduces the risk of rupture for children during the early years. In Denmark, however, it is customary for children under the age of 3 years to attend family day care, and then transit toward centre-based care, conducted by pedagogues, as they become older. The potential for transition difficulties is diminished, however, by the close training links established between the local early childhood centre and the municipal family day carers, who will often attend weekly or monthly training sessions, with their children in their care, at the early childhood centre.

The possibility of transition difficulties is greater in many other countries in the review. As outlined in the previous chapter, fundamental differences in goals and means can characterise the "child care" and "early education" sectors in countries operating split or two-tiered early childhood systems. The result can be a lack of coherence for children and families, with a confusing variation in objectives, funding streams, operational procedures, regulatory frameworks, staff-training and qualifications. Initiatives to provide continuity when children move from the childcare sector into early education seem to be few, unless the ECEC sector has been integrated or a common pedagogical approach is used in both sectors. In addition, many child care services are private, and may use a broad range of models and approaches to young children in their programmes quite unlike the approach used in the public early education domain. In this situation, it would seem important to train public early education personnel in the use of open pedagogical frameworks into which the previous experiences of young children can fit. It would also be helpful for children if public pre-school staff had some exposure to the pedagogical approaches most used in the child care and private sector, such as, Froebel, Montessori, Steiner, High/Scope, Reggio Emilia, Experiential Education and other recognised approaches.

Examples of co-operation to meet the challenges posed by transitions from crèche to kindergarten were noted in several of the reviews. Co-operation in Flanders between the Ministry of Education and the child care agency, *Kind en Gezin*, has generated over the past decade a seamless network of daylong services that young children can access from the earliest age. A fundamental aim is to ease transitions for children and families between different services. In Ghent, for example, the municipality promotes close collaboration between crèches and the local infant schools. In this initiative, care staff can move from the crèche to the infant school, a mechanism that is expected to increase the integration of programmes and services. A common pedagogical approach – Experiential Education – in which the well-being and involvement of children are fundamental aims – is frequently used in both sectors.

Many US states also make strong efforts to integrate early education standards into child care settings. Twenty-nine states now fund pre-kindergarten programmes both in schools and community-based child care settings (Schumacher *et al.*, 2005). These states or their school districts contract the child care settings to deliver pre-kindergarten programmes according to agreed standards, such as: teacher-child ratio; group size, teacher qualifications, curriculum and other service requirements. Such agreements, if properly funded, help to break down traditional barriers between early education and childcare, and strengthen the quality of community-based childcare by introducing higher programme standards, supported by additional resources, technical assistance and monitoring.

The transition from kindergarten to school

The transition from kindergarten to school is generally a stimulating experience for young children but can present a challenge to some children, particularly in countries where the routines and expectations of kindergarten and school differ widely. In school, for example, children may not be encouraged to move freely about and activities are generally chosen and directed by the teacher. The daily routine is programmed, frequently with all children involved in the same activity at the same time.[8] According to a survey by Elkind (2003), teachers expect social skills rather than cognitive abilities from children coming into school: the ability to listen and follow instructions given by an adult; the ability to start a task and bring it to completion without help; the ability to work co-operatively with other children, take turns, stand in line, and so on.[9]

If the school atmosphere and its routines seem constraining to children coming from kindergarten, they will be more so for children entering directly from home. These children are unlikely to have experienced group routines or even to have had sustained social contact with other children.[10] To prevent this situation, all countries in the review provide at least one year of pre-school or kindergarten preparation to children before they enter school. Mexico (see Box 3.1) and Hungary have made particular efforts in this respect: the former through legislating for compulsory early education from 3 years, and the latter through making the senior year of kindergarten compulsory. The Hungarian measure was introduced to ensure that all children would attend kindergarten, at least for one year before formal schooling. The measure has been reinforced by regulations providing priority places and free meals for disadvantaged (including large families and Roma[11]) children in kindergartens.

Box 3.1. **Education and care policies in Nuevo Leon, Mexico**

The OECD team's visit to Nuevo Leon coincided, not only with the new compulsory early education law but also with elections and the entry of a new State Secretary for Education. The Secretary explained the basic policy lines that the government proposed to follow. Initial education would be a priority for the new government, to be achieved in three ways:

- Attention to 0- to 6-year-olds of age will be treated as a continuum and from an educational perspective. This marks a profound change in current thinking, particularly for 0- to 3-year-olds.

- The main form of educational attention will be in centres, both public and private.

- The education and qualification of personal will be the key element driving the changes that are envisioned by the government.

The new government is aware that in order to develop these priorities it will have to study in depth the existing situation. Based on this knowledge, it will elaborate a financial proposal to expand the present educational offer and to improve the current quality of services.

During the visit, the team had the opportunity to explore further the context in which the major transformations proposed by our hosts would take place:

- In Nuevo Leon, changes in the family structure and the ever more general presence of mothers as well as fathers in the labour force, means that families need a long school day in order to meet both work and family responsibilities. This emerging reality contrasts with the reality of the present offer, which, in general provides just one morning or evening session to the children. To expand this offer will require audacious planning and an important budgetary pledge.

- In the future, school offers for 0- to 6-year-olds will be developed and administered by private and social organisations as well as by government. This open policy requires that the new government should establish criteria to guarantee educational quality. In addition, a balance will need to be found between quality and potentially large enrolments (often well in excess of 30 children per teacher), as well as between coherence and diversity.

- In Nuevo Leon, the process of changing from a closed to a professional system will certainly confront the weight of tradition. Finding an acceptable equilibrium between traditional hygienist views of early education and the freedom of enquiry needed by young children; between the traditional rote-learning approach of older teachers to a more active, child-centred dynamic will be a concern In sum, the challenge is to contribute to a change of mentality among the professionals. This is perhaps the most important and most difficult goal to achieve.

Upstream policy initiatives

Continuities between kindergarten and school can be strengthened both through the upstream organisation of systems and through the pedagogical choices made by the kindergartens and schools themselves. In many countries early education services and schools work under the same ministry or management, a situation that facilitates co-ordination between the two sectors. In Australia, France, Ireland, Portugal (in the *Escolas Básicas Integradas* or Integrated Basic Schools) and the Netherlands, the transition between the pre-primary classes and primary school is eased by the fact that institutions often share the same building. Teachers and children from each section meet regularly, and there is little difficulty for a pre-primary class to visit their future classroom in the primary school. In addition, in France, the Ministry of Education has elaborated a common basic learning cycle (*cycle des apprentissages fondamentaux*), that begins in the last year of the *maternelle* and continues into the first two years of primary school. In Belgium also, the ministries have elaborated *Developmental Objectives* that are considered attainable by children in both pre-school and primary classes. In other countries, without a pre-primary section within primary education, it may be necessary to introduce a regulation imposing co-operation between the two sectors as traditionally, they have tended to work apart, and the access of ECEC personnel to the school has not been ideal in many school districts.

Continuities between kindergarten and school: centre-based initiatives

Some other initiatives seen in centres visited by OECD teams include:

- *Preparing children in advance for change*: Positively discussing the change with children, and letting them know that the transition is a sign of their progress and maturation. Preparation can involve discussions with the new teacher, and visits to the new classroom.

- *Briefing the primary school*: In so far as deontology and regulations allow, it can be helpful if child records and work portfolios from kindergarten can be consulted by the primary teacher, and lessons shared as to how to support children and their families effectively.

- *Organising common professional development courses*: Courses including early childhood and primary staff, and participation by primary school principals, can help to focus on transition issues.

- *Clarification of the expectations of parents, pre-school, and school teachers about transition* (and about the first year in primary school): Schools in many countries (France, Germany, Ireland, etc.) organise end of year meetings to discuss the transition from pre-school to primary school. Many parents need guidance about smoothing children's transition and on how to support their child's first attempts at formal reading and writing. These meetings can lay the ground for co-operative work between the adults involved during the latter part of the school year.

- *Preparing the school for young children*: Primary schools are expected to provide a supportive setting for children entering school for the first time, and have staff who are committed to the success of each child. It was not always possible for OECD review teams to visit primary school classrooms, but in Canada, Denmark, Finland, Norway, Sweden and the United States, teams noted that first grade classrooms frequently had furniture and materials familiar to kindergarten children and used an adapted pedagogy and curriculum.

Continuity in subject fields and pedagogical methods

Another method of providing continuity of learning experience for young children, employed extensively in pre-primary education, is to focus, particularly in the last year of kindergarten, on specific learning areas that are then carried over into primary school. As mentioned above, almost all countries have published curricula or structured learning areas for young children from the ages of 4 to 6 years (EUROSTAT, 2000). The preferred domains of knowledge proposed are: nature and the environment; emergent literacy and numeracy; general knowledge; scientific concepts and reasoning. The learning areas that receive most focus in curricula – particularly in countries where child assessments are used shortly after entry into primary school – are emergent literacy and numeracy.

In Denmark, Finland and Sweden, the authorities aim also at continuity in pedagogical method. They have put into place a special preparatory year, or pre-school class, for 6- to 7-year-old children in the year before they enter compulsory school. This class prolongs the learning approaches of the kindergarten into the first years of the primary school. In Denmark, the pre-school class, which takes place in the local primary school, is led by a pedagogue from the originating kindergarten centre. He or she works alongside the primary teacher who is responsible for the class in the coming year. This bridging period is followed up by a curriculum for first and second grades of primary school that is designed to incorporate active learning and child initiative, as found in the pre-school learning environment.

In schools in Flanders, continuity is ensured through a common approach to children, guided by the Experiential Education programme, which is used increasingly in child care settings, the kindergarten school, the primary school and other educational settings. The aim of this approach is to start from the perspective of the children, ensuring their well-being and involvement at all stages in their school career. Other countries, such as the United Kingdom and the United States, ensure continuity through focusing on early literacy, math and science in early education as in primary school, and use methods associated with the term "teaching", *e.g.* adult-initiated activity, clearly stated learning objectives, group work, instruction, and enriched learning environments. Both the British EPPE study (Siraj-Blatchford *et al.,* 2003) and the United States *Eager to Learn* committee (Bowman *et al.,* 2001) favour a mixture of self-directed learning and teacher-directed instruction in early education.

Whatever the method used to ensure continuity in programmes, it is well to give attention to the meaning of "continuity" for a child. According to work by the National Center for Early Development and Learning (NCEDL, 2002) and Dockett and Perry (2001), continuity for a child means primarily continuity of relationships: the possibility for a child to move upward with his or her friends; to have a bridging period with a kindergarten teacher in familiar surroundings, and continued support from his or her family.

Notes

1. The *rapporteur* for the German review was Professor Peter Moss, Thomas Coram Research Institute, Institute of Education, Universities of London.

2. Generally, French, mathematics, science and technology, geography, sport, art and music.

3. There is also the issue of child-staff ratios in these countries, as high ratios hinder teachers wishing to use more child-centred methodologies.

4. International Standard Classification of Education (ISCED) Level 0 programmes are defined as centre or school-based programmes that are designed to meet the educational and developmental needs of children at least 3 years of age, and that have staff that are adequately trained (*i.e.* qualified) to provide an educational programme for the children. Programmes devoted to early childhood care or play are not included in this definition. When these programmes are considered to be "pre-primary education", they are further defined as the initial stage of organised instruction. As the "instructional" or "educational" properties of programmes are difficult to identify, different proxy measures are utilised by countries to determine whether a programme should be classified at this level.

5. Tobin *et al.* (1987, 1989) argue, however, that there can be no universal quality or programme standards in early childhood education. These anthropologists affirm that many of criteria of "good" programming are ethnocentric, and often reflect specific cultural beliefs about children and education underlying American research.

6. Structural standards are important: when ratios exceed 20 children per one adult in small classrooms, and a prescriptive curriculum is to be "delivered", it can be difficult for educators to practise an inter-relational, play-based curriculum in which young children are free to pursue their own interests and learning agendas (see Weikart et al., 2003).

7. In the case of England, this wider view of ECEC services rejoins a much older (pre-1980s) tradition of the nursery school that emphasised the individual child's interests, free play, firsthand experience and integrated learning. The *Birth to Three Matters* curriculum seemed to return to that tradition. The new draft *Early Years Foundation Stage* DfES (2006) curriculum for children 0-6 years, which replaces *Birth to Three Matters* still retains a unified approach to care and education, but focuses on teachers rather than on children and is consequently, far more prescriptive.

8. Early years classrooms have changed much in the last decade, but in some of the pre-primary education countries, a traditional ordering of space and of children's movements is still in evidence. In the majority of these countries, according to the IEA Pre-Primary Project (High/Scope) (Weikart et al., 2003) teacher initiated activities and whole class instruction still greatly predominate.

9. Teachers also assume that children will be physically and emotionally mature according to their age, and if coming from kindergarten, will have acquired certain language and cognitive skills (Murphey and Burns, 2002).

10. The study of over 1 800 young children in Australia (Thorpe et al., 2004) found that moving from home directly into school was a predictor of poor performance on early measures of social, cognitive and language skills.

11. The Roma population is a distinctive ethnic group, spread across many European countries. In the various European languages, they are often referred to as Gypsies. For centuries across Europe, Roma have been persecuted and discriminated against on racial grounds. Current laws in Hungary and other countries now protect and promote Roma children, but their access to and participation in mainstream education poses many challenges.

References

AAP/APHA (2002), (American Academy of Pediatrics/American Public Health Association and the National Resource Center for Health and Safety in Child Care), *National Health and Safety Performance Standards: Guidelines for Out-of-Home Child Care*.

Barnett, W.S., J.T. Hustedt, K.B. Robin and K.L. Schulman (2004), *The State of pre-school: 2004 State pre-school Yearbook* (http://nieer.org/yearbook/).

Bowman, B.T., M.S. Donovan and M.S. Burns (eds.) (2001), *Eager to Learn: Educating our Pre-schoolers – Committee on Early Childhood Pedagogy*, National Research Council Commission on Behavioral and Social Sciences and Education, National Academy Press, Washington DC.

Children in Europe (2003), *Early Years Services: Understanding and Diversifying the Workforce*, Issue 5.

Cleveland, G. and M. Krashinsky (2003), *Financing ECEC Services in OECD Countries*, OECD, Paris.

DfES (2005), *Birth to Three Matters*, London, Department for Education and Skills, Sure Start Unit.

DfES (2006), *Early Years Foundation Stage Curriculum 0-6 Years (draft)*, London, Department for Education and Skills, Sure Start Unit.

Dockett, S. and B. Perry (eds.) (2001), *Beginning School Together: Sharing Strengths*, Australian Early Childhood Association.

Education Week (2005), *Quality Counts, 2006*, 10th Edition, Bethesda, MD.

Elkind D. (2003), "The First Grade Challenge: Transition Stress", November 2003 *Exchange Magazine*, www.childcareexchange.com.

EPPE (1997-2007), *The Effective Provision of Pre-School Education (EPPE) Project. A Longitudinal Study*, http://k1.ioe.ac.uk/schools/ecpe/eppe/index.htm.

EUROSTAT (2000), Key Data on Education in Europe, 1999-2000, European Commission, Luxembourg.

International Social Survey Programme (1994 and 2002), *Family and Gender Roles II and III*, Zentralarchiv für Empirische Sozialforschung, University of Cologne.

Laevers, F. (2003), *Experiential Education: Making Care and Education More Effective through Well-being and Involvement*, Leuven, Belgium.

Leseman, P. (2002), *Early Childhood Education and Care for Children from Low-income or Minority Backgrounds*, OECD, Paris.

Lpfö (1998), *Laroplan for forskolan*, Utbildningsdepartementet, Stockholm, Sweden.

Martin-Korpi, B. (2005), "The Foundation for Lifelong Learning", in Children in Europe, Issue 9, September, Edinburgh.

Murphey, D.A. and C.E. Burns (2002), "Development of a Comprehensive Community Assessment of School Readiness", *Early Childhood Research and Practice*, Vol. 4(2), p. 22, *http://ecrp.uiuc.edu/v4n2/murphey.html*.

National Center for Early Development and Learning (NCEDL) (2002), *Transition to Kindergarten*, NCEDL, FPG Child Development Institute, Chapel Hill, NC.

NICHD (1997), "The Effects of Infant Child Care on Infant-mother Attachment Security, Results of NICHD Study of Early Child Care", *Child Development*, Vol. 68(5), pp. 860-879.

Oberheumer, P. and M. Ulich (1997), *Working with Young Children in Europe: Provision and Staff Training*, Paul Chapman Publishing, London.

OECD (2001), *Starting Strong: Early Childhood Education and Care*, OECD, Paris.

OECD (2003), *Babies and Bosses: Reconciling Work and Family Life*, Vol. 2, OECD, Paris.

OECD (2004), "Starting Strong: Curricula and Pedagogies in Early Childhood Education and Care – Five Curriculum Outlines", OECD, Paris.

Petriwskyj, A, K. Thorpe and C. Tayler (2005), "Trends in the Construction of Transition to School in Three Western Regions, 1990-2004", *International Journal of Early Years Education*, Vol. 13(1), pp. 55-69.

Rinaldi, C. (2006), *In dialogue with Reggio Emilia: Listening, Researching and Learning*, Routledge, London and New York.

Schumacher, R., D. Ewen, K. Hart and J. Lombardi (2005), "All Together Now: State Experiences in Using Community-based Child Care to Provide Pre-kindergarten", Centre for Law and Social Policy (CLASP) Policy Brief No.5, May, *www.clasp.org/publications/cc_brief5.pdf*.

Sinko, P. (2006), "pre-school in Finland", PowerPoint presentation, Morelia, March.

Siraj-Blatchford, I., K. Sylva, B. Taggart, P. Sammons and E. Melhuish (2003), "The EPPE Case Studies", Technical Paper 10, University of London/Department for Education and Employment, Institute of Education, London.

Skolverket (2004), *pre-school in Transition: A National Evaluation of the Swedish pre-school*, National Agency for Education, Stockholm.

Thorpe, K., C. Tayler, R. Bridgstock, S. Grieshaber, P. Skoien, S. Danby and A. Petriwskyj (2004), "Preparing for School", Report of the Queensland Preparing for School Trials 2003/4, Department of Education and the Arts, Queensland Government, Australia.

Weikart, D. (1992), "Appropriate Developmental Early Childhood Education", *Educare in Europe*, UNESCO, Paris.

Weikart, D., P. Olmsted, J. Montie, N. Hayes and M. Ojla (eds.) (2003), "A World of Pre-school Experiences: Observations in 15 Countries", The IEA Preprimary Project Phase 2, High/Scope Press, Ypsilanti, Michigan.

ISBN 92-64-03545-1
Starting Strong II: Early Childhood Education and Care
© OECD 2006

Chapter 4

A Universal Approach to Access, with Particular Attention to Children in Need of Special Support

Chapter 4 outlines the complexity of the notion of access and provides a rationale for universal and appropriate access. It includes tables of current enrolment rates for children 3 to 6 years old and repeats the recommendation of Starting Strong (OECD, 2001) to interpret international access rate tables for early childhood education and care (ECEC) with caution. Questions about what is included or excluded in these figures need to be asked, and in all instances, it is necessary to link raw figures with the notion of appropriate access. The chapter addresses also the field of out-of-school time care, and the efforts being made by countries to increase provision.

The need to increase licensed service provision for children under 3 still remains a critical issue. A comparison is drawn between employment rates of women with children under 3 and the actual uptake of licensed services. A conclusion to be drawn is that many women work part-time during this period, and that a large proportion of children are still placed in informal or unlicensed child care. The chapter also raises the issue of parental leave policies and sketches the policy approaches of different countries to child care and parents. Finally, the issues of ensuring equitable access for all children to attend quality ECEC is discussed, in particular, in regard to children with special needs, and children with additional learning needs due to socio-economic, cultural and/or linguistic factors. Many examples of initiatives taken by countries in this field are referenced.

Some of the major tables in the report are provided in this chapter: the main institutional forms of ECEC in the participating countries; the present access rates to ECEC services; the entitlements to ECEC provision provided by OECD countries; maternity, paternity and parental leave policies; policy approaches to children under 3 and their parents.

In 2001, *Starting Strong* noted the movement in many countries towards universal access to early childhood education for children from the age of 3 or 4 years. Universal access does not necessarily entail achieving full coverage, as at different ages and in different family circumstances, variation in need and demand for ECEC will necessarily occur. Universal access can be said to exist in Finland, for example, as children have an unconditional right to day care. At the same time, enrolments are relatively low compared to Belgium or France. This may be due to municipalities preferring to encourage the use of the home care allowance, rather than the more expensive alternative of creating early childhood services. A similar policy is seen in German municipalities, creating the paradoxical situation of public authorities encouraging parents not to use public services which research shows provide gender equality and real benefit to children from disadvantaged backgrounds. Universal access implies provision that is available to all children whose parents wish them to participate. This approach to access is contrasted with a targeted approach to ECEC, whereby a government provides public funding primarily to ensure programmes for certain groups of children, with significantly less support for the mainstream.

Enthusiasm for universal access is not shared by all countries. Questions are raised about whether a universal approach is equitable, and if so, how provision should be expanded in a fair and efficient way. For example, rather than requiring all taxpayers (including low and moderate-income families) to fund programmes for the children of middle-class parents who can afford to pay for services, is it not fairer to channel funding towards targeted programmes for children at-risk of school failure? In addition, universal early education programmes tend to take place within state school systems. In many instances, this may be a real advantage: early education systems generally organise services more equitably, observe higher standards and employ more qualified personnel than child care programmes. A major weakness, however, is the lack of evaluation of state pre-school programmes. Critics of government-sponsored programmes affirm that few States have undertaken evaluations that enable parents to be sure that attendance in public early education programmes actually benefits their children (Currie, 2004). In addition, whatever research exists tends to focus on children from "at-risk" backgrounds and ignores outcomes for the (majority) middle-class children.

In answer, proponents of universal services point out that targeting is costly and inefficient. Programmes, such as Head Start, miss most poor children, and at the same time, exclude by regulation low-income families just above eligibility for subsidised services. These children would also benefit greatly from free state services. In addition, their presence would provide the mix of social class and diversity in classrooms and on parent committees that programmes for children from poor or immigrant families need (Barnett *et al.*, 2004). In the targeted access option, publicly funded ECEC remains a selective arrangement for children at-risk rather than a social good for all children, *e.g.* in the United States, Head Start receives full government funding,[1] while state funding for universal early education for three- and four-year-olds is far from achieved.

What did Starting Strong recommend?

Starting Strong (OECD, 2001) encouraged countries to engage in a universal approach to access, with particular attention to young children below the age of 3 years and to children with special or additional learning needs: While access to ECEC is close to universal for children from age three or four in the European countries, more attention needs to be devoted to:

- *Providing universal and appropriate access for all 3- to 6-year-olds:* Appropriateness becomes an issue when available provision does not meet the needs of a particular child or his or her parent(s), *e.g.* a child may have special or additional learning needs, and an inclusive programme is not available in the local centre or pre-school. Another common example is when the early childhood service available does not meet the needs of working parents, *e.g.* when kindergarten – or the traditional junior school attached to primary school – opens on a half-day basis and only during term-time.

- *Expanding provision for infants and toddlers, including through parental leave:* Country reports from the reviews indicate that the demand for child care services for young children is high and insufficiently met, even in countries that provide long parental leaves. Increasing numbers of women wish to combine child-rearing and a career. Services available to them are often informal or unlicensed, and of doubtful quality. When a network of licensed, affordable child care services exists, the use of relative or unlicensed family day care diminishes. More highly educated parents in all countries show a preference for formal centre-based services.

- *Ensuring equitable access, such that all children have equal opportunities to attend quality ECEC,* regardless of family income, parental employment status, special educational needs or ethnic/language background. The role of government is to research needs, to set targets for equitable access and to develop strategies to meet these targets.

The concept of access

Before analysing access data across countries, it is well to recall that the concept of access is a complex one. Data tables supplied by the international organisations need to be read with caution, as they generally use a narrow definition of early childhood services (International Standard Classification of Education [ISCED] Level 0), and fail to explain or take into account important internal factors of the ECEC field, *e.g.*:

- *The conditions of access:* Is access free or fee-paying? If fee-paying, is access affordable for all parents? Is access equitable? Is it governed by eligibility criteria? Are children from low-income homes subsidised in fee-paying services? Do children with special learning needs receive first call on services and additional resources? At what age does obligatory free schooling begin?

- *The scope of access:* Is access typically sessional, half-day or full-day? Is there access to a continuum of services for parents and children across the whole working day, throughout the year? Is provision convenient for families, including families in rural areas and travelling families?

- *The kind of access:* Do access rates refer to just one type of service, and are other services, such as parental leave, family day care, playgroups and after-school care, also considered in the overall picture of provision? Table 4.1 below, showing the main institutional types of provision across the participating countries, illustrates the complexity of ECEC provision.

Table 4.1. **Main institutional arrangements for provision of ECEC in OECD countries**

Age of children	0 (birth)	1	2	2.5	3	4	5	6	7
AUS	Accredited centres and FDC cover up to 61.5% of children at 4 years and c. 24.6% between 0-3, figures include sessional and long-day periods					Kindergarten or reception classes: c. 17% of age 4, 84% of age 5		Compulsory school at 6	
AUT	*Tagesmutter* (FDC) and *Krippen* (crèches) care for 8.9% of children 0-3				Kindergartens enrol 80% of children 3-6			Compulsory school at 6	
BEL (FL)	*DOGs* (family day care – predominant in Flanders) and *Kinderdagverbliif* (centre-based crèches) together care for 34.2% of children 0-3; 31% of 0-1s; 42% of 1-2s and 32% of 2-3s			*Kleuterschool* (infant school) from 2.5 years: enrolment 90% at 2.5 years reaching nearly 100% from age 3				Compulsory school at 6	
BEL (FR)	*Gardiennes encadrées* (FDC) 12%. *Crèches* for children 0-1 (12%) and centres for 1-3 (21.5%) together cover on average 18% of children 0-3			*École maternelle*: from 2.5 years: enrolment 90% at 2.5; reaching nearly 100% from 3 years				Compulsory school at 6	
CAN	Lack of precise data on children 0-4 years. Excepting Quebec, state support is weak, many private and unsupervised arrangements. Quebec enrols 38% of 0-4s. Centre based and family day care cover 24% of children 0-6 years					Junior K: 40% of 4-5s in Ontario; 50%+ in Quebec	Kindergarten: 95% of 5-6s enrolled in most P/Ts	Compulsory school at 6	
CZE	Few crèche services				*Materska skola* (kindergarten) covers 76% from age 3; 98% at 5-6 years			Compulsory school at 6	
DEU	*Krippen* (centre-based crèche) cover 37% in former E.Germany, and c.3% of children 0-3 in former W.Germany (8.6% of 0-3 children nationally)				Kindergarten covers 90% of children 3-6, generally full-day in former E. Germany. Mostly under social/family services, but sometimes local ministry of education.			Compulsory school at 6	
DNK	Daycare services (*dagtilbud*) care for children from 6 months to 6 years. Services are: *Dagpleje* (family day care) covering 45% children to age 3; *Vuggestuer* (crèches) and *Adlersintegrer* (age-integrated) facilities which together enrol a further 15% of children under 3, and c. 38% of children 3-6 years. *Bornehaver* (kindergartens) enrol c. 58% of children 3-6 years.							Kgarten classes (*bornehaver-klasser*) enrol 98% of 6-7s	Compulsory school at 7
FIN	*Perhepaivahoito* (FDC) and *Paivakoti* (municipal early development centres) together cover 27.5% of children 1-2, 44% of 2-3, and 73% by age 5, with 54% in family day care and 46% in centres							*Esiopetus* (pre-school): enrols 96% of 6-7s	Compulsory school at 7
FRA	*Assistantes maternelles* care for 18% of 0-3s, crèches 8% and other licensed arrangements provide for 6% of children			*The école maternelle enrols 35% of children from 2 years and almost all children from 3 years. An entitlement to this free service exists from 3 years*				Compulsory school at 6	
HUN	*Bolcsode* (crèches) and some family day care cover 9.3% of children 0-3				Ovoda (kindergarten) cover 85% of children 3-5s, 97% of 5-6s		Compulsory K from age 5		
IRL	Licensed family day care and nurseries cover 10-15% of children from birth to 4 years. Most children are in family or unregulated informal child-minding arrangements				Pre-primary education covers 4% at age 3; 56% of children 3-6 years. Enrolments approach 100% from age 5 years			Compulsory school at 6	
ITA	*Asili nidi* (crèches) cover 18.7% of children 0-3. Most children either in family or other informal settings				The *scuola dell'infanzia* covers 70-90% of children from age 3 (depends on region); 96% at age 5-6 years			Compulsory school at 6	
KOR	Much family and informal care. Parallel systems under different ministries: child care centres cover 10% of children 0-3, 31% of 3-5s, 23% of 5-6s				MOE kindergartens cover 12% of children 3-4, 27% of 4-5, and 45% of 5-6, that is, c.70% of children 5-6 years in licensed services			Compulsory school at 6	
MEX	*Educación inicial* (centre-based crèche) covers about 3% of children 0-3				(Future compulsory) *educación prescolar* will begin from age 3, but covers at present: 81% of children 3-6 (55% 3-5; 88% from age 5)				
NDL	*Gastouderopvang* (family day care) and *Kinderopvang* (child care centres) enrol 23% of 0-4s. A further 5-10% are enrolled in municipal early education services for disadvantaged children. In total, 89% of 2-4s are enrolled in play groups or other service types.					Pre-primary 4-6 years: almost all children are enrolled at 4	Compulsory pre-primary school from age 5		
NOR	*Barnehager* (kindergartens), including rural *familiebarnehager* and both private (majority) and public, enrol about 48% of children 0-3, and 88% of 3-6s							Compulsory school at 6	
PRT	*Crèche familiare* (1.5%) and centre-based *crèches* (11%) cover 12.5% of age 3				*Jardims de infancia* enrol 60% children at age 3 and 90% from 5-6. National average for 3-6s is 76.3%			Compulsory school at 6	

Table 4.1. **Main institutional arrangements for provision of ECEC in OECD countries** (cont.)

Age of children	0 (birth)	1	2	2.5	3	4	5	6	7
SWE	*Familiedaghem* (family day care) care for 8% of children, esp. in rural areas. Full-day *forskola* enrol 45% of children 1-2, 86% of 2-3 and 91% of 4-5, and 96% of children 5-6 years							Preschool class – 91% enrolment. Other 9% are enrolled in school	Compulsory school at 7
GBR (Engl.)	Predominantly private nurseries, child minders and playgroups care for 26% of children 0-3, but under MOE responsibility				Playgroups and nurseries provide for 95% of children 3-4	Reception class and nursery schools enrol c.100% of 4-5s	Compulsory primary school begins at 5 years		
USA	Predominantly private child care centres and family day care cater for c. 50% of children 0-3 (38% of these in licensed services)				40% of children 3-4, and 70% of 4-5s enrolled in educational programmes, incl. pre-K, private kindergartens, Head Start, purchase-of-service. Head Start covers 11% of 3- and 4-year-olds. From age 5, over 80% of children are enrolled in state-funded kindergarten (education auspices)			Compulsory school at 6	

Key:

Family day care, crèches under social welfare, health, family services.

Preschool and other services under education ministry or agency.

Free and compulsory primary or pre-school educational service.

Mix of services, some under education ministry or agency.

● *The appropriateness and quality of access*: Are services flexible, yet suited to the needs of young children (not merely "slot" services but environments where children are cared for by trained professionals able to offer a sustained developmental programme)? Is access appropriate for young children, or is it a part of the primary school system with conditions and pedagogy more suitable for older children? Are the basic quality indicators – child-staff ratios; group size; the qualifications levels and certification of the educators, the quality of materials and environments – respected for all children in the services to which access is offered? Is access appropriate for children requiring special support?

1. Providing universal and appropriate access for all 3- to 6-year-olds

ECEC access rates across the OECD countries for children 3 to 6 years old

In Europe, the concept of universal access for 3- to 6-year-olds is generally accepted. Most countries provide all children with at least two years of free, publicly-funded provision before they begin primary schooling. In fact, with the exception of Ireland and the Netherlands, such access is generally a statutory right from the age of 3 years, and in a handful of countries from an earlier age. Early education programmes in Europe are often free, and attached to schools. In OECD countries outside Europe, most provide free access to early education only from age 5. In Australia, Korea and in some American States, many children are enrolled in free state programmes at the age of 4 years, but provision is generally much weaker than in European countries.

The move towards universal provision in Europe has been given a further stimulus by the 2010 objectives set by the European Union at its Barcelona meeting in 2002, encouraging member countries to supply subsidised full-day places for one-third of 0- to 3-year-olds, and for over 90% of all 3- to 6-year-olds. The *Starting Strong* recommendation of moving towards universal and appropriate access does not set a target or benchmark, but addresses also the internal constituents of access, as outlined above, and sees high coverage as only one aspect of country performance. To date, about five countries – Belgium (Flanders), Denmark, France, Norway, and Sweden – have reached the Barcelona targets for both groups of children, although at different levels of quality. Finland also may be said to have reached the target as although the coverage rate for children under 3 (municipal and private) is 24.7%, if children under 1 are left out (in Finland, almost all parents take leave) the percentage rises to 36.7%. Several other countries are on the way to achieving similar coverage.

Although strong access rates are shown for almost all countries in Figure 4.1, the graphs hide some basic weaknesses. Research and the experience of the OECD reviews suggest that the children who do not have access are often children with special or

Figure 4.1. **Enrolment rates in regulated ECEC and pre-primary education of children 3 to 6 years**

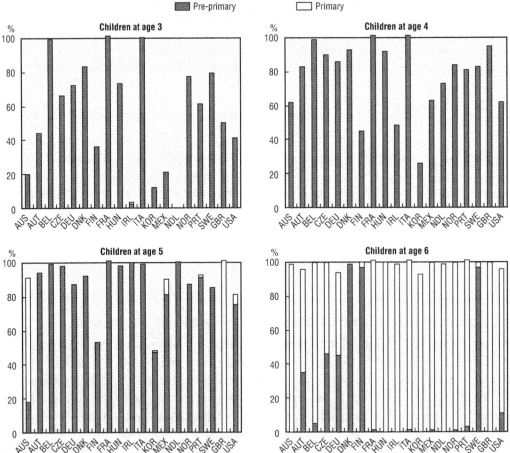

Notes: The dark bars in the figure refer to enrolments in optional, centre-based pre-school provision (sometimes within a primary school setting), designed to foster the cognitive and socio-emotional development of children from 3 years to compulsory school age. The lighter bars refer to enrolments in formal primary schooling.
Korean rates are for Ministry of Education kindergarten enrolments only. In the parallel child care system, 44.9% of 3- to 4-year-olds, 36.7% of 4- to 5-year-olds and 31.7%of 5-year-olds are enrolled in child care centres. Total enrolment rates in Korea (kindergarten and child care centres combined) are 3-year-olds: 59.5%, 4-year-olds: 66.4%, and 5-year-olds: 78.9% in 2004.
Source: OECD education database, 2005 and national *Background Reports.*

additional educational needs, that is, children with disabilities; children from disadvantaged backgrounds, or children from ethnic or cultural minorities (Leseman, 2002). In addition, the quality and duration of the services provided to young children are not made explicit in the figure, *e.g.* the coverage rate for the United Kingdom at age 4 often denotes in reality an entitlement for two-and-a-half hours per day for about nine months per year, in contrast to Swedish provision which provides, according to the parent's wishes, the possibility of full-day coverage for eleven months every year.

The age at which young children normally access services varies considerably across countries (see Table 4.2). The extent of remunerated parental leave and the age at which free early or primary education begins are two critical factors. The majority of children are enrolled in free early provision from the age of 30 months in Belgium, and increasingly in France from the age of 2 years; from the age of 3 years in Austria, the Czech Republic, Germany, Hungary, Italy, Norway (majority), the United Kingdom; from the age of 4 years in Ireland (majority), and the Netherlands; and from the age of 5 years in Australia, Canada, Korea (majority), Mexico and the United States, but with an increasing number of places for 4-year-old children.[2] In the Nordic countries (except Norway), municipalities have an obligation to provide families who demand it a place in a fee-paying centre or family day care, not just at 3 years but from the end of parental leave. For children in need in these countries, parental fees are generally waived. In Mexico, States are now obliged by law to provide early education services for children over 3 years, and attendance has been made compulsory for all children from this age. In most school districts in Canada and the United States, legal or *de facto* access entitlements to half-day, term-time kindergarten exist for children from the age of 5 years, where between 80% to 100% enrolment rates are achieved for the age group. The access of younger children (under 5 years) to public programmes is much more reduced, although within the United States, a strong move towards public (state-funded) pre-kindergarten provision can be observed in the majority of States (see Annex E for the United States profile). In Canada, the province of Quebec has increased significantly the number of licensed child care places available to children living in the province. By itself, Quebec accounts for almost all the increase in regulated ECEC places in Canada since 1998. In Australia, responsibility for pre-school provision rests with States and Territories. The majority of children aged 4 (average of 83%) and approximately 17.1% of children aged 3 years attended a state funded pre-school in 2003-04. Additionally, in 2002, 47.4% of children aged 3-years-old, 35.8% of children aged 4 years and 9.2% of children aged 5 years attended formal child care (Long Day Care, Family Day Care and Occasional Care).

In Portugal, a notable expansion in public investment in the pre-school network meant that between 1996 and 1999, coverage increased dramatically, from 57% to 72% of children over 3-years-old. Over 90% of 5-year-olds benefit from a free daily five-hour session in the *jardim de infância* (kindergartens). The story is similar in Germany for the 3- to 6-year-olds, but development has taken place over a longer period: from less than a 30% base in the 1970s, enrolments in kindergarten now stand at about 90% in largely half-day places in the West and all-day places in the East. In 1996, a statutory right to a place in kindergarten was legislated. In Korea, likewise, the State is investing far more in early childhood services: all 5-year-olds have now a right to free kindergarten, but as demand far outstrips supply, only about 50% of children have access. Another 20% of 4-year-olds from low-income families have also been given recently a right to access.

Table 4.2. Entitlements to ECEC provision across OECD countries

	Nature of entitlements	Age covered	Length of day	Duration of entitlement	Free or fee paying
AUS	– No legal right to services for children aged 0 to 4 years. Child Care Benefit for families using an approved service – No legal right to pre-school although most States provide free or almost free pre-school for 4 to 5-year olds	4 to 6 years	Usually half-day	No entitlement but pre-school generally available for 1- to 2-year-olds, depending on State	Generally free (depends on State)
AUT	– No legal right to services for children aged 0 to 3 years – Legal right to kindergarten from 3 to 6 years	3 to 6 years	Increasingly full day	3 years	Fee-paying
BEL	– No legal right to ECEC for children under 2.5 years, but supervised, subsidised services are broadly available (supply does not meet demand): in the French Community, services are mainly creches; in the Flemish Community, mainly family day – Legal right to universal pre-school from 2.5 to 6 years	0 to 3 years 2.5 to 6 years	Increasingly full day with OSP	3.5 years	Free
CAN	– Legal right to ECEC (kindergarten) varies between provinces, for most legal entitlement starts at age 5 or 6 – Legal right to ECEC (pre-kindergarten) at age 4 in Ontario. Legal right to ECEC 0- to 6-year-olds in Quebec (educational child care for 0- to 5-year-olds, kindergarten for 5- to 6-year-olds)	6 years 4 years 0 to 6 years	Half-day or full-day Half-day Varies	1 year 1 year Up to 6 year	Free Free Fee paying
CZE	– No legal right to ECEC for children under 3 – No legal right to pre-school (3 to 6 years), but access is generally broad, with priority given to 5-year-olds	3 to 6 years	Full-day	No entitlement but places available in most communes from 3 years	Free Free for 4 to 6 years
DNK	– 87% of municipalities guarantee places for all children aged 1 to 5 years – Legal right to a place in free, pre-school class in centres and primary schools – Legal right to place in out-of-school provision	0.5 to 6 years 6 to 7 years	Generally full-day	6 years	Fee-paying, except for pre-school class which is free
FIN	– Legal right to a place in centre-based or home-based ECEC from birth – Legal right to a place in a free pre-school class in centres and primary schools – No legal right to a place in out-of-school provision	0 to 7 years 6 to 7 years	Full-day Half-day After school	All early childhood + 1-year (half-day) free	Fee-paying Fee Fee-paying
FRA	– No legal right to ECEC services under age 3, but supervised, subsidised services are broadly available 35% of 2-year-olds have access to free *école maternelle* services, and over 90% of 3-year-olds – Legal right to school-based ECEC from age 3	3 to 6 years	Full-day (8 hours)	3 years	Free
DEU	– No legal right to ECEC for children under 3 – Legal right to ECEC services from age 3	3 to 6 years	Full-day in NBL (East)	3 years	Fee-paying
HUN	– Legal right to ECEC services for working parents from the age of 6 months. In practice, there is not universal access until the age of 3 years in the kindergarten (*Ovoda*) service	0 to 3 years 3 to 6 years	Full-day (10 hours) Full-day	3 years in practice	Free Free
IRL	– No legal right to services for children under 4 – Legal right to a place in school-based pre-school from 4 years	4 to 6 years	Half-day	2 years	Free
ITA	– No legal right to services for children under 3 – Legal right to a place in school-based ECEC	3 to 6 years	Half-day or full-day	3 years	Fee-paying Free in public system
KOR	– No legal entitlement for children 0 to 5 years, except from 2006, for 4-year olds from low-income backgrounds (20% coverage) – Legal entitlement from age 5. Demand exceeds supply: 20% of 5-year-olds covered in 2004, 30% in 2005, going towards 50% in 2006	5 to 6 years	Full-day in CC centres Increasingly full-day in kindergartens	1 year	Free

STARTING STRONG II: EARLY CHILDHOOD EDUCATION AND CARE – ISBN 92-64-03545-1 – © OECD 2006

Table 4.2. Entitlements to ECEC provision across OECD countries (cont.)

	Nature of entitlements	Age covered	Length of day	Duration of entitlement	Free or fee paying
MEX	– No legal right for children under 3				
	– Free and compulsory attendance at school-based centre for children from age 3 by 2009	3 to 6 years	Half-day	3 years	Free
NDL	– No legal right to services for children under 4 years, but high investment in subsidies for children "at-risk"	2 to 4 years	Half-day	2 years	Free
	– Legal right to a place in primary school, from 4 years	4 to 6 years	School-day		
NOR	– No legal right to services but 80% enrolment has been reached for children over 4 years. As soon as universal enrolment has been reached, an entitlement will be introduced	0 to 6 years	Full-day	No entitlement but places available in most communes from age 3	Fee-paying
PRT	– No statutory right to services for children				
	– Legal right to free *jardim* enrolment from 4 years under 3	4 to 6 years	5 hours, 5 days/week	2 years	Free
SWE	– Legal obligation to provide a place for children of working or studying parents from 12 months	1 to 6 years	Full-day	3 years of a free half-day service available to most children	Fee-paying
	– Legal right to free pre-school class for bilingual children from age 3 being extended progressively to all 5-year-olds and 4-year-olds	3 to 6 years	Half-day		Free
GBR	– Legal right of all 6- to 7-year-old children to a free pre-school class	6 to 7 years	Half-day		Free
	– Legal right to a place in after-school services for 1- to 12-year-olds	6 to 12 years	After-school		Fee-paying
	– No legal entitlement for children under 3				
	– Universal, free part-time early education for all 3- and 4-year-olds prior to the start of compulsory schooling	3 to 5 years	Legal entitlement to a free *part time* place for all 3- and 4-year-olds. 12.5 hours per week, for 33 weeks	2 years prior to compulsory schooling (which in England begins at age 5)	Free
USA	– No legal right for 0- to 5-year-olds				
	– Two States – Georgia and New York – provide universal pre-kindergarten to all 4-year-olds. Pre-kindergarten for children at risk in several States	4 to 5 years	Half-day, term-time (varies)	1 year across country	Free
	– Most school districts offer free kindergarten class to all 5-year-olds as part of primary schooling	5 to 6 years	Half- day, term-time (varies)		

In the United States, state authorities tend to target their programmes towards low-income families or towards children who are considered to be at risk of school failure, such as children of teen parents or with a disability or having limited English proficiency. Low- and moderate-income families, who do not have the means to pay private fees and earn too much to qualify for publicly-funded services or subsidies, often experience difficulties of access (Fuller *et al.*, 2005). Over the years, however, a notable increase in federal and state subsidies (in some States only) has taken place, *e.g.* in Missouri, in favour of low-income families. In addition, the number of state-funded pre-kindergarten programmes for 3- and 4-year-olds has grown considerably in the United States in recent years (Schulman *et al.*, 1999; NIEER, 2004). As many of these programmes are sessional or half-day, States try to co-ordinate pre-kindergarten with child care assistance programmes that help cover the costs of the extra hours for parents who work full-time. States may also offer pre-kindergarten programmes in child care centres (including private centres) so that children can remain at the same setting for the extended hours (NIEER, 2003).

Appropriate access

Despite these positive signs, there remains the challenge of appropriate access in many countries. Access is often inappropriate for children with special needs and/or additional learning needs, so much so that directors of centres may not allow them to enrol, or parents – seeing the difficulties involved for their children – simply desist. If access is achieved, classes may be far too large for these children, or appropriately trained staff may not be available to take them in charge. Similarly, group sizes, care and pedagogical approaches may be unsuitable for very young children in early education systems established along school lines. In addition, junior classes often do not meet the needs of working parents, *e.g.* when kindergarten – or the traditional junior school attached to primary school – opens on a half-day basis and only during term-time. Services may be closed for the summer for winter and spring breaks, and for teacher professional development days. Unless this service is augmented by after school care or another wrap-around service, the situation forces many mothers of young children either to reduce their work to part-time or to drop out of employment for a number of years.

Out-of-school time provision[3]

Out-of-school time provision for children of working parents is still not a policy priority in most OECD countries. Demand for it is growing rapidly as most school-based ECEC does not cover the full working day, and many parents – over 30% in some countries – work non-standard hours. A more coherent approach is needed for out-of-school provision. Currently, Denmark (and former East Germany), and Sweden, are the only countries that provide enough places – generally in early childhood centres or on school premises – to meet demand. In Sweden, all children under 12 years have a legal entitlement to provision. Leisure-time services are closely linked in concept and organisation to ECEC provision and stress social competence and the interests of children. Staff engaged to work with the children are trained to university degree level, specifically for this form of care. In most other countries, out-of-school provision is loosely regulated, with a range of different services, variably qualified staff and few reliable statistics. The 2002 Quality Decree in Flanders, Belgium stipulated, however, that by 2010, half of the workforce in the centres for out of school child care must hold a diploma in child care.

Several of these issues were raised in *Starting Strong* (OECD, 2001), in particular, how out-of-school provision was to be understood and organised. Critics point out that a clear concept of leisure-time activities is often absent, and that much out-of-school time provision takes place in schools where there is a tendency for the service to become a homework club. In addition, school buildings may not be ideal for leisure purposes. At the same time, when operated outside schools, children have to travel. In addition, provision may rely – often exclusively – on parent management and contributions, which again opens up issues of professionalism and sustainability. In sum, this form of care is not yet sufficiently recognised and supported, and is often inappropriately organised. An opportunity is lost for families and young children, as the research indicates that free-time services, out-of-school care and study support help particularly children from disadvantaged families, and contribute to tackling child poverty by enabling parents to work (United Kingdom Interdepartmental Childcare Review, 2002).

What have countries been doing to increase out-of-school provision?

Recent years have seen promising national initiatives in out-of-school provision. In the Netherlands, the quality regulations for ECEC in the welfare sector also apply to this provision, including staff qualifications, although these requirements have been considerably loosened in the new marketised system. However, by an Act of Parliament in 2005, school boards will be obliged from January 2007 to organise out-of-school provision for all parents who need the service. They are free to contract child care organisations, to use community school provision or to provide care and leisure activities on their own premises. In 2006, EUR 35 million will be reserved for the development of this care and from 2007, EUR 27 million will be made available annually for this activity. In Belgium, in both language communities, the issue of regulation has also been raised and new initiatives have taken place, *e.g.* the 2001 survey by the French Community of all leisure-time activities for children up to 12 years (Observatoire de l'Enfance, 2003), or the legal framework and charter of quality for out-of-school time provision formulated in the Flemish Community. Austria and Germany are also tackling the issue, in general, through extending both kindergartens and schools towards full-day provision (these services were traditionally half-day only). Although at first raising fears of educational pressure on young children, classes are still confined to the morning period, while afternoons are reserved for relaxation, leisure, social and learning activities including sports, music, arts and crafts. Both parents and non-statutory bodies are involved – the latter often as operators of programmes. New in-service training has been introduced in some *Länder*, bringing teachers, leisure-time educators and sports instructors together. Costs to parents are generally very reasonable, ranging from EUR 30-50 per month in publicly subsidised services.

In France, *écoles maternelles* and schools have traditionally operated for eight hours a day (except Wednesdays) from 8.30 to 16.30. To meet the demand for out-of-school time provision, the country has generated a network of accredited support services around the *école maternelle*. *Centres de loisirs* (leisure-time centres) run by non-profit associations or the communes operate on Wednesdays, after-school and during the shorter holiday breaks; and *garderies périscolaires* (out-of-school child care), run by municipalities and parents' associations operate before and after school hours generally on school premises. French children also go to the homes of accredited or informal family day carers for after-school care. Scotland also has made a contribution to out-of-school care through the New Opportunities Fund which has provided both a framework document and funding to these services (Scottish Executive, 2003). In the United States, Head Start is implementing a major initiative to expand full-day/full-year services through partnerships with other early childhood programmes and funding sources. National surveys of provision have been carried out by the National Centre for Educational Statistics (2004), the Afterschool Alliance (2004) and by the Harvard Family Research Project.[4]

However, until societies and education systems adopt a more caring attitude towards children, these efforts may remain marginal. In many countries, the education system plays no formal role in out-of-school provision, and if it does, the accent may be placed on custodial care or homework rather than on developmental leisure-time activities. Teachers also can be reluctant to take on extra hours before or after the official school-day. For this reason, many after-school clubs are run by parent-led management committees on a voluntary basis, with little steady funding from public authorities. Despite their public status, school premises frequently remain closed to children outside official school hours, and are not at the disposal of the groups who volunteer or are nominated by local authorities to facilitate out-of-school care. In addition, these premises (in particular, the assembly and out-door areas) have not been constructed with young children's leisure-time activities in mind.

2. Increasing public provision for children under 3

Relative to services for pre-school children, less attention has been given in most countries to provision for children under 3, although sufficient provision for this age group is an iron test of government policy in favour of equality of opportunity for women (see Box 4.1). Hard data on access is often difficult to obtain. A sentence from the Background Report of Germany (2004) provides an indication of the general situation in many countries:

"Until the beginning of the nineties in the West (Federal Republic of Germany) there were places in public or publicly-promoted facilities for fewer than 2% of children under 3 of age, supplemented by another 2% of places in family day care – as against an unknown number of private arrangements."

Through household and other surveys, estimates can be made of the use of child care in general, but with little knowledge of the duration of its use or of the type and quality of the services offered. As a result, national data on child care services are often not useful for policy makers. The statistical picture improves greatly when governments provide services directly to the younger children or when parent subsidies are linked to the use of licensed services. Table 4.2 above provides information on entitlements to ECEC across the participating countries, and Figure 4.2 below provides an estimate of enrolments in licensed child care in the OECD countries reviewed.

Services for 0- to 3-year-olds

Publicly subsidised services for the younger children take several forms (see also Table 4.1 above). The core services are: family day care; centre-based crèche services and integrated centres (with 1- to 6-year-olds). Most of these services charge parental fees, which, in many countries, are highly subsidised. Professional core services are often augmented by: drop-in centres for mothers where infants and young children can play and where the carers can avail of professional advice; information centres; mother and baby clinics; family centres and parent-led playgroups, the aim being to provide a continuum of services that matches the different needs of different families. When they are available, higher socio-economic

Box 4.1. **Developing new services for children under 3**
Csemete Gyermekcentrum (Children's Centre), Szekesfehervar, in Hungary

The history of child care services in Central Europe is one of changes of direction. In the 19th century, the countries in the region had the earliest large-scale early childhood systems in Europe. In Hungary, the first kindergarten (*óvoda*) was founded in 1828, and first child care centre (*bölcsöde*) was opened in Pest in 1852. The founding documents of these institutions formulated very progressive ideas for the time. After the Second World War, the development of early childhood services became a state responsibility. Along with supporting women's equality and right to study and work, policies adopted in the region sought to increase the number of places in early childhood services as a means of encouraging women's participation in the labour market and public life. During the 1960s and 1970s, many new centres for children under school-age were designed and built. Between 20-30% of children aged 0 to 3 years were enrolled and more than 60% of children aged 3 to 6 years. Service provision became exclusively the duty of State, but though often of high quality, the curriculum was centralised and services made insufficient allowance for different family requirements.

Since 1989, the process of transition has resulted in the dismantling of state property and the sale of many public centres. In Hungary, between 1984 and 2003, more than half the child care places and a substantial number of kindergarten places disappeared. Today, the child care system provides for about 8-9% of children under the age of three, and the kindergarten system for about 90% of children between the ages of 3 and 6. In the Czech Republic, the organised child care network – which covered over 20% of 0- to 3-year-olds before transition – collapsed: only 60 crèches (in 2004) have survived from the previous regime. The former crèche buildings have been sold or allocated to other purposes. Fertility rates dropped even further in the region, and population/employment ratios declined. In this context, governments have provided protected maternity leaves of up to 3 years. The change to a liberal economy also brought about changes in the structure of employment, resulting in different work structures, atypical hours of work, different demands on the part of employers, and different needs in terms of public services.

The *Csemete Gyermekcentrum* child care centre in the municipality of Szekesfehervar has followed a similar evolution. It was established as a child care centre (*bölcsöde*) at the end of the 1970s, at first maintained by the town council and later, after the creation of local authorities in 1989/90, by the Szekesfehervar local authority as a service provided directly for young children under 3. In 2000, the centre was privatised and subsequently taken over by a non-profit foundation. It provides a wide range of services for young children and their families. The centre is open between 7 a.m. and 5 p.m. every day. In 2003, it offered full-time day care for 72 children, and the following additional services: occasional crèche services; home care services; mother-toddler groups between 8 a.m. and 4 p.m.; advisory services and organised talks for parents; accredited courses for prospective family day care providers; advisory services for working family day care providers; advisory service for local authorities interested in family day care. Children receiving fulltime care pay only the cost of meals and some additional services (see below). The cost of meals is reduced or waived if the family is assessed as having difficulties or if they have more than three children.

All this shows remarkable powers of survival and adaptation, but new challenges are emerging. The situation of the workforce is becoming more and more problematic. Most of the staff working with children are qualified (all kindergarten teachers, and 89% of child care workers are trained in Hungary – in kindergarten to tertiary level, and in child care to upper secondary vocational level). The proposed reform of higher education, in line with the Bologna Declaration, is likely to improve the training of kindergarten staff but is unlikely to help those with lower qualifications. The average age of child care workers is increasing, and the younger generations do not wish to take on this role. A major priority is to find ways to improve the status, pay, education and working conditions of the workforce to ensure that new staff can be recruited.

Source: Dr. Marta Korintus: Background Report of Hungary, OECD, 2005; Care work in Europe study, 2005.

Figure 4.2. **Employment rates for mothers with children under 3 and access rates for children under 3 in licensed ECEC services**

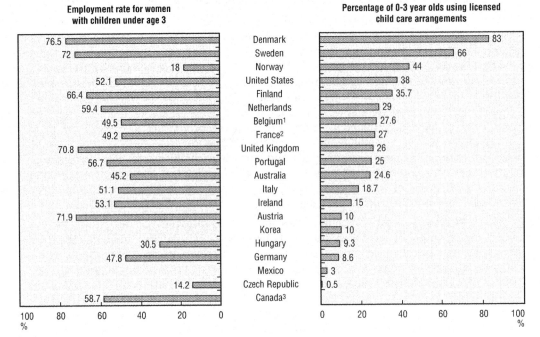

1. Enrolment in the infant school in Belgium begins at 2.5 years when about 90% of children are enrolled. The percentage of children in regulated child care in Belgium (Flanders) is 34.2%.
2. Enrolment in the infant school begins at 2 years. 35% of children enter between 2-3 years.
3. For Canada, the coverage rate for children aged 0-5 years is 24%. Data on the coverage rate for children aged 0-3 years are not available.

Notes: In reading this figure, caution is advised.

● The definition of "licensed service" differs widely from country to country, going from mere registration of an activity to programmes that follow a curriculum and are regularly inspected and evaluated. Again, information is not available in most countries concerning the length of use of the child care places available, whether the rate recorded refers to sessional, half-day or full-day usage.

● Likewise employment rates are open to different interpretations. In this figure, no distinction is made between part-time and full-time employment, and in some instances, the figures include women who are taking parental or other leave, *e.g.* the employment rate given for women in Austria includes women on Child Care Benefit leave, whereas the percentage of women actually working is closer to 30%.

● The low enrolments rates recorded in several countries may hide parental leave policies that play an important role in reducing demand for infant provision. Again, rates do not reveal the numerous informal or unlicensed arrangements that exist.

Source: Employment rates provided by EUROSTAT, United States Bureau of Labor Statistics and OECD, *Babies and Bosses* (Volumes 1-4). Information on access rates provided by OECD countries, 2004.

groups tend to use professional, centre-based services more than lower socio-economic groups, *e.g.* in Norway, 41% of university educated women use centre-based child care services for children under 3 compared to 21% of mothers with secondary education, who, in general, show a preference for home care by mothers, or informal care by family members and relatives. In France, a similar situation exists. The preference for home or extended family care is often cultural, but it is also influenced by the cost of services and the considerably greater difficulty for immigrant mothers to find work.

Costs to parents

For children under 3, costs for services are generally shared between parents and public authorities (in the Netherlands, with employers also). Public authorities subsidise services through direct local authority provision (Denmark, Finland, Norway, Sweden), or through indirect subsidies, such as family cash benefits (Australia, the United States), tax credits (Belgium, the United Kingdom) and employer contributions (Belgium, Italy, the Netherlands, etc.). In only three of the twenty countries reviewed (Denmark, Finland and Sweden) is the public provision of high quality ECEC for children from their first year considered an entitlement for a child, on an equal footing with services for the older children.

For services for children under 3, parents contribute on average 25-30% of the costs, varying from a 9-15% parental contribution in Finland, Norway and Sweden, to up to full service costs charged by private providers, who in several countries, such as Ireland, the United Kingdom or the United States, take in charge the majority of children under the age of 3 years. Other countries, such as Belgium and the Netherlands, may have relatively high costs for infants and toddlers but they then provide universal and free access for older children: from 2.5 years in Belgium, and from 4 years in the Netherlands. The Nordic countries generally retain some parental charges up to the year before entry into compulsory schooling, but charges decrease in relation to family income (or at a low, universal flat-rate in Norway and Sweden), and are often waived completely for low-income and second-language families.

Levels of enrolment

The highest levels of enrolment of children under 3 in subsidised provision are seen in Denmark and Sweden,[5] countries with a long history of publicly funded ECEC, combined with long-standing gender equity and family policies. With the exception of these countries (and Finland), reports from all review countries indicate that the demand for services for young children is significantly higher than the available number of places – including in countries that provide long parental leave, a measure that helps to reduce demand, especially in the first year. In countries where public funding for provision is limited, most working parents must either seek solutions in the private market, where ability to pay often determines accessibility and quality, or rely on informal arrangements with family, friends, and neighbours. In the United States, for example, a lack of paid parental leave and limited public investment in services means that many low- and middle-income parents struggle to find affordable arrangements for infants as young as six weeks old (Capizzano, 2000a, 2000b). However, ECEC policies are currently developing, with more generous fee subsidies being made available to enable low- and middle-income families to purchase ECEC in the private market.

Figure 4.2 illustrates that, with the exception of the Scandinavian countries, licensed coverage for the youngest age group is appreciably lower than for 3- to 6-year-olds. At the same time, the percentage rate of working women is far higher in many countries than the percentage enrolment rate for young children. This suggests that much informal care is taking place and/or that many women work part-time. Only in Denmark and Norway are there more places available to children than the proportion of women working. The ratio is probably correct in Sweden also as access to services is a right enshrined in legislation, and enrolments are relatively low during the first 18 months because of effective parental leave policies. Subsidised provision for children under 3 is most developed in Denmark, Finland, Norway and Sweden, countries with a long history of supporting publicly funded ECEC as part of broader gender equity and family support policies. Most services are full day, with parents paying fees on a sliding scale according to income. In these countries, services are integrated under the auspices of one ministry. Provision takes place predominantly in professional centres, excepting Denmark where most children under three are cared for in family day care homes managed by the municipalities.

Belgium (Flemish Community) and France provide for about one third of children under 30 months, in family day care, crèches and other services. In these countries, pre-school education begins at two (France) or 2.5 years (Belgium). Children of that age, enrolled in pre-school, are not included in the figure; if they were, French enrolment figures would be similar to those of Sweden, although in very different conditions. In the past five years, the Netherlands, Norway, and, more recently, the United Kingdom have significantly expanded publicly-funded provision for infants and toddlers. As a result of recent incentive schemes in the Netherlands, for example, 20% of children under four now have a place in ECEC, in addition to the 50% of 2- to 4-year-olds who attend part-day playgroups.

That many young children are being placed in informal or unlicensed child care can be seen for the majority of countries covered, where maternal employment rates far outstrip the rates of licensed child care use. Data from national household surveys and other sources confirm that the actual use of child care is much higher than enrolments in licensed child care. In Ireland, for example, the Pre-school Services Regulations require that when a child minder cares for more than three children under the age of 6 years in her home, she should notify the local Health Board, and become subject to certain regulations. According to figures provided by the National Childminding Association, 95% of child minders in Ireland operate outside this framework. It is estimated that 70% of long-day care is provided through private child-minding. The arrangements are generally unsupervised and escape health, safety, developmental and programmatic regulations (OECD Country Note for Ireland, 2003). Excepting Australia and the United States, similar figures can be cited for the majority (unlicensed) of child care arrangements in the other liberal economies, and in the United States licensing standards can be low and subject to many exemptions.

More positively, signs are emerging from all countries that the concept of services for the children under 3 is broadening from a labour market perspective to the inclusion of quality objectives. There is an increasing focus on the developmental and educational role of services for very young children, which is supported by research showing that the first 3 years of life are extremely important in setting attitudes and patterns of thinking (Shore, 1997; Shonkoff and Phillips, 2000). This new understanding of young children can be seen in the national curricula of several countries, *e.g.* Finland, Norway and Sweden, which make little distinction between the learning capacities of infants/toddlers and older children. In Australia, all child care services are required to participate in the Quality Improvement Assurance System, meet certain opening hours and adhere to a priority of access before parents can receive Child Care Benefit payments. To assist families searching for quality care, the National Childcare Accreditation Council (NCAC) also provides assistance to families through a search facility on their Web site that provides the names of Quality Assurance (QA) providers. In yet other countries, registered and accredited services are increasingly considered as a public good that can benefit both children and parents, and can serve public objectives such as child development, gender equality, social integration, and family support. In Italy, government proposals in 1998 described the shift in understanding of the *asilo nido* (crèche services) as a service on "individual demand" to "an educational and social service of public interest". As a result, flexible services for families with young children – full-time, part-time, drop-in centres, playgroups – have been developed, which support parents regardless of whether they are or are not in paid work. However, an Italian government commitment to expand child care through building 2 500 centres across the country has never materialised.

Parental leave policies

As noted in Chapter 1, remunerated parental leave is an essential element in effective ECEC policies, and is associated with better child and maternal health, lower infant mortality rates, fewer low-weight babies, less maternal depression, and more breast-feeding (Chatterji and Markowicz, 2004; Tanaka, 2005). In European countries, parental leave normally includes a period of absence from work for six months to about a year, on an adequate replacement wage or benefit, with the guarantee of a return to the same or similar position at work. Such leave responds to the needs of babies, mothers, and fathers around the critical moment of birth. It also provides a choice to parents to care for their child at home for a certain period, without excessive penalty to the family budget or to working careers. If fathers are included, greater bonding between men, their partners and offspring has been noted, and a fairer sharing of care and household tasks. Costs to public budgets incurred by the measure can be reduced by employment insurance and employer contributions, which in many countries provide a supplement to low-wage replacement levels or flat-rate benefits (see Table 4.3).

Brooks-Gunn *et al.* (2002), analysing data on 900 European American children from the NICHD sample, controlling for child care (*e.g.*, quality, type), home environment (*e.g.*, provision of learning), and/or parenting effects (*e.g.*, sensitivity) concluded that, unless the service is of high quality, the placement of infants under 1 in child care outside the home can have negative developmental effects. Likewise, the *Neurons to Neighbourhoods* committee found "overwhelming scientific evidence" of the central importance of early relationships for children's development. "Indeed, young children who lack at least one loving and consistent adult often suffer severe and long-lasting developmental problems. But the reality of life in the United States today makes it difficult for many working parents to spend sufficient time with their children. The committee therefore recommends policies that ensure more time, greater financial security, and other supportive resources to help parents build close and stable relationships with their young children" (Shonkoff, 2000).

As outlined in Chapter 1, appropriately licensed child care use and parental leave rights (excepting Canada and recently the United Kingdom) are weakest in the liberal economies.[6] In the more traditional sections of these economies (and also in the conservative continental economies, *e.g.* Italy) the demand for children's services can be relatively weak, as family members or other groups may be available to look after young children. However, as more women enter the labour market, government engagement in the sector grows, if only to organise labour market flows more effectively. In addition, the traditional informal solutions adopted by parents gradually become untenable, as grandparents are now obliged to work more years before pension rights are granted, and other family members continue in education or engage in salaried work. In sum, the pool of informal child minders, generally of the older generation, who assisted young parents – for example, in Ireland, Italy, Korea, and the former socialist countries of Central Europe – may diminish in future years as attitudes change and female employment grows (Ireland Background Report and Country Note, 2004).

The liberal economies are spared, however, from severe child care shortages by (temporary) withdrawal of mothers from the labour market and by informal child care arrangements. In these countries, with the exception of Korea, large immigrant populations exist. In Australia, Canada, the United Kingdom and the United States,

Table 4.3. **Maternity, paternity, and parental leave policies**

	Duration of maternity leave entitlement	Percentage of wage replaced[1]	Duration of parental leave entitlement	Benefit paid	Supplement leaves
Australia	[2]		12 months (family-based leave)	Unpaid	
Austria	16 weeks	16 weeks at 100%	30 months or 36 months if both parents share in ECEC duties	Flat rate of EUR 426 monthly, EUR 181 supplement for low-income families	
Belgium	15 weeks	82% 1st month and 75% thereafter	3 months (6 months part-time) before 4 years	+/- EUR 500 monthly flat rate	Paternity 10 days (3 days paid by employer, 7 days by social security) Possibility of career break for child-rearing, at a low flat rate (over EUR 300) with a small supplement added by the Flemish government
Canada	15 weeks	55% with upper limit	35 weeks; up to 50 weeks for eligible new parents	55% with upper limit, up to 65% for low-income	Leave for sick children
Czech Republic	28 weeks	69%	Until age 4	Flat rate	
Denmark	18 weeks	100% for most mothers (or unemployment benefit)	32 weeks (family-based)	100% or unemployment benefit	Paternity, 2 weeks "use it or lose it" at 100% of earnings Child Care Leave for 13 (or 26) weeks for each parent at 60% of unemployment benefit
Finland	18 weeks	66%	6 months	66%	Paternity, 3 weeks Child Care Leave until age 3, or partial leave until age 6 at EUR 253 per month with supplement for low-income, etc. Leave for sick children
France	16 weeks	84% with upper limit	Until age 3	EUR 485/month flat rate, income-tested	Paternity, 14 days
Germany	15 weeks	100%	3 years	Up to EUR 300/month for 1st 6 months, next 1.5 year income-tested, 3rd year unpaid	
Hungary	24 weeks	70% for 2 years Thereafter, flat rate	36 months	For uninsured: flat rate of HUF 23 200 (2004) For insured: 70% of wage for 24 weeks, flat rate up to age 3 (2004)	
Ireland	15 weeks	70% for 1st 14 weeks with upper limit (EUR 232/week), 4 weeks unpaid	6.5 months	Unpaid	
Italy	21 weeks	80% (paid by employer)	10 months	30% (paid by employer)	Parental leave is extended to 11 months if father takes 3 months leave
Korea	3 months	100% for 3 months	1 year including maternity entitlement	Flat rate USD 500/month	
Mexico	12 weeks	100%	None		
Netherlands	16 weeks	100% with upper limit	6 months leave for each parent who must also work at least 20 hours/week	Unpaid	Child Care Leave for 2-18 months. EUR 430/month

STARTING STRONG II: EARLY CHILDHOOD EDUCATION AND CARE – ISBN 92-64-03545-1 – © OECD 2006

Table 4.3. **Maternity, paternity, and parental leave policies** (cont.)

	Duration of maternity leave entitlement	Percentage of wage replaced[1]	Duration of parental leave entitlement	Benefit paid	Supplement leaves
Norway	Included in parental leave		43 or 53 weeks of which 30 days for father (use or lose)	80% with upper limit or 42 weeks at 100% with upper limit	
Portugal	16 weeks at 100% or 20 weeks at 80%	100% or 80%	3 months to 4 years	Unpaid	Paternity, 5 days simultaneous with mother or up to 120 days instead of mother at 100%. Grandparent Leave, 30 days if parent is less than 16 years at 100%
Sweden	Parental leave only	80%	240 days for each parent	390 days at 80%, 90 days at flat rate of SEK 60/day	Parental leave equally shared. Paternity, 10 days at birth at 80% with upper limit and 30 days of parental leave available to fathers (use or lose)
United Kingdom	26 weeks plus a further 28 weeks impaid if employed for 26 weeks with same employer	6 weeks at 90%, 20 weeks at a flat rate of GBP 100 or 26 weeks at 90% of wage, whichever is lower	13 weeks (or 18 weeks for parents of child with disability)	Unpaid	Paternity, 1-2 weeks at GBP 100 weeks or 90% of wage, whichever is lower
United States	[3]		12 weeks in firms with 50 or more workers	Unpaid, job-protected[4]	

1. In almost all countries, benefits are financed as part of social insurance or social security, that is, governments and employers bear the major costs. In some countries, direct employee contributions form part of the financing. With the exception of Finland and Sweden, the total costs of maternity and parental leave schemes do not exceed 1% of GDP (Kamerman, 2000).
2. Only 17-38% of mothers are eligible for paid maternity leave (depending on workplace agreement).
3. Some paid maternity leave depending on workplace agreement. Five States provide paid disability leave which, since 1977, is required to cover pregnancy and maternity.
4. Provided by 1993 Family and Medical Leave Act at time of pregnancy, childbirth or illness. Employers can require that employees use vacation and sick leave before claiming family leave.

Source: Data provided by countries.

significant groups of younger women from developing countries engage in housework and child-minding, and may remain available for child care for some years to come if immigration levels are maintained. However, this option may also be a temporary solution to easing the demand for child care, as access to education raises the skills and work expectations of all groups, including immigrant women, and helps them to enter other forms of employment with better wages and working conditions (the average working wage in child care in the United States in 2000 was less than in house-cleaning, coming to "roughly USD 6 per hour or about USD 12 000 a year" Shonkoff, 2000). In addition, as knowledge about child-rearing and early education grows in a society, parents seek out better quality for their children than informal child-minding solutions. Even in countries with a plentiful supply of regulated family day care of acceptable quality, parents increasingly choose professional centre-based care for their children when places are available, *e.g.* in Belgium, France or Norway (Norway, 2005).

Figure 4.3 seeks to present in visual form the policy approaches of different country groups to child care and parental leave. We are conscious, however, that the whole field is changing rapidly, as evidenced, for example, by the raft of ECCE policies promised in the United Kingdom (traditionally, a liberal economy), by the progress being made by Korea in expanding access in both child care and kindergarten, or by the adoption of a remunerated parental leave policy in Canada. In sum, despite a very low base in many countries, provision for children under 3 is undergoing profound change, and receives growing government attention and funding. Since *Starting Strong*, countries have introduced or made progress in policies that: introduce or improve parental leave (Canada, Italy, Norway, the United Kingdom); increase family-friendly work practices (Ireland, the Netherlands, Norway); introduce public-private partnerships into the provision of ECEC (Denmark, Sweden, Finland); and provide significantly greater access to early childhood services (*e.g.* Australia, Finland, Korea, Mexico, Portugal). Strategies have also been employed to address access barriers to centre-based services especially for low-income families (Belgium, France, Ireland, Korea) or to address supply-side barriers in low-income neighbourhoods (Australia, Canada, Germany, Ireland, Korea and Mexico).

3. Ensuring equitable access for all children to attend quality ECEC

Efforts to improve equitable access target primarily two categories of children: children with special needs due to physical, mental or sensory disabilities; and children with additional learning needs derived from family dysfunction, socio-economic disadvantage, or from ethnic, cultural or linguistic factors.[7] In practice, many children in need of special or additional educational support have accumulated both physical and socio-cultural at-risk factors. Early childhood services are particularly important for such children, and contribute strongly to their health, social and cognitive development, as well as to the social inclusion of their families and their future participation in society. Moreover, these services fulfil an early screening function in detecting special needs which, if identified sufficiently early, can be treated more effectively, including the provision of support to families.

Improving access conditions for children with physical and intellectual disabilities

Before the 1980s, care for young children with special needs was generally provided by their families, supported by health and medical services. Frequently, this is still the case for infants and toddlers, as for example, in the Netherlands with its comprehensive network

Figure 4.3. **Policy approaches to the children under 3 and their parents**

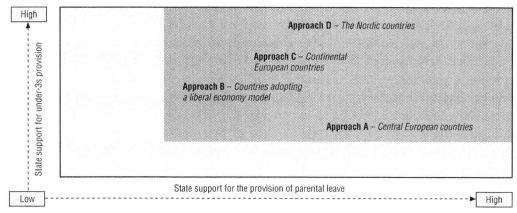

Approach A. Strong state support for parental leave but weak support for services for children under 3. For example, policy in Austria, the Czech Republic, Germany (excepting NBL – former East Germany) and Hungary favours parents (meaning mothers) caring for their child until age 3, with few publicly-supported child care alternatives. Child benefits are significant in these countries, and as they are not tied to the use of child care, they do not stimulate the provision of services or provide an incentive for women to seek work. Child care services remain few or, as in the former Communist bloc, were allowed to run down during the transition years. In the Czech Republic in 2001, for example, only 67 public crèches remained, serving less than 1% of children, compared to a 20% coverage in 1989. The question as to whether women who stay at home to rear their children (and hence forego careers, wages and pension rights) should have the right to more equitable employment opportunities is not a major issue in public debate.

Approach B. Weak support for parental leave with modest to moderate state support for services for children under 3, targeted especially towards low-income families. In the liberal economies, there is moderate state support for licensed services for children under 3, and weak support for parental leave except in Canada, Korea and the United Kingdom where both the duration of leave and its remuneration have been increased. Access rates of children under 3 to regulated services are weak; e.g. in Canada and Ireland, where much informal child care exists. Since 1998, the situation has improved radically in the United Kingdom, bringing the current British pattern of access closer to – and in some instances surpassing – European continental patterns. Although enrolment rates in registered centres in Australia are lower than in the United States, greater financial support is given to parents to access services. In Mexico, the shape of the economy is liberal, with health care, insurance and pensions being predominantly a private responsibility. Public social welfare is relatively weak and is strongly linked to occupation and formal employment. Fertility rates, population distribution and labour market conditions differ also from those holding in most OECD countries. 90% of Mexican child care is domestic, informal or private, but state employees and some working women have access to well-organised services. Women in formal employment (the minority) have a right to at least 12 weeks maternity leave at 50% pay, and to both pre- and post-natal medical attention.

Approach C. Moderate state support to parental leave and moderate support to provision for children under 3, especially for low-income groups. A third approach, offered in the majority of countries reviewed, is moderate support from government to family day care or centre-based education and care, with families still viewed as primarily responsible for providing or finding child care for their children. There is a period of paid statutory parental leave moving towards one year (Italy, Portugal), with very modest levels of publicly funded child care services in several countries, generally insufficient to meet public demand. Child care is subsidised primarily for working or disadvantaged parents. Belgium has a relatively weak parental leave regime, but with better subsidisation and organisation of care services and free access to early education for all children from 2.5 years. France offers also good support to services for children under 3, and in recent years, provides a wider range of parental choice through offering the possibility to parents (that is, mothers) to take a longer low-paid leave for three years.

Approach D. Strong state support for parents with well developed services for children under 3. The fourth model has two different emphases. In Finland and Norway, a main objective is parental choice, supported by strong government investment in child and family services where demand exists. Child care leave or cash benefit schemes allow one parent to stay out of the workforce to care for their child up to three years (Norway, Finland), and provision for children under 3 is publicly subsidised. In Finland, there is a statutory right for every child to a place in a publicly subsidised service, while in Norway addressing shortages in provision for children under 3 is a political priority. In Denmark and Sweden, policy emphasises parental employment after a comparatively well-paid parental leave of 11 months and 18 months, respectively. A guaranteed place in a quality publicly subsidised ECEC service is available from the end of parental leave on a sliding-scale, fee-paying basis. Few infants attend ECEC settings before the end of the parental leave period.

Source: Bennett (2002), *OECD Education Policy Analysis*, updated 2005.

of well-child clinics for young children. For the older children, the education sector has become today a strong ally of the health services and a key agency in tackling disability and learning difficulties. According to IEA/High/Scope research (Weikart et al., 2003), about half the centres reviewed in Phase 2 of the International Association for the Evaluation of Educational Achievement (IEA) Pre-Primary Project offer health and developmental screening to children in ECEC settings.[8] In so doing, education sectors have modified considerably their former practice of segregating children with special needs into specialised educational institutions. In this regard, the UN Convention on the Rights of the Child and the American legal requirement of placement in the "least restrictive environment" have become safeguards for these children and their families. In former Eastern Europe, the practice of separate institutions for children with special needs was also deeply rooted, but a more inclusive approach can now be seen in the New *Länder* of Germany and in Hungary. Today, the New *Länder* (East Germany) reserve 3% of places in their mainstream early childhood services for children with special needs, compared to 0.84% of places in the Old *Länder* (West Germany). In Hungary, the practice of classifying Roma children as children with special needs has given away to policies stressing equity (more resources for these children), poverty reduction, early intervention and inclusion. A gap remains, however, between the directives of central government concerning discrimination and the actual practice of municipalities.

The United States is among the leading countries in providing services for children with disabilities. According to Barnett et al. (2004), pre-school special education programmes are by far the best-funded ECEC programmes across the States:

> *"Federal law requires States to provide children with disabilities a 'free appropriate education' beginning at age 3. However, the federal government caps its spending for the program, and federal pre-school special education funding has steadily declined for many years on a per-child basis. 32 States and local school districts have had to bear the vast majority of the costs of this program. One lesson from this experience might be that adequate funding depends on strong legal entitlements enforced by the courts. In this regard, it is noteworthy that the best funded state pre-school programme for disadvantaged children is in New Jersey, where the state Supreme Court intervened to require high-quality pre-school education"* (Barnett et al., 2004).

The American experience merits attention from other OECD countries. Although an overwhelming case can be made for early intervention in the case of children with special needs (Guralnick, 1998), appropriate taking in charge, not to mention access to mainstream programmes, still remains a challenge. While national laws or government policy allow or encourage access to mainstream services, the official position may not be followed up by an adequately funded national plan to provide structured early learning programmes for children with disabilities and ensure their systematic and appropriate inclusion in mainstream pre-school services. Except for a handful of countries, a picture emerges of public support to these children and their families being irregular, under-funded and non-inclusive (OECD, 2001). Yet, despite neglect or segregation, the policy favoured by most countries – and recommended by the United Nations Convention on the Rights of the Child – is the inclusion of young children with physical and intellectual disabilities into mainstream ECEC services, if this is determined to be best for the child. In several countries, *e.g.* Denmark, Finland, Norway, Sweden, there is a conscious policy to ensure that such children have priority in enrolment in mainstream services and that additional staff resources are allocated to provide more individualised attention by specialised staff. At this young age, there is in fact no categorisation of these children, *e.g.* in the Nordic countries and Italy, but it is taken for granted that the great majority will have a place in the mainstream kindergarten services. Expenditure figures to support the inclusion of special needs children and of children at-risk are also high in the Netherlands and the United States. Early intervention services focus on early detection of problems; prevention of disabilities or further difficulties; stimulation of development; aid and support to families. In Hungarian kindergartens, in addition to the focus on Roma children, there is a concern to identify and prevent dyslexia or other cognitive processing disorders from an early age.

As noted in *Starting Strong* (OECD, 2001), successful inclusion requires attention to the organisation and management of ECEC settings, in particular the adaptation of premises to the needs of children with disabilities, the hiring or allocation of specialised staff, and more flexible organisation of group sizes and rooms to cater for specialised sessions. Access to centres and classrooms can still be difficult for children with impaired sight or movement, and services often lack the specialised personnel needed to support children with additional learning needs. In turn, greater public funding is necessary, based on realistic assessments of the numbers of children with special needs (approximately 5% in all populations, but greater in contexts of high child poverty and weak public health systems).

Successful inclusion of children with special or additional educational needs requires responsive pedagogical approaches and curricula, *e.g.* more intensive team planning and careful management of activities as staff endeavour to adapt constantly to the learning needs presented by individual children. To reach the learning goals that children can realistically achieve, individualised educational plans (IEPs) – determined by children, parents and teachers together – are formulated and implemented (*e.g.* Canada, Finland, Flemish Community of Belgium, Hungary, the United States). By necessity, staff ratios – both teachers and classroom assistants – are higher for children with special educational needs and special training is necessary, factors that still inhibit inclusion in some countries. In Canada (some provinces), Finland and Italy, special education staff provide on-the-job training to their mainstream colleagues.

Parental involvement is desirable in all programmes for young children, but particularly in programmes that include children with special educational needs. In addition, ECEC centres that receive children with disabilities or other educational differences must also put into place co-operative agreements with community health and social services agencies, an activity that demands expertise and much investment of time. Such agreements and co-operation with other services are characteristics of special needs services in Canada and the United States.

Children with additional learning needs deriving from low socio-economic or ethnic backgrounds

For children with additional educational needs deriving from low socio-economic or ethnic backgrounds, special programming within universal services can help address the barriers that hold back these children in education or prevent their families from making full use of services. Most countries provide (to different degrees) comprehensive ECEC services in poor neighbourhoods, with differentiated pedagogy, improved staff resources and outreach to families and communities. As outstanding programmes show – *e.g.* the Mo.Ki Project in Monheim, Germany (Box 4.2), Rinkeby in Sweden, Sheffield in the United Kingdom, or the Freinet schools in Ghent, Belgium[9] – whenever early childhood programmes acknowledge and welcome cultural diversity, they are more acceptable to

Box 4.2. **The pilot project Mo.Ki (Monheim für Kinder) – Monheim for Children in Westphalia, Germany**

Monheim is a city of 44 000 inhabitants, situated in Nord-Rhein Westphalia. Approximately 11.5% of the population is foreign born, and the overall unemployment rate is almost 8%. The Mo.Ki project – Monheim for Children – is located in Berliner Viertel, a district of 11 000 inhabitants, many of them immigrants. Before entering school, 82% of the children from this district showed cognitive and language delays that could be attributed to socio-economic and cultural factors. The Youth Welfare Office (Jugendamt) of the city and the Workers' Welfare Service (Arbeiterwohlfahrt) came together in 1999 to launch the pilot project "Mo.Ki", with the financial help of the State Youth Welfare Office. The main objective of the project is to prevent and overcome the consequences of poverty on young children from birth and throughout the education period. The project is based on the co-operation of many agencies, *e.g.* school, health, police, social pedagogy, family and employment services. The ISS, a research institute for social work and pedagogy, undertakes the scientific documentation of the project. It supports and follows the project from a participatory research perspective, and has contributed to the development of the child development and poverty prevention concept. It also collects and analyses the data, documents and tests the effectiveness of activities and approaches, and puts forward new hypotheses for consideration.

Mo.Ki adopts a comprehensive approach to poverty, and has developed a series of inter-connecting programmes. In sum, three main fields of action can be discerned:

● *Preventive programmes for children:* care and early promotion. Preventive programming for children has been expanded so that the demand for quality institutional day care is met. This includes more flexible hours, and more personnel provided to centres with a high percentage of poor and socially excluded children.

● *Strengthening the competences of parents:* Measures for parental counselling and education are included in order to strengthen the resources of families. Parents are informed about the factors that contribute to their child's well-being: regular common activities within the family; good atmosphere in the family; at least one parent with a good knowledge of German; no family debts; adequate living conditions.

● *Building up a network of co-operation "Monheim for Children":* The city of Monheim has developed an extensive programme to improve the image of Berliner Viertel as a place for living. This has meant co-ordinating and connecting existing programmes in the district as well as supporting new initiatives.

Child care centres were chosen as the first line of action, not only because poor families use them at one time or another but also because of the greater impact of poverty on infants and young children. In this regard, good quality early childhood services have a proven preventive effect, and provide not only security, care and early education for young children but also improve family functioning and the social participation of their parents, many of whom are unemployed.

For more information: *www.monheim.de/stadtprofil/moki/index.html.*

immigrant communities. However, comprehensive programming is still not the rule: evaluations in several countries (*e.g.* the Netherlands, Portugal, the United Kingdom, the United States) suggest that when disadvantaged children participate in ECEC, they often do not receive the full range of child development, health and family services that are needed to optimise their learning (*Starting Strong*, OECD, 2001). These children need not only equal access to services but also services with enhanced funding, better child-staff ratios, innovative and adapted pedagogies. Care should also be taken to acknowledge positively the multiple identities of children and families in keeping with the UN Convention on the Rights of the Child (Murray, 2006). Public provision will also address issues of prejudice and discrimination, which children from low-income and/or ethnic families can encounter both within and outside schools (Derman-Sparks, 1989).

As outlined in Chapter 1, it is also important to tackle the larger issue of child poverty at a more upstream level, through supportive employment incentive policies, income support, social services and child benefits. ECEC does make an important contribution to the development of young children from "at-risk" backgrounds, but it cannot inoculate against subsequent educational experiences or substantially address structural poverty (Zigler *et al.*, 1996). As Figures 1.7 and 10.1 show, participating OECD countries evaluate and approach the issue of disadvantage in different ways, with Denmark, Norway, Finland and Sweden being most successful in preventing child poverty.

Notes

1. Head Start is a federally-funded programme in the United States that provides comprehensive developmental services for America's low-income, pre-school children aged 3 to 5, and social services for their families. Approximately 1 400 community-based non-profit organisations and school systems develop Head Start programmes to meet the needs of this target group. It is estimated that the programme provides sessional services to about 3% of American children from birth to 5 years and to about 60% of eligible children from 3 to 5 years (Kagan and Rigby, 2003).

2. In Italy, pre-primary education is free only in state-run and municipal schools, not in private schools, although in general, only modest fees are required in the majority of voluntary schools. In the Netherlands, voluntary schools are fully subsidised, and cannot demand fees. The daily and annual duration of provision varies widely from country to country.

3. Also known as "wrap-around care" in the context of part-day pre-school, or "school-aged child care" for children in primary school, or preferably "free-time services" as these services should ideally be recreational for young children.

4. The Harvard Family Research Project makes available a valuable Out-of-School Time (OST) Programme Evaluation Database containing profiles and evaluations of a wide range of American OST programmes. It can be accessed at: *www.gse.harvard.edu/hfrp/projects/afterschool/ evaldatabase.html*

5. In Sweden, because of the long and generous parental leave scheme, infants are rarely seen in day care services, and are normally enrolled between the ages of 15 to 18 months.

6. Canada introduced in the federal Employment Insurance Act of 2001, a parental leave scheme of almost one year, remunerated at 55% of salary to a ceiling of CAD 413 per week. However, use of licensed child care is extremely weak, except in Quebec.

7. The OECD Directorate for Education classifies special educational needs in the following manner:
   - Category A: Refers to educational needs of students suffering from organic disorders attributable to organic pathologies, related to sensory, motor or neurological defects, *e.g.* blind and partially sighted, deaf and partially hearing, severe and profound mental handicap, multiple handicaps, etc. These are conditions that affect students from all social classes and occupations, generally around 5% of any population. Typically, adequate measuring instruments and agreed criteria are available.
   - Category B: Refers to educational needs of students who have difficulties in learning which do not appear to be directly or primarily attributable to factors which would lead to categorisation as "A" or "C". For instance, students with learning disabilities, as defined in the United States, are classified here. These difficulties are often temporary in nature, and afflict a small percentage – around 1% – of any population.

● Category C: Refers to educational needs of students that are considered to arise primarily from socio-economic, cultural and/or linguistic factors. There is present some form of background, generally considered to be a disadvantage, for which education seeks to compensate. This is a large group in many countries ranging from 15% to 25% of children in any given urban population.

8. The IEA Pre-Primary Project was a study conducted in 15 countries (Belgium, Finland, Greece, Ireland, Italy, Spain, Poland, Romania, Slovenia, China (People's Republic), Hong Kong, Indonesia, Thailand, Nigeria, and the United States) in an effort "to identify the settings in which young children of various nations spend their time, to assess the 'quality of life' for children in these settings, and to determine how these settings affect children's intellectual, social, and academic development at age 7" between 1986 and 2002.

9. For a description of the Ghent schools, see *Children in Europe*, No. 4, 2003.

References

Afterschool Alliance (2004), "America After 3 PM: A Household Survey on Afterschool in America", Afterschool Alliance, Washington DC.

Austalian Government Productivity Commission (2006), "Report on Government Services 2006", *www.pc.gov.au/gsp/reports/rogs/2006/index.html*.

Barnett, W.S., K. Brown and R. Shore (2004), "The Universal vs. Targeted Debate: Should the United States Have Pre-school for All?", *Preschool Policy Matters*, Vol. 6. National Institute for Early Education Research, Rutgers University, New Brunswick, NJ.

Bennett, J. (2002), "Strengthening Early Childhood Programmes: A Policy Framework", *Education Policy Analysis*, OECD, Paris.

Brooks-Gunn, J., W. Han and J. Waldfogel (2002), "Maternal Employment and Child Cognitive Outcomes in the First Three Years of Life: The NICHD Study of Early Child Care", *Child Development*, Vol. 73(4), pp. 1052-1072.

Capizzano, J. and G. Adams (2000a), "The Hours that Children under Five Spend in Child Care: Variation across States", Series to Assess Changing Social Policies, No. B-8, March, The Urban Institute, Washington DC.

Capizzano, J. and G. Adams (2000b), "The Number of Child Care Arrangements Used by Children under five: Variation across States, New Federalism National Survey of American Families", Series to Assess Changing Social Policies, No. B-12, March, The Urban Institute, Washington DC.

Currie, J. (2004), *Combining Early Care and Education: Is Universal Pre-K the Best Way?*, UCLA, Los Angeles, CA.

Chatterji, P. and S. Markowicz (2004), "Does the Length of Maternity Leave Affect Maternal Health?", Social Science Research Network, National Bureau of Economic Research Working Paper No. W10206, Harvard Medical School/Rutgers Department of Economics.

Derman-Sparks, L. (1989), *Anti-bias Curriculum: Tools for Empowering Young People*, NAEYC, Washington.

Fuller, B.C., A. Livas and M. Bridges (2005), "How to Expand and Improve Pre-school in California: Ideals, Evidence, and Policy Options", PACE Working Paper 05-1, Policy Analysis for California Education (PACE), Berkeley, California.

Guralnick, M.J. (1998), "The Effectiveness of Early Intervention for Vulnerable Children: A Developmental Perspective", *American Journal on Mental Retardation*, Vol. 102, pp. 319-345.

Hungarian Ministry of Youth, Family, Social Affairs and Equal Opportunities and the Hungarian Ministry of Education (2005), Background Report of Hungary, Budapest.

Kagan, S.L. and E. Rigby (2003), "Policy Matters: Setting and Measuring Benchmarks for State Policies. Improving the Readiness of Children for School. A Discussion Paper", Center for the Study of Social Policy, Washington DC, February.

Kamerman, S.B. (2000), "Parental Leave Policies: An Essential Ingredient in Early Childhood Education and Care Policies", *Social Policy Report*, Vol. 14, No. 2, ICFP Publications, NY.

Leseman, P. (2002), "Early Childhood Education and Care for Children from Low-income or Minority Backgrounds", OECD, Paris.

Murray, C. (2006), *The Dominant Walk: A Training Practice*, Pavee Point, Dublin.

National Centre for Educational Statistics (NCES) (2004), "Before- and After-school Care. Programs and Activities for Children in Kindergarten through Eighth Grade: 2001. Statistical Analysis Report", April, *http://nces.ed.gov/pubs2004/2004008.pdf*.

NIEER (National Institute for Early Education Research) (2003), "The State of Pre-School Yearbook", NIEER, NJ, *nieer.org/yearbook/pdf/yearbook.pdf*.

NIEER (2004), "Pre-School Policy Matters", Issue 6, NIEER, Rutgers University, NJ, *nieer.org*.

Observatoire de l'Enfance (2003), *État des lieux de l'accueil des enfants 2.5 à 12 ans en dehors des lieux scolaires*, ONÉ, Bruxelles.

OECD (2001), *Starting Strong: Early Childhood Education and Care*, OECD, Paris.

OECD (2003), Ireland Country Note, OECD, Paris.

OECD (2004a), Germany Background Report, OECD, Paris.

OECD (2004b), Ireland Background Report and Country Note, OECD, Paris.

Schulman, K., H. Blank and D. Ewen (1999), "Seeds of Success: State Pre-kindergarten Initiatives: 1998-1999", The Children's Defence Fund, Washington DC.

Scottish Executive (2003), "Integrated Strategy for the Early Years", Scottish Executive, Edinburgh.

Shonkoff, J.P. (2000), "Science, Policy, and Practice: Three Cultures in Search of a Shared Mission", *Child Development*, Vol. 71, pp. 181-187.

Shonkoff, J.P. and D.A. Phillips (eds) (2000), "From Neurons to Neighbourhoods: The science of Early Childhood Development", National Academy Press, Washington DC.

Shore, R. (1997), "Rethinking the Brain: New Insights into Early Development", Families and Work Institute, Washington.

Strategy Unit (2002), "Delivering for Children and Families: Interdepartmental Childcare Review – November 2002", Strategy Unit, London.

Tanaka, S. (2005), "Parental Leave and Child Health across OECD Countries", *Economic Journal*, Vol. 115, pp. F7-F28, February 2005.

United Kingdom Interdepartmental Childcare Review (2002), "Government Review of Childcare – Good News for Children, Parents and Communities", *www.dfes.gov.uk/pns/DisplayPN.cgi?pn_id=2002_0209*.

Weikart, D., P. Olmsted, J. Montie, N. Hayes and M. Ojla (eds.) (2003), "A World of Pre-school Experiences: Observations in 15 Countries, The IEA Preprimary Project Phase 2", High/Scope Press, Ypsilanti, MI.

Zigler, E., S.L. Kagan and N. Hall (eds) (1996), *Children, Families and Government: Preparing for the Twenty-First Century,* Cambridge University Press, New York.

ISBN 92-64-03545-1
Starting Strong II: Early Childhood Education and Care
© OECD 2006

Chapter 5

Substantial Public Investment in Services and the Infrastructure

Chapter 5 explores the critical issue of public investment in services for young children, including investment in the infrastructure of governance and support services. The benefits of public investment in early childhood education and care (ECEC) services are discussed, and the extent of investment by countries in ECEC services is gauged. Strategies employed by some countries to bring additional funding into the field are listed and information is provided on how governments fund ECEC services. A discussion is engaged on whether funding modalities – in particular, direct funding to services or, in contrast, subsidies paid to parents – have an impact on the overall quality of the system. A conclusion reached is that direct public funding of services brings, for the moment at least, more effective control, advantages of scale, more even national quality, more effective training for educators and a higher degree of equity in access and participation than parent subsidy models. This may be a question of the newness of the parent subsidy model and the relative inexperience of administrations in requiring equity and accountability of private providers. Effective policy in the early childhood field requires today – as it is still a relatively new field – significant investment in administration and support services. Without a critical mass of experienced administrators to offer advice and draw attention to research evidence, public policies with regard to early childhood can be short-sighted and wasteful.

Evidence from the OECD thematic reviews suggests that significant public funding is necessary to support a sustainable and equitable early childhood system. Without that investment, a shortage of good quality programmes, unequal access, and segregation of children according to income follows. When the main burden of costs falls on parents, children from disadvantaged backgrounds become less represented in ECEC provision or the quality of provision at their disposal is inadequate. In addition, a major barrier to the access of women to work is created, with mothers of young children either leaving the labour market or being obliged to take low-paid, part-time work[1] in order to rear their children (OECD, 2002). This chapter will describe how services for young children are funded in different countries, outline some of the funding options open to governments, examine the impacts of funding modes on the organisation and management of services, and recommend that government funding should also be channelled towards the governance and management structures of early childhood systems.

What did Starting Strong recommend?

- *Substantial public investment by government is necessary to support a sustainable system of quality, accessible services.* Limited public investment has negative effects, leading to provision shortages, low quality (generally for children from less affluent backgrounds), unequal access and the segregation of children according to income.

- The coherence and quality of the early childhood system requires not only funding for services but also investment in the management infrastructure that is responsible for planning, regulation, evaluation, in-service training, monitoring and research.

1. Who benefits from investments in ECEC services?

The international evidence on the benefits of high quality ECEC is outlined in Annex D of this report. This literature is based on research coming from both OECD and developing countries, and is provided by a wide range of researchers: public health administrators, nutritionists, neuro-biologists, psychologists and education researchers. As noted by Myers (2004), this vast research effort can be cited to support:

"*The position that the early years constitute a key period for the development of intelligence, personality and behaviour.*

The idea that early childhood learning and development can be enhanced.

The way in which early learning and development happens is sensitive to differences in cultural, social and economic contexts."

Governmental domains that benefit from the widespread provision of early childhood education and care services are: the national economy (short-term, through the contribution of working women, and long-term through more effective human capital formation); health (better mental and physical health for children and families, less at-risk behaviours, etc.); social welfare and criminal justice (less dependency of families on social welfare; higher earnings for families; more gender equality; less family violence, less criminality, etc.); education (better integration of young children at-risk into primary school, better grade progression, less participation in special education, etc.). Some of these benefits are graphically shown in findings from the High/Scope Perry Pre-school Study of participants and the control group at age 40 (Figure 5.1).

Figure 5.1. **Major findings of Perry Pre-school Study at age 40**

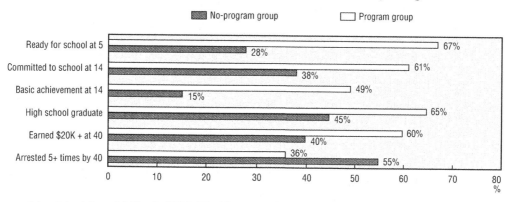

Source: Schweinhart, L. and J. Montie (2004), "Significant Benefits: The High/Scope Perry, Pre-school Study through Age 40", High/Scope Educational Research Foundation, World Bank Presentation, November 17.

In summary, the research suggests that the investment in young children is a sound one, bringing significant benefits not only for children and families but also for society at large. On the other hand, the consequences of under-investment can be seen all too clearly, particularly in the case of youth where crime figures are consistently high among the control group and their education achievement level at age 14 is extremely low. Though not illustrated by Figure 5.1, lack of investment also results in: child care shortages; low quality, especially in services for children from less affluent backgrounds;[2] unequal access and the segregation of children according to income (Prentice, 2005; Sadowski, 2006; Waters Boots, 2005). Unavailability of services raises barriers against women's full-time employment and also channels women towards low-paid, part-time jobs (Lee, 2004, Immervoll and Barber, 2005).

2. How much are countries spending on ECEC services?

Current investments of OECD countries in early childhood education and care services are difficult to calculate, as reliable figures for child care expenditure by governments are often not available. In addition, the available International Standard Classification of Education (ISCED) Level 0 figures supplied to the OECD by countries for pre-primary education are not comparable because of the different interpretations of "pre-primary" by countries which supply these data. The problem is raised also in Chapter 8 on data and research, where we indicate that *Education at a Glance* (OECD, 2005) provides an expenditure figure per child (3- to 6-year-old) in France of USD 4 512, in Sweden USD 4 107, and in the United Kingdom USD 8 452. Even a slight acquaintance with services in these countries suggests that the Swedish figure is grossly underestimated: child-staff ratios are significantly lower in Sweden than in the other countries; and 50% of pre-school staff (1- to 6-year-olds) are trained (and paid) to university level. The duration of work is also much longer than in Britain or France, as centres open 10 hours per day, during the whole working year.

Figure 5.2, based on OECD data sources, provides an indication of what countries are investing in services for families and young children in percentages of GDP. The white lines referring to early education and care need to be interpreted with caution, as the note indicates.

Figure 5.2. **Public investment in services for families and young children in percentages of GDP**

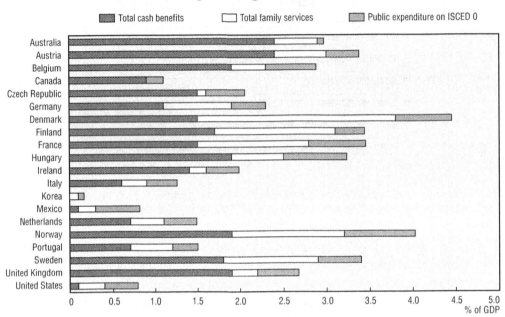

Note: For Denmark and Sweden, expenditure levels on ISCED Level 0 – as represented on this figure (white portion of the bar) – cover only a small proportion of their actual ECEC expenditure on children 1 to 6 years old. Similarly for Korea, where only Ministry of Education expenditure is included.

Source: OECD (2005), *Education at a Glance.*

From the figures supplied to the OECD for the ECEC country profiles, we have generated Figure 5.3 that provides a more realistic picture of public investment by selected countries in ECEC services (including out-of-school services but excluding family benefits and parental leave). The figure indicates that investment in early childhood services per country ranges from about 2% of gross domestic product (GDP) in Denmark to about 0.3% of GDP in Canada. This is a significant difference, which can also be seen in the quality and range of services available to parents.

In recent years, countries with comparatively low public expenditure on children's services in the past (*e.g.* Ireland, Korea, Portugal, the Netherlands, the United Kingdom, etc.) have increased spending significantly. In Portugal, for example, the budget for pre-school education has more than doubled since 1996, and has tripled in Korea. In the United Kingdom, according to official projections, government expenditure will have quadrupled in the ten years from 1997-2007, from GBP 1.1 billion in 1996/7 to GBP 4.4 billion by 2007/8. Despite these investments in families and young children, significant shortcomings still exist, particularly in services for children under 3. This is partly the result of an unprecedented demand for ECEC services, as increasing numbers of young women join and continue to stay in the workforce. Many governments were unprepared for the rapid rise in demand and have chosen to rely on the market to provide rapidly a

Figure 5.3. **Public expenditure on ECEC services (0-6 years) in selected OECD countries (%)**

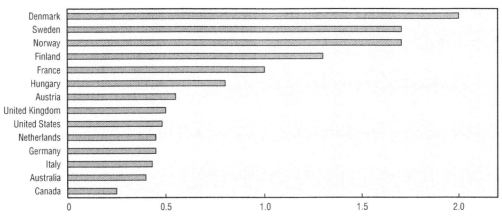

Note: This figure is comprised of expenditure estimates, based on replies provided by country authorities to an OECD survey in 2004. The figures provided suggest that Denmark spends 2% of GDP on early childhood services for 0- to 6-year-olds, and Sweden 1.7%. These countries – and Finland – also allocate an additional 0.3% (approximately) to the pre-school class for children 6 to 7 years.

sufficient number of services. The experience of the OECD reviews suggests that the market can help in quickly providing services but that quality in services will not be built up without considerable government investment and effort. (Discussion of service quality, a key to reaping the benefits of these investments, is taken up in Chapter 6.)

The support services offered to parents also differ widely from one country to another. This has already been noted in regard to parental leave, but it is also the case with respect to other allowances and facilities that encourage parents, especially with low or modest incomes, to use services and attempt to join the workforce. Box 5.1 refers to measures put into place over decades in France. Critics point out that some of these measures are not work or gender-friendly, *e.g.* the APE or prolonged parental leave is taken almost exclusively by mothers. However, the effect of the entire "package" makes it easier for French parents with young children both to work and to find quality solutions for their child care needs.

How much should countries be investing?

In 1996, the European Commission Network on Childcare (EC Network on Childcare, 1996) recommended to European countries an investment level of at least 1% of GDP. As can be seen from Figure 5.3 only five countries of the twenty reviewed have clearly reached this investment level: Denmark, Finland, France (the 1% investment attributed includes local authority investments; *école maternelle* for children from age 2; and child care services), Norway and Sweden. It is probable also that Belgium (Flanders) approaches the level of 1%, as in addition to the *kleuterschool* from 2.5 years, both child care and diversity expenditure are significant. Hungarian investment is also probably just beneath the 1% mark, but although investment in kindergarten is strong, child care services are still relatively few (parental leave payments are not included in the figure). However, the case can be made that 1% of GDP is a minimum figure if adequate quality is to be maintained. In this regard, France's relatively high investment of about 1% does not ensure adequate child-staff ratios, for although the system employs only graduate level teachers, it enrols almost 100% of children from 3 years. In addition, it depends almost entirely on public financing, with no

---

Box 5.1. **ECEC subsidies to French families**

There are currently five types of allowances to help offset the costs of early childhood care and education (ECEC) in France.

Allocation parentale d'éducation (APE) or parental leave allowance: Parents with at least two children who are not working or are working part time are eligible for the APE. For those with two children, the parent must have worked two of the past five years, and for those with three children or more, the parent must have worked two of the past ten years. The full rate is EUR 484.97 and can be received by eligible families until the child's third birthday. It cannot be cumulated with the APJE (described below) and is not included in the calculation of housing allowances.

Aide à la famille pour l'emploi d'une assistante maternelle (AFEAMA) or family day care allowance: Families with children under six who place their children with a licensed family day care provider (*assistante maternelle*) are eligible for this allowance which covers social insurance contributions. An additional allowance that varies according to the age of the child and to family income helps offset other costs. For a child under three, the allowance was EUR 203 monthly for those with annual incomes under EUR 12 912; EUR 160 for incomes between EUR 12 912; and EUR 17 754, and EUR 133 for those with incomes greater than EUR 17 754. For children between the ages of three and six, the subsidies are divided in half.

Allocation de garde d'enfant à domicile (AGED) or in-home caregiver allowance: Parents who use an in-home caregiver to care for one or more children under age six in their homes while they are at work may benefit from a subsidy which is given directly to the social insurance agency (URSSAF). The subsidy varies according to the age of the child and family income. For a child under three and a family income less than EUR 34 744, the subsidy covers 75% of social contribution expenses up to EUR 1 548 per trimester.

Allocation pour jeune enfant (APJE) or child benefit: This allowance is considered both an income subsidy and a child care allowance. The child benefit may not be received at the same time as the parental leave allowance (APE). This income-tested benefit may be received from the fifth month of pregnancy until the child's third birthday. Currently, 80% of families with children under three receive the benefit (EUR 156.31 monthly).

Tax benefits: Parents also can benefit from tax deductions to offset costs of ECEC. Specifically, parents can be reimbursed up to 25% of out-of-pocket expenses up to EUR 2 300 per year. The maximum tax reduction is EUR 575 per year. To offset the costs of hiring an in-home caregiver, parents can receive a tax reduction equivalent to 50% of out-of-pocket expenditures up to EUR 6 900. Thus, the maximum tax reduction is EUR 3 450 per year.

Source: French Background Report and Country Note for France, 2003, 2004.

---

support from parental fees. In contrast, the system in Finland spends over 1% of GDP on ECEC services for 30% fewer children, charges a small parental fee and employs a more mixed workforce.

Another way of looking at ECEC investment is to ask: what is the average investment per child in a good quality programme or in a public ECEC system known to have good services. A figure of this nature may perhaps be a more concrete benchmark for early childhood managers. From the evidence at our disposal – for example, average child costs in Denmark, Finland, Norway and Sweden; estimated average costs per child in the American Abecedarian[3] and Head Start projects; and estimates made by the Committee for Economic Development

(CED, 2002, 2006); or as proposed by Kagan and Rigby (2003) – the figure works out at over USD 8 000 per child per year in early education (3-6 years) for a school year, full-day programme in which reasonable child-staff ratios are practised, and a majority of certified educators are employed. The Committee for Economic Development (CED, 2006) proposes USD 5 000 as a rough starting point for a child attending a part-day, part-year programme. Again, from an American perspective, the independent researchers, Kagan and Rigby (2003), propose that States should allocate at least USD 8000-12 000 per child enrolled in a full-day pre-school (early education) programme, and from USD 4000-6 000 per child enrolled in a half-day programme. Table 5.1 summarises the evidence referred to.

Table 5.1. **Investment estimates per child in high quality early childhood programmes**

Country or programme	Half-day, school year programme	Full-day, school year programme	Full-day, year round, with integrated child care	Reference
Denmark, 2004			USD 19 500 (this figure includes a parental contribution of c. 30%). The net public investment is USD 13 650	BUPL, 2005
Finland, 2004			Over EUR 10 248 (not including parental contribution)	STAKES, 2005
Norway, 2005			EUR 12 520 (not including parental contribution)	BFD, 2005
Sweden, 2004			USD 12 097 (not including parental contribution)	Ministry of Education and Culture, 2005
Abecedarian Project, North Carolina		c. USD 13 000 in 2002 costs		Masse and Barnett, 2003
Committee Economic Development, 2006	USD 5 100	USD 8 800	USD 12 970	CED, 2006 www.ced.org
Head Start, 2005	USD 8 626 (federal and local contributions combined)			NIEER, 2006
Kagan and Rigby estimates	USD 4 000-6000	USD 8 000-12 000		Kagan and Rigby, 2003

No doubt, countries would have to judge these figures in light of their particular level of wealth,[4] but across the programmes and countries cited, there is a remarkable consensus on per child costs for a quality programme. The unit costs in Head Start seem high but in fact, many Head Start programmes are full-day, year long. Unit costs in Denmark, Norway and Sweden for children aged 1-6 years are all in excess of USD 10 000 per child and reach USD 13 650 in Denmark, being more expensive at the beginning of the cycle and less so towards the end. The higher proportion of university-trained pedagogues working in the Danish system than, for example, in Finland may explain the differences in costs between these countries. In contrast, across the OECD countries, the average investment per child in pre-primary programmes (ranging from 2.5 to 8 hours) is USD 4 294 per child (OECD, *Education at a Glance*, 2005), that is, significantly less than investments per pupil in primary or secondary education, not to mention tertiary education, which in many countries receives the greatest share per student of education budgets. The situation gainsays the economic returns analyses of Cunha *et al.* (2005) and other authors (see Chapter 1, Figure 1.9) showing that investments in young children have a more profound and lasting effect on learning potential than at any other age – in Heckman's phrase: "learning begets learning".

3. Bringing new resources into the ECEC field

Among the various strategies or mechanisms used to bring new financing into ECEC systems, OECD teams noted the following in the country reviews:

● A *pooling of resources and sharing of costs across ministries, social partners, local communities and users*, whenever common objectives are being attained for young children and their families. If wrap-around education and care for young children improves social inclusion and labour market expansion, there is little reason why the capital and operational costs of services should not be shared across a range of ministries and other interest groups. In Belgium, France and Italy, for example, a significant part (about 1%) of social security and/or corporate tax is channelled towards children's services. In Denmark, Finland, Korea, Sweden and the United Kingdom, local authorities raise taxes, which are used to supplement the state allocation for health, social welfare and early education services.

● A *reallocation of resources within education budgets*: All parts of the education systems have their importance but a better apportioning of educational resources towards young children needs to be considered. This is not only a question of an equitable distribution of educational resources towards children at the base but also of the efficiency of education investment (Cunha *et al.*, 2005 – and see Chapter 2). For a good return on investment, programmes for young children must provide quality, which in turn requires favourable child-staff ratios and appropriate pedagogy. In addition, more than any other group, young children spend a longer period each day in their centres.[5]

● *The creation of markets in child care*: This is a strategy found mostly – but not exclusively – in the liberal economies. Rather than the State being the sole purveyor of ECEC services, policy makers in Australia, Canada, Ireland, the Netherlands, the United Kingdom and the United States involve for-profit groups in the provision of services alongside state or community providers. The rationale is to supplement public expenditure, widen the sources of service supply, introduce competition into the provision of services and provide parents with more provider choice and greater flexibility in services. In crises of supply, for-profit providers, such as small family day carers, are able to react more rapidly to demand, particularly if regulation is kept low. In the United States, for example, there is a long-standing tradition of encouraging markets and competition in all fields. About 90% of child care in the United States is provided by private providers, over half of whom work on a for-profit basis. Australia has also pursued the privatisation of services, and from 1996 to 1998 removed – under a "level playing field" strategy – direct operational subsidies to community non-profit services (see Australian profile in Annex E). Currently, many Australian policy makers consider the strategy successful as it brought new investment into a field that had remained under-funded.[6] They argue that without this new investment, even greater shortages of provision might have continued to exist (Purcell, 2001). More recently, the Netherlands has transformed its public child care service (led by the municipalities) into a demand-side, parent subsidy child care system. However, concern is expressed in Dutch early childhood circles that in order to facilitate the operation of market forces, the new Youth and Child Care Act (2005) has abandoned structural regulations regarding group size, child caregiver ratios and deprives caregivers of further education and training[7] – leading, it is feared, to a lowering of quality standards. In addition, Dutch middle-class parents are currently paying a far greater share of costs than hitherto, and well in excess of the European Union average of one-third (Vermeer *et al.*, 2005).

- *Cost-effective co-ordination of early childhood policies at central level and integration of services at local level*, in particular for the 3- to 6-year olds. The co-ordination of early childhood management at central level has been discussed in Chapter 2. Integration under one ministry is more efficient in terms of vision and planning, and removes the duplication of administrative and regulatory frameworks that split or multiple auspices impose. At local level, a rationalisation of services can also be operated, again at administrative level (in the Nordic countries, local integration preceded the unified ministerial auspices). At local level also, it seems more sensible to invest significantly in school infrastructure, and to bring early education and care, full-day and out-of-school time provision together in one location, rather than to engage separate investments in rented and other premises. Concentration of centre-based services can help to reduce costs and create new synergies. Having services on one site also reduces daily transitions for young children and facilitates the schedules of working parents.[8] Criticisms have been voiced in Denmark, however, of over-concentration of services at school level, as insufficient attention may be given to the smaller services, such as free-time services. According to DLO (2001), early childhood services and out-of-school time provision need well-designed buildings for their own particular needs, and independent parent boards to ensure acceptable programming for the children involved in these services.

- *Public-private partnerships – a sharing of tasks with the voluntary, community and private sector*, and the incorporation of non-public providers into a publicly funded and professionally managed system. The contribution made by non-governmental organisations and local private providers to the state network is often significant, even essential. Many countries, *e.g.* Australia, Canada, Denmark, Finland, Hungary, Ireland, Norway, Sweden, the United Kingdom, and the United States, grant operating licenses to providers that maintain quality standards and reward them either directly with operational subsidies or indirectly through subsidising parental fees. In granting subsidies, governments may require voluntary early education bodies to accept an appropriate quota of children from disadvantaged or special needs backgrounds, and to keep fees within the range defined by the public authorities. In the liberal economies, however, governments sometimes grant providers a derogation from the standards expected of public services, *e.g.* Section 108 of the new Washington State law (2006) in the United States affirms: "Except for licensing as required by Washington State law and to the extent permitted by federal law, the director of the department of early learning shall grant waivers from the rules of state agencies for the operation of early learning programmes requested by non-governmental private-public partnerships to allow for flexibility to pursue market-based approaches to achieving the best outcomes for children and families."

- *Enlisting support from the corporate and business sectors*. In some countries, employers and corporations are important providers or funders of early childhood services. In the Netherlands, for example, companies above a certain number of employees are expected to pay a third of the costs of child care places in accredited centres for the young children of their employees. In Korea and Mexico, firms employing a certain quota of young women are required by law to establish an on-site day care centre or subsidise child care and early education expenses for their employees. More in keeping with seeing ECEC as a public good, employers in France must contribute to the *Caisse d'allocations familiales* (the family benefits treasury) which, in turn, subsidies child care costs in the region to an average of 25%. Belgium (0.05% of the company's wage bill) and Italy have similar levies on employers to meet the costs of local child care. In other countries, *e.g.* Australia,

Ireland and the United Kingdom, builders are expected to include in their costs for housing estates, the construction of appropriately-designed crèches and schools. Local communities and industry are also expected to contribute.

- *Other funding sources*: In the United States, grants from the large corporations towards early childhood services are common, as tax concessions can be granted by the public authorities for large donations. Other funding sources include special taxes, such as in Arkansas, where the excise tax on packaged beer is used to fund the state-wide Better Chance programme, or in Los Angeles County, where a tax on tobacco is used to fund early childhood programming. In Georgia, state lottery proceeds fund early childhood services and provide subventions to needy stage-three students wishing to enter college. A lesser but similar use of lottery money is practised in the United Kingdom through the New Opportunities Fund. It may be noted that governments in some countries would judge these means to be dubious and unnecessary, as they consider early childhood education and care to be the foundation stage of public education and hence, the direct responsibility of government.

4. How do governments fund ECEC services?

For this discussion, a distinction should be drawn between pre-primary and early education for 3- to 6-year-olds, and child care. Broadly speaking, governments in all countries take in charge the major costs of public early education from the age of 3, 4 or 5 years. Figure 5.4 provides a comparison across the countries in the review between public and private expenditure at ISCED Level 0.[9] When these public services are under ministry of education auspices, funding may be taken in charge almost completely by the central government: Belgium, France, Italy,[10] the Netherlands, and the United Kingdom are examples. With the exception of Mexico in the review, the non-European liberal economies provide free public early education at a later age than in other countries. Thus, in Australia, Canada, Korea and the United States, governments provide free pre-school educational services for children, from about the age of 5 years, although in some instances, efforts are made to provide free half-day services for 4-year-olds either under state/provincial auspices or through targeted central government programming. The Nordic countries still charge for services up to the age of 6 years, but charges are modest (parents fund between 9-15% of service costs). Certain parts of the day ("early education periods") may be free of charge, and costs are waived for poorer parents. Readers will note that Figure 5.4 shares the same weakness as other figures in the OECD, *Education at a Glance* series: the public financial contributions made by Denmark, Finland and Sweden are greatly under-estimated. The relevant figures refer only to the pre-school class, or to free morning sessions which offer "educational" programming.

With the exception of the Nordic countries, the picture in child care is different: the main costs of child care are taken in charge by parents, with subsidisation to a greater or lesser extent by government, depending on the country and on the income level of parents. For example, middle-class parents in Ireland, the United Kingdom and the United States pay most of the costs of child care, whereas in the continental European countries, public subsidies take in charge well over half the costs. In the Nordic countries, state and local government subsidies take in charge over 85% of costs (excepting Denmark). In addition, in Finland and Sweden a *de facto* right to highly subsidised child care services from the end of parental leave exists, with parents paying much less than 15% of costs (9% in Sweden).

Figure 5.4. **Public and private expenditure on pre-primary education (3- to 6-year-olds only) as a percentage of GDP**

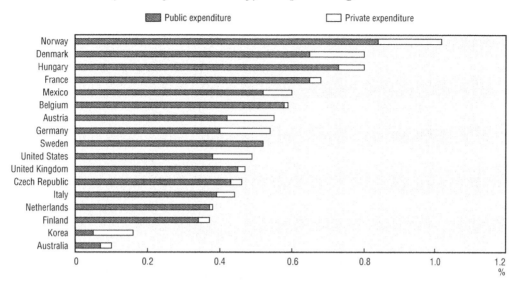

Note: Early education expenditure for Belgium and France is higher than this figure indicates, and significantly higher for Denmark, Finland and Sweden. In Belgium and France, early education begins before 3 years. For Denmark, Finland and Sweden, it is probable that this figure identifies expenditure only for what is considered free educational provision, *e.g.* the Finnish figure includes pre-primary education programmes for 6-year-old children (pre-school year preceding compulsory education) and centre-based day care for 3- to 5-year-old children, based on an expenditure estimation of 50%. Canada is absent from this figure as data are not provided in OECD, *Education at a Glance*, 2005. The last data received from Canada are for the year 2000, when Canada spent 0.2% of GDP on pre-primary education, for 3- to 6-year-olds. Data for Korea cover only kindergarten education and do not include public expenditure in the parallel child care system.

Source: OECD (2005), *Education at a Glance.*

Funding modalities used

The modes of funding adopted by countries differ greatly in detail (see Table 5.2), but in general, countries adopt public, supply-side, government funding in early education services for children from 3 years, or, as indicated above, in Australia, Canada, Ireland, Korea, the Netherlands and the United States from the age of 4 or 5 years. In Denmark, Finland, Norway and Sweden, public supply-side funding is the dominant form of funding for all services, although in these countries, parental fees are also charged. With the exception of Denmark, fees are set at a low flat-rate, with the education component of services (the morning session) being free in Sweden from 4 years. For the child care sector, mixed funding mechanisms are used, but in some countries, a significant proportion of parents receive no public support to defray the costs of child care (for more details, see below).

Funding in public early education services for children over 3 years

The funding of public education services for children over 3 years (or older in the liberal economies) is similar across all the countries in the review. Supply-side funding is the major mechanism used, and the sector is dominated by publicly financed services, generally centre-based and staffed by qualified, certified personnel. The majority of these services are provided directly by central government, or State (in the case of federal countries) or local authorities, or by government dependents, that is, voluntary or private organisations that receive more than 50% of their funding from government and who have agreed to run services according to government regulations or specific contractual obligations.

Table 5.2. **Main forms of funding for ECEC services (0 to 6 years)
in selected countries**

	Supply funding to services	Subsidies to parents	Employer contributions
Australia	Limited to public kindergarten	Main form	Yes, tax
Belgium	Main form	Mixed in child care	Yes, employer levy
Canada	In public kindergarten and community services mainly (Provinces and Territories, to varying degrees, use also supply-side grants, operational funding, wage supplements, etc., in support of other services) Main form in Quebec	Mixed. Supply-side funding to community services is usual.	No
Denmark	Main form	No	No
Finland	Main form	Mixed	No
France	Main form	Mixed for ECEC outside the *école maternelle*	Yes, employer levy
Germany	Main form	Mixed in child care	No
Hungary	Main form in child care and kindergarten	No	No
Ireland	Limited to social nurseries and public early education	Limited, mostly parental contributions	No
Italy	Main form	No	Yes, employer levy
Korea	Limited to public kindergarten, and to public targeted programme in child care centres	Main form of government support, but parental contributions are high	In some cases
Netherlands	Main form in pre-primary and targeted	Main form in child care but high parental contributions	Yes, tax to nearly 30% of costs
Norway	Main form	Mixed	Yes, tax
Portugal	Main form	Yes	Yes
Sweden	Main form	No	No
United Kingdom	Limited to public early education, social nurseries and targeted programmes	Main form for child care, but mostly parental contributions	Yes, tax
United States	Limited to public kindergarten, targeted programmes and Head Start	Main form but mostly parental contributions	Yes, tax

Source: OECD, Country Background Reports.

The variety of accredited voluntary or private organisations used by governments to deliver services in this way is varied. Possibly, the largest accredited government dependents in the early education field for 3- to 6-year-olds – as in compulsory education – are faith-based organisations, *e.g.* in the Benelux countries, Germany, Ireland and Italy where church groups take in charge a third or more of all early education services.

In these public or contractual services, governments (either central, state or local) provide funding directly to providers, linked to the numbers of children being served. These supply-side grants generally take the form of operational subsidies, staff wages (or wage-enhancement grants), grants for capital equipment and supplies, supplementary grants made to services serving children with additional or special educational needs, and grants for the enhancement of quality or other public objectives. In general, government dependent services in early education come under strict regulation and enjoy adequate government funding, although in many of these services in Europe (excepting the Nordic countries) child-staff ratios can be high, and shortages of provision occur, particularly in growth urban areas. Services are also supported by a governmental or local authority management infrastructure, which in turn, *e.g.* in Austria, Belgium, Germany, Ireland and the Netherlands, may also be supplemented by management units of the large government-dependent providers. In most countries, governmental departments prepare legislation or regulatory frameworks; license programmes; set group sizes and staff qualifications; Depending on the country, government services may be helped also by provider management groups in monitoring quality and programme standards; providing for educator support and professional development; and encouraging parental participation; etc.

Funding for children under 3

For children under 3, both supply-side (funding to services) and demand-side funding (subsidies to parents) or a mixture of both models are used. In general, a division can be seen between the liberal economies and other countries. Countries in the former group (Australia, Canada, Ireland, Korea, the Netherlands, the United Kingdom and the United States) tend to use, as the main mode of financing services, child care subsidies to parents, such as cash benefits, vouchers, tax reductions and the like. In contrast, the European continental countries use supply-side subsidies paid directly to services as their main mode of financing, although some countries, *e.g.* Belgium and France, may also use tax credits to help parents meet child care costs. In the social democratic countries, supply-side funding – and tax credits – are predominantly used. Direct municipal provision of day care services (including family day care) is also the rule in these countries, except in Norway where in 2004, private kindergartens already provided for the majority (57%) of children (Moser, 2005). However, family day carers in Denmark and the contracted private providers in Finland and Norway are not the independent (and often unregulated) operators found in the liberal economies, but are licensed and regulated by the local municipality.

5. Child care costs to parents

In all countries, costs for all forms of child care are shared between parents and governments (and with employers, as in Belgium, France, Italy and especially, the Netherlands). In only three of the twenty countries reviewed (Denmark, Finland and Sweden) is the public provision of high quality ECEC for children from their first year considered an entitlement for a child, on an equal footing with services for the older children. In these countries, and in Norway also, parental fees are charged up to the year before entry into compulsory schooling, though since 2002, Sweden provides a free three-hour session daily for 4- to 6-year-olds. Costs to parents are low and though based on means testing are capped, with low-income groups paying only token fees. In Finland, the average parental contribution is about 15% of costs, and in Norway and Sweden about 10%, since these countries introduced maximum fees.

In the continental European countries, public child care programmes also largely predominate, and parents contribute on average 25-30% to their costs. Countries, such as Belgium, France and the Netherlands, subsidise costs for infants and toddler services in a variety of ways. In addition, they provide universal and free early education services to children from a young age: from 2 years in France, 2.5 years in Belgium, and from 3 years in the Czech Republic, Hungary, Italy, etc.; and from 4 years in the Netherlands. In the liberal economies, with the exception of state programmes provided to disadvantaged groups, the parental share of funding is significantly higher, up to 82% of costs in some Canadian provinces and full costs in many American services.[11] In Canada, for example, the median annual fees for a family with an infant and a pre-schooler in full-time centre care were approximately GBP 12 000 per year or 23% of the median 1998 family income of GBP 52 500 for all double income families (Statistics Canada, 2000). In Ireland, also, child care costs – borne on average by families to some 51% of costs – have become a real disincentive to women remaining in the labour force, particularly if a second child is born (Background

Report on Ireland and Country Note for Ireland, OECD, 2002). Australia is unusual among the liberal economies in that fee support (the Child Care Benefit and a new 30% child care tax rebate) is available to 98% of parents, with low-income parents receiving a higher benefit. This means that approximately 60% of expenditure on all early childhood services is public, with parents contributing in total about 38% of costs. The general picture then is that in Europe, governments contribute from about 66% to 90% of child care costs, and parents less than a third. In most liberal economies, the situation is reversed with parents paying the major share and governments providing about a third of costs (Australia about 60%).[12]

6. Does the modality of funding chosen impact on system quality?

Despite current economic orthodoxy, the experience of the OECD reviews suggests that for the moment at least, a public supply side investment model, managed by public authorities, brings more uniform quality and superior coverage of childhood populations (1- to 6-year-olds) than parent subsidy models. The more uneven quality in marketised systems may be due to weaker regulation of private provision, the predominance of family day care, and to the reluctance of private providers to employ sufficient numbers of highly qualified staff.[13] It may also be caused by the newness of parent subsidy models, and the relative inexperience of administrations in dealing with marketised child care services. The 2004 evaluation of the Swedish ECEC system would also suggest that variability in quality may come from displacing management control from central government towards municipalities or parents. Direct or earmarked funding from the centre allows more direct control and steering by government. Governmental control can be weakened by block grant systems (the case of Sweden) that do not earmark funds for educational purposes, leaving it to municipalities to decide what and how to fund (Bjorklund et al., 2004).[14] A fortiori, the stratagem of directly funding parents, while politically attractive, may further weaken governmental steering of the early childhood field. Whatever the reason, the OECD reviews suggest that direct public funding of services brings, in the majority of countries reviewed, more effective control, advantages of scale,[15] better national quality, more effective training for educators and a higher degree of equity in access and participation than consumer subsidy models. The comparison is striking when the organisation of public early education – generally a public education responsibility – is compared with that of child care. A similar difference in coverage and quality is also apparent, when marketised child care models are compared with the predominantly public service model of the Nordic countries. The experience of Norway and Sweden also suggests that a public service model can accommodate private providers when they are properly contracted, regulated and supported by public funding.

Public authorities opting for supply-side funding – supplemented in some countries by parental fees – provide operating costs to centres and generally provide wage supplements or pay the salaries of personnel (the latter about 70% of the real costs of ECEC services). In the publicly managed systems, services regulation is the norm, with group sizes and staff qualifications being subject to legislation and enforcement by the responsible ministry or local authority. Services receive also the supervision and support of ministry or local authority management units, or are guided by public child agencies. For this reason, more efficient mapping of services, more coherent training, and benchmarking are likely to be attained. The mixing of children, valued in public education, can also be achieved more easily in public services, unless (which is often the case) there is a high degree of spatial segregation in neighbourhoods served by public provision.

The main critique made of the public investment model is that it is expensive, although the argument that high public investment in early childhood services necessarily implies significant tax increases is simplistic (see for example, the discussion by Kvist, 2002). Another criticism, cited in *Early Childhood Education and Care for Children from Low-Income or Minority Backgrounds*, Leseman (2002), is that the presence of well subsidised public programmes like *Head Start*, tend to lead to a crowding out effect, and reduce initiatives by private providers to increase their ECEC activities in the neighbourhood, as they cannot compete in quality with the better-funded public programmes. This critique may explain also a major weakness in public ECEC systems in the conservative European countries (with the exception of Belgium and France) *viz.*, the failure of many countries to create sufficient numbers of licensed, publicly supported, child care places for children under 3. It seems more likely, however, that the reason for this failure lies with inaction on the part of government. Yet another criticism often heard is that publicly financed systems create dependency on the State, whereas a competitive child care system based on private markets and incentives produces more self-reliant families, and is economically more efficient than equity requirements, controls and standards set by government.

Demand-side or consumer subsidy funding

The marketisation of early childhood services has been promoted in recent years in OECD countries (OECD 2002, 2003, 2004). To limit public expenditure, and allow greater choice and control by parents are among the reasons advanced. Vouchers and parent subsidies are favoured over direct funding of services in the expectation that parental purchase of services will bring private entrepreneurs, new funding and greater dynamism into the provision of services – all this with lesser cost to government. In parallel, deregulation occurs to facilitate commercial suppliers in dealing with child-staff ratios and the qualifications of contact staff. State or local government monitoring is replaced, at least to some degree, by the basic market principle that more information to consumers, and competition among providers will eventually bring quality at lower cost. Some governments consider that choice will be increased if parents are free to opt for the service provider that meets best their child's particular needs. To achieve equity, large targeted programmes, such as Head Start (United States) or Sure Start (United Kingdom), are maintained, which provide in principle low-income families with child care and early education to meet their needs.

As an approach, consumer subsidy funding corresponds well to the current, dominant "third way" social welfare model, which sees the creation of markets within the public services as a means of having lighter, less expensive and more responsive public services (Giddens, 2003). Because they are set below actual costs, demand-side subsidies to parents are less costly to the public budget, and at the same time, bring new suppliers and competition into the child care systems. Through tying subsidies to the use of licensed providers only, consumer payments can also encourage the unlicensed child minders to enter the formal economy and taxation system. The experience of Australia suggests that if sufficient voucher and subsidy money is made available, independent family day carers and commercial providers will respond to the business opportunity and quickly expand provision. The rapidity of the small private provider in starting up a service is a considerable advantage, as public systems, can take a number of years to plan and build each new early childhood centre.[16] Independent family day carers – and commercial providers with a sound capital base – can come on stream more quickly, a fact appreciated by parents seeking places desperately for their young children, and by governments searching for expedient solutions to child care shortages.

Proponents of choice also argue that the range of programmes presented to parents is more innovative and responsive to parental wishes than that supplied by public services. In the Czech Republic and Hungary, for example, some of the newer private centres offer English immersion, computer programmes, music lessons, swimming and other extras to young children, with yoga, art and education courses for parents. For affluent parents, in particular, such programming is attractive, but they are often beyond the budgets of the great majority of people in these countries. Commercial services have also shown themselves to be successful in certain niche areas of ECEC, in particular, in employer sponsored, on-site child care. Commercial services – aiming at consumers – also offer "flexible places", that is, the possibility of placing children for a few hours or for a few half days in a service, allowing a parent to work part-time or shop at irregular hours. Similar flexibility is generally unavailable in public services, which tend to keep to the foreground the well-being and development of young children. Thus, many public services refuse to provide "slot" services and require that each child should be given the opportunity to bond with staff and other children, and to follow integrally a developmental programme.

The advantages of the market approach are often tempting for governments trying to respond quickly to child care shortages. In addition, the current economic culture seeks to cut back on public services, and many government finance departments would prefer to have a mixed market of services. This is a legitimate aim if inequities can be avoided and if private services can be held to appropriate public standards. However, in early development and education – not a repeatable process for any child – a careful and long-term view needs to be taken. Unlike material commodities in a market, parents cannot easily obtain a refund or a new model if they are dissatisfied with their child's outcomes. An error at country level in the choice of organisation of early childhood services may carry serious penalties for certain groups of families and children. Some of the concerns raised about the market model by early childhood policy experts and planners are as follows:

● *A purely market system moves away from the principle of universality in education*, that is, of providing equal opportunity for all children within a universal system in which values of citizenship are inculcated, and a democratic and multicultural mixing of children is practised. In contrast, targeting and special supports can be effectively achieved within a universal system, and the educational mix of children from all backgrounds is generally positive for both at-risk and mainstream children (Jensen and Saint-Martin, 2003).

● *Demand-side funding is, in general, under-funding*, and the burden of costs in market-led systems falls essentially on parents, who, in the market economies pay fees ranging from 35% to 100% of the costs of child care, unless they belong to low-income groups. Families with modest resources, who are not eligible for public funding, are often unable to pay such a proportion. As a result, their children can be excluded from participation in early childhood services (Fuller *et al.*, 2005).

● When public funding to the child care system takes the form of subsidies paid directly to parents, *the steering capacity of governments services is considerably weaker than in funding-to-services systems*. Tax rebates and parent subsidies do not support system co-ordination or universal provision or even necessarily, improve in-service training and salaries for staff. When parental vouchers are used to support informal and unlicensed child care as well as licensed providers, the result can be a diffuse network of small-scale organisations and individuals offering an array of child care services (Fuller *et al.*, 2005). Negative practices tend to appear, *e.g.* the growth of unregulated services; the selling of services on appearance and the practice of offering "slot" services to parents, which undermine all notion of continuity of relationship for young children, of programming or of developmental progress.

● *Parent subsidies can be problematic in that they may not be used efficiently on behalf of children:* In sum, it given directly to parents, may not be passed on fully to providers. On the other hand, parents with low educational levels and unemployed parents have difficulties in claiming what is due to them (United Kingdom Inland Revenue, Analysis and Research, Child and Working Tax Credits, 2004).[17] From a planning perspective, demand side subsidies can also be problematic, as financial flows in a parent subsidy system depend not on the number of eligible children (which can be foreseen) but on how many parents claim tax credit.

● *The reluctance of market providers to invest in poor neighbourhoods incurs the risk of inequity towards low-income families with young children*, which undermines a major rationale for public investment in early childhood services, viz. to provide a certain equality among young children at the starting gates of school. This risk is answered to some extent by increased subsidies to parents and providers in low-income areas, as in Australia and the United Kingdom, or through parallel, publicly funded, targeted programmes, such as Head Start (United States) or Sure Start (United Kingdom). However, these programmes miss not only a significant proportion of the children whom they are supposed to serve, but also the large group of moderate income families who are unable to afford the programmes that are on offer in a market system. In addition, targeting is generally inaccurate – that is, it does not respond to children who move in and out of risk, whatever their social, cultural or linguistic status. (NIEER, 2004 ; Fuller *et al.*, 2005). As noted by the Daycare Trust analysis of 2003, fully one half of children at-risk live outside designated disadvantaged areas in the United Kingdom.

● *Parent subsidies for child care generally give rise to a significant increase in family day care,* which statistically provides significantly lower quality compared to professional ECEC centres (NICHD, 1997b). A further difficulty about family day care – unless organised into a public system as in Denmark – is that financial control of the system is taken out of the hands of management, making planning and steering problematic.

● The conclusion reached in the PricewaterhouseCoopers report (2004), on financing a universal ECEC system for England by the year 2020, finds that: "*Supply-side funding tends to be the dominant form of finance in countries with the best developed systems of early years education and care, such as Sweden, Denmark, France and New Zealand, whereas means-tested, demand-side funding is more typical of countries with less well-developed systems, such as the United Kingdom and the United States*" (PricewaterhouseCooper, 2004). The liberal economies adopting a market model of child care seem to do little better than the conservative (European continental) countries in increasing licensed provision for younger children because of "churning", that is, a high turn-over of providers, unless they set licensing standards at a low level. This can be seen quite readily from the provision statistics that are available. The liberal economies often fail to achieve adequate regulation, monitoring structures and quality standards in their child care sectors (Kagan and Rigby, 2003).

A more focused review of the economic arguments can be found in the PricewaterhouseCoopers report referenced above or in the work of the Canadian economists, Cleveland and Krashinsky (2003), who remark: "The debate over demand-side and supply-side (funding) is often really a debate over what kind of quality will be provided and what kind of standards will be set." According to this team, early childhood services are not appropriate for marketisation. For them, ECEC is a public good, delivering externalities beyond the benefit of immediate, personal consumption. Important national goals are achieved through early education and care, in particular, a significant contribution to the health, development and learning of a nation's children. If this is the case, it is appropriate for governments to intervene in the field, through funding and quality control, particularly if the benefits gained by society are greater than the costs incurred.

More recent work by social policy analysts advocates "active social policy" in response to new risks emerging in the post-industrial economy (Martin and Pearson, 2005). In this context, key policy levers include a paradigm shift in the definition of "equality", which should be anchored firmly in the notion of equality of opportunity and equivalence of outcomes, thereby focusing on prospective life chances. This shift in thinking calls for the universal provision of ECEC, and investment geared towards the collective good. Jensen and Saint-Martin (2005) characterise this as a change from a consumption paradigm (which drives free markets) to a future oriented investment paradigm where the most threatening social risk is identified as poverty, and in particular, child poverty.

Conclusion to this discussion

Starting Strong (OECD, 2001) recorded that a range of different funding sources – public, private, business, parents – is the current reality of early childhood funding. Differences of approaches are likely to remain, not least because of path dependence, that is, because ECEC systems are embedded within powerful socio-economic models (Mahon, 2006). In both supply-side and demand-side systems, governments seek to ensure access to services for all children whose parents require it, and in particular, for children who need these services most. The overwhelming evidence from the reviews of twenty countries suggests that without significant public investment in policy, services and management, both affordability to parents and the quality of services are likely to be undermined. This is true not only for public services but also for licensed private providers. Without sustained public funding (either directly to services or indirectly through parent subsidies) and public regulation of all providers, ECEC services are destined to be patchy and of poor quality in all but the more affluent neighbourhoods. This defeats a main purpose of early childhood systems, that is, to provide quality care, development and learning for all children, and in particular, to improve opportunity for children living in at-risk situations.

Whatever system of funding is chosen by a country, the best interests of young children should remain a primary guideline. In the early childhood field, market laws are insufficient as the time-span to eliminate poor quality providers is generally much longer than the few years that a child will be present in these services. The consequences of unregulated marketisation can be serious for the education and development of young children. As in other markets, government intervention is amply justified in the case of market failure, which, in fact, occurs too frequently in child care systems. Ball and Vincents (2005) conclude, for example, that the child care market "does not work as markets are meant to do; it does not guarantee quality or efficiency, and in fact dispenses services in a highly inequitable fashion." Despite the attractions of lower public spending and more rapid service provision brought by marketisation, governments need to fund, supervise and regulate private providers, if they wish to maintain quality for all young children, including children with special and/or additional learning needs. The evidence from cost-benefit analyses does not indicate that any expenditure will generate benefits greater than costs, but rather that the benefit-to-cost ratio is greatly influenced by the quality of services provided (Lamb, 1998).

Commercial services have shown themselves to be successful in certain niche areas of ECEC, in particular, in employer sponsored, on-site child care, but again, the appropriateness of such services needs to be examined in the light of equity and the public good. Since *Starting Strong* was published in 2001, much discussion about independent schooling and choice for parents has taken place, particularly in the United Kingdom and the United States. New evidence has emerged about ways to maximise choice, and at the same time curtail the (sometimes high) inequity produced by private schooling (Loveless and Betts, 2005). Some of these lessons – such as regulating admissions at district level; limiting selection; setting socio-economic quotas; providing targeted vouchers, enhancing financing for schools, capping fees, and enrolling at-risk students, etc., could also be applied to marketised child care systems. Another option is to avoid complicated regulation of dispersed systems, and opt for a well-funded, universal public system based on decentralisation and democratic participation, including the participation of private providers within the public system. In our view, consideration should also be given to the Nordic policy of preventing upstream the reproduction of child poverty and disadvantage, and thus avoid the plethora of palliative measures and programmes that characterise more unequal societies.

That being said, the benefits of greater choice should not be overlooked. In this regard, the relative stagnation – in terms of innovation and development – of public ECEC systems in some countries needs to be examined, for example, unfavourable child-staff ratios for 3- to 6-year-olds and totally inadequate services for families with younger children. Further research is needed on how to create effective *social markets*, that is, networks of mixed provision in which choice and innovation exist, while maintaining a sense of national and community responsibility for services. Widely different levels of purchasing power may be acceptable in the case of commodities or personal convenience, but they undermine equity and social solidarity in the fields of public health and education.

7. Effective policy includes investment in administration, and support services

OECD review teams noted the in-depth strength of administrations – at both central and local authority levels – in countries with mature systems in place, and the relative weakness of administrations in countries that have only recently begun to face the challenge of providing quality throughout their ECEC systems. Without a critical mass of experienced administrators to manage the national, state or municipal systems, public policies with regard to early childhood often remain inequitable and fragmented. In many countries, significant numbers of local managers with experience and expertise in early childhood policy and management are employed by local administrations. Situated mostly at municipal level, these managers undertake needs assessments, map services, co-ordinate with health, family and other services, provide information to parents and stakeholders, monitor the inputs and outputs of the local system, provide financial and other incentives to raise quality, and organise the support services that centres and staff need.

Encouraging signs of investment in administration are seen in the countries or States that are intent on improving policy and performance in the early childhood field. The Sure Start department in the United Kingdom has a significant group of administrators actively involved in what is a radical reform and strengthening of early childhood services – this is in addition to the many experienced officials in local authority offices across the country. A similar move to consolidate valuable expertise in the early childhood field and to measure up to the challenges raised by current expansion can be seen in several States in the United States. For example, the State of Massachusetts has merged the Department of Education's Office of School Readiness with the Massachusetts' Office of Child Care Services into a consolidated office for early education and care in the State, with, according to ECS reports, a strong team of administrators to staff this new office. These are encouraging signs that ECEC policy and planning are coming of age, and are no longer overlooked or subsumed under larger administrative units which are not directly concerned with early child development and education.

Notes

1. Much of this low-paid work is concentrated in the 4Cs: cleaning, caring (including ECEC), catering and cashiering – professions that are staffed in general by women.

2. A basic premise in the research on cost-benefits from ECEC services is that these services are of high quality. Where poor quality is the rule, the returns from investment are lost (Schweinhart and Weikart, 1996; Lamb, 1998).

3. Abecedarian costs run to USD 63 476 per child over 5 years. See also Gormley and Philips (2004) on Oklahoma pre-kindergarten costs, and the analysis of Barnett et al. (2005) of pre-kindergarten costs across five States.

4. USD 8 000 per child far exceeds the annual family income in many non-OECD countries.

5. Funding per student at the university level is, on average, almost 2.5 times greater than for a child in early education service (OECD, 2004). Although politically a difficult aim to achieve, the rolling back of free university places for all students can be justified in terms of achieving greater equality of opportunity for young children at the base, when they are beginning education. Because of enhanced earnings that tertiary education brings to graduating students, it is reasonable to require from at least some university students a personal contribution to costs. It is also more likely that tertiary education will benefit from private sector investment and sponsorships than early childhood services, where returns on investment are by definition long-term. Moreover, free university places for all provides a subsidy for middle and high income groups at the expense of students from low socio-economic (SES) backgrounds, whose participation in tertiary education remains low in most countries. Research from Australia suggests that charging student fees has little effect on enrolments if appropriate fee exemptions are introduced to support low SES students, and loans are made available on favourable terms for other students, e.g. reimbursement schemes that are contingent on attaining appropriate income thresholds after completing education (Gallagher, 2003).

6. At this time, Australia hosts the world's largest publicly quoted child care group, ABC Learning Centres. "The Brisbane based company is on track to post a full-year profit of at least USD 88 million after more than doubling its interim net profits to USD 44 million" (The Australian, 28 February, 2006). A significant proportion of ABC income comes from taxpayer-funds through supply of the Child Care Benefit.

7. These elements of regulation are seen as "the iron triangle" which assure the structural quality of child care (Mooney et al., 2003).

8. Respect for the rhythms and interests of young children, and consultation of parents and the community or voluntary sector need to be ensured in services attached to schools.

9. ISCED Level 0 programmes are defined as centre or school-based programmes that are designed to meet the educational and developmental needs of children at least 3 years of age, and that have staff that are adequately trained (i.e. qualified) to provide an educational programme for the children. Programmes devoted to early childhood care only are not included in this definition. When these programmes are considered to be "pre-primary education", they are further defined as the initial stage of organised instruction. As the "instructional" or "educational" properties of programmes are difficult to identify, different proxy measures are utilised by countries to determine whether a programme should be classified at this level.

10. A strong municipal system of communal *scuole materne* covering about 15% of the age group 3 to 6 years exists also in Italy, the costs of which are taken in charge by the municipalities. Reggio Emilia is an example.

11. Only 45% of 3- to 5-year-olds from low-income families in the United States are enrolled in pre-school programmes, compared with almost 75% from high-income families. A contributory factor is cost (Fuller *et al.*, 2005).

12. In calculating which countries best support parents, other factors need to be taken into account such as taxing patterns and the treatment of female partners in the tax system, wages and the range of family supports.

13. Quality services depend to a great extent on being able to retain experienced, certified staff. This can be difficult if salaries are pushed down.

14. The argument in favour of decentralisation of ECEC management is strong (see Chapter 2): decentralisation strengthens enormously administrative capacity across a country, is (in principle) more sensitive to local need and corresponds better to contemporary notions of democratic participation. Weaknesses appear when local authorities cater primarily for majority interest groups at local level, and neglect state goals for equity and quality. As the Swedish evaluation above, the OECD review of Hungary called attention to such weaknesses at municipal level in Hungary.

15. To be distinguished from "economies" of scale. Some, but rather few economies of scale can be achieved through the purchase of supplies in public ECEC systems, but these economies are minor. Most expenditure in ECEC is devoted to salaries (about 70%). "Advantages" of scale can be considerable, however: public systems make it easier to enforce regulations, support educators, monitor quality and communicate good practice within the system.

16. That this is not a necessary characteristic of public systems can be seen from the speed with which Early Excellence and Children's Centres have been constructed and put into operation in England.

17. The argument is often made that child care subsidies should not be paid to unemployed parents, who, in principle, can look after their child at home. However, withdrawal from care can be disruptive for the child, and does not support parents in finding new employment.

References

Ball, S.J. and C. Vincent (2005), "The 'Childcare Champion'? New Labour, Social Justice and the Childcare Market", *British Educational Research Journal*, Vol. 31(5), pp. 557-570.

Barnett, W.S., C. Lamy and K. Jung (2005), "The Effects of State Pre-kindergarten Programs on Young Children's School Readiness in Five States", NJ, NIEER, Rutgers University.

Bjorklund *et al.* (2004), "Education, Equality and Efficiency: An Analysis of Swedish School Reform during the 1990s", IFAU Report, No. 1, Stockholm.

Carnegie Corporation (1994), "Starting Points: Meeting the Needs of our Youngest Children", available: *www.carnegie.org/starting_points/startpt1.html*.

CED (2002), *Pre-school for All: Investing in a Productive and Just Society*, New York Committee for Economic Development, New York.

Center of Excellence for Early Child Development (2005), online encyclopaedia, *www.excellence-earlychildhood.ca/*.

Cleveland, G. and M. Krashinsky (2003), "Financing ECEC Services in OECD Countries", OECD, Paris.

Cunha, F., J. Heckman, L. Lochner and D.V. Masterov (2005), *Interpreting the Evidence of Life-Cycle Skill Formation*, IZA Discussion Paper Series, No. 1575, Institute for the Study of Labor, Bonn, Germany, July.

Daycare Trust (2003), "Costs and Benefits of Universal Childcare. A Preliminary Economic Analysis for the United Kingdom", *www.daycaretrust.org.uk/mod/fileman/files/Cost_benefits_universal_childcare.pdf*.

DLO (2001), Daginstitutionernes Lands-Organisation, Communication on SFOs (*skolefritidsordninger* or school-based leisure-time facilities), Copenhagen.

EC Network on Childcare (1996), *A Review of Services for Young Children in the European Union 1990-1995*, European Commission, DGV, Brussels.

Fuller, B.C., A. Livas and M. Bridges (2005), "How to Expand and Improve Pre-school in California: Ideals, Evidence, and Policy Options", PACE Working Paper 05-1, Policy Analysis for California Education (PACE), Berkeley, California.

Gallagher, M. (2003), "Higher Education Financing in Australia", OECD, Paris.

Giddens, A. (2003), *The Progressive Manifesto*, Cambridge Polity.

Gormley, W.T. and D. (2004), "The Effects of Universal Pre-K in Oklahoma: Research Highlights and Policy Implications", DC, Georgetown University.

HM Treasury (2004), "Choice for Parents, the Best Start for Children: a Ten Year Strategy for Childcare. Summary of Consultation Responses", *www.hm-treasury.gov.uk*.

Immervoll, H. and D. Barber (2005), "Can Parents Afford to Work? Childcare Costs Tax Benefit Policies and Work Incentives", OECD Social Employment and Migration Working Paper 31, Paris, December.

Jensen, J. and D. Saint-Martin (2003), "New Routes to Social Cohesion? Citizenship and the Social Investment State", *Canadian Journal of Sociology*, Vol. 28(1), pp. 77-99.

Jensen, J. and D. Saint-Martin (2005), "Building Blocks for a New Social Architecture: The Lego[TM] Paradigm of an Active Society", Paper from the project Fostering Social Cohesion: A Comparison of New Policy Strategies, Social Sciences and Humanities Research Council of Canada.

Kagan, S.L. and E. Rigby (2003), *Policy Matters: Improving the Readiness of Children for School: Recommendations for State Policy*, The Children's Project, Washington DC.

Keating, D.P. and C. Hertzman (1999), *Developmental Health and the Wealth of Nations*, Guilford, London.

Kvist, J. (2002), "Changing Rights and Obligations in Unemployment Insurance", in: R. Sigg and C. Behrendt (eds.), *Social Security in the Global Village*, International Social Security Series No. 8, Transaction Publishers, New Brunswick, pp. 227-245.

Lamb, M.E. (1998), "Nonparental Child Care: Context, Quality, Correlates and Consequences", in W. Damon, I.E. Sigel and K.A. Renninger (eds.), *Handbook of Child Psychology* (Vol. 4), *Child Psychology in Practice* (5th ed.), Wiley, New York.

Lee, S. (2004), "Women's Work Supports, Job Retention and Job Mobility", *Research-in-Brief*, Institute for Women's Policy Research, *www.iwpr.org*.

Leseman, P. (2002), "Early Childhood Education and Care for Children from Low-income or Minority Backgrounds", OECD, Paris.

Loveless, T and J.R. Betts (eds.) (2005), *Getting Choice Right: Ensuring Equity and Efficiency in Education Policy*, Brookings Institution Press, Washington.

Mahon, R. (2006), "The OECD and Reconciliation Agenda: Competing Blueprints", in J. Lewis (ed.), *Children, Changing Familie and Welfare State*, Edwin Elgar.

Martin, J. and M. Pearson (2005), "Time to Change. Towards an Active Social Policy Agenda", *OECD Observer*, March.

McCain, M and F. Mustard (2002), *The Early Years Study. Three Years Later*, Ontario Founders Network, Toronto.

McKay, H., L. Sinisterra, A. McKay, H. Gomez and P. Lloreda (1978), "Improving Cognitive Ability in Chronically Deprived Children", *Science*, Vol. 200.

Mooney, A., C. Cameron, M. Candappa, S. McQuail, P. Moss and P. Petrie (2003), *Early Years and Childcare International Evidence Project: Quality*, Thomas Coram Research Unit, Institute of Education, University of London, London.

Moser, T. (2005), Communication, Sofia Education Conference, 2005.

Myers R. (2004), *In Search of Quality in Programmes of Early Childhood Education and Care*, UNESCO EFA Global Monitoring Report, 2004.

NICHD Early Childcare Research Network (1997a), "The Effects of Infant Child Care on Infant-mother Attachment Security, Results of NICHD Study of Early Child Care", *Child Development*, Vol. 68(5), pp. 860-879.

NICHD Early Childcare Research Network (1997b), "Familial Factors Associated with the Characteristics of Non-maternal Care for Infants", *Journal of Marriage and Family*, Vol. 59, pp. 389-408.

NIEER (2004), "Pre-School Policy Matters", Issue 6, NIEER, Rutgers University, NJ.

OECD (2002), *Employment Outlook*, Chapter 2: "Women at Work: Who are they and how are they Faring?", OECD, Paris.

OECD (2003), *Babies and Bosses: Reconciling Work and Family Life*, Vol. 2, OECD, Paris.

OECD (2004), *Babies and Bosses: Reconciling Work and Family Life*, Vol. 3, OECD, Paris.

OECD (2004, 2005), *Education at a Glance: OECD Indicators*, OECD, Paris.

Prentice, S. (2005), "For Profit Child Care: Past Present and Future", Occasional Paper 21, Childcare Resource and Research Unit, Toronto, Canada.

PricewaterhouseCoopers (2004), "Universal Early Education and Care in 2020: Costs, Benefits, and Funding Options", A Report for Daycare Trust and the Social Market Foundation.

Purcell, G. (2001), Personal communication during the Starting Strong meeting in Stockholm, June.

Ramey, C.T. and S.L. Ramey (1998), "Early Intervention and Early Experience", *American Psychologist*, Vol. 53, pp. 109-120.

Rutter, M., H. Giller and A. Hagell (1998), "Antisocial Behavior by Young People", Cambridge University Press, New York.

Sadowski, M. (2006), "Degrees of Improvement", *Harvard Education Letter*, Vol. 22(1), pp. 1-4.

Schweinhart, L.J. and D.P. Weikart (1996), "Lasting Differences: The High/Scope Pre-school Curriculum Comparison Study through Age 23", Monograph of the High/Scope Educational Research Foundation, No. 12, High/Scope Press, Ypsilanti, Michigan.

United Kingdom Inland Revenue (2004), *Quarterly Statistics: Tax Credit*, IR, London.

Vermeer *et al.* (2005), *Quality of Dutch Child Care Centres: Trends in Quality in the Years 1995-2005*, University of Leiden, Netherlands.

Waters Boots, S. (2005), "Building a 21st Century Economy: The Case for Investing in Early Childhood Reform", Early Childhood Initiative Issue Brief, New America Foundation, December.

Werner, E.E. and R.S. Smith (1982), *Vulnerable but Invincible: A Longitudinal Study of Resilient Children and Youth*, McGraw-Hill, New York.

Young, M.E. (2002), *From Early Child Development to Human Development*, World Bank, Washington.

Youth and Child Care Act (2005), Ministry of Health, Welfare and Sport, The Hague, Netherlands.

Zeitlin, M., H. Ghassemi and M. Mansour (1990), *Positive Deviance in Child Nutrition: With Emphasis on Psychosocial and Behavioural Aspects and Implications for Development*, United Nations University Press, Tokyo.

ISBN 92-64-03545-1
Starting Strong II: Early Childhood Education and Care
© OECD 2006

Chapter 6

A Participatory Approach to Quality Improvement and Assurance

To maintain or improve quality standards, Starting Strong (OECD, 2001) recommended effective government steering of early childhood education and care (ECEC) systems on the one hand, and participatory and voluntary approaches to quality on the other. In examining these approaches, Chapter 6 reviews the state of regulations across countries – in services for children under 3, in countries with integrated services and in the early education sector. Some examples of progress in the field of regulation are outlined.

The chapter then examines the issue of curriculum frameworks, a key instrument for both democratic consultation and governmental guidance. Two different approaches to curriculum can be identified: the early education approach and the social pedagogy approach. Features of both approaches are compared along a number of criteria.

Another issue examined in Chapter 6 is that of parental involvement in early care and education. When parents are encouraged and trained to carry our specific reading tasks with their children, positive effects on children's language and pre-literacy skills are reported. The Effective Provision of Pre-school Education (EPPE) project in the United Kingdom concludes that parental support for emergent literacy in this period of development has a greater impact on child outcomes than social class: what parents do is more important than who they are.

The chapter ends with a discussion of monitoring practices that support and engage staff in maintaining and improving quality. A brief review of what countries are doing to promote a culture of quality discussion and evaluation in ECEC services is also provided – information that can be supplemented by consultation of the "developments" section in the different Country Profiles.

Increased investment by governments in early childhood education and care (ECEC) has been accompanied by a growing concern about quality. For governments, improving quality means ensuring that necessary programme standards are in place and that children are developing and learning in accordance with government objectives for the sector. To ensure quality, *Starting Strong* (OECD, 2001) recommended two policy strategies: on the one hand, effective government steering of ECEC systems, and on the other, participatory and voluntary approaches to quality improvement. The strategies are complementary and necessary. NAEYC accreditation in the United States, the documentation processes of Reggio Emilia programming, or the reflective practice of the Nordic countries are examples of what can be accomplished through voluntary attention to quality. However, the experience of the review suggests that the voluntary efforts of providers need to be underpinned by a commitment on the part of government or local authorities to define, fund and enforce basic standards across the board. Without a proactive approach on the part of government, it is unlikely that voluntary quality initiatives at provider level can survive.

In parallel, the enforcement of regulations is more likely to succeed when the authorities engage in consultative policy-making and management, and build up a general consensus about the need and relevance of standards. The belief that quality improvement can be left to market competition is naïve. The market is efficient where the market is well implanted. Except for some niche areas, such as the provision of early childhood services in large enterprises, market provision is weakly implanted in most OECD countries, in particular in poorer areas where ECEC services are most necessary. The experience of the ECEC policy reviews suggests that governments have a pivotal role in defining and ensuring programme standards and in creating strong and equitable early childhood systems.

What did Starting Strong *recommend?*

- To formulate regulatory standards for all forms of provision, supported by co-ordinated investment.

- To promote participatory processes in defining and ensuring quality. Beyond the minimum standard ensured by the basic regulations, defining and assuring quality should be a participatory and democratic process, involving different groups including children, parents, families and professionals who work with children. Participatory approaches can take many forms. *Starting Strong* (OECD, 2001) recommended two policy approaches:

  - In consultation with stakeholders, to generate a guiding curriculum framework for the country that focuses on the norms and values governing early education and care.

  - Monitoring that engages and supports staff, parents, and children.

1. Quality and regulation in ECEC

In attempting to evaluate early childhood systems, different aspects of quality can be examined (see, for example, Dahlberg *et al.*, 1997; Myers, 2004; Tietze and Cryer, 2004):

- *Orientation quality*: By orientation quality is meant the type and level of attention that a government brings to early childhood policy, *e.g.* through national legislation, regulation and policy initiatives. For example, it is clear that in the last decade, government orientation in Sweden and the United Kingdom has been particularly high. Among the issues that arise in the area of orientation are the following: is orientation towards a market or public system or some combination of both; is the focus on the basic care and protection of young children while parents work or is a more developmental and educational approach envisaged; is the focus on the readiness for school of older children or towards creating a more integrated system in which care, upbringing and the education of young children becomes an important national goal? Government orientations influence the training and the pedagogical concepts of the educators, as well as parental understandings of early childhood care and education. They are most likely to win consensus and respect when they result from a broad consultation of the major stakeholders in the early childhood field, including parents, and are founded on evidence-based research.

- *Structural quality* (often referred to in the United States as *programme standards*): Primarily a responsibility of administrations, it refers to the overarching structures needed to ensure quality in early childhood programmes, and is ensured by the clear formulation and enforcement of legislation or regulations. Structural requirements may define the quality of the physical environment for young children (buildings, space, outdoors, pedagogical materials); the quality and training levels of the staff; an appropriate curriculum properly trialled, and covering all the broad areas of child development; acceptable child-staff ratios; adequate work conditions and compensation of staff, etc. Typically, a selection of structural standards forms the substance of national licensing requirements. In the United States, reference is often made to subsets of *programme standards*, such as *classroom standards* (referring primarily to space, group size and child-staff ratios) and *teaching and curriculum standards* (referring to pedagogical approaches, curriculum aims, etc.).

- *Educational concept and practice*: The educational concept and practice of centres are generally guided by the national curriculum framework which sets out the key goals of the early childhood system. These goals differ widely from country to country, and no doubt from decade to decade, but a common conviction is emerging across countries that lead staff need to be trained to a high level to achieve the broad goals of early childhood programming, *e.g.* the five goals proposed by the American National Education Goals Panel (NEGP) in 1997,[1] or the general goals proposed for education in the 21st century by the Delors Report (Delors, 1996), which seem particularly appropriate for young children: learning to be (forming one's self identity); learning to do (through play, experimentation and group activity); learning to learn (through a learning environment providing interest and choice and that includes well-focused pedagogical objectives); and learning to live together (within the early childhood centre, in a democratic way, respectful of difference). The fostering of experiential, self-motivated learning in each of these fields requires a practice that puts children's participation at the centre of curriculum, and calls for the specific training of early childhood educators in the competences that allow this to happen. New training and new competences are required. Traditional professional training focusing on the classroom is no longer sufficient to respond to new responsibilities in relation to parents, families and communities, and vis-à-vis the growing diversity that educators find within centres.

● *Interaction or process quality*: The warmth and quality of the pedagogical relationship between educators and children, the quality of interaction between children themselves, and the quality of relationships within the educator team figure among the process goals most frequently cited. Decades of research converge on "relationship quality" as a key variable determining child outcomes (see for example, AAP/APHA, 2002; NICHD, 2004; Rutter *et al.*, 2003). The pedagogical relationship between children and educators seems to be most effective when the relationship includes care, upbringing and concern for the general well-being of each child, as well as expert support for the children's learning. This integrated approach and relationship is found in the concept of pedagogy, encountered in the social pedagogy tradition of Nordic and Central Europe (see also Country Note for Germany, OECD 2004a, Cohen *et al.*, 2004).

● *Operational quality*, in particular, management that focuses on responsiveness to local need, quality improvement and effective team building: Operational quality is maintained by leadership that motivates and encourages working as a team and information sharing. It includes regular planning at centre and classroom level; opportunities for staff to engage in continuous professional and career development; time allowed for child observation, assessments and documentation; support to staff performance in the form of accompaniment and mentoring. Operational quality may also include flexible and appropriate (for children) opening hours and the integration of core programming with other necessary services, *e.g.* out-of-school provision, social and medical services; arrangements for special needs children. The quality of operational standards depends largely on the professional competence of local administration and leaders of centres.

● *Child-outcome quality or performance standards*: ECEC services are founded not only to facilitate the labour market or other aims, but above all, to improve the present and future well-being of children. Positive child outcomes are a major goal for ECEC programmes in all countries. Differences between countries arise about the outcomes to be privileged. A child-outcome approach privileging language and logico-mathematical skills is characteristic of France and the English-speaking countries (excepting New Zealand), countries that adopt a "readiness for school" approach. The approach often includes addressing the knowledge and skills that children should acquire by the end of each year. Children may be evaluated in early education classes or at entry into primary school to test their progress, generally in emergent literacy and numeracy but also in socio-emotional development and general health. Undoubtedly, it can be tempting for administrators to have an objective instrument to measure the developmental curve of young children from year to year in the above areas, but this may lead to a focus on the assessment content and distract teachers from the intense relational and pedagogical work that young children need. Supporters of assessment argue that regular assessments are part of formative evaluation, and give valuable information to teachers about the effects of their teaching on individual children, allowing them to improve their practice.

● The approach is not followed to the same extent by other countries, and in fact, formal assessment is often considered unsuitable for young children.[2] Several countries, such as Sweden, prefer to evaluate centre performance and are extremely reluctant to use child measures or to announce detailed learning standards for young children. At the same time, national sample evaluations and centre-based performance assessments are used, to measure the performance of staff and centres. Within the centres, the progress of each child is measured as unobtrusively as possible, *e.g.* through systematic daily observation, ongoing documentation, child portfolios, parent interviews, learning stories, sample national surveys, etc. An example of centre evaluation is the national examination of the Swedish pre-school, published by the National Agency for Education in 2004 (Skolverket, 2004).

● *Standards pertaining to parent/community outreach and involvement*: This area is mentioned less than other quality standards in national regulations and curricula, but can emerge strongly in the requirements for targeted and local ECEC programmes. Among the tasks of centres in disadvantaged neighbourhoods are: outreach to parents and efforts to improve the home-learning environment; the capacity to relate well, without bias, to local cultural values and norms; support to women's and parent groups, and to the parent groups involved in centre management; participation in integrated programming with the employment, social, health and adult education authorities; and the ability to make referrals. It is not clear whether countries will opt for a new type of educator to undertake this kind of work or whether it is sufficient that early childhood personnel should be trained on the job to work in inter-disciplinary community teams. The issue is treated more in detail in Chapter 7.

2. The state of ECEC regulation in OECD countries

As early care and education outside the home expands, the regulation of services becomes inevitably a public responsibility. All countries impose a preliminary health and safety check on centres or homes licensed to look after young children. Thereafter, the extent and manner of regulation differs widely from country to country, and often varies within countries according to region or the type of service concerned. An appropriate degree of regulation helps not only to define and enforce health, environmental and programme standards but also ensures some degree of equity for parents and children in poorer neighbourhoods. Such neighbourhoods should be able to expect structural inputs (financing, buildings, educational materials, child-staff ratios, qualified teachers, etc.) at a level at least equal to the national average. The effectiveness of regulation is greatly assisted by the following factors:

● A national definition of minimum programme standards in key fields, and their acceptance by the sector.

● Adequate funding and support of the ECEC system (or programme), so that providers can comply with expected programme standards.[3]

● A participatory and democratic approach to standards definition, implementation and quality improvement.

● The provision by government or a national agency of leadership, technical assistance, professional development and other incentives to help providers and staff move the quality agenda forward.

● The presence of effective supervisory and support agencies at local level.

Regulations in services for 0- to 3-year-olds

In many OECD countries, the level of regulation of services for children under 3 gives rise for concern. A programme standard survey conducted by the OECD showed that the minimum requirements defined for licensed family day care services vary widely across the countries reviewed (OECD, 2004b) (see Table 6.1). Requirements ranged from registration with an initial (only) health and safety check, through registration with annual safety and health checks (the most usual form of licensing imposed on providers), to – in the most advanced cases – registration with requirements for staff and curriculum standards, annual pedagogical inspection, in-training requirements, and pedagogical supervision ensured regularly by an accredited supervisory body. In many countries, the majority of day care providers remain unregistered, and are free to exercise without any licensing requirement, except for a legal restriction on the number of children to be cared for.

Table 6.1. **Requirements in selected OECD countries for licensed family day care, crèches, and public early education**

	Licensed family day care	Licensed crèches	Public early education
Australia	Level 2/3	Level 3	Level 4
Austria	Level 2/3	Level 3	Level 4
Belgium (French Community)	Level 2/3	Level 4	Level 4
Canada	Level 1/2	Level 2/3 or 4 (depending on Province)	Level 4
Hungary	Level 3	Level 4	Level 4
Ireland	Level 1	Level 2	Level 4
Korea	Level 2	Level 2	Level 4
Portugal	Level 1	Level 3	Level 4
Sweden	Level 4	Level 4	Level 4

Level 1: Registration with an initial health and safety check.
Level 2: Registration with annual health and safety checks.
Level 3: Registration with annual checks, obligation to follow an official curriculum or developmental programme, and a minimum staff certification requirement.
Level 4: Registration with annual checks, curriculum or quality standards, staff certification, in-training and pedagogical supervision ensured regularly by an accredited supervisory body.
Source: Information provided by countries to the OECD (2004b).

Weakness of regulation is a particular concern in countries where the majority of young children attend unlicensed or weakly licensed settings before public early education begins. Although State Boards of Education in most American States set minimum operational standards for public pre-kindergarten and kindergarten programmes (children of 3, 4 and 5 years) the licensing of child care settings can be weak, 37 States in the United States require no or minimal training for child care providers in the private sector who supply the majority of services for children under 3 (Kagan and Rigby, 2003). The educational levels and working conditions of the majority of staff in this sector are low, and annual staff turnover rates of 35% are not uncommon.[4] The situation is paralleled in other OECD countries whenever public authorities do not legislate sufficiently for the child care sector, or do not enforce quality standards or fail to provide sufficient incentives for providers to comply. In fact, in several countries, *e.g.* in Canada and Ireland among the countries recently reviewed, much of the private provision in the child care sector tends to be exempt from all but minimal health and safety rules. At the same time, research from the United States suggests that appropriate governmental regulation, licensing and programme standards in ECEC consistently lead to improvements in quality (see, for example, the *Cost, Quality and Outcomes* studies in 1995 and 1999, Helburn and Howes, 1996; and Phillipsen *et al.*, 1997).

The situation is more reassuring in the public, integrated ECEC systems of Denmark, Finland, Norway and Sweden. Because government is firmly in control through legislation, and local authorities are in an influential position because of their funding, licensing and monitoring role *vis-à-vis* all ECEC services, there is much less discussion about regulation in these countries. Core understandings of programme standards and the purposes of ECEC are actively shared, and sufficient funding is allocated to providers to enable them to observe expected standards.

Regulation in early education systems

Clear national or state regulations are more a feature of public early education systems than in the child care sector. The basic structural standards or profile of quality decided by each country, such as adequate premises, child-staff ratios, curriculum frameworks, adequate professional education and certification of staff, and organised parental involvement are generally respected in early education. However, variations in the understanding of these indicators can exist, in particular with respect to buildings, child-staff ratios, educator qualifications and the role of parents. From the experience of the OECD reviews, regulations for child-staff ratios for 3- to 6-year-olds vary from about 7:1 in the Nordic countries to more than 25:1 in France, Ireland, Korea and Mexico. In addition, compliance with regulations varies, and derogations from required staff qualifications are found in many countries. Yet, no large scale derogations were reported from the early education sector, except in certain States in the United States, where, according to Kagan and Rigby (2003), fourteen states allow exemptions from licensing for nursery schools, pre-schools or pre-kindergarten, and thirteen States allow exemptions from licensing for faith-based centres.

3. Initiatives to improve regulation and quality standards

During the reviews, OECD review teams encountered many positive initiatives to improve regulation and quality standards in ECEC services:

- *The tying of financing to programme standards*: Some national and state governments tie funding levels to the achievement of programme standards that exceed basic licensing requirements. In Australia providers are required to satisfactorily participate in Quality Assurance to maintain eligibility for Australian Government funding support. The Quality Assurance regime encompasses all long-day care, family day care and outside school hours care services. Unless services are registered and undergo the quality accreditation process (NCAC, 2006), eligibility for the Child Care Benefit is denied. Several of the American States, *e.g.* Georgia, New Jersey, New York use "tiered subsidy reimbursement" to encourage providers to surpass basic licensing requirements, that is, higher rates of child care subsidy payments are paid to providers that provide higher quality care. States, such as California, uses contracts to improve the standards and performance of child care centres. In parallel, the Korean government has recently offered voucher funding to the quality *hakwon* system (private learning academies), if providers accept the national kindergarten curriculum, kindergarten teacher certification, and the national supervisory and environmental regulations. Such strategies require a strong commitment on the side of government, as the achievement of high standards (and especially to raise educator qualifications or to lower child-staff ratios) requires significant funding.

- *The combination of regulation and fiscal measures to discourage unlicensed provision*: In Australia and Belgium, for example, parents can benefit from tax relief or vouchers only when they use day care services – public or private – registered and supervised by public authorities. Danish law simply forbids unlicensed remunerated care of more than one child by a non-family member.

- *Improved organisation of family day care*: In most countries, family day care lacks adequate supervision and training. Some governments do formulate specific licensing requirements for this sector, and encourage individual carers to belong to municipal networks or child minder associations. These associations are then contracted and funded by local authorities to take in charge quality improvement and the professional training of the family day carers. This is the case in Austria, Belgium, Canada, Denmark, Finland, France, Germany, Hungary, Norway and Sweden, although in several of these countries, professional child care services are still few, and unlicensed non-parental care arrangements still continue to be widely used.

- *The creation of voluntary standards, codes of ethics, and guidelines*: e.g. in the Netherlands, and the United States. Voluntary guidelines developed in the United States by the National Association for the Education of Young Children (NAEYC), the National Early Childhood Program Accreditation (NECPA) and the National Association for Family Child Care (NAFCC) positively impact a wide range of service types. In particular, NAEYC Accreditation Performance Criteria have become a standard for centre-based ECEC across the States, and are also used widely at international level.

- *The use of regulatory frameworks*: Strong and detailed regulatory frameworks are in force in many countries. In 2001, the United Kingdom introduced national standards for early childhood services for children under age 8, setting a national benchmark of quality below which no provider may fall. Following the Childcare Bill of 2005, these standards are currently under review and will now cover all provision for children and young people. A new integrated inspection framework is also being developed to enforce these standards. In the United States, several States have recently legislated comprehensive regulatory frameworks for early childhood services that are in receipt of public financing either directly or indirectly. In Arkansas, the regulation, Rules Governing the Arkansas Better Chance Programme (for children from "at-risk" situations), shows a determination to raise programme standards well above the licensing or minimum operational standards set by most States (see Box 6.1).

- *The use of rating systems*: Other American States, *e.g.* Arizona, Iowa and Wisconsin, have introduced rating systems to encourage providers to improve their services and to give parents the information they need to choose a quality programme for their children. These rating systems (often based on Head Start or NAEYC work) provide information on programme standards, that is, indicators such as child-staff ratios, caregiver or teacher educational level. They provide valuable information to parents, and lead to enhanced funding for the better providers, which receive more state child care financing to serve children from low-income or at-risk backgrounds.

Box 6.1. **Rules governing the Arkansas Better Chance Programme (ABC), in the United States**

In addition to defining child and provider eligibility for the programme, the rules governing the ABC programme address five key areas:

Child-staff ratios and group sizes: Child-staff ratios in the classroom shall not exceed: 4:1 for infants up to 18 months; 7:1 for toddlers 18 months to 3 years; 10:1 for 3- to 5-year-olds. Maximum group sizes for these age groups are respectively: 8, 14 and 20 children.

Staff profiles, staffing patterns and professional development: Staff are divided into three categories, each being required to have minimal certification: Lead teachers with a Bachelor's or Master's degree in early childhood education (or other relevant degree with an emphasis on child development); Classroom teachers with an Associate Arts degree (2 years tertiary) in early childhood education; and paraprofessional aides with a child development associate credential. ABC staff should also reflect the ethnic diversity of the children participating in the ABC programme. Lead teachers are responsible for curriculum, programme planning and supervision of aides, and should have 30 hours annually of professional development; aides have a right to 20 hours. Each classroom should be staffed by one teacher and one aide. Centres with four classrooms must employ two lead teachers, two classroom teachers and four paraprofessional aides.

Programme standards and curriculum: Programmes shall be developmentally appropriate and individualised to meet the needs of each child. Centres follow NAEYC guidelines and the Arkansas ECE Framework. In addition to enriched environments (equipment and materials for children; interest areas and learning corners; appropriately planned outdoor areas), programmes will have thematic units and goals related to: cultural diversity, socio-emotional learning; creative-aesthetic learning; cognitive development; physical development and language. Teachers shall implement and maintain individual child portfolios, including samples of children's work, teacher and parent observations. The daily schedule should reflect a balance between indoor/outdoor; quiet/active; individual/small group/large group; gross motor/fine motor; child initiated/teacher initiated. A free meal and snacks are provided free to children in need, and mealtimes and other routines are used as opportunities for incidental learning. Attention should be given to easing transitions for children from one programme or age grouping to another, with particular concern for the transition to public school kindergarten.

Child assessment, developmental and health screening: All children in ABC programmes shall receive comprehensive health and developmental screens to determine their individual needs. Health screening will cover: growth and nutrition, developmental assessment, neurological and cardiac status, vision, hearing, teeth, immunization status, blood and urine lab tests. The developmental screen will cover the following areas: vocabulary, visual-motor integration, language and speech development, fine and gross motor skills, social skills and developmental milestones. A comprehensive longitudinal study shall also be implemented to evaluate the ABC programme over time and ensure that it meets its goals.

Parent/community involvement: Each programme shall have a parent handbook and a plan for parental involvement that will include opportunities for parental inputs into programme operation and design. The plan will include parental reviews of programmatic plans, parent conferences and a method to involve the parent in the child's educational experience. There will also be an "open door" policy for parents that encourages visiting and participation in classroom activities.

4. The use of pedagogical frameworks and educational plans

In the last decade, a major policy change has taken place in the early childhood field, with the publication of a rash of new national or state curricula (Germany has one for each of its 16 *Länder*). Unlike the centrally imposed curricula of traditional primary schooling, ECEC curricula often take the form of short pedagogical frameworks. These frameworks, based on consultation allow local interpretation, identify general quality goals and indicate how they may be attained. They also encourage the formulation of a more detailed curriculum by each centre. Many governments have introduced curricula in services for children over 3 years (Korea 1969, Australia QL 1997; England in 1999, 2000 and 2002; Scotland 1999; Ireland 2004; Germany 2004-05). Some countries have also developed a common curriculum or pedagogical framework for 0- to 6-year-olds (Denmark 2004, Finland 1996[5] and 2003, Norway 1996 and 2005, Sweden 1998); and some countries have developed guidelines for work with children from birth to three (England 2005). Such curricula help to promote a more even level of quality across age groups and provision; to guide and support professional staff in their practice; to facilitate communication between staff and parents; and to ensure pedagogical continuity between ECEC and school. France, Ireland, Korea, and Mexico are among the countries that have begun, revised or completed national curricula since 2000. In 2006, Korea is revising its 7th National Kindergarten Curriculum, and England is formulating a new *Early Years Foundation Stage* curriculum for children 0-6 years.

National pedagogical frameworks can include a broad range of elements, but in general, they identify the key goals of early childhood services for a particular country. Without such guidelines, inexperienced or untrained staff may easily revert to direct instruction as their default mode or – presuming that children learn intuitively when placed with other children in enriched learning environments – adopt a *laissez-faire* approach to programming and the acquisition of basic skills. At the same time, frameworks need to be flexible enough to allow staff to experiment with different methodological, didactic and pedagogical approaches. An agreed framework is useful in guiding practice across a country and, if addressed primarily to local administrations and centres, can ensure consistent standards across different forms of early childhood services. They can also ensure continuity in children's learning as they approach compulsory school age.

Depending on the country, curricular frameworks cover and emphasise different fields. They may focus on the social and civic attitudes that a country may wish to see inform early education (Swedish Ministry of Education, 1998), or identify important learning areas (England, Department for Education and Skills [DfES], 2002) or emphasise the physical, relational and programmatic requirements of quality learning environments (US Bredekamp and Copple, 1997; Harms et al., 1998) or again, as in France, the United States and other English-speaking countries, set standards for children in literacy and numeracy. A move can be seen in several countries and programmes towards including the environment and its protection as an important theme for young children.

In several countries, national guidelines have been formulated after a wide process of consultation, a procedure that seems more democratic and respectful of educator and parental wishes. Defining quality for ECEC programmes can be viewed from an expert perspective, but the meanings given to quality by the children involved, their parents, local practitioners, early childhood experts, and national child agencies are essential inputs. Goal setting in the quality field that aims to receive the assent of practitioners and parents will attempt to embrace these viewpoints. In sum, curricula seem to work best when their value base commands widespread consent, and key goals have been defined with a wide range of stakeholders including staff, parents, and other members of the community (Lindberg and Välimäki, 2004).

5. Dominant understandings of the ECEC curriculum

Most OECD countries now use a curriculum in early childhood services, especially as children grow older, that is to say, that some structuring and orientation of children's experience towards educational aims is generally accepted. Analyses by EUROSTAT show that European countries generally introduce structured learning areas to young children from the ages of 4 to 6 years (EUROSTAT, 2000). The preferred domains of knowledge proposed are: nature and the environment; emergent literacy and numeracy; general knowledge; scientific concepts and reasoning. The learning areas that receive most focus in official curricula – particularly in countries where child assessments are used shortly after entry into primary school – are emergent literacy and numeracy. It is precisely at this point that countries begin to diverge in their understandings of curriculum. Countries in the social pedagogy tradition do not exclude emergent literacy and numeracy but seek to maintain an open and holistic curriculum until children enter school and sometimes, until well into the early classes of primary school. On the other hand, countries in which early education has been part of, or closely associated with, the primary school tend to privilege readiness for school and a more academic approach to curriculum and methodology.

In curricular design terms, the difference in approach may be characterised as the adoption of a sequential learning approach in pre-primary classes, while the social pedagogy tradition favours more holistic learning. In the former, different developmental areas are selected, including emergent literacy and numeracy, and teachers are expected to help children advance their knowledge and skills level in each of these domains, in accordance with carefully sequenced steps. The teacher knows where the children are at a given moment in the year (she is aware of the zone of proximal development) and can raise the level of complexity whenever she judges the children are ready to advance. However, as van Kuyk (2006), author of the Piramide programme extensively used in the Netherlands, comments:

"The sequential approach is primarily teacher directed and offers limited opportunities for children to develop self-regulation. Activities often fail to tap into children's intrinsic motivation, because they do not authentically meet the needs and interests of children. When this intrinsic motivation is missing, the teacher will have to work harder to engage the children in learning… learning becomes artificial and uninteresting. Children seek a meaningful context for learning, and when learning activities are decontextualised, the teacher has to entice the children with functional contexts and playful activities. Even though the learning goals are very clear in the sequential approach, the developmental areas lack natural connection and integration."

In the holistic approach, all developmental areas are addressed through play and broad project work that encourage active learning and multiple experiences in the major developmental domains. With the help of experienced teachers (and parents and older children), young children can choose their activities and organise the projects, an excellent experience in self-regulation and agency, and one that is highly motivating. Project work also provides an authentic opportunity to teachers to challenge and extend the meaning-making of children in different developmental domains. Language, negotiation and communication are also fundamental in group project work. Certain projects also lend themselves investigation, measurements and hypotheses, such as nature and environment activities, and other project themes to familiarity with concepts such as responsibility for one's own health or with numbers and simple mathematical operations, such as projects about food supply and shopping.

The early education tradition

In France and the English-speaking countries (excepting the *Te Wharike* curriculum in New Zealand), national and state early education programmes for young children tend to focus strongly on cognitive development, early literacy and numeracy. Economic and labour market reasons may drive this focus, as literacy, numeracy and technology proficiency are seen as indispensable elements of education in modern economies. Another explanation is that the greater heterogeneity and social differentiation of populations in these countries requires a teaching or instruction approach, as in many early childhood centres there can be a high proportion of children at risk of school failure. In such circumstances, an emphasis on language and school readiness may be understandable, although limitations of space and large group sizes, especially in urban areas, may also be a factor inhibiting more child-centred processes. In early childhood centres in these countries, much evidence of literacy activity can be seen. Teacher-initiated and large group activities predominate, and a language hour or more may be scheduled each day.

In the United States, contractual federal programmes for young children, such as Head Start, have been required to formulate programme standards and to define expected outcomes for children (Head Start Bureau, 2001). This culture has grown with the No Child Left Behind (NCLB) initiative (see Box 6.2), which requires States to publish every year achievement standards in reading/language, mathematics and sciences from Grade 3 (ages 8-9) up to Grade 12 (ages 17-18). School districts in charge of the public kindergarten services have also adopted learning standards and introduced more focused learning strategies in public kindergarten services. Today, the great majority of the American States have published early learning standards for young children, four of them also covering children under 3 (Scott-Little *et al.*, 2003). Many States follow either Head Start or the NAEYC/NAECS/SDE[6] guidelines and include broad developmental areas for assessment.[7] However, in practice, the priority areas privileged by States for assessment are often language/literacy and cognition/general knowledge areas. Massachusetts, an influential State in educational matters, speaks only of content areas in its *Guidelines for pre-school Learning Experiences*: Learning in English Language Arts; Learning in Mathematics; Learning in Science and Technology/Engineering; Learning in History/Social Science; Learning in Health Education; Learning in the Arts.[8]

The movement in the United States towards learning standards in pre-literacy and numeracy is defended on several grounds. Firstly – a point sometimes overlooked by critics of early literacy and numeracy – children are genuinely interested from an early age in reading and writing. Again, underlying the formulation of standards for literacy and numeracy in early education, there is a genuine democratic concern that all young children should have a fair start in life, be supported in their early development, and enter school "ready to learn". The great diversity in the composition of the child population in the United States (as in many of the large European cities) requires special attention to basic language skills and to general knowledge relevant in the host society. These areas can be taken for granted in more homogenous societies, but become, in multi-cultural societies, an issue of equal educational opportunity for children from low-income and immigrant

---

Box 6.2. **The American No Child Left Behind (NCLB) framework**

Part of the NCLB policy framework, the Good Start, Grow Smart (GSGS) initiative calls on school districts to set expectations for young children that are research-based and that align with the standards set for literacy and numeracy in elementary and secondary education. The initiative is clearly marked by the NCLB framework, which promotes accountability, adequate yearly progress; more highly qualified teachers and a more focused preparation of young children before kindergarten entry (5 years) in early literacy and pre-mathematics skills. Spurred by the initiative, most States have established voluntary early learning guidelines that are clear statements of what children should know and be able to do when they enter kindergarten. As in Head Start, accountability systems are being put into place, although testing of children below Grade 2 is not mandated and is generally discouraged.

Professional development for teachers and caregivers

Good Start, Grow Smart. NCLB does not include early childhood and pre-kindergarten teachers in its "highly qualified" teacher requirements. In most States, in fact, training requirements for child care staff are minimal, and many States do not require pre-service training beyond a high school diploma. The field is "plagued by high teacher turnover, low pay and a lack of meaningful career paths. The problem cannot be solved without significantly more public funding. NCLB does not provide substantial funding increases to improve the quality of teaching in early childhood and pre-kindergarten programmes" (Kauerz and McMaken, 2004). The law includes an Early Childhood Educator Professional Development Program, which provides grants to partnerships providing high quality professional development to educators working with children from low-income families in high need districts.

Early reading first

NCLB includes a reading programme Early Reading First for young pre-school-age (3- to 5-year-olds) children designed to prepare them to start school with the language, cognitive and early reading skills they will need to become proficient readers. The programme targets children from low-income families, focuses on professional development activities and requires research-based curricula and assessments

Reliance on research

GSGS recognises early learning as a critical contributor to academic success in school, and emphasizes the importance of using the latest early literacy research to help families and teachers promote early literacy with young children. A United States USD 45 million, five-year research initiative, will seek to identify the most effective early pre-reading and language curricula and teaching strategies for early childhood educators and caregivers. To date, researchers understand that language development and, in particular, phonemic awareness and vocabulary are the foundations for later reading success. Reading researchers have identified reading skills, such as the ability to link letters with sounds, and practices such as interactive reading techniques, that are keys to children's success.

Source: Kauerz and McMacken (2004).

---

backgrounds. Learning standards also provide necessary benchmarks in an early childhood "system", which in many instances is a patchwork of services and programmes with uneven regulatory and staffing requirements, multiple auspices and a wide variety of aims (Fuller *et al.*, 2005). The standards-based approach also corresponds to the quality assurance mechanisms at work in the larger education system in the United States, that is, an emphasis on outputs, the naming of clear objectives and their measurement, regulation and a focus on the importance of instructional practice.

This approach is generally greeted with caution in other OECD countries. For many early childhood experts and managers, to define learning standards primarily in the logico-mathematical field presents a challenge to traditional understandings of early childhood programming and gives rise to fears of the "schoolification" of early childhood services. Moving the focus of early learning towards a staircase of pre-specified cognitive skills runs counter to the insights of the founders of early childhood methodology and to the strong social pedagogy tradition that exists in Nordic and Central Europe. More research and socio-cultural sensitivity are needed in this field. What young children are expected to know and do influences strongly the nature of ECEC programming and consequently, the daily experience of young children in services. Consensus is lacking across countries concerning the critical skills, knowledge and pedagogical approaches that serve best the development of young children.

The social pedagogy tradition

Countries coming from the social pedagogy tradition pursue societal aims in their early childhood programmes that go beyond preparation for school. Already reference has been made to the participatory democratic goals of the Swedish curriculum. Another aspect of this curriculum – and of curricula in neighbouring countries – is that it is not a prescriptive or normalising curriculum in the traditional sense. Nordic curricula are statements of principle outlining the main values and requirements of kindergarten education. They do not address primarily what children should learn, but provide guidelines for local authorities and the centres about the values, purposes and processes of early childhood education and care.

The Norwegian curriculum or Framework Plan (Ministry of Children and Family Affairs, 1996), the first of its type in Europe and now revised (2006, see Chapter 10), builds on a holistic concept of learning.[9] "This is in contrast to a view in which education primarily involves structuring and imparting a specific body of knowledge in the course of a limited period of time" (Norway Background Report, 1998). An emphasis is placed on basic competence acquired by children through the informal learning processes of the kindergarten (barnehage). Basic competence is defined as the development of social interaction skills, and the development of language and communication skills in the broadest sense. "Children's play is important both as a content in itself and as a working method" – a point of view upheld by research (see, for example, Winnicott, 1971; Bruner, 1990; Michelet, 1999). Objectives are formulated for children's development and learning, both in basic competences and in five broad learning areas: society, religion and ethics, aesthetic subjects; language, text and communication; nature, environment and technology; physical activity and health.

In Denmark, kindergartens also emphasise "the free and creative development of the child in a social context" (Lund, 2005). The formulation of a national curriculum was resisted by pedagogues until 2004, when the Law on Pedagogical Curriculum[10] was introduced. The new curriculum focuses attention on six areas: the personal development of the children; social competences; language; body and movement; nature and natural phenomena; and understanding culture, one's own and others'. In addition, each centre must specify the competences and experiences that the children are to acquire. Staff must also recognise and make allowance for younger children (under 3 years) and older children (3- to 6-year-olds). The notion of *competence* is more important in the Danish approach than the acquisition of knowledge, although competence will include knowledge appropriate to the child's understanding. The belief is strong in Denmark that early childhood centres are social pedagogical institutions, which should adopt a broad and holistic approach to children's development that should not be confused with educational institutions. According to many Danish pedagogues interviewed: "You cannot teach competence. Each child has to learn it through experience." For this reason, Danish kindergartens generally provide to children a welcoming environment, which allows them a wide range of experiences. The concept of pedagogy is considered a critical element – an active relationship with children that embraces the care of children, their upbringing and education (see also Chapter 3).

The Danish fear that an emphasis on learning or "education" will come to dominate the pedagogical work of the kindergarten and undermine its basic objective (to support the holistic development of the child) is not necessarily a view shared by either the Reggio Emilia schools or the Swedish authorities. The Reggio Emilia schools have been famed not only for their democratic vision of society, but also for the level and complexity of learning generated by children in these centres. Through projects freely chosen with their teachers, children experience aspects of the surrounding world (including their experience of life in the city) and explore their inter-connectedness. Their thinking and learning are expressed through many modes of expression (their words, projects, paintings, photos, constructions, etc.) and captured in pedagogical documentation. The wealth of expression – going far beyond a literacy/numeracy curriculum – reflects the central place given to freedom of inquiry, culture and imagination in Reggio *progettazione* (Rinaldi, 1998). These centres achieve an education of the senses, imagination and creativity of young children.

A strong Reggio movement also informs pre-school practice in Sweden, a country that in recent years has laid greater emphasis on learning and education, while retaining the social pedagogic emphasis on social competence and the holistic development and well-being of children. ECEC is seen as the foundation stage of lifelong learning and since 1996 has been incorporated into the education system. Initiatives taken since then have sought to build closer links between pre-school, free-time services (school-age child care) and school, treating all as equal parts of the education system. An aim announced by the Swedish authorities is that early childhood pedagogy with its emphasis on care, upbringing and learning should influence at least the early years of compulsory school. Current development work is focusing on the integration of pre-school pedagogy and leisure-time activities into primary education, and on creating pedagogical "meeting places" between all three services. Unlike the English or French systems, children are not graded or assessed in Swedish pre-schools or early primary:

> "... all children should develop a desire and curiosity for learning, and confidence in their own learning, rather than achieving a pre-specified level of knowledge and proficiency. The pre-school should be a place for play, exploration and love of learning, with practice that has the image of a competent child and takes seriously listening to children and respecting their thoughts, theories and dreams. This should lay a strong foundation for lifelong learning" (Martin-Korpi, 2005a).

However, this holistic approach to early childhood development should not be interpreted to mean that standards are absent. On the contrary, pre-school centres need to demonstrate through annual reporting on quality how they are fulfilling their aims and objectives. In this exercise, the views of parents and the wider community have an integral part. Within the centres, children's progress is regularly – if unobtrusively – assessed through observation, documentation and parent interviews. Staff performance is also regularly assessed, through documentation or other internal process, but also externally by the municipal pedagogical advisors and inspectors, and by regular surveys carried out by the National Education (Sweden) or Social Welfare Agency (Denmark, Finland). One of the most stringent national evaluations of early childhood services that we know was undertaken by the Swedish National Agency for Education in 2003 (Skolverket, 2004).

Understandings of the child are also important for the shaping of curricula (Soto Guzmán and Reveco, 2004, Rayna and Brougère, 2000, Rayna et al., 1996). For example, the Norwegian *Framework Plan* sees childhood as a phase in life with intrinsic value. There is an explicit acknowledgement of the right of the young child to well-being, autonomy and freedom. Childhood does not merely involve acquiring sufficient knowledge and skills to be able to participate in the adult community as quickly as possible. It entails growth on the child's own premises. *Starting Strong* (OECD, 2001) also made reference to seeing the child in the here and now, and repeats a phrase often heard in the Nordic countries: "there is a time for childhood that can never be repeated." This approach contrasts to seeing ECEC as primarily an investment in the future, strongly linked to utilitarian ends, *e.g.* preparation for school (and later work), in which the child is considered as a person to be formed rather than as a citizen who actively participates in the life of the ECEC centre. In the utilitarian perspective, state purposes are strongly foregrounded, and the actual desires and natural learning strategies of the child may be overshadowed.

In contrast, curricula in the social pedagogy tradition place trust in young children as agents of their own learning, as competent persons who desire to engage with the world. Educators are encouraged to create, not only enriched learning environments, but also an affective environment that nurtures growth and confidence. The natural learning strategies of the child – play, relationships, curiosity and the desire to make meaning – are encouraged, and channelled towards activities valued both by children and educators. The emphasis is on co-construction with young children and respect of their free choices and centres of interest. As noted by Rinaldi of Reggio Emilia, "The task of the teacher is to create a context in which children's curiosity, theories and research are legitimated and listened to…" (*Children in Europe*, 2005). Respect for the imaginative freedom, creativity and pleasure of the individual child is given primary importance, but within a learning environment where the requirements of society are also met.

Some of the contrasting features of the pre-primary and social pedagogy approaches are presented in Table 6.2.

A further development of the social pedagogy approach can be seen in the "educational plans" recently produced by several German *Länder*.

"Second generation" early childhood curricula in Germany

"Second generation" curricula or education plans, developed in some of the German *Länder*, build essentially on the social pedagogy approach to early childhood. They are called "second generation", as designed from 2003 to 2005, they are inspired by the "first generation" curricula for young children that were produced in OECD countries in

Table 6.2. **Features of two curricular traditions**

	Readiness for school tradition	The Nordic tradition
Understandings of the child and childhood	The child as a young person to be formed, as an investment in the future of society: the productive knowledge worker, the compliant well-behaved citizen… A benevolent, utilitarian approach to childhood in which State and adult purposes are fore grounded. Pedagogy focused on "useful" learning, readiness for school… A tendency to privilege indoors learning.	The child as a subject of rights: autonomy, well-being… the right to growth on the child's own premises. The child as agent of her/his own learning, a rich child with natural learning and research strategies… The child as member of a caring community of peers and adults, in which the influence of the child is sought. An outdoors child of pleasure and freedom. A time for childhood that can never be repeated.
The early childhood centre	Generally (though by no means always), the centre is seen as a service based on individual demand, a matter of "choice" for the individual parents. It is viewed as a place for development, learning and instruction. Children will be expected to reach pre-defined levels of development and learning (goals to be achieved).	The centre is seen as a public socio-educational service, in which the community interests as well as the interests of individual parents must be taken into account. It is viewed as a life space, a place in which children and pedagogues learn "to be, to know, to do and to live together" (Delors Report, 1996). Centre goals are to support child development and learning and provide experience of democratic values. Little pressure placed on children who are expected to strive for general goals.
Curriculum development	Frequently, a prescribed ministerial curriculum, with detailing of goals and outcomes. Assumption that the curriculum can be "delivered" by the individual teacher in a standardised way whatever the group or setting.	A broad national guideline, with devolution of curriculum detailing and implementation to municipalities and the centres. Responsibility falls on the centre staff, a feeling of collegiality… a culture of research about what children want to learn and how they learn.
Focus of programme	A focus on learning and skills, especially in areas useful for school readiness. Mainly teacher directed (Weikart *et al.*, 2003). Teacher-child relationships may be instrumentalised through large numbers of children per teacher and the need to achieve detailed curriculum goals.	Focus on working with the whole child and her/his family broad – developmental goals as well as learning are pursued. Programmes are child-centred – interactivity with educators and peers encouraged and the quality of life in the institution is given high importance.
Pedagogical strategies	A balanced mix of instruction, child initiated activities and thematic work is encouraged, generally managed by each teacher. The national curriculum must be "delivered" correctly. An emphasis placed on individual autonomy and self-regulation.	The national curriculum guides the choice of pedagogical themes and projects. Confidence is placed in the child's own learning strategies and centres of interest, that is, on learning through relationships, through play and through educator scaffolding at the appropriate moment.
Language and literacy development	A growing focus on individual competence in the national language. Oral competence, phonological awareness and letter/word recognition are valued. Emphasis on emergent literacy practices. Standards may be established for language skills pre-reading knowledge, pre-mathematical knowledge, cognitive skills and social development.	A growing focus on individual competence in the national language, in terms of language production and the ability to communicate. An emphasis also on symbolic representation and the "100 languages of children". Promotion of family literacies and inter-generational language experiences.
Targets and goals for children	Prescribed targets – generally pertaining to cognitive development – may be set at national level to be reached in all centres, sometimes translated by each year of age.	Broad orientations rather than prescribed outcomes. Goals are to be striven for, rather than achieved. A diffusion of goals may be experienced, with diminished accountability unless quality is actively pursued.
Indoor and outdoor spaces for young children	The indoors is considered to be the primary learning space, and resources are focused here. Outdoors is generally seen as an amenity, a recreational area and perhaps as important for health and motor development.	Indoors and outdoors have equal pedagogical importance. Much thought and investment is given to the organisation of outdoor space and its use. Young children may spend three or four hours daily out of doors, both in winter and summer. The environment and its protection is an important theme.
Assessment	Learning outcomes and assessment often required, at least on entry into primary school. Goals for the group are clearly defined. Graded assessment of each child with respect to pre-defined competences may be an important part of the teacher's role.	Formal assessment not required. Broad developmental goals are set for each child by negotiation (educator-parent-child). Goals are informally evaluated unless screening is necessary. Multiple assessment procedures are favoured.
Quality control	Quality control based on clear objectives, inspection, and frequently, on pre-defined learning outcomes. Standardised testing may be used – on a sample basis – in programme evaluation, but in most centres, child testing is not allowed. Assessment of skills mastery is generally ongoing and the responsibility of the lead teacher. An external inspectorate may also validate, but may be under-staffed (especially in child care) or staffed by personnel without training in ECEC pedagogy.	Quality control is more participatory, based on educator and team responsibility and, depending on country, supervised by parent boards and municipalities. Documentation used not only to mark child progress but also as a collegial research on staff pedagogical approaches. A wide range of child outcomes may be sought, and assessed informally in multiple ways. External validation undertaken by municipal pedagogical advisors and/or inspectors. The focus is on centre performance rather than on child assessment.

Source: Bennett (2005) revised.

the 1980s and 90s. The new curricula adopt a holistic approach to early development with regard to:

- *The pedagogical concept*, which brings together *Bildung* (education), *Betreung* (care) and *Erziehung* (nurturing or upbringing). This comprehensive concept of pedagogy ensures that all the basic needs of young children are more adequately met, regardless of the child's family background (OECD, 2004).

- *The content of educational work with young children*: the educational plans embrace all the main developmental areas. Knowledge acquisition in selected areas is considered less important at this age than the holistic development of children, and their involvement in learning. For this reason, the goals put forward in these plans do not privilege the mastery of sequenced knowledge in readiness-for-school subjects, but seek to respect the interests of children and their parents. At the same time, the interests of society are served: for example, these curricula place a strong emphasis on socially skilled and competent children, on language an communication abilities in the many languages of children, and on democratic participation.

- *The pedagogical approach*: German pedagogues privilege holistic group projects in which a range of developmental areas and the different intelligences of children – cognitive, socio-emotional and physical – are simultaneously involved.

The German education plans adopt also a strong socio-constructivist approach to curriculum, both at the *Land* and institutional levels. In Bavaria, Berlin and Hesse, the educational plans were developed, as in the Nordic countries, after widespread consultation of teachers, parents, and providers, as well as of administrators and curriculum experts (Fthenakis, 2006, Prott and Preissing, 2006). The plans also address different places where children learn, and not just the early childhood centre: they include home learning and the role of parents, leisure-time activities, the primary school, the potential contribution of local communities and youth welfare to social learning and culture. In this sense, the focus is on the learning biography of the child, and not simply on the early childhood institution (Fthenakis, 2006). Within the early childhood centre, education is increasingly understood as a social process, involving staff, parents and above all, the agency of children. It is also a process which can respond flexibly to the social context of children, and engage the local community in the care, upbringing and education of young children.

The fundamental aim of the Berlin curriculum is to assist young children in building up competencies – ego competencies, social competencies, knowledge competencies and learning method competencies in seven selected areas of education: body, movement and health; social and cultural life; communication: languages, writing culture and media; artistic activities; music; basic mathematical experiences; basic experiences in natural sciences and technology. Each of these competencies is further divided into aspects concerning: the child in its world; the child in the children's community; and the child experiencing and discovering the world. In this sense, the German curricula depart from the simplicity (and perhaps clarity) of the "first generation" curricula of the Nordic countries, in that they are far longer and outline in much detail the learning goals to be addressed by children in the different areas and the tasks to be undertaken by the pedagogues. Their prescriptiveness may stem from a lack of confidence in the current training of pedagogues or from the need to address a perceived "looseness" in pedagogical work in German kindergartens or simply from the wish to provide pedagogues with a comprehensive curricular document (see OECD, 2004).

In Bavaria and Hesse, the goals selected for children are influenced by the English "Birth to Three" curriculum, which in 2005 put forward four simple but powerful goals: a strong child; a skilful communicator; a competent learner; and a healthy child. The more elaborate Hesse curriculum, addressing the education of young children from 0-10 years, speaks of: strong children; communicating and media-competent children; children as creative and imaginative artists; children as active learners, explorers and discoverers; responsible children whose actions are based on value systems (Fthenakis, 2006). Activities, competences and orientations for pedagogues are outlined in all these domains.

Important features emerge from these new educational plans.

- *A focus on learning processes (meta-cognition) and their regulation.* Children's self-regulation of their own lives (socio-emotional development) is regarded as a necessary precondition of effective learning, for example, their ability to play and work with other children; their growing recognition of organisation and time needed; their appreciation of effort and perseverance; their ability to transfer knowledge or skills acquired in one area to another... Regulation or mediation by teachers is also stressed, for example, encouraging holistic pedagogies and active group work for the age group 3-6 years; sensitising children to learning styles and learning moments; the use of appropriate scaffolding and teaching methods, such as challenging and extending the child's understanding, demonstrating and modelling skills or behaviours; and an emphasis on relationships, language and communication.

- *A focus on values, including respect for diversity.* In many respects, the focus on learning processes and styles favours individuation and awareness of difference, with regard to sex, age, individual approaches to learning and personal interests. The curricula also refer to values systems and awareness of others. The Berlin curriculum includes a chapter on educational tasks and methods, which has a section on *Designing everyday life with children.* It enumerates the tasks of the *Erzieher* (pedagogues) in ensuring that life in the centre will strengthen the children's autonomy and their ability to live responsibly and democratically in diverse groups:

  ❖ They (the pedagogues) stimulate children to design everyday life themselves, to be active for and in the community and to take responsibility.

  ❖ They enable independent access to materials and technical media, and discover their possible uses together with the children.

  ❖ They help children to discover their neighbourhood and the local surroundings of the facility in an independent and self-determined way.

  ❖ The Erzieher take account of the common interests and special features of children who have different cultural backgrounds.

  ❖ They ensure that the different languages and dialects of children receive due respect and attention in everyday life.

  ❖ They ensure that the cultural background of the children is represented in the design of spaces and the selection of materials and books;

  ❖ They cultivate an atmosphere of mutual respect and esteem.

  ❖ They develop rituals and structures that provide structure and orientation in the children's daily routine and strengthen the children's sense of community.

The section on social and cultural life is equally democratic in tone. Many of the competencies, including at ego level, encourage democratic reflexes and attitudes, *e.g.*"forming an opinion and having a standpoint"; "developing ideas, taking the initiative, inspiring others, 'asserting oneself'"; "having the confidence to stick up for one's own rights and defend oneself against injustice", "forming an opinion and accepting other views"; "expressing and accepting criticism"; "being able to distinguish between one's own experiences and those of media productions", "knowing and using decision-making processes" (Prott and Presing, 2006).

● *A search for consistency in education environments and procedures*: It is well-known that unless a "schoolification" of pre-primary education has taken place, the transition from kindergarten to primary school can challenge some children (see Chapter 3, section 3 above: Facilitating transitions for young children). For this reason, the Nordic countries (excepting Norway) have introduced a "pre-school" class to serve as a bridge between the two sectors and to ease the gradual transition from a holistic approach to knowledge acquisition to a more sequential one. In this way, the learning experiences of the early childhood period can be revisited and amplified in line with the more linear, learning topics of the primary school. The new German curricula all speak about the transitional phase and the need for greater consistency in education environments and procedures between kindergarten and the primary school. Even more striking is the case of Hesse, where a unified curriculum for all children 0-10 years has been designed, with common goals (strong children, etc.) announced for all age groups, and attention given to age-related and individual developmental processes. In sum, a conceptual framework is advanced to eliminate transition and to achieve consistency in educational processes and regulation - not as in the pre-primary education tradition based on primary school processes, but on more holistic goals and learning experiences, and on learning processes more appropriate for young children.

Table 6.3 provides an overview of ECEC curricula in use in selected OECD countries (*Children in Europe*, 2005). From the table, it can be seen that prescription is not fully avoided, as several of these curricula are long and detailed (Belgium [French community], England). Other curricula may be less long, but stress selected learning areas such as language or numeracy, *e.g.* in France, in a week of 26 hours, French language (10 hours) and mathematics (5h30) take up the greater part of the curriculum in the senior section of the école maternelle (CNDP, 2002). Some teachers feel that a prescriptive curriculum provides a sense of purpose and structuring; they know which content areas should be addressed and to what degree for each age cohort. At the same time, prescription can take the initiative out of the hands of both children and educators, may set too many goals and competences within a narrow range, and above all run the danger of focusing on children's shortcomings. Direction of this kind is unnecessary if the system employs a stable, well-educated workforce, capable of planning and evaluating children's progress through the use of organised observation processes and a variety of informal assessment tools (Claxton and Carr, 2004; Martin-Korpi, 2005b). According to some research, the prescription of detailed learning goals linked to formal teaching may place children in a situation where they experience prolonged feelings of inadequacy, and may impact negatively on their self-esteem and motivation to learn (Sylva and Wiltshire, 1993; Schweinhart and Weikart, 1997; Sharp, 2002; Skolverket, 2004).

Table 6.3. **ECEC curricula in selected OECD countries**

	Age group covered	Length of CR (in pages)	Level of government responsible	Assessment related to curriculum	% of staff with tertiary level training	Child:staff ratio for age group covered by curriculum
Belgium Flemish Community	2.5 to 6 years	30 pages	Regional	None	100% in both Communities Excluding assistants	No national regulation Average for both Communities = 20:1 Excluding assistants
French Community	2.5 to 6 years	498 pages	Regional	None		
Denmark	0 to 6 years	2 pages	National + Individual centres	None	65%	No national regulation. Average = 3.3:1 (under 3) 7.2:1 (3 to 6 years)
France	2.5 to 6 years	Approx. 150 pages	National	Yes	100% of teachers Excluding assistants	No national regulation Average = 25.5:1 Excluding assistants
Germany	Mostly 3 to 6 years	18-320 pages (varies between *Länder*)	Regional	Mostly none	2%	No national regulation Ratios vary but approx 12-15:1 (3 to 6 years)
Italy	3 to 6 years	24 pages	National + regional + local	None	None (new law requires tertiary qualification in the future)	25-28:1 or 12-14:1 if school open 8 hours
Korea	3 to 6 years (in kindergarten)	39 pages	National	None	100% of teachers (in kindergarten)	Average = 1:20 (2004 National statistics)
Mexico	3 to 6 years	142 pages[1]	National	Informal assessment encouraged	Approximately 70%	No national regulation Average is 20:1 but classes in excess of 30:1 can be found in urban areas
Norway	1 to 6 years	139 pages in 1996 29 pages in 2005	National + local	None	32% trained pedagogues. Remaining staff are assistants with secondary vocational training	No national regulation: For 3 to 6 years, average = 15:1 (pedagogue); under 3, average = 8:1 Excluding assistants
Sweden	1 to 6 years	Guideline (22 pages)	National + local	None	50%	No national regulations Average = 5.4:1 (teachers and assistants included)
United Kingdom						
England[2]	3 to 6 years	128 pages	National	Yes	All teachers in schools are graduates. Other workers in schools and other services have lower level training No information on % of total who are graduates.	1:13 (schools); 1:10 (other services)
Scotland	3 to 6 years	60 pages	National	None		1:13(schools); 1:8 (other services) No information

1. *Programa de educación preescolar* (2004), Secretaría de Educación Pública, Mexico.
2. The new draft *Early Years Foundation Stage Curriculum* (DfES, 2006) has 142 A4, double-columned pages.
Source: *Children in Europe* (2005) and OECD (2003, 2004).

6. What are countries doing to promote a participatory culture of quality in ECEC services

Starting Strong (OECD, 2001) recommended that in addition to regulation and curriculum development, governments should support participatory processes to improve quality, which involve both staff and parents.

Developing quality through staff participation

Among the many initiatives noted by OECD teams in the countries visited, the following merit consideration in all countries:

- *Documentation*: The practice of documentation is most closely associated with the Reggio Emilia pre-schools, but has spread extensively into Sweden and other countries. Frequently, as the 2004 evaluation of the Swedish pre-school noted, the understanding of documentation may be narrowed in many centres to the simple tracking of children's activities and progress. In this understanding, documentation will be concerned primarily with work sampling, child portfolios, note-taking, teacher and parent observations of each child's progress and the like. As such, the practice is valuable and goes beyond the current practice of many centres, but understood in this way, documentation may remain superficial. Seen in this fashion, documentation may be used to provide only products, a visible trace for parents of what children have been doing, or more disquietingly, as an instrument to evaluate children's acquisition of various skills. In its fuller sense, documentation includes both the notion of research and the collegial evaluation of teacher concepts and attitudes. The selection of the artefacts (graphic, visual, iconic) or the video footage is meant to record significant sequences of child or group learning processes that both children and educators can revisit and reflect upon. Having the children reflect on what they have done becomes then an important element in the pedagogy. In turn, the artefacts reflect back to teachers their own values, concerns and readings of children's learning at that particular moment, and submits their organisation of the event and the learning environment to collegial discussion and analysis. In short, documentation in its full sense brings research into the process of education, where it properly belongs: "Pedagogical documentation is central to our idea of assessment – making learning visible. Assessment is understood as reflection and research – a shared experience concerned more with understanding learning and creating new knowledge than measuring whether children have achieved some education goal or developmental norm" (Rinaldi, 2006).

- *Formative centre evaluation* is a process wherein early childhood services undertake regular and systematic self-evaluation that is supported and validated externally by trained professionals. A major purpose of this type of evaluation is to raise the awareness of staff concerning different aspects of quality. Various participatory evaluation instruments of this nature have been developed in the United Kingdom for this purpose, *e.g.* the EEL (Effective Early Learning) instrument supports centres performing self-evaluations by encouraging discussion and reflection by staff on their programme, their attitudes and practice towards children and parents, as well as on the more technical aspects of administration, finance and planning. Through the EEL process, which normally takes place over several months, centres define their own programmes and activities, which are appropriate to their community circumstances. (Bertram and Pascal, 1997; see also *Starting Strong*, OECD, 2001, p. 68 ff). *Starting Strong* also called attention to the country-wide formative evaluation instrument and process used in Australia, today known as the National Quality Assurances System.

- *Rating systems* such as the Infant/Toddler Environment Rating Scale (ITERS), the Early Childhood Environment Rating Scale (ECERS) or the NAEYC/NAECS/SDE[11] guidelines, have also been transformed into instruments of self-evaluation and quality improvement. These scales and guidelines are used most widely in the United States, but some 20 other countries, such as Australia, the Flemish Community in Belgium, Germany and the United Kingdom, have also adopted these instruments. Rating scales and detailed central curricula are sometimes criticised as normalising, decontextualised instruments that may undermine more participatory and democratic reworking of quality by local communities (Dahlberg and Moss, 2005). It seems important that staff are trained sufficiently to understand the theory and cultural assumptions behind these scales and adapt them to their own needs and circumstances.[12] Used in a participatory way, expert scales and guidelines can provide a shared understanding and language to professionals and parents alike.

Similar formative quality improvement instruments are used in other countries (readers are referred to the section on *Developments* in the country profiles collected in Annex E). As might be expected, investment in quality improvement is most evident in the countries that have resolved, in the main, issues of access. Interesting quality initiatives are also taking place in countries that have begun, only in the last decade, to plan the early childhood field in a systemic way. The following are some examples from the second round of the OECD review:

- *Germany:* Germany has a strongly developed kindergarten sector for children aged 3 to 6 years, but with the exception of the *Neuebundesländer* (former East Germany), services for 0- to 3-year-olds are few. In 1999, a National Quality Initiative was begun, which involved five projects each focused on the development of methods for assessing and improving quality in different parts of the ECEC field, viz. services for children under three; kindergarten; school-age child care; the situation-approach to pedagogical work; and the work of the municipalities and providers, that is, the *Träger* (the six voluntary welfare providers recognised across Germany). Today, almost all *Träger* have engaged in quality improvement policies.

- *Ireland:* Although recent evaluations of ECEC policy are not positive (NESF, 2005), progress has been made since the OECD review in 2002 in terms of awareness of the need for greater quality in children's services. The Irish National Childcare Strategy, published in 1999, had identified five key clusters of quality indicators: child indicators (structural indicators such as child-staff ratios and group size; appropriate programming, broad developmental goals...); staff indicators; physical environment indicators; social welfare indicators such as affordability, accessibility, parent and community involvement, etc.; national indicators, that is, national policies for legislation, provision, supervision, co-ordination of policies and services, etc. Based on that work, the Centre for Early Childhood Development and Education (CECDE, 2005) has developed a quality framework for all early childhood services in Ireland, covering full and part-time day care; sessional services; infant classes in schools; child-minding.

- *Mexico:* In Mexico, a quality project initiated in 2001 (SEP, 2001), has led to the development and field testing of a quality instrument for use in early education centres (*Proyecto intersectorial*, 2004). Consultation and negotiation have led the process. Several dimensions of quality are included, such as the availability of resources; safety and health; the way in which the educational process is carried out, the management process and the relationship of centres to parents and the community (Myers, 2004).

● *Korea:* In Korea, the Child Care Act of 2004 has been revised to introduce several regulations to improve quality, *e.g.* more stringent conditions concerning child-staff ratios and employment conditions are now required to gain a license to open a child care centre. A national accreditation system has been introduced recently, as well as a national child care curriculum. A new Early Childhood Education Act was passed in 2004 recognising early education as a sphere apart from primary education. State investment in ECEC has more than doubled since 2002. However, public funding does not extend to private pre-schools, many of which provide an excellent service. As shown by the following example, the Han-Mi Reggio Emilia centre (see Box 6.3), their inclusion into the public network could bring many advantages.

Developing quality through parental involvement

Although *Starting Strong* (OECD, 2001) made no particular recommendation about parental involvement, the topic received an extended presentation in the report. The key points of this treatment were as follows:

"Parents are the first and primary educators of children, and despite some decline in both nuclear and extended family forms, their formative influence on young children remains central. Supporting young children's early development and learning requires ECEC staff to form a partnership with parents, which implies a two-way process of knowledge and information flowing freely both ways. After children themselves, parents are the first experts on their children. Parents can much assist programme staff to tailor programmes to the needs of particular children or particular groups."

"Parent engagement seeks to: a) build on parents' unique knowledge about their children, fostering continuity with learning in the home; b) promote positive attitudes and behaviour towards children's learning; c) provide parents with information and referrals to other services; d) support parent and community empowerment."

Patterns of parental, family, and community engagement in ECEC differ from country to country. Several formal and informal mechanisms are used to foster full participatory and managerial engagement. Some of the challenges to active engagement of parents include, cultural, attitudinal, linguistic, and logistical barriers, including lack of time. It is particularly difficult to ensure equitable representation and participation across families from diverse backgrounds.

The primary role of families in rearing children is protected in international law. Both the Universal Declaration of Human Rights (1948) and the UN Convention on the Rights of the Child (1989) make explicit reference to their role, *e.g.* the Preamble to the Convention on the Rights of the Child states:

"The family, as the fundamental group of society and the natural environment for the growth and well-being of all its members and particularly children, should be afforded the necessary protection and assistance so that it can fully assume its responsibilities within the community…"

This legal protection of society's basic unit indicates the important nurturing and educational role that families play. While earlier research suggested that parental involvement in educating their children brings only a weak or temporary contribution to

Box 6.3. **The Han-Mi "Reggio Emilia" centre in Korea**

The Han-Mi Kindergarten caters for 275 children aged between 3 and 5 years, in a suburban setting outside Seoul. The families are from middle- and lower-middle income bands. Parents fund the programme entirely through fees, as no government subsidy is available for a private kindergarten. A feature of this centre is that it applies the Reggio Emilia pedagogical approach. The director assured the OECD team that the goal was not to adopt a foreign programme.* The centre follows the National Curriculum and uses the Reggio Emilia principles of constructive education, staff reflection and documentation, to provide a programme of high quality.

In the kindergarten, children are at work in voluntary groups supported by trained adults. The majority of staff (16/22) have a four-year university qualification. The school also engages teachers trained in science/computing as well as a gymnastics specialist. The staff work as a team, and continually reflect together about what they do and why. The work of the children and the centre is continually documented, with a strong emphasis on using the artefacts that the children produce. Documentation indicates not just what happened but focuses on the value and meaning to the children of what was said and done. "We are showing a philosophy", the staff informed us, "of making children's intellectual work visible, not just keeping records of what happened". In this way, the centre has been able to move beyond a dominant paradigm in Korean education, explained to us as "giving recipe type lessons to passive children based on set topics".

A visit to the classroom found children absorbed in activities, with a high level of social and language interaction. Children were free to form their own small groups, which decide on a particular centre of interest and then seek teacher direction or support to achieve their plan. They were also free to spend time alone in thought or in concentration on a personal task or one engaged with a friend.

Although this was a Reggio Emilia style programme, the team noticed in the classrooms more artefacts and symbols of Korean culture than in many other centres. As well as the customary Reggio Emilia artistic and communication equipment, the environment was rich in natural materials that were available for selection by the children. In the classrooms, laughter and physical movement were evident.

Recognising that parents want the best for their children, staff emphasise parent participation and continually explain to parents what is being attempted and why. Monthly parent meetings are held in all classes to show specifically the educational value of the work in progress and to illustrate the children's ways of thinking. This has paid off handsomely in the past few years with parents becoming convinced of the benefits of learning through relationships and working with other children. In a country focused on academic attainment, this has been no small achievement.

The teachers of this centre have become a real resource for the district. They organise mini-conferences for other teachers, showing how they develop programmes and quality assessment in this kindergarten. A collaborative of 65 teachers now take part and visit each other's centres. It is acknowledged that the children in this centre have become active participants in their own learning and are warmly welcomed by the local primary schools. The director commented: "It takes two months to change children's attitudes from passive observer to active participant, and two years to change the teachers'." With public funding, the centre could become an important in-service training centre for the district.

* As is well known, Reggio Emilia schools do not follow an external curriculum. The curriculum, or content of the work, is said to be "emergent", that is, it is chosen primarily by the children and is negotiated with their teacher, whose main task is to support the children in realising and reflecting on their project.

Source: Country Note of Korea, 2003.

children's cognitive development, as compared to centre-based early education programmes (White *et al.*, 1992), intuitively, the recommendation to involve parents in their children's learning seems well-founded. Bronfenbrenner's (1986) ecological model of early childhood development emphasised that child-rearing is a joint endeavour between the family and the early childhood centre, local school and community surrounding the family.

More recent research on the issue corroborates Bronfenbrenner's insight, and the major American research compendiums, Shonkoff and Philips (2000) and Bowman *et al.* (2001), advocate outreach from centres to parents during the early childhood period. Likewise, French research has turned to this question, in an effort to develop parent-school partnerships across child care and early education (Rayna and Brougère, 2005), although in France, the century-old separation between the public and private spheres has hindered the involvement of parents in public education. The continuity of children's experience across environments is greatly enhanced when parents and staff-members exchange regularly and adopt consistent approaches to socialisation, daily routines, child development and learning. Again, when parents provide information to professional staff concerning their children's development, more accurate assessments of children's strengths are made, and parent-teacher relationships based on mutual trust and respect are enhanced (Reveco *et al.*, 2004). Information allows educators to respond more accurately to children's strengths and needs. The new NAEYC accreditation standards propose, for example, about 30 standards that centres should fulfil *vis-à-vis* parents, *e.g.*:

- Programme staff establish intentional practices from the first contact with families designed to foster strong reciprocal relationships and maintain them over time.

- Programme staff engage with families to learn from their knowledge of their child's interests, approaches to learning, and the child's developmental needs, and to learn about their concerns and goals for their children. This information is incorporated into ongoing classroom planning.

- Programme staff use a variety of formal and informal methods to communicate with families about the programme philosophy and curriculum objectives, including educational goals and effective strategies that can be used by families to promote their children's learning. They implement a variety of methods, such as new family orientations, small group meetings, individual conversations, and written questionnaires, for getting input from families about curriculum activities throughout the year.

- Families may visit any area of the facility at any time during the program's regular hours of operation as specified by the procedures of the facility.

- The programme's governing or advisory groups include families as members and active participants. Family members are mentored into leadership roles by staff or other families in the program.

- Programme staff provide families with information about programmes and services from other organisations. Staff support and encourage families' efforts to negotiate health, mental health, assessment, and educational services for their children (NAEYC, 2005).

In a comprehensive summary of research on the effects of parental involvement, Olmsted and Montie (2001) conclude that when parents are encouraged to intervene in children's programmes, at least modest positive effects on children's cognitive development are obtained. When parents are encouraged and trained to carry out specific reading tasks with their children, positive effects on children's language and pre-literacy skills are reported. This research is corroborated by the longitudinal EPPE project in the United

Kingdom, which shows that cognitive and language gains are strongly supported by parental involvement in children's literacy at home (Siraj-Blatchford *et al.*, 2002; Sylva, 2000; and Sylva *et al.*, 2003). Parental support for emergent literacy in this period of development has, according to EPPE, an even greater impact than social class: what parents do is more important than who they are. Parents who actively engage in reading and other activities with their children promote also their intellectual and social development. Some French research (Tijus *et al.*, 1997) also suggests that parental involvement in crèche activities alongside children promotes more complex cognitive interactions and helps mediate the effects of social disadvantage.

Olmsted and Montie also examine parent staff communications. The frequency of parent-staff relationships is linked positively with the quality of care provided in centres (Ghazvini and Readdick, 1994), although a subsequent High/Scope study (Schweinhart and Weikart, 1997) suggests that much depends on the content of the contact. Drop-off and pick-up meetings, for example, can remain routine, and focused only on immediate concerns. For this reason, Endsley and Minish (1991) suggest that if these encounters do not provide opportunities for mutual learning, they should be supplemented by focused parent-staff meetings, newsletters and home visits. Brooks-Gunn and Markman (2005) suggests that parental involvement should have a larger part in the kindergarten: "We estimate that about one-third to one-half of the variation in school outcomes between poor and not-poor children can be accounted for by differences in parenting" (in Harvard Family Research Project, Winter 2004/5). Language and learning materials in the home are the parenting behaviours most highly linked with vocabulary and early school achievement; discipline and nurturance are most closely associated with behaviour problems, attention, and impulse control. Attention to parents and home-visiting from centres have significant effects on parenting behaviour. The Harvard Family Research Project (2005) recommends not only engaging in dialogue with families and making use of family knowledge of their children, but also training parents for leadership. Centres should also facilitate for parents connections across the broad range of learning contexts that children experience.

Experience from the OECD reviews in regard to parental involvement

Experience from the OECD reviews suggests that appreciations of parent-staff collaboration (see Box 6.4) vary from country to country and across different institutions, unless ministries and research give a strong lead in the field. Education institutions seem to have greater difficulties in involving parents than child care centres or than centres in the social pedagogy tradition. This may be due to the age of the children involved, but also to the formality, structures and daily routines of education services compared to the flexibility of drop-off and pick-up times practised in child care centres. Schools still struggle to engage families on a large scale, while parents express their desire for greater participation in their children's learning. More research is needed on the issue, and perhaps, more professional development of teachers to undertake parent involvement effectively. Likewise, more socio-historical analysis is needed in this field. Certainly, 19th century attitudes to social child care (that is, child care for children of working-class women or from families considered "at-risk") were shot through with class and gender assumptions about the "ignorance" and "neglectful practices" of working-class mothers. Rather than seeing the need to change the deplorable economic situation and harsh working conditions of the poor, societies tended to undertake educational and moral crusades to change the child-rearing practices of working-class mothers (Hobsbawm, 1975, 2000).

Box 6.4. **Parental involvement in early education – examples from the United States**

Since at least the 1980s, the large Head Start project in the United States has stressed the importance of parental involvement. Performance standards for the project require parent involvement in programme making and curriculum development. Frequent parent-staff meetings must be held, and parents regularly participate in programmes and home-visiting. In addition, Head Start programmes must offer parents educational programmes in health, nutrition and child development; provide information about community resources and encourage parents to participate in community activities (Head Start Bureau, 1984).

Parental involvement is not just a recipe for targeted programmes. As evidence of the importance of parental involvement in education accumulates, many American States have enacted legislation designed to increase the involvement of parents in kindergarten programmes. 17 States have directed all school districts, boards of education and schools to implement parental involvement policies; 17 States have grant or award programmes to encourage schools or districts operating programmes involving parents in their child's education; and 15 States encourage or direct employers to enable parents to attend school activities, such as parent-teacher meetings and conferences. In addition to these policies, numerous States require parental involvement in early literacy programmes and for programmes targeted at student sub-groups, such as children at-risk or English-language learners. These provisions tend to supplement core commitments already formed by States to involve parents in education, *e.g.*:

● *Connecticut:* Full-day kindergarten programmes participating in the early reading grant programme must provide for parental involvement. In particular, proposals for intensive early intervention reading programmes, including after-school and summer programmes, must ensure that parents have access to information on strategies that may be used at home to improve pre-reading or reading skills.

● *Kentucky:* Local school districts must provide a developmentally appropriate half-day pre-school programme for each at-risk child who is 4 years old by October 1st of the year. All proposals must include a plan to facilitate active parental involvement in the pre-school programme, including provisions for complementary parent education when appropriate.

● *Michigan:* Each school district board must adopt and implement a parent involvement plan designed to encourage parental participation. A copy of the plan will be provided to the parent or guardian of each student. The department of education will review parental involvement practice and will post information about successful parental involvement polices and practices on the department's Web site. Special grants will also be provided to school districts that run programmes for parents with pre-school children that provide parents with 1) information on child development; 2) methods to enhance parent-child interaction; 3) examples or learning opportunities to promote intellectual, physical and social growth of pre-school children, and 4) access to community services through a community-school-home partnership.

● *Ohio:* Each board of education must adopt a policy on parental involvement for the schools of its district… The policy must provide the opportunity for parents and guardians to be actively involved in their children's education and to be informed of: 1) the importance of the involvement of parents in their children's educational efforts; 2) how and when to assist their children and support their classroom learning activities; 3) techniques, strategies, skills to be used at home to improve their children's academic efforts at school and their development as future responsible adult members of society.

● *South Carolina:* The education oversight committee, in co-operation with the department of commerce, the department of revenue and the SC chamber of commerce, will develop recommendations for employer tax credits as incentives towards: 1) providing release time for parent-employees to participate in parent-teacher conferences or to attend their children's academic-related events without loss of pay, and 2) developing workplace policies that enable parents to improve their literacy, assist their children with academics, and become more involved in their child's education, as a result of employers working with local school officials.

Source: Education Commission of the States, March 2005.

Notes

1. The National Education Goals Panel (NEGP) – dissolved pursuant to congressional mandate in 2002 – was a bipartisan and intergovernmental body of federal and state officials created in July 1990 to assess and report state and national progress towards achieving the National Education Goals. In 1997, the NEGP identified five goals as contributing to the young child's overall development and later success in school, *viz.* health and physical development; emotional well-being and social competence; positive approaches to learning; communication skills; and cognition and general knowledge.

2. Bowman *et al.* (2001) explain that though there is overlap in the use of the words "test" and "assessment", the former refers to a standardised instrument, formally administered and designed to minimise all differences in the conditions of testing. Assessments tend on the contrary to use multiple instruments (observations, performance measures, interviews, portfolios and examples of children's work…) and take place over a longer period of time.

3. The quality of staff is perhaps the basic programme standard, but the retention of qualified and experienced staff requires adequate salary levels. If child care subsidies or government grants per child are inadequate, providers are tempted to cut corners on other quality indicators, such as child-ratios.

4. It is important for the psychological development of young children that significant caregivers do not change repeatedly. The retention of experienced staff is critical for the quality of care and early education in centres (van Gevers Deynoot-Schaub and Riksen-Walraven, 2002). In addition, the costs of staff attrition are high, as new recruitment and training become necessary. In the education sector in the United States, with three times less staff attrition than in the early childhood sector, these costs are coming under increasing scrutiny.

5. Finland's 1996 curriculum was in fact for the pre-school class (6- to 7-year-olds) education, renewed in 2000. A new curriculum for day care (1- to 6-year-olds) was formulated in 2003. These curricula form an educational continuum for the child as they are linked together in many parts.

6. (American) National Association for the Education of Young Children, and the National Association for Early Childhood Specialists in State Departments of Education.

7. The guidelines recommend that early learning standards should include: Incorporation of all developmental domains Emphasis on content shown to be important for children's learning and development Grounding in knowledge of the processes through which children develop in the early years Inclusion of cultural, linguistic, community, familial, and individual perspectives

8. The introduction to the text does underline that the Guidelines "focus on what staff should do to help young children develop needed skills and knowledge, rather than on what children are expected to know at the age of 3 or 4".

9. The 2006 revision was not available to us at the time of writing. For this reason, citations are from the 1996 version.

10. The word "pedagogical" has a different connotation in Danish to the usual English meaning of "pertaining to the science of teaching". The word "pedagogical" in the social pedagogy tradition refers to a holistic approach to children encompassing care, upbringing and learning.

11. (American) National Association for the Education of Young Children, and the National Association for Early Childhood Specialists in State Departments of Education.

12. ECERS, for example, examines personal care routines, furnishings, language, reasoning experiences, motor activities, creative activities, social development and staff needs (Harms *et al.*, 1998).

References

AAP/APHA (2002), (American Academy of Pediatrics/American Public Health Association and the National Resource Center for Health and Safety in Child Care), *National Health and Safety Performance Standards: Guidelines for Out-of-Home Child Care.*

Bennett, J. (2005), "The OECD Thematic Review of Early Childhood Education and Care Policy", *Learning with Other Countries: International Models of Early Education and Care*, Daycare Trust, London.

Bertram, A.D. and C. Pascal (1997), "A Conceptual Framework for Evaluating Effectiveness in Early Childhood Education", in M. Karlsson Lohmander (ed.), *Researching Early Childhood*, Vol. 3, Göteborg, Suécia, Universidade de Göteborg, , pp. 125-150.

Bowman, B.T., M.S. Donovan and M.S. Burns (eds.) (2001), *Eager to Learn: Educating our Pre-schoolers*. Committee on Early Childhood Pedagogy, National Research Council Commission on Behavioral and Social Sciences and Education, National Academy Press, Washington DC.

Bredekamp, S. and C. Copple (eds.) (1997), *Developmentally Appropriate Practice in Early Childhood Education* (revised ed.), National Association for the Education of Young Children, Washington DC.

Bronfenbrenner, U. (1986), *Reality and Research in the Ecology of Human Development*, American Psychological Association.

Brooks-Gunn, J. and L.B. Markman (2005), "The Contribution of Parenting to Ethnic and Racial Gaps in School Readiness", *Future of Children*, Vol. 15(1), pp. 139-165.

Bruner, J. (1990), *Acts of Meaning*, Harvard University Press, MA.

Claxton, G. and M. Carr (2004), "A Framework for Teaching and Learning: the Dynamics of Disposition. Early Years", Vol. 24(1), pp. 87-97.

Centre for Early Childhood Development and Education (CECDE) (2005), *Early Childhood in Ireland. Evidence and Perspectives*, CECDE, Dublin.

Children Act (2004), The Stationery Office, London, United Kingdom.

Children in Europe. (2005), *Curriculum and Assessment in the Early Years*, Issue 9, Children in Scotland, Edinburgh, Scotland.

CNDP (2002), *Qu'apprend-on à l'école maternelle ?*, Centre national de documentation pédagogique, Paris.

Cohen, B., P. Moss, P. Petrie and J. Wallace (2004), *A New Deal for Children? Reforming Education and Care in England, Scotland and Sweden*, Policy Press, England.

CQO Study Team (1995), *Cost, Quality and Outcomes in Child Care Centres*, Public Report, Denver, University of Colorado.

CQO Study Team (1999), "The Children of the Cost, Quality and Outcomes Study Go to School. Executive Summary".

Dahlberg, G. and P. Moss (2005), *Ethics and Politics in Early Childhood Education*, RoutledgeFalmer, London and New York.

Dahlberg et al. (eds.) (1997), *Beyond Quality in Early Childhood Education and Care*, Routledge, London.

Delors, J. (ed.) (1996), *The Treasure Within*, UNESCO, Paris.

DfES(2002), *Curriculum: the Foundation Stage*, DfES, London, *www.standards.dfes.gov.uk/primary/foundation_stage/*.

Endsley, R.C. and P.A. Minish (1991), "Parent–staff Communication in Daycare Centers during Morning and Afternoon Transitions", *Early Childhood Research Quarterly*, Vol. 6, pp. 119-135.

EUROSTAT (2000), *Key Data on Education in Europe, 1999-2000*, European Commission, Luxembourg.

Fuller, B.C., A. Livas and M. Bridges (2005), "How to Expand and Improve Pre-school in California: Ideals, Evidence, and Policy Options", PACE Working Paper 05-1, Policy Analysis for California Education (PACE), Berkeley, California.

van Gevers Deynoot-Schaub, M. and M. Riksen-Walraven (2002), "Toddlers' Interactions with their Parents and Caregivers in Child Care: A Longitudinal Study", University of Amsterdam, The Netherlands.

Ghazvini, A.S. and C.A. Readdick (1994), "Parent-caregiver Communication and Quality of Care in Diverse Child Care Settings", *Early Childhood Research Quarterly*, Vol. 9(2), pp. 207-222.

Harms, T., D. Cryer and R. Clifford (1998), *Early Childhood Environment Rating Scale*, Teachers College Press, New York.

Head Start Bureau (1984), *Child Outcomes Framework*, Washington.

Helburn, S. and C. Howes (1996), "Child Care Cost and Quality", *The Future of Children: Financing Child Care*, Vol. 6, pp. 62-82.

Hobsbawm, E. (1975, 2000), *The Age of Capital*, Weidenfeld and Nicholson History, London.

Kagan, S.L. and E. Rigby (2003), *Policy Matters: Improving the Readiness of Children for School: Recommendations for State Policy*, The Children's Project, Washington DC.

Kauerz, K. and J. McMaken (2004), *No Child Left behind Policy Brief. Implications for the Early Learning Field*, Education Commission of the States (ECS), *www.ecs.org/clearinghouse/51/82/5182.pdf.*

Van Kuyk, J. (2006) "Holistic or sequential approach to curriculum: what works best for young children?" in *The quality of early childhood education* van Kuk (ed.) Arnhem, CITO.

Lindberg, P. and A.-L. Välimäki (2004), *ECEC Curricular Process in Finland: An Open Dialogue* EECERA communication, Malta.

Lund, S. (2005), "Denmark 'Progress or pitfall?'", in *Children in Europe, Curriculum and Assessment in the Early Years*, Issue 9, September, Children in Scotland, Edinburgh.

Martin-Korpi, B. (2005a), "The Foundation for Lifelong Learning", in *Children in Europe, Curriculum and Assessment in the Early Years*, Issue 9, September, Children in Scotland, Edinburgh.

Martin-Korpi, B. (2005b), "Early Childhood Education and Care in Sweden – A Universal Welfare Model", *Learning with Other Countries: International Models of Early Education and Care*, Daycare Trust, London.

Michelet, A. (1999), *Le jeu de l'enfant: progrès et problèmes*, OMEP, Québec.

Moss, P., C. Owen and J. Stantham (1998), "Informing Ourselves about Early Childhood Services", *Children and Society*, Vol. 12, pp. 263-274.

Myers, B. (2004), *In Search of Quality in Programmes of Early Childhood Care and Education. Background Paper*, EFA Global Monitoring Report 2005.

NAEYC (2005), New Accreditation System, Washington, *www.naeyc.org.*

NCAC (National Childcare Accreditation Council Inc.) (2006), *Child Care Quality Assurance,www.ncac.gov.au/.*

NEGP (National Education Goals Panel) (1996), *The National Education Goals Report. Building a Nation*, Government Printing Office, Washington DC.

NEGP (1997), *The National Education Goals Panel Report: Building a Nation of Learners, 1997*, Government Printing Office, Washington DC.

NESF (National Economic and Social Forum) (2005), "Early Childhood Care and Education", NSEF Report No. 31, NESF, Ireland.

NICHD Early Child Care Research Network (2004), "Family and Childcare Predictors of Mother-child Interaction and Children's Developmental Outcomes", Symposium presented at 18th Biennial Conference on Human Development, Washington DC.

Norwegian Ministry of Children and Family Affairs (1996), *Framework Plan for Day Care Institutions*, Oslo.

OECD (1998), "Background Report from Norway – Thematic Review of Early Childhood Education and Care Policy", OECD, Paris.

OECD (2001), *Starting Strong: Early Childhood Education and Care*, OECD, Paris.

OECD (2004a), Country Note for Germany, OECD, Paris.

OECD (2004b), "Starting Strong: Early Childhood Education and Care Data and Information Survey", OECD, Paris.

OECD (2004c), "Starting Strong: Curricula and Pedagogies in Early Childhood Education and Care – Five Curriculum Outlines", OECD, Paris.

Olmsted, P.P. and J. Montie (2001), "Early Childhood Settings in 15 Countries: What are Their Structural Characteristics?", High/Scope Educational Research Foundation, Ypsilanti, Michigan.

Phillipsen, L.C., M.R. Burchinal, C. Howes and D. Cryer (1997), "The Prediction of Process Quality from Structural Features of Child Care", *Early Childhood Research Quarterly*, Vol. 12, pp. 281-303.

Proyecto Intersectorial (2004), "Escala de Evaluación de la Calidad Educativa en Centros Preescolares" (Versión 3), Departamento General de Evaluación Educativa, mimeo.

QCA/DfEE (2000), *Curriculum Guidance for the Foundation Stage*, Qualifications and Curriculum Authority/ Department for Education and Skills, London.

Rayna, S., F. Laevers and M. Deleau (eds.) (1996), *L'éducation préscolaire : quels objectifs pédagogiques ?*, Nathan/Pédagogie, Paris.

Rayna S. and G. Brougère (2000), *Traditions et innovations dans l'éducation préscolaire : perspectives internationales*, INRP/CRESAS, Paris.

Rayna S. and G. Brougère (2005), *Accueillir et éduquer la petite enfance : les relations entre parents et professionnels*, INRP, Paris.

Reveco, O. et al. (2004), *Participación de las familias en la educación infantil latinoamericana*, OREALC, Santiago de Chile.

Rinaldi, C. (1998), "Projected Curriculum Constructed through Documentation – Progettazione: An interview with Lella Gandini", in C. Edwards, L. Gandini and G. Forman (eds.), *The Hundred Languages of Children: The Reggio Emilia Approach – Advanced Reflections* (2nd ed.), Ablex, Greenwich, CT, pp. 113-125.

Rinaldi, C. (2006), *In Dialogue with Reggio Emilia: Listening, Researching and Learning*, Routledge, New York, NY.

Rutter, M., K.J. Thorpe, R. Greenwood, K. North and J. Golding (2003), "Twins as a Natural Experiment to Study the Causes of Language Delay: Examination of Obstetric and Perinatal Environment", *Journal of Child Psychology and Psychiatry*, Vol. 44(3), pp. 326-341.

Schweinhart, L.J. and D.P. Weikart (1997), *The High/Scope pre-school Curriculum Comparison Study*, High/Scope Press, Ypsilanti, Michigan.

Scott-Little, C., L. Kagan and V.S. Frelow (2003), "Creating the Conditions for Success with Early Learning Standards: Results from a National Study of State-level Standards for Children's Learning prior to Kindergarten", *Early Childhood Research and Practice*, Vol. 5(2), pp. 1-21.

SEP (2001), *Proyecto Intersectorial sobre Indicadores de Bienestar en la Primera Infancia*, Secretaría de Educación Pública, Mexico.

Sharp, C. (2002), "School Starting Age: European Policy and Recent Research", paper presented at the LGA seminar "When Should Our Children Start School?", LGA Conference Centre, London.

Shonkoff, J.P. and D.A. Phillips (eds) (2000), *From Neurons to Neighbourhoods: The science of Early Childhood Development*, National Academy Press, Washington DC.

Siraj-Blatchford, I., K. Sylva, S. Muttock, R. Gilden and D. Bell (2002), *Researching Effective Pedagogy in the Early Years*, DfES Research Report 356, DfES, London.

Soto, V. and O. Reveco (2004), *Problematicas del curriculum educacional, hoy*, Editorial Arcis, Santiago de Chile.

STAKES (2005), information supplied to the OECD by the STAKES Early Childhood Education and Care Team, Helsinki.

Swedish Ministry of Education (1998), *Lpfö 98:Curriculum for the Pre-School*, Stockholm.

Sylva, K. (2000), *Effective Provision of Pre-school Education* (EPPE Research Project), Oxford.

Sylva, K., B. Taggart and I. Siraj-Blatchford. (2003), *Assessing Quality in the Early Years*, Trentham Books, London.

Sylva, K. and J. Wiltshire (1993), "The Impact of Early Learning on Children's Later Development", *European Early Childhood Education Research Journal*, Vol. 1(1).

Skolverket (2004), *pre-school in Transition: A National Evaluation of the Swedish Pre-school*, National Agency for Education, Stockholm.

Tietze, W. and D. Cryer (2004), "Comparisons of Observed Process Quality in German and American Infant/toddler programs", *International Journal of Early Years Education*, Vol. 12(1), pp. 43-62.

Tijus, C.A., A. Santolini and A. Danis (1997), "The Impact of Parental Involvement on the Quality of Day-care Centres", *International Journal of Early Years Education*, Vol. 5(1), pp. 7-20.

Weikart, D., P. Olmsted, J. Montie, N. Hayes and M. Ojla (eds.) (2003), *A World of pre-school Experiences: Observations in 15 Countries. The IEA Preprimary Project Phase 2*, High/Scope Press, Ypsilanti, Michigan.

White, K., M. Taylor and V. Moss (1992), "Does Research Support Claims about the Benefits of Involving Parents in Early Intervention Programs?", *Review of Educational Research*, 62.

Winnicott, D. (1971), *Playing and Reality*, Tavistock Publications, London.

ISBN 92-64-03545-1
Starting Strong II: Early Childhood Education and Care
© OECD 2006

Chapter 7

Appropriate Training and Working Conditions for Early Childhood Education and Care Staff

Chapter 7 reviews the situation of staff in early childhood education and care. Countries recognize implicitly that early childhood educators are the key to high quality services. As brought out forcibly in the OECD teachers' review (OECD, 2005), education systems need to provide intensive teacher training and good working conditions if teachers are to deliver high-quality outcomes. Such goals have still not been achieved for early childhood professionals in many countries.

The chapter examines the issue of staff profiling across the countries reviewed, and a simple typology of professional profiles in early education is outlined. It describes existing professional preparation both in the early education and the licensed child care sectors, and provides an overview of remuneration and conditions of work. A link is made between public attitudes towards women's work (including the rearing of children) and the low levels of remuneration practised in the child care sector. The issue is also raised concerning the opportunities provided to staff to participate in professional development and in-service training. Finally, strategies to recruit a mixed-gender, diverse workforce are discussed. Despite good intentions, most countries fail to recruit at professional level into early childhood education and care (ECEC) services, either sufficient numbers of men or sufficient numbers of women from minority and ethnic communities.

The importance of children's learning, development and social participation is widely recognised across OECD countries. Increasingly, governments see life-long learning as the key to human capital formation, the foundation of which is laid in early childhood. Despite this recognition, the professional standing of the early childhood workforce tends to remain low. Training and working conditions for ECEC staff often contradict public rhetoric about the value placed on young children and the importance of their early development and learning. This is particularly true of the child care sector, where recruitment levels can be inadequate and salaries remain well below those of teachers, at times being pegged at minimum wage levels.

Typically, early childhood educators working closest to the school gate are better trained and rewarded. Across the countries reviewed, staff serving children in three to six age are more likely to hold three- or four-year university (tertiary type A) or two-year college (tertiary type B) degrees. In contrast, staff in settings serving the youngest children are more likely to have varied backgrounds, ranging from no training whatsoever to a post-baccalaureate 3-year professional education (tertiary type B) or a two-year college degree (see Table 7.1 below). Preparation for the role of ECEC pedagogues, educators and teachers also varies substantially, and the considerable gender imbalance within the profession reflects deeply-held cultural beliefs about child-rearing and the roles of women and men in society.

What did Starting Strong recommend?

- Quality in ECEC depends on high quality staff training and fair working conditions across the sector.
- Strategies are needed to recruit and retain a well-qualified, diverse, mixed-gender workforce and ensure a satisfying, respected and financially viable career in this field.

1. The quality of ECEC systems requires effective staff training and fair working conditions

Research from many countries supports the view that quality in the early childhood field requires adequate training and fair working conditions for staff. The situation is summarised in *Starting Strong* (OECD, 2001):

"Staff working with children in ECEC programmes have a major impact on children's early development and learning. Research shows the links between strong training and support of staff – including appropriate pay and conditions – and the quality of ECEC services (Bowman et al., 2000; CQCO Study Team, 1995; EC Childcare Network, 1996; Whitebook et al., 1998). In particular, staff who have more formal education and more specialised early childhood training provide more stimulating, warm, and supportive interactions with children" (CQCO Study Team, 1995; NICHD, 1997; Phillipsen et al., 1997, EPPE 2004).

Table 7.1. Overview of trained staff in centre-based ECEC

	Main type of staff	Initial training	Age range covered	Main field of work	Work in primary?	Men in ECEC? % of staff	In-service opportunities	% primary teacher salary
AUS[1]	Teacher	3-4 year tertiary type-A[2] degree	0-8	Pre-school/preprimary, kindergartens	Yes	< 3.3% in care	Teachers – several funded days/year	100%
	Child care worker	2-3 year tertiary type-B[2] to 4-year tertiary Type A (a minority)	0-5	Long day care	No	< 2% pre-primary	Child care – limited to some services	~75%
AUT	Kindergartenpädagoginnen (kindergarten pedagogues)	5 years secondary level training diploma in kindergarten pedagogy	3-6	Kindergarten	No	2.7%	Funded by Land authorities. 3-5 days per year	
	Erzieherinnen (social pedagogues)	Vocational secondary education diploma in Sozialpädagogik	0-6	Essentially in Krippen and Hort (after-school care) and in Kindergarten as assistants			Vary considerably across the different Länder. Pedagogues express concern about the lack of professional development and career opportunities.	
	Kindergarten assistants	In several authorities, no training is required, but often Erzieherinnen work as assistants	3-6	Kindergarten				
BEL-FR	Institutrice de maternelle (kindergarten teacher)	3 years pedagogical – tertiary type B	2.5-6	École maternelle	No	Less than 1%	Funding decentralised to schools	100%
	Puéricultrices (child care nurses)	3 years post-16 vocational secondary	0-3	Crèches (or assistant in école maternelle)	No			
BEL-FL	Kleuterondervilzer(es) (kindergarten teacher)	3 years pedagogical – tertiary type B	2.5-6	Kleuterschool	No	Less than 1%	Funding decentralised to schools	100%
	Kinderverzorgster (child care nurses)	3 years post-16 vocational secondary	0-3	Kinderdagverblijf or crèches	No			
CAN	Teacher	4 year tertiary type-A (except PEI)	0-5/5-10	Kindergarten, pre-kindergarten and primary school	Yes	2%	Provided for kindergarten teachers	
	Early childhood educator	2-year ECE, Type B	0-12	Child care, nursery school, pre-school	No			
CZE	Uéitel mateske koly	4 years secondary pedagogical or 3 years tertiary type-B or tertiary type-A	3-6	Mateská kola	No	Less than 1%	Voluntary – offered by regional centres	75%
	Detska sestra	4-year secondary nursing school	0-3	Crèche	No			
DNK	Pædagoger (specialised in kindergarten pedagogy)	3.5 years in specialised tertiary level colleges type B, but shorter depending in prior experience	0-100	Pedagogues make up 60% of staff in centre-based services for children from 6 months to 7 years	Yes – 6- to 7-year-olds in the pre-school class and in teams with 6-to 10-year-olds	14% in Dagtilbud. 3% in preschool class and 25% in leisure-time services	Funding decentralised to municipalities	
	Pædagogmedhjaelpere (nursery and child care assistants)	Senior secondary vocational training. Some assistants undertake 18 months adult education in the social care field; some have no formal qualifications		Crèches, kindergartens, age-integrated services (Dagtilbud) and SFOs				
FIN	Lastentarhanopettaja or day care centre teachers with a bachelor/ masters in education	Education degree – university tertiary type A	0-7	Päiväkoti or day care centres. One-third of staff must have tertiary degree, but multi-disciplinary work with Lähihoitaja is the rule. Day care teachers with an education degree can also teach in the vuotiaiden esiopetus or pre-school class	Yes, with 6-7 year olds	4%	Funding decentralised to municipalities. Municipal obligation to provide 3-10 days annual per person – all staff	81%
	Sosionomi (social pedagogues) with a tertiary degree in social sciences	Social science degree – polytechnic tertiary type B	0-6	Päiväkoti and pre-school class. The majority of staff in Päiväkoti are trained children's nurses				
	Lähihoitaja (practical nurses)	Senior secondary vocational training of 3 years in practical nursing	0-7					
	Trained day care assistants	Day care assistants must also have training	0-7					
FRA	Professeurs d'écoles	4-year university degree A + 18-24 months post-graduate professional training	2-6	École maternelle (pre-primary education)	Yes, can teach in all primary classes			
	Puéricultrices (child nurses)	Nurse/mid-wife diploma + 1-year specialisation	0-3	Crèches services	No			
	Éducateurs de jeunes enfants	27-month post-Bac in special training centres	0-3	Crèches services	No			
	ATSEM (école maternelle assistants)	Secondary level certificate in early childhood studies. Older ATSEM may not have training	2-6	ATSEMS work as assistants in écoles maternelles, especially in urban centres				
GER	Erzieherinnen (kindergarten pedagogues)	2-year post-18 vocational training + 1-year internship	3-6	Kindergarten, Hort (leisure-time and home-work programmes)	No			
	Kinderpflegerinnen (child carers)	2-year secondary vocational training + 1-year internship	0-6	Krippe (crèche), Hort and kindergarten				
HUN	Óvodapedagógus (kindergarten pedagogues)	3-year tertiary degree	0-7	Óvoda (kindergarten for 3-6). Over two-thirds of staff are tertiary pedagogues, the rest trained assistants				
	Gondozó (child care workers)	3-year post-secondary vocational training – specialist certificate	0-3	Bölcsóde (for under 3). Over 90% of staff are fully trained				

Table 7.1. Overview of trained staff in centre-based ECEC (cont.)

	Main type of staff	Initial training	Age range covered	Main field of work	Work in primary?	Men in ECEC? % of staff	In-service opportunities	% primary teacher salary
IRL	Teacher	3-year tertiary type A – primary focus	4-12	Schools	Yes	Less than 1%		100%
	Child care assistant	Wide variation – many untrained	0-6	Child care centres				c. 60%
ITA	Insegnante di scuola materna	4-year tertiary type A	3-6	Scuola materna	No	Less than 1%	Municipality or director/inspector decides	c. 100%
	Educatrice	Secondary vocational diploma	0-3	Asili nidi	No			
KOR	Kindergarten teacher A	4-year tertiary type A	3-6	Kindergartens	No		Offered by regional teacher centres to all kindergarten teachers and child care teachers	
	Kindergarten teacher B	2-year tertiary type B	0-6	Child care centres				
	Child care worker	1 year training after high school	0-6	Hakwon (private learning academy)				
MEX	Docentes or early childhood teachers	University degree tertiary type A – licentiatura	3-6	Educación preescolar	No		Severa funded days/year with an obligatory 3-day professional development before each work year	
	Child care staff	Mostly untrained or with in-service training (e.g.madres communales – community mothers). In the CENDIs, a variety of health (children's nurses) and social care-personnel	0-3	Educación inicial				
NLD	Leraar basisonderwij	3-year vocational tertiary education – tertiary type B	4-12	Bassischool	Yes	25% in primary, but few men work with the 4- to 6-year-olds.	Funding decentralised to municipalities	100%
	Leidster kinder centra	2-year post-18 training	0-4	Kinderopvang	No			
NOR	Pedagogiske ledere	3-year college professional education – tertiary type B	1-6	Barnehager, SFOs (about one-third staff in kindergartens hold a tertiary qualification)	Yes, grades 1-4 with 1 year extra training	7%	A plan for access is part of public sector labour agreement	88-96%
	Assistents	2-year post-16 apprenticeship	1-6	Two-thirds of staff in Barnehager, a significant proportion without training.				
PRT	Educadoras de infância (or early childhood teachers)	4-year university or polytechnic	3-6	Jardim de infância	No	Less than 1%	56 hours minimum annually, offered by regional teacher centres and universities to all teachers. Not mandatory but necessary for career progression	100%
	Educadoras, nurses and social workers	Tertiary-level B professional qualifications	0-3	Crèches				
	Auxiliary staff	Training is now mandatory, but many still untrained		Jardins and crèches. Ratio of educadoras and auxiliary staff is not available				
SWE	Lärare (teachers[3]) composed of Förskollärare (pre-school teachers) Fritidspedagog (leisure pedagogues) and primary school teachers	3.5 years in university college, professional education – tertiary type A	1-7	Pre-school teachers work in pre-school centres (50% of staff, the rest being trained child assistants), open pre-schools, pre-school classes and in multi-disciplinary teams in the primary school.	Yes	5%	Funding decentralised to municipalities	100%
	Barnskötare or child assistants (are fully part of the pedagogical teams)	2-year vocational senior secondary (compose nearly 50% of staff in pre-schools – almost all trained)						
UKM	Qualified teacher (QTS – qualified teacher status) including nursery teachers with a similar qualification	4-year university tertiary type A	3-11	Nursery and reception classes for 3-5 years. Although mandatory, the requirement is not always observed in pre-schools outside the state-funded system	Yes	1% in non-school ECEC	Regular access for teachers	100%
	Nursery assistants	Level 3, vocational diploma	0-5	Assistants work in child care settings or as assistants in nursery and reception classes. 30% of assistants are without any diploma			Limited in child care	
	(Foreseen: A 4-year graduate Early childhood professional in each Children's Centre, and Senior practitioners with a 2-year type B qualification)	Tertiary level A						
USA[1]	Public school teacher	4-year university – tertiary type A	4-8 (0-8)	Public schools	Yes	3%	Most states require a certain number of hours per year	100% school
	Head Start teacher	CDA = 1-year tertiary type B	0-5	Head Start	No			42% in child care
	Child care personnel	1 course to 4-year university	0-5	Child care centre	No			

1. Except for official federal services, qualification and staffing requirements vary according to the regulations of each state or territory.

2. Tertiary-type A corresponds to Level 5A of ISCED, tertiary-type B corresponds to Level 5B of ISCED. An important difference is that Type A colleges are financed and mandated to undertake research.

3. In the new professional education regime in Sweden, these professions have merged into a single "new teacher" professional profile, serving children from 1-12 years. The new graduates now take a common core course together and then specialise in primary teaching, pre-school teaching or free-time pedagogy. Composite teams (including child assistants) can now work together across the age range, whenever different competences are needed.

Source: OECD Country Reports; Oberhuemer and Ulrich (1997).

However, governments often fear the funding consequences of raising staff qualifications. Higher qualifications can be followed by increased wage demands, which, in turn, contribute significantly to the costs of services. Although the evidence is strong that improved training and qualification levels raise the quality of interaction and pedagogy in ECEC services – similar evidence exists in favour of teacher qualifications (OECD, 2005) – governments tend to ask: Is this the best way to spend available budget? The issue was raised, for example, in California in 2005, when discussions were taking place on a universal pre-school system staffed by teachers, with a professional level equivalent to primary teachers, that is, teachers with a tertiary, four-year degree and certification to teach. A team of researchers, Fuller, Livas and Bridges (Fuller et al., 2005) argued that in present circumstances in California – where severe service shortages exist and many moderate income families can access only low quality services – it may be better to aim first for a two-year college degree. Budget saved could then be spent on subsidising families who face serious cost and quality constraints. A brief overview of the situation of early childhood personnel in OECD countries may help to put such issues into context.

2. Staffing profiles in the ECEC sectors

As can be seen from Table 7.1, countries have adopted two main approaches to staffing in early childhood services:

- In countries with split regimes (child care/early education), qualified teachers work in early education with children over 3 years,[1] while in the child care sector (services for 0- to 3-year-olds), a mixture of lower-trained staff are employed. In early education, there is a cross-national trend towards at least a three-year tertiary degree for lead professional staff (generally teachers) who have the main responsibility for pre-school children. These teachers are often trained as part of the primary school teacher corps (France, Ireland, the Netherlands, etc.) and may not have a dominant training or adequate certification in early childhood studies. In services for the younger children, it is difficult to identify across the different countries a core professional who works directly with infants and toddlers. In many countries, child care services tend to remain hierarchical with a few professionals (often trained nurses) managing the majority auxiliary staff who care for and interact with the children.[2]

- In countries with integrated services[3] for 1- to 6-year-olds, a core lead professional profile has emerged across the services for 1- to 6-year-olds. Tertiary trained pedagogues or early childhood educators work directly with children right across the age range. Trained child assistants, with primary responsibility for care, work alongside these pedagogues. They are not considered as auxiliaries but as equal and valuable members of the work team (Martin-Korpi, 2005).

Worker profiles

To simplify a complex situation, there are basically three types of lead professionals working in early childhood education centres (see Table 7.2), and many levels of child care workers and auxiliary staff (Oberhuemer and Ulich, 1997; Oberhuemer, 2000, 2005).

The early childhood specialist (pedagogue or teacher) (Oberhuemer [2004] prefers the term "early childhood pedagogue"). This profile is found in Austria, Belgium, Czech Republic, Finland, Hungary, Italy, Mexico and Sweden. Significant differences exist between the pre-school specialists from these countries with regard to profiling and training, but a common characteristic is that they are trained specifically to work with young children in the three

Table 7.2. **A simplified typology of lead professionals in early childhood education**

Profile	Country	Education
The early childhood specialist, either pedagogues or teachers	Austria, Belgium, Czech Republic, Finland, Hungary, Italy, Mexico and Sweden	Except Austria and Czech Republic, tertiary degree with dedicated training in ECEC for children 1 to 6 years old or 3 to 6 years old
Teachers, either pre-primary or primary	Australia, Canada, France, Ireland, Netherlands, United Kingdom, United States	Tertiary degree with predominant training in primary education.
Social pedagogues	Austria, Denmark, Finland, Germany and Norway	Tertiary diploma or degree with training in social pedagogical care, and specific training for pre-school early education and care

or more years prior to entry into primary school. Generally, pre-school specialists practise only in early childhood centres, and depending on the country, they work full-day, full-year, except in the case of Belgium, Italy and Mexico where they work only during the academic year. When they have tertiary level diplomas (which is not the case in Austria and the Czech Republic), early childhood specialists receive salaries roughly similar to or somewhat below those of primary school teachers.

In Austria, Czech Republic, Finland, Hungary and Sweden, the approach of the early childhood specialist is founded on the notion of pedagogy, that is, a view of interaction with the child that includes care, upbringing and education:

"The pedagogue sets out to address the whole child: the child with body, mind, emotions, creativity, history and social identity. This is not the child only of emotions, the psycho-therapeutic approach; not only of the body, the medical approach; nor only of the mind, the traditional teaching approach" (Moss and Petrie, 2002).

Emphasis is placed on forming educators who can sensitively support the learning trajectory of children (individually and as a group), undertake research and reflect with efficacy on their own practice.

The pre-primary/primary teacher (or kindergarten/pre-school teachers in Australia, Canada and the United States): Although they work in pre-primary schools, pre-primary teachers are generally trained at the same level and in the same training institution as primary school teachers. The profile is found in Australia, Canada, France, Ireland, the Netherlands, the United Kingdom and the United States.[4] Readiness-for-school is a primary aim of early education in these countries, and pre-primary classes will include a focused introduction to literacy and numeracy through whole and small group experiences. Traditionally, teachers are responsible for the children in their classes only during school hours and the school year.[5] In several of these countries, *e.g.* France, Ireland, the Netherlands, the pre-primary teacher is trained both for the pre-school and primary sector, but predominantly in primary school methods and pedagogy. In others – Australia, Canada and the United States – more focused training in early childhood education theory and methodologies may be provided, but training is part of the certification route for elementary school teachers, with, it is said, an insufficient focus on the early years (AACTE, 2004). Kindergarten teachers are licensed to teach kindergarten and early primary grades, usually pre-school through grade three, although licences in jurisdictions may extend to teaching all the primary grades. A national or state curriculum is generally prescribed for pre-primary classes, although detailed content may be defined only in the learning areas deemed important for school readiness. According to an informal survey carried out by the OECD in 2004, salaries of pre-primary teachers are equivalent to or slightly below those of primary teachers.

The social pedagogue: The social pedagogue has a wider remit than the early childhood specialist, and may be trained to work in various settings outside the kindergarten, most notably in youth work and work with the elderly. In the social pedagogy tradition – found in Denmark, Finland,[6] Germany and Norway[7] – an important study option is to become a social pedagogue specialised in the care, upbringing and learning of young children. The social pedagogue is trained to take a wider view of early learning, and is trained to understand the role of ECEC in the wider field of society. Early childhood services are seen as a framework both for educational work with children and social support to families. According to Oberhuemer and Ulich (1997), the desired professional role is that of "social network expert with a clear educative function." This educative function includes the organisation of the early childhood centre for care and learning purposes and the generation of the centre curriculum. Curriculum work is guided by national pedagogical frameworks and in consultation with the parents of participating children. Social pedagogues may also be mandated to contribute to the professional development of family day carers and offer them advisory services. The salaries of social pedagogues are slightly below primary school teachers, but the working day and year are significantly longer for social pedagogues.

The free-time pedagogue: To complete the picture, a new profile or profession is emerging in the Nordic countries, that of "free-time" or "leisure-time pedagogues" who work in kindergartens, schools and out-of-school provision with 1- to 12-year-olds, and in some countries, as Denmark, with adolescents and elderly people.[8] Their role is to take primary responsibility for children's free-time activities and to work in teams with pre-school specialists and teachers in schools. To date, only Sweden requires obligatory tertiary level training for these pedagogues, but interesting training initiatives for leisure-time pedagogues can be seen in the other Nordic countries, Belgium and the United States. The salaries of free-time pedagogues in Denmark and Sweden are roughly similar to primary school teachers, but in other countries they are often well below this level, due to lack of qualifications, temporary work or the poor organisation of these services.

Staffing profiles in the care sector

In child care services, whether in the public or private sector, the profiling of lead professional staff is often blurred. Different types of staff may intervene, but a large proportion of staff are in auxiliary positions and poorly paid, due perhaps to the work being conceived as being primarily a question of physical care which can be carried out by women without training. A similar situation is experienced in public split systems, where the hiring of a high proportion of unskilled, low paid women is common in child care. Another reason for the low level of qualifications is the lack of a framework clearly linking skills development with career progression.

Child care workers

The qualifications of child care workers differ greatly from country to country and from service to service. In countries with split services, no dominant core professional profile for work with infants and toddlers has emerged. This may be due to seeing the work as primarily a question of care, or in collective situations, as a question of maintaining health and hygiene. In countries with integrated services, conditions for workers are considerably better as, in general, thought has been given to making clear professional profiles with fixed salaries and work conditions. In most countries, lead child care workers have a vocational level diploma, generally at children's nurse level (upper secondary, vocational level), although many countries will also have specialist staff trained to secondary level graduation, plus a one- to two-year tertiary level vocational diploma. France, for example, has made it obligatory for large crèche services to employ early childhood educators (*éducateurs de jeunes enfants*) with a 27-month post-baccalaureate training, and more recently, a *licence* or three-year university degree. In Korea and Australia, the usual qualification for a lead educator in the child care services is a two-year college diploma in early childhood studies. Ireland, too, introduced in 2002 an agreed qualifications framework for early years workers that provides a co-ordinated vision for initial and in-service professional education and sets down core values, occupational profiles and professional standards. Significant differences in remuneration exist from country to country, but from our calculations, the starting wage in several of these profession is about 50% to 75% that of teachers at the same stage.

Auxiliary staff

There are many types of auxiliary staff working in centres who are trained to different levels. In countries where government interest and funding are weak, the majority of auxiliary staff in child care services may have only a one-year, post-16 vocational qualification, or be composed of women with no qualification in this field, employed at low wage levels and with poor working conditions. Such low qualifications in auxiliary staff may not be without consequence as research indicates that young children emerge with better language skills from early childhood settings staffed by well-educated personnel (Shonkoff and Philips, 2000; EPPE, 2004). In countries where there is strong governmental support for early education and care, auxiliary staff are better trained and work in teams with qualified pedagogues. In Sweden, for example, auxiliaries or child assistants have qualifications in ECEC similar to the lead social pedagogues working in kindergartens in Austria, or as lead child care workers in the Netherlands, that is, an upper secondary three-year vocational diploma.

Family day carers

Family day care (FDC) is the dominant form of child care provision for children under 3 in a diverse range of countries: Austria, Belgium/Flanders, Denmark, Finland, and in Canada, Ireland, the United Kingdom and the United States. In the first group of countries, family day care is well regulated and integrated into the state early childhood system (not in all *Länder* in Austria). For example, in Finland, child minders must have appropriate training but, in practice, variations in the length and content of their training occur. In 2000, the National Board of Education presented a recommendation for a new competence-based qualification for child minders (Further Qualification for Child Minders, 2000). Training requirements are rigorous (perhaps the most demanding across the OECD countries), but in practice, the length of the training may vary according to the competence and work experience of the child minder. The schools offering the training, and responsible for competence tests, must make an individualised learning plan for each student. The qualification gained can then be a basis for further upper secondary or tertiary work. In Austria also, family day carers organised by the provincial federations must have not only a licence to practise but also must complete a basic training course in: personal development and communication; developmental psychology and pedagogy; special didactics of day care; household management; first aid and accident prevention;

organisational and legal basics (Austrian Federation of Foster Parents, Adoptive Parents and Childminders' Association, 2004). However, in countries outside this group, family day carers have minimal or no training in early education and care. Frequently, they constitute a largely unlicensed child care sector, although there may be strong encouragement from child minder associations for their members to take national vocational qualifications in early education and care. In addition, according to the country survey carried out by the OECD in 2004, supervision of FDC in these countries is often lacking (see Table 6.1, Chapter 6). Furthermore, even when they are supervised by the public authorities, the inspectors – often drawn from primary education or the health services – may have little knowledge of appropriate early childhood pedagogy or of the special challenges encountered by family day carers.

In the family day care field, it is useful to distinguish between family day carers who belong to a municipal or agency scheme and those who operate as self-employed providers. Among the self-employed are family day carers who are licensed and regulated by public authorities, but the great majority in many countries operate privately without any external supervision. Belgium, however, has effectively put a stop to this practice by denying tax breaks and child care subsidies to parents who do not use licensed day carers. With regard to family day carers attached to a municipality, the scheme or agency in charge will generally have the responsibility to provide some training for these carers (sometimes compulsory, as in France), to guarantee a living wage and ensure social and health insurance. In Denmark, for example, family day carers are attached to a municipality, are trained at the local kindergarten every one or two weeks (allowing the children also to experience the resources of the kindergarten) and are well considered as a profession, especially in country areas. They are, in effect, municipal employees, and the municipality not only ensures salaries and social insurance, but also organises the distribution of children to each family day care.

3. New thinking about the core professional in early childhood services

These wide differences in staffing profiles across the sectors calls attention to the need to have a suitable profile and specific training for early childhood educators. If the task of the early childhood professional includes social care and well-being, differs from instruction and yet is focused on children's learning, then further reflection on how to profile and train this new professional seems necessary. At least, this is the viewpoint taken by the Department for Education and Skills in the United Kingdom as they attempt to integrate child care, early education services and children's social work, and to break down organisational and professional boundaries. The project is part of the ambitious reform of the early years system in the United Kingdom, which has become one of the more noteworthy projects in the ECEC field since the first OECD reviews:

> "The ten year strategy for child care sets out the Government's vision of child care services in this country with the aim of becoming among the best in the world, with a better qualified workforce and with more workers trained to professional level, including all those leading full day care provision. To achieve this, the strategy envisages radical reform of the early years' (and broader child care) workforce, recognising the crucial role it plays in determining the quality of provision. And we know from the Effective Provision of Pre-School Education Project (EPPE) that the better the quality of child care and early education, the better it is for the child's development" (DfES, 2005a).

As currently there are not enough teachers or highly qualified personnel available to early years settings in the United Kingdom, particularly to private, voluntary and independent settings, the opportunity is present to rethink the role of the workforce and identify a lead professional role, around whom care workers, teaching assistants and other professionals would work in multi-disciplinary teams. A single qualifications framework with a common core of skills and knowledge would be used for professional education across the sector. According to the document, to move forward on the project implies resolving three issues: First, to decide on the most appropriate model(s) for the sector – whether that is qualified teachers, or other professionals working with children with appropriate training in child development. Second, to develop a sufficient supply of these professionals to meet the needs of the sector. Third, to ensure that providers across the sector have incentives to employ professional level staff, including the means to pay the higher salaries that such workers command. Having reviewed lead professional models in other countries in Europe, the government seems to favour "new" teachers and "pedagogues" as the two models (see below) that may be suitable for the reformed organisation of early childhood services in Britain, in which 3 500 polyvalent children's centres will be established by 2010 across the country. According to the consultation document, "the pedagogue's holistic way of working with children would seem to fit particularly well with the increasing integration of children's services, as exemplified by children's centres":

- *The pedagogue model* favoured by the report is the graduate social pedagogue. This professional is the main worker in early childhood settings in Denmark and other countries, but works also in out-of-school provision, youth work, residential and foster care for children, with the elderly and in services for persons with severe disabilities. Pedagogues, however, are not teachers but have a distinctive identity: their approach to children is through the concept of pedagogy in which care, upbringing and learning have equal shares. For them, the early childhood centre is not a junior school, but a socio-educational centre, a site for human relationships and for learning that springs from social interaction. A central understanding is that the early childhood institution should contribute, alongside the parents, to the individual child's development and well-being, which is generally interpreted as learning to live in society and sharing a society's fundamental values, including respect for autonomy and independence. It is an approach prompted more by family and social life than by education (Lund, 2005). According to Boddy *et al.* (2005), social pedagogy "provides a strong basis for an approach to both children and young people that embodies ideals of active citizenship, rights and participation, and for working with the whole child and her family".

- *The "new teacher"* or *"early childhood specialist" model*, also uses the "pedagogy" approach (care, upbringing and learning) with children. In Sweden, following the integration of early childhood services into education in 1996, the profession of pedagogue continued until reform in 2001 when it was combined with free-time pedagogues and primary school teachers into a unified profession "teacher". These branches of the same profession receive common core training for 18 months at tertiary level. Then, for a further two years, teachers in each branch specialise intensively in their own field. This constitutes an obvious strength of this particular profile – intensive training in child development and pedagogy, which pre-primary teachers in the United Kingdom and other countries often lack. After graduation, all three branches work together in teams in the pre-schools, on school sites in the pre-school classes, in the primary school classes, and in free-time services, each branch taking the lead whenever it is appropriate. This integration of training is intended to serve the interests of children – integrating the child's journey through education, with care at all levels of the system, all taking place in the same setting and with staff working in teams right across the system from 1 to 16 years. The child's day is integrated through having the same teams of teachers (pre-school, primary teachers and leisure-time staff) working together daily within the same setting, and through following a unified curriculum from kindergarten into secondary school. It is too early yet, to assess the effects of this innovation.

At this stage, it is difficult to forecast which profile will be preferred in Britain. In the English-speaking world, a strong emphasis is laid on the educational role of services, with a focus on the teaching role. A new and powerful public discourse on early learning has emerged from the United States, encouraging early childhood professionals to support school learning more effectively. The comprehensive EPPE study in England – and in particular, the section dealing with Research in Effective Pedagogy in the Early Years (Siraj-Blatchford et al., 2002) – suggests also that effective pedagogy includes adult and child involvement, cognitive (co-constructive) engagement and the use of instruction techniques such as modelling, explanation, questioning and the channelling of the child's interest towards socially desirable learning objectives, without dominating the child's freedom of choice. This is a challenging agenda for early childhood educators, requiring high educational standards, theoretical knowledge and regular professional development. On the other hand, there is a need for early childhood centres to respond to the changing social context – to high levels of child poverty in the English-speaking world, to the far greater diversity in families and child-rearing; to the large numbers of children and families in need of social and psychological support, to the needs and expectations of working parents, etc. Working with diversity in particular milieus is a feature of ECEC professional work, to which traditional teacher training has responded insufficiently. In the future, practitioners will be required to play an enhanced role in developing social cohesion, for which new skills and understandings about community and society will be critical.

The choice between the educator and the pedagogue for the lead role in early childhood services is a complex one, but it may not be an either/or choice in which one profile is preferred and the other rejected. In Finland, emphasis is increasingly placed on multi-disciplinary teams, including children's nurses educated at secondary level, who are considered not as assistants but as full members of the pedagogical (care, upbringing, education) team. In all countries, it may be possible to imagine profiling teams according to the needs of the milieu, with more social pedagogues, second language specialists and special needs educators practising (with lower child-staff ratios) in disadvantaged, multi-cultural milieus; and more "new teachers" (educated in the care, upbringing and learning of 1- to 6-year-olds – including high-level language and project work) practising in the mainstream districts, with higher child-staff ratios, and with, at least, one social pedagogue working in the centre team. Trained children's nurses will be essential contributors in both types of pedagogical team. Some profiles used in the Reggio Emilia pre-schools could also be envisaged: an atelierista in every pre-school to work with teachers and children on material modes of expression, and a pedagogista shared across several schools to encourage quality development based on documentation and dialogue within and across the different schools.

4. Initial and in-service education

Starting Strong (OECD, 2001) describes the contents of initial professional education programmes, and noted some of the training gaps, such as work with parents, work with infants and toddlers, bilingual/multi-cultural and special education, and research and evaluation. In split systems, the training of lead child care workers who work with 0- to 3-year-olds tends to remain at secondary vocational (Austria, Czech, Republic, Germany[9]) or college B or associate level (Australia, Korea, the Netherlands, the United States Head Start, etc.). In contrast, the professional preparation of the educators of 3- to 6-year-olds is confided increasingly to university departments or to degree-level training colleges. Austria (and to a lesser extent, the Czech Republic and Germany) is now alone in training lead personnel for the age group 3 to 6 years to vocational secondary level only. University-level training of early childhood educators is resisted, partly because ministries fear that early childhood pedagogues educated to tertiary level may drive up the costs of services. Experienced early childhood trainers in these countries also fear that university professional education may be too theoretical or may not practise an experiential and co-constructive model of education, suitable for work with young children. They point to the fact that even when university graduates certified in early childhood studies are recruited, several outstanding curricular schools insist on further training to ensure that new teachers understand well a particular curriculum and are guided by its principles in their work, *e.g.* Montessori and Froebel; the Reggio Emilia schools in Italy; High/Scope or Bright Start in the United States; Piramide or Kaleidescope in the Netherlands; Freinet in Belgium.

Opportunities to participate in professional development and in-service training can vary greatly across countries and between education and child care in the split systems. Staff with the lowest levels of initial training in the child care sector have the least access to in-service education, including, as noted, family day carers. On the other hand, in much of Belgium, Italy and Hungary, educators can set aside about 10% of their time to non-contact work, including to their own professional development. In Korea, a statutory requirement exists on the local authorities to fund a minimum level of staff development, for example, every 3 years, kindergarten teachers must take 80 hours of in-service training to raise the level of qualifications, and child care teachers must take 40 hours of professional development. In Hungary, every pedagogue has the personal obligation to take 120 hours of professional development each seven-year period, paid for by the State. Maintainers (providers) of services – generally, the local municipalities – will also frequently provide in-service sessions for their staff. Professional development can also take the form of attendance – if the maintainer authorises – at one of the many topic courses provided by methodological centres.

5. Remuneration and conditions of work

Initial education, on-going professional development and conditions of work such as salary, leave, contact hours and preparation time are most varied in mixed or free market systems. As in the public split systems, conditions of work are least favourable in service provision directed towards children below the age of 3 or 4. As noted by Oberhuemer (2005), "The market model of child care, in particular, generates highly differentiated systems of training, payment and employment conditions." Many of the community or voluntary bodies who are part of the mixed market system are also seriously under-funded and despite a courageous stance, are unable to offer sufficient compensation to their staff. In the commercial sector, some companies try to match wages and conditions towards the top end of the market, but as noted by Brown (2001), many companies consciously drive down labour costs and downplay quality, "usually meeting only minimal state-licensing laws".

Salaries earned by family day carers vary widely across countries, and are much influenced by the regulations in force. In our estimation, unless family day carers operate in a market with weak supply and high demand, compensation in this field is considerably less than an average family wage. In schemes or agency-supported services, parental fees are often capped, and a small wage is provided to the carer, often below a living wage. In Germany, for example, it is understood that a family day care wage is insufficient to live on, and even today is considered as a supplement to the main salary earned by a working spouse. In countries where a large proportion of family day carers are unlicensed, the laws of demand and supply determine both costs to parents and the day carer's earnings.

Figures from various countries reveal the wide gap between child care pay and teacher compensation. From the information received from OECD countries in 2004, child care staff in many countries are poorly trained and are paid around minimum wage levels. For example, average gross hourly pay for staff in child care settings in England range between GBP 4.80 and GBP 5.30 per hour, compared with hourly pay rates for nursery and primary teachers of GBP 13.76. Average gross annual pay for child care workers is GBP 7 831, compared with GBP 22 662 for primary teachers (Sure Start, 2004). Figure 7.1 is taken from the British Labour Force Survey of 2003 (DfES, 2005b):

Figure 7.1. **Average hourly pay for early childhood workers (including nannies but not teachers) compared to similarly qualified occupations**

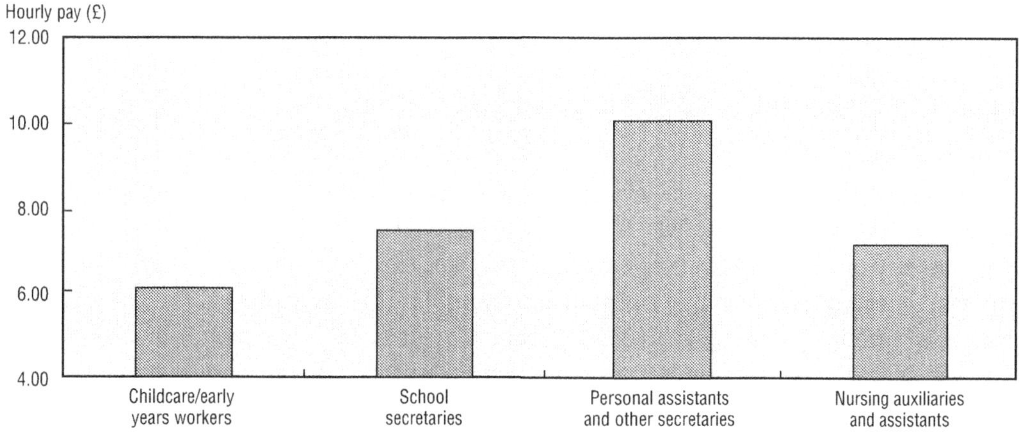

Source: Labour Force Surveys, Winter 2003.

With regard to the United States, Kagan and Rigby (2003) raise the issue starkly in the following comment:

"Research has indicated that teachers' wages are associated with the quality of care provided. Professional quality ECE is hard to find in a market place where ECE providers do not earn as much as funeral attendants (USD 17 320) or garbage collectors (USD 25 020). Despite having higher levels of formal education than the average American worker, ECE professionals earn dreadfully low wages – on average, only USD 16 980 per year. In addition, they rarely receive benefits or paid leave. Not surprisingly, given the low salaries, staff turnover is high in early childhood programmes outside the public schools. Some estimate it to be around 36% a year."

Undoubtedly, attitudes towards women's employment influence ECEC staffing and compensation. In this regard, Chapter 1 outlined some of the common attitudes towards female employment and remuneration, viz.: to give less recognition and less status to what is considered "women's work"; to pay women significantly less for equal work; to tolerate gender segregation and low pay in the caring professions; and to expect greater engagement of women in part-time work. No doubt, some of these tendencies are century-old reflexes but they prevent a clear-sighted view of the new requirements of ECEC, that is, as a place where well-trained professionals can support the language and social development of young children and the child-rearing skills of parents. Decisions about staffing are in reality, decisions made about the level of quality that a State wishes to provide to young children (Phillips, 1988 cited in Kontos et al., 1995:9, Blenkin et al., 1996; Oberhuemer and Ulich 1997:3, Abbott and Pugh, 1998; Feeney and Freeman, 1999).

Another element influencing decisions about the status and training of staff are views about the function of ECEC services. Policy makers and managers who view children's services as primarily child-minding can be content with the physical care and safety of young children, and hire staff accordingly. However, once the learning and social potential of early childhood[10] is recognised,[11] then the nature and level of staffing changes. If one takes into account also the new responsibility given to ECEC services, namely, to provide social and educational support to parents, it becomes clear that staff in many settings need a robust knowledge of child psychology, learning theory, adult education and social work. As *Starting Strong* (OECD, 2001) observed, all countries in the coming years will have to address the professional education, status, pay and working conditions of ECEC staff. If not, the sector will remain, at least in some countries, unproductive where quality and child outcomes are concerned, and non-competitive with other sectors for the recruitment and retention of staff.

6. Strategies to recruit a mixed-gender, diverse workforce

Gender

Whatever the type of service encountered in the early childhood field, almost all staff are women. In *Starting Strong* (OECD, 2001), the issue was raised, and reasons put forward to promote a greater gender-mix among the workforce, *e.g.* the positive effects on children's development in having dual role models in their lives; or the added value brought to caring and pedagogy in early childhood centres by the presence of men. On the negative side, as discussed in Chapter 1, gendering reinforces the notion that child-rearing is essentially "women's work", with the traditional reflex of paying the profession less and regarding their work as being of small importance.

Some few countries take the challenge seriously, convinced of the benefits that a male presence can bring to young children and to the working environment. The United Kingdom has tried to reach a certain percentage of male recruits in training colleges and services, but it seems without any real breakthrough. Since the publication of *Starting Strong* (OECD, 2001), Flanders has engaged in several poster campaigns to inform the public that aspects of child care work, such as free-time pedagogy, are areas to which young men can make a real contribution. Today, about a third of the candidates for this course are male. Likewise, the enrolment rate of about 25% of men in *paedagog* courses in Denmark is keeping up (Jensen and Hansen, 2003), and Norway is making renewed efforts to meet its 1997 target of having 20% of men as active pedagogues in ECEC services. However, the issue is not even discussed in most countries, and gendering is so pervasive as to have become "invisible" (Moss, 2001). Few countries have set targets for the recruitment of men into ECEC or sought to rethink this work in ways that would make gendering less pervasive.

Diversity

Working with diversity is also a growing challenge for ECEC services in most OECD countries. Researchers in the field – and the leaders of many comprehensive services visited by OECD teams – underline that ethnic diversity in the ECEC workforce is not only a question of equality of opportunity but also an issue of quality (Vandenbroeck, 2003). An ECEC system in which multi-cultural recruitment and an appropriate emphasis on diversity are practised can be formative for young children, and give confidence to their families. However, the workforce in ECEC services, at least in Europe, remains highly homogenous in terms of gender and ethnicity. Greater diversity exists in the United States, but as noted by Starting Strong (OECD, 2001), at the lower levels of recruitment:

> "Data from the United States indicate that family day care providers match the children they serve in terms of ethnic and linguistic background; out-of-school provision is more diversely staffed than ECEC centres; and centres are more diverse than public schools" (p. 106).

It is noteworthy that the higher the qualifications required and the more institutionalised the service, the less likely it is to have a representative workforce. Minority ethnic women are found predominantly in the least qualified positions with the lowest wages in the least considered professions. Staff patterning of this kind does not send out positive messages of inclusion and respect. Ethnic minority children need positive role models and a mix of professionals from their own backgrounds. Further, there is the probability – though this is disputed by some – that professional carers and educators from their own communities will understand the particular needs of ethnic children, and will be able to support their learning and language development with authentic experiences close to the reality of children's lives. For this reason, successful community services focus closely on issues of diversity. These efforts can be greatly helped by government policies.

Among policies and regulations to address issues of diversity, Starting Strong (OECD, 2001) noted the following initiatives: the requirement of the United States Head Start programme to employ parents and volunteers from the local community; recruitment policies in several countries encouraging the employment of ethnic minority staff either as fully qualified staff (Australia, Denmark, Norway, Sweden, the United Kingdom) or bridging staff (Belgium, the Netherlands). Since that time, policies in Belgium have developed considerably beyond bridging personnel, and strong efforts are being made in the Flemish Community to recruit early childhood educators and crèche personnel from different ethnic groups. Several of the larger cities, such as Antwerp and Ghent, fund diversity initiatives. Some excellent inclusive programmes also exist in the eight new countries reviewed but their programmes tend to remain isolated and seldom go to scale across the system. Strong equal opportunity policies are in place in Canada, and the better educated immigrant women are well represented across all areas of Canadian life. However, outside the reservations, First Nations representation – in terms of professional presence and culture – seemed to the OECD review team to be extremely weak in Canadian ECEC services, not least in cities where First Nation children constitute a significant minority population (OECD Canadian Country Note 2004). In Hungary, the OECD review team noted a committed stance by government to redress the balance in favour of the Roma community, which has long suffered discrimination and isolation from mainstream society across Central and Eastern Europe. The review team met several Roma women in kindergarten training, and noted a real effort at government level to consult Roma representatives and make their presence visible. Several government committees and institutions exist with a focus on minority questions, a state secretary for Roma issues sits in the Prime Minister's cabinet, while the Ministry of Education has appointed from the Roma community a commissioner for Disadvantaged and Roma Children. Yet, improving the representation of ethnic minority groups among ECEC professionals continues to be slow. Despite far-reaching educational reforms in Hungary, only 33% of Roma who enter primary school subsequently enrol in secondary school, and a mere 0.2% progress to higher education (Katz, 2005). Comparable figures can be cited for the children from the Traveller community in Ireland. The representation of these communities among teachers or at administrative level could hardly be lower.

Similar difficulties are encountered by immigrant women to enter early childhood services at professional level, as their initial qualifications are often low or unrecognised in the host country. Satisfactory means are yet to be found to adapt recruitment regulations to allow local adults into the child care workforce and at the same time, maintain quality levels by intensive in-service training and upgrading of staff in child care centres. In Belgium (Flanders), the *Decree on the recognition of child care services*, passed in 2001, envisages such a strategy: municipalities will be required to ensure that staff in centres reflect the ethnic mix of their neighbourhoods, but municipalities will be supported to raise the qualifications of staff in centres and free-time services. In addition, licensed training centres are requested to facilitate the entry of ethnic minority candidates through assessments that take into account existing training and experience. Local governments in the larger Flemish cities have extended existing diversity programmes and several municipalities pursue equal opportunity policies that encourage diversity (see Vandenbroeck, 2003).

Notes

1. In Australia, Canada and the United States, where public education services are not accessed by a majority of children until age 4 or 5, professionals working with children up to that age have a lower level of qualification.

2. In France, a development can be seen with the creation of "early childhood educators" (*éducateurs de jeunes enfants*).

3. Early childhood in the United Kingdom is, in principle, integrated under ministry of education auspice. Cohen *et al.* (2004) point out, however, that integration is relatively new and that neither conceptual nor sector integration has been yet achieved.

4. In federal countries, variation exists across different states or provinces, but the predominant type of training is in primary school-oriented pedagogy.

5. Because of present labour market conditions, schools in many countries are now evolving towards full-day and full-year opening hours.

6. Finland appears in both the early childhood specialist and social pedagogue groups, as both profiles are found within the Finnish ECEC system.

7. Social pedagogues are also found in child care services in split systems, such as in many of the countries ranged above under pre-school teaching, *e.g.* France and the Netherlands, where training in social care is a strong part of initial training.

8. In Denmark, pedagogues work in early childhood settings, pre-school classes, out-of-school services, residential care, and settings for persons with special care and support needs. Their

initial education emphasises the social and cultural role of the pedagogue in Danish society (Jensen and Hansen, 2003).

9. *Erzieherinnen* (social pedagogues trained to work in the kindergartens) in Germany form 64% of the staff in kindergartens, and receive a 2-year upper secondary vocational training plus a one-year apprenticeship in a kindergarten.

10. Early childhood does not refer only to 5-year-olds. Babies learn to interact with others, talk, walk and create complex theories about their world in the first three years of life.

11. James Heckman identifies two key concepts with regard to investments in early childhood: *self-productivity* (skill attainment at one stage of the life cycle raises skill attainment at later stages) and *complementarity* (investment in early childhood facilitates the productivity of later investments in education).

References

Abbott, L. and G. Pugh (1998), *Training to Work in the Early Years: Developing the Climbing Frame*, Open University Press, Buckingham (England).

AACTE (American Association of Colleges for Teacher Education) (2004), *The Early Childhood Challenge. Preparing High-quality Teachers for a Changing Society*, AACTE, Washington DC.

Austrian Federation of Foster Parents, Adoptive Parents and Childminders' Association (2004), *Berufsbild Childminder*, Salzburg.

Blenkin, G., J. Rose and N. Yue (1996), "Government Policies and Early Education: Perspectives from Practitioners", *European Early Childhood Research Journal*, Vol. 4(2), pp. 5-19.

Boddy, J., C. Cameron, P. Moss, A. Mooney, P. Petrie and J. Statham (2005), *Introducing Pedagogy into the Children's Workforce, Children's workforce Strategy Consultation Response*, TCRU, London.

Bowman, B.T., M.S. Donovan and M.S. Burns (eds.) (2001), *Eager to Learn: Educating our pre-schoolers. Committee on Early Childhood Pedagogy*, National Research Council Commission on Behavioral and Social Sciences and Education, National Academy Press, Washington DC.

Brown, R. (2001), "How We Built a Strong Company", *Harvard Business Review*, Cambridge MA, February.

Cohen, B. P. Moss, P. Petrie and L. Wallace (2004), *A New Deal for Children: Reforming Education and Care in England, Scotland and Sweden*, Polity Press, United Kingdom.

Cost, Quality and Child Outcomes [CQCO] Study Team (1995), "Cost, Quality, and Child Outcomes in Child Care Center", Department of Economics, University of Colorado at Denver, Denver, CO.

DfES (2005a), Children's Workforce Strategy (CWS) Consultation, DfES, London.

DfES (2005b), *The Children's Workforce in England: A Review of the Evidence, Version 1*, DfES, London, April.

EPPE (2004), *The Final Report*, Technical Paper 12, Institute of Education, University of London, London.

European Commission Childcare Network (1996), *A Review of Services for Young Children in the European Union 1990-1995*, Brussels.

Feeney, S. and N. Freeman (1999), *Ethics and the Early Childhood Educator*, National Association for the Education of Young Children, New York.

Fuller, B, A. Livas and M. Bridges (2005), *How to Expand and Improve pre-school in California: Ideals, Evidence, and Policy Options*, PACE Working Paper, UC-Berkeley.

Jensen, J.J. and H.K. Hansen (2003), "The Danish Pedagogue – A Worker for all Ages", in Children in Europe, Vol. 5, pp. 9-14.

Kagan, S.L. and E. Rigby (2003), "Policy Matters: Setting and Measuring Benchmarks for State Policies" (Discussion Paper), Centre for the Study of Social Policy, Washington DC.

Katz, S.R. (2005), "Emerging from the Cocoon of Roma Pride: First Graduates of the Gandhi Secondary School in Hungary", *Intercultural Education*, Vol. 16(3), pp. 247-261.

Kontos, S., C. Howes, M. Shinn and E. Galinsky (1995), *Quality in Family Child Care and Relative Care*, Teachers College Press, New York.

Lund, S. (2005), "Denmark 'Progress or Pitfall?'", in Children in Europe, *Curriculum and Assessment in the Early Years*, Issue 9, September, Children in Scotland, Edinburgh.

Martin-Korpi, B.M. (2005), "The Foundation for Lifelong Learning", in Children in Europe, *Curriculum and Assessment in the Early Years*, Issue 9, September, Children in Scotland, Edinburgh.

Moss, P. (2001), *The UK at the Crossroads: Towards an Early Years European Partnership*, Daycare Trust, London.

Moss, P. and P. Petrie (2002), *From Children's Services to Children's Spaces: Public Policy, Children and Childhood*, Routledge Falmer, London, United Kingdom.

NICHD (National Institute of Child Health and Human Development) (1997), *Mother-child Interaction and Cognitive Outcomes Associated with Early Child Care: Results of the NICHD Study*, Society for Research in Child Development meeting symposium, NICHD, Washington DC.

Oberhuemer, P. (2000), "Conceptualisng the Professional Role in Early Childhood Centers: Emerging Profiles in Four European Countries", *Early Childhood Research and Practice*, Vol. 2(2), pp. 1-7.

Oberhuemer, P. (2004), "Controversies, Chances and Challenges: Reflections on the Quality Debate in Germany", *Early Years*, Vol. 24(1), pp. 9-21.

Oberhuemer, P. (2005), "Conceptualising the Early Childhood Pedagogue. Policy Approaches and Issues of Professionalism", *European Early Childhood Research Journal*.

Oberheumer, P. and M. Ulich (1997), *Working with Young Children in Europe: Provision and Staff Training*, Paul Chapman Publishing, London.

OECD (2001), *Starting Strong: Early Childhood Education and Care*, OECD, Paris.

OECD (2004a), Canadian Country Note, OECD, Paris.

OECD (2004b), "Starting Strong: Curricula and Pedagogies in Early Childhood Education and Care – Five Curriculum Outlines", OECD, Paris.

OECD (2005), *Teachers Matter. Attracting, Developing and Retaining Effective Teachers*, OECD, Paris.

Phillipsen, L., M. Burchinal, C. Howes and D. Cryer (1997), "The Prediction of Process Quality from Structural Features of Child Care", *Early Childhood Research Quarterly*, Vol. 12, pp. 281-303.

Shonkoff, J.P. and D.A. Phillips (eds.) (2000), *From Neurons to Neighbourhoods: The science of Early Childhood Development*, National Academy Press, Washington DC.

Siraj-Blatchford, I., K. Sylva, S. Muttock, R. Gilden and D. Bell (2002), *Researching Effective Pedagogy in the Early Years* (DfES Research Report 356), DfES, London.

Sure Start (2004), *Childcare and Early Years Workforce Survey 2002/3. Day Nurseries and other Full Day Care Provision*, DfES, London.

Vandenbroeck, M. (ed.) (2003), *Diversity and Training in Early Childhood Training in Europe*, DECET, VBJK, Ghent, Belgium.

Whitebook, M., C. Howes and D. Phillips (1989), *Who Cares? Child Care Teachers and the Quality of Care in America: Final Report of the National Child Care Staffing Study*, Child Care Employee Project, Oakland, CA.

ISBN 92-64-03545-1
Starting Strong II: Early Childhood Education and Care
© OECD 2006

Chapter 8

Systematic Attention to Data Collection and Monitoring

Chapter 8 explores the situation of data collection in the early childhood education and care (ECEC) field. Overall, data collection remains weak, especially for children under 3. Even for 3- to 6-year-olds, data in the major international and national collections are often insufficient. In the UNESCO/OECD/EUROSTAT (UOE) data collection, the underlying model of early childhood education is limiting, and information provided on young children lacks comparability and analysis. More positively, many countries have been able to provide comprehensive data to OECD review teams, and several countries are developing their data collection procedures. In addition to supplying first-rate national data, the Nordic countries take a consultative approach to policy-making, and encourage the municipalities and ECEC centres to engage in data collection on their own behalf. Section 2 puts forward some proposals for the improvement of data collection in the ECEC field.

Monitoring an ECEC system includes continuing evaluation of system performance for accountability and policy purposes, and involves also tracking general trends and parental expectations. Monitoring is generally the responsibility of government through its statistical agencies, evaluation and research units, but in many countries, central or state governments involve other actors, such as local administrations, ECEC staff, parents, and independent research and survey groups. The chapter outlines government approaches to system monitoring and some initiatives to make the process more responsive to parent, educator and children's needs.

To achieve evidence-based policy-making, government administrations need to organise ECEC data collection in the ECEC field, and cover annually important areas of ECEC policy, *viz.* demand, supply and utilisation of ECEC places; the volume and allocation of public financing; the status of the children (demographic, health, socio-economic, etc.) within and outside services; the recruitment and training levels of staff, etc. However, data collection systems dedicated to the ECEC field exist only in a handful of OECD countries. Information relevant to early childhood policy is often derived from data sets created for other age groups and purposes. Such limitations lead to uncertain policy-making at national level and to a lack of reliable comparative data at international level.

What did Starting Strong recommend?

● *A need exists in most countries for a systematic procedure* to collect and provide consistent and comparable information on ECEC. Currently, the ministries responsible for young children use different indicators and diverse methods in collecting data on young children.

● *Future data collections need to cover 0- to 6-year-olds*, and include all forms of provision (including parental leaves), regardless of administrative responsibility (education, health, welfare, etc.), funding source (public, private or mixed), or setting (home, family day care, centre or school). Today, large data gaps appear in statistics addressing young children, and especially children under age 3, as whatever data does exist is generally focused on 3- to 6-year-olds.

1. Creating comprehensive data collections for young children and their services

The coherence and co-ordination of data sets continue to pose challenges for ECEC researchers. Many countries are only now beginning to modify their information systems to include data on young children. The large scale information systems on population, households, social policy or education that are routinely managed by national statistical bureaus were not initially set up to deliver the kinds of data needed to advance ECEC policy and provision. These systems often service the traditional needs of the larger ministries, and ignore major indicators of the early childhood field. Examples are many: social welfare databases have traditionally failed to treat young children as a separate category, or have used age groupings that bear little relationship to the age groups commonly found in ECEC services. In parallel, education ministries often restrict data collection to children over 3 years who are enrolled in instructional programmes recognised by ministries – a small proportion of the early education programmes that exist in many countries.

During the reviews, reliable data on 0- to 3-year-olds were particularly hard to access, especially in countries in which significant numbers of children in the age group were committed to care in unregulated services or with child minders. Information was sketchy, most notably with respect to the actual numbers of children under 3 in services, their patterns of participation, their socio-economic backgrounds or the extent of informal care arrangements.

These gaps in knowledge about young children undermine policy-making in the early childhood field, and have implications not only for international comparability, but also for national issues such as child protection.

The UOE data collections

The insufficient nature of national ECEC statistics is reflected in the UOE data collection.[1] This collection, based at the OECD, is sponsored by the Institute for Statistics (UNESCO/UIS), the Organisation for Economic Co-operation and Development (OECD), and the Statistical Office of the European Union (EUROSTAT) – hence the acronym UOE. The objective of the data collection is to provide internationally comparable data on key aspects of education systems, specifically on enrolments and completion of education programmes, as well as the cost and type of resources dedicated to education. The Member countries co-operate to gather information, to develop and apply common definitions and criteria for the quality control of the data, to verify the data and to provide the information necessary to interpret and report the submitted data.

In principle, the UOE provides a favourable framework for the collection and analysis of early childhood data. Yet, it must be recognised that pre-primary education remains a minor focus in UOE work plans. Data are collected in only a few relevant domains, and until very recently, little analysis of this data was not provided. The dynamic analytic procedures of the Programme for International Student Assessment (PISA) – linking socio-economic status, student characteristics, financing variables and the like – are not applied to services for young children. ECEC researchers have to be content with raw figures of enrolment or unit costs per child. In sum, ECEC is subsumed into a primary education framework as if services organisation, objectives, group sizes, staff-child ratios, staffing and training domains were similar to those pertaining in schools.

Again, although member countries are committed "to making all reasonable efforts to report according to the definitions, classifications, and coverage specified in the current document, and to report deviations from these standards in their data collection protocols", data supplied for pre-primary education often lack comparability. For example, the current *Education at a Glance* (OECD, 2005) provides expenditure figures per child aged from 3 to 6 years in early education centres: in France, USD 4 512 per child, in Sweden, USD 4 107 per child, and in the United Kingdom, USD 8 452 per child. For the lay reader, this may seem reasonable until one considers that child-staff ratios are significantly lower[2] in Sweden than in the other countries, that the Swedish pre-school is a full-day, full-year (11 months) service, and that over half the staff are trained pre-school teachers educated to tertiary level (International Standard Classification of Education [ISCED]-level qualification 5A). How then can unit costs per child come to less than half the expenditure of the United Kingdom, a country that provides two-and-a-half hours free early education per day during the academic year to 3- and 4-year-old children? Clearly, countries interpret the category ISCED Level 0 (pre-primary education) in different ways and use different protocols to report expenditure and other data.

Part of the difficulty for countries lies in the 1997 ISCED definition of early childhood education. ISCED Level 0 programmes are defined as "centre or school-based programmes that are designed to meet the educational and developmental needs of children at least 3 years of age, and that have staff that are adequately trained (i.e. qualified) to provide an educational programme for the children. These programmes are further defined as the initial stage of organised instruction". Such an understanding does not correspond to how early childhood programming is conceived in many countries or as described in *Starting Strong* (OECD, 2001). A basic confusion is found in the distinction drawn by ISCED between "education" and "care" and on that basis, its decision to begin data collection at the age of 3 years or to treat certain forms of kindergarten education as outside the ISCED definition. To our knowledge, there is no valid pedagogical reason for such distinctions – and in fact, several countries begin early education at earlier ages and often practise age-mixing in ECEC centres. A 1998 government publication from the United Kingdom affirmed that in the early years there is "no sensible distinction between education and care" (DfES, 1998). In addition, the "instructional" properties of programmes are difficult to identify. ECEC programming in its better manifestations relies to a great extent on the child's natural learning strategies (*viz.* play, interaction with others, the exploration of the wider environment) and seeks, in addition to cognitive development, other aims, such as social competence, which cannot be taught only through instruction.

In sum, on the basis of UOE figures, direct comparisons of countries in regard to the volume of ECEC provided, enrolment rates, public expenditure on ECEC and unit costs per child, remain unsafe:

- The definition of the population group considered to be in pre-primary education is arbitrary. Brain research, developmental psychology, and the actual practice of countries provide no cogent reason why 3 years should be a cut-off point.
- The programme criterion "centre or school-based programmes that are designed to meet the educational and developmental needs of children" is confused. What is clear is that countries use different proxy measures to determine whether a programme should be classified as educational or not. Variation in these proxy measures undermines comparability.
- The weekly and annual duration of ECEC sessions are rarely taken into account.

Despite these shortcomings, current work by UOE is useful. With some caution, it is possible to compare countries with similar ECEC organisation, and discern trends in enrolments and investments. Work is ongoing also at the OECD to improve definitions, and to standardise data collection methodologies, in particular through the OECD International Indicators of Education Systems (INES) Technical Group. For example, a reflection is taking place on ECEC teacher definitions and qualifications in an effort to obtain more accurate information about child-staff ratios across the member countries states. It is hoped that these discussions will involve consultations with ECEC experts as the design of data collection for the early childhood field remains a challenge in terms of scope, basic definitions and comparability.

What countries are doing

Despite the general picture of inadequate data systems in support of early childhood policy-making, several positive examples exist. Countries with long established early childhood services, and in which unlicensed services are actively discouraged, have been able to shape data collection and surveys to the needs of early childhood policy. The Nordic countries, with specific policy units at national and local levels responsible for children's affairs, excel in producing data relevant to the early childhood field. A number of other countries have also assigned responsibility to dedicated agencies to collect data and provide comprehensive information to governments and the public on young children and their families. The Flemish Community in Belgium, for example, publishes yearly a comprehensive compendium of statistics on young children: *The Child in Flanders* (*Kind en Gezin*, 2004). The publication (also available in English) contains a broad spectrum of data: demographic data (such as birth rates, the number of young children per age cohort, the number of ethnic minority children, adopted children and minors who come to Flanders as asylum seekers); data on family circumstances (such as family composition, ethnicity, age of parents, roles within the family, income and deprivation in families and parental participation in the labour market); data on child care, out-of-school care and on children receiving special support; data on the health and physical development of young children; and finally, data on issues relating to the question of whether children are living healthy lifestyles. The clarity and level of analysis can be seen in Table 8.1.

Table 8.1. **Use of child care by sub-groups in Flanders**

	Regular use (2002)	Regular use (2004)	Limited use (2004)	No use (2004)
Ethnic minority children	19.6	23.8	6.7	69.5
Children in underprivileged families	18.8	21.9	5.9	72.3
Of which:				
Children in underprivileged Belgian families	26.8	29.7	3.4	66.9
Children in underprivileged ethnic minority families	8.1	12.7	7.9	79.4
All children	52.2	55.7	10.1	4.2

Note: Ethnic minority children and children in underprivileged families make far less use of child care, but use by these groups has increased significantly. Only 23.8% of ethnic minority children and 21.9% of children in underprivileged families use child care on a regular basis. The lowest rate of use is noted for ethnic minority children who also belong to underprivileged families (12.7%). Compared with autumn 2002, regular use of child care by ethnic minority children and children in underprivileged families has also increased significantly.

Source: Kind en Gezin: Survey on the use of child care for children aged under 3, Autumn 2002 and February 2004.

2. Steps to improve ECEC data collection

If a national database on children does not already exist, a necessary first step is to establish one. An integrated, interoperable data system for all children is desirable and allows professionals who deal with young children (including the police, social welfare and other departments) access to vital information. In normal conditions, central responsibility increases professionalism and scope, and reduces the burden on local authorities to fund stand-alone data collections systems or buy expensive data management technologies. A central database can also monitor effectively the large-scale publicly funded ECEC programmes and achieve a more coherent and consistent picture of the national or state scene. At the same time, care will be taken to increase local professional capacity. An interactive database with clearly defined sections, *e.g.* general statistics, administrative information on provision and participation; evaluation research; summaries of mainstream ECEC research; news and current concerns; centre support measures; and parent information, should be feasible sections for most local governments to supply. Countries will assign clear responsibilities at each level of administration (federal, regional, local, ECEC centre or provider) for data collection and management in relevant sections. Adequately designed, a comprehensive data collection can be a powerful management tool not only for government but also for municipal authorities and centre directors. In addition, it can be a valuable source of information for researchers and for parents, educators and the general public. For the early childhood section, the scope of data collection would include in so far as possible private centre-based provision and family day care.

A second step – and one which is mentioned in different contexts throughout this text – is to establish ECEC policy units (if they do not already exist) to take in charge policy guidance, data collection, quality and curriculum matters in this growing field. Without formal recognition of early childhood policy at administrative level, and of the specificities and needs of the field, there is little reason for central statistical units to change their mode of working, or to employ statisticians with a working knowledge of ECEC organisation.

A third step would be a focus on the key issues of demand, supply, equitable access and quality (Olmsted and Montie, 2001). As these issues have still not been satisfactorily resolved for early childhood services in most countries, particularly for the lower age group 0 to 3 years, the data collected should be capable of providing adequate information to policy makers to forecast and plan provision, and in parallel, to measure the quality and appropriateness of services offered to different groups of children. The experience of the OECD early childhood review suggests that much information on these issues is available, but that the data may not be well organised or easily accessed.

Fourth, would be the redefinition and expansion of data collection beyond the present ISCED "level zero" perspective, to include all early education and care services for young children. Within the enlarged perspective, pre-primary education for the 3- to 6-year-olds would continue to be examined, but so also would other registered provision if it has sufficient intensity and provides effective cognitive and social development for children. Recognised categories, such as family day care; day nurseries; day care centres; age-integrated day care centres; playgroups; nursery/pre-school education; after-school care; and special services, would be monitored and reliable data collected on each. The Danish researchers, Rostgaard and Fridberg (1998), basing their research on official documents and national experts' advice, have already made a start in defining service types and comparing them across countries in terms of full-time equivalents.

Fifth, it would be helpful for early childhood policy makers in countries with mixed delivery systems to have reliable figures on public and private subsidies towards young children, disaggregated to cover key elements of expenditure, child-staff expenditure on the various ECEC service types; expenditure on maternity and parental leave; expenditure on child allowances and other transfers towards families with young children, including cash benefits, tax credits and employer contributions to cover child care expenses.[3] Financial tracking and monitoring contribute to accountability, and help to inform planning and resource allocation. For example, where efficient use of resources is concerned, it would be useful for ministries to know the comparative unit costs for a child in a public crèche, as compared to a place in publicly funded family day care or age-integrated centre, or as compared to being looked after at home, through the provision of paid parental leave.[4]

Sixth, the harmonisation of data collection with the goals of ECEC, that is, the holistic development of young children. Each country will identify the important goals for it to achieve with regard to young children, and generate indicators to measure that achievement. Following the education model, there is a tendency to measure the effectiveness of early childhood interventions through a narrow selection of outcome or impact indicators, focused on the child, *e.g.* early literacy measures as children exit kindergartens or enter the first year of compulsory schooling. The practice has its uses but it may overlook other important outcomes for children in this age group, and underplay the need to gather information also on structural and process standards. Where outcomes are concerned, the United States National Education Goals Panel (1997) has identified five dimensions that contribute significantly to children's success in school: health and physical development; emotional well-being and social competence; positive approaches to learning; communication skills; cognition and general knowledge. Countries may wish to develop measurable indicators within each of these dimensions, or decide on outcomes important for their societal needs. Just as major targeted programmes such as Head Start and Sure Start, undergo evaluations on a regular basis, it would be useful if mainstream programmes were likewise evaluated on agreed outcomes.

Lastly, more dynamic methods of statistical analysis in the early childhood field need to be created. By dynamic is meant the ability to treat data as interactive variables, whose impact on system goals can be measured with some degree of accuracy. An example from lower secondary education is the PISA (Programme for International Student Assessment) exercise carried out by the OECD across 32 countries (OECD, 2001, 2004). PISA allows a dynamic relationship to be established between student-related data, e.g. family and socio-economic background, and learning environment data, child-staff funding or staffing levels of the school system, instruction strategies and the like, revealing the intersecting impacts of different variables on selected goals of the school system. A similar analysis based on sound data could introduce more rigour into programming for young children, and provide reliable information on the environmental features that make a difference. The EPPE research project in the United Kingdom is an example of such an approach.

3. Establishing a national procedure to collect and provide reliable ECEC data

While the collection of ECEC data is well organised in some of the countries reviewed, other countries have been less successful. A challenge in all but a handful of countries is that the basic organisation of data collection in the ECEC field has not really begun in any rigorous way. There is no procedure in place to collect relevant data for early childhood policy-making. In one sense, this is not surprising as in many countries early childhood policy-making is only beginning to emerge as a separate field, and early childhood policy units have been either inexistent or weak. Until these units grow in strength, it is unlikely that regular data surveys will be organised to provide essential information on young children, for example, numbers of children in each age cohort, numbers and type of services, numbers and quality of staff, etc. If such data are not collected on a regular basis to serve the needs of policy makers, researchers and families, they have to be retrieved painstakingly from a variety of sources and surveys, such as from household surveys, health, social welfare, education or labour force statistics. More specific questions, such as the number of children from immigrant backgrounds enrolled in early education and care at the age of 3 years may require the addition of new questions in forthcoming national surveys, or supplementary small-scale sample surveys. Micro-surveys can be helpful in eliciting rapid information on current issues, such as, parental fees, children in need of special support, etc. An active and energetic ministry will ensure that such questions are regularly surveyed, and that the data are published for public scrutiny and comment. Micro-surveys, such as the Austrian initiative described in Box 8.1, can be helpful in eliciting rapid information on current issues, such as, parental fees, reasons for lack of uptake, socio-economic background of children, etc.

The level at which data on outcomes are reported is often a matter of contention, involving debates about ideology, privacy, and ethics. In England, the Children Act (2004) has made the legal changes necessary to ensure a central and shared data collection,

Box 8.1. **Statistics Austria – the role of the national statistics bureau**

Since 1972, Statistics Austria has collected data annually on early childhood facilities throughout Austria. Uniform data collection forms are filled out by all crèches, kindergartens, after-school day care facilities, mixed age day care facilities and all other types of day care facilities. After completion, they are then submitted to Statistics Austria for processing via the competent inspectorate of the provincial governments. Information is collected on the day care facilities (providers, opening hours, facilities, equipment, whether lunch is served, medical care, possibilities for using a playground area), on the children (length of stay, disabilities, age, employment of the mother, whether they eat lunch there, nationality) and on the staff (employment relationship, marital status, level of education/training, age, scope of employment). After treatment and analysis, the results are made available for local policy and administrative purposes to the statistical offices and inspectorates of the provincial governments. These data serve primarily as a basis for decisions that affect early childhood education and care in Austria.

Special data collections through Austrian micro-censuses

In addition to this annual data collection, special data collections and surveys are also made. Micro-censuses in 1995 and 2002 included a special section entitled "Household Management, Day Care and Nursing Care". These micro-censuses contain items on day care, including questions on the lack of provision and other reasons for not taking advantage of day care facilities.

Statistics on family day care and parent-toddler groups

Statistics Austria does not have uniform statistics on child minders and parent-toddler groups. The provincial child minder associations do collect some data, but their data are not standardised, nor do they include the child care institutions that are not members. They also document the scope of child care on a continual basis, as the remuneration for child minders and the parent contribution depend on the scope of care. Likewise, the Federation of Austrian Parent-Toddler Groups has collected data annually since 1995 on parent-toddler groups organised via the provincial associations, using a questionnaire that is filled out by the groups. The aims of this data collection are to determine: "the location of the parent-toddler groups and playgroups in each of the federal provinces, how the different framework conditions impact on these institutions (legislation and funding) compared among the provinces, identifying the needs and current situation of the parent-toddler groups and playgroups, current situation and needs assessment for initial and continued training programmes as the basis for planning BÖE training courses, statistical material for public relations work and funding agencies, documentation and development progress" (Naderer, 2000).

Source: Background Report of Austria, 2004.

which should reduce the burden on the local authorities and individual services. In the United States, further development of data management technologies is taking place, spurred by the No Child Left Behind (NCLB) initiative. Since its enactment, NCLB requires States to monitor rigorously the progress of children, teachers and schools. To this end, States are mandated to establish systems that will store and analyse data on diverse aspects of school life from student achievement and school expenditure to student health records and family history. Although some difficulties are reported about financing these complex state-wide data systems, and about the lack of capacity of teachers to exploit the data fully, state administrators consider that the new information systems will facilitate mandated reporting, provide monitoring of group and individual student achievement, improve budgeting and make possible rational policy decisions based on data. Suggestions for programme improvement and effective teaching strategies are also included in these databases, as a resource for teachers. This data-based monitoring approach has been extended to Head Start, and in most States, to early education.

4. Monitoring ECEC systems

By monitoring is meant not only the continued evaluation of the performance in ECEC systems for accountability and/or for country- or state-wide policy purposes, but it also involves tracking general trends and parental expectations. Monitoring is generally the responsibility of government through its statistical agencies, evaluation and research units, but in many countries, central or state governments involve other actors, such as local administrations, ECEC staff, parents and independent research and survey groups.

The role of government

As indicated in the first part of this chapter the annual collection of reliable data on ECEC and its analysis by governments is an essential task in monitoring ECEC systems. System monitoring is further reinforced by national or state inspectorates, whose work presupposes that a regulatory framework has been agreed, and, in the area of pedagogical quality, that a national curriculum or framework has been published setting clear goals for the system as a whole. In the United States, for example, the goals or standards[5] adopted for public programmes in different States derive essentially from NEGP, Head Start or NAEYC guidelines. Thus, they are broad in scope, covering seven identifiable domains: motor development; health, safety and nutrition; general cognitive development; numeracy, language; socio-emotional development; and aesthetics (Bowman et al., 2001). Many States also use programme standards to ensure that an adequate pedagogy can be employed, for example, child-staff ratios of 10:1 or better; adequately trained and certified teachers; rich learning environments with adequate space, learning materials and indoor/ outdoor layout to meet the work and play needs of young children. The work of administration and inspectorates (referred to also as "pedagogical support" or "coaching") is to ensure that standards are met in all centres and that each centre strives for high quality in its pedagogical work.

As already indicated, such monitoring has not always been satisfactory in traditional pre-primary systems in Europe because of the placing of pre-school under primary school administration and the ensuing "schoolification" of the system. The situation has led to inadequate formulation of specific goals for the pre-school sector; to programme standards based on primary school criteria, and to low levels of certification in early childhood pedagogy among both teachers and inspectorates. In the United States, monitoring weaknesses are also apparent. Examples are the irregular monitoring of (the majority) private provision in the child care sector, and derogations to public and faith-based pre-kindergarten programmes from both licensing and monitoring requirements.

Pedagogical advisory services

Countries seeking to ensure quality standards across the board in early childhood services provide, in general, an external inspectorate or local advisory corps to ensure that pedagogical and programme standards are known and respected across early childhood services. It seems obvious that such support services should be certified in early childhood studies and pedagogy, but as noted above, this is not always the case. Hence, the relative neglect of pre-primary classes in inspections in traditional school services, even when a "whole school" approach is taken. Again, the pedagogical advisory corps in the Nordic countries stand out by their professionalism and presence on the ground: pedagogical advisors are drawn from the ranks of practising pedagogues and work comprehensively at local level to upgrade the quality of pedagogy in all services (with in some countries a lesser interest in family day care). Local pedagogical advisors ensure that minimal standards in services for young children are maintained, and that pedagogical work progresses. In several instances noted by OECD review teams, advisors provided staff with up-to-date information on new forms of pedagogy, and supported the organisation of internal quality improvement processes, such as team-evaluations and documentation.

National or programme evaluations

Another means of monitoring ECEC systems, or at least, large programmes within a national system, has been the use of large-scale evaluation studies. The question is taken up in more detail in Chapter 9. The United States is a leader in this field and carries out many comprehensive, research-based evaluations of large-scale programmes, because of the requirement to present performance results and justify management of public funds. The re-authorisation evaluations of Head Start are an example of the approach. The United Kingdom has carried out several similar studies of its flagship Sure Start programme, for example in 2005, a study of the impacts on children and families of Sure Start local programmes (NESS Impact Study, 2005). In addition, the Department for Education and Skills is funding a longitudinal study Effective Provision of Pre-school Education (EPPE), which measures young children's development (intellectual and social/ behavioural) between the ages of 3 and 7 years in different types of ECEC settings. To investigate the effects of pre-school education for 3- and 4-year-olds, the EPPE team collected a wide range of information on over 3 000 children, their parents, their home environments and the pre-school settings they attended. The study has provided much valuable information to the ministry and policy makers. Such studies are less common in European countries, but are replaced by inspections and ongoing monitoring, with the limitations noted above. With the exception of a few countries, OECD teams encountered few comprehensive national evaluations of early childhood systems, possibly because, until recently, the social and pedagogical goals of these programmes were poorly defined in most countries. In contrast, the 2003 national evaluation of Swedish pre-schools is an impressive piece of work. Published by the National Agency for Education in 2004, it provides policy makers at central and local levels with many valuable insights into how the national pre-school framework curriculum is understood and implemented by administrations, centres and staff. More regular national evaluations of this type are needed across the OECD countries.

5. More participatory approaches to system monitoring

Involving local administrators and centres

It has long been noted that though expert data and monitoring systems provide necessary information for government purposes, they may fail to involve local administrators and parents in their concerns. Conscious that these partners are a valuable source of information and that they merit consultation, some countries rely, as in Austria, on local administrations and centres to provide annually the raw data on enrolments, family background, demand needs and patterns. Central statistical offices may use also their statistical and research capacity to focus on matters of concern to the public, while ensuring the participation of municipalities and centres. For example, when faced with the challenge of after-school care in the early 1990s, the Swedish authorities, in addition to collecting statistical data to measure the scope of the challenge, sponsored also a network of centres (with parents) to analyse the issue from a user perspective. The work of this network provided qualitative information on the precise needs of children and families: What do parents need? What do parents consider is good quality in free-time services? Is the school a good location for free-time services? What are the actual and desired qualifications of staff in these services? In general, the reflex of ministries in the Nordic countries is to take a more consultative approach to policy, and through legislation and information, encourage municipalities and centres to engage in data collection and to pursue their own quality assurance and monitoring.

Involving parents and teacher associations in monitoring

In addition to local administrations and centres, parents also need to be part of the monitoring and information process and their opinions sounded regularly in national review mechanisms and at the level of services. Several countries, *e.g.* Denmark, Norway, and more recently, the United Kingdom, undertake surveys on parent opinion and consult parents on a regular basis about their difficulties and desires with regard to ECEC services. The involvement of parents is also achieved through granting parents significant management rights in ECEC centres, a practice that assists parents to make informed judgements about early childhood programming. Not only can parents inform staff of parental needs and their expectations of services, but their presence may also be critical in maintaining quality, affordability and transparency in the spending of budgets. National surveys and parent ("client", "consumer" or "service user") consultations were also mentioned in *Starting Strong*. In this approach, information on many variables can be collected: such as ease of access, convenient hours of opening, efficient administration and distribution of places, sensitivity to family background (socio-economic, cultural, religious, linguistic, etc.), quality standards, parents' perception of the happiness and well-being of children, the provision of meals and normal healthcare to children, relationships with teachers, etc. Such information is also useful for parents in choosing the centre suitable for their child(ren). Teacher surveys carried out by researchers or by the major unions also provide valuable monitoring information, especially if undertaken on a regular basis.

Involving the research community

The contribution of independent researchers is also important in gathering information about ECEC systems. An example is the work undertaken in the United States by the National Institute of Early Education Research (NIEER), which has begun to collect annual data on the state of pre-kindergarten. The NIEER yearbook, *The State of pre-school* (NIEER, 2003, 2004, 2005) shows, in a readable and graphic form, the extent of state investment in pre-school, the numbers of children enrolled at ages three and four, group sizes and child-staff ratios, the qualification of teachers, and data on other important quality indicators. Information from independent research sources is a useful means of monitoring the performance of administrations and political leaders.

Notes

1. UOE data refer to UNESCO/OECD/EUROSTAT data collection. See also, *OECD Handbook for Internationally Comparative Education Statistics* (2004).

2. Lower child-staff ratios mean, of course, higher costs.

3. In Norway, the Ministry of Children and Family Affairs compiles the annual expenditure on children across all Ministries into one document to show what share of the budget is spent on children, as well as to formulate government objectives and policy for children across sectors.

4. In addition to cost efficiency measures, the quality provided to children, the child's best interests and parental choice need also to be taken into account in policy decisions.

5. "Standards" are defined by Bowman *et al.* (2001) as "the values, expectations and outcomes of education".

References

Ball, S.J. and C. Vincent (2005), "The 'Childcare Champion'? New Labour, Social Justice and the Childcare Market", *British Educational Research Journal*, Vol. 31(5), pp. 557-570.

Bowman, B.T., M.S. Donovan and M.S. Burns (eds.) (2001), *Eager to Learn: Educating our pre-schoolers*, Committee on Early Childhood Pedagogy, National Research Council Commission on Behavioral and Social Sciences and Education, National Academy Press, Washington DC.

Children Act (2004), The Stationery Office, London, United Kingdom.

Dahlberg, G. and P. Moss (2005), *Ethics and Politics in Early Childhood Education*, Routledge Falmer, London.

DfES (1998), "Consultation Paper on the Regulation and Inspection of Early Education and Day Care", DfES, London, *www.dfes.gov.uk/consultations/downloadableDocs/37_1.doc*.

DfES (1997-2007), "Effective Provision of pre-school Education – A Longitudinal Study Funded by the Department for Education and Skills", DfES, London, *http://k1.ioe.ac.uk/schools/ecpe/eppe/index.htm*.

Kind en Gezin (2004), *Child in Flanders*, available at: *www.kindengezin.be/KG/English_pages/default.jsp*.

Naderer, E. (2000), *Elternverwaltete Kinder- und Spielgruppen in Österreich. Datenerhebung 1999/2000*, A study commissioned by the BÖE, Vienna.

NIEER (2003), *The State of Pre-School Yearbook*, NIEER, Rutgers University, NJ, available at: *nieer.org/yearbook/pdf/yearbook.pdf*.

NIEER (2004), *Pre-School Policy Matters*, Issue 6, NIEER, Rutgers University, NJ.

NIEER, (2005), *2005 State pre-school Yearbook*, by W.S. Barnett, J.T. Hustedt, K.B. Robin and K.L. Schulmann, *http://nieer.org/yearbook/*.

OECD (2001), *Starting Strong: Early Childhood Education and Care*, OECD, Paris.

OECD (2004), *Learning for Tomorrow's World: First Results from PISA 2003*, OECD, Paris.

OECD (2005), *Education at a Glance: OECD Indicators*, OECD, Paris.

Olmsted, P.P. and J. Montie (2001), *Early Childhood Settings in 15 Countries: What are their Structural Characteristics?*, High/Scope Educational Research Foundation, Ypsilanti, Michigan.

Rostgaard, T. and T. Fridberg (1998), *Caring for Children and Older People: A Comparison of European Policies and Practices*, The Danish National Institute of Social Research, Copenhagen.

Sylva, K., B. Taggart and I. Siraj-Blatchford (2003), *Assessing Quality in the Early Years*, Trentham Books, London.

ISBN 92-64-03545-1
Starting Strong II: Early Childhood Education and Care
© OECD 2006

Chapter 9

A Stable Framework and Long-Term Agenda for Research and Evaluation

Chapter 9 examines the status of early childhood education and care (ECEC) research, which is still at a rudimentary stage in several of the countries reviewed. Some of the more common types of research undertaken in the ECEC field are outlined: country-specific policy research; large-scale programme evaluations; longitudinal studies; comparative; cross-national research; neuroscience and brain research. In most of these fields, North American research predominates. The expanding agenda of ECEC research can also be seen in post-modern and socio-cultural analyses, in growing practitioner-research; and in the burgeoning of research on particular topics, such as, diversity, children's spaces and environments.

Some critical issues for research in the ECEC field are also briefly outlined: for example, the failure of different language groups to make their research known abroad. This tends to leave the field free to English language research. Because of strong links with education research, a high proportion of ECEC research in the English language tends to debate education questions that are often not central to the early childhood concerns of other countries. The issue of how to expand local participatory modes of research is also raised. Another challenge is to progress original research towards greater public dissemination – initially through peer reviewed academic and, professional journals, and then to media reports and parent information channels.

Since the publication of *Starting Strong* in 2001 and the review of a further eight countries, there has been considerable development in ECEC research carried out at national level in support of policy-making. Both longitudinal research and point-in-time evaluations play an important part in this process. So too, has there been an expansion in research methodologies and in the scope of studies across this transdisciplinary field. Despite these encouraging developments, there is still more progress to be made, as ECEC research in many countries has started from a low base. The following is a citation from one of the OECD Country Notes that describes an ECEC research situation that is not unique:

"… (in the early childhood research field), few university chairs in early childhood studies exist, fewer we were told than in Japanese Language, and only a small fraction of the number of chairs in other fields of education. This is matched by few postgraduate programmes, few dissertations and no academic journals with an early years focus. In consequence, the research base in early childhood is unduly small, with no obvious means in current conditions of increasing its size. As one researcher put it, the area 'lacks critical mass' while a former government funder of research remarked that the shortage of specialist researchers presented problems when wanting to develop new projects."

Another consequence is that such research as there is has become highly dependent on funding from government (either central or local). It is focused on policy or evaluation-driven projects, where funders define the research questions, and there is little opportunity to undertake other forms of research. Most researchers we met agreed that there was 'simply no university-level basic research to speak of in the area of early childhood pedagogy'. Furthermore, the small size of the ECEC research base makes it difficult to break into the main source of university research funding, which is highly competitive and where the few early years researchers are competing with well established fields including large numbers of university-based researchers. This perpetuates a dependency on government funding.

In addition, information on ECEC services at a national level is poorly developed. According to several informants at ministry and research levels, there are no regular or comparable data collected on use of ECEC services by children and families across the country, either their numbers or their backgrounds. The result is that the exact number of children actually attending services is not known, nor are the characteristics of users and non-users sufficiently researched. The same goes for comparable information on the costs of services and how these costs are met; one expert added that only a handful of people have an overall understanding of the funding system. As we have seen above, this is certainly linked to the looseness of the present system where no clear responsibility exists for the research and monitoring infrastructure, on which effective systems must to a great extent rely."

What did Starting Strong recommend?

● *Research frameworks and sustained investment to support long-term policy goals:* Starting Strong (OECD, 2001) proposed strengthening the essential elements of national research processes: a stable research infrastructure and long-term funding, combined with a planned agenda and training opportunities. Enhancing the links between research, policy and practice, as well as increasing investment in research and development were seen as important.

- *Expanded research agendas to include disciplines and methods currently under-represented.* *Starting Strong* (OECD, 2001) noted the dominance of concerns and methodologies derived from programme evaluations and developmental psychology in ECEC research. While this focus was deemed important for ECEC, a wider research perspective using other disciplines was needed also. Anthropology, sociology, public policy, gender studies and learning theory were cited as disciplinary bases to be researched and from which pertinent policy and practice could be developed. Cross-country studies were also seen as useful for assessing the impact of different policy initiatives.

- *The development of a range of instruments and evaluation procedures sensitive to the complex dynamics of early childhood environments, and to user and staff needs: Starting Strong* (OECD, 2001) drew attention to the importance of self-evaluation procedures and action-research at local level. Cost-benefit analyses of different approaches were encouraged, along with strategies to help the dissemination of findings within and across countries.

1. What types of research are most common?

Despite the penury of research in some countries, early childhood research is growing rapidly. Countries, such as Belgium, Finland, France, the Netherlands, Norway, Sweden, the United Kingdom and the United States, have established well-coordinated research agendas, linked to extensive data systems and government-university agreements. The following types of research are most usually undertaken – although the favoured research methodologies and themes can vary greatly from country to country.

Country-specific policy research

Country-specific policy research examines, for example, broad policy issues and policy choices faced by national administrations. This type of research, often sponsored directly by governments, frequently focuses on evaluating the features or effects of particular programmes or policies. Many OECD countries produce good research on their own systems, but undoubtedly, the United States leads in this field. American research in the early childhood field influences policy decisions in many countries all over the world, and is the most often cited in research journals.[1] Not only do several powerful national research agencies exist but also a large number of university departments and private agencies engage with the early childhood field and provide research on every facet of policy and organisation.

Some caution needs to be exercised in using research from another context, country or culture. An example often cited is that of developmental psychology which, through tracing the development and maturation of young children at different ages, made a valuable contribution to early childhood education practice. From the findings of developmental psychology, a programmatic approach to young children – developmentally appropriate practice (DAP) – was formulated in the United States during the 1980s and 90s. The approach helped to inform early childhood practice throughout America and in many other countries. However, inferences drawn from the research often went beyond the actual findings. The contents, behaviours and centre environments recommended by DAP strongly reflected urban white American cultural and educational values. The linking of these values to "universal" psychological schemas came under criticism from both minority groups and researchers, and appeals were made for more sensitivity to social environment and socio-cultural factors (Dahlberg *et al.*, 1999; Tobin *et al.*, 1989; Woodhead, 1998).

Comparative, cross-national research

Comparative, cross-national research identifies specific policies and practices from which people in other countries can draw inspiration. Its intention is not to identify "models" for imitation or to construct league tables, but to assist policy makers to think more broadly and critically about ECEC. To this end, the thematic reviews of ECEC, conducted under the auspice of OECD Ministers for Education, contribute to knowledge and understanding of this field. Comparative research links well with educational anthropology and socio-cultural theory, and provides a prism or lens to identify the unquestioned assumptions, discourses and practices of one's own country (Moss, 2001). It reveals important differences in management and practice, for example, the wide range of public funding or child-staff ratios practised across different OECD countries. The awareness of such differences can lead to a reassessment of domestic policy, and provide an impetus to further research on important issues, *e.g.* on the cultural underpinnings of ECEC practice (see, for example, Tobin *et al.*, 1989, Rayna and Brougère, 2000), on funding patterns or the relative importance across countries of literacy and numeracy practices.

Longitudinal studies

Longitudinal studies have been initiated in several OECD countries, but are funded more frequently in the United States. Recently, the report of the "High/Scope Perry Pre-school Study through Age 40" (see Chapter 5, Figure 5.1) has been published (Schweinhart and Montie, 2005). The findings of American longitudinal studies – such as the NICHD studies, or the earlier "Cost Quality and Child Outcomes study" – have been influential and widely read by researchers and policy makers all over the world. They have helped to clarify, for example, quality parameters and their effects, or the relationship between family characteristics and children's health, educational or employment outcomes. Reiterative data, collected at different intervals on a representative national sample or on a population cohort of a certain type, allow researchers to study – in depth and over time – many of the important issues for children in contemporary society. A typical study of this kind may assess whether exposure to particular types of early childhood programmes is associated with different outcomes. The temporal aspect of longitudinal research allows time for both children and programmes to mature, showing how immediate outcomes from programmes may change over time (Chatterji, 2004). Almost all the larger countries in the OECD review have their own longitudinal national studies, with the United Kingdom (the Millenium Cohort Study) and the United States (the National Children's Study) recently undertaking new ones. Likewise, Australia (LSAC) and Korea have recently commissioned longitudinal studies of children, and Ireland has proposed a similar venture. How closely these initiatives will be linked to gaining knowledge about children in ECEC services is open to question. The development of national longitudinal studies is costly, and in small countries, the designers of these studies may be required to cater for several constituencies or apply, with little or no adaptation, study measures and protocols developed elsewhere. The resulting data may be well or poorly linked to ECEC policy and practice, depending on the strategic direction that has guided the longitudinal research framework.

Large-scale programme evaluations

Again, the United States is an acknowledged leader in this type of research, due not only to the inherent strength of the American research community but also to the requirement that publicly funded programmes in the United States should present performance results and justify management of public funds. The re-authorisation evaluations of Head Start are an example of the approach. Some critics allege that frequent evaluations put pressure on managers and educators in these programmes to produce easily measurable results, such as math and literacy gains, at the expense of other important but less quantifiable goals (Meisels *et al.*, 1996; Clark Wortham, 2004). With the exception of the United Kingdom, evaluations of public programmes are less common in Europe, and are generally replaced by regular monitoring and inspection processes. However, a comparative study by Cryer *et al.* (1999) showed poor results for the quality of care in public early education programmes in several European countries, which suggests that more research evaluations of public programmes in Europe could provide useful feedback to the responsible government departments.

In Britain, the resources invested by DfES in research to address policy and quality issues in ECEC are impressive. Sure Start has a large research and evaluation programme in place (with an annual budget of approximately GBP 6 million, or USD 10 748 400) to provide evidence related to the effectiveness of Sure Start centres. Recent results have already been noted in Chapter 1 (NESS, 2005). Another major evaluation programme in Britain supporting quality improvement processes is the "Effective Provision of Pre-School Education" (2000-2004), a further study tracking the effect of pre-school provision on children's outcomes from start-of-school to age 11 (see Box 9.1). Other national evaluations include the "Neighbourhood Nursery Programme Evaluation." The evidence from these evaluations helps to inform ECEC policy in Britain and lead the development of the new Children's Centres in England. In contrast, the volume of government-sponsored research on national early childhood issues coming from other countries, including those with long-established early childhood systems, seems rather less, though it may be possible that research from these countries is not being accessed internationally because of language (Boocock, 1995).

Neuroscience and brain research

Over the past decades, research on young children and their learning has greatly developed, moving from a behavioural genetics perspective in the 1960s and 1970s, to a more developmental and interactionist paradigm with strong attention to environments. In line with Bronfenbrenner's (1986) critique of behavioural genetics, recent neuroscience research shows that complex skill development is essentially "experience dependent" and requires structured experience through social interaction. In sum, a child's development requires positive interaction, modelling, and support from the outside by parents and other care-givers (Leseman, 2002). Owing to media interest in brain research, many popular ideas about the early development of the brain – synaptogenesis, left side/right side brain development, critical periods, etc. – are in circulation, but in many instances, their relevance for early childhood practice is far from proven (Bruer, 1999, OECD 2002).

Box 9.1. **The EPPE (Effective Provision of Pre-School Education) Project in the United Kingdom**

The Effective Provision of Pre-School Education (EPPE) project is the first major European longitudinal study of a national sample of young children's development (intellectual and social/behavioural) between the ages of 3 and 7 years. To investigate the effects of pre-school education for 3- and 4-year-olds, the EPPE team collected a wide range of information on over 3 000 children, their parents, their home environments and the pre-school settings they attended. Settings (141) were drawn from a range of providers (local authority day nursery, integrated* centres, playgroups, private day nurseries, maintained nursery schools and maintained nursery classes). A sample of "home" children (who had no or minimal pre-school experience) were recruited to the study at entry to school for comparison with the pre-school group. In addition to investigating the effects of pre-school provision on young children's development, EPPE explores the characteristics of effective practice (and the pedagogy which underpin them) through twelve intensive case studies of settings with positive child outcomes. EPPE has demonstrated the positive effects of high quality provision on children's intellectual and social/behavioural developmental. The key findings are:

The impact of attending a pre-school centre

- Pre-school experience, compared to none, enhances children's development.
- The duration of attendance is important with an earlier start being related to better intellectual development and improved independence, concentration and sociability.
- Full time attendance led to no better gains for children than part-time provision.
- Disadvantaged children in particular can benefit significantly from good quality pre-school experiences, especially if they attend centres that cater for a mixture of children from different social backgrounds.

The type of pre-school attended

- Good quality can be found across all types of early years settings. However, children tended to make better intellectual progress and quality was higher overall in integrated settings, nursery schools and nursery classes.

The quality and practices of pre-school centres

- The quality of pre-school centres is directly related to better intellectual/cognitive and social/behavioural development in children.
- Settings that have staff with higher qualifications, especially with good proportion of trained teachers on the staff, show higher quality and their children make more progress.
- Where settings view educational and social development as complementary and equal in importance, children make better all round progress.
- Effective pedagogy includes interaction traditionally associated with the term "teaching", the provision of instructive learning environments and "sustained shared thinking" to extend children's learning.

The importance of home learning

The quality of the learning environment of the home (where parents are actively engaged in activities with children) promoted intellectual and social development in all children. Although parent's social class and levels of education were related to child outcomes the quality of the home learning environment was more important. The home learning environment is only moderately associated with social class. What parents do is more important than who they are.

* "Integrated" settings fully combine education and care and are referred to as "combined" centres in EPPE Technical Papers.

Source: DfES Brief, No: RBX15-03, October 2003.

However, it is known from research, as summarised by ECS (1998) and the National Research Council/Institute of Medicine (2000) that:

- The development of the capacity to learn is most receptive during the first years of life, and these are the years that traditionally receive the least attention from the education world.

- Interactive environments enhance development of brain and neural connections. Yet, many infants are in day care centres for too many hours with employees who lack training in early childhood development and may be responsible for too many children.

- With intense early intervention, some adverse effects can be reversed or even prevented for much less than it costs to provide special services later. The tendency for education systems is to wait for students to fall behind and then place them in special-education programmes at a high cost to States.

- Learning in young children is impeded by emotionally stressful home or school environments. ECEC centres and school should maintain a relaxed, focused atmosphere that offers options for learning in individually satisfying ways. Children's emotional and social development is as important to school readiness as their cognitive and language development.

- The old notion of students as empty vessels waiting to be filled with knowledge is giving way to a more credible working hypothesis that children continuously build understandings in interaction (including with well-trained educators) based on their own activity, prior experiences and new information. The idea of a fixed intelligence is giving way to a more flexible perception of gradual intellectual development dependent on external stimulation and interaction.

From Neurons to Neighbourhoods (Shonkoff and Philips, 2000) summarises much of the research in this field. Many findings are relevant to the ECEC field, such as the focus on the importance of relationships to healthy human development. The feelings of children are reported to need the same level of attention as their thinking, and learning to manage emotions can be more difficult for young children than learning to count or read. Successful relationships with adults and other children provide a solid foundation of capacities that children will use over a lifetime. These reciprocal learning interactions afford children ways to define who they are, what they can become and how and why they are important to other people. The emotional development of young children is a "critical aspect of the development of overall brain architecture that has enormous consequences over the course of a lifetime".

2. Expanding ECEC research agendas

In addition to the above areas of research, a wider research perspective using other focuses, disciplines and approaches can be seen emerging in the ECEC field. The following is a small sample of some of the more promising avenues of research found in recent years in ECEC literature.

Socio-cultural analysis and post-modernist research

Socio-cultural and socio-economic analyses contribute towards understanding the contexts of ECEC in different countries, and provide useful insights into the social, organisational and policy environments of early childhood systems. They show how the organisation of early childhood services can be "path dependent", embedded within larger socio-economic structures (Esping Andersen, 2002) or produced by current labour market organisation (Morgan, 2005). Some of this research is designed cross-nationally, using mechanisms and sampling processes that give attention to issues of the comparability of concepts and linguistic equivalences (Osborn, 2004). Diversity is valued and cultural differences with regard to child-rearing and education are identified. Analysts and writers who adopt the approach seek to clarify the meanings given – within and across cultures and language groups – to essential concepts used in early childhood policy-making, such as "childhood", "early education" or "children's services".

Socio-cultural analyses also link with gender studies and cast light on societal constructs of child-rearing and the role of women. ECEC policy and thinking is underpinned by (often unacknowledged) theories and beliefs about parenting, childhood and the role of women in raising children (Mahon, 2006). As we have seen, women predominantly take the parental leaves and part-time work necessary to rear young children in dual-earner families. There are few men represented in ECEC, a field maintained by women who receive limited recognition or reward. This organisation of services sends out a clear message about who is considered to be responsible for children. Issues such as family function, maternalism, the role of the state in child and family matters are important themes in this research.

Post-modernists push the analysis further and note the co-existence of different points of view from which to describe ECEC. They attempt to identify the assumptions that underlie policy-making and to challenge "regimes of truth", that is, taken-for-granted, normalising approaches to reality. For example, Dahlberg et al. (1999) call into question the notion of a value-free, technical definition of ECEC quality, based on the specification of quality criteria by experts or a central authority. If justice is to be done to the range of cultures and child-rearing ideals, to the wishes of stakeholders (communities, parents, educators and children as well of governments), to the diversity of children and childhoods, then the prevailing governmental "discourse on quality" should be replaced by participation and a "discourse of meaning-making" in which ethical and (minor) political choices are recognised (Dahlberg and Moss, 2005). From this perspective, early childhood institutions should be considered not just as centres that supply "services" to consumers (child care, early education, preparation for school; etc.), but as "children's spaces", "domains of negotiated social practice and relationships".

Unlike RCTs (Randomised Controlled Trials), which use experimental designs and complex statistical methods to analyse massive data entries,[2] socio-cultural studies and post-modernist theories use more ethnographic and qualitative methods. Post modern and other recent approaches are enriched also by perspectives from other disciplines, such as economics, history, anthropology, and sociology.[3] Some of the important questions asked include: How does a particular nation or culture view childhood and child-rearing? What are its understandings of family function and gender equality? What are the purposes of early childhood institutions? Are these purposes valid for all ethnic groups in a society? How are quality criteria and outcome goals arrived at? How do societies understand knowledge, learning and care? What power relations and societal visions underlie technical discourses on education and childhood?

The post-modern critique is useful in calling attention to the fact that "common sense" discourses about education are a product of a certain vision of human activity. Currently, an economic competition discourse is common, in which OECD countries push for higher educational levels for their (future) workforces. Arguments, such as future competition with China and India, or the need for higher productivity to pay pensions in the future, are used to come to a dubious conclusion: that children should acquire competency in literacy, math and other measurable skills at an ever-earlier age. Post-modernists point out that other scenarios for young children are possible and valid, *e.g.* widening the experience and knowledge of young children (particularly from poor or diverse backgrounds) in order to make technical skills operational and meaningful; cultivating the creativity and joy in learning of young children by introducing them to nature, culture and the arts to which they so readily respond; conceptualising the school as a space for child participation and inter-culturalism, where young children and their families acquire democratic and positive attitudes; paying attention to young children's natural research and learning capacities, so that education becomes a question of meaning-making and understanding.

Many of the proposals made by post-modernists – while utopian in some early childhood systems – are being currently achieved within others:

- The co-construction of new democratic institutions and meeting places around early childhood issues and service organisation.
- Teaching and learning as an ethical practice, including egalitarian and respectful approaches to young children.
- An enriched concept of pedagogy in early childhood centres, that embraces care, upbringing and education.
- Listening, project work and documentation as major means of working with young children.
- Parental involvement and the valuing of diversity.

Research on practice and process

Research on practice and process, sometimes referred to as "action- or practitioner-research", is a valuable mode of research in that it enables staff to reflect systematically on their own practice. Some researchers express reserves about this type of research, saying that its methods are rudimentary and that it lacks rigour and reliability. However, if carried out by practitioners with the support of university research departments, methodology and reliability can be ensured. As a practice, it also models a major aim of ECEC, *viz.* to encourage participants to build theories, and to experiment and reflect on their environment in a democratic and mutually supportive way. Some countries, such as Norway, have integrated research methodology and practice into the pre-training of ECEC professionals. In other countries, reflection on practice is encouraged through government- or agency-funded renewal programmes (Belgium), through the practice of documentation (*e.g.* Reggio Emilia in Italy) or through participatory self-evaluation instruments (*e.g.* the United Kingdom). In yet others, staff research is led by local university early childhood departments or agency expert centres (*e.g.* Finland); pedagogical advisors (*e.g.* Denmark); or by various model programmes that encourage ongoing research and team training (*e.g.* Reggio Emilia education in Sweden). Research-led professional development has a strong tradition in Belgium, Finland, Norway and Sweden, and, increasingly, in the United Kingdom. Practitioner research has a high value as a tool for professional development, because of the clear methodological links to pedagogy, reflection and quality improvement processes. A possible weakness is that many of its valuable findings and insights remain at local level, and are not passed upward to ministries in a systematic way, unless ministries are proactive in keeping open lines of communication.

Participant observation and child research

One of the current strengths of early childhood education research lies in embracing new ways of viewing the child (Kilderry, Nolan and Noble, 2004). Recent acknowledgement of young children as capable learners has brought an increase in the involvement of children in research, not only as subjects but also as participants. Research deontology is being strengthened in this area. Participant observation and questioning of children is bringing new respect for the learning strategies naturally adopted by young children, such as play, social interaction and sustained shared thinking either one-to-one or within groups.

Two developing areas of research

Research on issues of diversity

The migration of people within and across countries impacts ECEC service provision in almost all OECD countries. Increasing population diversity within countries has highlighted the need for responsive ECEC policy and provision, and has given new importance to research on inter-cultural and diversity concerns. Issues of access and equity become important in countries where high levels of diversity exist – diversity in culture, language, religion, ethnicity and geographic location, as well as in health status and income. Research on local demographic patterns and on cultural expectations about early childhood services gives important planning and policy information. Data on access rates by specific groups of children, *e.g.* according to linguistic and ethnic diversity, age and special needs, can help administrations to provide sufficient information to families and ensure that their children have reasonable and appropriate access to essential services. The research network, Diversity in Early Childhood Education and Training (DECET) provides an example of an action-research project at European level (see Box 9.2).

Research on children's spaces and environments

The study of children's spaces and environments is a growing area of research in both the United States and Europe (Finland, Italy, the Netherlands, Norway, the United Kingdom, etc.). Cross-country comparisons have been useful in calling attention to this issue, *e.g.* questioning the assumption that "serious" learning and education of young children can only take place indoors, compared to the strong outdoors approach of the Nordic countries. Again, the growing inclusion of children with disabilities has woken up school designers and architects to the fact that in many countries few buildings have access for disabled children, and are often poorly designed for group work and children's activities. In sum, early childhood environments often fail to fulfil the role of "the third teacher" as proposed by Malaguzzi.

An important indicator of quality is the level of investment in and the appropriateness of early childhood buildings and learning environments, both indoors and outdoors. This is generally admitted from a health and hygiene perspective but is not always understood from an educational perspective, although at least two of the great founders of early childhood education and care, Friedrich Fröbel and Maria Montessori, had decided views on the organisation of space and materials. Two Finnish researchers, Bergstrom and Ikonen

---

Box 9.2. **Diversity in early childhood education and training**

The research network "Diversity in Early Childhood Education and Training", or DECET as it is known, brings together researchers and practitioners interested in resolving issues of appropriate access to ECEC for families and children from diverse cultural backgrounds. The goals of the network are:

● To facilitate exchange among trainers, practitioners, researchers and policy makers throughout Europe.

● To promote actively equity and respect for diversity in early childhood education and care services.

● To develop new insights and knowledge in this field.

● To work in collaboration with other networks in and outside Europe.

DECET research and action focuses essentially on methods, training, and quality evaluation, from the perspective of diversity. Eight European countries are represented in the network: Belgium, Germany, Greece, France, Ireland, the Netherlands, Spain and the United Kingdom (England and Scotland). The DECET network has undertaken a number of projects with different national and regional governments, for example, in Flanders, it has been engaged in training early childhood personnel in diversity practice. This means training educators to have effective dialogues with parents, and to counter stereotypical thinking and institutional discrimination. With policy makers and managers, the challenge is to work towards equal access for children, and to undo unequal power relation in ECEC services.

The DECET network is funded by the Bernard van Leer Foundation (*www.bernardvanleer.org*), and also seeks supplementary funding from EU programmes and foundations to support the aims of the network.

Source: www.decet.org.

(2005) bring these insights up to date, and show the links between appropriate spaces for children and brain development. They argue that "nature's empty space is the best environment for young children's learning" (Children in Europe, April, 2005). The same journal quotes the 1995 report of the EC Network on Childcare, which found that in some countries and in many programme types, there existed:

"... clear views about how pedagogic aims should determine the environment for children. In others, buildings were strictly functional, poorly pre-fabricated or inadequately converted from other uses. The report commented that too much emphasis sometimes put on the size of rooms and number of toilets, but pointed out that 'space is liberty' and that children need to have the space to explore their environment, inside and outside" (Children in Europe, April 2005).

In its ten action points for teachers, the well-researched curriculum, "Experiential Education", in Flanders (Laevers, 2003), consecrates no fewer than four points to the organisation of space within the classroom:

● Rearrange the classroom in appealing corners or areas.

● Check regularly the content of the corners and replace unattractive materials by more appealing ones.

● Introduce new and unconventional materials and activities.

● Observe children, discover their interests and find activities that meet these orientations.

It is understood in "Experiential Education" and similar programme that teachers must also interact intensively with the children as they use and move through their spaces. An active adult presence enhances the interest and learning potential of the environment.

Where outdoor space is concerned, yards attached to centres can be planned with more than recreational purposes in mind. Recreation and physical play are of course necessary for young children: they need space to move and enjoy themselves in informal games and play. Moreover, given current concerns about child health and obesity, it seems fitting to build opportunities for vigorous exercise into the child's environment (Penn, 2004). In addition, an outdoor environment intelligently constructed, e.g. a discovery garden – can be a rich learning environment for young children. Plants, trees, flowers, water, clay, sand, mud, animals, insects and birds present innumerable possibilities for manipulation or observation. Nature offers to children high levels of variety and interest, and invites longer and more complex play. Because of its interactive properties, it stimulates observation, discovery, dramatic pretend play, and imagination.

In the outdoors, children learn about the cycle of life through observing living things, and if carefully guided, will learn respect for both life and nature. A natural or intelligently constructed outdoor environment places the focus on "experiencing" rather than "teaching". Young children learn much through discovery and self-initiated activities, particularly when engaged with responsive others. Their learning is multiplied through active involvement – hands-on manipulation, sensory engagement, and self-initiated explorations. Natural elements provide for open-ended play and creative exploration with diverse materials.

In some countries, architectural competitions have proved a useful catalyst for developing appropriate premises, most notably in Denmark, Finland, Germany, Italy and Scotland. In certain parts in these countries, ecologically sensitive designs have been encouraged – where exploration of the environment and nature is easily possible for children and teachers. In Norway, there is also the belief that familiarity with the outdoors, and mastery of one's own climate and weather is important for children. Contact with the natural world contributes to the emotional health of children, to their sense of independence and autonomy. Children benefit from the opportunity to imprint themselves in an experiential way on an environment, to endow it with significance, and to experience their own actions as transformation.

In terms of readiness for school, children need also the concepts and vocabulary to formalise their experience of nature – and to symbolise it in speech, writing, movement and the other languages of children. In the forest and nature schools of the Nordic countries, well-trained professionals ensure the necessary support to children to enable then to re-express their experiences in language and other creative media. Guided by experienced staff, children learn colours, numbers and vocabulary experientially in natural settings, and can experience the basic principles of scientific enquiry in manipulating and collecting natural objects and in observing plant, animal and bird life.

3. Some challenges in the research field

The predominant role of state-sponsored research

In the countries actually undertaking research in the early childhood field, the State is often a major sponsor. Its support to ECEC research is essential, and does much to stimulate needed research and to establish university research chairs in this field. A balanced funding of independent research also needs to be found. State-sponsored research tends to favour research on issues that are important for administrations, such as, programme evaluations, financing, standards and outcomes. In addition to this strong focus on utilitarian issues, state funding of research can also run the danger of becoming partisan – excluding from public funding critical studies or research that runs counter to current orthodoxy. A legislated, national research framework can do much to preserve the place of independent and basic research and ensure fairness in the allocation of research funds.

The dominant role of the English language

Given that paradigms underpinning research questions and approaches are determined by particular understandings of the early childhood field, the current dominant place of English-speaking countries in research dissemination is a concern. The research focuses of the English-speaking countries reflect concepts and definitions of early childhood that do not necessarily correspond to the traditions of other countries or to their aspirations for young children (see the discussion in Bowman *et al.*, 2001 on this subject). In addition, many of the themes circulating in English-language ECEC research are derivatives of education research, as ECEC services are often subsumed under education in the English-speaking world. In this situation, a predominant focus on standards, instruction methods, cognitive outcomes, the mastery of literacy and numeracy skills at an early age, targeted programming and the like tends to occur – themes that may not be of central interest to ECEC in countries with different socio-economic organisation and traditions.

Although Canada plays an important role in communicating North American research to the French-speaking countries, the reciprocal flow of information from European languages towards the English-speaking world remains weak. OECD teams have suggested in several Country Notes that European ministries might wish to consider sponsoring from time to time the publication in English of a compendium of their national ECEC research. For example, some interesting German research on quality, with concepts not commonly discussed in English, has accumulated since 1999, when the national Quality Initiative was launched in Germany. Access to this research would be welcomed by all OECD countries, and would provide an insight into the German social pedagogy tradition and its concepts.

At the European level, the work of Moss and his colleagues has been exemplary in soliciting and publishing research from different countries and language groups. Currently, the bi-annual magazine, *Children in Europe*, is becoming a forum for European practitioners. As it is published in eight language editions, it promotes a strong cross-fertilisation of ideas across different language groups. Likewise, EECERA (European Early Childhood Education Research Association) and the Asian PECERA (Pacific Early Childhood Education Research Association) bring together each year researchers from a wide range of countries and language groups for exchanges on topics important for their regions. More initiatives of this nature are needed.

Expanding participatory modes of research

Another challenge is that much research remains external to practitioners and parents. Already reference has been made to expert-driven data collection, focused more on the immediate needs of government than on building up in-depth knowledge within the early childhood field at local level. Except for a handful of countries, funding of research on process and practice involving practitioners is weak. In Belgium (Flanders), for example, practitioner research is directed towards practical applications that improve quality at the point of services. Through a series of research studies, Flanders has developed a number of participatory measures to assess quality from a child-experience perspective, with the

Box 9.3. **A process oriented self-evaluation instrument for care settings (PSIC) in Belgium (Flanders)**

As part of its policy to improve the quality of child care provision (in Flanders, care signifies full day care for 0- to 3-year-olds, and sessional out-of school provision for older children), *Kind and Gezin*, the national agency responsible for care care policy and settings, decided in 2003 to develop an instrument that could be easily used as a self-assessment tool in early childhood settings. The instrument was developed by the Research Centre for Experiential Education (Leuven University – Belgium), and takes the child and his or her experience of the care environment as the main criterion of quality.

The conceptual framework of PSIC is set firmly within the work carried at by Professor Laevers and his team over the past decades, which has produced the well-known Experiential Education model (see OECD, 2003), now used at pre-school, primary, secondary and higher education levels. At the centre of this framework stand the process variables, well-being and involvement. Well-being is defined by enjoyment, feeling at ease, spontaneity, vitality and, at a deeper level, self-confidence and being in touch with ones own emotions and experience. Involvement refers to engagement, concentration and persistence, intense mental activity, satisfaction of the exploratory drive and being active at the very limits of ones capabilities. Well-being and involvement are regarded as critical indicators for quality. The first is seen as a condition to secure mental health, the second as the condition for deep level learning and development.

The procedure for self-evaluation as defined in the instrument, starts with an assessment of the actual levels of well-being and involvement of the children. For both indicators a five-point scale serves as a tool to code observations conducted in each of the groups that are part of the provision. To collect these scores, a preliminary scanning procedure is used by the head of the setting or by an internal co-ordinator. Individual children are observed one after the other, each for two minutes. In a second stage, the scores are analysed in order to identify the conditions that explain the recorded levels of well-being and involvement of the children. This analysis is guided by a framework in which five dimensions of the pedagogical approach are distinguished: the infrastructure and offer of activities, group climate, child initiative, adult style and organisation. Each of these dimensions is further defined by a series of items that can be rated on a three-point scale ("this is o.k." – "this could be improved" – "this needs to be addressed").

The analysis of the pedagogical approach is a shared activity in which the practitioners as a group work towards setting priorities for action. These serve as a guide to define possible interventions, to implement them and to reflect on their impact. This whole cycle of observation, analysis and action can be repeated several times in a year.

Since 2004, *Kind and Gezin* has introduced PSIC to managers of settings and practitioners through a series of in-service training sessions. Although a full-scale evaluation of the instrument has not yet taken place, significant changes have been observed in the settings using the self-evaluation instrument. Practitioners are also enthusiastic and feel that the use of the instrument contributes to their professional development and teamwork. In their pedagogical approach, they learn to take into account the perspective of the child and because of this, to create optimal conditions for social-emotional and cognitive development.

Source: Kind en Gezin, 2005.

well-being and involvement of children as key guidelines (Laevers, 2003). This research attends, in particular, to developing participatory, self-assessment instruments that may be used by parents and educators to gauge the quality of provision at local level (see Box 9.3).

The practitioner research culture in the Nordic countries is also noteworthy. Professional research is becoming an important part of teacher/pedagogue training, and frequently continues to be practised by pedagogues during their working careers. In some cities, educator-researcher networks assist in identifying practical issues at local level, and disseminate the knowledge generated through published papers. Practitioner research is considered to contribute to professional reflection, team evaluation and on-going quality development. These local research activities are encouraged by new policies to move from a quality control perspective to quality development through information and promotion. Attention is given also to extending "added-value" in these systems, *e.g.* identifying what can be changed attitudinally and practically within the existing system in order to improve quality outcomes for children. The practice of self-assessment and practitioner research is not so deeply rooted in other countries, due perhaps to staff educational levels, or to weaknesses in pre-service education, or to the predominance of family day care, a service type in which training is often insufficient. The "research-policy-practice" paradigm has a better chance of success where training in research methodologies are built into pre-and in-service education courses, linked with promotion or career incentives for staff who engage in these activities.

Dissemination of research

The dissemination of research findings has improved markedly since the publication of *Starting Strong* in 2001. Search and analysis facilities have undergone rapid development, and the multiplication of ECEC Web sites and search engines bring new power to parents and professionals in search of information about children's development, about the programmes available and the policies in place in different localities, regions or nations. However, useful information may remain difficult to obtain because it has not been prepared for different audiences, or access may be restricted to the agency or group who funded the work. The step of moving original research and development to public dissemination through peer reviewed, professional journals, and then to media reports and parent newsletters is often not organised effectively. The work of the Canadian Childcare Resource and Research Unit, in Canada *www.childcarecanada.org* is exemplary in this domain, and provides freely to researchers and practitioners up-to-date information on major policy and research initiatives across a broad range of countries.

Notes

1. The funding policies of the international agencies, such as the World Bank, are deeply influenced by American research results and approaches to early childhood organisation.

2. A *randomised controlled trial* study randomly assigns individuals to a treatment group or to a control group. When certain assumptions are met, the intervention is interpreted as causing group differences on outcomes.

3. Doubts are often raised about the paradigms and methods used in trans-disciplinary research and whether "soft" research should be used in policy-making. Policy makers – particularly in the English-speaking countries – place higher value on large-scale research that generates policy options based on quantified information. Increasingly, RCTs (randomised controlled trials) using massive data inputs are favoured by government agencies. A challenge raised by this development

is that research becomes concentrated in large institutes dependent on government funding, as few independent bodies have the capacity to fund RCTs.

References

Bergstrom, M. and P. Ikonen (2005), "Space to Play, Room to Grow", in *Children in Europe*, Vol. 8, pp. 12-13.

Boocock, S.S. (1995), "Early Education Programs in Other Nations: Goals and Outcomes", *The Future of Children*, Vol. 5(3), pp. 1-19.

Bowman, B.T., M.S. Donovan and M.S. Burns (eds.) (2001), *Eager to Learn: Educating our pre-schoolers*, Committee on Early Childhood Pedagogy, National Research Council Commission on Behavioral and Social Sciences and Education, National Academy Press, Washington DC.

Bronfenbrenner, U. (1986), "Ecology of the Family as a Context for Human Development: Research Perspectives", *Developmental Psychology*, Vol. 22, pp. 723-742.

Bruer, J. (1999), *The Myth of the First Three Years*, The Free Press, New York.

Chatterji, M. (2004), "Evidence on 'What Works': An Argument for Extended-term Mixed-method (ETMM) Evaluation Designs", *Educational Researcher*, Vol. 33(9), pp. 3-13.

Children in Europe (2005), *Curriculum and Assessment in the Early Years*, Issue 9, Children in Scotland, Edinburgh.

Clark Wortham, S. (2004), *Assessment in Early Childhood Education*, 4th Edition, Prentice Hall/Pearson, New York.

Cryer, D., W. Tietze, M. Burchinal, T. Leal and J. Palcois (1999), "Predicting Process Quality from Structural Quality in pre-school Programs: A Cross Country Comparison", *Early Childhood Research Quarterly*, Vol. 14(3), pp. 339-361.

Dahlberg, G., P. Moss and A. Pence (1999), *Beyond Quality in Early Childhood Education and Care: Postmodern Perspectives*, Falmer Press, London.

Dahlberg, G. and P. Moss (2005), *Ethics and Politics in Early Childhood Education*, RoutledgeFalmer, London and New York.

DECET (Diversity in Early Childhood Education and Training) (2006), DECET projects, *http://decet.org/*.

ECS (Education Commission of the States) (1998), *Brain Research*.

EPPE project (1997-2007), "The Effective Provision of Pre-School Education Project. A Longitudinal Study Funded by the DfES", *http://k1.ioe.ac.uk/schools/ecpe/eppe/index.htm*.

Esping Andersen, G. (2002), "A Child-centred Investment Strategy", in G. Esping-Andersen, D. Gallie, A. Hemerick and J. Myles (eds.), *Why we Need a New Welfare State*, Oxford University Press, Oxford, England.

Kilderry, A., A. Nolan and K. Noble (2004), "Multiple Ways of Knowing and Seeing: Reflections on the Renewed Vigour in Early Childhood Research", *Australian Journal of Early Childhood*, Vol. 29(2), pp. 24-28.

Kind en Gezin (2005), *www.kindengezin.be/KG/*.

Laevers, F. (2003), *Experiential Education: Making Care and Education More Effective through Well-being and Involvement*, Leuven, Belgium.

Leseman, P. (2002), "Early Childhood Education and Care for Children from Low-income or Minority Backgrounds", OECD, Paris.

Mahon, R. (2006), "The OECD and Reconciliation Agenda: Competing Blueprints", in J. Lewis (ed.) *Children, Changing Families and Welfare State*, Edwin Elgar.

Meisels et al. (1996), *Assessment of Social Competence, Adaptive Behaviour and Approaches to Learning with Young Children*, Washington, NCES.

Morgan, K.J. (2005), "The Production of Child Care: How Labor Markets Shape Social Policy and Vice Versa", *Social Politics*, Vol. 12, p. 243-263.

Moss, P. (2001), *The UK at the Crossroads: Towards an Early Years European Partnership*, Daycare Trust, London.

National Research Council and the Institute of Medicine (2000), *From Neurons to Neighborhoods: The Science of Early Childhood*, by J. Shonkoff et al., National Academy Press, Washington.

NESS Impact Study (2005), *Early Impacts of Sure Start Local Programmes on Children and Families*, Birbeck, University of London.

OECD (2001), *Starting Strong: Early Childhood Education and Care*, OECD, Paris.

OECD (2002), *Understanding the Brain: Towards a New Learning Science*, OECD, Paris.

OECD (2003), *Babies and Bosses: Reconciling Work and Family Life*, Vol. 2, OECD, Paris.

Osborn, M. (2004), "New Methodologies for Comparative Research? Establishing 'Constants' and 'Contexts' in Educational Experience", *Oxford Review of Education*, Vol. 30(2), pp. 265-285.

Penn, H. (2004), in Country Note for Canada, OECD, Paris.

Rayna, S. and G. Brougère (2000), *Traditions et innovations dans l'éducation préscolaire : perspectives internationales*, INRP/CRESAS, Paris.

Rayna, S. and G. Brougère (2005), *Accueillir et éduquer la petite enfance : les relations entre parents et professionnels*, INRP, Paris.

Schweinhart, L. and J. Montie (2005), "Significant Benefits: The High/Scope Perry Pre-school Study through Age 40", High/Scope Educational Research Foundation, World Bank Presentation, November 17, 2004.

Shonkoff, J.P. and D.A. Phillips (eds.) (2000), *From Neurons to Neighbourhoods: The science of Early Childhood Development*, National Academy Press, Washington DC.

Tobin, J.J., D.Y.H. Wu and D.H. Davidson (1989), *pre-school in Three Cultures: Japan, China, and the United States*, Yale University Press.

Woodhead, M. (1998), "'Quality' in Early Childhood Programs: A Contextually Appropriate Approach", *International Journal of Early Years Education*, Vol. 6(1), pp. 5-17.

ISBN 92-64-03545-1
Starting Strong II: Early Childhood Education and Care
© OECD 2006

Chapter 10

Concluding Policy Observations

In the light of the reviews of the 20 countries, Chapter 10 proposes ten policy areas for consideration in the early childhood field: to attend to the social context of early childhood development; to place well-being, early development and learning at the core of early childhood education and care (ECEC) work, while respecting the child's agency and natural learning strategies; to create the governance structures necessary for system accountability and quality assurance; to develop with the stakeholders broad guidelines and curricular standards for all ECEC services; to base public funding estimates for ECEC on achieving quality pedagogical goals; to reduce child poverty and exclusion through upstream fiscal, social and labour policies, and to increase resources within universal programmes for children with diverse learning rights; to encourage family and community involvement in early childhood services; to improve the working conditions and professional education of ECEC staff; to provide autonomy, funding and support to early childhood services; to aspire to ECEC systems that support broad learning, participation and democracy.

The preceding chapters of this text have given a broad overview of ECEC policy-making in OECD countries. After the foreword, Chapter 1 examined some of the important economic and social contexts that influence early childhood policy, such as child poverty and the changing role of women in service economies. The report then considered in Chapters 2-9 the implications of the eight key elements of policy-making identified in *Starting Strong* (OECD, 2001), and examined how countries have responded to them. Given the mixed picture of progress made across different OECD countries in responding to these proposals (for example, ECEC financing has continued to stagnate since the first reviews, and the recruitment and professional education of staff are still matters of concern), this final chapter identifies ten policy areas that some OECD countries have approached with good effect, and that may merit attention in all countries.

The conclusions to the chapter underline that these policy areas are provisional, drawn, it is true, from a detailed analysis of the OECD reviews but influenced strongly by a governance perspective. They are proposed for consideration by governments and stakeholders, but are not intended to be normalising orientations. A major underlying lesson from the OECD reviews is that sound policy cannot be a quick fix from outside but more a matter of democratic consensus generated by careful consultation with the major stakeholders. Official policy in the early childhood field can meet resistance or be ignored unless it is based on prior consultations with the major stakeholders, and provides a space for local initiative and experimentation.

1. Policy areas for consideration

1. *To attend to the social context of early childhood development*

- An understanding of social and economic context is fundamental for policy-making in the early childhood field. ECEC programmes not only address the care, nurturing and education of young children but also contribute to the resolution of complex social issues. Social inclusion, family well-being, and gender equality can be served through intelligent, comprehensive policies. An integrated vision of early childhood services will promote parental leave entitlements, affordable quality services for children 0 to 3 years; improved wages and work conditions in the ECEC sector, support for parents and measures to promote the social inclusion of low-income and immigrant families.

- Social equity: The reduction of child and family poverty is a precondition for successful early childhood care and education systems. Early childhood services do much to alleviate the negative effects of disadvantage by educating young children and facilitating the access of families to basic services and social participation. However, a continuing high level of child and family poverty in a country undermines these efforts and greatly impedes the task of raising educational levels. Governments need to employ upstream fiscal, social and labour policies to reduce family poverty and give young children a fair start in life.

● Family well-being and involvement: In proposing policy, governments need to attend to the actual needs of contemporary families, *e.g.* to provide and organise services to allow parents the opportunity for full- and part-time employment, according to their wishes. Again, the provision of remunerated parental leave of about a year, followed by a child entitlement to a place in an early childhood service, allows parents to be with their child in the critical first year, supports the family budget and also facilitates the return to employment. This is a human support to family life and bonding that advanced industrial economies should consider. Research suggests that parental leave of at least nine months brings many benefits: lower infant mortality, more breast-feeding, less maternal depression, more use of preventive health care (Chatterji and Markowicz, 2005; Tanaka, 2004, 2005). Unpaid leave does not seem to have the same protective effects (Tanaka, 2005). To link the end of parental leave to an entitled place in a publicly supported early childhood service seems to be a critical element in parental leave policy that adds considerably to the well-being and security of families and infants. Within early childhood services, family involvement should also be encouraged and valued, especially the involvement of low-income and immigrant parents, who face the added challenge of segregation and exclusion.

● Equality of opportunity for women: The United National Convention against All Forms of Discrimination against Women (CEDAW) and other equity agreements at international and national levels require that women should have equal opportunities *to* work and *in* work, in particular, with regard to formal work contracts, equal pay, the right to full-time work and equal promotion opportunities. Flexible work hours and the provision of early childhood services facilitate the reconciliation of work schedules and child-rearing responsibilities. In couple-based families, a more equitable division of child-rearing and household work facilitates women in taking on full-time employment.

2. To place well-being, early development and learning at the core of ECEC work, while respecting the child's agency and natural learning strategies

● Children's learning is a core goal of early childhood services, but within a context that ensures the child's socio-emotional development and well-being. In the past, services for children under 3 have been seen as an adjunct to labour market policies, with infants and toddlers assigned to services with weak developmental agendas. In parallel, traditional early education services have placed children 3 to 6 years old in pre-primary classes, characterised by high child-staff ratios, the employment of teachers without early childhood certification, poor learning environments, and the quasi-absence of care personnel. A challenge exists in many countries to focus more on the child, and to show greater understanding of the specific developmental processes and learning strategies of young children.

● Two principles, selected from the country reviews, seem to support the child's personal learning and well-being:

  ❖ A focus on the agency of the child, including respect for the child's natural learning strategies (Norway, Sweden).

  ❖ Listening, project work and documentation as major means of working with young children (Reggio Emilia).

These approaches counter the tendency of seeing the school as the benchmark and of imposing external targets and skills on young children. The first approach promotes the child's influence and shows confidence in the child's own learning strategies, that is, play, active learning, expression in media other than language, learning from relationships with significant others, informal but intense research on matters of interest or concern to the child. In the second approach, "listening to young children" is also a sign of respect for the child's capacity to guide his or her own learning, when supported by well-trained educators within a rich learning environment. Project themes or specific topics, influenced by the surrounding environment, are determined by dialogue between children and teachers. "The main aim is that children should develop a desire and curiosity for learning, and confidence in their own learning, rather than achieving a pre-specified level of knowledge and proficiency" (Martin-Korpi, 2005). Underlying the approach is also the desire to introduce young children to democratic values and reflexes — learning to live together (adults and children) in a respectful, dialogic manner.

3. To create the governance structures necessary for system accountability and quality assurance

- The experience of the OECD reviews suggests that active governance of the ECEC system leads consistently to improvements in access and quality. To achieve effective steering, central ECEC policy units with critical mass need to be created, supported by legislation and financing powers. The growing importance given to such units can be seen in the United States, where, among others, Georgia (2004), Massachusetts (2005) and Washington State (2006) have brought together under one central agency the varied child care and early education services spread across these states. Active, integrated policy units can also be seen at work in the United Kingdom or in the large Nordic cities, which continuously improve their provision structures, adapting them to new needs and challenges.

- Decentralisation is necessary for effective governance, in particular in a field so localised and diverse as early childhood services. In the decentralisation process, it is important to ensure that early childhood services are part of a well-conceptualised state policy, which on the one hand, devolves real management powers and funding to local authorities and on the other, ensures a unified approach to regulation, staffing criteria, and quality assurance. In the interests of equivalent access and quality across a country, clear agreements need to be reached between central and local authorities about system aims, funding processes and programme standards.

- Support (sub-)systems and agencies are a necessary part of well-performing ECEC systems, for example, active policy units, a training and curriculum authority; independent monitoring and evaluation agencies; a research council, a corps of pedagogical advisors (coaches or inspectors); a monitoring and/or statistical unit, etc. Specialised support agencies undertake specific system tasks and maintain equivalent standards and accountability across large and diverse systems. Many such support structures are already present in education systems, but for lack of expertise, they may not to be fit for purpose in the early childhood field, e.g. inspection corps who lack pedagogical certification in early childhood, or data collection offices that are badly informed about the organisation and statistical needs of the early childhood field.

- There is a need in many countries to have a national research council or research association to organise early childhood research, and improve links between research, policy and practice. This need is felt most keenly in countries where early childhood university research is weak, for example, in countries where the training of educators remains at secondary level, or is confined to colleges of education, devoid of research funding or even a mandate for research. In many countries, the binary nature of tertiary education, which divides institutes into either research or vocational colleges, does not help early childhood research.

- For system accountability and quality development, programme evaluations are necessary. Such evaluations are common in the United States, and recently have been undertaken in Sweden (2004) and the United Kingdom (ongoing: 1997-2007). A national pedagogical framework for early childhood services that includes both agreed goals and a regulatory framework for the different programme types (family day care, centre-based care, integrated services, etc.), facilitates programme evaluation. For many reasons, programme evaluation is more suitable in the early childhood field than the use of standardised tests or assessment scales within early childhood centres, which, in fact, is forbidden or discouraged by many early childhood authorities. Programme evaluations focus on structures (the quality of funding, staffing, programme standards, etc.), processes (both relational and pedagogical) and the achievement of curriculum goals. The centre of attention is on administrative accountability and on the (formative) assessment of the educators' work, rather than on testing young children.

4. To develop with the stakeholders broad guidelines and curricular standards for all ECEC services

- In the last decade, many countries have published national curricula for ECEC services, mostly for services dealing with children over 3 years: England in 1999, 2000, 2002 and 2006; Scotland 1999; France 2002, Ireland 2004; Germany 2004-05 (state-level only); and Mexico 2005. In 2006, Korea published its 7th National Kindergarten for children 4 to 6 years, based on an original curriculum from 1969. Some countries have also developed a common curriculum or pedagogical framework for children 0 to 6 years: Denmark 2004, England 2006, Finland 2003, Norway 1996 and 2006, and Sweden 1998. Such curricula help to promote a more even level of quality across age groups and provision; to guide and support professional staff in their practice; to facilitate communication between staff and parents; and to ensure pedagogical continuity between ECEC and school.

- Many pedagogical frameworks are broader than a traditional curriculum, and may include a regulatory framework and an explicit values base. A guiding framework can define, for example, the legal status, pedagogical goals, pedagogical orientations and the regulatory framework (including programme standards) for early childhood services. When formulated in consultation with educators and other stakeholders, including parent associations, ownership and knowledge of the curriculum is deepened. An important aim is to identify the holistic goals a country wishes to set for its young children. Frameworks, based on consultation, allow local interpretation, identify general quality goals and indicate how they may be attained. They may also encourage the formulation of a more detailed curriculum or pedagogical plan by each centre. Box 10.1 provides an example from Finland, which, from 2000 to 2003, undertook a wide national consultation in order to develop a new ECEC curriculum.

- The consultative curriculum framework will normally name goals to strive for in all areas of development. Readiness for school is important, but so also are objectives such as the health and well-being of young children, socio-emotional development, physical intelligence (motor development, rhythm, dance, music, spatial awareness, art, gestual and symbolic communication, etc.), and shared values, such as democracy, and knowledge and environment, etc.[1] Respect for the successful curriculum implementation, *contextual*

Box 10.1. ECEC curriculum development in Finland 2000-2003

In 2000, STAKES established an expert Steering Committee to prepare a strategic framework draft for a new curriculum for ECEC services in Finland. This framework was based on the best research available and focussed on principles and process rather than on content areas. The opening document was intended as a stimulus for discussion with the various stakeholders, and in particular to institute dialogue with the municipalities, educators and parents. Local perspectives on the framework were collected, analysed and made available across the country on a dedicated Web site. The process provided a country-wide platform around which comprehensive discussions about quality and how to achieve it were generated.

Subsequently, successive drafts of the strategic framework were published on the Web for discussion and critique. In parallel, municipalities were encouraged to train curriculum mentors and to begin dialogue with educators, parents and the elected officials.

At local level, staff and parents have the responsibility of elaborating each centre's more detailed curriculum and pedagogical plan, based on the national pedagogical framework and local municipality objectives. In addition, an individual development and learning plan is drawn up for each child in collaboration with the child's parents. Staff are given support by municipalities to implement the pedagogical plan and to assess their performance regularly.

Source: STAKES (2005).

(*e.g.* funding, regulation and support by the state, etc.), *structural* (*e.g.* programme standards, stimulating learning environments, teacher certification, strong staff supports, professional development, etc.) and *process* variables (the relational and pedagogical skills of educators) are important.

- In several countries, curricular standards refer primarily to programme standards, that is, the structural and process standards required of high quality early childhood provision, such as educator or caregiver qualifications and child-staff ratios. More focused learning standards are named by other countries, but many administrations prefer to see these as goals *to strive for* rather than requirements for young children. More research and socio-cultural sensitivity are needed in this field. What young children are expected to know and do influence strongly the nature of ECEC programming and consequently, the daily experience of young children in services. Consensus is lacking across countries concerning the critical skills, knowledge and pedagogical approaches that serve best the development of young children.

- At classroom level, comprehensive pedagogical skills are fundamental: well-trained educators will attend to the affective involvement of children and their cognitive engagement. They will also use a repertoire of modelling and instructional skills in handling issues of personal safety, health, social interaction (*e.g.* how to share, handle feelings, resolve conflict, etc.) and other knowledge, skills and attitudes considered important by a society for young children to acquire. The role of the educator is critical both in one-to-one interactions with the individual child, and in generating with children and parents learning projects that motivate; that have a certain density and duration; that cover all areas of development; that lead to collaboration, and stretch the knowledge and understanding of each and every child. Educators will recognise also that young children develop along varied paths and at different rates of maturation. Although it is important to have high expectations for children, including what they can know and do, too great an insistence on stantards can undermine the quality of pedagogical work, that is, the relationships and pedagogical activities that support positive outcomes for children.

● A characteristic of the framework documents or curricula that have been formulated in recent years is that they propose broad pedagogical orientations rather than a detailed list of what should be taught or learned.[2] The approach encourages municipalities and centres to generate local programmes, based on the guiding principles and ground rules of the national curriculum. It also allows the use of time-tested curricular approaches, such as Froebel, Montessori, Freinet or Steiner or more recent open framework approaches as High/Scope, Experiential Education, Reggio Emilia, etc. Such openness requires of administrations confidence in their teachers, rather than opting for teacher control and the imposition of detailed early learning goals that do little to foster understanding. Trust in educators and local management is critical in open systems: it is based generally on high quality initial and in-service professional education, and on continuous information flows and support.

5. To base public funding estimates on achieving quality pedagogical goals

● *Starting Strong* (OECD, 2001) noted that while ECEC may be funded by a combination of sources, substantial government investment is necessary to support a sustainable system of high quality, affordable services. In well-functioning systems, governments develop clear and consistent strategies for efficiently allocating resources, including investment in an infrastructure for long-term planning and for ongoing quality initiatives. Without strong government investment and involvement, it is difficult to achieve quality pedagogical goals and broad system aims (social inclusion, child health and well-being, gender equality).

● In the area of funding, the results from the reviews are disappointing (see Figure 5.3 in Chapter 5). As far as can be estimated, investments in services have increased only marginally in most OECD countries in the years from 1999 to 2004, with the exception of Korea, Mexico, the United Kingdom and the United States, where investments have primarily been directed to expanding early education programmes. Apart from the Nordic countries, Belgium, France and Hungary, few countries approach an ECEC investment level of 1% of GDP, as recommended by the former European Commission Network for Childcare. The reality is that investment per child in many OECD countries remains at a rate lower than or roughly equivalent to investments in primary school children, although younger children need more staff than older children, and generally spend eight to ten hours per day in the services they attend. Funding "places" that cannot deliver pedagogical quality seems extraordinarily short-sighted. Other things being equal, investment per child in the pre-school years should be at least equivalent to investment per child in primary schooling.

● Estimates made by a number of authoritative sources (CED, 2006; Kagan and Rigby, 2003; NIEER, 2003; Head Start, 2004; Barnett and Robin, 2006, etc.) indicate that costs per child in a high quality early education service, with child-staff ratios equal to or less than 10 children per trained adult, range from USD 8 000 to USD 14 000 annually per child 1 to 3 years, and between EUR 6 000 to EUR 10 000 per child 3 to 6 years. In terms of hours in services with qualified educators, the best estimates suggest the following figures:

❖ At least USD 5 000 per child, per year for a half-day, school year programme.

❖ Around USD 9 000 per child per year for a full-day, school year programme.

❖ Around USD 13 000 dollars per child, per year for a full-day, year round programme with integrated child care.

These figures suggest public expenditure of between two and three times the amount allocated on average by OECD countries to pre-primary education (OECD, *Education at a Glance*, 2005).[3] In sum, costs per child in ECEC services will become a troubling issue in the years to come. To move from an average OECD investment per child of USD 4 294 (OECD, *Education at a Glance*, 2005) to double that amount (the Head Start investment, including a 20% local contribution) will demand a significant financial effort on the part of governments.

● Various strategies are used in the OECD countries to bring new financing into ECEC systems. Essentially, as in other social and education services, the ratio of qualified educators employed sets the level of ECEC costs. In many cases, countries limit these costs through allowing child-staff ratios in early education to rise (among the second round review countries, child-staff ratios are around 25:1 in France, Ireland, Korea, and Mexico). In the child care sector, costs are contained through the employment of poorly qualified and poorly paid staff – a feature found often in privatised child care in the liberal economies. Neither approach is adequate if the aim is to have services that provide high quality education and care for young children.

● A more positive approach to keeping costs at a reasonable level is to build up team teaching. In some of the Nordic countries, university trained, kindergarten educators form approximately a third (Finland) or half (Sweden) or 60% (Denmark) of the ECEC staff in centres. They work in teams with trained children's nurses or child assistants. In this way, these countries can provide appropriate child-staff ratios and quality programmes. At the same time, staff knowledge and morale are maintained – especially for the lesser qualified staff – by acceptable work conditions and ongoing professional development tied to professional advancement.

● Another possible solution is the "quasi-market" approach, whereby private providers are brought into the provision network through public-private partnerships. This is the predominant approach, for example, in New Zealand. The approach may bring down the costs of services[4] and enlarge the choice of provision offered to parents. It can be acceptable also to ECEC workers, when the state supports a policy of high qualification and a maintains a guaranteed wage structure for all qualified personnel, whatever their place of work. A similar situation pertains in the formal education system, where "government dependents" are contracted to deliver primary and secondary education. In many instances, for example in the Netherlands and Sweden, these providers receive full government funding, but are not allowed to charge fees or (in the case of Sweden) fees greater than those charged by the public services. Energetic government supervision and policy-making is necessary it the quasi-market approach is to work efficiently and equitably.

● A more radical means of lowering costs is for governments to encourage an open, deregulated market in child care services. Up to the moment, results from such policies have not been encouraging (Mitchell, 2002; Prentice, 2005; Cleveland and Krashinsky, 2004, 2005). A possible reason is that state disengagement and a loosening of regulations generally accompany the marketisation of services. In turn, weak government engagement leads to a fragmentation of provision, a decline in quality, and clear inequalities in access and outcomes. The crux of the matter is that when public funding of the child care system takes the form of subsidies paid directly to parents, the subsidies are generally too low to employ high quality staff or to finance system infrastructure. In addition, the steering capacity of governments *vis-à-vis* parents subsidy services is considerably weaker than in funding-to-services systems.

● In recent decades, consumer choice has become a key approach in the theory and practice of market economies. When applied to parents and the early childhood field, the term needs analysis and deconstruction. "Choice for parents" can sometimes hide a patchwork of children's services, since choice in this field bears a close relationship to the quality offered, to the availability of information on quality measures and to the financial means of different families. In this regard, the OECD Country Note for France (OECD, 2004) makes a useful analysis of the discourse on choice and of policies adopted to expand family day care services in lieu of opening more professionally staffed centres. To enhance parental choice is an admirable aim for policy makers, but the discourse becomes less convincing when it promotes the cheapest form of child care, while professional services are cut back or made less accessible to moderate and low-income families.

6. To reduce child poverty and exclusion through upstream fiscal, social and labour policies, and to increase resources within universal programmes for children with diverse learning rights

● A central aim in all countries is to improve the development and learning of young children, and not least, of children from disadvantaged and second language backgrounds. Early childhood programmes make an important contribution to this aim: they contribute to the development of young children and to their school-related achievement and behaviour (Brooks-Gunn, 2003; Thorpe *et al.*, 2004; Takanishi, 2004). They are particularly important for children with diverse learning rights, whether these stem from physical, mental or sensory disabilities or from socio-economic disadvantage. The former group generally constitute about 5% of the child population, and the second group from 2.4% (Denmark) to over 20% (one child in five) in other countries (see Figure 10.1).

● Although providing care and education to children from "at-risk" backgrounds, early childhood programmes cannot substantially address issues of structural poverty and institutional discrimination (Zigler *et al.*, 1996; Dearing *et al.*, 2006). The challenge of reducing child poverty needs also to be tackled upstream by governments through energetic social, housing and labour policies, including income transfers to low-income groups, comprehensive social and family policies, and supportive employment schemes and work training. Preventive, anti-poverty measures can significantly reduce the numbers of children arriving at early childhood centres with additional learning needs.

● While measures of child poverty by UNICEF are based on the income level of parents, other factors are generally present in poverty situations, and serve to aggravate its impacts. Among the factors usually mentioned are unemployment, lone parent families, low education and poor skills of parents, discrimination, high-crime and anti-social neighbourhoods, poor housing, ill health and family breakdown. For this reason, programmes for children from disadvantaged background cannot focus on cognitive development alone, but need a strong concept of pedagogy, that embraces care and nurturing as well as education.

● New thinking about diversity refuses to diagnose young children in terms of what they lack, or on the grounds of race, religion, second language, etc. All individuals have multiple identities and qualities that cannot be captured by broad labels. Each child is talented and competent in his or her own way, and when born into adverse backgrounds

Figure 10.1. **Relative child poverty rates in rich countries**
(source years range from 1997-2001)

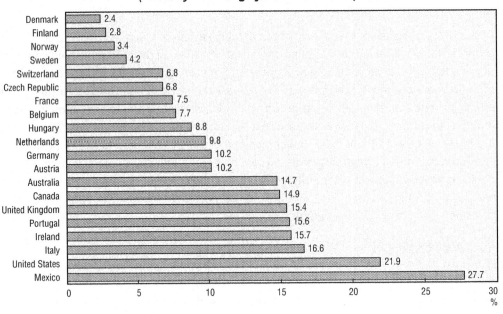

UNICEF comments:

● At the top of the child poverty league are Denmark and Finland with child poverty rates of less than 3%. At the bottom are the United States and Mexico, with child poverty rates of more than 20%.

● Over the latest 10-year period for which comparable data are available, the proportion of children living in poverty has risen in 17 out of 24 OECD countries. Norway is the only OECD country where child poverty can be described as "very low and continuing to fall".

● Higher government spending on family and social benefits is clearly associated with lower child poverty rates.

● Four out of 13 OECD countries for which 1990s data are available saw a decline in earnings for the lowest-paid 25% of fathers. Seven countries saw a decline in earnings for the lowest-paid 10%.

● On average, government interventions reduce by 40% the rates of child poverty that would theoretically result from market forces being left to themselves.

● Governments in the countries with the world's lowest levels of child poverty reduce "market poverty" by 80% or more. Governments in the countries with the world's highest poverty rates reduce "market poverty" by only 10% to15%.

● Variation in government policy appears to account for most of the variation in child poverty levels between OECD countries.

● No OECD country devoting 10% or more of GDP to social transfers has a child poverty rate higher than 10%. No country devoting less than 5% of GDP to such transfers has a child poverty rate of less than 15%. There is no fixed ratio between levels of government support and child poverty rates.

● Many OECD countries appear to have the potential to reduce child poverty below 10% without a significant increase in overall spending.

● In most OECD countries, increases in social spending over the decade of the 1990s appear to have been allocated mainly to pensions and to health care.

● Agreed definitions and measures of poverty are essential if policy targets are to be set and met.

● Relative income poverty measures need to be supplemented by direct measures of material deprivation.

Source: Poverty in Rich Countries, UNICEF Innocenti Research Centre, Florence, 2005.

can show extraordinary inner strength and resilience. Successful programmes do not categorise young children as having developmental or language needs, but believe that these children will learn and develop quickly if given a supportive, pedagogical environment. The inclusion of these children in universal programmes seems the most acceptable and effective approach, as targeting can segregate and stigmatise, and generally fails to provide for many of the children eligible for special programmes (Barnett *et al.*, 2004). At the same time, centres in poor neighbourhoods need enhanced funding and supplementary staff to provide young children with the full range of child development, health and family services that are needed to optimise their learning.

7. To encourage family and community involvement in early childhood services:

- The primary role of families in rearing children is protected in international law. Both the Universal Declaration of Human Rights (1948) and the UN Convention on the Rights of the Child (1989) make explicit reference to their role, *e.g.* the Preamble to the Convention on the Rights of the Child states:

  "The family, as the fundamental group of society and the natural environment for the growth and well-being of all its members and particularly children, should be afforded the necessary protection and assistance so that it can fully assume its responsibilities within the community…"

- Families play a critical nurturing and educational role toward their children, particularly in the early childhood period when brain and personality continue to form (Gerhardt, 2004). As the first educators of children, parents would like to support their child's development and learning. Many are prevented, however, by lack of time, or by underestimating the importance of the responsibility or by not knowing how they can effectively support their children's learning. Yet, it is important that they invest in their children's socialisation and learning, especially in the early childhood period. Along with providing a stable and loving home environment, parents can greatly help their children's learning by monitoring their programmes in early childhood settings, providing them with interesting learning experiences, and in particular, by daily conversation and out-loud reading of children's literature.

- The continuity of children's experience across environments is greatly enhanced when parents and staff-members exchange information regularly and adopt consistent approaches to socialisation, daily routines, child development and learning. Early childhood staff should be trained to listen to parents. They will encourage parents to support the learning of young children, and will share with families the values on which early childhood services are based, including participation and respect for diversity. Staff will endeavour to engage parents in centre activities. Parent engagement will build on parents' unique interest in and knowledge about their children. It will promote positive attitudes toward children's learning, provide parents with information and referrals to other services, and include parents in centre committees and management. Efforts will be made to ensure equitable representation and participation of families from diverse backgrounds.

- Performance standards for the large Head Start project in the US require parent involvement in programme making and curriculum development. Frequent parent-staff meetings must be held, and parents regularly participate in programmes and home-visiting. In addition, Head Start programmes must offer parents educational programmes in health, nutrition and child development; provide information about community resources and encourage parents to participate in community activities. Such programmes not only provide expanded services[5] and referrals where necessary, but can become a space for partnership and the democratic participation of parents.

- In speaking with parents, an awareness of power relations is necessary. Despite the unique interest and knowledge of parents in regard to their children, the tendency to know better than parents is difficult to overcome. Sensitivity to socio-cultural difference is also needed: many families maintain cultural beliefs and behaviours that do not necessarily match the expectations of centres (Ryan and Grieshaber, 2005). To avoid prejudice, gender assumptions, class attitudes or ethnocentrism, more anthropological and socio-historical analysis of child-rearing and early childhood practice is needed (Tobin, 1989; Vandenbroeck, 2006), and of course, more rigorous training of educators and administrators in anti-bias attitudes (Derman-Sparks, 1989).

● Community involvement in the pre-school is growing in importance, not only for providing expanded services and referrals where necessary, but also as a space for partnership and the democratic participation of parents. When opportune, communities and education authorities will provide adult education, information, services and social activities for parents, if possible from the early childhood centre.

8. To improve the working conditions and professional education of ECEC staff

● A strong link exists between the training and support of staff – including appropriate pay and conditions – and the quality of ECEC services. Recent research from the United Kingdom confirms the earlier American research on the subject:

"Settings that have staff with higher qualifications, especially with a good proportion of trained teachers on the staff, show higher quality and their children make more progress... The higher the qualification of staff, particularly the manager of the centre, the more progress children made. Having qualified trained teachers working with children in pre-school settings (for a substantial proportion of time, and most importantly as the pedagogical leader) had the greatest impact on quality, and was linked specifically with better outcomes in pre-reading and social development" (Sylva et al., 2004).

● Close attention needs to be paid to the level of recruitment of early childhood workers, their initial and ongoing training, and even in some countries, to the long-term sustainability of recruitment into early childhood services. Because of poor wages, lack of professional development and long hours, staff turnover can be high and the quality offered to young children clearly inadequate. These shortcomings are exacerbated in child care markets that operate without sufficient state support or regulation.

● In order to enhance the status and quality of early childhood work, governments may wish to consider introducing equal working conditions (salaries, benefits and professional development opportunities) for equivalent qualifications across the early childhood and primary education fields. Care should be taken that dead-end jobs are eliminated from early childhood systems, and that in-service training is linked to career progression and to obtaining further qualification.

● A number of weaknesses in ECEC staff policies emerge from the OECD reviews: low recruitment and pay levels, particularly in child care services; a lack of certification in pre-primary education systems; the feminisation of the workforce; and the failure of pedagogical teams to reflect the diversity of the neighbourhoods they serve. Professional development and the allocation of non-contact time can also be insufficient. Collective agreements between public authorities and staff unions would seem a helpful approach to resolving such issues.

● Opportunities to participate in professional development and in-service training vary greatly across countries, and between education and child care in the split systems. Consistent with trends in other sectors of employment, workers with the lowest levels of basic training are the most likely to have the least access to in-service training (OECD, 1999). Staff in child care, in particular, face many practical challenges to accessing in-service training, *e.g.* to obtain release time with pay to attend courses. In countries where devolution of responsibility to the institutional level has occurred, management staff need to develop budgeting, organisational, and human resources skills. Currently, there are too few professional development opportunities available in the public sector and in parts of the commercial and private sectors.

- Where diversity is concerned, *Starting Strong* (OECD, 2001) commended the requirement of the Head Start programme to employ parents and volunteers from the local community. It also noted the recruitment policies in other countries that encourage the employment of ethnic minority staff. In recent years, the Flemish Community in Belgium has taken a lead, and its "Decree on the recognition of child care services" envisages funding support to municipalities to raise the qualifications of staff in centres and free-time services, but on condition that centres ensure that the workforce should reflect the ethnic mix of the surrounding neighbourhood. In addition, the licensed training centres are requested to facilitate the entry of ethnic minority candidates through assessments that take into account existing training and experience.

- Education is a key to development, and educators are the key to successful early childhood programmes. The realisation is growing that the work of early childhood professional staff is complex, and that sound training is required. Whatever the qualification provided, professional training should include knowledge of child development and learning processes and an awareness of the rights and potentialities of young children. Staff morale benefits greatly from consistent support and engagement in participatory approaches to quality development. The practice of team documentation seems to be particularly suited to bringing research and reflective practice into early childhood services.

9. To provide autonomy, funding and support to early childhood services

- Once the ground rules, goals and outcomes for young children have been decided in the national framework documents and sufficient funding provided, educators and services should have the autonomy to plan, to choose or create curricula that they find appropriate for the children in their care. In many countries, well-trained staff are fully capable of taking responsibility for the programmes and the pedagogical choices that appropriately serve the children in their care. An independent budget and freedom to achieve the national outcomes for children in their own way is motivating for staff and can assist quality development.

- An important element of educator support is continuing professional development, in particular, when a new curriculum or other major change is introduced. The engagement of staff in team management and team planning is also important. Another strategy used successfully in some countries is to form and support local research networks that bring together researchers, local administrators and educators. A primary purpose of these networks is to investigate and resolve local challenges and to raise awareness among educators about the importance of team reflection, supported by data and evidence. Programme quality can also be reinforced by participatory and formative approaches to quality.

- Among the many approaches to participatory quality development, the Reggio Emilia practice of documentation is highly influential. Documentation focuses on the learning and research of young children, irrespective of age, developmental stage, content areas or the like. Through words, drawings, photos, videos, etc., documentation chronicles the ideas and significant learning experiences of children, and the observations made by teachers on the dynamics of children's enquiry and social interactions. In the practice of documentation, teachers are seen as "reflecting practitioners", that is, professionals who continually review and reflect on their own practice and learning theory. The purpose of documentation is not to evaluate children against external norms, either developmental or academic, but to lead to a common reflection by professionals, parents and children on pedagogical practice and the processes of learning.

● Because the path of early child development is highly individual, educators will not undertake the assessment of children's progress through testing or grading.[6] A more supportive and participative approach to children's progress is necessary, for example, through observation, documentation of children's activities, portfolios, parent-child-educator contracts. Early childhood assessments should enhance children's sense of themselves as capable people and competent learners. They should take place within meaningful activities and relationships; families should be part of the process, and assessments should be reciprocal, giving children a say. Programmes will always provide a positive, non-judgmental learning environment so that children can develop their natural curiosity and pleasure in learning.

● In their approach to children, early childhood educators will not require individual children to reach a standard at a given age, but will take an unhurried approach to human development, which is a long process reaching into adolescence and beyond. Learning will be experiential and cover broad areas, as recommended by the NEGP[7] or the 1996 Delors Report (UNESCO, 1996): *learning to be, learning to do, learning to learn and learning to live together.* Educators will identify and respect the natural learning strategies of young children (play, enquiry, exchange with other children, modelling adult behaviour, etc.), encourage project work to match the children's interests and provide them with the experience of working in teams. The well-being and involvement of young children are important daily goals.

● As every child has a right to access formal education in the best possible conditions, educators will ensure preparedness and a smooth transition to school as children approach school age. Several elements combine to provide a smooth transition for children from an early childhood service to school: firstly to ensure free access to a kindergarten or pre-school class for every child from at least one year before obligatory education begins. A second strategy is to prepare children for school through appropriate social and cognitive development programmes, including exposure to literacy and numeracy environments. A third important strategy is to prepare schools for young children. In some countries, government regulations encourage dialogue and partnership between school staff and local early childhood programmes. The aim is to secure a positive transition for each child. The holistic goals and active pedagogies of early childhood are carried into primary school, as well as appropriate outreach to parents. Some of the newer curricula attempt to address this issue, and seek to align the goals, processes and learning areas of kindergarten and the junior school.

10. *To aspire toward ECEC systems that support broad learning, participation and democracy*

● An early childhood system founded on democratic values: The spirit and articles of the United Nations Convention on the Rights of the Child offers a common values base to guide the development of early childhood services in most cultures. Governments will provide services to all children within their jurisdiction without discrimination of any kind (Art. 2). They will direct the education of children toward the fullest development of each child's personality and abilities; towards peace, tolerance and solidarity with others; toward knowledge and respect for the natural environment: and toward the preparation of children for a responsible life in a free society (Art. 29). The first chapter of the Swedish curriculum begins as follows:

"Democracy forms the foundation of the pre-school. For this reason, all pre-school activity should be carried out in accordance with fundamental democratic values. Each and everyone working in the pre-school should promote respect for the intrinsic value of each person, as well as respect for our shared environment.

An important task of the pre-school is to establish and help children acquire the values on which our society is based. The inviolability of human life, individual freedom and integrity, the equal value of all people, equality between the genders as well as solidarity with the weak and vulnerable are all values that the pre-school should actively promote in its work with children."

- In addition to learning and the acquisition of knowledge, an abiding purpose of public education is to enhance understanding of society and encourage democratic reflexes in children. Today, societies seem to be less concerned with such ideals. Reflecting the growing marketisation of public services, consumer attitudes toward education and knowledge are increasing. Individual choice is put forward as a supreme value, without reference to social cohesion or the needs of the local community. In many schools, a focus on "test-prep" knowledge threatens the broad liberal arts tradition that sustained in the past informed and critical thinking. In the early childhood field, an instrumental and narrow discourse about readiness for school is increasingly heard. Faced by this challenge, it seems particularly important that the early childhood centre should become a community of learners, where children are encouraged to participate and share with others, and where learning is seen as primarily interactive, experiential and social. *Learning to be, learning to do, learning to learn and learning to live together* are each important goals for young children.

- It is important that Ministries should become a powerful and influential voice for young children. For example, the new Norwegian *Framework plan for the content and tasks of kindergartens* (Norwegian Ministry of Education and Research, 2006) retains a strong emphasis on local centre autonomy, parental participation and the agency of the child. Following the United Nations Convention on the Rights of the Child, it emphasizes that children are entitled to express their views in all matters that affect them, and that their views should be solicited by staff and taken into consideration. The children's right to influence is also strongly reflected in Section 3 of the *Kindergarten Act* (Norway, 2005), which underlines the children's right to participation: in all aspects of life in the *kindergarten*:

  ❖ Children in kindergartens shall have the right to express their views on the day-to-day activities of the kindergarten.

  ❖ Children shall regularly be given the opportunity to take an active part in planning and assessing the activities of the kindergarten.

  ❖ The children's views shall be given due weight according to their age and maturity.

- Pragmatic results are often sought from parental involvement, such as, to ensure home support for the child's learning. The democratic dimension is also important, that is, the exercise by parents of their basic right to be involved in the education of their children. In neighbourhoods with diverse populations – the majority in many of the major cities – it is helpful to conceptualise the early childhood centre as a space for participation and inter-culturalism, where young children and their families can experience a welcoming, democratic and tolerant environment. Examples from many of the countries reviewed suggest that participation in kindergarten activities is highly affirmative for parents, providing them with recognition and perhaps, the motivation and experience to participate in other community institutions. Continuing dialogue with teachers can also lead to awareness in multi-cultural societies that although different viewpoints on children's education legitimately exist, acceptable compromises between parental viewpoints and the institution can be reached.

- The vision of early childhood services as a life space where educators and families work together to promote the well-being, participation and learning of young children is based on the principle of democratic participation. This principle can also work effectively in management. The decentralisation of management functions to local authorities is a gauge of participatory democracy. At the same time, the experience of the ECEC policy reviews suggests that central governments have a pivotal role in creating strong and equitable early childhood systems, and in co-constructing and ensuring programme standards. In sum, there is a strong case to be made for the ministries in-charge to retain significant influence over both legislation and financing within a framework of partnership. Through these instruments, democratic governments can ensure that wider societal interests are reflected in early childhood systems, including social values such as democracy, human rights and enhanced access for children with special and additional learning needs.

- In this vision of administration, the state can become the guarantor of democratic discussion and experimentation at local level, instead of simply applying policies from the centre (Dahlberg and Moss, 2005). An example is given by the National Agency for Education in Sweden, which, having drawn attention to a misunderstanding of pedagogical documentation in some municipalities, advises dialogue:

"… There is a risk that development plans (or other types of mapping), despite the fact that the original intentions were different, will in practice increasingly focus on the child's shortcomings and become an instrument of normalization, where the individual child is assessed on the basis of what a child should be expected to accomplish… Here, there is a risk of focusing excessively on the individual child's performance, where no account is taken of different conditions of pre-schooling, nor how children function in a social and pedagogical context… It is thus important to have a more meaningful dialogue between those responsible for management functions and the professionals concerning what the terms 'development' and 'learning' mean for children between the ages of 1-6 in the pre-school. Such a discussion would contribute to stimulating the pedagogical development of the pre-school in the future" (Skolvernet, 2004).

The advice coincides with the Reggio Emilia notion of "social management", that is, regular consultation and discussion at community level about the development of young children and the role of the city pre-schools.

2. Concluding remarks

The chapter has outlined ten policy areas for consideration by governments and the main stakeholders in the early childhood field: to attend to the social context of early childhood development; to place well-being, early development and learning at the core of early childhood education and care (ECEC) work, while respecting the child's agency and natural learning strategies; to create the governance structures necessary for system accountability and quality assurance; to develop with the stakeholders broad guidelines and curricular standards for all ECEC services; to base public funding estimates for ECEC on achieving quality pedagogical goals; to reduce child poverty and exclusion through upstream fiscal, social and labour policies, and to increase resources within universal programmes for children with diverse learning rights; to encourage family and community involvement in early childhood services; to improve the working conditions and professional education of ECEC staff; to provide autonomy, funding and support to early childhood services; to aspire to ECEC systems that support broad learning, participation and democracy. Their selection emerges from the themes identified in the first round of the review, and from the subsequent reviews that took place from 2002 to end 2004.

The selection of these policy areas, based on a detailed analysis of the OECD reviews, is influenced strongly by a governance and children's rights perspective. They are proposed for the consideration of ministries and stakeholders, and are not intended to be normalising orientations. Each country has its own strengths and its own concerns, and in general, sufficient expertise to address the major challenges confronting its early childhood services. In addition, a strong lesson emerges from the OECD reviews, namely that early childhood policy should not be elaborated from the outside. A sound policy process must include consensus-building, within a country, based on carefully prepared discussion and collaborative analysis. Official policy in the early childhood field can meet resistance or be ignored unless it is based on prior consultations with the major stakeholders, and provides a space for local initiative and experimentation.

Other equally important or perhaps more synthetic themes, might have been proposed for discussion. For example, population diversity is increasing in all countries, and many societies seem ill-prepared for the cultural and economic changes that diversity will bring. OECD countries are not only a favourite destination for immigration, but also face themselves an accelerated ageing and population decline. Immigrant populations may not have the same qualification levels, and children from minority groups currently fall behind in school (OECD, 2005). Education systems find it difficult to supply sufficient numbers of language teachers in the official language for these children, not to mention tutors in the many foreign languages that immigrant or indigenous children may speak. In the circumstances, it is probable that a major onus will be placed on early childhood services to resolve some of these issues. Public early childhood centres will be expected to prepare diverse children for school, and provide comprehensive and responsive services for families from marginalised or new populations, and assist their social inclusion in local communities. Within this challenge, there is the issue of language: how to immerse young children in the host-country language in a respectful and effective manner. Some hopeful signs are emerging from Reggio Emilia programmes in both Italy and Sweden that this can be achieved through the "100 languages of children", without resorting to literacy and numeracy drilling which does little for the self-esteem or understanding of young children (Barsotti *et al.*, 2004).

Another policy theme that may emerge in coming years is that of globalisation and its effects. For decades, postmodernists have argued that the old certainties of history, culture, structures and knowledge are weakening. Under globalisation, the world is entering a moment of accelerating change in which time and space are compressed, populations move and diversify, science and technology advance with remarkable speed, but within a world marked by wars, trade competition and political instability. Hargreaves (1994), in his critical work on teachers, is at pains to point out that the response of public education systems to this cultural revolution has been deeply anachronistic. Organisation, curriculum and decision-making in schools continue to resemble 19th century patterns: curricula imbibed with the certainties of the past, formal testing of discrete skills and knowledge items, and the "balkanisation" of teachers into separate classrooms and disciplines. The school as an education institution cannot continue in this way. Knowledge is inter-disciplinary and increasingly produced in small networks. In the future, it will be constructed through personal investigation, exchange and discussion with many sources, and co-constructed in communities of learning characterised by team teaching. This approach to knowledge can begin in early childhood and, in fact, fits well with the child's natural learning strategies, which are fundamentally enquiry based and social.

Globalisation raises important questions about education and early childhood services. In particular, there are issues of direction and focus: whether countries should opt for training and the pursuit of technical skills in their education systems in order to survive in a world characterised by ever greater economic competition; or whether to support in young children creativity and openness to others in preparation for a world marked by diversity, the explosion of knowledge and expanding opportunity. Faced by this dilemma, the emergence of two-tiered systems in early education along income lines is a distinct possibility.

Openness to others, and the possibility of learning from and with others is a red thread running through this review. The diverse approaches of countries to the eight themes advanced in *Starting Strong* (OECD, 2001) can help inform policy makers in all countries about the existence of different approaches to services for young children. The meetings organised throughout the reviews have provided opportunities to discuss policies in detail and for countries to learn with each other. The aim is not fast-track policy transfer, as most experienced administrators would agree that policies should not be transferred from one context to another without due reflection and adaptation. Rather, the various processes of this review – with its country visits, reports and regular meetings of the national co-ordinators – open up a range of policy options and allow participants to discuss and question taken for granted assumptions.

Although not all the recommendations of *Starting Strong* (OECD, 2001) have been achieved, most countries participating in the review can look back on their efforts with satisfaction. An overview of the many fine initiatives launched by ministries and other stakeholders can be gleaned from the section in each Country Profile devoted to developments (see Annex E). Some countries have managed to maintain and even expand services under very tight budgetary restrictions, while others have undertaken ambitious system-wide reform. Many challenges, of course, remain. By its nature, early childhood policy is a complex field covering both social and educational issues. Child poverty, family well-being; gender and labour force issues, the professional education and professional development of educators, the needs of diverse children within services, the interface between early childhood services and the school, are all challenges that early childhood policy makers must face while focussing on the central task of enhancing the well-being and learning of young children in services. This complexity is likely to continue. It is hoped that the OECD project has provided information and support to ministries in confronting these challenges, and that it can contribute in the future to strengthening policy-making for families and young children.

Notes

1. In Queensland, Australia, an early education centre, Campus Kindergarten, has undertaken a now decade-long *Sustainable Planet Project* (see Davis *et al.*, 2005). A variety of curriculum and pedagogical activities have led to improvements in play spaces, reduced waste, lowered water

consumption and improved biodiversity with a culture of sustainability now permeating the centre. One way that this is reflected is that children's ideas provide much of the motivation and inspiration for changing to more sustainable practices in the centre. A whole centre project on water conservation, for example, was sparked when pre-schoolers (aged 4 years) articulated their concerns to staff about water use in the sandpit. Creating a culture of sustainability has been a slowly evolving process requiring a large vision that incorporates small but realistic goals and achievements.

2. Although administrators responsible for learning standards in the United States and other countries stress that readiness for school should include broad goals (such as the NAEYC recommendation to "implement a curriculum that fosters all areas of child development – cognitive, emotional, language, physical and social"), a recent analysis of these standards suggests that, in practice, they privilege language and cognitive domains (Scott-Little, Kagan and Frelow, 2005).

3. Such estimates are corroborated by financing costs provided by Head Start, the Nordic countries and several municipalities interviewed during the reviews. In OECD *Education at a Glance* (2005), the average expenditure per child in pre-primary services is unrealistically low as figures provided for Denmark, Finland and Sweden pertain only to the pre-school class or other hours deemed to be "educational".

4. The experience in Sweden with public-private partnerships in the education system shows that costs are not reduced by the introduction of a quails-market, when a guaranteed wage structure for teachers is maintained (Bjorklund *et al.*, 2004).

5. *Expanded services* can be found in kindergarten, pre-school or public pre-primary programmes. Following the definition of NIEER (2004), an expanded service would include at least three of the following: 1) Snacks and at least one meal provided on site; 2) An extended day of seven hours minimum on the same site; 3) Health screening and medical referrals; 4) Regular liaison with social and/or family services for children considered to be at risk.

6. Bowman *et al.* (2000) explain that though there is overlap in the use of the words "test" and "assessment", the former refers to a standardised instrument, formally administered and designed to minimize all differences in the conditions of testing. Assessments tend on the contrary to use multiple instruments (observations, performance measures, interviews, portfolios and examples of children's work, etc.) and take place over a longer period of time. The term evaluation is generally used with reference to programmes. In national evaluations, it is generally considered legitimate for a national agency to test a small sample of young children across the broad developmental domains defined in curriculum, but with due regard for the children and the interpretation of results.

7. The American National Education Goals Panel (NEGP) – dissolved in 2002 – was a bipartisan and intergovernmental body of federal and state officials created in July 1990 to assess and report state and national progress toward achieving the National Education Goals. In 1997, the NEGP identified five goals as contributing to the young child's overall development and later success in school, viz. health and physical development; emotional well-being and social competence; positive approaches to learning; communication skills; and cognition and general knowledge.

References

Barnett, W.S. and K.B. Robin (2006), *How Much Does Quality Pre-school Cost?*, NIEER, Rutgers, N.J.

Barnett, W.S., K. Brown and R. Shore (2004), *Universal Versus Targeted Debate. Should the United States have pre-school for all?*, NEIIER pre-school Policy Matters, April.

Barsotti *et al.* (2004), *Multiculturalism and Communication: Interim Report*, Stella Nova pre-school, Stockholm.

Bowman, B.T., M.S. Donovan and M.S. Burns (eds.) (2001), *Eager to learn: Educating our pre-schoolers. Committee on Early Childhood Pedagogy*, National Research Council Commission on Behavioral and Social Sciences and Education, Washington DC, National Academy Press.

Bjorklund, A., P.A. Edin, P. Frederiksson and A. Krueger (2004), *Education, Equality and Efficiency: An Analysis of Swedish School Reforms during the 1990s*, IFAU Report, No. 1.

Brooks-Gunn, J., W. Han and J. Waldfogel (2002), *Maternal Employment and Child Cognitive Outcomes in the First Three Years of Life*, The NICHD Study of Early Child Care, Child Development, 73(4), 1052-1072.

Brooks-Gunn, J. (2003), "Do you Believe in Magic? What we Can Expert from Early Childhood Intervention Programs", *Social Policy Report*, XVII (1), 3-7.

CED (2002), *pre-school for All: Investing in a Productive and Just Society*, New York, New York Committee for Economic Development.

Chatterji, P. and S. Markowitz (2005), "Does the Length of Maternity Leave Affect Maternal Health?", *Southern Economic Journal, 72*(1), 16-41.

Cleveland, G. and M. Krashinsky (2004), *The Quality Gap: A Study of Non-Profit and Commercial Child Care Centres in Canada.* Toronto, Ontario: University of Toronto at Scarborough.

Cleveland, G. and M. Krashinsky (2005), *The Non-profit Advantage: Producing Quality in Think and Thin Child Care Markets,* Toronto, Ontario: University of Toronto at Scarborough.

Dahlberg, G. and M. Moss (2005), *Ethics and Politics in Early Childhood Education*, RoutledgeFalmer, London and New York.

Davis, J.,, M. Gibson, R. Pratt, A. Eglington and N. Rowntree (2005), *Creating a Culture of Sustainability: From Project to Integrated Education for Sustainability at Campus Kindergarten*, in Walter Leal Filho (ed.), *Handbook of Sustainability Research*, Vol. 20, pp. 563-594, Germany: Peter Lang.

Dearing, E., D. Berry and M. Zaslow (2006), Poverty during Early Childhood, in K. McCartney and D. Phillips, *Blackwell Handbook of Early Childhood Development*, pp. 399-423.

Edwards, C., L. Gandini and G. Forman (1993), *The Hundred Languages of Childhood*, Norwood NJ: Ablex.

Gerhardt, S. (2004), *Why Love Matters. How Affection Shapes a Baby's Brain*, London: Palgrave Macmillan.

Hargreaves, A. (1994), *Changing Teachers, Changing Times: Teachers' Work and Culture in the Post-modern Age*, London, Cassell.

Head Start (2004), *Research and Statistics, www.acf.hhs.gov/programs/hsb/research/2004.htm*.

Kagan, S.L. and E. Rigby (2003), *Policy matters: Setting and Measuring Benchmarks for State Policies. Improving the Readiness of Children for School. A Discussion Paper.* Washington, DC, Center for the Study of Social Policy, Washington, DC. February.

Martin-Korpi, B. (2005), "The Foundation for Lifelong Learning", in Children in Europe Issue 9, September 2005: *Curriculum and Assessment in the Early Years*, Edinburgh, Children in Scotland.

Masse, L.N. and W.S. Barnett (2003) *A Benefit Cost Analysis of the Abecedarian Early Childhood Intervention*, NIEER, Rutgers, N.J.

Mitchell, L. (2002). *Differences between Community Owned and Privately Owned Early Childhood Education and Care Centres: A Review of the Evidence.* New Zealand Council for Educational Research Occasional Paper 2002/02. Wellington, NZ: NZCER.

NAEYC (2006), National Association for the Education of Young Children, *New NAEYC Program Standards and Accreditation Criteria, www.naeyc.org/accreditation/standardscriteria/*.

NIEER (2005), *2005 State pre-school Yearbook*, by W.S. Barnett, J.T. Hustedt, K.B. Robin and K.L. Schulmann, *http://nieer.org/yearbook/*.

Norway (2005), Act No. 64, June 2005, relating to Kindergartens, Oslo, Government Publications.

Norwegian Ministry of Education and Research (2006), *Framework Plan for the Content and Tasks of Kindergartens*, Oslo, Author.

OECD (1999), Training of Adult Workers in OECD Countries: Measurement And analysis. *Employment Outlook 1999* (pp. 133-175), Paris: Author.

OECD (2001), *Starting Strong: Early Childhood Education and Care*, Paris, OECD.

OECD (2004), *Country Note for France*, Paris, Author: *www.oecd.org/document/3/0,2340,en_2649_201185_27000067_1_1_1_1,00.html*.

OECD (2005), *Education at a Glance*, Paris, OECD.

Prentice, S (2005). *For Profit Child Care: Past Present And Future,* Childcare Resource and Research Unit, Occasional Paper 21, Toronto, Canada.

Rinaldi, C. (2006), *In dialogue with Reggio Emilia: listening, researching and learning*, London and New York, Routledge.

Ryan, S. and S. Grieshaber (2005), Shifting from Developmental to Postmodern Practices In Early Childhood Teacher Education. *Journal of Teacher Education, 56*(1), pp. 34-45.

Scott-Little, C., L. Kagan and V.S. Frelow (2003), "Creating the Conditions for Success with early Learning Standards: Results from a National Study of State-Level Standards For Children's Learning Prior to Kindergarten", *Early Childhood Research and Practice*, 5(2), pp. 1-21.

STAKES (2005), National Research and Development Centre for Welfare and Health, Helsinki: Information supplied to the OECD by the STAKES Early Childhood Education and Care Team.

Sylva, K., E. Melhuish, P. Sammons, I. Siraj-Blatchford and B. Taggart (2004), *The Effective Provision of Pre-School Education [EPPE] Project. Final Repor,*. November, London: Sure Start.

Takanishi, R. (2004), "Levelling the Playing Field: Supporting Immigrant Children from Birth to Eight", Children of Immigrant Families, 14(2) pp.61-79, *www.future of children.org.*

Tanaka, S. (2005), "Parental Leave and Child Health Across OECD Countries", *Economic Journal*, Vol. 115, No. 501, pp. F7-F28, February.

Thorpe, K., C. Tayler, R. Bridgstock, S. Grieshaber, P. Skoien, S. Danby and A. Petriwskyj (2004), "Preparing for School", *Report of the Queensland Preparing for School Trials 2003/4*, Department of Education and the Arts, Queensland Government, Australia, *www.education.qld/etrf.*

UNESCO (1996), *Learning: The Treasure Within*, J. Delors (ed.), Paris, Author.

UNICEF (2005), *A League Table of Child Poverty in Rich Nations*, Innocenti Report Card, Florence.

Vandenbroeck, M. (2006), Globalisation and Privatisation: the impact on child care policy and practice, Bernard van Leer Foundation, The Hague, Netherlands.

Zigler, E., S.L. Kagan and N. Hall (eds.) (1996), *Children, Families and Government: Preparing for the Twenty-First Century,* Cambridge University Press, New York.

ISBN 92-64-03545-1
Starting Strong II: Early Childhood Education and Care
© OECD 2006

ANNEX A

Terminology Used in the Report

- *Accreditation* is a voluntary process proposed to providers by government, agencies or professional associations in order to help them achieve higher standards in key domains of early childhood programming. The Quality Assurance Accreditation Process in Australia and the NAEYC accreditation programme in the United States are examples. Centres wishing to be accredited must undergo evaluation from the agency in charge to confirm that they have reached the quality standards formulated by the agency, which, in general, far exceed minimum licensing standards.

- *Ages of children: Starting Strong II* again follows the convention set by the European Union Early Child care Network and adopted in *Starting Strong*. Age digits refer to birthdays: *e.g.* 1-3 years covers young children from their first birthday (12 months) to their 3rd birthday (36 months); 3- to 6-year-old children means children from their third (36 months) to their sixth birthday (72 months only). It does not include children who are six years and one month, who are classified as 6-year-olds and who are in schools in most countries.

- *Certification* or teacher licensing: A process used in the United States and some other countries, where teachers – after obtaining the minimum degree or diploma – should also obtain a certificate or license to teach. A significant number of personnel in early childhood services remain uncertified. A similar process exists in Europe, but certification is generally part of the degree or training course, and takes the form of specialised didactics or methodological modules, with *practica* in the early childhood services.

- *Children's services.* The main children's services referred to in *Starting Strong II* are:
  - *Family day care (FDC):* Family day care exists when a child (or children) is (are) looked after in the private home of a carer on a sessional, half-day (less than 20 hours per week) or full-day basis. The carer may be self- or municipally employed. Family day care is regulated and licensed, according to the country, to varying degrees (see licensing regimes below). The term also may include a licensed *child minder*, who looks after a child in the child's own home. In many countries, child-minding in the child's home is considered a private agreement and is not subject to any regulation.
  - *Centre-based ECEC:* Centre-based ECEC is collective (more than 5 children) early education and care for young children from 6-12 months to 6 years, distinguished from services provided in households or family settings. The centres may be public or private, and normally cater to toddlers and/or older children until entry into

kindergarten or perhaps up to school age. Many countries still operate a split between services for children 0-3 years and those for children 3-6 years, but current trends favour *age-integrated centres*. Programmes are typically full-day or part-day (less than 20 hours per week), and are in all cases conducted by a minimum number of qualified professionals. Centres open either for the academic year only (with scheduled school holidays), or for the longer work year, that is for about 11 months. In our definition of centre-based ECEC, we include crèches, kindergartens, pre-school (normally 3-6 years) and publicly provided pre-primary classes, but not playgroups, or out-of-school care.

❖ *Crèche:* A crèche is a professional centre-based service primarily for infants and toddlers.

❖ *Kindergarten or pre-school programmes* are professional centre-based ECEC programmes, primarily for children from 3-6 years, with a predominantly educational aim. Kindergartens attempt to nurture holistic development, learning dispositions and in some countries specific competences in pre-defined learning areas. Kindergartens may also have a "readiness for school" objective and may focus on pre-literacy and numeracy activities. Kindergarten and pre-school programmes are distinguished from playgroups in being daily, more focussed on education, and with more highly qualified staff.

❖ *Out-of-school provision, after-school care or free-time services for children.*[*] "Free-time" is a professionally organised care service for children aged 3-12 years before and/or after early education/primary school hours. The service can take place either on the school premises or outside.

❖ *Playgroup:* A playgroup is a service offering toddlers (and perhaps, older children) the opportunity – generally on a sessional basis, once or twice a week – to play with each other, supervised by a qualified playgroup supervisor or parent. Large differences exist between countries with regard to regulation, programme, staff qualifications, pedagogical supervision, etc., in this type of programme.

❖ *Public pre-primary education* (and *kindergarten* in Australia and the United States) is defined as the initial stage of *organised instruction*, designed primarily to introduce young children to a school-type environment. This professional service is generally free, funded directly by the Ministry of Education or local school district. Classes are conducted by fully trained teachers, but can be characterised – particularly in European countries – by unfavourable child-staff ratios and a pedagogy oriented to the acquisition of pre-defined competences in cognitive fields.

❖ *Comprehensive services:* A comprehensive services approach to early childhood education and care goes beyond curriculum and activities for children and focuses also on the home and community environments. Typically, a comprehensive services centre works in co-operation with other community services and pays particular attention to parents. The centre will provide when necessary courses and advice on parenting (in particular, how to support child development), employment and job training, and leisure activities. See also the definition of *expanded services* below.

---

[*] These services are known in various countries as out-of-school provision, after-school care, and leisure-time services. The term "free-time service" underlines that this time is *free* time for children, to be used for recreation and leisure (as well as for homework or sports), taken in secure and stimulating environments and facilitated by trained personnel.

● *Early childhood education and care (ECEC):* The phrase is used throughout the volume as a global term encompassing all arrangements providing care and education for children under compulsory school age, regardless of setting, funding, opening hours or programme content. ECEC includes also out-of-school provision (OSP) for young children up to their 12th birthday. When referring to government policy, ECEC also encompasses parental leave (with a replacement income) and family-friendly policies, as these policies have a major impact on early childhood provision, promote the involvement of parents with their children, and assist towards gender equality. "Education" and "care" are combined in the phrase to underline that services for young children should combine care, developmental and learning opportunities, and that education and care should not exist apart in approaches to young children. An alternative term is *pedagogical service* as used in Nordic and Central Europe, which denotes a service for young children that combines care, upbringing and learning. (The term raises some difficulties in English, as the word "pedagogical" is understood more narrowly as referring to "teaching" or "teaching methods" – see note on "pedagogy" below.) Another term growing in popularity, particularly in the United States, is *early childhood education* (ECE), used in an effort to promote learning in all services and as a claim on universal services (White, 2002).

● *Expanded services* can be found in kindergarten, pre-school or public pre-primary programmes. Following the definition of Barnett (2003), an expanded service would include at least three of the following: 1) snacks and at least one meal provided on site; 2) an extended day of seven hours minimum on the same site; 3) health screening and medical referrals; 4) regular liaison with social and/or family services for children considered to be at risk. A further degree of outreach to other services is *provided* by *comprehensive services* (see above).

● *Formal/informal services:*

   ❖ *Informal services* are services supplied on a non-monetary basis – generally in the child's home, but also in the carer's home – by other family members, relatives, family employees and friends.

   ❖ *Formal services* are services supplied on a paying basis by unlicensed or licensed persons or centres.

● *Full-day, half-day and sessional services:* Definitions of full-day, half-day and sessional services differ across countries. We have chosen one that is commonly used. A service that is *full-day* is in operation from 25 to 50 hours per week, that is, a child is considered to be in full-time ECEC if s/he is present at least five hours per day; *half-day* is attendance from 12.5 hours weekly to 25 hours, that is, a child should be in attendance for at least 2.5 hours daily over five days; attendance for less than 12.5 hours weekly is described as *sessional*. Often associated with these terms are: *academic year* (normally 8-10 months only) and *working year* (11 months in most OECD countries).

● *Income groups:* Income groups within a population are often divided into quintiles. This text refers to them in the following terms: very high income groups; high income groups; mid-income groups; moderate income groups and low-income groups.

● *Integrated services* are services for young children delivered in co-operation with health, social and human services, in particular in areas of disadvantage. The definition and concept overlap to some extent with the notion of *expanded services* (see above).

● *Licensed/unlicensed services:*

  ❖ *Unlicensed* child care takes place without notification or reference to the relevant public authorities. In most OECD countries, unlicensed *centres* are rare, and generally illegal. Unlicensed family day care is, however, common, the most usual form being child care provided by unregulated, untrained local child minders. The activity is often in the "grey-market"/cash economy, and some countries, such as Denmark, have made the practice illegal. Where unlicensed child care continues to exist, consumers are more likely to be moderate income families, especially in countries where government investment in child care has been weak and licensed subsidised services are scarce or confined to low-income groups. More affluent families, with higher educational levels, tend to choose centre-based, licensed services for their children (see for example, Hirshberg, Huang and Fuller, 2005).

  ❖ *Licensed* child care centres include services that have notified the recognised licensing authority, and have been certified as acceptable (sometimes only from a child density, and/or fire and health hazard perspective – see below). The three major types of licensed services are: *family day care* (FDC), *centre-based ECEC* (including crèches, kindergarten, early education, age-integrated services, pre-primary classes, etc.), and *out-of-school provision.*

● *Licensing regimes:* Licensing regimes differ widely from country to country. OECD reviews have identified four levels or degrees of licensing:

  ❖ Level 1: Registration with an initial and health and safety check.

  ❖ Level 2: Registration with annual health and safety checks.

  ❖ Level 3: Registration with annual checks, obligation to follow an official curriculum or developmental programme, and a minimum staff certification requirement.

  ❖ Level 4: Registration with annual checks, curriculum or quality standards, staff certification, in-training and pedagogical supervision ensured regularly by an accredited supervisory body.

● *Pedagogue, pedagogy and pedagogical:* In English, the word "pedagogue" means a teacher (and often a pedantic teacher); "pedagogy" normally means "a teaching method" and the adjective "pedagogical" can be interchanged with "didactic". The connotations attached to these words in the social pedagogy tradition of the Nordic and Central European countries are broader and more positive: "pedagogy" is an approach to young children that addresses the whole person and the pedagogical relationships is one that includes integrally care, upbringing and education.

● *Service integration:* Occurs when services are merged *structurally* across government departments, and enjoy common funding, regulation and staffing regimes. In such a move, *conceptual* integration is also desirable, which involves shared goals and values, as well as common understandings of children, children's services and learning.

Readers will also note expressions such as *child care services* and *early education services.* Such terms are difficult to avoid in English, as a longstanding division between child care and early education still operates in most of the English-speaking world. In this review, five of the 20 countries were predominantly English speaking.

Information in figures, tables and boxes

Throughout the text, many figures, tables and boxes are presented, a full listing of which can be found in the table of contents. Care has been taken to ensure that the information they contain is accurate and up-to-date. The sources used were chosen for their reliability, and participating countries have been given the opportunity to cross-check the data. By its nature, however, the ECEC field is a complex one. Due to the variety of agencies involved, the diversity of services, both licensed and unlicensed, the simultaneous enrolment of the same child in different child care and early education settings, and the well-known weaknesses of data collection in the early childhood field, it can be difficult to have a clear picture of provision and its effectiveness in some countries.

The boxes in the text are taken from the OECD Country Notes, or derived from new information supplied by countries. The purpose of including them is to lighten a descriptive text and to provide readers with further knowledge of individual countries. They are not intended to be taken as examples of "best practice" that can be applied in a de-contextualised way outside their country of origin.

References

Barnett (2003), *The State of Preschool*, National Institute of Early Education Research (NIEER), N.J.

Hirshberg, D., D. Huang and B. Fuller (2005), "Which Low-income Parents Select Child-care? Family Demand and Neighborhood Organizations", *Children and Youth Services Review*, Vol. 27(10), CA, pp. 1071-1162.

White, L.A. (2002), "Ideas and the Welfare State: Explaining Child Care Policy Development in Canada and the United States", *Comparative Political Studies*, Vol. 35(6), pp. 713-743.

ANNEX B

The Scope and Methodology of the ECEC Review

Early in the process, the OECD Secretariat and the participating countries reached agreement about the framework, scope and process of the review, and identified the major policy issues for investigation. As was agreed, the review adopted a broad, holistic approach concerning early child development and learning so as to examine thoroughly what children experience in the first years of life. To this end, the review studied policy, provision and programmes for children from birth to compulsory school age, including the transition period from ECEC to primary schooling. Consideration was also given to the influence of families, communities and other environmental influences on children's early learning and development, and several forms of comprehensive programming explored. Concerns about *access, quality,* and *equity* were explored in each country, with a focus on policy development in the following areas: governance, regulations, staffing, programme content and implementation, family engagement and support, funding and financing. A particular focus was maintained on fair and equitable access for children in need of special attention: children with organic disabilities; children with additional learning needs stemming from disadvantaged socio-economic milieus, or from indigenous and second-language backgrounds. A focus was maintained too on services for children under 3. As the accumulating brain research testifies, it is equally critical for these younger children to have access to high quality services, where their great potential for reasoning, creativity, language development and social interaction can be developed (Goswami, 2004; Lindsey, 1998, Ramsburg, 1997, Shonkoff and Phillips, 2000). In their visits to ECEC centres, reviewers focused on the basic structural indicators of quality and on the overall issue of the well-being of young children and their free involvement in learning.

The review objectives

The goal of the review was to provide cross-national information to improve policy-making and planning in early childhood education and care in all OECD countries. With the aid of ministries and the major stakeholders in each country, the review aimed to:

- distinguish and investigate the ECEC contexts, major policy concerns, and policy responses to address these concerns in participating countries;
- explore the roles of national government, decentralised authorities, NGOs and other social partners, and the resources devoted to planning and implementation at each level;
- identify and evaluate feasible policy options suited to different contexts;
- highlight particularly innovative policies and practices; and

- contribute to the OECD INES (Indicators of Education Systems) project by identifying the types of data and instruments to be developed in support of ECEC information collection, policy-making, research, monitoring and evaluation.

Following the publication of *Starting Strong* in 2001, the OECD held a series of international workshops on issues pertinent to ECEC policy. These meetings were organised by the Secretariat, in co-operation with a host country, and were held specifically for the national early childhood co-ordinators; they provided an opportunity for administrators to discuss common challenges in the policy-making field. These workshops addressed, the particular role of ECEC for children from low-income or minority backgrounds (Oslo, June, 2002), the need for additional data in the field of early childhood education (Paris, October, 2002), the financing of ECEC services (Rotterdam, January, 2003), and outstanding pedagogies in the ECEC field (Stockholm, June, 2003).[1]

According to meeting feedback received, this systematic exchange of ideas on policy issues and their implementation was helpful and allowed participants to establish their own "critical friend" networks. Comparative policy research in the early childhood field is still relatively rare and difficult to access. In many countries, early childhood policy-making units at ministerial level still lack the critical mass to engage in regular meetings with the research community. Like the practitioners they direct, time may not be written into contracts for professional development and involvement in research activities. The meetings organised by the OECD provided an opportunity for administrators to meet with some leading researchers in the early childhood field and to continue their engagement with international comparative research.

The review procedures

The procedures of the OECD review were similar for each country. Five phases can be distinguished: *i)* a preparatory phase in which the theoretical framework of the review is worked out and agreed; *ii)* preparation of the core quantitative and descriptive information for the review, which is prepared by each country and written up in its Background Report; *iii)* the review team visit and evaluation; *iv)* the discussion, publication and dissemination of the evaluation report, or Country Note as it was named; and *v)* the writing and dissemination of a final, synthetic report such as the present text.

The preparatory phase is critical as during it, the theoretical framework, review procedures, and the areas to be covered by the Background Report (the preliminary report on early childhood policy and organisation prepared by each country before a review takes place) are explained and agreed upon. This phase requires a short pre-visit from the Secretariat to the country to be reviewed, in order to discuss with ministries the documents governing the OECD early childhood review, namely, the content framework (OECD, 1998), the questionnaire to guide the preparation of the Background Report, and the various protocols governing meetings and visits (OECD, 1998).

The production of the Background Report is the key output of the second phase of the review, namely, the preparation of the core quantitative data and descriptive information necessary for the visiting review team. The ministry responsible for this task is free to organise its research and writing as it sees fit. The Secretariat advises, however, a wide consultation of stakeholders about the preparation of the Background Report, and a participatory approach to its writing. Broad consultation promotes awareness of the review, provides ownership of the national report, and leads to dialogue between stakeholders and greater objectivity (Gallagher, Clifford and Maxwell, 2004; Moss, Owen and Stantham, 1998). Another aspect suggested by the Secretariat is that the report should be descriptive and based on the best data available. External review teams need hard data before undertaking the more hazardous task of interpretation and evaluation.

The third phase is the actual field visit, which is undertaken to ensure that data interpretation by the external experts corresponds – to an acceptable degree – to the reality on the ground. Occasions for misunderstanding abound, both in terms of context and concepts. For example, it can be surprising for outside reviewers to visit a country such as Norway, and find little discussion of compensatory educational programming for young children. At first sight, this might indicate insensitivity to issues of disadvantage. However, a visit to the Norwegian *barnehager* (kindergartens) suggests the contrary. Although there are few children from low-income backgrounds, they receive priority in enrolment and free places. Because of effective income redistribution policies at national level, Norwegian society prevents child poverty before it becomes a serious issue in the *barnehager* (kindergartens). The targeting of low-income groups is not therefore a priority focus for Norwegian ECEC policy, even though public *barnehager* are considered a front-line preventive service for young children who may be at-risk, and additional resources and educators are supplied to centres receiving more children from migrant or low-income families.

Another source of possible misunderstanding stems from translation inaccuracies between the national languages and English. Here again, field visits are critical in avoiding misinterpretation. Frequently, the concepts and terminology used by other language groups may have no near equivalent in the English language and can be poorly translated. Examples are the key concepts "pedagogy" and "pedagogue", which in English have the meaning of "the art or science of teaching" and "a pedantic or dull teacher". Frequently, the words are translated into English as "education" and "teacher", which is equally misleading, and can lead to a basic misunderstanding of the philosophy and practice of early childhood centres in the Nordic and Central European countries. Field visits to these countries reduce the probability of such misunderstandings.

The review methodology

The methodology of the review is both quantitative, based on statistical data, and phenomenological, that is, based on actual visits to countries to experience their early childhood systems in a personal and experiential manner. Much care was given to choosing review team members with strong policy backgrounds in early childhood administration and research – sometimes with an intimate knowledge of the country being visited. The reviewers chosen conducted interviews with ministry officials, stakeholder groups, national researchers, and the personnel of the early childhood services that they visited. Because of the time available for review visits, the sample of persons interviewed and the number of early childhood services observed were relatively small – on average: from 15 to 20 stakeholder interviews per visit, one hundred or more non-directive, individual interviews by review team members combined, and visits to 20 to 25 centres in each country. The information obtained from these sources was rich and varied, as it was gathered essentially from professionals with long experience of the management of national systems and/or of conducting programmes on the ground.

However, what is concluded from observations in a centre or understood from a qualitative interview incorporates the subjectivity of the observers and their personal values, which may be effective or ineffective in refining and validating evidence (Howe, 2005). Conclusions must therefore be validated from other sources. The OECD review methodology links quantitative data with observations, moderating the individual subjectivity of reviewers and maintaining a level of reliability through triangulation, semi-directive group interviewing and other measures (Elliott, Fischer and Rennie, 1999; Richards, 1985). During the OECD review, triangulation of what was seen and heard was achieved through:

- regular cross-checking of individual team member impressions against the observations of other team members;
- cross-checking of the statements of government officials and interviewees against other opinions, and against hard data already provided to the team either from OECD sources or from the country Background Reports.

Review teams found that open exchanges and ongoing triangulation were necessary if a balanced evaluation of a socio-cultural situation was to be achieved. At times, during the review, the method was reinforced by semi-directive interviewing, that is, through using a framework of questions that focuses the enquiry on pre-defined areas, such as, the core elements of policy-making, *e.g.* governance and financing; regulations and patterns of operation; staffing and work conditions. Such a framework is useful in comparative work, and helps to ensure that the most important areas in early childhood policy are covered.[2] In addition, if communicated in advance, a framework allows interviewees – for whom English was rarely their first language – to prepare information and answers more fully. At the same time, care was taken to ensure that questions remained sufficiently general to allow information from outside the frame to be added. The process was greatly helped by the positive attitudes of national officials and their willingness to provide information to the OECD teams.

The fourth phase in the OECD review comprises the discussion, publication and dissemination of the evaluation report, or Country Note as it is named. In general, ministries were open and accepting of the OECD evaluations, and after discussion, proposed only minor changes to the draft Country Notes submitted for their approval. On three occasions out of the 20 countries reviewed, ministries or agencies showed less enthusiasm for the publication or dissemination of reports.

Dissemination of reports depended on the countries themselves. In the majority of cases, ministries went to the trouble of publishing the OECD documents, launching them officially in the presence of a minister or other high-ranking official. How the reports were used to forward the agenda for children again depended on the country. Some ministries used the reports to promote parliamentary discussions and to push through reforms and new policies for young children. In many cases, as the various chapters of this text show, the reviews helped countries to renew attention to certain aspects of policy, to adopt better practices and move towards established standards in the early childhood field.

The comparative report

The fifth stage in the OECD review process is the writing and publication of the final comparative report. The aim of this report is to communicate the experiences and "findings" of the reviews, and to draw some lessons of use to *all* participating countries.

Cross-national comparative work can provide countries with an insight into common trends in policy and system organisation. If comparison does not lead to emulation, at least it can lead to critical thinking and a consciousness of the relativity of one's own cultural and family norms. Moreover, if studied carefully, experiences from abroad can save time and costly piloting, although saving time does not absolve local policy makers from analysing their own situation adequately. Context – with all its painful realities – is important, and external models are not always transferable. Learning from each other is possible but policy transfers pass through a number of "filters" before being absorbed by the receiving society. The experience of the review suggests that the following needs to be taken into account in considering policy transfers in the early childhood field:

- *The values and concepts surrounding family and childhood in a given society.* Societal notions about child-rearing have always been subject to change (Ariès, 1962). What seems "the natural way" of rearing children changes significantly both in time and space, from century to century and from country to country. Chapter 1 makes reference, for example, to the dominant male bread-winner family model of the post-Second World War period throughout the OECD countries. Child attachment to the biological or substitute mother was promoted as a value, and almost all publics held the view that mothers should remain at home to rear their young children until kindergarten or school age.[3] Frequently, values and views about childhood or women's roles in society are latent or are not expressed openly. Careful analysis of government and public discourses is necessary to bring them to light and evaluate their compatibility with aspects of a contemporary early childhood policy.

- *Current social and economic concerns* are also a barrier or a fillip to a proposed new policy. Early childhood services – and indeed the employment of women – are placed under pressure during periods of economic recession. On the other hand, an election in which child care issues come to the fore can help to prioritise early childhood issues and lead policy makers to look outward to other countries for new, workable ideas.

- *Socio-economic structure or the customary way in which responsibility for social welfare and education is distributed in a society between the State, the market and households.* This issue is analysed further in Chapter 1. Countries tend to react to new discourses, either by rejecting them as incompatible with their own values and ways of doing things or by considering them well-suited and then absorbing them progressively into their own socio-economic reality. For example, the notion of a universal early childhood service funded primarily by the State has evolved more rapidly in Europe than in the United States, where public intervention in the early childhood sphere may be perceived as interfering with both family prerogative and a free market in services.

- *The organisational structures and receptivity of the existing early childhood field.* New policy initiatives cannot afford to unduly disturb the present order in the receiving country, particularly if significant gains and losses are incurred. For example, a proposal to professionalise and regulate early childhood services will be resisted almost certainly by unlicensed providers, who form a significant group in several countries, unless some incentive can be offered to bring them into the public system. The move towards putting into place higher quality services will need to include in some way the recognition and upgrading of these providers, and better information to parents about quality in services.

The writing of the *Comparative Report* is entrusted to the Secretariat – a logical choice in some respects, as Secretariat members take part in all the country reviews and by reason of this work are able to take a strong comparative perspective. The task places a considerable burden on OECD administrators, but also bestows an agenda-setting influence. Safeguards are built into the process in that the reports go through a peer-review process at the OECD, and through one or two editorial reviews by the countries involved. However, the process could perhaps be strengthened by wider consultation and the organisation of reading committees. Certainly, in the early childhood or family policy fields, it would be useful to have policy recommendations proofed from the perspective of the best interests of young children, and for gender equality and equity. Moreover, several commentators have warned against attempts at "fast" policy transfer, where the research and practices of the larger countries, the concepts of a dominant language group, or the analytic framework of an OECD division may predominate (Cohen *et al.*, 2004; Mahon, 2005; Porter and Webb, 2004; Rinne *et al.*, 2004).

OECD review and cross-national research

Positive assessments of the ECEC review and the cross-national research that it has generated are not infrequent, and countries continue to ask for comparative evaluations in the early childhood field. The sharing of experience and practice across countries in areas of common concern is generally useful, and can be a stimulus for policy learning and innovation. Even when countries did not agree with opinions expressed by reviewers, the occasion offered further opportunity for discussion and clarification of criteria. Sometimes differences of opinion were due to different contexts and investment possibilities, for example, when defining and assessing quality, but in general, disagreements stem, not from different appreciations of a particular standard to be used, *e.g.* child-staff ratios for young children, but from divergent social and economic philosophies. Countries that have active gender policies and effective redistribution strategies to support families with young children will often provide widespread and high quality children's services.

Understandings of the role of the State families, of the place of young children in society, of the notion of early childhood services as a public good can differ widely from country to country. In this respect, one may note that the emergence of young children from the private sphere into the public policy domain has taken place only in recent decades, and in some countries only in recent years, *e.g.* in the United Kingdom in 1998 with the launching of the National Child care Strategy, and in Germany in October 2002, when the government first called for the creation of places for approximately 20% of young children below the age of 3 years. OECD teams have found that if the context is not right, calls for greater public investment in children's services can be met with incomprehension, even with the suspicion that family life or a market-approach to services is being undermined. It is only when contemporary changes in family function and child-rearing have been acknowledged, and when early childhood services are recognised as a cornerstone of family, social and educational policy that public responsibility for the quality of services received by young children can be invoked with some credibility.

In general, administrations and stakeholders in the countries visited have appreciated the OECD early childhood review. The various reports present a comprehensive analysis of national systems through which country actors can evaluate their policies and identify assumptions or blockages that may be impeding progress. In addition, the participatory nature of the review process allows national policy makers to debate with the review experts, and become familiar with principles, standards and practices that are current in the early childhood policy field in other countries. Information of this nature can widen choice, but still needs to be followed by the mobilisation of assent and energies at national level. In some instances also, officials from the country under review welcomed the review as a means of pushing forward a reform agenda, of revealing hard policy choices, and happily, of announcing new measures to facilitate the lives of parents and improve quality for children.

Notes

1. Papers that were written subsequent to each workshop are available online at: *www.oecd.org/edu/earlychildhood*.

2. Frameworks introduced from the outside have also their pitfalls, as they may induce an external definition of the situation that ignores local definitions of the same reality, and the possibility of conflicting readings. See, for example, Richards (1985) or Moss and Pence (1994).

3. Many countries have introduced policies to reconcile the rearing of young children by parents during the critical first year and the desire of women to participate fully in society through their work. Parental leaves of one year are now common, considered as part of the employment regime and linked to a guaranteed child care place when parental leave is ended.

References

Ariès, P. (1962), *L'enfant et la vie familiale sous l'ancien régime*, Paris, Éditions du Seuil, Paris, translated into English: *Centuries of childhood*, Vintage Books, New York.

Cohen, B., P. Moss, P. Petrie and L. Wallace (2004), A *New Deal for Children: Reforming Education and Care in England, Scotland and Sweden*, Policy Press, United Kingdom.

Elliott, R., C.T. Fischer and D.L. Rennie (1999), "Evolving Guidelines for Publication of Qualitative Research Studies in Psychology and Related Fields", *British Journal of Clinical Psychology*, Vol. 38(3), pp. 215-229.

Gallagher, J.J., R.M. Clifford and K. Maxwell (2004), "Getting from Here to There: To an Ideal Early Preschool System", *Early Childhood Research and Practice*, Vol. 6(1), *http://ecrp.uiuc.edu/v6n1/clifford.html*.

Goswami, U. (2004), "Annual Review. Neuroscience and Education", *British Journal of Educational Psychology*, Vol. 74(1), pp. 1-14.

Howe, K. (2005), "The Question of Education Science: Experimentism *versus* Experimentalism", *Educational Theory*, Vol. 55(3), p. 307.

Lindsey, G. (1998), "Brain Research and Implications for Early Childhood Education", *Childhood Education*, Vol. 75(2), pp. 97-103.

Mahon, R. (2005), "The OECD and Reconcilation Agenda: Competing Bleuprints", in J. Lewis (ed.) *Children, Family Policies and Welfare State Change*, Edwin Elgar.

Moss, P., C. Owen and J. Stantham (1998), "Informing Ourselves about Early Childhood Services", *Children and Society*, Vol. 12, pp. 263-274.

Moss, P. and A. Pence (1994), *Valuing Quality in Early Childhood Services: New Approaches to Defining Quality*, Paul Chapman, London.

OECD (1998), "Early Childhood Education and Care Policy: Proposal for a Thematic Review", OECD, Paris.

Porter, T. and M. Webb (2004), "The Role of the OECD in the Orchestration of Global Knowledge Networks", paper for the *Annual Meeting of the International Studies Association*, March 17-20, Montreal.

Ramsburg, D. (1997), *Brain Development in Young Children: the Early Years Are Learning Years*, *www.nldontheweb.org*.

Richards, H. (1985), *The Evaluation of Cultural Action*, Macmillan, London.

Rinne, R., J. Kallo and S. Hokka (2004), "To Eager to Comply? OECD Education Policies and the Finnish Response", *European Education Research Journal*, Vol. 3, No. 2.

Shonkoff, J.P. and D.A. Phillips (eds.) (2000), *From Neurons to Neighbourhoods: The science of Early Childhood Development*, National Academy Press, Washington, DC.

ANNEX C

Data for Figures

Data for Figure 1.1. **Employment/population ratio of 25- to 34-year-old women and men in OECD countries, 1980 and 2004**

	Women		Men	
	1980	2004	1980	2004
Australia	49.8	66.7	91.7	85.9
Austria		74		89.1
Belgium	57.9	74.9	88.5	85.9
Canada	63.5	76.6	89.2	85.3
Czech Republic	66.7	60.1	94.1	90.1
Denmark	78.4	78.1	85.5	84.5
Finland	78.4	71.1	89.2	83.7
France	63.5	68.7	93.6	84.2
Germany	57.9	69.2	89.2	85.1
Hungary	55	60.1	81.7	84.4
Ireland	34	73	92.9	87.6
Italy	49.5	58.6	90.7	80.9
Korea	35.3	54.6	90.5	83.6
Mexico	37.6	47.1	94.8	93.6
Netherlands	59	75.3	90.1	92
Norway	61.5	77.3	88.6	83.9
Portugal	57.8	78.3	91.8	86.3
Sweden	79.5	76.1	93.4	87.5
United Kingdom	64.8	72.2	89.5	86.9
United States	60.7	69.5	88.8	85.9

Source: OECD labour force statistics database, 2005.

Data for Figure 1.2. **Female part-time and full-time employment as proportion of total female employment, 2004[1]**

	Part-time	Full-time
Netherlands	60.2	39.8
Australia[2, 3]	40.8	59.2
United Kingdom	40.4	59.6
Germany	37	63
Ireland	35.1	64.9
Belgium	34.1	65.9
Norway	33.2	66.8
Austria	29.6	70.4
Italy	28.8	71.2
Mexico	27.6	72.4
Canada	27.2	72.8
Denmark	24.3	75.7
France	23.6	76.4
Sweden	20.8	79.2
United States[4]	18.8	81.2
Finland	18.2	81.8
Portugal	14	86
Korea[2]	11.9	88.1
Czech Republic	5.2	94.8
Hungary	5.1	94.9

1. Part-time employment refers to persons who usually work less than 30 hours per week in their main job. Data include only persons declaring usual hours. Because of its non-contractual nature, the "marginal" or "non-regular" work mentioned in the text is not covered in these official figures.
2. Data are based on actual hours worked.
3. Part-time employment based on hours worked at all jobs.
4. Data are for wage and salary workers only. Part-time work on a casual is not included.
Source: OECD (2005), OECD Employment Outlook, OECD, Paris.

Data for Figure 1.3. **Effective parental leave provision**

	Maternity leave (in weeks)	Total parental leave (in weeks)	Effective parental leave (weighted by level of payment)
Australia[1]		52	17
Austria	16	104	71
Belgium	15	26	18
Canada[1]	15	35	20
Czech Republic	28	180	73
Denmark	18	32	36
Finland	17.5	145	99
France	16	156	48
Germany	14	156	64
Hungary	24	104	114
Ireland	18	28	11
Italy	22	48	24
Netherlands	16	26	11
Norway[1]		43	43
Portugal	17	52	20
Sweden	12	156	119
United Kingdom	26	26	25
United States[1]		52	17

Note: The degree of parental leave effectiveness is calculated by weighing the length of parental leave by the level of payment. Effective parental leave = [(maternity leave in weeks – 14 weeks) * % payment benefit) + (total parental leave in weeks * % payment benefit].
1. Data taken from Cleveland and Krashinsky (2003).
Source: Deven and Moss (2005); Platenga and Siegel (2004).

Data for Figure 1.4. **Part-time employment as proportion of total employment: men and women, 2004**[1]

	Men	Women
Australia[2, 3]	16.1	40.8
Austria	3.7	29.6
Belgium	6.3	34.1
Canada	10.9	27.2
Czech Republic	1.5	5.2
Denmark	11.6	24.3
Finland	7.7	18.2
France	4.8	23.6
Germany	6.3	37
Hungary	2.2	5.1
Ireland	6.9	35.1
Italy	5.9	28.8
Korea[2]	5.9	11.9
Mexico	8.1	27.6
Netherlands[4]	15.1	60.2
Norway	10.3	33.2
Portugal	5.8	14
Sweden	8.5	20.8
United Kingdom	10	40.4
United States[5]	8.1	18.8

1. Part-time employment refers to persons who usually work less than 30 hours per week in their main job. Data include only persons declaring usual hours. Marginal or non-regular work in which women form a large majority is not included in this figure.
2. Data are based on actual hours worked.
3. Part-time employment based on hours worked at all jobs.
4. Data on population/employment ratios for the Netherlands is for the population aged 15-64, as opposed to the total population.
5. Data are for wage and salaried workers only.

Source: OECD (2005), *OECD Employment Outlook*, OECD, Paris.

Data for Figure 1.5. **Employment/population ratios for men and women (25-54 years), 2004**

	Women	Men	All
Australia	68.9	85.7	77.2
Austria	75.8	87.4	81.7
Belgium	68.8	85.7	77.3
Canada	76.8	86	81.4
Czech Republic	73.4	89.2	81.4
Denmark	80.6	87.3	84
Finland	78.1	83.7	81
France	72	86.7	79.2
Germany	74.6	84.2	79.5
Hungary[1]	67	80.5	73.6
Ireland	65.8	87.6	76.7
Italy	57.8	86.5	72.1
Korea	58	88.4	73.4
Mexico[2]	48.3	94.3	69.6
Netherlands	74.5	90.2	82.5
Norway	80	86.2	83.1
Portugal	74.9	87.4	81.1
Sweden	80.8	85	82.9
United Kingdom	74.2	87.5	80.7
United States	71.8	86.3	79

1. The year 1990 refers to 1992.
2. The year 1990 refers to 1991.
Source: OECD (2005), *OECD Employment Outlook*, OECD, Paris.

Data for Figure 1.6. **Ageing and immigrant populations in the OECD world**

		Ratio of population 65 and over to the total labour force	
	% change in foreign population between 1993 and 2002	2005	2020
Australia	0.5	25.2	36.2
Austria	1.3	33.4	43.7
Belgium	−0.7	39.2	47.2
Canada	2.3	24.9	35.8
Czech Republic	18.9	28.2	44.8
Denmark	4	28.4	39.3
Finland	8.4	31.2	48.1
France	−1.1	37.6	50.5
Germany	1.2	36.7	44.5
Hungary	−2.2	36.5	49.7
Ireland	7.1	22.6	28.2
Italy	5	46.0	55.7
Korea	16.3	19.4	36.1
Mexico		12.7	17.0
Netherlands	−0.8	27.2	38.0
Norway	2.5	27.4	34.8
Portugal	12.8	31.1	35.2
Sweden	−0.5	35.0	47.5
United Kingdom	3.1	31.6	39.0
United States	5.8	24.7	33.8

Note: In the case of Australia, Canada, Mexico, New Zealand and the United States, the data concern the foreign-born population only. Annual average change between 1993 and 2002, except Canada (1991 and 2001), France (1990-1999) Hungary (1994-2002), the Slovak Republic (1995-2002), and the United States (1994-2002).
Source: OECD (2005), *OECD Factbook* and *OECD Society at a Glance*, OECD, Paris.

Data for Figure 1.7. **Impacts of social transfers on child poverty**

	Relative child poverty rates	
	Before government taxes and transfers	After government taxes and transfers
Australia	m	m
Austria	17.7	10.2
Belgium	16.7	7.7
Canada	22.8	14.9
Czech Republic	15.8	6.8
Denmark	11.8	2.4
Finland	18.1	2.8
France	27.7	7.5
Germany	18.2	10.2
Hungary	23.2	8.8
Ireland	24.9	15.7
Italy	m	m
Mexico	29.5	27.7
Netherlands	11.1	9.8
Norway	15.5	3.4
Portugal	16.4	15.6
Sweden	m	m
Switzerland	18.0	4.2
United Kingdom	25.4	15.4
United States	26.6	21.9

Source: Poverty in Rich Countries, UNICEF Innocenti Research Centre, Florence, 2005.

Data for Figure 1.8. **Lone parents as a percentage of all families in selected OECD countries**

	Single-parent households for selected OECD countries	
	1980	2000
Canada	12.7	13.9
Denmark	13.4	18.4
France	11.9	17.1
Germany	15.2	21.2
Ireland	7.2	16.7
Japan	4.9	8.3
Netherlands	9.6	13
Sweden	11.2	23.1
United Kingdom	13.9	20.7
United States	19.5	26.5

Notes: Data from 1981 were used for Canada, Ireland, and the United Kingdom, data from 1985 were used for Sweden, data from 1988 were used for France and the Netherlands and data from 1991 were used for Germany.
Data from 2001 were used for the United States, Denmark, and the United Kingdom, data from 2002 were used for Ireland.
Source: Clearinghouse on International Developments in Child, Youth and Family Policies at Columbia University, 2005.

Data for Figure 4.1. **Enrolment rates in regulated ECEC and pre-primary education of children 3 to 6 years**

	Enrolment rates based on head counts							
	Children at age 3		Children at age 4		Children at age 5		Children at age 6	
	Pre-primary	Primary	Pre-primary	Primary	Pre-primary	Primary	Pre-primary	Primary
AUS	20	0	62	0	18	73	0	99
AUT	44	0	83	0	94	0	35	61
BEL	99	0	99	0	99	0	5	95
CZE	66	0	90	0	98	0	46	54
DEU	72	0	86	0	87	0	45	49
DNK	83	0	93	0	92	0	99	0
FIN	36	0	45	0	53	0	97	3.3
FRA	101	0	103	0	101	0	1.2	101
HUN	73	0	92	0	98	0	72	28
IRL	2.3	1.2	1.5	47	0.8	99	0	99
ITA	100	0	102	0	99	0	1.3	102
KOR	12	0	26	0	47	1	0	93
MEX	21	0	63	0	81	9	1	99
NDL	0	0	73	0	100.2	0	0	99
NOR	77	0	84	0	87	0	1	99
PRT	61	0	81	0	91	1.5	3	101
SWE	79	0	83	0	85	0	97	3
GBR	50	0	95	0	0	101	0	100
USA	41	0	62	0	75	6	11	85

Source: OECD education database, 2005.

Data for Figure 4.2. **Employment rates for mothers with children under 3 and access rates for children under 3 in licensed ECEC services**

	Women employment rates with children under 3	% of children aged 0-3 in regulated child care
Australia, 2000	56.7	24.6
Austria, 2001	71.9	10
Belgium, 2004[1]	59.4	27.6
Canada, 2001[2]	58.7	m
Czech Republic, 2004	14.2	0.5
Denmark, 1999	76.5	83
Finland, 2002	52.1	35.7
France, 2004[3]	49.5	27
Germany, 2004	47.8	8.6
Hungary, 2004	30.5	9.3
Ireland, 2002	51.1	15
Italy, 2004	45.2	18.7
Korea	m	10
Mexico	m	3
Netherlands, 2004	66.4	29
Norway	18	44
Portugal, 2001	70.8	25
Sweden, 2003	72	66
United Kingdom, 2003	49.2	26
United States, 2004	53.1	38

1. Enrolment in the infant school begins at 2.5 years when about 90% of children are enrolled. The percentage of children in regulated child care in Belgium (Flanders) is 34.2%.
2. For Canada, the coverage rate for children aged 0-5 years is 24%. Data on the coverage rate for children aged 0-3 years are not available.
3. Enrolment in the infant school begins at 2 years. 35% of children enter between 2-3 years.

Source: Employment rates provided by EUROSTAT, United States Bureau of Labor Statistics and OECD, *Babies and Bosses* (Volumes 1-4). Information on access rates provided by OECD countries, 2004.

Data for Figure 5.2. **Public investment in services for families and young children in percentages of GDP**

	Total cash benefits	Total family services	Public expenditure on ISCED 0	Total public spending as % of GDP
AUS	2.4	0.5	0.07	2.97
AUT	2.4	0.6	0.42	3.42
BEL	1.9	0.4	0.58	2.88
CAN	0.9	0	0.2	1.1
CZE	1.5	0.1	0.43	2.03
DEU	1.1	0.8	0.40	2.55
DNK	1.5	2.3	0.65	4.14
FIN	1.7	1.4	0.34	3.75
FRA	1.5	1.3	0.65	3.2
HUN	1.9	0.6	0.73	3.23
IRL	1.4	0.2	0.39	1.85
ITA	0.6	0.3	0.39	1.29
KOR	0	0.1	0.05	0.15
MEX	0.1	0.2	0.52	0.82
NDL	0.7	0.4	0.37	1.47
NOR	1.9	1.3	0.84	4.04
PRT	0.7	0.5	0.30	1.55
SWE	1.8	1.1	0.52	3.42
GBR	1.9	0.3	0.45	2.65
USA	0.1	0.3	0.38	0.78

Note: For Denmark and Sweden, expenditure levels on ISCED Level 0 – as represented on the figure (white portion of the bar) – cover only a small proportion of their actual ECEC expenditure on children 1 to 6 years old. Similarly for Korea, where only Ministry of Education expenditure is included.
Source: OECD (2005), *Education at a Glance*; OECD/DELSA/ELSA (2004)8.

Data for Figure 5.3. **Public expenditure on ECEC services (0-6 years) in selected OECD countries**

	Public expenditure as % of GDP
Canada	0.25
Australia	0.4
Italy	0.43
Germany	0.45
Netherlands	0.45
United States	0.48
United Kingdom	0.5
Austria	0.55
Hungary	0.8
France	1
Finland	1.3
Norway	1.7
Sweden	1.7
Denmark	2

Note: Expenditure estimates, based on replies provided by country authorities to an OECD survey in 2004. The figures provided suggest that Denmark spends 2% of GDP on early childhood services for 0- to 6-year-olds, and Sweden 1.7%. Each country – and Finland – also allocates an additional 0.3% (approximately) to the pre-school class for children 6 to 7 years.

Data for Figure 5.4. **Public and private expenditure on pre-primary education (3- to 6-year-olds only) as a percentage of GDP**

	Public expenditure as % of GDP	Private expenditure as % of GDP	Total expenditure as % of GDP (public and private)
Australia	0.07	0.03	0.1
Austria	0.42	0.13	0.55
Belgium	0.58	0.01	0.59
Canada	m	m	m
Czech Republic	0.43	0.03	0.46
Denmark	0.65	0.15	0.81
Finland	0.34	0.03	0.38
France	0.65	0.03	0.67
Germany	0.4	0.14	0.53
Hungary	0.73	0.07	0.79
Ireland	0.39	n	n
Italy	0.39	0.05	0.44
Korea	0.05	0.11	0.16
Mexico	0.52	0.08	0.61
Netherlands	0.37	0.01	0.38
Norway	0.84	0.18	1.02
Portugal	0.30	m	0.35
Sweden	0.52	0	0.52
United Kingdom	0.45	0.02	0.47
United States	0.38	0.11	0.49

Note: Early education expenditure for Belgium and France is higher than this table indicates, and significantly higher for Denmark, Finland and Sweden. In Belgium and France, early education begins before 3 years. For Denmark, Finland and Sweden, it is probable that this table identifies expenditure only for what is considered free educational provision, *e.g.* the Finnish figure includes pre-primary education programmes for 6-year-old children (pre-school year preceding compulsory education) that takes place in day care centres or in comprehensive schools, and centre-based day care for 3- to 5-year-old children, based on an expenditure estimation of 50%. Canada is absent from this table as data are not provided in OECD, *Education at a Glance*, 2005. The last data received from Canada are for the year 2000, when Canada spent 0.2% of GDP on pre-primary education, for 3- to 6-year-olds. Data for Korea cover only kindergarten education and do not include public expenditure in the parallel child care system.
Source: OECD (2005), *Education at a Glance*.

Data for Figure 10.1. **Relative child poverty rates in rich countries**

	Relative child poverty rates % of children living below national poverty line
Australia	14.7
Austria	10.2
Belgium	7.7
Canada	14.9
Czech Republic	6.8
Denmark	2.4
Finland	2.8
France	7.5
Germany	10.2
Hungary	8.8
Ireland	15.7
Italy	16.6
Mexico	27.7
Netherlands	9.8
Norway	3.4
Portugal	15.6
Sweden	4.2
Switzerland	6.8
United Kingdom	15.4
United States	21.9

Source: *Poverty in Rich Countries*, UNICEF Innocenti Research Centre, Florence, 2005.

ANNEX D

A Summary of International Evidence in Favour of Public Investment in ECEC

Over the past decades, cost-benefit analyses have been a significant feature of early childhood research, perhaps more so than in any other area of education or social policy. In an effort to spur government investment in early childhood services, and particularly in services for the younger children, numerous investigations have been made to justify public expenditure. The paragraphs that follow outline some of the international evidence, indicating that investment in early childhood services brings not only proven benefits to the children and families they serve, but also to governments and national economies. Two OECD research papers not included here, Leseman (2002), Cleveland and Krashinsky (2003), can be accessed on the OECD Web site: *www.oecd.org/edu/earlychildhood*.

Cost-benefit research is particularly intense in the United States. We describe briefly below some of the direct studies of particular programmes, but readers may also wish to consult a compendium of this research: the Economic Policy Institute summary by Robert G. Lynch (2004), *Exceptional Returns: Economic, Fiscal and Social Benefits of Investment in Early Childhood Development*. More recent research continues to be published from the United States, *e.g.* the Rand Corporation research reports: *The Economics of Investing in Universal Pre-school Education in California* (Karoly and Bigelow, 2005) and *Early Childhood Interventions: Proven Results, Future Promise* (Karoly, Kilburn and Cannon, 2006).

Doubts have been expressed concerning the validity of the research methods used in many of these studies, *e.g.* that samples are too small, or that children in some studies were not randomly assigned to a particular ECEC programme, making it difficult to separate out family effects from programme effects.* Again, the risk of extrapolating results from American studies (the majority) to other countries is raised by Penn *et al.* (2006), but studies from European countries (six European studies are cited below), Australia, Canada and New Zealand corroborate these findings. According to Penn and the EPPI research team (part of the Social Science Research Unit, Institute of Education, University of London), among the many hundreds of studies that have looked at the question of costs and benefits, only three studies are valid: "We found only three studies which deal with the long-term economic outcomes of early childhood interventions"; and

---

* As in other areas of human endeavour, research too creates its own orthodoxies. Currently, education research favours a methodology borrowed from the medical field, that of randomised field trials.

these American studies do not allow the extrapolation of results from the United States to other countries:

> "Given the much wider range of policy initiatives on early childhood care and education in the United Kingdom, and in OECD countries, than in the United States, the longitudinal cost-benefit studies of early childhood interventions add little to understanding outside of a United States context, and are often misleadingly cited… The results of the three studies here can only be cited with caution. Whilst there may well be long-term outcomes from early childhood interventions, these studies are based on cost estimates and projections, which do not directly apply outside of a United States context… There seems little point in trying to replicate longitudinal studies in the United Kingdom. Apart from the expense of such studies and the difficulty of obtaining conclusive results, the notion of targeted intervention is itself problematic. On the other hand, it is important to explore different models of providing and costing services."

One of the members of the EPPI Peripheral Review Group, Professor Gordon Cleveland (University of Toronto), has published a critique of the EPPI methodology, calling attention to the inclusion and exclusion criteria used by the team, which allowed only three studies to be considered from among so many. The three studies selected are: the Perry High Scope study, the North Carolina Abecedarian Early Childhood Intervention, and the Chicago Child-Parent Centres study (see below for a brief description of each). As a result, the EPPI team did not examine:

> "… the careful statistical analyses (NICHD, 2005; NICHD and Duncan, 2003) about effects on children from the NICHD (National Institute of Child Health and Human Development) longitudinal study in the United States, nor did they look at similar positive results from the Cost, Quality and Child Outcomes Study (Peisner-Feinberg et al., 2001), or other United States studies. They did not take into account recent studies (Lefebvre and Merrigan, 2005) of the very strong maternal labour supply effects of the Quebec (Canada) child care reforms of 1997, with very positive effects on society's tax revenues (Baker, Gruber and Milligan, 2005). They did not take into account the positive academic and behavioural findings by Andersson (1992) from Sweden. They did not take into account positive results from the EPPE study in the United Kingdom (Sylva et al., 2003). They did not take into account the above-mentioned longitudinal studies of the Head Start programme in the United States. They did not consider cost-benefit studies (Cleveland and Krashinsky, 1998) that were not based on a specific longitudinal experiment, but instead gathered cost and benefit data from numerous sources" Cleveland (2006).

It may be noted that, in general, cost-benefit analyses are technical, post factum exercises that examine the economic returns from the programmes being reviewed, but up to fairly recently, they have not analysed more fundamental questions, e.g. how early childhood services should be conceptualised or what is the place of children and families in these services. In a sense, also, cost-benefit studies address a question that has already been decided: family life has changed radically in the past three decades, and in many OECD countries, most children do not have a parent at home to look after them full time. Dual-earner families are now the rule, and the economic advantages for both families and societies brought by this change are unlikely to be surrendered in the immediate future. Willy-nilly, societies are now obliged to create extra-domestic ECEC programmes that contribute to child well-being (basic health and cognitive, social and emotional development); family well-being (employment and parental choice); gender equity; and social inclusion. For this reason, the more recent studies that attempt to identify which are the kinds of programme that merit government investment may be more useful for policy makers. However, there is little doubt about the main findings of the cost-benefit studies listed below: they make an overwhelming case for strong government investment in early childhood services.

Analyses showing social, economic and labour market returns from investment

The Perry Pre-school study (ongoing)

The ongoing Perry Pre-school study (Berrueta-Clement et al., 1984, and Schweinhart et al., 2005, Belfield et al., 2005) evaluates the educational and economic returns of a high quality pre-school programme, High/Scope, on a sample of Afro-American children. Key findings were that the children from the Perry Pre-school programme had better school records, improved labour market entry and higher incomes than the control group of similar children. In a cost-benefit analysis of the data, Barnett (1996) estimated that the cost-benefit ratio for the investment in the programme was 1:7.

The Zurich study by Müller and Kucera-Bauer (2001)

The Müller Kucera-Bauer study, *Costs and Benefits of Child care Services in Switzerland – Empirical Findings from Zurich* (2001), shows that the city's public investment of CHF 18 million annually in child care services is offset by at least CHF 29 million of additional tax revenues and reduced public spending on social aid (Müller Kucera-Bauer, 2001). Where affordable child care was available, the rate of hours worked by mothers almost doubled, especially for single-headed households with one or more children. In sum, publicly funded child care resulted in: 1) higher productivity and earnings due to maintaining productive workers in work; 2) higher contributions to social security and savings; 3) less dependency on social assistance during both the productive and retirement ages (without affordable child care, many families would fall below the poverty line).

The North Carolina Abecedarian Early Childhood Intervention (2003)

The North Carolina Abecedarian Early Childhood Intervention, which began in 1972, has been subject to numerous studies. The various researches show positive cognitive and social results for the children (mostly disadvantaged) in the project, some of whom gained entry into four-year university programmes. A cost-benefit study by the National Institute for Early Education Research (Masse and Barnett, 2002) was published in 2003. It finds that every dollar invested in high quality, full-day, year-round pre-school generated a four-dollar return to the children, their families and all taxpayers. Among the study's findings:

- Participants are projected to earn about USD 143 000 more over their lifetimes than those who did not take part in the programme.
- Mothers of children who were enrolled can also expect greater earnings – about USD 133 000 more over their lifetimes.
- School districts can expect to save more than USD 11 000 per child because participants are less likely to require special or remedial education.
- The next generation (children of the children in the Abecedarian project) are projected to earn nearly USD 48 000 more throughout their lifetimes.

Two Californian studies (2001)

The first study, *The Economic Impact of the Child Care Industry in California* by the National Economic Development and Law Centre, quantifies the economic contribution the licensed child care industry makes to California's economy. Examining factors such as the industry's revenues, job generation, and employee productivity gains, the report paints the picture of the child care field as a multi-billion dollar industry that plays a key role in the State's economic health. Apart from enabling parents to work and earn higher incomes, the child care industry contributed USD 65 billion to the total value of goods and services produced in California – just over four times as much as the motion picture industry. Licensed child care directly employed 123 000 people, including teaching and non-teaching staff, and maintained a further 86 000 jobs in transportation, publishing, manufacturing, construction, financial services, real estate and insurance (NEDLC, 2001).

The 2001 report on the benefits produced by child care in California has been reinforced by a recent study on universal pre-school sponsored by the Rand Corporation: *The Economics of Investing in Universal Pre-school Education in California* (Karoly and Bigelow, 2005). The authors find that if only the poorest 25% of children in California benefited from a year of pre-school – meaning there was no benefit to the other 75% – Californians could still expect to gain nearly USD 2 for every USD 1 invested. Children who attend pre-school are likely to do better in school and go on to graduate high school, are less likely to be convicted of crimes and are more likely to earn higher salaries as adults. All this saves governments money and boosts tax revenues. The authors also analyse the probable effects on working-class families and middle-class children, who face many of the same problems as children in poverty. Half of all children who repeat a grade in school, and half of all high school drop-outs, come from families in the middle 60% of the income ladder. Any benefits of pre-school realised by children from these families push the return from investing in pre-school even higher – from USD 2.62 to USD 4 depending on the assumptions of pre-school benefits.

The authors claim that their estimate of USD 2 to USD 4 in benefits in California is conservative because they do not count savings that would result from such favourable effects of universal pre-school as lower lifetime welfare use and improved lifetime health. Even if early gains in achievement scores eventually fade, other benefits still remain at older ages, including better high school graduation rates, less delinquency and crime and higher adult earnings.

The Canadian cost-benefit analysis (1998)

The Canadian cost-benefit analysis issued in 1998 by a team of economists at the University of Toronto estimates the costs and benefits of establishing a national quality child care system for Canada (Cleveland and Krashinsky, 1998). Although the authors make conservative assumptions about the extent of positive externalities, they conclude that the substantial public investment envisaged would generate important net benefits for Canadian society, the benefits exceeding costs by about 2 to 1. The benefits to children using the service and the benefits to mothers and families from continued employment were each equal to about half the benefits obtained.

Labour market/taxation studies: examples from Norway, the United Kingdom and Canada

Labour market/taxation studies. The provision of education and care services has allowed most OECD countries in the last decades to maintain the labour market participation of women, with a corresponding widening of the tax base. In Norway, the increase has been from about 50% female participation in 1972 to well over 80% in 1997 (Statistics Norway, 2002). In particular, women of 25 to 40 years have greatly increased their participation.

The recent PricewaterhouseCooper (2004) estimation of future economic benefits to the British economy, brought about by expanding ECEC services in the United Kingdom, suggests a rise in GDP of between 1 and 2% through higher rates of female employment (at present at 69%) and by increased lifetime employment rates.

Low-fee (USD 5/day/child) regulated child care policy and the labour supply of mothers with young children: A natural experiment from Canada (Lefebvre and Merrigan, 2005). In 1997, the provincial government of Quebec initiated a new child care policy, offering day care spaces at the reduced parental contribution of USD 5 per day child for children aged 4 years, in child care services licensed by the Ministry of the Family. In successive years, the government reduced the age requirement. By September 2000, the low-fee policy applied to all children aged 0 to 59 months (not in kindergarten) and the number of partly subsidised spaces increased from 77 000 in 1998 to 163 000 spaces, totally subsidised by the end of year 2002. Using annual data (1993 to 2002), drawn from Statistics Canada's Survey of Labour and Income Dynamics (SLID), this study estimates the effect of the policy on the labour supply behaviour of Quebec mothers with pre-school children, aged from 0 to 5 years. The analysis examines the impact of the policy on the following outcomes: labour force participation, annual number of weeks and hours at work, annual earned income and whether the job was full-time for mothers who declared having a job during the reference year. The results support the hypothesis that the child care policy, together with the transformation of public kindergarten from a part-time to a full-time basis, had a large and statistically significant impact on the labour supply of Quebec's mothers with pre-school children.

Analyses showing educational returns from early childhood investment

Sweden: Andersson study (1992)

Andersson's pioneering study of Swedish children in 1989 and 1992 provides information about the long-term cognitive and social effects of a high quality ECEC system on children. The original study, when children were aged 8, was based on a sample of 128 families drawn from low and middle-resource areas of Sweden's two largest cities. This follow-up study when the children were aged 13 controls statistically for family background, gender of the child, child's native intelligence, and child's achievement at aged 8. With these factors controlled, the study shows that the earlier a child entered centre or family day care, the stronger the positive effect on academic achievement at age 13. For children entering child care in their second year of life or earlier, the academic benefit was found to be an improvement of between 10-20% in academic performance at age 13, compared to children cared for exclusively at home. Andersson's conclusion was that "early entrance into day care tends to predict a creative, socially confident, popular, open and independent adolescent" (pp. 32-33).

The French National Survey (1992)

In France, a national survey comparing children who had attended a kindergarten for one, two, or three years before beginning primary school found that performance in primary school is correlated with the length of time spent in pre-primary education, even after controlling for background characteristics (Jarousse, Mingat and Richard, 1992). Every year of *école maternelle* (kindergarten) attended reduced children's likelihood of retention in the first grade of primary school, especially for children from the most disadvantaged homes.

The United States "Success For All" study (2002)

"Success For All": Long-term Effects and Cost-effectiveness (Borman and Hewes, 2002). "Success For All" is a comprehensive elementary school reform programme designed to promote early school success among at-risk children. It is widely replicated in the United States, and serves over 1 million children in 2 000 schools. In addition to offering intensive, pre-kindergarten and kindergarten programmes, it provides mechanisms to promote stronger links between the home and the school, and to address social, behavioural and health issues. Relative to control groups, and at similar cost, "Success For All" children complete elementary school at an earlier age, achieve better learning outcomes, have fewer retentions or special education placements. The authors underline that for success to continue, similar programmes need to be used throughout primary and lower secondary schooling.

The Chicago Child-Parent Centres study (2002)

The Title I Chicago Child-Parent Centres (Reynolds *et al.*, 2002). Opened in 1967, the Centres are located in public schools and provide educational and family support to low-income children from ages 3 to 9 years. Using data from the Chicago Longitudinal Study, and comparison group children born in 1980, Reynolds and his team show that participation in the Centres was significantly associated with greater school achievement, higher rates of school completion, with significantly lower rates of remedial education, juvenile delinquency and child maltreatment. Cost-benefit analyses indicate that the programme provides a strong return per dollar invested, through increasing economic well-being and tax revenues; and reducing public expenditure on remedial education, criminal justice treatment and crime victims.

The longitudinal New Zealand survey "Twelve Years Old and Competent" (1992 ongoing)

The latest (2004) iteration of the ongoing New Zealand survey "Twelve Years Old and Competent" – a part of the longitudinal study "Competent Children/Learners" begun in 1992 – shows that at age 12, children who have had high quality early childhood education are better readers and mathematicians than those whose early education was of a low standard. Importantly, there was also evidence that these gaps widened as children got older, even after family income and parental education levels were discounted (New Zealand Council of Educational Research, 2004, *www.nzcer.org.nz*).

The United States National Evaluation of Early Head Start (2003)

The congressional mandated National Evaluation of Early Head Start (EHS) – a large-scale, random assignment evaluation published in 2003 – reached the conclusion that EHS made a positive difference in areas associated with children's success in school, family self-sufficiency and parental support for children's development. The evaluation underlined that EHS produced statistically significant measures of children's cognitive and linguistic development, and that EHS children had more positive interactions with their parents. EHS helped parents to move towards self-sufficiency. In particular, participation in EHS increased parental involvement in education and job-training activities.

The longitudinal British EPPE study (1997-2007)

The Effective Provision of Pre-school Education (EPPE) project is a British longitudinal study of a national sample of young children's development (intellectual and social/behavioural) between the ages of 3 and 7 years. In addition to investigating the effects of pre-school provision on young children's development, EPPE explores the characteristics of effective practice (Sylva et al., 2003). Key findings are:

- *Pre-school experience, compared to none, enhances children's development.* The duration of attendance is important with an earlier start being related to better intellectual development and sociability. Full-time attendance led to no better gains for children than part-time provision. Disadvantaged children in particular benefit significantly from good quality pre-school experiences, especially if they attend centres that cater for a mixture of children from different social backgrounds

- *The quality of programmes is directly related to better intellectual/cognitive and social/behavioural development in children.* Settings that have staff with higher qualifications, especially with good proportion of trained teachers on the staff, show higher quality and their children make more progress. Effective pedagogy includes attention to social development and also to interaction traditionally associated with the term "teaching", the provision of instructive learning environments and "sustained shared thinking" to extend children's learning.

- *The type of pre-school is important.* Children tend to make better intellectual progress in fully integrated centres and nursery schools.

- *The importance of home learning.* The quality of the learning environment of the home (where parents are actively engaged in activities with children) promotes intellectual and social development in all children. Although parent's social class and levels of education were related to child outcomes, the quality of the home learning environment was more important than social class. What parents do is more important than who they are.

Summary

Strong social, economic and education rationales exist in favour of establishing and maintaining national networks of early childhood services, including research from leading economists or institutes (ESO/Swedish Finance Ministry Report, 1999; Sen, 1999; Urrutia, 1999; Van der Gaag, 2002; Vandell and Wolfe, 2000; Verry, 2000; Heckman and Carneiro, 2002, NEPI, 2004, etc.). By establishing these services, significant employment is generated, tax revenues increased, and important savings made in later educational and social expenditure, if children – especially from at-risk backgrounds – are given appropriate developmental opportunities early enough in life, and careful academic programming is continued through primary and secondary schooling. More recently, OECD (2005) showed some correlations between years spent in early education and subsequent school outcomes.

However, the question of the *quality* of the early childhood services provided is critical (see, for example, Sylva et al., 2003, Vandell, 2004). The following summary from *From Neurons to Neighbourhoods: The Science of Early Childhood Development* by the United States

National Research Council and Institute of Medicine (Shonkoff and Phillips, 2000) presents an assessment of the effects of child care quality, and indicates some of its key features. The assessment is based on a critical review of a wide range of recent studies:

"... the positive relation between child care quality and virtually every facet of children's development that has been studied is one of the most consistent findings in developmental science. While child care of poor quality is associated with poorer developmental outcomes, high-quality care is associated with outcomes that all parents want to see in their children, ranging from co-operation with adults to the ability to initiate and sustain positive exchanges with peers, to early competence in math and reading... The stability of child care providers appears to be particularly important for young children's social development, an association that is attributable to the attachments that are established between young children and more stable providers. For cognitive and language outcomes, the verbal environment that child care providers create appears to be a very important feature of care (pp. 313-314)."

The consequences of not investing sufficiently in services can also be considered. Without strong state investment and steering of this field, the result will be an insufficient supply of services for those who need them most, leading to increased numbers of children with special needs and learning difficulties; a lack of equity for poorer families; and overall poor quality of provision.

At the same, it is unreasonable to expect early childhood programmes – even the best ones – to ensure either personal success or social equality. Although early childhood is an important phase in the life cycle, even a bright head start can be quickly dimmed by poor primary schooling, dysfunctional family conditions, troubled communities or social and employment prejudice. In sum, it is more realistic to see early childhood education and care from a societal perspective, as a small but important variable in the complex, interconnecting systems that govern outcomes for individuals, economies and societies.

References

Andersson, B.-E. (1992), "Effects of Day care on the Cognitive and Socio-emotional Competence of Thirteen-Year-Old Swedish School Children", in *Child Development*, Vol. 63, pp. 20-36.

Baker, M., J. Gruber and K. Milligan (2005), "Universal Child care, Maternal Labor Supply, and Family Well-being", National Bureau of Economic Research Working Paper 11832, Cambridge, Massachusetts (*www.nber.org/papers/w11832*).

Barnett, W.S. (1996), *Lives in the Balance: Age-27 Benefit-cost Analysis of the High/Scope Perry Preschool Program*, Monograph of the High/Scope Educational Research Foundation, 11, High/Scope Press, Ypsilanti, MI.

Belfield, C., M. Nores, W.S. Barnett and L. Schweinhart (2005), *Updating the Benefit-cost Analysis of the High/Scope Perry Pre-school Programme through Age 40*, Educational Evaluation and Policy Analysis, Vol. 27(3), pp. 245-262.

Berrueta-Clement et al. (1984), *Changed Lives: the Effects of the Perry Pre-school Programme on Youths through Age 19*, High/Scope Educational Research Foundation, Ypsilanti, MI.

Borman, G.D. and G. Hewes (2002), "The Long-term Effects and Cost-effectiveness of *Success for All*", Educational Evaluation and Policy Analysis, Vol. 24, pp. 243-266.

Cleveland, G. (2006), Personal communication, May.

Cleveland, G. and M. Krashinsky (1998), *The Benefits and Costs of Good Child Care: the Economic Rationale for Public Investment in Young Children*, University of Toronto Centre for Urban and Community Studies, Child care Resource and Research Unit, Toronto.

Cleveland, G. and M. Krashinsky (2003), *Financing ECEC Services in OECD Countries*, OECD, Paris, *www.oecd.org/document/3/0,2340,en_2649_201185_27000067_1_1_1_1,00.html*.

ESO (1999), *Day care and Incentives – A Summary*, Swedish Finance Department, Stockholm.

van der Gaag, J. (2002), *From Child Development to Human Development*, University of Amsterdam, Faculty of Economics and Econometrics, Amsterdam.

Heckman, J. and P. Carneiro (2002), "Human Capital Policy", NBER Working Papers 9495, National Bureau of Economic Research, Inc., Cambridge, MA.

Jarousse, J.P., A. Mingat et M. Richard (1992), "La scolarisation maternelle à deux ans : effets pédagogiques et sociaux", *Education et Formation*, ministère de l'Éducation nationale et de la Culture, Paris, April-June.

Karoly, L.A. and J.H. Bigelow (2005), *The Economics of Investing in Universal Pre-school Education in California*, RAND Corp, Santa Monica.

Karoly, L.A., R.M. Kilburn and J.S. Cannon (2006), *Early Childhood Interventions: Proven Results, Future Promise*, RAND Corp, Santa Monica.

Lefebvre, P. and P. Merrigan (2005), *Low-fee ($5/day/child) Regulated Child Care Policy and the Labor Supply of Mothers with Young Children: A Natural Experiment from Canada*, Centre Interuniversitaire sur le Risque, les Politiques Économiques et l'Emploi (CIRPÉE Working Paper 05-08).

Leseman, P. (2002), *Early Childhood Education and Care for Children from Low-income or Minority Backgrounds*, OECD, Paris, *www.oecd.org/document/3/0,2340,en_2649_201185_27000067_1_1_1_1,00.html*.

Lynch, R.G. (2004), *Exceptional Returns: Economic, Fiscal and Social Benefits of Investment in Early Childhood Development*, EPI, Washington DC.

Masse, L.N. and S. Barnett (2002), *A Benefit Cost Analysis of the Abecedarian Early Childhood Intervention*, NIEER, NJ.

Müller Kucera, K. and T. Bauer (2001), *Costs and Benefits of Child care Services in Switzerland – Empirical Findings from Zurich*.

National Economic Development and Law Centre (NEDLC) (2001), *The Economic Impact of the Child Care Industry in California*, Oakland, CA.

NICHD, Early Child Care Research Network (2005) (ed.), *Child Care and Child Development: Results from the NICHD Study of Early Child Care and Youth Development*, The Guildford Press, New York, NY.

NICHD, Early Child Care Research Network and G.J. Duncan (2003), "Modeling the Impacts of Child Care Quality on Children's Pre-school Cognitive Development", *Child Development*, Vol. 74(5), pp. 1454-1475.

OECD (2005), *Education at a Glance: OECD Indicators*, OECD, Paris.

Peisner-Feinberg, E.S., M.R. Burchinal, R.M. Clifford, M.L. Culkin, C. Howes, S.L. Kagan, and N. Yazejian (2001), "The Relation of Pre-school Child care Quality to Children's Cognitive and Social Developmental Trajectories through Second Grade", *Child Development*, Vol. 72:5, pp. 1534-1553.

Penn, H. *et al.* (2006), "What is Known about the Long-term Economic Impact of Centre-based Early Childhood Interventions?", EPPI-Centre, Social Science Research Unit, Institute of Education, University of London, London.

PricewaterhouseCooper (2004), *Universal Pre-School Child care Provision: Towards a Cost-benefit Analysis for the United Kingdom*, PWC, London.

Reynolds, A.J., J.A. Temple, D.L. Robertson and E.A. Mann (2002), "Age 21 Cost-benefit Analysis of the Title I Chicago Child-Parent Centres", *Educational Evaluation and policy Analysis*, Vol. 24(4), pp. 267-303.

Schweinhart, L.J., H.V. Barnes and D.P. Weikart (1993), *Significant Benefits: The High/Scope Perry Preschool Study through Age 27*, monographs of the High/Scope Educational Research Foundation, 10, High/Scope Press, Ypsilanti.

Schweinhart, L.J., J. Montie, Z. Xiang, W.S. Barnett, C.R. Belfield and M. Nores (2005), *Lifetime Effects: The High/Scope Perry Pre-school Study through Age 40*, High/Scope Educational Research Foundation, Ypsilanti, MI.

Sen, A. (1999), *Investing in Early Childhood: its Role in Development*, Inter-American Development Bank, Washington.

Shonkoff, J. and D. Phillips (2000) (eds.), *From Neurons to Neighbourhoods: The Science of Early Childhood Development*, National Academy Press, Washington DC.

Sylva, K., E. Melhuish, P. Sammons, I. Siraj-Blatchford, B. Taggart and K. Elliot (2003), *The Effective Provision of Pre-School Education (EPPE) Project: Findings from the Pre-School Period*, Institute of Education, University of London and Sure Start, London.

Urrutia, M. (1999), *The Impact of Early Childhood Intervention Programmes on Economic Growth and Equity*, Inter-American Development Bank, Washington.

Vandell, D.L. (2004), "Early Child Care: The Known and the Unknown", *Merrill Palmer Quarterly Journal of Developmental Psychology*, Vol. 50:3, pp. 387-414.

Vandell, D.L. and B. Wolfe (2000), *Child Care Quality: Does it Matter and Does it Need to be Improved?*, United States Department of Health and Human Services, Washington DC.

Verry, D. (2000), "Some Economic Aspects of Early Childhood Education and Care", *International Journal of Educational Research*, Vol. 33, No. 1, pp. 95-122.

ANNEX E

Country Profiles
An Overview of ECEC Systems in the Participating Countries

Introduction

The aim of this Annex is to provide a short, comparative account of ECEC in the countries that participated in the review. In so far as possible, a common profile of each country is presented, using the following descriptors:

- *Auspices* or ministries in charge.

- *Context* in particular female employment rates (full-time and part-time, and the participation rates of women with children under 6 years), and parental leave measures.

- *Access and provision*: This section includes information on operational features; rates of provision for different age groups and different categories of children, *e.g.* special needs, low-income and second-language children.

- *Quality*: The section on quality is the most substantive in most profiles. The quality profile on which information is made available includes: licensing and regulation; funding; staffing and training requirements; work conditions; child-staff ratios; curriculum and pedagogy; monitoring, evaluation and research; and parent and community involvement.

- *OECD policy issues* as reported in the different Country Notes.

- *Developments* as recorded by OECD review teams in the case of the countries in the second round, or as supplied more recently for all countries by the country authorities.

It is hoped that the descriptors used in the profiles will give an insight into country characteristics and, if read in conjunction with the chapters in the volume, provide an indication of the qualities of ECEC in each country. Each profile is preceded by a short overview, which provides a quick snapshot of the major indicators of ECEC in the countries concerned.

The main sources of information for these profiles are: the Background Reports on ECEC policy and organisation, contracted by each country in preparation for the OECD reviews; the OECD Country Notes written by the OECD expert teams that visited each country; the ECEC Country Survey of 2004, carried out by the OECD Education Division; the OECD database on labour force statistics; EUROSTAT figures on fertility rates (*www.europa.eu.int*); the OECD annuals, such as *Society at a Glance; Education at a Glance; Employment Outlook*; and the UNICEF 2005 report on *Child Poverty in Rich Countries* (Innocenti

Centre, Florence). These sources can be easily consulted on their respective Web sites. An overview of terms is provided in Annex A, while Chapter 4 describes the main forms of ECEC provision in the countries reviewed (see in particular Table 4.1).

The different rubrics chosen

Auspices

The first rubric in the profiles, *auspices*, provides information about which ministries have responsibility for ECEC matters, and whether decentralisation of responsibilities is in place. Apart from giving information about the responsible ministry, auspices indicate whether unified policies for 0- to 6-year-olds are the rule, or whether the traditional division between care and education is perpetuated through administrative structures. The issue is important as a move towards co-ordination or unified auspices generally implies that countries wish to take a more coherent and rigorous approach to the early childhood field. The integration of services for children 0-3 and 3-6 years under one ministry or agency is associated with a clearer policy vision in ECEC, and more effective funding and management of the system.

Context

Several context indicators that influence the organisation of early childhood services have been chosen. The *country population*, its *fertility rate* and *current child population under 6 years* provide readers with an idea of the pressures particular governments face, *e.g.* Mexico, in their efforts to provide access to services. The wealth of a country is also important, the indicator chosen being *GDP per capita*. The *age of compulsory schooling* is also another element to take into account when planning early childhood services, as well as *the level of social expenditure* and the *rates of child poverty*. To allow child poverty rates to rise disproportionately is not only a failure of social democracy, but also counteracts the efforts of early childhood and formal education systems. Another essential indicator of the success of ECEC policy is the effects that these policies (or their lack) have on outcomes for women and gender equality.

The levels of female participation in the labour force: Although women are still taking up a far greater proportion of part-time work than men, the participation rates of women in the labour market show a remarkable progression in the last decade, ranging from 42.8% in Mexico (formal employment) to 76.6% in Sweden. Women's work has an important impact on family budgets, and contributes to the general well-being of families and young children. At the same time, societies are slow to recognise that equality of opportunity *to* work and *in* work should become a reality: women are still three times more likely to be in part-time work than men and, in general, make all the sacrifices of careers, salaries and pensions in order to rear children. Enforcement of women's rights to equal wages, the provision of early childhood services and the recognition of the need for paid parental leave are some of the measures being taken by countries to redress the situation.

The provision of maternity and parental leave: Though problematic in certain regards, a developed maternity and parental leave provision improves the quality of care provided to an infant in the critical first year of life. Without it, mothers are obliged to have recourse to informal, unregulated arrangements or to leave the labour market, particularly in countries with under-developed ECEC provision for children 0-3 years. In contrast, countries that fund adequate parental leave seem to offer greater parental choice, reduce unregulated child care and, in some countries at least, achieve high participation rates of women in the labour market. There is a question here of achieving *effective* parental leave policies – an issue examined in the main text.

Access and provision

The section in the profiles on *access and provision* includes a description of *ECEC service structures and characteristics*: Countries provide ECEC in ways that reflect the auspices of those services, *e.g.* under split auspices, the organisational and conceptual divide between "child care" and "early education" runs deep. In marketised systems with large private for-profit groups, inequalities of access, quality differences and disparities in pay and professional training are constant challenges. Without firm management of the sector from a governmental level, families may experience markedly different level of access and quality depending on country, locality and income. The contrast is probably most striking in the large federal countries, such as Canada, where differences in access opportunities between provinces/territories can be extremely wide. In most countries, increasing attention is being given to integration across ECEC services in order to provide more coherence between the horizontal dimension of care, education, health and welfare domains, or between the vertical levels of central, decentralised, private and voluntary provision. The level of coherence achieved is often a predictor of quality and indication of government interest (or lack of interest) in the sector.

Rates of provision: Under this rubric, rates of provision for young children at different ages are given. Readers will note that some countries have comprehensive data by year of age; other countries will have data only for the age group 3-6 years, and can be vague about the participation of young children 0-3 years. One of the reasons is because unlicensed private provision, particularly in family day care, still dominates child care in some countries. A pattern of coverage is emerging across the industrialised countries: a coverage rate of between 10-30% for the 0-3 age group (in licensed services), and after this period, reaching over 80% coverage in full-time places, some time in the fourth year (see Chapter 4). Many factors can influence demand, such as the attitudes of a society towards child-rearing, the presence or absence of high quality services that parents can actually see in operation, affordability, or the participation rate of mothers with young children in the labour market.

Countries are sometimes judged by the level of access that children have to ECEC services or by their rate of progress towards universal service provision. Such indicators are important in light of research evidence on the positive impact of effective ECEC programmes on children's development and learning. However, information about the percentage of children in each age cohort for whom either full-day or part-day services are provided does not reveal the base from which a country is starting or the level of demand. In addition, rates of coverage give little indication of the appropriateness or the quality of services.

Access rates of children with diverse needs: An important element in a country's access performance is whether it provides adequately for children with special education or additional learning needs. Important criteria in services for these children are *appropriate access* and *social equity*. Access figures provided in the profiles are taken from the national Background Reports, the OECD update survey (2004), further literature researches and, in the case of child poverty, from the UNICEF analysis *Child Poverty in Rich Nations* (UNICEF, 2005). Most countries give attention through targeted programmes to children from low-income and immigrant families who are most at risk of school failure. In addition, as the figures on child poverty in each profile show, some countries are successful in preventing disadvantage (through taxes, transfers and social policies) and are able to establish universal systems in which social cohesion is achieved and disadvantaged children can find the services they need.

Quality

A broad range of indicators has been adopted in the country profiles in order to provide readers with some means of assessing *quality* in services across the countries reviewed. In the quality profile proposed, the following indicators are found:

● *Licensing and regulation*: Licensing and regulation are governance tools used in many countries to maintain acceptable standards across provision. If enforcement is real, licensing laws can ensure that providers maintain basic structural standards for the children in their care.

● ECEC *funding*: This rubric is sometimes treated apart when the country situation is complex or important changes in funding have taken place, *e.g.* in the Netherlands. A few simple indicators are generally used under this rubric: such as the unit cost per child in ECEC services; the overall government spending on ECEC in terms of percentage of GDP. These are essential indicators. In highly complex societies, a satisfactory level of ECEC quality will not be achieved across a country's child population without substantial government expenditure. As available data about ECEC funding is unsatisfactory in the UNESCO-OECD-EUROSTAT (UOE) collections, we provide where possible supplementary financing data from country sources (see Chapter 5 or a discussion of this issue).

● *Staffing and training* are among the more important issues of the review, which are treated comprehensively in Chapter 7. Wide differences can be seen between countries in their recruitment and training of staff, ranging from countries with 98% of staff fully trained, to countries in which less than a third of contact staff have a recognised early childhood qualification. Yet, well-motivated, professional staff are perhaps the key to quality in a system. Early socialisation and the stimulation of children's learning in out-of-home environments is a complex task, ideally entrusted to well-trained, professional staff. The positioning of ECEC as the first phase of lifelong learning carries also the implication that the staff of early childhood centres should also be pedagogues or educators. As children approach school age, the professionals should be able to ensure young children a smooth entry into primary school classes, which in turn, should employ methodologies appropriate to the age of these children. The major source of information for this section is the Background Report of each country.

● *The work conditions* of staff in services form a fundamental part of quality. A well-paid motivated staff can be retained and provide continuity and growing expertise for the children in their care. In contrast, high staff turnover rates, low levels of team work and psychological withdrawal among children have been recorded in centres where staff morale is low. Remuneration, the number of hours worked per week and the availability of professional development opportunities are important elements in analysing work conditions.

● *Child-staff ratios*: Much research and discussion of this quality indicator has taken place. The general consensus is that low child-staff ratios are associated with successful early childhood programmes. In early education programmes for young children 3-6 years, ratios range from 5.7 children per adult (Sweden) to an average of 25:1 in Ireland. In the United States, a growing number of States have a requirement of a ratio of 10 children to one staff member (often a qualified teacher) in all public pre-school programmes.

- *Curriculum and pedagogy*: There is a growing trend in OECD countries to have curricula or curriculum standards for early childhood centres, or at least in early education programmes for children 3-6 years. Curricula help prioritise certain content areas and provide common goals for educators and centres to reach. Early childhood curricula can be general frameworks or they may require standards and outcomes to be achieved in language, numeracy, science concepts, etc. In many curricula, socio-emotional development, health, physical exercise, healthy diet, contact with nature and the outdoors, and other elements may also be emphasised. The debate is still open concerning whether curricula should prescribe learning content or remain open frameworks that allow child autonomy and interest to develop. What seems important is that, on the one hand, the natural learning strategies of young children should be respected, and on the other, that some structuring of learning and clear pedagogical aims be formulated and implemented. A more comprehensive discussion of the issue is provided in Chapter 6. Where available, we have also included information on the pedagogical concept employed in services: whether for example, it is holistic in nature and brings care, upbringing and education to young children in an integrated way.

- *Monitoring, evaluation and research*: This indicator emphasises the quality of the data collection and upstream (governmental, local authority) monitoring and evaluation of the ECEC system. The question of ECEC research is treated more generally in Chapters 8 and 9.

- *Parent and community involvement*: Parents play an important role in ensuring the responsiveness of services to child interests and needs. Their crucial contribution to children's early learning and language mastery is also shown in research, such as EPPE (DfES, 2004). The recognition is growing that centres should involve parents. Similarly, involving the local community can enrich early childhood programming and the child's view of how society works. In other instances, in particular in disadvantaged neighbourhoods, a comprehensive services approach to early childhood education and care may be needed. Typically, a comprehensive early childhood service works in co-operation with other community services to provide additional supports to young children and their families. For example, the centre may provides when necessary, courses and advice on parenting (in particular, how to support child development), employment and job training, and leisure activities.

OECD policy issues

OECD policy issues are the various policy, provision or organisational challenges identified by OECD in the course of the country reviews. The issues vary from country to country and reflect the variety and the wide range of concerns that country-wide ECEC systems can present. Because of the nature of the profile format, the issues are presented in these profiles in a very abbreviated manner, but a fuller and more adequate treatment can be found in each Country Note.

Developments

The section on *developments* describes advances made in the past five years by countries in the review, starting from very different bases and levels of provision. From the evidence presented, it is clear that countries have made strong efforts to expand and improve services in the ECEC field. Developments since 2001 demonstrate a continued interest in ECEC policy-making in most countries. Some countries have announced and implemented far-reaching policy reforms. Even countries that have enjoyed decades of extensive service provision have refocused their efforts in light of recent research on the importance of ECEC to child well-being and education outcomes. It should be noted that the extent and accuracy of the developments recorded depend on information provided by the country authorities, who were invited by the Secretariat to participate in a survey in 2004, and to comment on the draft country profiles in 2005.

Australia

Population: 20 m. Fertility rate: 1.7. GDP per capita: USD 28 100. Children under 6 years: 1.5 million (ABS Population Estimate, June 2003).

Female labour force participation: In October 2005, 68.5% of women aged 15-64 years were in the labour force, 43.3% of whom were in part-time employment (male part-time: 13.3%).

Labour force participation rate of women with a child under 5 years: 16.2% are employed full-time, 35.5% part-time. (Australian Government, December 2005). (Data are not available for women with children under 6.)

Maternity and parental leave: In Australia, there is a statutory entitlement to 52 weeks of parental leave, starting from childbirth, but this leave is unpaid, unless employers agree to pay a salary or support sum. 30.6% of employees in their main job have access to maternity/paternity leave (26% of males and 36% of females) (ABS 6310.0). At the birth of a child, 38.8% of leave taken by women is unpaid leave and 32.2% is leave paid by employers. 5.9% of men take unpaid parental leave and 18.7% take paid parental leave (ABS 6254.0). National data on the duration of these leaves are not available. In addition to the statutory entitlement to parental leave, the Australian Government provides a Maternity Payment – a lump-sum payment of AUD 4 000 from 1 July 2006. The payment is non-means tested and is designed to assist with the costs associated with the birth or adoption of a child, including the loss of income while on unpaid maternity leave. Other financial support to assist with the costs of children is available through the means-tested payments Family Tax Benefit (Part A and Part B). For example, a single income family on low income (below AUD 33 361 per annum) having their first child may receive a maximum of around AUD 10 700 (combined Family Tax Benefit and Maternity Payment) in the child's first year of life.

Compulsory school age: c. 6 years.

Social expenditure: 18%. Child poverty rate: 14.7% (OECD average is 11.2 %).

Funding of pre-primary educational services (ISCED Level 0): 0.1% of GDP – 0.7% public and 0.3% private (OECD, *Education at a Glance 2005*), which is 1.7% of the education budget for 2.9% of educational enrolments (OECD, *Education at a Glance 2005*). (This percentage does not include expenditure on child care services or a substantial number of primary school students aged 5 years who are counted in ISCED Level 1 figures.) Australia spends 4.3% of GDP on primary, secondary and post-secondary (non-tertiary) institutions (OECD, *Education at a Glance*, 2004). Enrolments in pre-primary education institutions represent 4.4% of enrolments in all education institutions in Australia (2002). The Level 0 expenditure covers mainly children aged 3-5 years old who attend pre-school (called *kindergarten* in Victoria, Queensland, Western Australia and Tasmania). Australian National Accounts evidence (2002-03) indicated that expenditure on ECEC, including child care and pre-school by both public and private sources was 0.45% GDP.

Funding of services for children under 3: 0.45% of GDP – all private and public expenditure. In the case of long day care, almost all the public expenditure is via subsidies to parents.

Major service types and duration: *Family day care* (FDC) provided in the homes of caregivers, typically less than 10 hours per day. *Long-day child care centres* available for on average 11 hours daily for whole year. *Pre-schools or kindergartens:* normally available for 3-6 hours daily for the academic year. *Out-of-school care* (OSP) for children 6-12 years normally from 7:00-9:00 and 15:00 to 18:00 daily during school terms and 8:00 to 18:00 Monday to Friday during school vacations.

Unit cost per child: Data on unit cost per child consistent with OECD definitions are not available for children aged 3-6.

Average costs to parents: for *child care* – parents assume on average 31% of costs for child care; for pre-school/kindergarten, 22% of costs; and for OSP for children 6-12 years: 35% of costs.

Legal entitlement to a free service: 5 or 6 years (depending on jurisdiction).

Rate of access to regulated services (percentages reported here include varied service durations): Children 0-1 year: 6.9%; 1-2 years: 26.3%; 2-3 years: 40%; 3-4 years: 61.5%; 4-5 years: 80.9%; 5-6 years: 27.6%; OSP for children 6-12 years: 14.2%.

Designation and qualifications of key staff: Long day care centres normally engage a certified *Group Leader* with a post-secondary (2 years) professional diploma for every group of 20-25 children. In addition to a Group Leader other staff may have diplomas, or certificates, or be unqualified. Kindergartens/pre-schools normally engage tertiary qualified *Teachers* with a 4-year undergraduate degree. Qualifications regulations vary across jurisdictions. Nationally, Australian Productivity Commission data (2004) reported 51.3% of staff in approved child care services had formal qualifications.

Overall percentage of qualified staff in services: Family day care: 26%; long day care: 55%; pre-school: 57%. Long day care centres require 1 qualified staff per 20-25 children (depending on the State).

Child-staff ratios (ranges reflect state variations): Family day care: 4-5:1 for children not in school, and 7-8:1 for school-aged children; long day care 0-2 years: 5 or 4:1; 2-3 years: 12 or 10:1; for children 3-5 years: 10-15:1; community pre-school/kindergarten classes for 3-5 years vary from 20 to 26:1 with variable teacher assistant presence; out-of-school provision for children 6-12 years: 11-15:1, but several States do not have regulations.

Maximum group size: A number of jurisdictions do not set maximum group sizes. Regulated family day care: 6; pre-school and kindergarten class sizes up to 30 children; OSP up to 35 children (depending on jurisdiction).

Auspices

Australian early childhood education and care (ECEC) has separate and layered auspices involving both federal and state governments. At federal government level, ECEC auspices are shared by the Department of Family and Community Services and Indigenous Affairs (FaCSIA) and the Department of Education, Science and Training (DEST). FaCSIA administers national child care policy and strategic direction in all types of ECEC programmes except schools and pre-schools. Child care is viewed partly as an issue of employment, providing a support to working parents with young children. It is also understood as a developmental opportunity for children. FaCSIA oversees quality issues in long-day, family day and out-of-school hours care services by funding and supporting the National Child care Accreditation Council, which operates the Quality Assurance systems. All long-day, family day care and out-of-school hours care services take part in the quality assurance systems, involving a review of services every 2.5 years. The capacity of these quality assurance systems to achieve good quality services is often challenged by local evidence of poor service quality. However, the state and territory governments set the regulations and issue licenses for long day care services. Family day care services and out-of-school provision (OSP) are not regulated in all States.

DEST is responsible for formulating national policy in school and pre-school education, although school and pre-school provision is primarily in the control of the state and territory governments. DEST exerts influence through national agenda setting and funding. The national funding policy for financing government and non-government schools is based on maximising choice for parents and removing disincentives for schools to raise private income. The process has drawn strong criticism from some quarters for placing public schools, in terms of overall operating resources, at a disadvantage (see for example, Watson, 2004, "The Total Operating Resources of Australian Private Schools in 2004", Discussion Paper No. 4, Lifelong Learning Network). Within this funding regime, pre-school education is the responsibility of state and territory governments. DEST initiatives in the pre-school sector include Supplementary Recurrent Assistance (SRA). SRA provides supplementary per capita funding to education providers. The aim is to accelerate educational outcomes for Indigenous Australians, particularly in remote regions, beyond those which could reasonably be expected from mainstream and own-source funding alone, by focusing provider effort on the 8 Indigenous education priority areas of the Ministerial Council on Education, Employment, Training and Youth Affairs (MCEETYA). These are:

- Improving Indigenous literacy.

- Improving Indigenous numeracy.

- Increasing the employment of Indigenous Australians in education and training.

- Improving education outcomes for Indigenous students.

- Increasing Indigenous enrolments.

- Increasing the involvement of Indigenous parents/community members in education decision-making.

- Increasing professional development for staff involved in Indigenous education.

- Expanding culturally inclusive curricula.

Critics argue that Australia's complex and multi-layered system of policy development, funding and provision for ECEC may inhibit coordination, an issue also noted by the OECD review team in 2001. In response, various new administrative structures have been introduced to help unify ECEC issues nationally. At the federal level, an Australian Government task force has led co-ordination of early childhood issues, including ECEC, and has sponsored efforts to improve national coherence through the development of the National Agenda for Early Childhood. Many state governments have also established cross-agency working groups to oversee state early childhood initiatives. Education, child care and community services are administered through single departments in some States and separate departments in other States. Three States (New South Wales, Queensland, and Tasmania) have established Commissions for Children and Young People, giving high-level authority to Commissioners to monitor the administration of policies and services, and to act in the interests of children and young people. Two additional States (Western Australia and the Australian Capital Territory) have announced plans to have Children's Commissioners. The State of Victoria has recently established a Commissioner for Child Safety with a narrower remit.

Context

Labour force rates: Australian government data from 2001 indicated that the percentage of women with at least one child below six years who participated full-time in the labour force was 14.5% and part-time, 32.8%. The percentage of women with a child below 3 years who participated full-time was 11.6% and part-time, 30.8%. There was a 28% participation by lone mothers, of which 7% were in full-time employment. These percentages suggest that many children of working parents are cared for by relatives or informal carers during at least part of the day (see *Access and provision* below).

Parental leave: Parental leave in Australia is predominately unpaid. Employees, after twelve months of continuous employment with the same employer, are entitled to 52 weeks of unpaid leave, which can be shared between a mother and father at any ratio, but periods of leave cannot overlap. This is supported by a lump-sum Maternity Payment and means-tested family assistance payments. These "family payments" are provided to perform the function that maternity and parental leave do in other countries. In addition, around 30% of the workforce has access to employer funded paid maternity leave. Data on uptake and the percentage of remunerated salary are unavailable. However, the Australian Bureau of Statistics *Pregnancy and Work Survey*, as well as a study drawn from the Longitudinal Study of Australia's Children, will soon provide this information.

Access and provision

Operating hours and the annual duration of services vary according to service type. Services that open for a full day for the whole working year include regulated family day care, and centre-based ECEC. The services that open for sessional (short) hours for the academic year include, pre-school and accredited out-of-school care (during school terms). Public kindergarten classes operate for the length of the school day (normally 9:00-15:00) and year (40 weeks). School holiday programmes, run by private and community providers, offer care for the full day during breaks between school terms in all States and Territories.

Rates of provision

0-3 years: Based on 2002 ABS Population data, 46.8% of children aged 0-3 years are cared full-time by parents. 24.6% of 0-3 years spend at least part of their day in publicly licensed services while an estimated 36% are placed, for at least part of their day, in informal child care. Of infants (0-1 year) 6.9% are enrolled in licensed and regulated services; for 1-2 year-olds the proportion grows to 26.3%; for 2-3 year-olds: 40%.

3-4 years: Data on participation at 3-4 years vary substantially in the different States. In 2004, the Australian Productivity Commission reported 37.3% of children 0-5 years accessed child care services (2002-03). Almost two-thirds (61.5%) of the 3-4 year-olds in services are in licensed child care settings. Children in this age band may take part in more than one service type in a routine week. For example, some children attend sessional pre-school or kindergarten classes for some hours/days in the week and child care centres for other hours/days.

4-6 years: Wide variation exists across Australia in the age at which children access pre-school services. These services are generally attached to schools, use varied nomenclature (*e.g.* pre-school, kindergarten, reception), and operate for 5-6 hours daily, during each school term. For convenience, they are termed "pre-school" in this profile. The programmes that accept children one year prior to primary are free publicly funded provision in almost all of Australia. These programmes are also known by various terms in different parts of Australia, but are referred to here as "kindergarten" classes. The Australian Productivity Commission (2004), advising caution because of differing age criterion for access in different States, indicated that in 2002-03 some 83.5% of children attended funded pre-school in the year before they commenced school. For the same period, only 17% of children accessed pre-school programmes two years before they commenced school, this varying by jurisdiction.

Children with diverse needs

Children with disabilities: Of the population of children 0-4 years 3.77% have a reported disability. Data on the inclusion of this age group into ECEC services are not available. However, Australian Productivity Commission data (2004) report 2.3% of children 0-12 years with a disability access approved child care services.

Children from low-income families: The child poverty level in Australia is 14.7% after redistribution (OECD average is 11.2%). Data grouping 0-14 year-olds indicate in 2002 that 31.4% of children accessing child care services were from low-income families. Poverty is particularly marked in the Indigenous communities (in 2001, 2.4% of population).

Ethnic and bilingual children: 40% of the Indigenous population is under 15 years and life expectancy is nearly twenty years less than for the wider population. Representation of children from Indigenous background among children accessing child care services in 2002 varied across Australia, but was lower than overall Indigenous representation in the community. For example, 9.8% of the children who attended child care services in the Northern Territory (NT) were Indigenous whereas representation of Indigenous children in the NT population is 41.4%. ABS data (2001-02) indicate that in parallel, Indigenous children are over-represented in the child protection system. Incidence of Indigenous children being placed under care and protection orders is approximately six times higher than for non-Indigenous Australian children. Across jurisdictions, the proportion of Indigenous children attending pre-schools was broadly similar to their representation in the community.

Quality

Licensing and regulatory regimes: Different licensing and regulatory requirements apply in each State. State licensing with guaranteed annual health checks applies to family day care, crèche and centre-based care, and out-of-school care. These services are monitored also for quality through the national Quality Assurance system (normally every 2.5 years). Kindergarten/pre-school regulatory requirements (for 3-4 year-olds) vary even more widely than those in child care services. Some follow the monitoring and accounting processes used in public kindergarten services (generally for 5-year-olds) including registration and reviews, set curriculum standards, staff professional development and supervision. Others follow some of the requirements set for child care services, in particular licensing and annual health checks but do not take part in Quality Assurance.

Funding: Australian National Accounts evidence (2002-2003), published through the Australian Bureau of Statistics, indicate that expenditure on ECEC (including pre-school services) by both public and private sources is 0.45% of GDP. Sixty-six per cent of the expenditure is public funding for child care with 34% private spending (including parental). Parental contributions as a percentage of overall costs are reported to be 31% in child care and 22% in pre-school. Outside the school-based pre-school system, fees for ECEC services are set by the market. Fee support is available to over 98% of parents using child care services (both formal/approved and informal/registered) through Child Care Benefit (CCB). Low-income families receive a higher rate of CCB. In addition to CCB, the Australian government has announced the introduction of a 30% child care tax rebate for out-of-pocket expenses incurred by families using approved child care from 1 July 2004.

The Australian Productivity Commission (2004) indicated that in 2002-03, average expenditure by federal and state governments on children's services (including child care and pre-school), was AUD 650 (approx. USD 500/€380) per child (aged 0-12), varying in different States and Territories. Average state and territory government expenditure for the same range and type of services was less than USD 200/child (approx USD 140/€116), varying significantly by jurisdiction. For early education services, state governments normally fund the cost of one full-time year of school prior to Year One of primary. While all States have available a sessional pre-school year, this sessional pre-school year is free in some States while in others costs are only partially subsidised and parents pay fees.

Staffing: ECEC staffing varies according to the regulatory requirements of each State and Territory. In general, non-school services employ a mix of trained (often two-year vocational) and untrained staff. In family day care settings only 26% of carers have relevant formal qualification. In long day care services this figure is 55% and in pre-schools the derived estimate (excluding Tasmania) is 57%. In long day care centres, minimising staff costs to limit fee increases has worked against the employment of qualified staff whenever such staff are not a regulatory requirement. In some States, staff can be employed while in training for the minimum-level qualification. The estimated proportion of primary contact staff with qualifications in the system as a whole is 52.6%, a low percentage by OECD standards. School-linked pre-schools overseen by state education departments must employ fully trained teachers.

Training requirements: The minimum qualification required for teacher/child care group leader in care settings is a tertiary professional diploma. For trained assistants a post-secondary diploma is required. Qualification requirements for family day care staff (in addition to a First Aid Certificate) were only recently introduced. In school-linked pre-schools, the required qualification is an education degree (normally four years) but not necessarily with an early childhood specialisation in all States. Staff in child care settings who complete qualifications above minimum requirements frequently leave child care settings for employment in education-based ECEC services.

Work conditions: The percentage of part-time staff in ECEC settings is 27.5% for teachers/child care group leaders and 31% for trained assistants. Statutory working hours are 38 hours per week. There is neither a statutory requirement to fund a minimum level of staff development nor recommendations regarding annual hours of in-service training. The status of ECEC staff in non-school services is low. Compared with teachers in pre-schools and kindergarten classes, child care staff have longer contact hours (38 vs. approx 26 per week), greater responsibility, fewer holidays, less planning time and lower wages. Turnover rates are high and difficulties in recruiting care staff are reported extensively, especially in rural and remote areas. Men are hardly represented in care services or pre-school.

Child-staff ratios: Ratios vary, depending on state regulations and type of service. In long day care, ratios are: 5:1 or 4:1 for children 0-2 years; 12:1 or 10:1 for children 2-3 years, and range between 10:1 and 15:1 for children 3-5 years. In family day care, ratios are 5:1 or 4:1 for children not yet in school and 8:1 or 7:1 for school children. In pre-school and kindergarten classes delivered by communities and education departments, child-staff ratios vary according to local jurisdiction with group sizes ranging from 20-26. Teachers have varied amounts of support from teacher-assistants. For out-of-school care provision some States do not have regulations. Those with regulations vary in ratio from 15:1 to 11:1. The maximum group size allowable varies widely according to service type and the State in which it functions. In centre-based ECEC services, maximum group size is 35. In regulated family day care services, maximum size is 6. Pre-school and kindergarten class sizes vary from 15-30. The staff in ECEC services are not necessarily qualified. In general, long day care centres (depending on the State) are required to have one qualified staff member for every group of children, which, for children aged 3-5, could be 20-25 children.

Curriculum and pedagogy: Regulation and processes surrounding curriculum and pedagogy divide according to type of setting. Child care settings participating in Quality Assurance (all long day care, family day care, out-of-school care services) are required to provide a "developmentally appropriate" programme. There is no prescribed curriculum. Some States have a curriculum framework that is mandatory for pre-school aged children in centre-based child care services although normally, pre-school programmes located in child care centres are not required to follow a prescribed curriculum. In pre-school and kindergarten settings, the States and Territories have separate curriculum frameworks and guidelines. The most common provision is a detailed curriculum guideline for 3- to 5- or 4- to 6-year-olds. The framework in South Australia is designed to cover programmes for children 0-18 years. Most guidelines address socio-emotional, physical, cultural, cognitive and linguistic areas of development and include attention to early literacy and numeracy development. Play-based pedagogy is the most common recommended approach. Some recent curriculum guidelines articulate outcomes and are designed to link with the outcomes-based school education curriculum of early primary.

Monitoring, evaluation and research: Reference has already been made to licensing and regulation regimes, and to the Quality Assurance accreditation process. In addition, the role of parents is viewed as central to quality monitoring of all ECEC services, although critics suggest that parents may not always have the required knowledge or time, or choose to engage in this way with services.

National monitoring and reporting is targeted on the overall development, health and well-being of Australian children. The Australian Productivity Commission, through regular reviews of government services, provides coordinated information about child care and pre-school services in each State/Territory, and for the nation, based on existing data sets. A national minimum data set on Children's Services (0-12), focused on usage, provider and service-type statistics is under development and will help further identify ECEC provision when adopted. A focus of current national effort has been the creation of an Australian-relevant evidence base about child outcomes and effective prevention and early intervention approaches during early childhood. The Longitudinal Study of Australian Children (LSAC) was initiated in 2004. One wave of data has been collected and made available to researchers. In addition, the federal government is developing and testing an Australian Early Development Index for its usefulness as a community-level measure of children's development. Considerable national effort is going into evaluation of early childhood interventions at both state and federal levels. There is an active body of professional researchers in Australia with expertise in early childhood who are increasingly contributing to ECEC policy and service delivery.

Parent and community involvement: The current phase of the federal government's Stronger Families and Communities Strategy (SFCS) has a major focus on improving early childhood outcomes through engaging stronger community involvement and improving service delivery in disadvantaged communities. The National Agenda encompasses the importance of supporting parents in their child-rearing role, attention to maternal and child health, and building child-friendly communities. Under the SFCS, for example, there is a project establishing the information needs and preferences of parents to guide the way information about child development and parenting is targeted to parents. A new National Parenting Information Website is being developed in response to consultations from this project. Quality Assurance also fosters family involvement through encouraging family members to participate in the planning, programming and operation of child care services. Further evidence is being gathered on the needs and service experiences of parents in their child's early years. State and territory governments also support parent and community involvement through a variety of initiatives.

OECD policy issues

Among the issues for policy attention identified in 2001 by the OECD review team for Australia were:

- *Understandings of childhood and early education:* ECEC in Australia reveals a range of beliefs and policy directions depending on government philosophy, the government department or administrative body in charge, type of setting and community perception. It was felt that a clearer vision (including a strategy framework) of Australian ECEC policy should be elaborated, drawing from the views and interests of children, families, communities, professionals and researchers across the States and Territories.

- *System coherence and co-ordination:* Currently, real limitations on system coherence are imposed in Australia by the complexities of government in a federation of states, and the multi-layering of administration and regulation. Other difficulties arise from the vastness of the territory and the dispersion of populations.

- *Quality issues:* It was felt that the low pay, low status and training levels of ECEC staff undermine quality, and may counterbalance the investments governments are making in the sector, despite state regulation and national monitoring of quality through a Quality Assurance system. In addition, attention was drawn to the poorer work conditions experienced by staff in the early childhood child care sector, compared to other education sectors.

- *Training and status of ECEC staff:* The OECD team suggests that firmer regulations about the numbers of *trained* staff to be employed by long day centres and family day care would help to improve the quality of their services, and that comprehensive in-service training at a range of levels for staff in this sector is a necessity.

STARTING STRONG II: EARLY CHILDHOOD EDUCATION AND CARE – ISBN 92-64-03545-1 – © OECD 2006

● *Children with special educational needs:* Poverty and early education issues arise most acutely with regard to Indigenous children. The determined targeting of resources by recent governments towards Indigenous educational, economic, and health programmes is acknowledged. The key to the success of the new Indigenous programmes will be their respectful approach to issues of self-determination, cultural ownership, and for some, language. In addition to Indigenous children, children with special needs such as children with a disability, and children from culturally and linguistically diverse backgrounds are target groups for support by Australian Government programmes. Inclusion of these children is critical to a positive and equitable child care environment.

Developments

Over recent years, ECEC has been viewed as a competitive market service in Australia. Government funding of ECEC provision includes both public and non-government sector services (Australian Government funding is through subsidies to parents not to service providers). More recently, corporate, profit-based child care providers have listed on the stock exchange and currently occupy a significant place in the Australian child care sector. With few exceptions, direct operational subsidies to community, non-profit services were removed under a "level playing field" strategy in 1996 and 1998, although Indigenous and other special services, including family day care, retain subsidies.

In the education sector there is a major emphasis on learning outcomes, with national attention to literacy and numeracy skills, seen as vital for labour market participation. The commitment of the States to furthering an outcomes-based approach is evident through state funding of state authorities to engage in the development of curricula and quality standards.

Growing recognition of the importance of ECEC is evident in *The National Agenda for Early Childhood* (DFCS, 2004). The consultations with all levels of government and the non-government sector surrounding the development of the National Agenda revealed strong support for early learning and care as one of four action areas to improve outcomes for Australian children. Achieving greater national consistency in early childhood education and care systems has been recognised in the National Agenda document as a key objective. The National Agenda highlights the need for development of a skilled and knowledgeable workforce as a key consideration for ensuring an effective and sustainable early childhood system. The National Agenda has been endorsed by the Australian Government and is with States and Territories for their endorsement. Once endorsed, collaborative cross-government projects will be developed under the auspices of the National Agenda.

Austria

Population: 8.17 m. **Fertility rate:** 1.39. **GDP per capita:** USD 28 900. **Children under 6 years:** 487 000.

Female labour force participation: 63.5% of women (15-64) participate, 29.6% of whom are in part-time employment (male part-time is 3.7%) (*OECD in Figures*, 2004).

Labour force participation rate of women with a child under 6 years: 30% (Statistics Austria 2002/03).

Maternity and parental leave: 16 weeks of maternity leave paid at 100% of earnings. 3 years with funded benefit.

Average duration of parental leave: Not available.

Compulsory school age: 6 years.

Social expenditure: 26% GDP Child poverty rate: 10.2% GDP (UNICEF, 2005) after taxes and transfers (OECD average is 11.2%).

Funding of pre-primary educational services: 0.55% of GDP, 9% of education budget with 14% of education enrolments.

Funding of services for children under 3: Not available but very low. Less than 10% of children in licensed services.

Unit cost per child is USD 6 169 (OECD, *Education at a Glance*, 2005).

Average costs to parents: 20% maximum of service costs.

Legal entitlement to a free service: 5 years, but places in kindergarten are generally available from 3 years.

Major service types and duration: *Tagesmütter* or family day care; some few *Krippen* (crèches – in Vienna mainly) provide centre-based care for children 0-3, available for approx. 10 hours per day; *Kindergartens* provide programmes for 3- to 6-year-olds with over half of the centres offering all-day programmes; *Hort* are after-school day care centres (OSP), generally open before and after school – at 7:00 and up to 18:00; *Kindergruppen* (parent-toddler and playgroups – mainly in West Austria) are organised by parents as private initiatives, mostly offering a half-day (playgroups) or a full-day (parent-toddler groups) programme; *mixed age day care facilities* run as full-day kindergartens: in this type of service, children under the age of 3 may make up to a maximum one-third of the children.

Rate of access to regulated services: Children 0-3 years: 8.9%. Children 3-6 years: 80%. OSP for children 6-12 years: not available.

Designation and qualifications of key staff: *Kindergartenpädagoginnen* or kindergarten pedagogues are the main staff in kindergartens, while in crèches and *Hort*, *Erzieherinnen* are the majority staff. Over 60% of staff in both kindergartens and crèches have a professional diploma.

Child-staff ratios: Family day care: 3.4 children per caregiver and 5 children maximum per group; *Krippen:* 8.7 children per staff, and on average 12 children/group; *Kindergarten:* 16 children per adult and on average, 20 children/group, but a maximum group size of 25-28 children is permitted, unless young children under 3 are present; mixed age facilities: 13.6 children per pedagogue. In *Kindergruppen* organised by parents, the average ratio is 6.5 children per adult, and 15 children per group.

Maximum group size: The maximum group size allowed is 28 children (in most provinces 25 children per group), but in fact, the average group size practised in 2002 was 21 children per group, with 16 children per kindergarten educator (Background Report for Austria, 2004).

Auspices

Austria is a federal country composed of nine provinces or *Bundesländer*, each with its own parliament and government. Because of its federal nature and Constitution, full responsibility for social welfare and early education and care is devolved to each province. Within the context of social partnership and the social economy, the allocation of public responsibilities is further governed by the principle of subsidiarity, namely, that societal tasks are best undertaken by the smallest possible social unit, which, in the case of infants and toddlers is deemed to be the family. Care by the family is interpreted in most of Austria as requiring a traditional division of labour on gender lines with the majority of mothers taking leave from work to care for children, or – if the option is available – to combine part-time care and part-time work. Family and social policy provides fiscal incentives (such as the Child Care Benefit) during this period to encourage the second family earner to remain at home to rear young children. For these reasons, the demand for crèches and other child care services has remained weak, with these services catering for less than 10% of young children on a full-time basis.

The Federal Ministry for Social Security and Generations defines the framework that governs maternal, infant and youth welfare. A fundamental aspect of the work of this department is to maintain and strengthen the family influence in child-rearing and to create a framework for child development within this direction. The "child minder" system and child care services for young children are overseen by this department. The Federal Ministry for Education, Science and Culture is the competent authority for creating the legal foundation for kindergarten, issuing ordinances such as uniform frameworks, and allocating resources for the training of kindergarten pedagogues, both pre-service and in-service (Background Report for Austria, 2004).

De facto, the provincial (*Länder*) governments have full responsibility for the organisation and funding of ECEC services. The provincial governments set regulatory and funding frameworks that guide the planning and provision of ECEC services. The actual administration of ECEC within the different *Länder* may be through education or other child and youth ministries, or distributed across ministries. The Austrian system, therefore, is complex and highly decentralised.

Context

Labour force rates: In 2003, 63.5% of women participated in the Austrian labour force. 29.6% of women are in part-time employment compared to 3.7% of men (*OECD in Figures*, 2004).

Parental leave: Parents may take up to 3 years supported parental leave, if both parents take at least 6 months. Most fathers do not use this entitlement, reducing the leave in those families to 30 months, and since 1996 to 24 months. Mothers receive 16 weeks maternity leave, required to be taken before and after the child's birth. A cash benefit that replaces full wages is paid for this period. There is protection from dismissal during long parental leave (up to two years), and for up to four weeks after returning to former positions. Parental leave payments (EUR 426/month if income is less than EUR 14 600/year, until the child's third birthday) are funded under a family benefit scheme, enabling students, unemployed parents and parents not in the workforce wishing to care for a child full-time to obtain the leave. A generous Child Benefit is also paid to low-income families for 30 months – or to 36 months if both parents claim. Parents can also take paid, job-protected leave to care for a sick or a handicapped child under the age of 12. There are questions about women's labour market participation after parental leave. The effect of these accumulated benefits is twofold: they reduce effectively family and child poverty and simultaneously, provide an incentive for women – particularly in low-income families – to withdraw from the labour market for two or three years after the birth of a child.

Access and provision

Types of institutional ECEC differ primarily according to age of the children. *Krippen* (public crèches), kindergartens and parent-toddler groups are, in principle, available to 0- to 6-year-olds. Non-centre based services are also provided by child minders and *kindergruppen* (playgroups). Approximately 70% of all ECEC facilities are operated by local authorities, the remainder being offered by parishes, non-profit association, companies and private persons (Background Report for Austria, 2004).

Kindergarten is the most widespread service available, accounting for 86.7% of all children in institutional care settings. The remaining 13.3% are distributed across *krippen* (crèches) (5%); child minders (3.5%); mixed age facilities (3.1%); and parent-toddler groups (1.7%). Less than 9% of children below the age of 3 years access the available services.

Mixed-age facilities have developed in response to lower demand, given diminishing numbers of young children in Austria. A maximum of one-third of the children in these facilities may be in the 0-3 age range. Most of these facilities operate full day. The new mixed age grouping from 2 to 6 years led to a stronger focus on team work among pedagogues and the use of their natural strengths. This opportunity brought about by a declining birth rate – although threatening the viability of some kindergartens – is encouraging stronger investment in present institutions to increase the level of child care and out-of-school provision available to children.

Parent-toddler groups are independent initiatives where parents and caregivers work closely together in family-like environments, parents taking on both organisational and educational responsibilities. As parent-toddler groups are run by parents, the operating hours meeting the needs of local families, about half of such groups open 6-9 hours per day. The length of time children spend in the group during a day varies widely from province to province, with half-day services in west Austria and full-day services being more common in Vienna and the east.

0-3 years: Approximately 80% of mothers of children in crèche are in the paid workforce (Statistics Austria, 2002/03), of whom 29.6% are in part-time employment (male part-time is 3.7%). Child minders, either accredited or unregulated, provide the majority of extra-domestic care available for this age. In 2003, approximately 8 500 children were in the care of 2 500 child minders, predominantly on a half-day basis. *Krippen* (crèches) provide centre-based care for children 0-3 years, but few children access this service (approximately 8.9%). Parent-toddler group programmes are the main form of service to children in this age span, offering support for a few hours per day to a full-day (9-10 hours), depending on the province and locality.

3-6 years: Kindergartens provide programmes for children from three years to compulsory school age (at 6 years). Widespread acceptance of kindergarten programmes ensures most children (approximately 80%) attend, irrespective of the labour force participation of parents. As children move through this age span, a pre-primary school programme (*vorschulstufe*) is available at primary schools for children of compulsory school age who are deemed not mature enough for the first grade of primary school. Depending on local parental demand, this programme operates as a class of 10-20 children or as a group less than 10. More than half the kindergartens offer all-day operating hours with no break at midday, although widespread variation exists from province to province (Background Report for Austria, 2004).

Attention to children with diverse needs

Children with disabilities: Special needs kindergartens, operated by "special education kindergarten teachers", provide programmes promoting children and providing therapy. Children may also be served in through "integration groups", whereby children with special needs are included in mainstream kindergartens. In general integration groups contain 15 children, 3-5 of whom may have been medically evaluated to having special needs. However, there is no legal entitlement to inclusive child care and there is insufficient data available to document the level of access, need, or support to children with disabilities in either child care or kindergarten. In consequence, levels of access for these children differ widely across the provinces. Proactive federal involvement is lacking in this and other important fields.

Children from low-income families: Data are not collected on children from disadvantaged groups. The Background Report for Austria (2004) recognises the gap in information and the "fundamental lack of scientific studies" in this area.

Ethnic and bilingual children: In 2001, approximately 45% of non-Austrian residents in the country were nationals from former Yugoslavia and 17.5% were Turkish nationals. Other groups included Germans (10.5%), Poles (2.1%), and Romanians (2.5%), Czechs (1.9%) and Hungarians (1.8%). Approximately 11% of the children in kindergarten are immigrants, having mothers whose mother-tongue is a language other than German (Background Report for Austria, 2004). An overall plan for the support of these children in not in place.

Quality

Licensing and regulatory regimes: Provincial laws specify building standards, equipment for the programmes and the required training for staff. These requirements are more comprehensive for kindergartens and crèches than for facilities not regulated by kindergarten laws. Child care institutions are visited by inspectors, on average, once per year. Non-routine inspections may also occur if parents complain about a service. Inspectors may access the building and review operational records, acting as primary assessors of quality and indicate quality shortcomings. If problems are apparent, the agency receives written notification from the municipality and must initiate necessary improvements. However, differences among the provinces result in some inspectors being responsible for very large numbers of services and all aspects of inspection, including building standards (Background Report for Austria, 2004). Except in one province, child minders (operating form their homes) require a day care licence from the competent district administration authority. The licences prescribe the number of children a child minder may supervise. These child care programmes, and the activities of parent-toddler groups, are inspected at random intervals after licensing.

Funding: Since 1970, municipalities have provided the greatest share of funding towards ECEC services in Austria: 60-70% of costs are taken in charge by municipal budgets; 15-25% by the *Bundesländer* governments, and some 15-20% (including child care) is provided by parental fees, with again a fairly wide variation across provinces (OECD, *Babies and Bosses*, 2003), *e.g.* kindergartens in Lower Austria do not charge parental fees for the morning session, but parents contribute to lunch and the afternoon session. A usual form of funding is for the municipality to pay the salaries of qualified kindergarten educators. As a rule, facilities run by for-profit providers do not receive any financial support. Facilities maintained by recognised non-profit associations, parent groups and church organisations receive municipal subsidies under certain conditions. Expenditure on pre-primary institutions (kindergartens for children 3-6 years) as a percentage of GDP is 0.55% of GDP, which corresponds to 9% of the education budget for 14% of education enrolments. 76.2% of this expenditure came from public sources and 23.8% from private sources including 11.6% household expenditure. Generous family benefit payments, home care credits (called in Austria a Child Care Benefit) and long parental leaves are in place, leading to lesser service demand and availability, especially for children 0-3 years.

Staffing: Kindergarten and crèche groups are staffed by kindergarten pedagogues (60.4% of staff) and some 30% of *Erzieherinnen* (care assistants). Approximately 25% of the assistants are trained pedagogues. The remaining 10% of staff have completed different training or may have none. Kindergarten directors are responsible for admitting children, assigning them to groups, scheduling staff, creating the educational programme and conducting meetings with parents. Child minders and parent-toddler group staff, like staff in kindergartens, are normally trained, and must take into account age-specific and individual child needs.

Training requirements: Kindergarten pedagogues (*Kindergartenpädagioginnen*) receive a 5-year training in *Bildungsanstalten für Kindergartenpädagogik* at 24 ECEC Training Institutes or *Fachschulen* (secondary education level) across Austria. To work in kindergarten or crèche, candidates must have demonstrated success in the Diploma exam and secondary school leaving examination (matriculation). Kindergarten pedagogues generally work in kindergartens with children, 3-6 years. They may also work – often in positions of direction – in crèches for children 0-3 years, but the majority of staff in crèches are *Erzieherinnen* (educators, social pedagogues) who are trained in *Bildungsanstalten für Sozialpädagogik*. *Erzieherinnen* work essentially in crèches, kindergartens *Hort* (leisure centres or classes for children), which children attend in the afternoon to do their home work and spent some leisure-time. *Erzieherinnen* also work with adolescents, and they are trained to the same level as *Kindergartenpädagoginnen* but in 6 special schools for social educators in Austria. *Erzieherinnen* working in crèches have taken special modules to prepare them for work with infants and toddlers. *Special needs kindergarten pedagogues* have additional training, enabling them to work with children deemed to have developmental problems, or disabilities. *Kindergarten assistants* may work at kindergartens or crèches without training, but many kindergartens employ *Erzieherinnen*. In principle, child minders must also be trained in Austria. Child minders linked to the Austrian Federation of Child Minders complete a relevant, short training course, but training requirements differ widely across provinces. Training ranges from 30 hours in Lower Austria to 468 hours with a professional examination in Styria.

Although the training of both *Kindergartenpädagoginnen* and *Erzieherinnen* is of high quality in the *Fachschulen*, concern is expressed about the level of training – which, at secondary upper level, is among the lowest in Europe. Current demands on the profession, *e.g.* the greater diversity of children, higher education expectations of parents, and the need to promote equality of opportunity for women in work – all suggest that kindergarten pedagogues need a tertiary-level, professional education, which, in turn, would lead also to higher quality standards in services.

Work conditions: Graduates from the specialised *Fachschulen* are approximately 19 years of age when they begin their professional career, and most who leave the profession do so in the first 10 years (Background Report for Austria, 2004). There are few opportunities for professional advancement and development although attention to assuring acquisition of the secondary school leaving certificate suggests some improvement.

Child-staff ratios: On average, there are 12 children per group in crèche settings and 20 children per group in kindergartens (Background Report for Austria, 2004). The maximum group size allowed in kindergarten is between 25-28 children. In *Krippen,* crèches for children under 3 of age, the average ratio practised 8.7 children per trained staff member, not an outstanding ratio by international standards (Statistics Austria, Kindergartens and After-School Child care, 2002/03). Parent-toddler groups comprise 5-10 children, and child minders generally supervise a maximum of 5 children at any one time, the average child-adult ratio being 3.4:1. Mixed age facilities generally have a staff-child ratio of 13 or 14:1, with no more than a third of the children being under 3.

A 2004 study by the Charlotte Bühler Institute expresses concern about ratios. According to this study, the actual group sizes in Austrian kindergartens were near 25 children in two thirds of the groups and reached 28 or more children in 19% of the groups. Large groups with 28 or more children are found in those provinces, where special derogations for exceeding the legally determined group sizes are used in many instances. Kindergarten groups in village municipalities are typically smaller than those in cities.

With regard to staff structure, data are also available from the aforementioned study. Of the kindergarten teachers, 69% lead a group jointly with a non-qualified helper, and 14% of the kindergarten teachers lead a group completely alone. Only 7% of kindergarten teachers lead a paired group with a comparably qualified colleague, and only 3% of the kindergarten teachers are supported by a helper in addition to the paired group. In this study an overall teacher-child ratio of 1:23 was calculated. Only groups that were led by two qualified teachers jointly (therefore only 10% of all Austrian kindergarten groups), show a favourable care ratio of 1:12.

Curriculum and pedagogy: A strong social pedagogic tradition is in place supported by good buildings and outdoor spaces. There is a concern about space per child, recently regulated to 3 m^2 per child. Favourable (in practice) child-staff ratios support the curriculum and a policy emphasis on the holistic development of young children forms a key framework for activity. Pedagogues well-trained in the practical/aesthetic skills of kindergarten work operate in stable staff teams.

Monitoring, evaluation and research: Programmes in kindergartens and *krippen* are monitored by municipal inspectors, although the scale of duties and number of centres in the jurisdiction of each inspector is great. Data collected at federal level (by Statistics Austria) on providers, opening hours, facilities, child access, and staff provide the basis for decisions affecting ECEC services. No uniform statistics are available on child minders and parent-toddler groups. Data pertaining to children with additional needs are not readily available at federal level.

Parent and community involvement: Traditional views of the role of mothers and fathers in child-rearing prevail, whereby women take on the majority of responsibility for the care and education of children. Parents are expected to cooperate with kindergarten staff and become involved in activities related to the kindergarten.

OECD policy issues

Among the issues for policy attention identified by the OECD review team in 2004 were:

- *The social context, including women's status and family role:* Among the issues discussed under this heading were: current demographic trends; family supports and parental leave (in particular, the effects of the Child Care Benefit package, which favours a male, bread-winner family model and may also send out a signal to the *Bundesländer* governments not to invest in child care services); and women's status and role within Austrian society.

- *Governance and finance:* Among the issues discussed were: a more proactive role for central government (the involvement of a central ministry can bring much needed direction to an ECEC system, including defining common entitlements and requirements; funding, and the promotion of "impulses" or initiatives, which focus the attention of the stakeholders on important current issues); building up critical mass and ECEC expertise in the ministries; and increasing and stabilising the public funding of early childhood (it was felt that a real commitment from the Federal government is needed i) to bring additional resources into early childhood education and care; ii) to bring transparency and consistency into present funding arrangements; iii) to ensure equitable treatment for special needs and at-risk children across the country, and iv) to link funding to improved quality and access, for example, kindergarten hours that better match parents' work days; more transparent pedagogical aims).

- *The challenges of access:* In this field, the following was discussed: the quantitative expansion of ECEC in Austria (in particular for children from 1-3 years, and in poor neighbourhoods); and the appropriate access of children with special or additional educational needs (children with disabilities in Austria do not always have first call on services, and municipalities can be reluctant to take on the extra costs involved, such as extra staff or renovations of kindergarten buildings and classrooms to facilitate access for these children).

- *Strategies to improve quality:* Among the issues discussed under strategies to improve quality were: licensing and regulatory regimes (devolution of powers to the provinces is a positive step towards local democracy and to creating more responsive local services, but it seems excessive to find wide divergences in the regulations in force in different parts of a small country); staffing, training and work conditions (especially the need to review the present training level of the *Kindergärtnerinnen* and to improve significantly the working conditions of staff and their professional development opportunities – linked to career development); curriculum and pedagogy (a national curriculum framework to clarify common values and objectives for early childhood education and care across Austria; to promote an even level of quality across age groups and regional provision; to facilitate communication between staff, parents, and children; to help guide and support professional staff in their practice; and to ensure pedagogical continuity across the *Länder* and between ECEC and school.); improved data collection, evaluation and research; and parent and community involvement (the need to have a more proactive project towards parents from the kindergartens: children whose parents talk, negotiate and read aloud to them have generally little difficulty in expression, or and later in acquiring early literacy. In high poverty or immigrant areas, early childhood centres are very effective when they function as a hub of interconnected community services for families, and act as a frontline mechanism for child well-being, screening and prevention).

Belgium: French Community

Population: 4.3 million. **Fertility rate:** 1.7. **GDP per capita:** EUR 28 700 (Belgium).

Female labour force participation: 57.3% of women participate, 34.1% of whom are in part-time employment (male part-time is 6.3%).

Labour force participation rate of women with child(ren) under 6 years: 68%.

Maternity and parental leave: 15 weeks of maternity leave paid at c. 80% of earnings; paternity leave of 10 days (3 days paid by employers, 7 days by social security); parental leave of 3 months (6 months part-time) paid at a flat rate; time-credit breaks are possible for all workers.

Average duration of parental leave: Not available.

Compulsory school age: 6 years.

Social expenditure: 27.2% of GDP. **Child poverty rate:** c.10%. For Belgium as a whole, the figure is 7.7% after taxes and transfers (OECD average is 11.2%).

Funding of pre-primary educational services (ISCED Level 0): 5% of GDP.

Unit cost per child in early education: (in USD converted using PPP) USD 4 420 (OECD, *Education at a Glance*, 2005).

Funding of services for children under 3: (for Belgium) 0.6% of GDP; 9% of total education.

Average costs to parents: 0-3 years and OSP: parents contribute a maximum 28% of costs for public services. As fees are based on income, at-risk and low-income families have free access. In general, 10% of places in public services are provided freely to families in need. Children 3-6 years: free to parents from 2.5 years. OSP for children 6-12 years: not available.

Legal entitlement to a free service: From 2.5 years.

Major service types and duration: *Accueil familial* (family day care); *crèche*; *école maternelle* (kindergarten), *service d'accueil extra-scolaire* (OSP).

Rate of access to regulated services: Children 0-3 years: 18%. Children 3-6 years: 100%. OSP for children 6-12 years: 33%.

Professional qualifications of lead staff: In the crèches, children's nurses (*puéricultrices*) have a 3-year, post-16 vocational qualification; in the école maternelle, teachers (*institutrices*) have a specialised 3-year, tertiary level teaching diploma.

Designation of key staff: In crèches, *puéricultrices*; in écoles maternelles, *institutrices de maternelles*.

Child-staff ratios: Depends on type of service: family day care 4:1; crèches 7:1 (depends on age of child); école maternelle: 15:1; OSP for children 6-12 years: 14 children to one trained adult.

Maximum group size: Children 3-6 years: 32 children. OSP for children 6-12 years: centres decide themselves.

Auspices and context

In the French Community of Belgium, education and care are divided administratively, although brought together under the Minister of Childhood (Ministre de l'Enfance). The Minister has full competence for early care and basic education (the école maternelle and primary education) within the French Community. Some policy and funding responsibilities have been devolved to the two regions, Wallonie and Bruxelles-Capital. At the local level, local authorities organise services (including out-of-school provision) and provide additional funding. Policy with regard to taxes, state finances, employment, social affairs and social welfare falls within the competence of the Federal government.

For children from 0-3 years, the Minister relies on ONE (Office de la Naissance et de l'Enfance), a governmental, public agency responsible for mother and child health and protection, and for all aspects of child care policy and provision. All settings providing care to children under 6 years of age must declare themselves to the ONE, obtain its authorisation and bring their programme into conformity with the Code de qualité de l'accueil, decreed in May 1999.

The Minister of Childhood also designates the broad aims and objectives of basic education in the Community, which includes primary education and the école maternelle for children from 2.5-6 years. Most schools and educational services fall under one of three main umbrella organisations or networks: French Community Schools (non-confessional, covering 10% of children); the public network of non-confessional, Communal Schools, organised by local communes, covering 50% of children; and the Free or Private Schools (including the voluntary, state-aided Catholic system) covering 40% of pupils.

Labour force participation of women: Average female employment in Belgium stands at 57.3%, 34.1% of whom are in part-time employment (male part-time is 6.3%). The labour participation rate of women with children below the age of 6 years is significantly higher at 68%. However, fully a third of women work part-time, indicating – confirmed by the 2002 INS Survey of the Workforce (INS, Enquête sur les forces de travail) – that child care issues may be impeding full-time employment.

Maternity and parental leave: By European standards, parental leave is short. In summary, the law provides for 15 weeks of maternity leave paid at c. 80% of earnings; paternity leave of 10 days (3 days paid by employers, 7 days by social security); parental leave of 3 months (6 months part-time) paid at a flat rate; and unpaid time-credit breaks for all workers. In 2002, nursing mothers were allowed to take a daily break of half- to one hour to breast-feed their children. The salary loss for the nursing period is taken in charge to 82% by employers or social security.

Context: During the OECD visit in October 1999, it was clear that Belgium has one of the most comprehensive early education and care systems in Europe. In the care sector, ONE's wish to improve the access and quality of services has given rise to management reform, concertation and planning. A Quality Code for child services was decreed in 1999, based on the UN Convention on the Rights of the Child, and European Union recommendations. Emphasis is placed too on training and professional development. There is high take-up of training opportunities, particularly in Brussels where the FRAJE, a training association attached to the region, has been very active (see Box 3.1 of Chapter 3 in Starting Strong (OECD, 2001)). There are also efforts to create new municipal posts to co-ordinate early childhood services in different milieus.

The French Community sees child care and the école maternelle as a tool against social exclusion, and a privileged means of integrating "at risk" children. A universal right to early care and education exists in practice, through the *école maternelle*, which is open to all children from the age of 2.5 years. At the *école maternelle*, the focus on quality has given rise to official guidelines (*Décret mission*), drawing attention to fundamental goals, such as developing the creativity of children, early learning, socialisation and citizenship, and the early diagnosis of disability or special need. In-service training is also seen as a privileged instrument to improve the understanding and professional practice of personnel, and it is planned to bring together the different networks for common training sessions. The commitment of university researchers to the early childhood sector is high, and in collaboration with teachers and staff, they carry out many action-research projects on the ground.

Access and provision

0-1 year: Parental care predominates, although many infants – up to 12% – are enrolled from three months in the public crèches. Because of regulations and tax-credits paid to families for use of accredited services, there is little informal care (calculated at about 6.6%), unless by the extended family.

1-3 years: In this age group on average, 21.5% of children are cared for in full- or half-day day care centres and a further 12% in family day care. Further care is provided by drop-in services (*haltes-garderies*, etc.) and by informal, non-registered child minders. Normally, the registered services open 10-12 hours per day throughout the year.

2.5-5 years: Free, half-day coverage is provided to all children from 30 months in the *école maternelle*, with after-school care available if needed. Almost 100% of children are enrolled at 3-4 years. The pre-school opens daily (half-day Wednesday) from 8.30-15.30, with after-school care available if needed.

After-school provision: About 33% of children use after-school provision regularly in the French Community. Much effort has been invested in the domain in recent years.

Attention to children with diverse needs

Children with disabilities: In Belgium, the tradition has been to support these children when young in the home, and then in special education units. There is growing awareness, however, of the benefits of including children with light handicaps in ECEC, and today, children receiving subsidies because of special needs represent about 1% of enrolments. From the age of 3 or 4, special education is well funded in Belgium, but is generally separate from mainstream provision. Relatively few children with organics physical or mental handicaps are included in mainstream early education.

Children from low-income families: After redistribution mechanisms, the child poverty level in the French Community is reckoned to fall around 10%, greater than the 7.7% average for Belgium as a whole. Higher per capita grants and special subsidies are available for low-income children (often including immigrant children – see below), and their schools may receive increased funding for extra teachers and more intensive programmes.

Ethnic and bilingual children: Immigrant children constitute 12% of the basic school population, reaching 30% in Brussels. Strong government investment in social exclusion and priority education programmes exists. 6.4% of children enrolled in the *école maternelle* are recognised as having additional learning needs (immigrant children, low socio-economic background, etc.), and as such benefit from special attention.

Quality

Licensing and regulatory regimes: Although the system is one of mixed public and private provision, the licensing of children's services in Belgium is strict and closely supervised. In the provision of early education services (the *école maternelle*), the three main umbrella organs act in accordance with the laws governing public services, and provide free education that is open to enrolment from all sections of the public. In addition, community regulations, *e.g.* concerning quality or curriculum content, must be followed by all providers. Operating hours, internal regulations, annual duration of services and some content may vary, however, in function of the needs of families attending a particular centre or of the particular ethos of the umbrella organisation. In the care sector, public services are licensed, supervised and continually evaluated; private services are licensed and supervised.

Funding: In the education sector, services from 2.5 years are free, with special supports for low-income/ethnic areas and families. *Écoles maternelles* are operated by official, community and private networks – almost completely financed by the French Community government. With respect to actual funding, we have not been able to obtain disaggregated figures for the French Community alone. OECD's *Education at a Glance*, 2004, provides an average figure of 0.6% public investment in the infant school for both Communities in Belgium.

In the care sector, parents pay fees to recognised services, according to income, from 17-25% of actual costs. In turn, they are granted tax benefits to recuperate these costs, up to 80%. In the care sector, provision is publicly subsidised and supervised when supplied by community services, and supervised only when provided by private bodies, *e.g.* private family day care. In public services, 10% of budget must be reserved to meet the needs of families and children presenting particular needs.

Staffing: The division between care and education in the Community is reflected in the training and status of contact staff in each sector. The *puéricultrices* in the care sector have a secondary level, four-year general professional course, followed by two years (16-18 years) of child nursing, which comprises a number of paramedical courses and practical placements. Their salary level is low, about half that of pre-school teachers, who now enjoy a salary level equivalent to that of their primary school colleagues. Personnel in family day care or *maisons d'enfants* (children's centres) are required simply to have a "useful experience" although in the *maisons d'enfants*, many *puéricultrices* are found. In-service training is available, especially for personnel belonging to community services in Brussels. A lack of adequate training has been noted among staff working in private child care institutions.

In the *école maternelle*, teachers are trained at tertiary level for three years in one of 14 higher education colleges. The Community devolves in-training budgets to the level of the school, which must organise eleven days training per year. The umbrella organisations are also required to engage in training activities and inspection of quality.

Work conditions: Information on the number of part-time staff in ECEC settings for children 0-3 years was not available. Among the teachers (*institutrices*) of the *école maternelle*, almost a quarter work part-time. By statute, both professions work 38 hours per week. There is also a statutory requirement to fund a minimum level of staff development, where teachers are concerned, at least 6 half-days per year, with a proposal to extend the number of half-days to 10. Few men are employed in child care, except at managerial level, and among teachers, over 85% are women.

Child-staff ratios: In child care, ratios are as follows: in centre-based day care (*crèche*) 1 children's nurse (*puéricultrice*) for 7 children; in family day care, 1 adult for 4 children. Crèches (18-48 places) must also employ a medical nurse and trained social worker, one of whom is generally the manager. In the *école maternelle*, the maximal child-staff ratio is 19 to 1, but in most cases, it is much less. *Puéricultrices* are often employed to assist teachers with the younger children.

Developments

Increases in public investment to widen access to services and in infrastructure: Measures to increase public investment include more efficient use of resources through participation mechanisms, and a new ten-year plan for the development of out-of-school provision. For children aged 0-3 years, a new Stork Plan (le *Plan Cigogne*), adopted in 2003, represents a significant new investment in the sector. It aims to increase the number of subsidised places in the sector over a period of ten years, so as to reach the targets set by the European Union during the Barcelona European Council meeting, 16-17 March, 2002. These plans are written into the management contract of ONE, and are based on greater equality of coverage levels across regions, the creation of synergies with employers, the improvement of the conditions of family day care providers (first steps towards a recognised social status and the possibility of receiving up to 4 children), and a pilot experiment with parental crèches. Access to free public education is guaranteed to every child from the age of two-and-a-half years.

Strengthening relations with the education system: A common concern of child care and early education is the challenge of transition. This led ONE, in 2004, to devoting its choice of annual theme to the issue of the passage of each child from child care services (le *milieu d'accueil*) to the *école maternelle*. A renewal of pedagogy in the *école maternelle* classes has also taken place to take into account transition challenges, as also in the child care sector. In the recommended programme for the *école maternelle*, the psycho-motor development activities begun in the crèche services are now continued, and policies of positive discrimination in favour of children with special learning needs have been reinforced. Where the older children are concerned, transition between the *école maternelle* and the school is taken in charge by the organisation of a common 5-8-year-old cycle.

Improvements in regulation: By French Community Decree of 27 March, 2002, an Advisory Committee (*comité de pilotage*) for the French Community education system (of which the *école maternelle* is a part), was created. In the child care sector, from 2004, the regular care of any child under 12 years must be reported to ONE, and the provision receiving the child be subject to the Quality Code. In this context, ONE has developed a new professional profile "child care co-ordinators" (*coordinateurs accueil*) whose main function is the inspection of norms and support to pedagogical practice in child care services. Child care providers must also formulate a child care project in conformity with the Quality Code. The successful examination of these projects by ONE agents leads to the delivery of a certificate of quality. The evaluation is a condition for certification and for the payment of subsidies to the provider. A Decree of the 3rd July, 2002, covers out-of-school provision, in particular, the quality of the out-of-school project, the role of personnel, the reception and taking in charge of children, and the development of pedagogical practices.

Improvements in programme quality, e.g. the adoption of a valid pedagogical framework in all services for children 0-12 years, and the education of personnel to implement it. Service frameworks should take into account and conform to the Quality Code, which establishes a basis for reflection, and is turned actively towards the search for quality within the larger context of equality of opportunity. Every service should develop its own care and education project supported and guided by the Quality Code. Professional development courses will focus on the elaboration of these projects and their contents. In the early education sector, in addition to the reform of pedagogical quality in the *école maternelle*, a significant increase in school budgets (on which the *école maternelle* depends) took place in 2004, and a new mode of financing linked to the socio-economic status of the children attending particular schools was introduced.

Improvements in the education and working conditions of staff: Several governments decrees regulate the education of persons involved in the care and education of young children: the Decrees of 12 December 2000 and of 11 July 2002 govern the initial training and professional development of teachers and aides in the *école maternelle* while the Decrees of the 17th and 3rd July 2003 determine the requirements of recruitment, initial and in-training of personnel in the child care sector and out-of-school provision.

Improvements in the evaluation of programmes and pedagogical support: New agreed structural, pedagogical and process indicators are now applied by regulation (or recommended) to all forms of services. In addition, ONE is developing a new profile, that of "pedagogical advisor". These advisors will have as their mission the task of reinforcing the psycho-pedagogical dimension of child care. They have been mandated to construct evaluation instruments and processes to allow the new child care co-ordinators to undertake valid and reliable evaluations of child care projects.

Improvements in out-of-school provision: A new ten-year plan for the development of out-of-school provision was launched in 2003 with significant new funding. In addition, a Decree of the 3rd July 2002, covered out-of-school provision, in particular, the quality of the out-of-school project, the role of personnel, norms governing the reception and taking in charge of children, and the development of pedagogical practices. An education bill, voted 28 April 2004, has placed on a statutory basis the financing of homework clubs in schools. Some 4% of *école maternelle* children attend these clubs but their main contribution is towards better preparation of school work by primary school children and as a contribution to the range of services offered by out-of-school provision.

More attention given to data collection and monitoring:e.g. information systems have been established in both sectors to facilitate a more rational planning of access, quality improvement, and the taking into account of new family needs and of changes in the ECEC workforce. Where children from 0-3 years are concerned, the new information systems have allowed a more accurate calculation of the real rate of coverage, taking into account actual capacity, through including places assimilated to subsidised places. The new systems have allowed also the creation of indicators for a universal service and a fairer sharing of places, including positive discrimination in certain communes. The systems have also been able to identify imbalances between sub-regions, between subsidised and non-subsidised services and between crèche services and family day care – enabling a fairer balance to be achieved. Similar initiatives can be seen in the education sector, where likewise a more accurate calculation of children and places has been achieved, and more individualised data on children produced. At the request of the Advisory Committee on education, further uses of information systems and education indicators will be made.

Belgium: Flemish Community

Population: c. 6 million. **Fertility rate:** 1.6 **GDP per capita:** USD 28 700. **Children under 6 years:** 375 935.

Female labour force participation: 57.3% of women participate, 34.1% of whom are in part-time employment (male part-time is 6.3%).

Labour force participation rate of women with a child(ren) under 6 years: c. 74% either full- or part-time.

Maternity and parental leave: 15 weeks of maternity leave paid at c. 80% of earnings; parental leave of 3 months or 6 months part-time or 15 months time, all paid at a flat rate. Time-credit breaks are possible for all workers.

Average duration of parental leave: Not available.

Compulsory school age: 6 years.

Social expenditure: 27.2% of GDP. **Child poverty rate:** 5.2%. For Belgium as a whole, the figure is 7.7% after taxes and transfers (OECD average is 11.2%).

Funding of pre-primary educational services: 0.6% of GDP with 16% of education enrolments.

Funding of services for children under 3 and OSP: 0.12% of GDP, of which 74% is public subsidy.

Unit cost per child: Crèche: USD 13 483.40 per child; family day care (or registered child minder): USD 5 818.31; early education (for Belgium): USD 4 442 per child.

Average costs to parents: 0-3 years and out-of-school time provision (OSP): parents contribute 59.7% of costs in subsidised family day care and 26.2% of costs in subsidised centre-based care; children 3-6 years: the *Kleuterschool* is publicly funded and free. Parents pay only incidental costs, about 4%.

Legal entitlement to a free service: From 2.5 years in the *Kleuterschool*.

Major service types and duration: Family day care (covering 54% of places) and *Kinderdagverblijf* (state-subsidised child care centres covering about 22% of children 0-3 years) are the main service types. They both open 11 hours daily for whole year. Just over two-thirds of these services are licensed and subsidised by *Kind en Gezin*. In the education sector, the *Kleuterschool* (public pre-school provision) operates 7 horrs daily during the academic year; OSP (out-of-school time provision) operates from 7.00 a.m. (before school hours) and up to 18.00 (after school hours) daily, on Wednesday afternoon and during school holidays.

Rate of access to regulated services: Children 0-2.5 years: 38%; children from 2.5 to 6 years: almost 100% from 3 years; OSP for children 4-7 years: 28% and then declines. 53.2% of children 0-3 years are cared for by parents or family members (35.2% are cared exclusively by a parent; 18% make use also of care by grandparents or families, 0.4% make use of other informal care). The next largest carer of young children is family day care, which takes in charge 38% of the children not using parental care, that is, well over 54% of the places available.

Designation and qualifications of lead staff: Subsidised child care centres engage certified *kinderverzorgsters* (child carers) with a post-secondary (1 year) professional diploma; *Kleuterschools* engage *kleuteronderwijzers* (nursery school teachers) with 3-year tertiary qualification. These teachers receive salaries equivalent to primary and lower secondary teachers.

Overall % of qualified staff in services: 99% of teachers in early education are fully trained. In the child care sector, only about 25% of the child care jobs require a diploma or certificate (Peeters, 2005, "Childcare in Flanders: the Essential Reversal towards Professionalisation and Sustainability", VBJK Ghent University). Service managers are all required to have some qualification, and in the public subsidised crèches, a diploma or equivalent training is required for all staff. Training requirements for the private sector are much weaker. In public family day care, some training is required, but not a diploma or educational requirement. Over 30% of OSP workers have a diploma for this type of work.

Child-staff ratios: Average ratios practised are: FDC: 4:1 in full-time care (up to 8 children in part-time); centre-based day care: 6.5:1; pre-school: 17:1 (school year 2001-2002), but 17:2 in the first year, when a child carer works alongside the teacher; OSP: 14 children to one trained adult.

Maximum group size: FDC: 8 children; centre-based day care: centres decide themselves; pre-schools: schools decide themselves (the Department of Education does not impose a maximum group size); OSP for children 6-12 years: centres decide themselves.

Auspices

In the Flemish Community of Belgium, a clear division of responsibilities for education and care exists. Child care and out-of-school care provision is the responsibility of *Kind en Gezin* (Child and Family), a Flemish Government agency. The Ministry in charge is the Flemish Ministry for Welfare, Family and Equal Opportunities. The national agency, *Kind en Gezin*, oversees regulations and policies, foresees places and funding to the services. *Kind en Gezin* also determines, in consultation with the sector, the minimum level of quality, monitors the quality of care and stimulates and promotes quality in care. Local authorities and non-profit organisations run child care provision, a role that is partly historical and, in some cases, partly in response to initiatives developed by *Kind en Gezin*.

The Ministry of Education of the Flemish Community has competence for almost all education matters in Flanders (including children 2.5 years and above – see *Access and provision* section). This Ministry sets the broad aims and objectives of education in the Community. Considerable autonomy to organise schools exists, a freedom originally established to guarantee confessional choice. Most schools and educational services fall under one of three main umbrella organisations or networks: Official Community Education that is, non-confessional, Flanders Community education, covering 13.88% of children; Official Subsidised Education organised by local authorities, covering 22.25% of children; and Private Subsidised Education covering 63.86% of pupils.

The Federal Government intervenes with regard to minimum requirements for diplomas, beginning and end of compulsory education, pensions, tax benefits for child care costs, parental leave and career breaks, or with the regions, in employment policy.

Context

Labour force rates: In 2002, 76% of women with a child between 3 and 6 years were in paid employment, and 72% of women with a child under 3 were in paid employment. A rise of 600 000 in the active working population in the past 30 years is attributed to increased participation by women. Concurrently the male working population has decreased. One woman in three works part-time whereas one man in twenty works part-time. Despite the law (introduced in 1999) on equal treatment of men and women regarding access to labour and work conditions, women are often offered part-time work in a limited number of sectors and jobs. There is considerable salary differentiation between men and women deriving from the systems of job description and assessment. Women report that they feel guided into accepting reduced working hours because of the unpaid work-load which falls on them.

Parental leave: Universal paid maternity leave was set at 15 weeks in 1998, with partly-paid leave available for 3 months full-time or 6 months part-time or 15 months time before children are 4 years old. In 2001 some 75 250 mothers (take-up rate not available) availed of this leave. Payments are made through health and invalidity insurance. Data are not available on the uptake of leave by fathers, although all fathers have automatic right to 3 days (private sector) or 4 days (public sector) paid leave taken within 12 days of birth. Since 2002, ten working days of paid paternal leave are available through health and invalidity insurance. In 2002 the system of career breaks (including parental leave) was replaced by a system giving workers the right to a time credit of one year over an entire career, a right granted to all employees. The break can be taken in the form of total suspension of activity or part-time reduction for at least 3 months.

Access and provision

Operational features: Both day care and early education are characterised by mixed public and private provision, funded by the Flemish Government. Normally, day care centres are open 10-12 hours per day and pre-primary schools open daily (half-day Wednesday) from 8.30-15.30, with after-school care if needed.

Early education from 2.5 years is free, with supplementary investments given to schools catering for substantial family diversity. *Kleuterschools* (mainstream pre-primary provision) are operated by the school boards belonging to the different networks, each group being financed or subsidised by the Government.

Despite a great increase in capacity over the past five years the care structure does not yet meet the demand of parents. In 2003, some 65 547 places across crèche and family day care were available (43 874 places in subsidised care and 21 673 places in independent care). Services are mostly used by working mothers in dual-income families, although strategies are in place to balance access for children across the whole community. There is strong uptake by single-parent families.

0-1 years: In the first year, maternal and family care predominates, with 31% of the cohort in licensed public settings. Because tax relief is offered to families who use care supervised by *Kind en Gezin*, the use of non-supervised family day care is not common.

1-3 years: 42% of 1- to 2-year-olds and 32% of 2- to 3-year-olds are in licensed care services. (Children may access a free, full-time place in pre-primary education at 2.5 years). 35.2% of 0- to 3-year-olds are in the full-time care of parents. 34.2% of the 0-3 cohort access licensed care at least part of the day and a further 0.9% access unregulated care. More than 36 000 3-year-olds (over 85% of the 3-year-old cohort) attend pre-primary (infant) school.

2.5-6 years: There is an 85% uptake by 2.5 years old in the first year of free pre-primary school, with from age 3 onwards (98.4% in 1997-98). 11.2% of the 3- to 6-year-old cohort access, in addition, publicly licensed child care settings, and 17.1% access out-of-school care provision. The relative child care and out-of-school care figures for 4- to 5-year-olds are 11.7% and 16.1%, and for 5- to 6-year-olds, 11.6% and 18.2%.

Out-of-school provision: This care operates either as a) publicly licensed initiatives outside the school, or as b) care outside school hours by the school. For the former 11.7% of 4-year-olds, 11.6% of 5-year-olds and 8% of 6-year-olds access this care. For the latter 16.1% of 4-year-olds, 18.2% of 5-year-olds and 19% of 6-year-olds access care at their school (see details in the table below).

	Publicly licensed (initiatives for out-of-school care)	Out-of-school care by school	Total
4 years	11.7	16.1	27.8
5 years	11.6	18.2	29.8
6 years	8.0	19.0	27.0

Children with diverse needs

Attention to children with diverse needs: Accredited providers must give priority to children from single parent families, families with low income, children for whom care is desirable for social or pedagogical reasons and children of parents at work.

Children with disabilities: In Flanders, the tradition has been to support these children at home, but there is growing awareness of the benefits of including children with light handicaps in ECEC. Providers receive extra remuneration per child per day and may also receive a structural grant (since 2001) to support and ensure optimum facilities. In subsidised care, the amount of days of stay of children with disabilities increased with 8.5%. Subsequent special education is well funded, though often separate from mainstream provision;

Children from low-income families: Flanders makes significant investments in social exclusion and priority education programmes. The percentage of children born in 2003 into under-privileged families was 5.2% (based on low levels on three or more of the indicators: income, education level, work status, child development, home and health). The child poverty level is 4.3% after redistribution.* The participation of children 3 months to 3 years from underprivileged families is rising. In 2002, 18.8% accessed child care, increasing to

---

* *Kind en Gezin* defines poverty as a persistent state in which people are restricted in their opportunities to have a satisfactory share of socially highly valued goods such as education, home and work. Six selection criteria are derived from this definition on the basis of which, within Child and Family, it is established whether a family should be regarded as underprivileged: namely the monthly family income, the educational level of the parents, the development of the children, the working situation of the parents, the home and health. If a family scores badly in three or more criteria it is regarded as underprivileged.

21.7% in 2004. Strategies in place to increase the participation of this group include a revision of the parental contribution regulation, which in 2002 lowered the cost of child care for families with an income below the guaranteed minimum monthly salary. In addition accredited providers can also charge a lower social tariff and if necessary even a zero tariff. *Kind en Gezin* guarantees the accredited provider a fixed amount for working costs so that the charging of a low parental contribution does not disadvantage the provider. Since 2004, *Kind en Gezin* subsidies a number of "Neighbourhood and proximity services" to target minority groups.

Ethnic and bilingual children: In Flanders, 17.3% of children speak a language other than Dutch as their mother tongue. 4.4% of the children do not have Belgian nationality. The participation of children 3 months to 3 years from ethnic families is rising. In 2002, 19.6% accessed child care, increasing to 23.7% in 2004. Much effort is being devoted to integrating these children and to ensuring that they receive enhanced educational opportunities (*gelijke onderwijskansenbeleid* – see the section on *Developments* below).

Quality

Licensing and regulatory regimes: Licensing regimes in child care services are varied according to their subsidised or independent status. Subsidised services have to meet minimum quality standards and have to develop a quality handbook in which they describe the procedures of how they evaluate quality, how they engage parents, how child carers are trained. Independent services require registration only, but most of them choose to work under the supervision of *Kind en Gezin*. This means that they have to meet certain quality standards. Both types of services are subject to irregular checks by *Kind en Gezin*.

Funding: Subsidised crèches and family day care services (private and public) have two main sources of income, namely public subsidies and parental fees. In services supervised by *Kind en Gezin*, government subsidises are paid directly to child care providers. A fixed amount for working costs is guaranteed so that the charging of a low parental contribution does not disadvantage the provider. In this case, non-profit bodies have preferred status, receiving higher pro-rata subsidies than independent providers. Parents pay fees according to income. On average, in the subsidised care sector, parental fees amount to 26% of the actual care costs in centre-based care and 60% of costs in family day care. Fully independent providers do not receive a subsidy, and parents pay the full costs. Since 2001, small, independent crèches receive an annual subsidy per place to promote quality and management. In addition, when provision is under the supervision of *Kind en Gezin* (the majority case), tax benefits are granted to parents to recuperate the fees paid to services. The tax-deductibility of child care costs is limited to EUR 11.20 euro per day per child. The federal Parliament recently extended the tax deductibility to children younger than 12 years. Within the educational services, public funding provides 96.1% of costs with private (parental) expenditure contributing the balance. Expenditure on child care and early education from both public and private sources is over 0.1% of GDP.

Staffing: The division between care and education is reflected in the training and status of staff in each sector, although some initiatives are in place to address this. *Kleuterschools* engage *kleuteronderwijzers* (nursery school teachers) whose status parallels that of primary or secondary school teachers. Subsidised child care centres engage certified *kinderverzorgsters* whose training differs (see below) while family day carers in subsidised provision are selected by interview and may subsequently engage in training while in service.

Training requirements: Kleuteronderwijzeres (nursery school teachers) are trained at tertiary level for three years in teacher training colleges alongside primary and lower secondary teachers. In-service training is well developed in the education sector, and the Ministry of Education devolves substantial funding for training budgets to the level of the school. Outside the education sector, training remains low. In subsidised day care centres, staff are generally trained child care workers (*kinderverzorgster*), who have taken the professional stream in secondary education and are given one further year of specialisation in their field. According to reports, trainees do not receive a strong theoretical base for their future work. Family day carers receive "in-service" training of between 4 to 60 hours only, and need no qualification to be licensed. Afterwards, though regularly visited and guided by service managers, they benefit little from further in-training. In contrast, in-training of child care workers in the subsidised centres is provided within their contractual hours. Overall, the training situation is matter for concern: "only 25% of the child care jobs in Flanders require a diploma or certificate" (Peeters, 2005). *Kind en Gezin* has initiated a discussion on the proper educational requirements in the different services for young children. The most important result of these talks is the document *Beroepsprofiel van de Begeleider Kinderopvang* (Professional Profile of the Child care Worker) that was published by the Flemish Social and Economic Council (SERV) in 2001. The 2002 Quality Decree also stipulates that by 2010, half the child care workforce should have a diploma.

Work conditions: As is usual in split systems, salary and working conditions in the early education sector are correct, with nursery school teachers receiving pay largely equivalent to their colleagues in primary and lower secondary schools. In the social sector, the situation is very different, but improving. In 2003, agreement was reached to give child minders affiliated to a service a limited social statute. Since 2001, new child minders joining the sector receive a start-up allowance for installation costs. Efforts are underway to improve the career structure of child care workers. Since 2000, job profiles have been prepared for assistants and managers in child care services. Acknowledgment of competences acquired outside of formal education (EVC) aims to support the assistants to become certified workers.

Child-staff ratio: The child-staff ratio in regulated family day care is 4:1. Maximum group size is 8. In crèche the ratio is 6.5:1; in accredited out-of-school care 14:1, but a specified group sizes is not obligatory for either group. Providers in crèche may apply their own quality policy regarding maximum numbers of children per assistant. In the *kleuterschool*, government investment to increase staff for the younger children has reduced the child-staff ratio to 18:1 (1997-98), but numbers can be greater or lesser depending on the time of the year.

Curriculum and pedagogy: In Flanders there is no national curriculum. Each school can develop its own curriculum and method of teaching. A set of minimum developmental goals (*ontwikkelingsdoelen*) that are desirable and attainable for children in pre-school was ratified in 1997. All schools work to these goals. The *ontwikkelingsdoelen* emphasise a broad and harmonious approach to education, addressing: personal characteristics – positive self-image, motivation and initiative; general development – being autonomous, communicating and cooperating, determining own direction, creativity and problem solving; and specific skills in selected domains: physical education, expressive arts, language, environmental studies, mathematics. Cross-curricular teaching is stressed to achieve the broad objectives of social competence and lifelong learning skills.

Monitoring, evaluation and research: In 1997 the strategy for stimulating quality changed from one of control to one of information and promotion. Corresponding to this change, research was conducted in 2003, to develop an assessment instrument for the measurement of the experience and perceptions of the children 0-12 years. Further refinements of the process are underway. Monitoring processes for family day care and crèche reflect wide variation across the sector. *Kind en Gezin* is a three-fold approach to quality (determining, monitoring and stimulating). Minimum levels are determined in consultation with the sector. In the future, monitoring will be managed by a separate inspection agency following a new decree passed in 2004. For the moment, inspection is still part of *Kind en Gezin*. In the infant school, inspection is carried out by education inspectors, generally on a whole school basis.

Parent and community involvement as partners in child care is promoted. A quality decree for the subsidised services asks for users to be informed and involved in the service, and to assist in monitoring, and controlling the quality policy. Providers have to describe how parental involvement is established and how they deal with complaints from parents. They also have to describe how parental satisfaction is measured. A web-site on child care supports parents to choose quality care, understand the different types of care available, and survey the cost of care. This development is aimed at supporting parents to choose care from an informed base and to progress the quality of care available.

Community involvement is established by the creation of local consultative groups. These groups comprise all those involved in child care in one way or another (providers, parents and policy makers). The aim is to develop a local policy plan, to advise on the establishment of child care initiatives in the local authority and to create a permanent consultative structure through annual evaluation of the local care situation and of the policy plan. In education a new decree on participation (also parental participation) has come into force since September 2004.

Developments

Developments in the area of inclusion and social cohesion: In recent years, Flemish society has become increasingly multicultural, and there is growing public awareness of immigrant issues, poverty and the need for greater equality. Between 1995 and 1998, *Kind en Gezin* and the Research Centre for Early Childhood Education and Care (VBJK) set up a training and employment programme for women from ethnic minorities supported by the European NOW initiative. The project trained with success 25 women from ethnic minorities and all of them found a job in the Flemish day care centres. This project is now influencing ECEC recruitment policies in the large cities. Between 1999 and 2004, in collaboration with the European DECET Network (Diversity in Early Childhood care Education and Training), several diversity projects have been set up in Ghent, Brussels and Antwerp. According to the 2002 Quality Decree, ethnic, as well as gender diversity in the Initiatives for Out-of-school Care workforce represents an important condition for licensing. Diversity is no longer an option; facilities need to demonstrate that they are taking specific steps to ensure that their workforce reflects the ethnic mix in the neighbourhood, and that they have tried to recruit male employees.

Child poverty levels have also been reduced, and a main policy concern is to make regular care and early education accessible to all children who need it, irrespective of their family situation, their socio-economic background or their ethnic origin. Demand for child care has grown rapidly in the past five years. In education, the Equal Education

Opportunities Decree of 2002 aims at giving each child as many opportunities as possible. Each child can enrol in the school of the parents' choice, and schools receive extra teaching hours when the children enrolled come from disadvantaged backgrounds. Recently, elementary schools have been provided with care co-ordinators, who support the regular staff in supporting children with learning challenges. Several innovative programmes have been initiated, such as the Freinet schools in disadvantaged neighbourhoods in Ghent. These schools are developing diversity pedagogy with the parents from ethnic minorities and in consultation with the children (De Meyer, 2005, *Social Disadvantage: The Ghent Projects*, Pedagogische Begeleidingsdienst, Ghent).

Developments in the area of quality: A continuing quality challenge for ECEC in Flanders has been the relatively low government investment in professionals caring for young children, and the choice, during the 1980s and 90s, of low cost (in the short term) forms of child care and out-of-school provision (OSP). Much of the quality work in the last decade have been efforts to palliate for the inherent weaknesses of a large, poorly-qualified family day sector, a new (and fast-growing) commercial mini-crèche sector for which only a low vocational child care worker diploma is needed, and under-invested child care and out-of-school provision (OSP).

In 2001 the government proposed a more participative quality system that after long consultation with the sector was introduced in 2004. In the new approach, quality is seen as an ongoing construction, jointly determined by parents, the child care workers, the children and the management board of centres (Peeters, 2005). In addition, processes of local consultation designed to stimulate the quality of care are underway, focusing on out-of-school care, care outside office hours, emergency care and sick care. As policy is moving in the direction of de-regulation, ways are being sought to integrate consultation into policy development in order to achieve more strategic and integrated local care policies. Much effort is being invested in professional development, especially to promote management that is more effective. An additional subsidy is given to centres for management work and logistics, based on *per capita* enrolments.

The universities and training centres (though the VBJK, the tri-partite university Training and Resource Centre for Child Care) focus on including child care as a pedagogical discipline in higher education, giving special attention to diversity. In the larger cities, *e.g.* Antwerp, Ghent, local governments have brought the day care facilities under the responsibility of the alderman of the department of education. Crèches collaborate closely with local infant schools to ensure smooth transitions for children and families from one service to another. In this initiative, staff can move from the crèche to the school. The introduction of child care workers into pre-primary education is expected to enhance collaboration and increase integration of programmes and services.

The whole system is moving towards a coherent national quality system (Vandenbroeck *et al.*, 2004, "Diversity and Equity in Early Childhood Training in Europe", DECET Network, Ghent), but is still significantly under-financed. In 1992, *Kind en Gezin* introduced national quality scales for pedagogical functioning in all subsidised day care centres in Flanders based on the ITERS and ECERS quality scales. The impact on the daily practice in the centres of the introduction of these national pedagogical standards led to much improvement, with care settings becoming more educational and stimulating for infants and toddlers. In 2004, the agency and the Ministry of Education promoted the use of the *Experiential Education* scales developed by Prof. Ferre Laevers from the University of

Leuven. These scales focus on children and provide a simple measure of their well-being and involvement in the centre or classroom. Centres are very positive about these self-evaluation scales as they provide concrete guidelines on how to increase pedagogical quality and change daily practice.

In the education sector, efforts are also being made to reduce child-staff ratios, and to introduce a greater degree of care for the younger children. For this reason, a regulation is now in force to employ one *kinderverzorgster* (child carer) in all the first year classes of the *Kleuterschool*. Another important policy orientation is to bring pre-primary (the *kleuterschool*) and school closer together, to make basic education a cohesive unity. Goals are elaborated in the "Developmental Objectives" or minimum goals (knowledge, insights, skills and attitudes) that are considered desirable and attainable by children in primary and pre-primary classes. At the same time, there is widespread recognition that pre-primary has its own specificity, that of developing the total personality of the children.

Canada

Population: 32.2 m. **Fertility rate:** 1.53. **GDP per capita:** USD 30 700. **Children under 6 years:** 2 074 860 (2005).

Female labour force participation: 73.5% of women (15-64) participate in the formal labour market, 27.2% of whom are in part-time employment (male part-time is 10.9%) (OECD, *Employment Outlook*, 2005).

Labour force participation rate of women with children: 67.7% of women with a child under 6 years are employed, accounting for 30% of total part-time employment (OECD, *Society at a Glance*, 2005). 58.7% of women with a child under 3 are employed (OECD, *Babies and Bosses*, 2005).

Maternity and parental leave: 15 weeks of maternity leave paid at 55% of earnings, plus a 2-week unpaid waiting period; 35 weeks parental leave paid at 55% of earnings.

Average duration of parental leave: In 2003-04, the average duration of maternity leave was 14.5 weeks. The average duration of parental leave (mothers) was 23.8 weeks; of parental leave (fathers), 14 weeks; of parental leave (adoptive mothers), 28.1 weeks; of parental leave (adoptive fathers), 17 weeks.

Social expenditure: 17.8% of GDP. **Child poverty rate (2000):** 14.9% after taxes and transfers measured as the percentage of children living in families with income below 50% of the national median (OECD average is 11.2%) (UNICEF, 2005).

Compulsory school age: 6 years.

Funding of pre-primary education for 3- to 6-year-olds: about 0.2% of GDP; for all child care, 0-12, funding amounts to 0.4% of GDP.

Unit cost per child (in USD converted using PPPs): for 2004 and 2005, information is not available in *OECD Education at a Glance*. The figure for 2003 is USD 6 120 (OECD, *Education at a Glance*, 2003).

Funding of services for children under 3: Information on expenditure as a % of GDP is not available.

Average costs to parents: Excluding Quebec, costs to parents using community services amount to c. 50% of costs across the country.

Legal entitlement to a free service: 5-6 years of age, depending on jurisdiction.

Major service types and duration: Family day care homes, child care centres, pre-kindergarten (3-5 years) and kindergartens (5-6 years).

Rate of access to regulated services: Access is low and varies greatly depending on the province and district. Across Canada, approximately 24% of children aged 0-6 have access to a regulated place. Rates are considerably higher in Quebec, which in 2004, accounted alone for 43% of all regulated spaces. About 95% of 5-year-olds across Canada are enrolled in state-funded kindergarten, with access to junior kindergarten being assured in Ontario for almost all children from the age of 4 years.

Designation and qualifications of key staff: Ranges by province/territory. Kindergarten and pre-kindergarten programmes organised by provincial/territorial public education systems employ teachers with a 4-year university degree, generally specialised in primary education teaching. In regulated pre-school and child care centres, early childhood educators are likely to have a two-year ECE credential.

Child-staff ratios: Ranges by province or territory (2001): 1-year-olds: 3:1 to 8:1; 3-year-olds: 7:1 to 10:1; 5-year-olds: 8:1 to 15:1.

Maximum group size: Ranges by province or territory (2001): 1-year-olds: 6-18 children; 3-year-olds: 14-25 children; 5-year-olds: 16-25 children. Some provinces/territories do not regulate group size.

Auspices

Different levels of government have responsibilities for ECEC in Canada. Under constitutional arrangements, direct responsibility for social and educational programmes such as ECEC lies with the provincial and territorial governments, while the federal government assumes responsibility for specific populations, such as the Aboriginal people, military families and new immigrants or refugees. The federal government is also responsible for maternity and paternity leave benefits, and for the National Child Benefit.

Primary responsibility for ECEC programmes rests with the provincial and territorial governments. These governments, with the exception of Prince Edward Island, treat care and education separately. Child care regulation, policies, and fee subsidies and grants systems form one domain of engagement while public kindergarten policy and administration is another domain. In addition, provinces/territories are responsible for income support programmes for low-income families; health care; legislating length of job protected maternal and paternal leave; and training institutions for early childhood educators and kindergarten teachers.

Municipal governments and other local authorities are involved in ECEC at the discretion of the provincial governments. Municipal governments in Ontario have the delegated authority to provide and maintain ECEC services focused on child care at the local level; in almost all other jurisdictions there is no local authority involvement. Within education, local school boards operate under powers delegated by the provincial governments. These boards have responsibility for kindergarten programmes within schools.

Inter-governmental initiatives by the federal, provincial and territorial governments take place within a framework, the 1999 Social Union Framework Agreement (SUFA). SUFA establishes the partnership between governments within which specific social programme initiatives are developed, and the related financial transfers are enacted. Recent framework agreements between the federal government, provinces and territories, for example, the 2003 Multilateral Framework on Early Learning and Child Care (ELCC), have generated a clearer focus on early child development and learning. Federal funding will enable provinces and territories to improve and expand early learning and child care, based on the principles of quality, universal inclusion, accessibility and developmental. Funds are also being directed to enhancing early learning and child care for First Nations children living on reserve, and to extend the knowledge base and improve data collection so as to support better planning and accountability.

Context

Labour force rates: The labour force participation rate for females (15-64) is 73.5%, rising from 68.3% in 1990 (OECD, *Employment Outlook*, 2005). 27.2% of women are in part-time employment, compared to 10.9% of men. 67.7% of women with a youngest child under 6 are employed, accounting for 30% of total part-time employment (OECD, *Society at a Glance*, 2005). Women with a youngest child under 3 had an employment rate of 58.7% (OECD, *Babies and Bosses*, 2005).

Parental leave: Responsibility for maternal/parental leave is shared by the federal and provincial/territorial governments. Provincial/territorial legislation sets the length and conditions of job protected leave while partial salary replacement is provided by the federal government through its Employment Insurance Programme. Access to maternity and parental benefits in Canada is high. Remunerated parental leave for almost a year was enacted in the Federal Employment Insurance Act of 2001. 91.1% of paid employees in December 2003 had sufficient hours to qualify for Employment Insurance special benefits. Currently, the self-employed do not pay into the Employment Insurance programme and thus are not eligible for maternity and parental benefits. Federal benefits are provided as partial salary replacement – 55% of wages up to a ceiling of CAD 413/week (EUR 265/ USD 337) for up to 50 weeks for eligible new parents (many are not eligible) (Background Report for Canada, 2003).

Access and provision

Because of the private nature of much Canadian child care, systematic information on rates of provision for younger children is lacking at both federal and provincial levels. Access to services is dependent on available places, meeting eligibility criteria for subsidy assistance, ability to pay fees, and finding a programme that meets child/family need. Access is low and varies depending on the province/territory. Approximately 24% of children aged 0-6 have access to regulated child care spaces, the majority of which are provided by non-profit, community organisations. These centre-based community services (including a small number of publicly-operated services) account for 80% of regulated child care provision for children 0-12 years. Except in Quebec, access to regulated child care is not treated as an entitlement in any province/territory (Background Report for Canada, 2003). In Quebec, 34% of 0- to 3-year-olds, 48% of 3- to 4-year-olds, and 50% of 4- to 5-year-olds have access to licensed services (OECD, *Babies and Bosses*, 2005). From 4 years onwards, nearly all children in Ontario have access to state-funded pre-kindergarten and kindergarten. In 1995 (most recent data available) some 62% of children under 6 who received regular, non-relative care while parents worked or studied, received this care in an unregulated setting (Background Report for Canada, 2003). However, across Canada, there is a well-established early education network within the primary school system for children over five years; every province/territory provides a publicly funded kindergarten programme in the year before primary school, usually part-time but full-time in Quebec. This service is considered a public responsibility and a public good in all Canadian provinces. Approximately 95% of Canadian children attend kindergarten from the age of

5-6 years. Kindergarten benefits from stable funding, trained teachers, structured programming and regular monitoring and evaluation. Age eligibilities vary by service and province. In Ontario and Quebec (48% in 2003), most 4-year-old children also participate in junior kindergarten, while in other jurisdictions access is limited to a small number of children at risk. Compulsory schooling generally begins at age 6.

Children with disabilities: Legislation or policy in all provinces and territories guarantees children with special needs access to public school kindergarten programmes; this is usually (but not always) through inclusion in regular classrooms. No province/territory guarantees children with special needs access to regulated child care, but children frequently obtain sufficient support to enable participation in regular kindergarten programmes. The Background Report for Canada (2003) notes that in 1998, some 40% of child care centres indicated that they had been unable to enrol a child with special needs due to structural limitations and/or concern of staff regarding the adequacy of their training.

Children from low-income families: A limited subsidy system is available, with widely varying and complex eligibility criteria, accessed by 22% of lone parents and approximately 5% of married mothers from low-income families (1997 figures – Background Report for Canada, 2003). In 2001, 36% of children in regulated care, outside of Quebec, were receiving subsidies. These subsidies are not always effective at ensuring affordability for the low-income families towards whom they are targeted. A National Child Benefit (NCB) was introduced in 1998, combining two key elements: monthly payments from the Government of Canada to low-income families with children, and benefits and services designed and delivered by provinces and territories to meet the needs of low-income families with children in each jurisdiction. A key design element of the NCB is the flexibility it provides to provinces and territories to develop and deliver programmes and services that best meet the needs and priorities of their communities. As part of this flexibility, provinces and territories may adjust social assistance or child benefit payments by an amount equivalent to the National Child Benefit Supplement. This has permitted families on social assistance to maintain at least the same level of benefits as before, while providing additional funds for new or enhanced provincial and territorial programmes benefiting low-income families with children. Through this recovery/reinvestment mechanism, provinces and territories have allocated significant investments towards day care and child care initiatives (USD 225M in 2003-04), which include subsidies for low-income families with children.

Aboriginal children and diversity: In 2001 there were 33 155 children 0-4 years, and 36 945 children 5-9 years, living on First Nations reserves in Canada (Background Report for Canada, 2003). In the year 2001-02, 13 409 (95% of 4- and 5-year-olds) attended junior (pre) kindergarten or kindergarten programmes in schools on reserve, although these children may also seek access to kindergarten programmes in non-reserve schools. Child care may be funded for children living on reserve or in Inuit communities, but access to spaces has not been sufficient to meet demand. Expansion of programmes for First Nations children, primarily those living on reserve, has been underway since 2003. In the larger urban areas, where many of the low-income children are of Aboriginal or ethnic origin, specialised programmes for these children are often not available. In addition to children from Aboriginal communities, many other ethnic and racial groups live in communities of all sizes throughout Canada. Although there are no official policies regarding diversity in child care – a prominent feature of Canadian ECEC – Canada has an official policy of supporting multiculturalism.

Quality

Licensing and regulatory regimes: Education and child care are regulated separately. Responsibility for ensuring that kindergarten programmes comply with provincial/territorial legislation is generally delegated to school boards. In turn, these boards delegate responsibility to superintendents of education, who establish budgets, hire staff, supervise schools and ensure programmes meet children's needs (Background Report for Canada, 2003). Child care is regulated as a private enterprise (not-for-profit and for-profit). Regulatory policy rests with departments of social and/or community services. Requirements generally specify the physical space and training levels of staff, maximum numbers of children, staff- child ratios. The elements vary across provinces and territories.

Funding: With the exception of limited grants for specific purposes, regulated child care services are not publicly funded, except in Quebec. A market-determined fee structure (except Manitoba and Quebec) combines with high levels of parental contribution (ranging from 34% to 82%) to meet child care costs. The average parental contribution in public and community services across the country, excluding Quebec, is just under 50% of costs. A limited fee subsidy approach supports the participation of some low-income families. Overall, public child care expenditure for children 0-12 years averaged USD 500 per child, and USD 3 223 dollars per child care place (Background Report for Canada, 2001 figures revised for 2003/04). Public child care spending ranged between provinces/territories from USD 104 to USD 1 448 per child and USD 816 to USD 4 849 per space, compared to USD 6 120 per child in kindergarten (OECD, *Education at a Glance*, 2003). According to the same source, Canada spends 0.2% of GDP on pre-primary educational services from 3-6 years, but it is not clear what this figure includes. During the 2001-04 period, increased federal funding and attention to ECEC had an impact on the renewal of services in several provinces. Expenditure by provinces/territories on care for children 0-12 years in Canada came to about 0.17% of GDP, but new federal figures for 2003-04 suggest that all public expenditure on services for children 0-12 years comes to approximately 0.4% of GDP. It is not clear what proportion of this expenditure was spent on children 0-6 years.

Staffing and training: Staffing protocols divide according to the "education" or "care" designation of services. Pre-kindergarten programmes organised by the provincial/territorial public education systems and kindergarten programmes employ teachers with a 4-year university degree, generally with a specialisation in primary education. There are no requirements for kindergarten teachers to have specific training in the development or pedagogy of children under 6 years. In regulated child care settings in 1998 (most recent data available), 66% of early childhood educators have a two-year ECE credential or more, and 29% have one year or less of ECE training. With the exception of two territories, all jurisdictions have minimum qualification requirements for work in child care settings, but a Canada-wide standard for training does not exist. In general, educators receive their diploma from a community college. Typically, programmes include "coursework on health and safety, early childhood development, education theory, programming strategies, and strategies for behaviour guidance plus some supervised experience in a child care setting" (Background Report for Canada, 2003). Assistants in both kindergartens and child care settings are generally not required to hold formal qualifications. The required qualification for (school) principals is a 4-year-university degree but with no specific requirement to specialise in early education. Only Manitoba has a requirement for child care directors, set at community college level with a specialisation in ECEC. Family child care providers

– either those who are supervised by agencies in some provinces/territories or those who are individually licensed – are not required to have any post-secondary, early childhood training although some provinces may require limited training or orientation courses.

Work conditions: Substantial differences exist in work conditions of kindergarten teachers and child care staff regarding salary, sick leave, medical and dental insurance, disability insurance, retirement pension, life insurance and unionisation. Teachers view themselves, and are viewed as, professionals. During 2002 and 2003, an extensive consultation process reviewed proposed occupational standards for early childhood educators. These were endorsed and later ratified during the Canadian Child Care Federation's annual meeting in June 2004. Currently, the sector is engaged in awareness-raising and seeking endorsement from provincial and territorial government as certification and entry qualification requirements are determined at this level. Seven jurisdictions now take responsibility for ECE certification. In some jurisdictions, professional organisations have adopted voluntary codes of practice. The annual turnover rate for staff in Canadian child care centres is an average of 28% (range 15% to 45%). Almost all (98%) staff in child care settings are women, as are 81% of elementary school teachers. In proportion to their place in the population, cultural and racial minorities are not sufficiently represented among ECEC staff (Background Report for Canada, 2003).

Child-staff ratios: Considerable variation exists across provinces/territories. Child to staff ratios range from 3:1 to 8:1 for 1-year-olds, 7:1 to 10:1 for 3-year-olds, and 8:1 to 15:1 for 5-year-olds. Maximum group size varies by province/territory from 6-18 for 1-year-olds, 14-25 for 3-year-olds, and 16-25 for 5-year-olds.

Curriculum and pedagogy: In kindergarten, there is no national approach to curriculum although substantial consensus is reported across the expected learning outcomes articulated in provincial/territorial statements. Kindergarten curricula are generally linked to elementary school curricula and evidence is available of collaboration among some provinces in curriculum framework, assessment and performance standards. Evidence is not available about the pedagogical approaches in ECEC programmes although some provincial statements refer to desired pedagogical orientations. With the exception of Quebec, specific curricula are not required for child care programmes.

Monitoring, evaluation and research: Some national monitoring and reporting data are available from the *National Longitudinal Study of Children and Youth* (NLSCY), the *Understanding the Early Years* (UEY) study, and the annual series *Early Childhood Education and Care in Canada* researched by the CRRU unit of the University of Toronto. Provinces also collect a considerable amount of data, but according to the Background Report for Canada, "the methodology used differs and results in data that are not comparable from one jurisdiction to another. There is no regular collection of national data by government or others about the use and characteristics of kindergarten, nursery schools, regulated child care or family resource programmes, or about the children and families using them. Nor are data collected on the demand or need for ECEC services" (p. 85).

Parent and community involvement: The involvement of parents and communities in the design and delivery of early childhood education and care programmes and services varies across provinces/territories and within individual communities. Although a strong rhetoric of parental responsibility for children is heard in Canada, little information on actual policies to involve parents in ECEC is found in the public domain.

OECD policy issues

Among the issues for policy attention identified (in 2003) by the OECD review team for Canada were to:

- Strengthen the present federal/provincial/territorial agreements and focus them as much as possible on child development and learning.

- Encourage provincial governments to develop, with the major stakeholder groups, an early childhood strategy with priority targets, benchmarks and timelines, and with guaranteed budgets to fund appropriate governance and expansion.

- Build bridges between child care and kindergarten education, with the aim of integrating ECEC both at ground level and at policy and management levels.

- Substantially increase public funding of services for young children, ensuring the creation of a transparent and accountable funding system, and for parents, a fairer sharing of ECEC funding. Devise an efficient means of funding a universal early childhood service for children 1-6 years, delivered equitably by mixed providers, governed by public agencies.

Developments signalled by Human Resources and Social Development Canada

From 2000, significant ECEC policy and funding changes had begun to be initiated across the country. A 2003 federal/provincial/territorial agreement on early learning and child care (USD 350 million per year by 2007-08) has increased the level of investment in early childhood education and care services. Funds are also being directed to enhancing early learning and child care for First Nations children living on-reserve.

Czech Republic

Population: 10.24 m. **Fertility rate:** 1.18. **GDP per capita:** USD 15 100. **Children under 6 years:** 540 000.

Female labour force participation: Female labour force participation rate for women 15-64 is 62.2%, 5.2% in part-time employment (male part-time employment rate is 1.5%).

Labour force participation rate of women with children: 27% of women with a youngest child under 6 are employed and 16.7% of women with a child under 3 (OECD, *Society at a Glance*, 2005).

Maternity and parental leave: 28 weeks maternity leave paid at 69% of earnings, followed by a flat-rate, parental leave benefit paid until children reach their 4th birthday.

Average duration of parental leave: not available, but at least three years.

Compulsory school age: 6 years.

Social expenditure as % of GDP: 20.1%. **Child poverty rate:** 6.8% (OECD average is 11.2%).

Funding of pre-primary educational services (ISCED Level 0): 0.46% of GDP (0.43% public and 0.03% private), corresponding to 10% of the education budget, for 13% of education enrolments.

Unit cost per child: (in USD converted using PPP): USD 2 724 (OECD, *Education at a Glance*, 2005).

Funding of services for children under 3: Government funding is directed almost exclusively to parental leave policies. Child care services are a municipal responsibility.

Major service types and daily duration: Children 0-3 years: almost all children 0-3 years are cared for by their families or through informal care arrangements. Centre-based crèches, providing care for 0.5% of 0- to 3-year-olds are few. Children 3-6 years: public *mateřská škola* (kindergarten) is the predominant service; with 76-95% coverage from 3 years to 6 years – full day). Out-of-school provision (*školní družina*) for children 6-12 years, enrolling 36% of children, during the school year.

Average costs to parents: Fees are capped at 50% of costs for the first two years of the *Mateská škola*, with the last year being free. Fees are reduced or waived for families in need.

Legal entitlement to a free service: From age 6, when compulsory primary schooling starts.

Rate of access to regulated services: Children 0-3 years: almost no access. Children 3-6 years: 67-98% coverage.

Designation and qualifications of key staff: Child nurses staff the few remaining crèches. Their three-year, secondary/vocational level course has a strong health and hygiene orientation. Kindergartens are staffed by pedagogues, 95% of whom are trained through a specialised four-year secondary level course in one of 18 pedagogical vocational schools.

Child-staff ratios: In public kindergartens (*mateřská škola*), a ratio of 12:1 is recommended, at least during the core period of the day. A ratio of 23:1 is practised in out-of-school provision.

Maximum group size: 28 children.

Auspices

Early education in the Czech Republic is almost entirely a public service. *Mateská kola* (kindergartens) are part of the educational system, under the responsibility of the Ministry of Education, Youth, and Sport. Since transition, regional and municipal education authorities have increasing responsibilities, and centres enjoy much autonomy. Financing is drawn from multiple sources – the regional school authority (teacher's salaries, books and equipment), municipalities (running costs and capital investments) and from parental fees (capped at 50% of costs for the first two years and free for the final year), while funds to improve material conditions or purchase equipment and toys are often generated through sponsoring contracts with private enterprises. Some private and church kindergartens are now in operation, though on a small scale.

Crèches are administered by the Ministry of Health and therapeutic child care centres are part of the Ministry of Social Affairs. In practice, there is no longer an organised day care network for children from 0-3 years, compared to a coverage rate of 20% in 1989. The introduction of an extended period of maternal leave after transition reduced demand for public child care outside the home. Only 60 crèches (in 2004) have survived from the previous regime. Former crèche buildings have been sold or allocated to other purposes. However, children over 2 years of age can attend kindergartens (at the present time, only about 20 000 do so).

Context

Labour force rates: In 2004, 62.2% of women participated in the labour force (OECD, 2005). Of the women employed, 5.2% work part-time compared to 1.5% of men (OECD, 2005). 27% of women with a youngest child under 6 are employed and 16.7% of women with a child under 3 (OECD, *Society at a Glance*, 2005).

Parental leave: The Czech Republic offers universal, paid maternity leave of 28 weeks (69% of earnings) with a flat-rate, parental leave of 4 years. Parental leave is still taken almost exclusively by mothers. Only 16.7% of women with a child under 3 are in the workforce (OECD, *Society at a Glance*, 2005).

Access and provision

The operating hours and annual duration of services vary according to service type. In early education, 3-6 years, the system is almost entirely public. It is now decentralised, with a great deal of autonomy given to municipalities and to each centre. Helped by falling fertility rates, sufficient numbers of places are available, although access is said to be limited or inadequate in rural areas. Parental fees are capped at 30% of costs, and are reduced or waived for families in need. There are special supports for low-income/ethnic areas and families. Despite this, the families considered to be most in need are least likely to enrol their children in pre-school settings. From 2005, parental fees will be raised to 50% of costs, however with the exception of the last kindergarten year which will be free.

Rates of provision

0-3 years: The policy of long-term maternity leave has limited the availability of crèches for children of this age. Children in this age group are cared almost exclusively by mothers and/or by informal caregivers (about 20 000 of 2- to 3-year-olds attend kindergartens).

3-6 years: 76% of 3-year-old children enter public fee-paying, full-day pre-school, reaching 95% at 5-6 years. Children of this age group are entitled to a place in a public kindergarten. The average coverage rate for children aged 3-6 years is 88%. The State Social Support Act (No. 117/1995) limits kindergarten access of children in care of mothers on paid maternity leave to 5 days per month. Kindergartens remain open eight or more hours per day. The compulsory school age is 6 years, although a child deemed not developed enough may enter primary school at a later age. The average percentage of postponed education is at least 22%, more than half these initiatives coming from parents (Background Report for the Czech Republic, 2000). In principle, these children have preferential placement in kindergartens.

Children with diverse needs

Children with disabilities: There is growing inclusion of children with disabilities, though many special kindergartens and schools still exist, even for children with relatively light handicaps. Disabled children amount to 4.2% of the total number of children attending kindergarten; almost a half of them (48.8%) attend special kindergartens. A parent responsible for a chronically ill or long-term disabled or handicapped child is entitled to parental benefit until the child is age 7 years.

Children from low-income families: The child poverty level is 5.9% after taxes and transfers, and specific and means-tested benefits are available to families with young children. Some children from socially and culturally disadvantaged environments, with postponed entry to kindergarten at age 5, access preparatory classes where assistants have special knowledge of their specific environment and/or culture.

Ethnic and bilingual children: Problems of poverty, social exclusion and education under-achievement are most acute among Roma families. Other ethnic groups, *e.g.* Polish, German, generally organise education in their own language. It is estimated that the Roma community constitutes 0.7% of the population. High rates of unemployment are recorded among the group and levels of education are low compared to Czechs, 84% of whom complete upper secondary education. Since 1993, the government has invested in several pilot projects for Roma children, and preparatory classes for socially or culturally disadvantaged children of 6-7 years of age, whose entry into compulsory school had been delayed. In 2004, 126 preparatory classes with 1 779 children were in operation. The Ministry of Education provides grants to NGOs to support work with Roma parents and schools in order to increase the enrolment and adequate inclusion of Roma children.

Quality

Licensing and regulatory regimes: The state authorities, school authorities, municipalities, private entities or churches are each responsible for setting up and maintaining kindergartens. Legislation defines the rights and duties of kindergarten heads, sets the number of children per class, conditions for boarding and rules for health, care and security. However, it does not define basic standards of educational quality from the point of view of children or in terms of the goals of education.

Funding: Expenditure on pre-primary education as a percentage of GDP is 0.46%. Of this expenditure, 92.7% derived from public sources, 6.1% from household expenditure, and the remainder from private sources. 10.3% of all expenditure on educational institutions is allocated to pre-primary whereas 13% of the children/students are enrolled at this level of education (OECD, *Education at a Glance*, 2005). Public expenditure on services for children under 3 is for the moment very low.

Staffing and training: Both crèche and kindergarten staff are trained at upper secondary level. More than 95% of pedagogues in the *mateřská škola* have completed four years of training (15 to 19 years) in one of the 18 upper secondary pedagogical schools in the country. Particular emphasis is placed on skills in art, music and sports, areas that traditionally have been deemed important for Czech pre-schools. Further accreditation through in-service courses has not yet been organised. Though often of high quality, the location and level of training tends to keep early childhood studies separate from university support and research. More recently, some tertiary education programmes have been opened, leading either to a bachelor degree or a tertiary diploma. Graduates from the kindergarten pedagogical secondary schools are almost all female, but increasingly fewer of them actually enter the profession.

Work conditions: In 2004, the average wage of pedagogues in the *mateřská škola* was 76% of the average wage in the Czech Republic (the teacher wage in basic schools is 96% of the average wage). Statutory working time is 40 hours weekly, with 31 hours assigned for "direct, obligatory teaching" work. Pedagogues are entitled by the Education Staff Act (No. 563/2004) to 12 days of a study leave. Kindergarten pedagogue status is still lower than that of basic school teachers. Only few men work as a kindergarten pedagogue although they can study pre-school pedagogy.

Child-staff ratios: Child-staff ratios are 12:1, but classes will often have up to 25 children, looked after by more than one teacher for, at least, part of the day.

Curriculum and pedagogy: In 1989, the choice of the educational programme and teaching/assessment methods became the responsibility of the kindergarten head. Curriculum and programme strategies were no longer centrally defined, but kindergarten staff were to assess the local context and determine a relevant curriculum and select suitable strategies/pedagogy. However, concern was expressed about the lack of support for local curricula/pedagogical initiatives, in terms of expert advice, training or implementation support. In 2001 a Framework Programme for Pre-school Education was introduced defining the basic values, aims and goals of kindergarten education. The programme was again modified in 2004. Until 2007, every kindergarten will prepare its own *mateská kola* programme, based on the Framework Programme, with implementation being supported by focused in-service training.

Monitoring, evaluation and research: Evaluation in kindergarten is conducted within the frame of general indicators set by the Czech School Inspectorate for all types of schools, including respecting accepted pedagogical, psychological and health related principles defined by examiners/inspectors (Background Report for the Czech Republic, 2000). While helpful, these indicators are deemed insufficient by ECEC experts if early childhood expertise and practice is to be enhanced. With regard to ECEC research, the authors of the Background Report are critical of limited activity and feel that comparative research, with recommendations for programme improvement linked to such research is needed.

Parent and community involvement: The family is recognised as the most important educational environment for young children. Parental involvement in ECEC services is deemed important to the successful conduct of kindergarten education and good quality care. At the national level, the Union of Parents operates as an interest group to strengthen the influence of parents within the Czech education system. However, school boards made up of parents, municipality members, sponsors and others are not obligatory in the case of kindergartens. The Education Act (No. 561/2004) indicates that pre-school education should provide education support and help to parents as well as children. Access to kindergartens by parents differs from school to school. Their involvement in classes is a recent development in some kindergartens.

Policy developments in the areas identified by the OECD

● Since the "velvet revolution" of 1989, the Czech Republic has renewed its links with its long tradition of early childhood education. There has been an impressive increase in diversification and pedagogical freedom. The understanding of education as conformity to accepted knowledge and social norms has given away to a spirit of enquiry and innovation. There is a fresh appreciation of the child as a subject of rights, reflected both in the desire to lessen the pressures placed on children in pre-school institutions, and to integrate children with special needs. Pedagogical approaches and methods of work more suited to the young child's needs and mentality have been encouraged, and daily routines in kindergartens have been relaxed. Greater emphasis is placed on free play and creative expression. Age-integration in classes has become a common practice.

● Decentralisation has taken place, and great efforts have been made to change the relationships between the education partners. Outreach to parents as equal partners has improved immeasurably, and men have been invited into the previously female world of kindergarten teaching.

● Work on the preparation of a framework curriculum for the kindergarten was completed in 2001. The new curriculum orients kindergartens to offer systematic and appropriate programmes to young children, yet remain open enough to allow innovation and experimentation. The content of education is worked out in five spheres: biological, psychological, interpersonal, socio-cultural and environmental. General competences (personal, cognitive and operational) that children should acquire in the kindergarten are set, linked with behaviour and knowledge expected in the primary school. This well-conceived curriculum is inspired by the UN Convention on the Rights of the Child, and children's agency and participation are given a strong emphasis.

Denmark

Population: 5.4 m. **Fertility rate:** 1.76. **GDP per capita:** USD 29 200. **Children under 6 years:** 400 000.

Female labour force participation: (women aged 15-64, in 2004): 76.1% of women participate, 24.3% of whom are in part-time employment (male part-time is 11.6%) (OECD, *Employment Outlook*, 2005).

Labour force participation rate of women with children: Mothers with children 3 and below: 70%; children 3-7 years, about 80%, with the average employment rate from mothers with children under 6 at 74%. Share in part-time employment for mothers with children under 6 is 5% (OECD, *Society at a Glance*, 2005). Women out of work are generally students, parental leave, housewives working at home, etc. ("Børneforløbsundersøgelsen", 2000, 2004, Danish National Institute of Social Research and OECD, *Society at a Glance*, 2005).

Maternity and parental leave: 14 weeks maternity leave, followed by 14 weeks parental leave and 2 weeks paternity leave – all paid at full unemployment benefit rate, to which 26 weeks of child care leave may be added, paid at 60% of the unemployment rate. Total child care leave period may not exceed 52 weeks.

Average duration of parental leave: Women 43.2 weeks and men 3.4 weeks.

Compulsory school age: 7 years.

Social expenditure: 29.2%. **Child poverty rate:** 2.4% after taxes and transfers, the lowest rate in the world (UNICEF, 2005) (OECD average is 11.2%).

Funding of all kindergarten services and leisure time facilities (ISCED Level 0): 2.1% of GDP. The unit cost per child in centre-based day care amounts approximately to USD 10 200 per older child (USD 19 550 for the youngest), and in leisure-time services for 6-10 years USD 5 950. Net annual public expenditure for all children enrolled in services 0-6 years is approximately USD 7 650.

Average costs to parents: Costs are capped at 30-33% of costs with low-income families paying much less. Average parental contribution comes to approximately 22% of costs.

Legal entitlement to a free service: There is a legal entitlement to a place in the kindergarten class in the primary education system, generally at 6 years, but could be from 4 years and 10 months.

Major service types and duration: Day care facilities (*dagtilbud*) for children from 6 months to 6 years, which are divided into family day care (*kommunal dagpleje*), centre-based day care (*Vuggestuer*-crèche; *bornehaver*-kindergartens and *aldersintegrerede institutioner*-age-integrated centres). *Bornehaveklasse,* kindergarten classes for children 5-6 are led by pedagogues; after school care leisure time facilities (*fritidshjem and* free-time activities, SFOs) are led by pedagogues.

Rate of access to regulated services: 0-1 year: 12%; 1-2 years: 83%; 3-5 years: 94% (2004).

Designation and professional qualifications of key staff: Managers of services: all day care facilities, with the exception of municipal child minder facilities, have a manager and a deputy manager. Both must be qualified educators. Pedagogues (*pædagoger*) i.e. qualified child and youth educators (sometimes called social educators) work in day care facilities, kindergarten classes and SFOs. Pedagogues also work in the *Folkeskole* kindergarten classes that belong to integrated school start. Pedagogues have completed a three-and-half-year course at a specialised tertiary training college. Nursery and child care assistants (*pædagogmedhjælpere*) work mainly in crèches, kindergartens and SFO facilities. They receive secondary vocational training. Municipal child minders or family day care caregivers have no mandatory training but courses in child care are offered regularly since the early 1980s when municipal child minder facilities for children aged 0-2 years were placed on an equal footing with day care facilities. In ECEC services (excluding family day care), 60% of staff have a tertiary level qualification.

Child-staff ratios: 0- to 2-year-olds: 3.3:1; 3- to 5-year-olds: 7.2:1; mixed age 0-9 (or 0-13)-year-olds: 6:1 (2003); special day care: 1.4:1; OSP: 9.7:1 or 13.7:1, depending on organisation.

Maximum group size: There is no legal regulation of group size. Normally no more than 12 for 1- to 2-year-olds, 22 for 3- to 5-year-olds and with activity-dependant and flexible group size for 6- to 13-year-olds.

Auspices

Services for 0- to 6-year-olds are considered in Denmark to be an integral part of the social welfare system. Pre-school institutions comprise crèches, kindergartens, and, to a growing extent, integrated services for children 0- to 6-year-olds. A further option for children 0-3 years is public family day care. All these institutions are established in accordance with the 1998 Social Services Act. According to this law, the purpose of the institutions is pedagogical, social, and care-related. The pedagogical aims are to take care and to prevent; to ensure the opportunity for children to play and learn; to stimulate the fantasy, the creativity and the language of the child – in short, to ensure that children get a good and secure childhood.

The national authority for child care centres is the Ministry of Family and Consumer Affairs. The Ministry has responsibility for policy in the field, and for overseeing the principle of: admission criteria; the quality of the services provided, and the implementation of quality regulations and measures; work conditions and training of staff; parental involvement; funding and financing. A major aim is to support, in collaboration with parents, the development of young children and provide caring and learning environments for them while their parents are at work. The Ministry of Education, through the *Folkeskole* Act (covering the pre-school class, primary and lower secondary education), has policy responsibility for pre-school classes (-7 years) and SFOs (school-based, leisure-time) facilities.

Current administration and management is, however, the responsibility of the local authorities, *e.g.* to fund and establish services to meet parental demand; to supervise the quality and educational content of local services; to provide adequate staffing and sufficient support to staff, etc. Frequently, the municipalities establish unified departments, bringing together care and education. Local authorities determine the objectives and the framework for work carried out in day care facilities and schools, and are responsible for funding and supervision. They have overall responsibility for providing child care facilities for children, to ensure a sufficient supply of places and to take all necessary initiatives in relation to children in need of special supports. Within this arrangement, parents are free in principle to decide the kind of child care they want to use. Because of costs and facility, most Danish parents opt for family day care until children reach the age of 3 years. Parents may also be provided with a grant to use the services of a free-choice child minder, recognised by the municipality.

Context

Labour force rates: In 2004, 76.1% of women (15-64) participated in the formal labour market, decreasing from 77.6% in 1990. Of those employed, 24.3% were in part-time employment in 2004, compared to 11.6% for men (OECD, *Employment Outlook*, 2005). The employment rate for mothers with a youngest child under 6 is 74%, and their share in part-time employment is 5%.

Parental leave: Universal paid maternity leave of 28 weeks for mothers + 2 weeks paternity leave paid at 100% salary level (public sector employees and increasingly private sector). It is possible to obtain another 26 weeks at 60% of unemployment benefit. Total child care leave may not exceed 52 weeks. If child care leave is taken after the first year, children aged 3-8 may have part-time places in a child care facility. Special supplementary allowances are available for single working parents with children aged 6 months to 5 years when leave is taken to care for children. The sum of the leave allowance and supplementary allowance must not exceed 80% of the parent's previous income. In many municipalities, parents returning to work after 26 weeks have the guarantee of an immediate child care place for their child, but difficulties are sometimes experienced by parents at this stage. A new amendment to the law ensures child care for families when the child is 9 months old and will in 2006 be lowered further to children aged from 6 months.

Access and provision

The operating hours and annual duration of services vary according to service type. The system is predominantly one of mixed, public and private services, supervised and funded (from local taxes and central government grants) by local authorities. Major forms of provision are:

- Day care facilities (*dagtilbud*) for children from 6 months to 6 years, which are divided into family day care (*kommunal dagpleje*), centre-based day care (*Vuggestuer*-crèche; *aldersintegrerede institutioner*-age-integrated centres; and *bornehaver*-kindergartens) and independent day care facilities. About 70% of day care facilities are operated by public, community services. Public provision is supplemented by independent, non-profit providers and networks (about 30%), which offer parents another choice of service. There is no significant use of private for-profit operators, although in 2005, new legislation favouring the entry of private operators was proposed by the government. To receive municipal grants independent providers must work in conjunction with the local authority and observe local authority regulations and operating guidelines.

- *Kindergarten classes* (*bornehaveklasse*) for children -7 years (7 is the compulsory school age). The kindergarten class, led principally by a pedagogue, takes place in the primary school (*Folkeskole*) and is free. Teaching in the kindergarten class is expected to be play-based and linked to the developmental stage of the child. Approximately half of all public schools run a programme called "integrated school start" where pupils from pre-school classes and 1st and 2nd classes are taught to some extent in age integrated groups. In recent years, emergent literacy approaches have been gaining ground in the kindergarten class.

- *Leisure time* or out-of-school-time care in centres or schools, or in leisure time facilities (*fritidshjem and* SFO facilities). Out-of-school provision is fee-paying, but is massively enrolled, with approximately 80% of 6- to 10-year-age group (does not include 10-year-olds) involved (2004).

Rates of provision

0-1 years: Parental care predominates, but from the age of about six months parents begin to enrol their children in day care facilities. Informal care outside the family is little used. *Legestuer* – the playrooms and facilities shared by all municipal child minders (family day carers) – operate within the municipal child minder arrangements. Parents may also take their children to *Legesteder* to play with other children. In 2004 12% of 0-year-olds were enrolled, whereof 8% were in family day care and 4% in centre-based day care (crèche or age-integrated centres).

1-2`years: 83% of children are enrolled in day care facilities in this period (the highest rate in Europe). Family day care (45%) is most widely used in rural areas, while age-integrated facilities and *Vuggestuer* (crèche) are the most common day care facilities elsewhere (38%).

3-5 years: 94% of 3- to 6-year-old children were enrolled in 2004 – almost exclusively in centre-based day care (age-integrated centres or kindergarten). Furthermore, there are 15-hour programmes for bilingual children who are not attending the day care system.

5-6/7 years: 98% enrolments in free pre-school class in *Folkeskole*, with wrap around care provided for children in fee-paying, integrated services or leisure-time facilities.

Children with diverse needs

Children with disabilities: Inclusion of children with disabilities in all early services and schools is common. Mainstreaming is the general objective, but there is also a wide variety of specialised institutional settings.

Children from low-income families: The child poverty level after redistribution policies is 2.4%, the lowest in the world (UNICEF, 2005). However, as many as 11.4% of the children lived in families receiving social benefits because of low income or temporary loss of income (according to *Red Barnet* on the basis of a research report from the Danish National Institute of Social Research on the level of poverty amongst children in 2002).

Ethnic and bilingual children: Immigrants form 4.1% of the Danish population, and it is estimated that bilingual children will soon constitute 10% of enrolments. In February 2000, the government published an overall action plan for the improved integration of these children. It is now mandatory for local authorities to offer language-stimulation activities to bilingual children from 3 years. Language activities mostly take the form of intensified Danish language coaching in kindergarten and in the first years of primary education. When children are not in the kindergarten system, 15 hours per week of Danish language contact may be offered to families in their own home.

Quality

Licensing and regulatory regimes: It is the responsibility of local authorities to supervise and support all child care services within their area. Because of this decentralisation, disparities in access and quality have been noted between different municipalities, a situation which generally does not favour poor neighbourhoods and families.

Funding: Investment in ECEC is high in Denmark, owing to low child-staff ratios and relatively higher salaries for pedagogues and teachers than in other countries. Total expenditure on day care and leisure time facilities (*i.e.* all ECEC) is approximately 2.1% of GDP. Fees are capped for parents at 30-33% of running costs, with poorer families using services free of charge or at reduced rates. Fees will be lowered to an upper ceiling of 25% of costs through new legislation foreseen in 2006 and 2007. Gross costs for children under 3 come to USD 19 500 dollars per child; and for children 3-6 years, approximately USD 10 200 dollars per child; and in leisure-time services for 6-10 years (leisure time), USD 5 950 per child. Some of this expenditure is clawed back through high (for Scandinavia) parental fees. Net public expenditure for all children enrolled in services 0-6 years is approximately USD 7 650 annually.

Staffing: With the exception of family day care, all facilities have a manager and deputy-manager, both of whom must be qualified pedagogues. Pedagogues (social educators for children and youth), are the lead personnel in all facilities, including kindergarten class. With pedagogues accounting for 60% of staff, Denmark has the highest rate of professionals working in centres of all the Nordic countries. Nursery and child care assistants (*paedagogmedhjaelpere*) are also employed in crèches and kindergartens. Among qualified pedagogues, men make up 8% of employees in day care facilities for children aged 6 months to 6 years, and make up 25% of staff in out-of-school care.

Training requirements: The minimum qualification for pedagogues requires 3.5 years at tertiary level in Centres of Further Education. A small proportion of assistants undertake an adult education or vocational training course for 18 months. Qualified teachers with four years tertiary education are sometimes partly engaged in *Folkeskole* kindergarten classes linked to integrated schools. In-service training is also available. There is no mandatory training for family day carers, but all receive at least three weeks training, and have access to intensive supervision and in-service training.

Work conditions: Pedagogues and assistants working on a full-time basis, work 37 hours a week. Family day carers (child minders) work 48 hours per week. All of these staff are entitled to paid holidays, pay during periods of sickness, and parental and child care leave. Almost all pedagogues are members of the National Union of Child Care and Youth Educators (BUPL). Nursery and child care assistants are organised by the national trade union FOA – Trade and Labour. Nursery assistant positions are popular since this type of work is relatively well paid for unskilled workers and offers responsibility and team work with others.

Child-staff ratios: Child-staff ratios in 2003 per full-time adult are as follows: crèche (0- to 2-year-olds), 3.3:1; *kindergarten* (3-5 years), 7.2:1; age-integrated facility (0-9 or 13 years), 6:1; leisure time facilities (*fritidshjem and SFO* for 6-9 years) respectively 9.7:1 and 13.7:1; special day care, 1.4:1. The number of staff per child is highest for the youngest children. Staff intensity is highest in special day care facilities for children with physical and/or mental disabilities. There is no national regulation concerning child-staff ratios or about the involvement of qualified staff. A negotiated agreement (through collective bargaining) guarantees, however, that the manager and deputy-manager in child care centres must be qualified pedagogues.

Curriculum and pedagogy: The general purpose of ECEC as specified by the Act of Social Services is to further the well-being, development and independence of children in consultation with their parents, while also functioning for educational, social and care purposes. The children learn by playing, by observing committed adults and by interacting with them. The child's right to participation (UN Convention on the Rights of the Child) ensure that s/he must be listened to. Children are expected to play a participatory role and share responsibility for their own daily life. The programmes offer experiences and activities in an environment designed to stimulate imagination and creativity. Day care facilities must give children an opportunity to achieve a broad understanding of Danish culture as well as understanding of other cultures met in the daily life of the centre. In addition, children must be able to acquire knowledge about and experience of the natural environment.

Monitoring, evaluation and research: Monitoring, evaluation and research are normally the responsibility of the line ministry, the Ministry of Family and Consumer Affairs. The task is generally achieved through regular reporting and data collection, and through periodic surveys. Since the first OECD review in 2000, some confusion in central co-ordination seems to have occurred, as three separate ministries now share responsibility for services to children and families. To our knowledge, there is currently no national government agency providing or gathering systematic data on developments in local child care in Denmark. The close monitoring of kindergartens takes place at municipal level, where teams of pedagogical advisors monitor services and provide support to pedagogues to improve the quality of services or to implement special programmes, *e.g.* child participation in decision-making processes has been encouraged for more than a decade, though projects such as *Children as Citizens*. In the school system, the Ministry of Education is responsible for formulating learning objectives, monitoring quality and initiating research, including for the kindergarten class (6-7 years).

Parent and community involvement: Danish day care and the *Folkeskole* each operate with strong parent boards, obligatory since 1993, in all municipal and independent day care facilities. The parent boards define the principles for the educational work carried out and for the use of funds available through the budgetary framework. This activity is usually communicated in the form of a business plan. The business plans are used as a basis for evaluation of the work carried out in the centre. Centre staff are also board members although parent representatives must have the majority.

Features of the review period in 2000

Despite the high coverage rates achieved by Danish ECEC services, demand continued to rise, though not as rapidly in recent years. The law required that a place should be provided to parent(s) for each child within three months* of demand, but waiting lists existed in some ten municipalities. New investments by local authorities were being made available to meet the challenge, and it was expected that places for all children would be soon available. Attention was also focused on providing places and appropriate programmes for children at risk, *i.e.* children with low socio-economic status, immigrant children, children from dysfunctional families. A Danish language stimulation programme

---

* After parental leave, within four weeks, provided that parents have requested a place within the time framework set by the municipality.

was available to bilingual children and families in the years prior to compulsory school, and some excellent bridging work towards immigrant families was taking place, particularly in Copenhagen.

Qualitative developments were also taking place. The traditional division in Denmark between primary education and the kindergarten was being questioned, and seen as a challenge to be overcome through discussion and partnership. The debate was focused on the need to develop a common set of societal values and aims among pedagogues and teachers for the later years of kindergarten and the first stages of primary education. ECEC was seen to include "structured learning activities in a caring environment", as well as play, informal learning and social development. The non-compulsory kindergarten class at the start of the *Folkeskole* (the basic school) was to a large extent characterised by this approach, and were conducted by pedagogue-teacher teams.

Co-operation and cohesion between the day care system (*i.e.* the kindergartens), the school system and leisure-time activities were given special attention in the national *Folkeskole 2000* plan. With the help of their pedagogical advisors, some municipalities were pushing ahead with plans to make of their kindergartens and schools, active centres of learning which would develop their own learning plans. In addition, the Ministry of Social Affairs, in collaboration with the National Association of Local Authorities in Denmark, had created a working group in 1996 to improve quality, and develop new methods for educational work in kindergartens. Other initiatives were being considered, which included reforms in staff training and curriculum guidelines.

Current developments and issues

The new Law on Pedagogical Curriculum

The Law on Pedagogical Curriculum came into force on August 1st 2004 and it applies to all child care centres for the 0- to 6-year-olds as well as to public child-minding. Each individual child care centre must work out its own pedagogical curriculum, while a common curriculum is worked out for the public child-minding. The purpose of the pedagogical curriculum is to make the institution "support, lead, and challenge the learning of children" through, among other things, "spontaneous experiences and playing" with a focus on children's "potentials and competences". Before it became law, much discussion was evoked by this project. Many parents and professionals saw in it a risk that "learning" would come too predominate, and thus change the Danish view of childhood and the core of pedagogical objective of supporting the child in its development. BUPL, the national pedagogue trade union, expressed concerns about the lack of time to formulate, carry out, and evaluate the curriculum, and about the adequacy of funding to educate staff to take care of this new task.

The terms of the pedagogical curriculum deals with the following six topics: the holistic personal development of the children; social competences; language; body and movement; nature and natural phenomena; cultural expressions and values. The pedagogical curricula of the different centres must list the aims and intermediate aims regarding the competences and experiences the children are to "acquire". They should be divided into a section dealing with the younger children (0-3 years) and a section dealing with the older children (3-6 years). In regard to integrated institutions (*e.g.* children's houses) with 0- to 6-year-old children, a joint curriculum can be worked out, which makes allowance for both age groups.

The head of the child care centre is responsible to the Board of parents and the local authorities in seeing that a pedagogical curriculum is worked out. In practice, the curriculum is worked out in cooperation with the staff, whereupon it is to be approved by the Board of parents and the local authorities. In an appendix to the Law on Pedagogical Curriculum, examples of content, aim and focal point have been worked out in regard to each of the 6 topics, intended as an example for the child care centres when they are to work out their own curriculum.

Staff motivation

Over recent years, both parents and staff have expressed over financial cuts to day care centre budgets and public debate has occurred. A part of this concern, has been the transfer of administrative functions to the managers and pedagogues in centres, without the addition of administrative staff. Although the move is due in part to the further decentralisation of ECEC, attention to the issue is needed as professional time spent with children is a central aim of early childhood services. Without interaction, children's learning can become dispersed and unstructured. According to a study by the Institute of Local Government Studies (AKF) for Frederiksberg Municipality (part of the city centre of Copenhagen), the directors of ECEC facilities can allocate on average only 27% of their time to work with the children. These findings are consistent with similar surveys carried out by BUPL, the national pedagogue trade union.

Co-ordination at central level

In 2001, the OECD review team recommended attention to co-ordination of policies across municipalities. Since the review, progress has been made in this area through the work of the Association of Municipal Authorities. At central level, however, some confusion in co-ordination seems to have occurred, as three separate ministries now share responsibility for services to children and families. As a result, there is no national government agency currently providing or gathering systematic data on developments in local child care in Denmark. This is notably the case with respect to child-staff ratios and other quality parameters. It is possible, however, on the basis of data from the national statistical agency (Statistics Denmark) to calculate data concerning child-staff ratios, but as explained in the main body of this text (Chapter 8), national statistical offices are generally unable to provide adequately the data and qualitative information that ECEC policy makers and managers need.

Accountability

In Denmark, the local authorities are free to determine standards, and it seems that in some municipalities, there is no requirement for centres to report ratios or other matters. A legal or formal regulation of quality standards seems to be lacking. In sum, quality becomes a matter of opinion or a negotiation, without appeal to research evidence and the good practice in other municipalities. The situation weakens the possibility for parents or professionals to test in administrative or client hearings (and eventually in the courts) whether a particular local government is providing the necessary inputs to safeguard quality, unlike Norway where ratios and other quality standards are governed by law. Parental concern about the quality of services seems to be growing and surfaced clearly during the general elections at the beginning of 2005. At that moment, the issue of rising child-staff ratios was widely debated, until the government announced further financial support to early childhood services to the amount of DKK 2 billions over the period 2005-09. It is planned also to reduce maximum costs for parents from a 33% ceiling to 25%. This positive response is, however, a political one. The question here is one of administrative accountability: who is responsible for structural quality standards (sufficient funding; recruitment and training levels of staff and the proportion of lead professionals in services; child-staff ratios; the state of buildings and materials); and whether there is a possibility of redress for parents and centres, through recognised administrative procedures, when standards are breached.

Finland

Population: 5.21 m. **Fertility rate:** 1.7. **GDP per capita:** USD 26 500. **Children under 6 years:** 399 889.

Female labour force participation: 72% of women (15-64 years) are employed, 18.2% of whom are in part-time employment (male part-time is 7.7%).

Labour force participation rate of women with a child(ren) under 6 years: 49.6%, of whom 8% work part-time (OECD, *Society at a Glance*, 2005).

Remunerated maternity and parental leave: 18 weeks of maternity leave plus 26 weeks of parental leave paid at average 66% of earned income (gross). Utilisation almost 100%.

Social expenditure: 27.1% (2003). **Child poverty rate:** 2.8% after taxes and transfers in 2002 (OECD average is 11.2%).

Compulsory school age: 7 years.

Funding of day care services for 0- to 7-year-olds: (including family day care and centre-based care) is 1.1% of GDP. Including the pre-school class (6-7 years), the investment rises to 1.3% of GDP, and when expenditure on the home care allowance is added, the figure reaches 1.7% of GDP. The unit cost per child in day care services is over EUR 8 000 per year.

Average costs to parents: In day care about 15% of costs, and capped at EUR 200 per child per month. Pre-school education is free.

Legal entitlement to a free educational service: Begins at 6 years.

Major service types and duration: Day care centres (*päiväkoti*) open full-day, all-year round; family day care homes/places are also full time, full year. Most children are enrolled full-day. Pre-school classes for children 6-7 years are half-day for the academic year, and are wrapped around by day care.

Rate of access to regulated services: 27.5% of 1- to 2-year-olds; 43.9% of 2- to 3-year-olds; 62.3% of 3- to 4-year-olds; 68.5% of 4- to 5-year-olds; 73% of children 5-6 years; almost full enrolment in the pre-school class for children 6-7 years, about 70% of whom also attend day care.

Designation and professional qualifications of key staff: Children's day care services employ, in addition to heads of centres, kindergarten teachers (the official term), children's nurses, day care assistants, and child minders (family day carers). Kindergarten teachers have completed 3-4 years of study for a Bachelor degree in Early Childhood Education or in Social Sciences, many of them going on to Master's level.

Child-staff ratios: 1 trained adult for every 4 children under age 3 years; 1 trained adult for every 7 children over 3 years (with additional staff for children with special needs). In family day care, the ratio per day care parent is 4, plus one half day pre-school or school child including day care parents' own (under school age) children. In pre-school education, the maximum ratio is 1 teacher (with an assistant) for 13 children.

Maximum group size: In family day care, the maximum group is 4 full-day children, plus 1 half day child. In child care centres, there are no group size requirements. In pre-school education, the recommended maximum group size is 20 children. If the group exceeds 13, the teacher needs an assistant.

Auspices

In Finland, early childhood policy is intended to support the development and learning of young children and enable them to become ethically responsible members of society. Policy is built on clear understandings by all stakeholders that a creative cohesive society depends on social justice and concern for the rights and responsibilities of all, including children. Respect for mutuality (the possibilities of all different participants and stakeholders to be involved in the development process in an open dialogue) underpins the development of the national ECEC framework launched in 2002, which defines the main principles and guidelines to develop early childhood services across Finland.

Government responsibility for ECEC from 0-6 years rests primarily with the Ministry of Social Affairs and Health. The ministry is responsible for the *National Policy Definition Concerning ECEC*, allowances to parents and service providers, maternity grant, health care, child and family counselling, child welfare and home help services. The National Research and Development Centre for Welfare and Health (STAKES) has guided the formulation of the *National Curriculum Guidelines in ECEC* for children 0-6 years of age. The Ministry of Education has responsibility for pre-school education for 6-year-olds and morning and afternoon activities for school children. The National Board of Education has responsibility for the curricular orientation of pre-school education. The Ministry of Labour is responsible for parental and care leave.

Municipalities are fully responsible for the implementation and steering of the services in their own localities. In turn, Provincial State Offices monitor the activities of municipalities and provide an annual evaluation of social welfare services. The subjective right of each child to day care, following the parental leave period and until entry to primary school at age 7, is a powerful catalyst underpinning legislative and policy developments. This unconditional right to day care includes the right of parents to choose a home-care allowance instead of municipal day care for their child until the youngest child in the family turns 3.

Context

Labour force rates: In 2004, 72% of women participated in the Finnish labour force, down from 73.4% in 1990. 18.2% of this number are in part-time employment, compared to 7.7% of men in part-time work. (OECD, *Employment Outlook*, 2005). The percentage of women with at least one child below 6 years who participate is 49.6%, and their share in part-time employment is 8% (OECD, *Society at a Glance*, 2005). The percentage of women with a child below 3 years who participate in full-time employment is 42.7%, of whom 8.5% work part time. The relatively low participation rate may be a result of the 3-year child care leave that may be taken by a parent after the birth of a child (see below).

Parental leave and home care leave: Finland offers universal 18 weeks maternity leave, plus 26 weeks paid parental leave. The level of payment is determined according to income earned, being approximately 66% of an employee's pay, and includes a minimum set rate of EUR 15.20/day for 6 days per week (2004). Further, paternity leave of 3 weeks maximum is also granted, which can be taken by fathers during maternity and/or parental leave time. If the father also takes at least two weeks of parental leave he gets two extra weeks of paternity leave, which he can have after the parental leave period. For parents opting not to enrol their children in municipal day care, child care leave can be taken full time or part time until the youngest child turns 3, during which time a flat-rate benefit is paid to the parent at home. A partial child care leave can also be taken for children from birth to second grade in primary school, but with an allowance only when the youngest child is under 3 or in the first or second grades in primary school.

Access and provision

Every child in Finland under compulsory school age has a subjective right to day care, to be provided by the local authority once parental leave comes to an end. Family and centre-based day care offer full day, full year service, including round the clock care if needed. The Reform concerning morning and afternoon activities for school children entered into force on 1 August 2004. This out-of-school provision is targeted for children on the first and second grades in primary school, and for children in special education from grades 3 to 9. As the provision of out-of-school services is not an obligation, the State provides substantial subsidies to municipalities that offer a minimum of 570 hours annually per child. These services include a variety of municipally provided services, extended by services provided by the Lutheran Church and other voluntary organisations.

Operational features: The municipalities have the obligation to organise day care for all young children whose parents choose to have it. Provision, operating hours and the annual duration of services vary according to service type. Municipalities can opt for a mixed system of provision, combining public and private provision. In general, municipalities provide services directly through municipal day care centres (*päiväkoti*), family day care homes/places and the pre-school class (the main forms of provision). There are two types of private services in municipalities: the fully private services (7% of total) that parents can choose for their child, while accessing a private child care allowance; and secondly, services outsourced by the municipalities to selected private providers. These outsourced services are considered as part of the municipal network, and are partly administered by the municipality, *e.g.* in managing the delivery of places and in supervising quality. In addition, municipalities and voluntary organisations organise various open part-time or sessional ECEC services.

Access patterns

0-1 years: Almost all children are cared for by parents.

1-3 years: 27.5% of children 1-2 years, and 43.9% of 2- to 3-year-olds are in ECEC services, of which 54% in family day care and 46% in day care centres. Services are open 10-12 hours daily, and almost all children take full-time places.

3-6 years: 62.3% of 3- to 4-year-olds, 68.5% of 4- to 5-year-olds and 73% of 5- to 6-year-olds attend, generally full-day in day care centres or family day care.

6-7 years: Enrolments in pre-school education cover about 96% of children. 70% of these children also attend day care.

Out-of-school provision is accessed by 40.5% of the first grade children and 22.4% of children on the second grade in primary school. About 2 500 children in special education on grades 3-9 also attend these services.

Attention to children with diverse needs: In Finland, special services are not considered a separate system. The subjective right to access applies to all children. Many examples of inclusion can be seen in mainstream services all over Finland.

Children with disabilities: In ECEC services, 7% of children have special needs. 85% of the children who receive special support are in mainstream programmes, the remaining 15% being in special groups, these representing about 1% of children in ECEC.

Children from low-income families: The child poverty rate in Finland is 2.8% after taxes and transfers, the second lowest in the world (UNICEF, 2005).

Ethnic and bilingual children: Apart from the Swedish-speaking population (5.6%), there are 2.4% of children using Finnish as a second language. There are over 100 different immigrant groups, the largest of which come from Russia and Somalia. The municipalities in which there is some small concentration of immigrants, for example, in Helsinki and the surrounding municipalities, make policy to support immigrant families and to create experimental programmes for them. Also attention and investment are devoted to the small Indigenous Sami population in Lapland.

Quality

Licensing and regulatory regimes: Finland adopts a strongly decentralised style of regulation. At the same time, the legislation sets out strong and clear requirements, *e.g.* for staff qualification and adult-child ratios. These requirements apply to both public and private service providers.

Funding: According to OECD (*Education at a Glance*, 2005), expenditure in Finland on "pre-primary educational institutions" (ISCED 0) as a percentage of GDP for pre-primary is 0.4%, and expenditure per child per annum is USD 3 929. These figures, based on ISCED Level 0 definitions, are very partial. Public expenditure for day care services for children 0-6 years amounts to 1.1% of GDP. When the pre-school class (6-7 years) is included, the total expenditure for ECEC is 1.3% of GDP (family day care, centre-based care and pre-school class). When expenditure on the home care allowance is added, the figure reaches 1.7% of GDP. For parents, affordability is not an issue because of the relatively small parent contribution of about 15% of costs, the rest being subsidised by state and local authority taxes. In addition, parents pay eleven months only per annum, although their child's place is available during holidays also. No fee is charged for low-income families, while the highest fee cannot be more than EUR 200 per month. Pre-school hours for the 6-year-olds are free.

Staffing: In addition to heads of centres children's day care services employ kindergarten teachers, children's nurses, and day care assistants. Of staff working directly with children, about 30% have a tertiary degree (bachelor or master of education or bachelor of social sciences), and the rest an upper secondary level training. This percentage of tertiary trained pedagogues is low compared to Denmark (60%) or Sweden (51%). In the pre-school class, teachers must have at least a tertiary level training. Almost all staff are female and some concern is expressed about recruiting more men in ECEC services. Only 4.6% of teachers and 5.8% of children's nurses are employed part-time.

Training requirements: Day care centres (*päiväkoti*) are staffed by kindergarten teachers (at least, one-third of staff), trained children's nurses and day care assistants. Kindergarten teachers complete 3-4 years of study for a Bachelor degree in Early Childhood Education or Social Sciences, some of them going on to Master's level. Some heads of centres have further training. The other main staff in day care centres are trained children's nurses who have a secondary vocational training of 3 years in practical nursing. Day care assistants have also appropriate training. Present policy seeks to maintain multi-professional, team-working in centres, with staff carrying out different professional tasks and roles.

Child minders must also have appropriate training but, in practice, variations in the length and content of their training occur. In 2000, the National Board of Education presented a recommendation for a new competence based qualification for child minders (Further Qualification for Child Minders, 2000). Training requirements are rigorous (perhaps the most demanding across the OECD countries), but in practice, the length of the training may vary according to the competence and work experience of the child minder. The schools offering the training and responsible for competence tests must make an individualised learning plan for each student.

Work conditions: The recruitment of new child minders in family day care and a shortage of special educators in ECEC are current challenges. Several initiatives are in place concerning training, steering and wages for family day carers, focused on local and regional networking and the development of new training models, targeting early special education in particular. For 73% of kindergarten teachers, the bachelor degree is only an intermediate phase to a master's degree. However, many of these students move to work in other fields where better income and career opportunities exist, along with better working conditions and less stressful work. The statutory weekly hours worked by trained staff are 38.15, both for kindergarten teachers and children's nurses. There is no statutory requirement for a minimum level of staff development, although an initiative specifying 3-10 days per year for all social welfare staff (including ECEC) took effect on 1 August 2005. From that time, the municipalities will have a statutory obligation to provide sufficient staff development for all social welfare staff (including ECEC).

Child-staff ratios: Child-staff ratios are low in Finland. In centre-based care, there should be at least 1 trained adult for every 4 children under age 3 years, and 1 children's nurse or kindergarten teacher for every 7 children over 3 years. In family day care, the ratio is 4 full-day children and one part-time pre-school or school child per child minder. In part-day services for children 3-6, the ratio is 13 children per one children's nurse or kindergarten teacher. In the pre-school class (6-7 years), there is a recommendation for group size, but no requirement for the child-staff ratio. This means that when the pre-school class takes place in a day care centre, the ratio goes according to the day care regulations (part day 1 to 13, full day 1 to 7). When the pre-school is in a school, the ratio can be as high as 13 children to one teacher, but in excess of 13, the teacher must have an assistant.

Curriculum and pedagogy: The *Core Curriculum for Pre-school Education* (2000) initiative began a holistic process of curriculum reform in Finland. Since August 2000 local curricula for pre-school education for 6-year-olds have been drafted in each municipality (day care centres and schools) in consultation with providers, including private providers from which local authorities have purchased pre-school services. The *National Curriculum Guidelines on ECEC* was published in September 2003. The guidelines serve as a basis for the design of the municipal (local) curricula for children from 0 to 6. The core curriculum stresses the importance of care, upbringing and education as an integrated whole for young children. Beyond this focus, no requirement about specific pedagogies is imposed. The new guidelines stress the importance of ECEC in the educational continuum as part of lifelong learning. The ECEC curriculum is part of a comprehensive, integrated whole that ensures consistency and continuity in children's development. The evaluation of the effects of the core curricula for pre-school education is now in process. STAKES provides training for the municipal curricula process organisers, who in turn, lead the training in the municipalities. The centre has also provided an internet-based network to support the organisers during the different phases of implementation (*www.stakes.fi/varttua*)

Monitoring, evaluation and research: The government *Resolution Concerning National ECEC Policy* proposes an action programme for the development of ECEC, including the *Project on Quality and Steering in ECEC* (2000-2005) aimed at strengthening the local, regional and national systems of steering and assessment. Research on quality continues to expand, with clear cohesive links between several universities, the Ministry and STAKES. A tool to support ECEC staff across Finland is a comprehensive database (*www.stakes.fi/varttua*) containing the latest ECEC information on development projects and studies being conducted. This portal has a central role in the implementation of the new curriculum guidelines. Since 2002, information systems work has been guided by the Social Welfare and Health Care Data and Information Reform strategy. This strategy is designed to prepare a national social welfare and health care data information system comprising statistics, corporate data and information on regularly repeated studies and separate surveys. How ECEC planning, monitoring and evaluation activities are enhanced in the age of technology is a question for the future.

Parent and community involvement: Parents have a crucial role in ensuring the responsiveness of services to child interests and needs. Finland's *Government Resolution concerning the National ECEC Policy Definition* strongly raises the issue of parent involvement. National projects such as the *Educational Partnership* (2003-05) and *Early Support* (2004-05) seek to respond to parental needs, the former through staff training that enhances capacity to support parents and parenthood, the latter developing the role of parents in early intervention. In day care centres, it is customary to draw up an individual ECEC plan for each child in collaboration with parents. The implementation of the plan is assessed annually. This is a statutory obligation based on the *Act on the Status and Rights of Social Welfare Clients* (2000).

Developments

ECEC in Finland is a well-developed and stable system much appreciated by parents. Universal access to day care services has been a subjective right of each child under 3 since 1990 and of all pre-school children since 1996. Public investment is assured and quality regulations are clear and strictly enforced. The system is characterised by sensitivity to the rights of the child and an avowed concern for equality and fairness. Even for low-income families, fees are not a barrier either to access or to the labour market participation by parents. Day care fees are income-related, the variation being from EUR 18 to EUR 200 (USD 246) per month per child, depending on income level.

Parents have the freedom to use a private or public service. Competition from the excellent public services induces private providers to supply services at reasonable cost. Parents contribute 15.4% of the child care expenditure within public facilities (90% of the sector). With the private child care allowance and municipal supplements, the fees parents pay in private services do not significantly exceed fees in public facilities. Social welfare reform projects are a significant current state initiative with municipalities and regions having access to substantial funds (EUR 82 million/USD 101 245 400).

Mention has been made of the new *National Curriculum Guidelineson ECEC* (2003) developed by STAKES that guide the organisation and content of ECEC programmes for children 0-6. This curriculum was preceded by a similar initiative by the National Board of Education in formulating the *Core Curriculum for Pre-School Education*.

In addition, ECEC in Finland is gaining recognition as a teaching and research discipline in the universities and polytechnics. New Centres of Excellence in Social Welfare encourage research and development work, bringing together university researchers and ECEC personnel in common projects. A more recent focus for research and the early childhood field is the broader community and family context of a child's life. Greater outreach to parents is being practised, seeing them as not only clients but as valued pedagogical partners. Lifelong learning and transition from one educational setting to another have also received close attention. STAKES' promotion of learning-in-work has also encouraged activities to increase the competence of ECEC personnel in the application and use of information technologies. An outcome of this work is the creation of a new training and network model that enhances collaboration in and between municipalities.

France

Population: 60.42 m. **Fertility rate:** 1.89. **GDP per capita:** USD 27 200. **Children under 6 years:** 4.5 m.

Female labour force participation: For women aged 15-64, the labour force participation rate was 63.7% in 2004, 23.6% of whom are in part-time employment (male part-time is 4.8%) (OECD, *Employment Outlook*, 2005).

Labour force participation rate of women with a child(ren): 65% of women with youngest child under 6 are employed, accounting for 23% of total part-time employment (2002) (OECD, *Society at a Glance*). For mothers with youngest child under 3, the rate is 49.5% (2004) (EUROSTAT).

Maternity and parental leave: 16 weeks of maternity leave for 1st child and 26 weeks for subsequent children, paid at full earning. Further leave (*congé parental d'éducation*) is available until child's 3rd birthday, unfunded unless combined with the *Allocation parentale d'éducation* for parents with two or more children, when a flat rate stipend is paid. The allocation can also be combined with a salary for part-time work beginning at least 6 months before the end of the allocation. Fathers are entitled to 11 days of paid, job-protected leave (*congé de paternité*).

Average duration of parental leave: 30 weeks.

Compulsory school age: 6 years.

Social expenditure: 28.5%. **Child poverty rate:** 7.5% after taxes and transfers (OECD average is 11.2%).

Funding of pre-primary educational services (ISCED Level 0): 0.7% of GDP (0.65% public and 0.03% private), 11.7% of education budget and 17.3% of education enrolments. To this may be added public investment in crèches, family day care, école maternelle for 2- to 3-year-olds, leisure-time services for young children, and publicly subsidised home-based care – bringing the total investment to at least 1% of GDP.

Unit cost per child in pre-primary education: (in USD converted using PPP): USD 4 512 (OECD, *Education at a Glance*, 2005).

Funding of services for children under 3: Not available, but given the extent of coverage (27% in family day care or crèches, plus home-care funding, plus 35% of all children enrolled in the *école maternelle* by age 2.5 years), the figure is probably in the region of 0.5% of GDP.

Average costs to parents: Children 0-3 years: 27% of costs; children 3-6 years: free.

Legal entitlement to a free service: 3 years, but depending on the commune, can begin from 2 years.

Major service types and duration: Centre-based, public options include: crèches for children 0-3 years; *écoles maternelles* for children 3-6 years (in certain communities, 2 years). Individual options include: *assistantes maternelles* (literally "maternal assistants"), that is, family day care providers who care for one to three children in the provider's home on a regular basis; *garde à domicile* or home care giving is increasing in use, but though supported fiscally is not regulated in terms of training or programme standards.

Rate of access to regulated services: For children aged 0-3 years: accredited family day care providers take in charge 18% of young children 0-3 years, crèche services 8%, with a further 35% of 2- to 3-year-olds enrolled in the *école maternelle*. Figures for out-of-school provision for children (6-12 years) are not available.

Designation and professional qualifications of key staff: 75% of staff in crèches and child care services are required to have an appropriate diploma. In the *école maternelle*, all teaching staff must have, in principle, the diploma of *professeur d'école*. Auxiliary staff (ATSEM) are required since 1992 to hold a CAP or secondary level certificate in early childhood. Older ATSEM working in the services are often untrained.

Child-staff ratios: For child care, ratios and group sizes are recommended, but not for the *école maternelle*. Average ratios are: children 0-2 years: 5:1; children 2-3 years (except *école maternelle*): 8:1; *école maternelle* (children 3-6 years): 25.5:1; OSP for children 6-12 years: not available.

Auspices and context

In France, child care and early education fall under separate ministerial auspices. For children under 3, the *ministère des Affaires sociales, du Travail et de la Solidarité* and the *ministère de la Santé, de la Famille et des Personnes handicapées* develop the regulations for the different forms of non-school ECEC and define, with the national family allowance fund (*Caisse Nationale des Allocations Familiales* – CNAF), the goals and resources of the regional family allowance funds over a four-year period. The decentralised CAFs, or *Caisses des allocations familiales*, are the key actors in supporting local policy development. Over the past 30 years, their priority has been to develop ECEC settings in partnership with the *communes* and non-profit associations, and sometimes *départements*. The *Direction Générale de l'Action Sociale* is the administrative unit responsible for non-school ECEC and is jointly affiliated to both ministries.

In contrast, a single, universal model of pre-school education, the *école maternelle*, exists, and is available to all children from 3-6 years. The programme – fully funded and organised by the State – is part of the national education system, under the auspices of the *ministère de la Jeunesse, de l'Éducation nationale et de la Recherche*. The Ministry defines the curriculum, opening hours, and operations of the *école maternelle*. It recruits, trains, and remunerates the teaching staff and inspectorate. The physical infrastructure is the responsibility of the local commune: construction and maintenance of buildings; provision of class rooms and educational spaces; pedagogical materials; etc. A sub-ministry focused on youth affairs, *ministère chargé de la jeunesse*, works closely with the *ministère des Affaires sociales* in regulating and monitoring leisure-time centres and staff that serve children under 12 years.

Labour force rates: In 2004, the labour force participation rate was 63.7% for women aged 15-64, rising from 58.0% in 1990. Of those, 23.6% were in part-time employment, while male part-time is 4.8% (OECD, *Employment Outlook*, 2005). For mothers with a youngest child under 6, the employment rate was 65% in 2002, and constituted 23% of all part-time employment. For mothers with youngest child under 3, the employment rate was 49.5% in 2004.

Parental leave: At the birth of a first child, mothers in France have a right to 16 weeks of paid, job-protected *congé de maternité* (maternity leave), six of which is generally taken before the birth and ten weeks taken after the birth. From the second or later child, the maternity leave is 26 weeks, with eight weeks to be taken before the birth and 18 weeks taken post-partum. The leave is also extended by at least eight weeks for multiple births. Since 2002, fathers have been entitled to 11 days of paid, job-protected leave (*congé de paternité*). For many years, there was an unpaid parental leave until the child's third birthday, but this has recently been transformed into a three-year, paid parental leave, known as the *Allocation parentale d'éducation* or APE. In order to facilitate women's transition back to employment, it is now possible to receive both the APE and a part-time job income for a limited period starting at least six months before the end of the APE. The current level of the allowance is EUR 484.97 per month.

Access and provision

For children aged 0-3 years, the relevant ministries, aided by the CNAF and the decentralised CAFs activate and administer a diverse and decentralised care system. Publicly subsidised home-based care (64%), accredited family day care providers (18%), and crèche services (8%) form the basis of provision. Centre-based services take the form of *crèches collectives* (centre-based services run by municipalities, departments or non-profit organisations); *crèches parentales* (parent cooperatives) are similar services where parents are involved in the daily management; *crèches familiales* linked with *assistantes maternelles* (family day carers); *crèches d'entreprise* (company crèches, mostly in the public sector and in hospitals); *centres multi-accueil* (open centres) and *haltes garderies* (centres providing temporary care for a number of hours) are among the most usual models in use.

Children have a legal right to a place in an *école maternelle* (pre-school) from the age of three years, but in many communes, enrolments can be made from 2 years. By the age of two-and-half years, 35% of all children are enrolled. From 3 years, enrolments reach approximately 90% of the age cohort. The organisation of groups is by age: the *petite section* for 3-year-olds; the *moyenne section* for 4-year-olds and the *grande section* for 5-year-olds. Mixed age grouping is uncommon in urban centres but occurs frequently in rural centres. Those schools with 2-year-olds contain a *toute petite section*. The *écoles maternelles* are part of the primary school system, including church affiliated pre-schools under contract from the State. There are also private *jardins d'enfants* open for 3- to 6-year-olds. These vary in terms of opening hours and fees. Outside of school hours (and Wednesday afternoons) children may attend leisure time centres (*garderie* or *centre de loisirs sans hébergement*). *Halte-garderies* operated by municipalities and non-profit providers, offer part-time and occasional care, often for parents who work non-standard hours.

Individual child care options include: *assistantes maternelles* (literally "maternal assistants"), that is family day care providers who care for one to three children in the provider's home on a regular basis. Most work directly for the parents, although some work within a family crèche network (*crèche familiale*). In-home caregivers (*garde à domicile*) work in the child's home and are not subject to the same regulations as family day carers.

Some out-of-school provision (OSP) is provided when the pre-schools are not in operation. On Wednesdays, after-school, and during short vacations, *centres de loisirs sans hébergement* (CLSH – leisure centres) serve about 280 000 of the 2.2 million children aged 3 to 6. About 53% of CLSH are operated by non-profit associations, 42% by the communes, and 5% by businesses, the CAF or individuals. They are open about 100 days per year. *Écoles maternelles* and schools increasingly supply after school care, linked to recreational activities and guided home-work.

Rates of provision

0-3 years: Most children are cared for by parents (64%), followed by licensed family child care (*assistantes maternelles*) (18%), crèches (8%), grand-parents (4%) or through other arrangements (6%). Many children are cared for by multiple arrangements in any given week. *Assistantes maternelles* payments are minimum EUR 222/month (Background Report for France, 2003).

3-6 years: Almost 100% of 3-, 4-, and 5-year-olds and approximately 35% of 2-year-olds attend the free *écoles maternelles*.

Children with diverse needs

Children with disabilities: Although inclusion is a stated aim of education in France, and attention is given to the Convention on the Rights of the Child, the inclusion of children with special needs in mainstream early childhood groups has not been as widely practised as, for example, in Nordic or Italian pre-schools. According to informants, the tradition was to treat disability in children at this age in the home and through the health services and medical institutes. Data on the issue were difficult to obtain, perhaps because a number of ministries and bodies, which gather data in different ways, are involved. However, since 2001, an inter-ministerial policy has been put into place, and 3 400 school assistants (*auxiliaires de vie scolaire*, AVS) were recruited to provide help to individual children to participate in class activities. More than 7 000 assistants were employed by 2003, 6 000 of whom are remunerated by the State. They now assist 11 000 children with special needs, over half of whom are enrolled in the *écoles maternelles*. Different medico-social structures participate in this effort, especially the CAMSP (*les centres d'action médico-sociale précoce* or centres for early medico-social action), and provide advice and support to parents and the *écoles maternelles*.

Children from low-income families: The child poverty rate in France is about 8%, after the effect of fiscal transfers and social policies. Priority is generally given in the public crèche system to families in need, and *écoles maternelles* are encouraged to establish sections for 2-year-old children and upwards in education priority zones.

Ethnic and bilingual children: About 6% of pre-schoolers and elementary school children in France are non-French nationals, mostly from the Maghreb, West and Central Africa, and from Turkey, Portugal and other countries, but many more second language children attend the *écoles maternelles*. Districts of concentrated disadvantage are treated as priority education areas (*zones d'éducation prioritaire* or ZEPs), and their *écoles maternelles* receive extra posts and funding. Zones with a minimum of 20% immigrant children generally can open classes for young children at the age of 2 years.

Quality

Licensing and regulatory regimes: The child and maternal health services (*protection maternelle et infantile* – PMI) under the auspices of the *Conseil Général*, are responsible for licensing and monitoring services for young children outside the school system (including crèches, *assistantes maternelles*, *haltes-garderies*, CLSH, etc.). Regulations set out in *Décret 1/8/2000* and

Arrêté 26/12/2000 address capacity, building requirements, parent role, adult/child ratio, group size, staff qualifications and affiliations. All *assistantes maternelles* are required to be licensed by the PMI, but a significant number remain outside the system. Many parents recognise, however, that licensing provides assurance of safety and quality for children in this form of ECEC, and also ensures caregivers social security benefits and training. Family day care providers can care for up to 3 children in each home. The *école maternelle* programmes are supervised by the *Inspecteur de l'éducation nationale (IEN)*. The organisation and operation of the *école maternelle* is regulated under the *Code de l'Éducation Décret,* 6/9/90, while *Arrêté* of 25/1/02 governs schedules and curriculum.

Funding: According to OECD *Education at a Glance* (2005), France invests 0.7% of GDP in early education services (the *école maternelle*), representing 11.7% of the education budget, but with 17.3% of education enrolments. Unit costs per child approach that of primary education but are considerably less than unit costs at secondary and tertiary levels. Public *écoles maternelles* (covering over 90% of the age group) are completely free except for meals, which in turn are often fully subsidised for families in need. Public investment in crèches, family day care, *école maternelle* for 2- to 3-year-olds, and leisure-time services for young children are not included in this figure. Outside the school system, the financing of the ECEC system is relatively complex. Funding involves a number of different actors, direct and indirect grants to settings, as well as family subsidies and tax benefits. It is calculated that in centre-based care, families pay approximately 27% of costs, or about 12% of monthly income.

Staffing and training: The chief contact persons in the different service types are as follows. In *crèches, haltes-garderies* and other services supervised by the PMI, staff are generally *puéricultrices* or children's nurses assisted by *éducateurs de jeunes enfants* and *auxiliaires de puériculture. Écoles maternelles* are staffed by *institutrices* and increasingly by *professeurs des écoles*, that is, the newer cohorts of teachers who have a basic three-year university degree plus 18 months teacher training, allowing them to teach in both primary and early education. A weakness in this training – noted by the OECD review team – is that certification (specialised training) in early childhood studies and pedagogy is relatively weak.

Training requirements: All child care settings are required to meet the same staff qualification requirements. A minimum of 50% are required to have a diploma of *puéricultrice, infirmière, éducateur de jeunes enfants*, or *auxiliaire de puériculture*. A quarter of the staff need to have qualifications related to health, social work, or leisure, and a quarter of the staff are exempted from any qualification, as long as the employer provides support for them to perform their work. Teachers in the *école maternelle* are recruited by public examination, open to candidates with a *license*, that is, a 3-year university degree. They are trained for a further 18 months as *professeurs des écoles*. (The older pre-school teachers, *institutrices*, many of whom are still working in the system, were recruited at *Baccalaureat* level, followed by 2 years training). *Puéricultrices* have nurse or midwife qualifications + 1.5 years of specialisation and *éducateurs de jeunes enfants* are trained (for 27 months post bac) in a training centre. *Auxiliaires de puériculture* study 1 year post BEPC (*brevet d'école*).

Work conditions: As with qualifications, conditions vary greatly depending on the type of ECEC. *Instituteurs* and *professeurs des écoles* in *école maternelle* are state public employees (Cat. B/Cat. A respectively). *Puéricultrices* (2.1% men) and *éducateurs de jeunes enfants* (4.6% men) normally work for *collectivés locales* (communities) and non-profit associations as Cat. B (public) employees, having the right to professional development and sometimes to management training. *Auxiliaires de puériculture* (0.7% men) normally work for *collectivés locales* as Cat. C public employees, they are ineligible for regular professional development.

Child-staff ratios: In the *école maternelle*, there are no national regulations for staff-child ratios. In general the number of children per class has decreased over the years: from 30 in 1980, to 25.5 in 2001-02. In ZEPs (*zones d'éducation prioritaire*), schools receive additional posts and funds in order to reduce the child-staff ratios. In the *crèches*, the required staff-child ratio is 1:5 for children who do not walk), and 1:8 for toddlers (children who walk). In the *jardins d'enfants*, the ratio for children over 3 years is 1:15 children.

Curriculum and pedagogy: All pre-schools follow the same national curriculum (current version 2002) focused on five areas: oral language and introduction to writing; learning to work together; acting and expressing emotions and thoughts with one's body; discovering the world; and imagining feeling and creating. To bridge children's learning from pre-school to primary, competences are defined in learning cycles (*cycles d'apprentissage*), *e.g.* the cycle of *apprentissages fondamentaux* (foundation learning) bridges the last year of *maternelle* and the first two years of elementary school. Ministry of Education evaluation tools are used by teachers to follow the progress of children. There is no curriculum for child care settings although services are required to develop a *projet d'etablissement* including a description of the care, development and well-being of the children; services offered, special measures for children with handicaps or chronic illness and competences and backgrounds of the professionals. Family crèches need also to outline plans for the training plan for assistants, the professional support provided and the monitoring of children. The *projet d'etablissement* translates to a global vision of education and a child's development. Components include the *projet pédagogique,* translating these goals into practical daily activities; the *projet social,* situating the setting within the political, economic social and co-operative framework of the local area, reinforcing the centre's place in promoting social integration and civic engagement and preventing exclusion and inequality. The *projet d'etablissement also* addresses how the setting works with other partners – policy makers and other agencies.

Monitoring, evaluation and research: Within the framework of national policy objectives, the *inspecteur d'académie* has the mission of defining educational policy for primary schools, including the *écoles maternelles.* An inspector in charge of the primary schools evaluates each teacher through observations and discussions about once every three to four years. The national agency *protection maternelle et infantile* or PMI, under the auspices of the *Conseil Général* of the Department, has responsibility for licensing and monitoring services for young children outside the school system (including *crèches, assistantes maternelles, haltes-garderies,* CLSH, etc.).

Parent and community involvement: In the *école maternelles,* the loi *d'orientation* of 1989 recognised parents as members of the education community and encouraged their participation in school life. Parents are formally represented in the elected school council (*Conseil d'école*), but they are not involved in decisions about pedagogy, which are made by the teaching team. Parents, whose schedules allow it, can also have regular contact with teachers at the beginning and end of the day. Formal parent-teacher conferences take place at least once a year. In the crèche sector the decree of 1/8/2000 officially recognised the place of families in the operation of ECEC settings as well as the legal status of parent co-operatives. Staff in ECEC are expected to work on strengthening non-hierarchical relationships with parents, adapt to diverse family needs and circumstances, and generally make parents feel welcome.

OECD policy issues

Among the issues for policy attention identified by the OECD review team in 2003 were:

● *A focus on quality from the child's perspective:* The review team indicated a need to refocus policy debates on the rights and interests of young children. In the education sector, the current pedagogical approaches could be improved by giving greater attention to children's holistic development and their natural learning strategies, rather than excessively targeting cognitive skills and school outcomes. In the care sector, building on the *Guide d'accompagnement* to the Decree of 2000, the OECD team recommended the development of a *référentiel de qualité* that would open discussion to determine quality and strategies to improve it. The team also encouraged ministries, regions and employers to recognise their role in supporting the reconciliation of work and family life, *e.g.* by allowing parents to adapt their working hours in ways that meet the needs of their young children.

● *Rethinking the needs of young children* giving special attention to the conditions and practices in place in schools; and according more attention to their psychology, needs and learning patterns in pre-service and in-service training. Special consideration is needed to ensure that pre-schools provide quality care and education to the 2-year-olds from low-income and immigrant backgrounds living in ZEPs.

● *Ensuring a real choice for parents:* The review team commended the development of diverse forms of ECEC, but questioned the policy preference accorded to expanding individual care arrangements in national and often local policy (for both financial and ideological reasons). Given the superior staff qualifications and the known contribution of child care centres to children's early development and learning, it is important for places in *crèches* to be supported, along with other forms of ECEC, in all neighbourhoods. Even if individual arrangements are made available to families, the team contends that centres should be supported to provide critical quality support and training for family day care providers and in-home carers via family day care networks (RAM) and *crèches familiales*.

● *Encouraging mechanisms for coherence and co-ordination at various levels of responsibility:* At ministerial level, by reviewing the joint protocol signed between the Ministry of Education and the Ministry of Social Affairs to see how it could be better implemented both at the level of policy and practice. At the level of the sectors, more co-ordination is needed: between the care sector and the education sector, and between the *écoles maternelles* and the *écoles élémentaires*, and between *écoles maternelles* and leisure-time services, especially since quality of the latter is often unregulated. The *contrats éducatifs locaux* are a promising effort to strengthen co-ordination and quality at local level, as are the new early childhood commissions at the department level. The team recommended more financial incentives for local partners to offer joint in-service training and opportunities to exchange concerns and ideas that could help bridge the institutional and attitudinal gaps that exist in the field.

● *Support stable investment in ECEC and a comprehensive system of monitoring* to ensure equitable access to quality ECEC across the regions. One step that would help towards this goal would be to make the *fonds d'investissement* for facilities a permanent source of funding (rather than re-authorised on a yearly basis), in order to allow local authorities to plan more than a year at a time.

● *Strengthen the training of early childhood professionals,* placing greater emphasis on early childhood development and pedagogy. In the care sector, training for staff would benefit from more emphasis on early childhood development and pedagogy to balance the health orientation of the current preparation programmes. In addition, the lack of pre-service training and limited professional development opportunities for both the *assistantes maternelles* and those engaged in *garde à domicile* need to be addressed urgently. In the early education field, the general education level of the *professeurs d'école* is good, but certification in early childhood studies and pedagogy can be weak.

● *Build a career lattice for diverse early childhood staff:* Career progression is critical in order to retain strong expertise in early childhood in the management, guidance, and monitoring of the field. For example, it is important to create articulation agreements across training courses which would help *auxiliaires de puériculture* to become eventually *éducatrices de jeunes enfants* or even *puéricultrices*. This reform would help provide opportunities to improve the overall qualifications of those who work directly with children. To ensure representation of staff from diverse backgrounds, mechanisms should be created to enable staff and family day carers (*assistantes maternelles*) from ethnic backgrounds to be recruited and become qualified in the early childhood sector.

Germany

ABL = *Altebundesländer* (former West Germany). **NBL** = *Neue Bundesländer* (former East Germany).

Population: 82.42 m. **Fertility rate:** 1.34. **GDP per capita:** USD 25 900. **Children under 6 years:** 4.23 million.

Female labour force participation: 66.1% labour participation rate for women aged 15-64, of whom 37% work part-time (6.3% of men work part-time).

Labour force participation rate of women with a child(ren): 42.3% of mothers with a child under 6 are employed, accounting for 28.4% of all part-time employment (Statistisches Bundesamt, Mikrozensus 2004).

Labour force participation rate of women with a child under 3: 31.2% of mothers with a child under 3 were employed in 2004 (Statistisches Bundesamt, Mikrozensus 2004).

Maternity and parental leave: Maternity leave is for 6 weeks before birth and 8 weeks after, at average annual earnings. Parents then have the option of a period of parental leave (*Elternzeit*) lasting until 3 years after the birth of their child. Parents taking leave may work up to 30 hours per week, with a reduction to their child-rearing benefit paid.

Average duration of parental leave: Not available.

Compulsory school age: 6 years.

Social expenditure: 27.4%. **Child poverty rate:** 10.2% after taxes and transfers (OECD average is 11.2%).

Funding of pre-primary education (ISCED Level 0): 0.53% of GDP, of which 0.4% is public funding. This corresponds to 9.3% of the education budget (*Ausgaben für den Bildungsprozess*), with kindergarten representing 14% of education enrolments.

Unit cost per child (in USD converted using PPP): USD 4 999 (OECD, *Education at a Glance*, 2005).

Funding to children under 3: As of 2005, according to calculations of the federal government, the municipalities will have at their disposal an annual amount of EUR 1.5 billion for the development of ECEC services for children below 3 (from savings generated through the consolidation of unemployment and social welfare benefits), but these funds are not earmarked.

Average costs to parents: On average across Germany, parents pay about 14% of costs, but parental contributions differ widely across regions, and even within *Länder*, mainly according to income.

Legal entitlement to a free service: From age 3, until entrance into school, children are entitled to a kindergarten place but this place is not free.

Major service types and daily duration: For children 0-3 years, the *Krippe* or centre-based crèche is the norm, with some family day care – *Tagesmütter* – also existing in the ABL. *Krippen*

---

are full-day services. For children from 3 years until entrance into school, the *Kindergärten* is the main service, almost always a full-day service in the new *BundesLänder* and tending in that direction (now about a quarter of kindergartens) in the old *Länder*. *Hort* – or out-of-school provision – is the third major service, catering for school-age children up to 10 or 12 years of age. These types of provision can cover half or full day (normally with lunch). *Krippen*, *Kindergärten* and *Horte* can be run as separate centres but also as a mixed form for children of different age groups (below and above 3 years).

Rate of access to regulated services: Children 0-3 years: there are available places in *Krippen* for 2.8% of children under 3 in the ABL, and 37% in the NBL. There are available places in the *Kindergärten* for 89.9% of children in the ABL (24% full-time places) and for almost all children in the NBL (98.4% full-time places). In the ABL, there are available places in after school care for 6.4% of children 6-10 years, but the service is growing, with new services tending to be placed within full-day schools. In the NBL, 67.6% of children have places in the local *Hort*. The overall figure for out-of-school provision across Germany is 14.2%.

Designation and qualifications of key staff: Staff in children's services are almost all female. *Erzieherinnen* (kindergarten pedagogues) form 64% of the personnel in the different types of services. In the ABL *Kinderpflegerinnen* (literally, children's carers) play a greater role, especially in services for children under 3. They receive a two-year training course at a vocationally-oriented secondary school, followed by one year internship in a day care centre. The vocational training of *Erzieherinnen* and *Erzieher* is placed at *Fachschulen für Sozialpädagogik*. The training is spread on three years and has either an integrated intership or one year of internship in the third year. Finally, there are *Sozialpädagogen* and *Sozialpädagoginnen* (social pedagogues, 2 %) who have had a tertiary level education in a *Fachhochschulen*. They work most often as leaders of centres, especially larger ones, but also sometimes with children with disabilities. A higher proportion of this group are men. Data are not available concerning the percentage of staff coming from minority backgrounds.

Child-staff ratios and maximum group size: Child-staff ratios depend on varying factors, but in general, kindergarten groups do not exceed 25 children, and will have two adults in charge, one of whom must be a trained *Erzieherin*.

Auspices

Two fundamental political principles underlie the organisation, funding and regulation of early childhood policy in Germany, namely, *federalism* and *subsidiarity*. *Federalism* characterises Germany as a federal State with three levels of government: federal; the *Länder* (16 states/city-states); and the municipalities (some 13 000). The municipality level must plan and ensure the provision of ECEC services, but under the principle of subsidiarity, which requires that societal tasks should be undertaken by the smallest possible social unit – in this case the voluntary sector and the family – municipalities do not take in charge direct provision of early childhood services if private organisations are available. For this reason, the majority of services in the ABL are delivered by non-profit bodies (mainly religious), the *Freie Träger der Jugendhilfe*. They receive public money from *Länder* and municipalities to fulfil this task. The old *Länder* (11 of 16) have traditionally interpreted subsidiarity with relation to child-rearing as requiring a marked division of labour on gender lines with the majority of mothers taking leave to care for children, or taking part-time paid employment. Further, this principle endorses the provision of children's services by numerous small, non-statutory, non-profit providers of ECEC services, which generally cluster within six *Freie Träger*. In the new eastern *BundesLänder*, the NBL (5 former GDR areas), subsidiarity does not apply to the same extent.

The *Länder* governments normally regulate, provide funding and direct children's services both through the ministry responsible (usually child and youth services or education) and through the autonomous *Land* Youth Welfare offices (*Landesjugendämter*). The Federal government has the competence of concurrent legislation as well as a competence of stimulus in the area of child and youth welfare, including children's services. Funding, however, is the sole responsibility of the *Länder* and the municipalities, but the *Freie Träger* and the parents bear a part of the costs. The responsible Federal ministry, the *Bundeministerium für Familie, Senioren, Frauen und Jugend*, may influence the development of the early childhood field by initiating and funding projects (in collaboration with *Länder*) in areas deemed in need of more attention. The *Länder* governments fill in, complete and expand the frame which is set by the federal government in SGB VIII law. They set the regulatory and funding frameworks that guide the planning and provision of ECEC services, both by clusters within the *Träger* and directly by the *Länder*. Administration of ECEC within different *Länder* may be through education ministries or other child and youth services ministries. In all *Länder* special bodies (*Landesjugendämter*) exist. They are also responsible for the protection of children in the centres. The provision with day care facilities is task of the municipalities. The German system therefore, is complex and highly decentralised. The three layers of government intersect and communicate with the six *Träger*, allowing great scope for diversity (OECD Country Note for Germany, 2004). Constant debate and negotiation exist about the roles and responsibilities of different levels of government for ECEC, particularly regarding the application of the *subsidiarity* principle.

Context

Labour force rates: In 2004, the labour participation rate for women aged 15-64 was 66.1%, increasing from 55.5% in 1990. Of those, 37% work part-time, while 6.3% of men work part-time (OECD, *Employment Outlook*, 2005). Mothers with a youngest child under 6 years had an employment rate of 42.3% in 2004 (active working mothers), and constituted 28.4% of part-time employment (Statistisches Bundesamt, Mikrozensus 2004). Mothers with a child under 3 had an employment rate (active working mothers) of 31.2% in 2004 (Statistisches Bundesamt, Mikrozensus 2004).

Parental leave: There is a period of maternity leave – 6 weeks before birth and 8 weeks after, during which mothers receive, if applicable, maternity pay from public funds supplemented by an employer's allowance, which brings up their income to average annual earnings. After this period of leave, parents have the option of a period of parental leave (*Elternzeit*) lasting until 3 years after the birth of their child. Under Federal law, a "child-rearing benefit" (*Erziehungsgeld*), depending on income, may be paid during the first two years of this leave period and an additional child benefit (*Kindergeld*) is made for children up to the age of 18. Some four *Länder* continue the *Erziehungsgeld* payment in the third year using *Länder* budgets. Parents taking leave may work up to 30 hours per week, with a reduction in the benefit paid. In addition, the third year of parental leave may be taken any time until the child is 8 years. Parental leave is used primarily by mothers, only about 2% of fathers availing of the entitlement. A notable difference between the two parts of Germany is that in the NBL (new *Bundesländer* or former GDR), the leave policy of 1 year was closely connected with ECEC services, that is, after 12 months parental leave, a place was available for the child in an early childhood service. In the ABL (old *Bundesländer*), the 3-year period of leave is not generally co-ordinated with child services.

Access and provision

The *subsidiarity principle* as interpreted in Germany means that non-profit, private organisations are given priority in the provision of services, with local authorities stepping in only when private organisations are unable to provide. In the ABL in 1998, about two-thirds (64%) of kindergarten places and 55% of places for children under 3 were offered by private providers (*freie Träger*), while local authorities provide just over half (55%) of *Hort* places. The main private providers are churches – Catholic or Protestant – making Germany unique, at least within Europe, in the major role that religious bodies play in the provision of ECEC services. In the NBL, with its different history, the public sector was the main provider (*öffentliche Träger*) in 1998, with about two-thirds of places for children under 3 and from 3 to 6, and 86% of places in *Horte*. This figure, however, will have fallen since 1998, as most *Länder* and local authorities have encouraged a move to private, non-profit providers.

Centre-based services comprise three types: *Krippen,* that is centre-based crèche services for children under 3; *Kindergärten* or centres for children aged 3-6 years; and *Hort* services, which provide out-of-school provision for children from entry to school up to 10 or 12 years. *Krippen* and *Kindergärten* services are run in most NBL as full-day, mixed-age services, a change from the strict separation of *Kindergärten* and *Krippen* prior to unification. The old federal *Länder* are also following suit: one quarter of kindergartens are now full-day, and there is the emergence of the *Kindertaggesstätte*, that is, kindergartens taking in mixed-age children (below 3 years), and providing a range of services, including *Hort* and more intensive parent outreach. In the new *Länder*, the links between *Hort* and primary schools are now weaker, as they currently operate under separate ministries, although these services were under one ministry (education) prior to unification. Family day care services, normally made available by *tagesmütter* in their own homes, are also available. ECEC access and provision vary widely in western (ABL) and eastern (NBL) *Länder*, due to different development histories. Before unification, kindergarten (sessional) places in the west addressed 70% of the 3- to 6-year-old population, whereas there was almost complete full-time coverage in the east. For children under 3, the west had places for < 5% of the child population and there was 56% coverage in the east. A similar pattern was evident in school-age child care. Today, availability of centre-based places remains varied.

Rates of provision

0-3 years: Places for this group in all Germany cover only 8.6% of the children, although national data hide large regional differences. In 2002, ABL places catered for only 2.8% of the child population, while in the NBL, there were places for 36.9% of the age group. In the ABL, almost all children 0-3 years are cared for by their families (mothers), with the help of informal care arrangements. In the NBL, the situation is more flexible, as a strong link had been forged between a leave policy of 1 year and ECEC services; over one-third of children still have access to *Krippe* places.

3 years to school entry: Places for this group in Germany cover 93% of the child population. In 2002, places were available in the ABL for almost 90% of the child population (24% available as full-time places); in the NBL, places were available for all children (98.4% available as full-time places). Compulsory school age is 6 years. Children who are six at the end of June can begin school in September, but in practice, most children are well into their seventh year on commencement at school. Of the 5-6 year age group, 8% are not enrolled, but clear data are unavailable concerning who these children are. The 2001 Microcensus found that non-German children enter kindergarten less and later than German children.

Children with diverse needs

Children with disabilities: Children with special learning needs fall into two main categories: children with disabilities and children with learning challenges stemming for various at-risk indicators such as low-income, ill health, immigrant status, or family dysfunction. Data about these children are not readily available, and hence, the actual state of integration of the children is not always known. Official policy recommends integration of children with organic handicaps into mainstream services. In the old *Länder*, special integrative groups consisting of children with and without disabilities were established in many kindergartens, with more staff. Statistics available suggest, however, that little expansion in the supply of places has taken place in recent years, except in the NBL which now maintain almost 3% of integrated places for special needs children, compared to 0.84% in the old *Bundesländer*.

Children from low-income families: For children from poor, at-risk backgrounds, free or subsidised places are often provided, but data indicate that 36% of children from the lowest income families (EUR 500-900 monthly) do not attend a kindergarten. The downstream results from PISA also suggest that a challenge exists in this domain. The challenge is met in some municipalities by well-planned outreach programmes, *e.g.* MoKi in Monheim. A new federal-wide initiative in favour of these children is recommended by the OECD review.

Ethnic and bilingual children: The German Social Code sets out the right of young persons to promotion, conditional on foreigners having lawful habitual residence in Germany. However, data on progress achieved are generally not available. The Background Report for Germany indicates "children with a migration background enter kindergarten later than German children. Roughly 25% of foreign children between the age of 3 and 6 do not attend kindergarten at all, whilst this figure is almost 19% for German children (with a migration background)" (p. 71).

Quality

Licensing and regulatory regimes: Each *Länder* sets standards for children's services in its areas, these standards being monitored by the independent *Landesjugendamt* – the Youth Welfare Office. Standards generally cover number of places, opening hours, parent fees, building requirements and maintenance, group size, staff-child ratios and space, both indoor and outdoor. Space allocation and scope for outdoor engagement is substantial in most kindergartens. Pedagogical standards vary, however, between *Länder*, while monitoring depends on the focus, expertise and number of staff available to the *Landesjugendamt*. Family day care (*Tagesmütter*) services have a low level of regulation. *Tagesmütter* with 3 or fewer children do not need to be licensed and hence, are unregulated.

Funding: According to *Education at a Glance* (OECD, 2005), expenditure on pre-primary educational institutions as a percentage of GDP is 0.53%, with over 91% of this expenditure coming from public sources and 8.7% from private sources. 9.3% of total educational expenditure is allocated to pre-primary (kindergarten) whereas 14% of the children/ students are enrolled at this level of education (OECD, *Education at a Glance*, 2005). Federal government funding of ECEC is only possible in narrowly defined circumstances, and the *Länder* and municipalities determine how resources are deployed. Across the country, this leads to a significant difference in resources allocated to young children.

Staffing: Staff in children's services are overwhelmingly female (95% in 1998). *Erzieherinnen* (the name *Erzieherin* derives from the German term *Erziehung* – upbringing – and the term might best be translated as kindergarten pedagogue) form 64% of the personnel in the different types of services. In general, after obtaining the lower secondary school diploma, *Erzieherinnen* receive three years vocational training with either an integrated internship in a centre or one year of internship in the third year. In the ABL *Kinderpflegerinnen* (literally, children's carers) play a bit more bigger role, especially in services for children under 3. They receive a two-year training course at a vocationally-oriented secondary school, followed by one year internship in a day care centre. Finally, there are *Sozialpädagogen* and *Sozialpädagoginnen* (literally, social pedagogues) who have had a tertiary level education in a *Fachhochschule*. With their higher level qualification, they are most likely to be found working as leaders of centres, especially larger ones, but also sometimes with children with disabilities. A higher proportion of this group are men. Data are not available concerning the percentage of staff coming from minority backgrounds.

Training requirements: Training requirements are defined in each *Länder* although some common features are apparent. The three-year course for *Erzieherinnen* takes place in *Fachschule für Sozialpägagogik* (Colleges for Social Pedagogy), which are secondary level vocational colleges. In contrast, primary teachers are trained at tertiary level, generally in higher education institutions. A considerable gap exists, therefore, between *Erzieherinnen* and the teaching profession, in training, status and conditions of work. Moves to upgrade training are generally rejected on the grounds of cost, although it is generally recognised that current societal demands on *Erzieherinnen* and the framework of lifelong learning impose a re-thinking of their training. Early indications of change to this system are apparent in two *Länder* (Berlin and Brandenburg). *Kinderflegerinnen* complete a two-year course at a vocationally oriented secondary school, followed by a one year internship. *Hort* (out-of-school care) staff have similar training to *Erzieherinnen*. In the NBL this is a substantial cutback from the original (GDR) requirement that *Horterzieher* should be trained alongside primary teachers and receive specialist training. Staff in the NBL are generally older than staff in the ABL, because of differing histories and processes. The *Tagesmütter* (family day carers) may have no training although this is changing.

Work conditions: *Erzieherinnen* earn about the German average wage, a salary similar to those in other occupations who hold similar level qualifications. Promotion prospects are limited other than progressing to become a centre director. By comparison, school teachers achieve a similar salary to that of directors of kindergarten and benefit from lower social insurance expenses as they are deemed to be tenured staff. In Germany, less than half of ECEC staff work full-time and hence, do not rely on ECEC work alone for a living wage. Around 15% have temporary contracts only. Pay and conditions (*e.g.* health and employment insurance) for *Tagesmütter* are particularly low. ECEC staff are normally given a period of non-contact time each week, varying according to *Länder*, for completing administrative work.

Child-staff ratios: Child-staff ratios differ considerably across *Länder*. Apart from the *Länder* regulatory framework, the number of staff per group depends on the group size, the hours the group is open for, and other circumstances, for example staffing may be higher where there are children from non-German backgrounds or with disabilities. In general, groups do not exceed 25 children, and will in such cases have two adults in charge, one *erzieherin* and one assistant.

Curriculum and pedagogy: Situationsansatz, or situation-oriented pedagogy, in which learning, care and upbringing are inseparable activities, has been the guiding practice of working with children in Germany. Realising the increasing importance of the educational element of ECEC, and concerned that the situation approach lacked precision and rigour, the Federal Ministry for Family Affairs, Senior Citizens, Women and Youth funded a "model project" running from 1997 to 2000, "On the education task of children's day care centres" (*ZumBildungsauftrag von Kindertageseinrichtungen*). This was followed by a National Quality Initiative (*Nationale Qualitätsinitiative im System der Tageseinrichtungen für Kinder*), starting in 1999, which involved five projects each focused on the development of methods for assessing and improving quality in different parts of the ECEC field, viz. services for children under 3; kindergarten; school-age child care; the situation approach to pedagogical work; and the work of the providers (the *Träger* and municipalities). Today, almost all *Träger* have engaged in quality improvement policies.

Monitoring, evaluation and research: National monitoring and reporting at population level is managed by the *Federal Statistical Office* which compiles data on the basis of surveys to *Länder.* Structural characteristics of services (type of facility by age groups, and type of place by age-group) are primarily the focus of data collection. These data have limited application as places may be counted but without knowledge of the extent of occupation or whether new places are needed. In some *Länder, e.g.* Hamburg, 5-year-old children are allocated to the school system and are therefore not included. With respect to evaluation and accountability, pedagogical monitoring is often carried out by the providers, that is, not by an external body but by the *Träger* and communities themselves. In addition, there is limited research on ECEC in Germany, particularly as universities are removed from the training and supervision of ECEC staff. Only five university chairs exist in the discipline for the whole of Germany. A large number of project evaluations and small investigations are funded by the Federal government and by individual *Länder,* but access to reports is said to be difficult.

Parent and community involvement: There is a strong predominance of traditional ways of working co-operatively with parents, *e.g.* through information evenings and presentations by specialists. Recognising the importance of parent and community involvement, some *Länder* require parent committees or councils to be formed in conjunction with the services, and parent voices must be part of the strategic decision-making process.

OECD policy issues

Among the issues for policy attention identified in 2004 by the OECD review team for Germany were:

- *Defining the field broadly*: It is desirable to consider pre-school services in the context of surrounding services (including primary school and *Hort* or out-of-school provision), and to ensure cohesion between parental leave policies, children's services and social policy. In this respect, the social pedagogy tradition provides an admirably broad and integrative concept, with its outreach to families and communities, and its understanding of the inseparability of *Betreuung, Bildung and Erziehung.*

- *Opting for a long-term strategy*: The team encouraged construction of an agreed view of where Germany wants to be in 10-15 years in this broad ECEC field, and to set in place as early as possible the resources and processes to achieve this.

- *Developing the federal role*: The Federal Government has played an important role thus far in building a united ECEC service. The review team encouraged this role to be developed in areas related to ECEC entitlement, funding, equality of opportunity and policy initiatives.

- *Creating effective mechanisms for partnership*: Close collaboration between different levels of government and across the different areas of policy and provision is deemed essential for ECEC to build and assure services of quality. A wider and more difficult issue concerns whether there should be more standardised regulation of ECEC systems across Germany.

- *Supporting quality through in-service training, practice consultants and other well-tried quality measures*: Processes that could support the development and improvement of quality were suggested by many stakeholders: in-service training; more consultation centres; a strong network of practice consultants with a reasonable number of centres to support; emphasis on observations of children; training and work conditions of pedagogues. Development of these for systematic review and reflection is encouraged.

- *Increasing public funding to ECEC*: Public funding to ECEC at large is well below the target proposed by the EC Child care Network (1996) of 1% of GDP. The governments – and not least, the Federal Government – have an important role to play in raising the public contribution to ECEC funding.

- *Improving participation and outcomes for children with additional learning needs*: While recognising the policy of integration that is in place, the review team encourages more evaluation and follow-up on the appropriate inclusion of special needs children (children with organic handicaps and children at-risk) into the services. Encouragement of intervention for children at-risk is given on the basis of evidence of effective results demonstrated by research elsewhere.

- *Revaluing the workforce*: By European standards, the German ECEC workforce remains at a low level of training. The argument that higher recruitment and training will be too costly downstream is unsustainable in the longer term. Cost scenarios developed elsewhere demonstrate that if high quality is desired, it is necessary to upgrade professionals if they are to deliver improved outcomes for children across the system.

- *Improving the relationship between ECEC and school, while respecting the independence of each*: Encouragement was given to defining the age-range from 0 to 10 as a field for development. The issue of building the relationship goes far beyond preparing children for school.

- *Creating a focused learning environment in ECEC centres*: Research suggests that young children who have acquired basic competences in kindergarten – basic general knowledge (for the society in question); good social skills; aural and oral competence in the language of school instruction; and an understanding of the uses of literacy and numeracy – generally do well in school. These competences are particularly important for children from challenged backgrounds, and are most effectively acquired when part of the day is devoted to structured, early learning programmes or projects, complemented by individual learning plans. This implies: raising the pre- and in-service training of staff; improving goal setting and monitoring of services; and re-appraising situation pedagogy approach to take into account clearly defined outcomes.

● *Building up research*: The current research represents a range of interests and approaches but is extremely small in volume given the importance of the field and Germany's size. The review team encouraged development and improvement of data and information, and the establishment of a strong link between teacher education and research.

● *Ensuring critical mass, particularly in the policy and monitoring field*: The present position of ECEC services is more marginal than their importance to the economic, educational, social and cultural development in any modern society. Policy units for ECEC development are either small or non-existent at central and local levels. The review team argued for recognition of the field and enhancement of its place within government thinking and decision making.

● *Stimulating exchange*: Recognition was given to the value of sharing experiences between and among *Länder*, and between Germany and other countries. Outreach to other countries could enhance networks and developments, particularly for activities related to: initial training; a more gender-mixed workforce; more effective support in the field for practice and evaluation; and to linking ECEC services and schools. In addition, other OECD countries could profit from Germany's rich history and conceptualisation of early childhood education and care.

Hungary

Population: 10 m. **Fertility rate:** 1.3. **GDP per capita:** USD 13 900. **Children under 6 years:** data not available.

Female labour force participation: 54% of women (15-64) are employed, 5.1% of whom are in part-time employment (male part-time is 2.2%) (OECD, *Employment Outlook*, 2005).

Labour force participation rate of women with young children: For mothers with children under 6 years: 30%, who account for 8% of total part-time employment (OECD, *Society at a Glance*, 2005). For mothers with children under 3: 30.5% of mothers are in employment (2004) (EUROSTAT).

Maternity and parental leave: Insured (employed) women are entitled to a maternity leave period of 24 weeks, remunerated at 70% of the person's average salary, and then at a flat rate into the third year. Hungary provides also a universal (including mothers who were not employed) parental leave child care allowance (called GYES) for a maximum of 135 weeks (or 53 weeks if the mother has not previously taken maternity leave) at a flat sum equal to the minimum old age pension (HUF 23 200 in 2004).

Average duration of parental leave: Data not available.

Compulsory school age: 6 years, but final kindergarten year (5-6 years) is also compulsory.

Social expenditure: 20.1%. **Child poverty rate:** 8.8% after taxes and transfers (OECD average is 11.2%).

Funding of pre-primary educational services (ISCED Level 0): 0.79% of GDP (0.73% public and 0.07% private), that is, 14.7% of education budget with 16.9% of education enrolments.

Unit cost per child (in USD converted using PPP): USD 3 475 (public institutions only) (OECD, *Education at a Glance*, 2005).

Funding of services for children under 3: Data not available.

Average costs to parents: Relative to GDP per capita, the annual parental expenditure on ECEC amounts to 8.2% for child care and 3.5% for pre-school education (Hungarian Government, 2004).

Legal entitlement to a free service: In principle at 6 months, but not all children are able to access. Preference is given to children of employed parents.

Major service types: Two kinds of full-time services exist: *bölcsde* for under 3 (referred to as child care centres and/or crèche); and *óvoda* (referred to as kindergarten and/or pre-school and/or nursery school) for children between 3 and compulsory school. Both service types offer long-day (c. 10 hours) services for 50 weeks per year. Licensed family day care is only now beginning.

Rate of access to regulated services: Children 0-3 years: 8.5%; children 3-4 years: 85%; 4- to 5-year-olds: 91%; 5- to 6-year-olds: 97%; OSP for children 6-12 years: over 40% of all pupils attended these services (National Statistical Office, 2004).

Designation and professional qualifications of key staff: *Gondozó* (child care workers), *óvodapedagógus* (kindergarten pedagogues) and *napközis tanár* (school pedagogues). Each group undergoes separate training. Training models and arrangements are in a process of change, affected by the Bologna process, which is addressing the parity of education qualifications.

Percentage presence of tertiary qualified staff in kindergarten services: About 50% of staff in kindergarten are trained pedagogues, and other staff are trained day care pedagogues. Over 90% of total staff are fully trained.

Child-staff ratios: FDC (family day care): 7:2; crèche: 12:2; kindergarten: 22:2; OSP for children 6-12 years: 26:1.

Maximum group size: FDC (family day care): 7; crèche: 12; kindergarten: 25; OSP: 26.

Auspices

Responsibility for ECEC policy in Hungary is shared between two ministries: the Ministry of Youth, Family, Social Affairs and Equal Opportunities is responsible for centre-based care for under-3-year-old children. The Ministry of Education is responsible for the much larger kindergarten education system for children 3-6 years, which is seen as the first stage of public education.

Since transition, public administration in Hungary has been decentralised, and is shared across different levels. With regard to ECEC provision for children aged 3-6 years, the Ministry of Education oversees the preparation and issue of legislation and regulations, develops a national curriculum document and organises the associated inspection system. In addition, this Ministry develops and oversees schools of education and training for kindergarten pedagogues. However, different administrative, supervisory and political responsibilities are divided among several parties at central, regional (county), local (settlement) and institutional levels. At local and regional levels, education – including kindergarten education – is integrated into the general system of public administration. Public administration at these levels is under the control of elected bodies which enjoy political independence. The most substantial responsibilities including funding reside, however, with local governments at settlement level, which receive block grants from the central government.

For 0- to 3-year-olds, the 1997 Law 31 assigned child protection and child welfare provision, under the supervision of the Ministry of Health, Social and Family Affairs (currently, the Ministry of Youth, Family, Social Affairs and Equal Opportunities). For 0- to 3-year-olds, the Ministry develops and oversees legislation, and the training of child care workers. As in the kindergarten system, the regulation and inspection of day care provision is a state task supervised by the Ministry, but carried out by county guardianship authorities. The central government provides funding to local (settlement) authorities who are responsible for service provision and inspection. The Association of Hungarian Child care Centres (*Magyar Bölcsődék Egyesülete*, MBE) and the Democratic Trade Union of Child care Centre (*Bölcsődei Dolgozók Demokratikus Szakszervezete*, BDDSZ), take an active role in child care centre provision. The law also regulates co-operation between trade unions and the government, stating that it is obligatory to hold discussions with the representative trade unions of the affected groups prior to the formulation of legislation.

Context

Labour force rates: In 2004, the labour participation rate for women aged 15-64 was 54%, decreasing from 57.3% in 1990. Of those, 5.1% work part-time, while 2.2% of men work part-time (OECD, *Employment Outlook*, 2005). Mothers with a youngest child under 6 years had an employment rate of 30% in 2002, and constituted 8% of part-time employment (OECD *Society at a Glance*). Mothers with a youngest child under 3 had an employment rate of 30.5% in 2004.

Maternity and parental leave: A comprehensive series of support and leave measures are accessible to Hungarian mothers. In summary, two different regimes are available: the GYES or universal child-rearing allowance for uninsured (unemployed and not receiving unemployment benefit) women; and the GYED for insured (employed) women. For uninsured parents, the GYES child-rearing allowance (equivalent to the old age pension) is available for 2.5 years. Under certain conditions, this allowance is also available – but for a shorter period – to the grandparents of the child and to insured women who can combine it with their own regime. Insured women (women who have been working) receive a pregnancy-confinement and maternity leave allowance, paid up 70% of an average salary (capped at HUF 83 000 per month) for a period of 168 days (24 weeks). It can then be followed – for a period of 53 weeks – by the GYED – still remunerated to 70% but to a ceiling level. Thereafter, the beneficiary can avail of a year long GYES, paid at the flat rate.

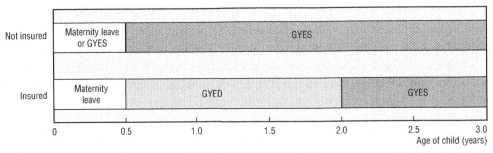

Notes: Maternity leave: 24 weeks, up to 4 weeks before birth. 70% of earnings.
GYES: Until the child's 3rd birthday. Flat-rate payment.
GYED: From the end of the maternity leave period until the child's 2nd birthday. 70% of earnings up to a ceiling.

The GYED is taxable income, and the period spent in it is considered to be part of the years in service and thus entitles the recipient to a pension. In sum, all mothers in Hungary have the possibility of State support for at least 36 months after the birth of their child, and in the case of most women, for nearly 3 years, when, in general, kindergarten becomes available. Existing legislation ensures that employers provide women returning from child care leave the same job or equivalent to that worked before childbirth. It is difficult to assess the effectiveness of the legislation because the low return to work levels may also be due to a depressed employment situation.

Access and provision

ECEC provision in Hungary in all types of services is offered as a full day programme for the working year. Kindergartens are open 10 hours per day, 50 weeks per year. Child care centres are open 8-10 hours per day, closing only for the summer holiday or 4-5 weeks. Opening hours are set by the maintaining authority, which is the local authority in most cases. Usually, the hours are adjusted to family needs and hence, they can vary from centre to centre. Access to a place in child care for all children under 3 whose parents cannot care for them during the day is assured under law. It is the duty of local authorities to provide the places needed. In practice however, access is often denied to parents who are unemployed, or live in poor municipalities or neighbourhoods that cannot afford to fund a crèche service. In addition, children of parents receiving the child care or other allowances are normally not accepted in services. Although child welfare services can refer children in need to attend child care services, priority criteria often deny access to at-risk children who need these services most of all. Payment (primarily for cost of food) can be waived based on the family socio-economic situation. Many families receive places at no direct cost to them.

Rates of provision

0-1 year: Almost all children are cared for by parents or, informally, by relatives at home. 0.2% of babies are in ECEC settings.

1-3 years: 4.3% of children aged 1-2 years attend services, the proportion increasing to 14.2% for 2- to 3-year-olds. Some 9.3% of 0- to 3-year-olds access a publicly licensed service for at least part of the day. After three years, access and involvement is much higher, corresponding to the end of parental leave.

3-6 years: Approximately 85% of 3- to 4-year-olds attend kindergarten, as do 91% of 4- to 5-year-olds and 97% of 5- to 6-year-olds. Enrolment of children in kindergarten depends on the parent until the first day of the academic year in which the child reaches the fifth birthday. From that point, parents are obliged to ensure each child takes part in kindergarten as a preparation for school. There are no separate educational programmes within kindergarten, but all children must attend regular kindergarten between 5-6 years of age. Overall 87% of 3- to 6-year-olds attend kindergarten, although some children older than six are in kindergartens because eligibility for this programme extends beyond a child's sixth birthday. 93% of eligible children attend kindergarten. Although there is little official data available, the children who are most likely to be absent from kindergarten or be retained there after they turn 6 years may come from low-income and Roma families.

Out-of-school care: Elementary schools organise after-school care services, for the children between the ages of 6-14, attending those schools. These services are available, in the morning before teaching begins and in the afternoon after teaching is over. Sometimes children are in small groups with the same *napközis tanár* (day care pedagogue), sometimes they have a choice of after school "club" activities. Among the 3 696 elementary schools 3 151 provided after school care in the 1999/2000 academic year. In 2003/04, 40.6% of all elementary school pupils attended these services according to National Statistical Office (KSH) data.

Summer camps can be organised by schools that have access to a recreation site somewhere in the countryside (sometimes in the same town, sometimes elsewhere). These sites are usually owned by the local authority where the school is located. Kindergarten children can attend such camps for different time periods, usually between 1-2 weeks. The camps provide day care and various leisure activities for children. Sometimes, the activities include, or are focused on school-related programmes such as mathematics, etc. In these camps, usually the teachers of the school and/or some parents take turns and reside with the different groups of children. Summer camps can also be organised by different voluntary and private sector organisations, although these may not be related to schools.

Children with diverse needs

Children with disabilities: Until the early 1990s, public policy encouraged segregated education for children with disabilities and other special needs, and a number of specialist institutions for specific conditions were in place. More recently, children are being integrated into mainstream child care settings with 173 of 532 centres (almost a third) working in an integrated or semi-integrated way. However, as coverage is weak in the child care sector, many children remain at home without accessing services that can provide sufficient support for their developmental levels. In kindergartens, segregation is still the norm, although change is evident. The 1996 revisions of the Public Education Act gave an impetus to kindergarten enrolment of children with additional learning needs: a child with a speech-based need or light mental disability should receive a normative grant equivalent to that of two healthy children, whereas, children with a physical or sensory disability, autistic children and children with medium severity disabilities should receive a grant equivalent to three children. In 1999, 0.6% of the total kindergarten population comprised children with designated disabilities (Country Note for Hungary, p. 32).

Children from low-income families: Child poverty in Hungary is concentrated on rural and Roma children. In 2003, some 18.6% of children 0-6 years live in poverty (TARKI, 2003, *Stabilizálódó Társadalomszerkezet, TÁRKI Monitorjelentések,* 2003 – TÁRKI is the Social Research Centre in Hungary), but more recent estimates indicate the level has declined, and is currently at 8.8% (OECD average is 11.2%). Since 2003, a free-meal policy is in place for all disadvantaged children in kindergartens, and early kindergarten enrolment of Roma children is improving.

Ethnic and bilingual children: Hungary has a comprehensive charter, under the Minorities Law of 1993, to ensure individual and collective minority rights. Hungarian minorities can establish self-government in settlements and districts, with children given in the law, priority status and particular advantages. These include special normative grants for language, and in the case of Roma, for transmission of Roma culture. Since 2004, Roma children in kindergartens also are eligible for free meals if parents so wish. Kindergartens may also receive grants attached to children from disadvantaged backgrounds and claim rights for integration education. Under this law, if parents of (at least 8) minority children so request, the local authority must arrange a special minority class or study group. In recent years kindergartens that develop programmes supporting inclusive education and/or fostering Roma culture and traditions are eligible for an additional normative grant (Country Note for Hungary, p. 34).

Quality

Licensing and regulatory regimes: Child licensing regimes vary according to the type of service. In family day care, registration is required and irregular health checks are conducted on the services. The local authorities provide monitoring and support to administrators and ECEC services. Licenses are issued under strict conditions and inspections occur every four years. A Register of Child Care Experts is maintained, and external evaluations commissioned as deemed necessary. In kindergartens, registration, health checks, and curriculum requirements are ensured by in-service training (professional development) requirements and pedagogical supervision provided by accredited supervisory bodies.

Funding: Expenditure on kindergarten for children aged 3-6 years is 0.79% of GDP. Almost 91.7% of this expenditure came from public sources, and 6.2% from household expenditure. 14.7% of all expenditure on educational institutions is allocated to pre-primary whereas 16.9% of the children/students are enrolled at this level of education (OECD, *Education at a Glance*, 2005). 90% of total ECEC expenditure in Hungary goes towards maintaining public provision. The remaining government funding is channelled towards the small non-profit sector, that is, to kindergartens provided by voluntary organisations and churches. Public subvention of child care and kindergarten exists in the form of set grants for ECEC from central government, alongside complementary funding from the local authorities. Overall, the central government provides 25-30% of costs; municipal local government provides about 60%, and parents the remaining 10-15%. Effectively, parents pay only for the cost of food. Fees are subsidised for all parents, leaving parents to contribute about 10% of the overall costs of child care and 12% of the costs of early education provision. Relative to GDP per capita the annual parental expenditure on ECEC amounts to 8.2% for child care and 3.5% for pre-school education (Hungarian Government, 2004). Public expenditure per child, based on full-time equivalents and expressed in USD is USD 2 758 for crèche and USD 3 475 for kindergarten. Spending has greatly increased since 1998 (indexed at 100), reaching 224 for child care and 172 for kindergarten. In calculating this expenditure, two kinds of full-time services are included: *bölcsde* for under 3 (referred to as child care centres and/or creches); and *óvoda* (referred to as kindergarten) for children between 3 and compulsory school age.

Staffing and training: In child care and early years settings, staff – both child care workers and pedagogues – are almost exclusively female. Staff are also ageing (the average age is now 41 years) and candidates for the training colleges are declining in numbers. Between 1986 and 1996, the proportion of child care workers aged between 19 and 25 dropped from 18.5% to 4.1% (Korintus, 2005, "Overview of ECEC in Hungary", *Children in Europe*, Issue 10, Edinburgh). Specific data on full/part-time appointment of staff are not available although most staff work full-time. Two-thirds of staff in kindergartens working directly with children are tertiary-trained pedagogues, and according to estimates, 60% of the remaining one-third are trained assistants. In centres for children under 3, 90.1% of child care workers (they are not nurses) working directly with children are qualified.

Training requirements: Kindergarten pedagogues and child care workers undergo separate training, the former being trained at tertiary level, the latter generally at secondary vocational level. One-year and two-year post secondary courses are also becoming available. Kindergarten training courses have also been available for decades and 98% of kindergarten teachers have a 3-year tertiary degree from an approved training college. The OECD visiting team noted particular expertise in music, handcrafts and the visual arts. Training models and arrangements are in a process of change, affected by the Bologna process, which is addressing the parity of education qualifications. Basic training for nursery workers is being moved up to a post-secondary level, and plans are underway to lift it to a tertiary level, which many would like to see integrated with kindergarten training. Where kindergarten training is concerned, concern is expressed that the number of hours spent in the field on teaching practice during study years may decrease, and that the new pre-service curriculum may not provide sufficient in-depth pedagogy and psychology for pedagogical work. There is also hope that the recent integration of teacher training colleges with universities will further improve the quality of training for kindergarten pedagogues. *Dajka* (kindergarten assistants) support the kindergarten teacher's work. The *Dajka* help the children with care routines, and ensure the cleanliness of the environment. There are no qualification requirements for these workers but if they wish, there is a 2 200-hour training (40% theory and 60% practice) secondary certificate developed specially for them, which they can obtain.

Work conditions: Statutory working hours are 40/week both for pedagogues and assistants, although the daily hours to be spent with children for child care workers have been reduced from 8 hours to 7 (Background Report for Hungary, 2004). Staff work in shifts, as kindergartens normally open for 10 hours per day, from 7 a.m. to 5 p.m. The organisation of shift hours varies, but the aim is to ensure full deployment of staff during the core hours of the day. For both child care workers and kindergarten pedagogues, there are statutory minimum levels of staff development. Child care workers receive at least 60 hours and kindergarten pedagogues receive 120 hours per 7 years of service. Courses taken must be accredited to be counted in the hours and funding is available to cover the full cost of recently accredited courses. A shortage of child care workers exists in centres for children below 3 years. This situation, combined with training colleges having few students because the prestige and salary of ECEC workers is low, will present a serious challenge to staffing in future years.

Child-staff ratios: For family day care the maximum group size is 7, requiring a child-staff ratio of 7:2. In *bölcsde* (crèche) the maximum group size is 12 with child-staff ratio at 12:2. *Óvoda* (kindergarten) provision has a maximum group size set at 25. In these settings, a child-staff ratio of 22:2 is in place. Regulations do not specify that the required ratios must be met at all times of the day.

Curriculum and pedagogy: A specific curriculum or pedagogical methodology is available for all 3- to 6-year-olds. A National Framework Curriculum has been formulated to support pedagogues in developing their programmes, but centres are free to use a number of alternative curricula. The modification of the Education Law in 2003 made it compulsory for kindergartens to review and adjust their educational programmes according to local needs, thereby formally involving parents in the process. As in the northern and other central European countries, an integrated concept of pedagogy, *nevelés*, permeates the approach to children. *Nevelés* has a meaning close to the concept of "upbringing" and involves the inseparable concepts of care, pedagogy, and education. Services are seen as providing a setting that meets children's physical and psychological needs as well as supporting their learning and development. The focus is on promoting children's autonomy and creating opportunities for active learning (Korintus, 2005). Child care workers in nurseries give priority to "teaching the children how to do everyday tasks and become self-reliant and autonomous" while pedagogues in kindergartens emphasise "passing on cultural values and preparation for school".

Monitoring, evaluation and research: The 2003 Education Law specifies that kindergartens should have in place a quality assurance programme which emphasises self-evaluation. Service providers (normally local municipalities) are required under the same law to inspect the work and effectiveness of public education institutions (kindergartens and schools) once every four years. However, it is alleged that kindergartens are assessed less often than schools.

Parent and community involvement: The Education Law of 1993 states the legal rights of parents and requires their participation in kindergarten education. The modification of the Law in 2003 strengthens this requirement further. The development of local quality assurance in accord with the recent Education Law (2003) will ensure that families are more directly involved in kindergarten education than they have been in the past. As far as child care for under 3 is concerned, Law 31 of 1997 also states the legal rights of parents and places the duty on bölcsde (child care centres) to set up a "forum" that deals with complaints and problems, and which involves representatives of parents.

OECD policy issues

Among the issues for policy attention identified by the OECD Review team were:

- *Addressing administration, co-ordination and decentralisation*: Two major challenges that hampered efforts to improve ECEC across the country were the division between early education and care and difficulties in implementing policies because of the highly decentralised nature of Hungarian administration. In particular, smaller settlements in low employment or rural regions faced the greatest challenges in providing and assuring quality ECEC services to young children in their jurisdiction.

- *Addressing challenges to access and quality*: Access to services is variable in Hungary, with rural areas often lacking services. Local authorities have many duties to fulfil, and the funding necessary for these tasks is often not enough. In particular, access for children below the age of 3 is limited and the need to improve access for children with additional educational needs – children with disabilities, children in under-serviced rural areas and Roma children – are aspects of current service provision needing development and increased funding. In addition, the ageing, training and status of the bölcsöde workforce are a major concern. Recruitment is becoming difficult as the economy expands, with training levels and remuneration too low to attract younger recruits.

- *Addressing weaknesses in quality*: The overall management of quality, sensitive and responsive programming for diversity groups, especially for Roma children, and more effective recruitment and training of staff were considered to be at the core of quality improvement. Such management could be further helped by greater attention to research on children's services from the research and evaluation facilities that exist in Hungary.

- *Strengthening general funding*: The favourable investment by Hungary in kindergarten education is beneficial to many young children. However local criteria for entry tend to keep out disadvantaged and Roma children despite the strong national laws in favour of these groups. Although economic circumstances may pose numerous challenges across social and educational programmes in Hungary, experiences in other countries call for caution in cutting back funding to early childhood services. In particular, reductions in staffing levels can result in substantial lowering of quality especially in services for at-risk children.

Developments

Significant recent developments include:

- The National Development Plan prepared for the EU, which proposed the aim of establishing bölcsde-s (child care centres for under 3) in every settlement with a population of at least 10 000.

- The modification of the Education Law in 2003, which now requires óvóda-s (kindergartens) to admit Roma children from the age of 3.

- The re-shuffle in government in 2004 resulting in the new Ministry of Youth, Family, Social Affairs and Equal Opportunities, which is strongly motivated to expand child care for children under the age of 3.

- Access to EU funding sources, which have increased the budgets for ongoing training, and for new buildings for children's services (both *bölcsde* and *óvoda*).

- New governmental allocations and designated funding for special needs children in *óvoda*-s.

Ireland

Population: 3.9 m. Fertility rate: 1.98. GDP per capita: USD 33 200. Children under 6 years: c. 330 000.

Female labour force participation: 58% of women (15-64) participate in the labour force, 35.1% of whom are in part-time employment (male part-time is 6.9%).

Labour force participation rate of women with child(ren) under 6 years: Women with youngest child 0-3: 51.1% (OECD, *Babies and Bosses*), women with youngest child 3-6: 52%.

Maternity and parental leave: 18 weeks maternity leave paid, 14 of which are paid at 70% of earnings (ceiling imposed) or a social security stipend. Maternity leave can be followed by 14 weeks unpaid parental leave.

Average duration of parental leave: 14 weeks.

Compulsory school age: 6 years.

Social expenditure: 13.8% (2001). Child poverty rate: 15.7% after taxes and transfers (UNICEF,2005) (OECD average is 11.2%).

Funding of public pre-primary education services: 0.44% of GDP (0.39% public and 0.05% private); 8.5% of the education budget is devoted to the education of 3- to 6-year-olds, who comprise 11.6% of education enrolments.

Funding of publicly financed services for children under 3 and OSP: 0.07% in 2002.

Legal entitlement to a free service: From 4 years.

Major service types and duration: (unregulated child-minding); regulated family day care and nurseries generally on a full-time basis; half-day pre-primary classes offered to children aged 4-6 in primary schools; playgroups and private pre-school working mainly on a sessional basis. Regulated OSP does not exist.

Average costs to parents: Children 0-3 years: the average cost to parents of child care is in the region of 51% of costs, or 30% of the disposable income of the average double income family, unless in community child care where subsidies exist; children 4-6 years: the morning session of pre-primary is free; other services (playgroups and pre-schools) are paying services.

Rate of access to regulated services: Children 0-3 years: from 10-15% of children have access to regulated services; children 3-6 years: 56% of the age-group enrol in public pre-primary.

Designation and qualifications of lead staff: Qualifications are not regulated in the child care sector. Family day care, nurseries and playgroups can have a variety of staff, ranging from no qualification to tertiary level. Key staff in centres are expected to have a 2-year, post-18 certificate. In pre-primary, all staff are tertiary trained primary school teachers.

Overall % of qualified staff in services: In the child care sector, no qualifications are required. It is estimated that 30% of staff are without any qualification. In early education, lead staff are primary school teachers, all trained to university degree level.

Child-staff ratios: Children 0-3 years: depends on type of service and age of child; for children aged 3-6 years in a non-pre-primary session, the ratio is 8:1; children 3-6 years in pre-primary: the average is 25 children to one teacher (no assistant), but 24% of children are in classes of 30 children or more. In *Early Start* sessional classes for at-risk children, the ratio is generally 15:2 (one teacher and child care worker).

Maximum group size: Children 0-3 years: 20 children; children 3-6 years: 29 children.

Auspices

Seven government departments have had responsibility for different aspects of early childhood and family policy in Ireland, although three ministries take major responsibility: the Department of Health and Children (DHC); the Department of Justice, Equality and Law Reform (DJELR); and the Department of Education and Science (DES). ECEC is clearly divided into child care and education sectors, the former two ministries being involved in child care for children under 3, and in principle, for out-of-school provision (OSP). The Department of Education and Science (DES) is responsible for the pre-primary sector, that is, for children aged 4-6 years, under the 1998 Education Act (1998), with in the last decades, sponsorship of some programmes for children experiencing disadvantage or special needs (Background Report for Ireland, 2002).

Child care services are administered under the Child Care Act (1991). Until the late 1990s public recognition and support for child care was vested with the DHC, whose focus mainly was on children at risk, including children in need of protection. A national agreement, *Partnership 2000*, involving government, trade unions, employers, and social and community organisations generated a broader focus. Child care administration and provision has since been consolidated under the remit of the Department of Justice Equality and Law Reform (DJELR). In order to implement the *National Child Care Strategy*, the DJELR has a *Child Care Directorate* within its Equality Division. This Directorate oversees the EU *Equal Opportunities Child Care Programme* (2000-2006). In addition, the National Children's Office and the Office of the Ombudsman for Children are the primary agencies that are oriented towards a children's rights approach, following ratification of the Convention of the Rights of the Child in 1992. The degree to which a rights-based approach has filtered into policy and provision developed in the different child care and education areas is yet unclear (Background Report for Ireland, 2002).

In December 2005, the Office of the Minister for Children was established by the government to maximise the co-ordination of policies for children and young people (including early childhood care and education, youth justice, child protection, children and young people's participation and research on children and young people). This new office will have a range of functions previously discharged under the Departments of Health and Children; Justice, Equality and Law Reform; and Education and Science.

A new Early Years Education Policy Unit has been established within the Department of Education and Science and will be co-located with the Office of the Minister for Children. This unit will oversee the development of policies and provision for early years education within an overall strategic policy framework to be developed with the Office of the Minister for Children.

These developments are designed to address the issues of fragmentation of policy development and service delivery in the sector and respond directly to related recommendations in the White Paper on Early Childhood Education and the OECD review of early childhood education in Ireland.

Context

Labour force rates: In 2004, the labour participation rate for women aged 15-64 was 58%, increasing from 42.6% in 1990. Of those, 35.1% work part-time, while 6.9% of men work part-time (OECD, *Employment Outlook*, 2005). Mothers with a youngest child under 6 years had an employment rate of 52% in 2002, increasing from 31% in 1990, and constituted 8% of part-time employment (OECD *Society at a Glance*).

Parental leave: The Parental Leave Act 1998, introduced for the first time in Ireland a statutory right to parental leave. Mothers may now take 18 weeks maternity leave, 14 of which are financed by social welfare payments. Payment is based on income, generally being 70% of the gross income, subject to a maximum of EUR 232.40 per week. In addition, parents may take 14 weeks unpaid parental leave from work to take care of children below 5 years of age. Because it is unpaid, there has been limited adoption of parental leave by Irish couples. Some large employers provide women with their full salary for 18 weeks, the women in return giving the welfare payment to the employer to offset costs (Background Report for Ireland, 2002).

Access and provision

Operational features: Provision of services is diverse and fragmented, spread across the child care and education sectors. Within the child care sector, paid child minders form the major component of services, predominantly from their own homes. This service is usually available year-round for the full day, according to the needs of the parents. Transactions between parents and child minders are generally conducted in the informal economy, with only those child minders caring for more than 3 children being required to notify the Health Boards. Centre-based child care (nurseries and crèches) caters for children 2-3 months to school age. These services are mainly privately owned and operated, or community-based services for lower income families. In addition, a small number of workplace crèches and drop-in crèches exist providing work-based and/or occasional care services. Further, playgroups and pre-schools, mostly privately owned, provide sessional services (< 3.5 hours/child/day) for children typically aged 3-5 years. Parent and toddler groups may be attached to crèches and nurseries, offering play for children and social interaction/support for parents. Montessori schools, privately owned and managed, also cater for children 3-6 years. *Naionrai* (Irish language) pre-schools also form part of this varied set of services, catering for children 3-6 years. Within the education sector, provision in pre-primary education is public, centre-based, universal and free. Four types of provision exist: morning infant classes in primary schools, catering for 4- and 5-year-olds; special needs facilities within a small number of schools; specific pre-school pilot programmes; and pre-schools for traveller children.

0-3 years: Evidence from the Economic and Social Research Institute (1998) indicates 38% of all parents with children 4 years and below, rely on paid child care arrangements. One-fifth of mothers with full-time jobs and 47% of mothers with part-time jobs use no paid child care, relying instead, on informal provision by partners, family, friends or neighbours (Background Report for Ireland, 2002). Based on the mix of data available, the OECD review team estimated that 10% to 15% of children 0-3 years access half-day or full day publicly subsidised services.

3-6 years: All 5-year-olds and just over half of 4-year-olds attend infant classes located in primary schools (Irish Background Report, 2002). Few children aged 3 years are enrolled, with net enrolment being around 4%. Overall access for the age-range 3-6 is about 56%, among the lowest in Europe. Junior infants (for 4-year-olds) and senior infants (for 5-year-olds) generally operate from 9:00-14:00.

Attention to children with diverse needs: Most measures to redress educational disadvantage come under the remit of DES, whose pre-school facilities cater for children from disadvantaged backgrounds and children with special learning needs. Some child care centres in disadvantaged areas receive support through EOCP (the EU Equal Opportunities Child Care Programme), while others receive support from Health Boards (Background Report for Ireland, 2002).

Children with disabilities: There is no national plan to provide from birth, public interventions in favour of children with disabilities. Children are to be included in regular infant classes (at age 4-5) wherever possible, but according to teachers, with insufficient support to provide appropriate access. With the exception of visual or hearing impairment, DES does not take responsibility for the great majority of children over 4 years with disabilities. Just over 2% of children with special needs are included in mainstream primary settings. When enrolled, children with special needs may receive periodic tuition from a specialist teacher. According to the specialists and voluntary bodies engaged in this field, major issues are priority entitlement for these children and appropriate inclusion.

Children from low-income families: Since the launch of the National Anti-Poverty Strategy, many recent initiatives are in place to support children from disadvantaged families and neighbourhoods. The *Early Start* programme in early education is based on assessments of children's cognitive, language and motor capacities in junior infant classes. However, early results have not been strong, possibly because of irregular attendance, inadequate support and insufficient specific training for staff, resulting in unfocused or inappropriate pedagogy. The initiative has not been expanded since its inception in 1996.

Pre-schools for Traveller children: Traveller children are among the poorest group of children in Ireland. They suffer from discrimination and the practical difficulties of regular school attendance. The 50 or so pre-schools established for them have generally been created by voluntary bodies, with DES providing 98% of teacher salaries and transport costs. The pre-schools offer play-based experiences based on active learning strategies to develop cognitive, language and social skills. These pre-school are separate from the primary school system, and rarely staffed by fully trained teachers. On the positive side, assistants are often drawn from the Traveller community, but the need to have fully-trained Traveller teachers has yet to be addressed.

Ethnic and bilingual children: The need for children without distinction to access appropriate ECEC provision is generally accepted. According to the National Child Care census, however, less than one-quarter of services have written policies on equal opportunity and non-discrimination. As with Traveller children, anti-bias training for teachers, children and adults is strongly recommended by the voluntary bodies.

Quality

Licensing and regulatory regimes: Child care is regulated through the Child Care (Pre-School Services) Regulations (1996); and the Amendment to these Regulations (1997). Any pre-school, crèche, day nursery, playgroup, day care or other service outside of primary schools are overseen by the regional Health Boards (Background Report for Ireland, 2002). The regulations for child care are designed to ensure the health, safety and welfare of the pre-school child. They do not address the quality-related issues of staff qualifications, curriculum and pedagogy. Annual inspection of services is dependent on staff availability and the number of notifications received. Department of Health inspectors are not required to undergo specific training to inspect early childhood centres. Current review of the regulations is focused on including a voluntary notification and support system for child minders. Early Start Units within primary schools are inspected under education system processes by inspectors who are trained primary or post-primary teachers (Background Report for Ireland, 2002).

Funding: Public expenditure on educational institutions for young children as a percentage of GDP is about 0.39%. For child care, total funding available is EUR 436.7 m (USD 580 m) for 2000-06, comprising 27% exchequer funds and 73% European funds (Background Report for Ireland, 2002). As provision in the child care sector is mainly private, parental fees are the major source of funding. Costs to parents are among the highest in Europe and average over 30% of disposable income for the Average Production Employee (Country Note for Ireland, 2004). In addition, according to recent reports, costs of child care are rising far more quickly than inflation.

Staffing and ratios: Staff in the child care sector may have one of a variety of qualifications of variable quality and length, but many (particularly in the case of child minders) have no formal preparation for their roles. The percentage of qualified staff working in the sector is currently not known, but estimates place the number of staff without any qualification at about 30%. Child-staff ratios in the child care sector are regulated and appear correct by international standards. In the education sector, services are staffed by trained primary school teachers, who normally have had little or no specialist preparation in early childhood education. Junior class ratios in the pre-primary sector (4- and 5-year-olds) have on average a child-staff ratio of 1:25. According to figures provided in the Irish Background Report (2002), 24% of infant class children are in class groups of 30 children or above, with one teacher without asistance. Such ratios are extremely difficult for teaching staff, and are unfavourable to child initiative or to individual attention being given to children.

Training requirements: Until recently there has been little state involvement in child care. This circumstance enabled a general low-level of training and the *ad hoc* development of training for child care workers. The sector comprises a large number of "qualification poor/experience rich" workers in the sector (Background Report for Ireland, 2002). A wide range of qualifications exists – from Froebel and Montessori teachers trained to international standards to child care workers with no formal qualifications in child development. Post-leaving certificate courses in child care have also been developed. The National Child Care Strategy has recently prompted a training framework through the *Model Framework for Education, Training and Professional Development in the Early Childhood Care and Education Sector* (Government of Ireland, 2002). Primary teachers are trained through state supported training colleges, generally to Bachelor of Education level. However, only in some programmes is there a significant core subject in early childhood education.

Work conditions: Low status, low rates of pay and high staff turnover are features of child care positions. Trade union representation for child care workers does not exist across the sector. Two surveys of nursery staff (1999) indicated the scale and range of earnings of this group was EUR 8 900-17 000/year for junior nursery teachers and EUR 11 900-24 000 for senior teachers (Background Report for Ireland, 2002). The relevant scales for Health Board employees are EUR 24 851-32 621 and for managerial staff EUR 35 178-42 430. However, the recent *Model Framework* (noted above) offers a vision of professional development and articulation of professional roles. Recognition and accreditation of learning through experience, and development of pathways to formal qualifications are included in the *Framework*. Work conditions for teachers are much better. The pay scale for primary teachers starts at EUR 23 096 per annum, progressing to EUR 44 891. The working day and year are shorter (generally 9 a.m. to early afternoon, for the academic year only) than in child care where 9-hour-days and an 11-month year are the rule for full-time workers. Junior class teachers are represented by the Irish National Teachers Association. There is no statutory requirement for annual staff development or training.

Curriculum and pedagogy: Wide differences are apparent in curriculum approaches to children in child care, pre-school groups (non-public early education) and public pre-primary classes. Some pre-school settings adopt approaches to learning such as High/Scope, Montessori and Steiner. In the public sector, the *Curriculum Guidelines for Good Practice in Early Start* shape curriculum and pedagogy in early start programmes. The National Council for Curriculum and Assessment (NCCA) is developing a non-mandatory *Framework for Early Childhood Learning* and the Centre for Early Childhood Development and Education (CECDE) is preparing learning goals for the 0-6 age span. These developments are intended to link with Department of Health and Children requirements set out in the Child Care Regulations.

Monitoring, evaluation and research: One of the measures proposed in the White Paper on Early Childhood Education concerns the development of minimum quality standards for some of the areas not covered by the Child Care (Pre-School) Regulation and the establishment of best practice in others. Meeting these standards will be obligatory for those receiving state funding for the provision of developmental/educational places. Non-State funded providers may voluntarily adopt these standards and apply for the Quality in Education (QE) Mark. The QE Mark or its equivalent is to be devised by the CECDE and will cover curricula, methodologies, staff qualifications and training. It is hoped that this development will lead to an increased recognition of the need for quality standards both to improve services and to guide parents in their choices. It is proposed that attaining a quality standard should be based on inspection and evaluation visits. A persisting challenge is how quality and quality goals will be implemented in children's services, as the broad goals outlined, for example, by the American National Education Goals Panel for kindergarten education – health and physical development; emotional well-being and social competence; positive approaches to learning; communication skills; cognition and general knowledge – are not always given equal weight in traditional services (NEGP, 1997, "Getting a Good Start in School", Government Printing Office, Washington DC).

Parent and community involvement: Under the Act parents are represented on primary school boards and may form parent associations, although a national parent association for early childhood does not exist. The recently established Centre for Early Childhood Development and Education (CECDE) is expected to facilitate strategies for enhancing parent involvement, which traditionally has not been strong in the education sector in Ireland. County Child care Committees include at least one parent representative and parent involvement in the management of community-based services. Evidence gathered by the National Child Care Census indicates that the concept of active parental involvement is not firmly anchored in this sector. Less than half (40%) of facilities have a policy on parental engagement, with only 19% having a written statement.

OECD policy issues

Among the issues for policy attention identified by the OECD review team in 2004 were:

Co-ordination of ministries, agencies and resources: In the interest of coherent policy-making and of the efficient funding of priority goals, it was proposed that consideration be given towards:

- Bringing together education and care policy under one ministry or designated agency.
- Formulating a national plan for early childhood services development.
- Decentralising the practical planning and management of ECEC services to integrated agencies or committees at country level.

Improving general access: Among the measures proposed to increase access were:

- Extending funded parental leave to one year after the birth of a child.
- Increasing the supply of places for children one year and older through accrediting and subsidising quality child minders.
- Removing barriers to affordability for low- and modest-income families.
- Increasing parent support and education through professional planning and management of local services from county level.
- Entitlement of a place in a free, accredited early education service for all children who have reached their 4th birthday.
- Development of a publicly funded morning education for all children of 3 years.
- Extension of the Early Start in areas where there is sufficient demand.
- Accreditation and financial support provided to voluntary, community and private organisations delivering high quality programmes.

Improving access for children with additional learning needs: Given the significant size of the group of children with additional learning needs, urgent consideration and implementation of National Forum recommendations in favour of children with special needs were recommended, with intensive quality programming for disadvantaged children from as early an age as possible.

Improving the quality of ECEC: Among the strategies put forward for consideration were:

- Formulation of a common quality framework for centre-based programmes and agreed standards for services.
- Introduction of a voluntary accreditation and quality improvement scheme for service providers.
- Restructuring the infant school to favour autonomy, quality and accountability.
- Reassessment of initial training for early childhood services at all levels.

Financing new measures: The financing measures proposed not only an increase in funding towards young children, but also a more equitable sharing of budgets between the ministries, parents and the private sector. Among the measures proposed were:

- Significant increase in ministry budgets for early childhood services.
- A pooling of resources and sharing of costs across ministries.
- Shifting educational financing towards quality ECEC.
- Cost-effective co-ordination of policies at central level.
- Sharing of tasks with the voluntary, community and private sectors.
- Enlisting the support of the corporate and business sectors.
- A study of international funding mechanisms.

Italy

Population: 58 145 360 (source ISTAT) **Fertility rate:** 1.30. **GDP per capita:** USD 26 347 (OECD, *Education at a Glance*, 2005). **Children under 6 years:** 3 842 256 (source ISTAT – central estimate 1-1-2004).

Female labour force participation: 50.6% of women aged 15-64, 28.8% of whom are in part-time employment (male part-time is 5.9%) (OECD, *Employment Outlook*, 2005).

Employment rates for mothers with children: For mothers with children 0-3: 45.2% (EUROSTAT), for mothers with children under 6: 53%.

Maternity and parental leave: 5 months of compulsory maternity leave usually paid at 100% of earnings. Both parents are entitled to leave in the first year of the child, and either parent can take up to 10 months parental leave until the child is eight years old.

Average duration of parental leave: Data currently not available.

Compulsory school age: 6 years.

Social expenditure: 24.4% of GDP. **Child poverty rate:** 16.6% after taxes and transfers (OECD average is 11.2%).

Major service types and duration: The *nidi d'infanzia*[1] for children 3 months to 3 years, open for 8 to 12 hours daily. The *scuole dell'infanzia* (Law No. 53 of 28 March 2003, art. 2, letter e) for the 3- to 6-year-olds open during the academic year with a flexible timetable, ranging from a minimum of 875 to a maximum of 1 700 annual hours (in most cases open from 8.30 a.m. to 4.30 p.m.). *Integrated services* – play areas, centres for children and families, in-home services – that supplement ECEC services. Besides 732 integrated services,[2] a growing number of recent pilot schemes ("in-home" and "company" services) enrich and diversify the provision.

Major providers of ECEC services: The State runs 55.2% of schools, the remaining 44.8% are run by non-state providers (non-state schools include schools run by municipalities, confessional providers, and private individuals). The recent reform aims at ensuring the generalisation of education provision and the possibility to attend *scuola dell'infanzia* and provides for diversification of providers to meet the diverse needs of families, with a view to progressively overcoming the rigidity of service provision (Government decree 19 February 2004, No. 59, art. 1, item 2).Continuing expansion, rather than balance distribution, has confirmed diversification at national level between areas and regions (Aldo Fortunati, *op. cit.*, p. 19).

---

1. Aldo Fortunati, "I servizi educativi per la prima infanzia come risorsa ed opportunità per bambini e genitori: tendenze e prospettive", in *Cittadini in Crescita*, 2004, pp. 18-29.
2. "I servizi educativi per la prima infanzia. Indagine sui nidi d'infanzia e sui servizi educativi 0-3 anni integrativi al nido al 30 settembre 2000", Florence, Istituto degli innocenti, 2002.

Funding of pre-primary educational services (ISCED Level 0): 0.44% of GDP (0.39% public and 0.05% private); 8.5% of the education budget is devoted to the education of 3- to 6-year-olds, who comprise 12% of education enrolments. Salary costs in the municipal and confessional *scuole dell'infanzia* are supported by state funding (data currently not available).

Unit cost per child (in USD converted using PPP): USD 5 445 (public institutions only) (OECD, *Education at a Glance*, 2005).

Average costs to parents: Children 0-3 years: fees are charged according to parental income level, but they are capped at a maximum of 18% of costs. Children 3-6 years: attendance is free in state and municipal services, except for meals and extra services.

Legal entitlement to a free service: At the age of 3 years in state and municipal *scuole dell'infanzia*; for all children at the beginning of obligatory schooling.

Rate of access to regulated services: Children 0-3 years: 18.7%[***]. Children 3-4 years: 98.1%. 5-6 years: 100%. ([***] *source*: Istat-Census 2001).

Designation and professional qualifications of key staff: *Insegnante* (teacher) in scuola dell'infanzia with a 4-year university education; *educatrice* (educator) in *asilo nido* with a secondary vocational education.

Child-staff ratios: For child-minding inside the home: 3:1. In *asilo nido* 7:1. In *scuola dell'infanzia* per 2 teachers: 20 children (if there are children with disabilities), 25 children (generally), 28 children (in exceptional cases), plus a teacher assistant (special needs teacher) and a religion teacher.

Maximum group size: *Asilo nido*: 10 children; *scuola dell'infanzia*: group size is a maximum of 25 children. Since at some points of the day there are several teachers in one section, it is possible to create groups with a variable number of children for lab activities, exploring, researching and playing outdoor.

Auspices

Policy responsibility for ECEC in Italy is separated according to governmental level, the type of service being offered and the age of focus. The Ministry of Education is responsible for the *scuola dell'infanzia*, catering for the 3- to 6-year-olds. This Ministry oversees the educational orientation, quality inspection and evaluation of the *scuola dell'infanzia* system.

Law No. 62 of 10 March 2000 introduced fundamental changes into the ECEC legislative framework. After the entry into force of the law, most non-state *scuole dell'infanzia* successfully applied for the recognition of equal status (*parità scolastica*). *Scuole paritarie* are non-state schools, including those run by local authorities, which, starting from the *scuola dell'infanzia*, follow the general education guidelines and meet families' educational demand, as well as observing quality and effectiveness requirements (Law No. 62 of 10 March 2000, art. 1, par. 2). In particular, they must: have an educational project in line with the principles of the Italian Constitution; have an educational plan (POF) consistent with regulations and provisions in force; have collective bodies based on democratic participation; guarantee access to all children whose parents apply for a place; implement current regulations for disabled or disadvantaged children; employ fully qualified teaching staff, with individual contracts in accordance with the national collective contracts for the sector.

The regions and municipalities are responsible for the *asili nido*, catering for the 3 month-3-year-olds. At local level, in response to community demand, municipalities may provide and operate services, using part of their own funding. Maternal and child health services, infant and toddler care, child welfare, and related social services are largely the responsibility of regional and local governments. The region supplements municipal budgets, through the distribution of the employer's 1% contribution to social funds (devoted, in principle, to infants and toddlers). Local authorities are also responsible for financing buildings. The bodies directly responsible for the *scuole dell'infanzia* organise in-service training activities for the staff:

- The State, through the Regional Institute for Educational Research (IRRE) and the National Documentation Institute for Educational Innovation and Research (INDIRE).

- The municipalities, confessional providers and private individuals (also through initiatives carried out by their associations).

Context

Labour force rates: In 2004, the labour participation rate for women aged 15-64 was 50.6%, increasing from 44.0% in 1990. Of those, 28.8% work part-time, while 5.9% of men work part-time (OECD, *Employment Outlook*, 2005). Mothers with a youngest child under 6 years had an employment rate of 53% in 2002, and constituted 29% of part-time employment (OECD *Society at a Glance*). In 2004, mothers with a youngest child under 3 had an employment rate of 45.2% (EUROSTAT).

Parental leave: Italy offers 5 months of job-protected maternity mandatory leave paid through the social security fund, paid at 80% of salary. Civil servants receive their full pay while on maternity leave and many collective bargaining agreements require employers to top-up the social insurance benefit and pay an additional benefit covering the remaining 20% of wage. Full-time working mothers are also entitled to two hours/day of rest time during the first year after birth, which if taken together, can effectively shorten their workday by two hours. Since 2000, either parent may take up to 10 months' leave at any time until the child is eight years old. Employers receive state incentives to offer part-time employment opportunities to parents following leave. Small firms, which have to replace workers, may receive a tax concession.

Access and provision

Three main types of provision are found in Italy, in which children are generally grouped according to age:

Nidi d'infanzia (child care centres) cater essentially for children from 3 months to 3 years, and are open from September to the following June/July. In recent years, they have increased in number (from 2 180 in 1992 to 3 008 in 2000 – a 27.5% increase) and provision (from 5.8% in 1992 to 7.4% in 2000). The potential of active services with respect to potential users was estimated at 6.75% in 1992; in 2000 the estimate increased to 8.6%.[1] Non-state providers have increased: from 146 centres in 1992 (6.7% of the total 2 180) to 604 centres in 2000 (20.1% of the total 3 008). The distribution of *nidi* is not homogeneous on the national territory and availability of places varies: northern regions provide 59.3% of places, central regions 25.4%, southern regions plus the islands 15.3% (*op. cit.*, p. 41). These centres may operate from 1st September to 31st August, but most (36%) are open 45-48 weeks, 34% are open 40-44 weeks, around 20% are open 49 weeks or more, and 105 are open

39 weeks (*op. cit.*, p. 72). They are open from Monday to Friday with variable daily working hours: the majority of them (36%) operate 11-12 hours, 34% operate 9-10 hours, 27% operate 7-8 hours, only about 3% operate 7 hours (*op. cit.*, p. 73). There are 2 404 (79.9%) public *nidi d'infanzia*, and 604 (20.1%) private ones (*op. cit.*, p. 127).

Scuole dell'infanzia cater for the 3- to 6-year-olds. The recent reform law of the school system (Law No. 53 of 28 March 2003 and Government decree No. 59 of 19 February 2004) provides for the possibility to enrol – on a gradual and experimental basis – children who will be 3 years old before 30 April of the academic year. This implies the introduction of new professional profiles and new organisational aspects. Presently only children who are 3 years old by 28 February are admitted to *scuola dell'infanzia* (C.M. No. 90 of 30 December 2004). About 55.2% of *scuole dell'infanzia* are now under the direct responsibility of the Ministry of Education, University and Research. *Scuola dell'infanzia* offers a full day programme, from 8.30 a.m. to 4.30 p.m. from September to June, with municipal services generally offering summer programmes. Attendance at state and municipal *scuola dell'infanzia* is free, except for meals. Modest fees are charged in confessional *scuola dell'infanzia*, as these services receive some regional and state funds. Other private providers may charge higher fees, but many private services are, in fact, non-profit.

Integrated services: Typically, these services cater for children from 1-6 years, and combine care and education. On 30 September 2000, besides 2 404 public *nidid'infanzia* and 604 private ones, 504 public integrated services for 0- to 3-year-olds and at least 228 private ones were calculated (31% of total).[2] The survey on public integrated services for 0- to 3-year-olds is a proper census, but for private ones the estimate may reflect only a small part of the actual provision. The so-called "new service typologies" of integrated services respond to the demand for differentiation of the *asili nido* provision and meet the diverse needs of families, women and children (*op. cit.*, p. 79). There are three types of integrated services (*op. cit.*, p. 79): *Centres for children and families*, catering for 0- to 3-year-olds not in an exclusive way, where children can be accompanied by their parents or other adults. The location for service provision is fixed and appropriate, but not necessarily exclusive. The activities are carried out on a regular and permanent basis. *Play areas* for children aged between 18 and 36 months: children are admitted either in the morning or in the afternoon for a maximum of 5 hours daily. Regulation provides for a diversified attendance according to users' needs. Extra services, like meals and afternoon rest, are not provided. *Educational services* for small groups of children younger than 3 years: These are typically provided by qualified staff, either in the home of one of the users' families or in the educator's home (*op. cit.*, p. 80). Among the best known are the municipal schools of Reggio Emilia, which combine infant, toddler and kindergarten care under the auspices of the municipal education system. Because the demand for places is greater than supply, Reggio Emilia programmes are part-day and part-week. Municipal services may also include new service typologies that are characterised by integrated, inter-generational approaches, with outreach to families and children who normally would not have opportunities to interact and socialise with others.

Rates of provision

0-1 years: Most care for infants is parental – linked to the parental leave system. Parental care is supplemented by informal (unregulated) family care, or *asilo nido* provision.

1-3 years: Children are cared for in the following ways: 27% in-home care; 48% relatives or informal care; 15% by a child minder in the home; 7.5% in *asili nido* (open full day for 11 months); and 2% father's and family care (Background Report for Italy, 1998).

4-6 years: 98% of children (depending on region) attend *scuola dell'infanzia* from the age of 3 years, reaching a national coverage of over 100% of children aged 5-6 years (the rate of access is slightly higher than 100%, since it includes children of non-registered foreigners).

Children with diverse needs

Children with disabilities: In Italy, general inclusion of children with disabilities into ECEC and schools is the rule, with reduced group sizes and special needs teachers at their disposal. In the academic year 2004-05,[3] 10 084 children with disabilities enrolled in state *scuole dell'infanzia*, that is 1.04% of the total number of students (968 399). They have different types of disabilities: mental and physical: 9 270 children; sight: 299 children; and hearing: 515 children. There are 4 898 posts for special needs teachers, not including extra teachers recruited in exceptional cases. Posts for general teachers are 79 370 (*ibid.*).

Children from low-income families: The child poverty level in Italy is 16.6% after taxes and transfers (OECD average is 11.2%), but the national figure covers wide regional variations. Children of low-income families and of single parents have priority of access to *nidi d'infanzia*.

Ethnic and bilingual children: The 2003-04 rate of attendance at state and non-state *scuole dell'infanzia* of foreign children is 3.83% of the total number of enrolled children.[4] Compared to 2002-03 the rate has increased by 0.43%, thus confirming a long-standing trend. Of the 54 947 foreign children enrolled in *scuole dell'infanzia*, more than six children out of ten are enrolled in state schools (64.61%). The national rate of foreign enrolments in the *scuole* is not homogeneous, ranging from: 6.19% in north-western regions; 6.24% in north-eastern regions; 5.4% in southern regions; 0.76% in the islands (*op. cit.*, p. 35). In origin, the 54 947 foreign children attending *scuola dell'infanzia* in the academic year 2003-04 come from diverse backgrounds: 1 547 come from EU countries, 20 435 from European countries outside the EU, 19 584 from Africa, 5 084 from America, 8 216 from Asia and 81 from Oceania or are stateless (*op. cit.*, p. 42).

Quality

Licensing and regulatory regimes: Because of a strong regional tradition in ECEC provision in Italy, compliance with national standards and regulations differs across regions. In principle, the State, primary school, head-teachers are responsible for monitoring the state system, as well as municipal and private schools in specific localities. A small group of inspectors visit state *scuola dell'infanzia* to regulate as necessary.

Funding: Expenditure on pre-primary educational institutions as a percentage of GDP is 0.44% of GDP. Almost 88.8% of this expenditure comes from public sources and 11.2% from private (household) sources. In the public sector, 9% of the total expenditure on educational institutions is allocated to pre-primary whereas 12% of the child/student population is enrolled at this level (OECD, *Education at a Glance*, 2005). The *scuola dell'infanzia* (pre-school for 3- to 6-year-olds) is universally provided. Attendance at state-run *scuole dell'infanzia* is free by law.[5] Fees are income-related to a maximum of 20% of the cost of provision. *Asili nido* (child care centres for children 3 months to 3 years) are also publicly funded, although a proportion of costs are funded by parents. Fees differ according to municipality and the ability of parents to pay, and range from EUR 90-460 monthly.

Staffing: Initial training for all teachers – from *scuola dell'infanzia* to upper secondary school – is provided by universities in second degree courses *(corsi di laurea specialistica)*. Access to these courses is regulated by Law No. 264 of 2 August 1999 (art. 1, par. 1), and its successive amendments. The programming of access to courses is regulated by art. 3 of the above law, on the basis of the estimate of places available in schools in each region (Law No. 53 of 28 March 2003, art. 5, item 1, letter a). The university course in "sciences of primary education", set up under art. 3, par. 2 of Law No. 341 of 19 November 1990, ends with a state exam which includes the assessment of a teaching practice period to be carried out as part of the training. This state exam gives Qualified Teacher Status to candidates for *scuola dell'infanzia* or primary school. It also entitles teacher trainees to be placed in the permanent lists of the school system (Law No. 53 of 28 March 2003, art. 5, item 1, letter g).

Training requirements: The current reform of the training system is a major national initiative. Two laws were enacted in 1997/1998 with the aim of raising the qualifications of pre-school and primary teachers to university level. Prior to this law, teacher training was undertaken in largely Catholic training institutes – *scuole magistrali* – or in state training institutes. This training was designed as mid-secondary level education. In future, co-ordinators of the *asili nido* will have a 4-year university degree, and other contact staff will require a 3-year tertiary diploma. Staff-training reform is still underway: teachers of the *scuola dell'infanzia* will have in the future a university degree.

The reform law contains a delegation of power to the government to define the general rules on education and the basic levels of performance in the field of vocational education and training (Law No. 53 of 28 March 2003, item 3). The law confirms that teacher training has to be undertaken in universities (second degree courses), and that the university degree obtained – which includes the assessment of the teaching practice – gives Qualified Teacher Status. Special needs teachers (teacher assistants) can be admitted to the university course in "sciences of primary education" (art. 3, par. 2, of Law No. 341 of 19 November 1990), under certain conditions: they must pass the relevant entry tests, have an upper secondary school diploma, and be awarded learning credits on the basis of their learning pathway (theory and practice) and the exams passed to obtain the two-year specialisation diploma as special needs teacher (*ibid.*).

Work conditions: In the *scuola dell'infanzia*, teachers are currently paid at the same rates as primary teachers, and conditions of work are good. The State provides them with many opportunities for in-service training. Conditions for staff in the *asilinido* are much less satisfactory. Although often as highly trained, these staff have less pay, longer working hours, and in some cases less access to in-service training than teachers in the *scuola dell'infanzia*.

Child-staff ratios: Maximum group size in *asili nido* is 10. The established ratios are: 7:1 in the *nido*, 8:1 for complementary services outside the home, and 3:1 for services inside the home. Ratios are higher in state *scuola dell'infanzia*: 20 children (if there are children with disabilities), 25 children (generally), 28 children (in exceptional cases) per 2 teachers (double staff, if working hours are more than 25 per week), plus a teacher assistant (special needs teacher) and a religion teacher.

Curriculum and pedagogy: The National Guidelines for Personalised Educational Plans in *scuole dell'infanzia*,[6] define the basic levels of performance that *scuole dell'infanzia* of the National Education System have to meet in order to guarantee the personal, social and civil rights of children to quality education and training. They exclude pedagogical approaches aiming at anticipating formal learning and define the essential elements of educational provision: personal relations between peers and with adults; enhancement of playing in all its forms and expressions; emphasis on productive making, and direct contact experiences with nature, things, materials, social environment, culture (*op. cit.*, p. 2).

The National Guidelines set out the general objectives of the educational process: developing personal identity, autonomy and competences. They also classify specific learning objectives in four areas: 1) the self and others; 2) body, movement and health; 3) receiving and producing messages; 4) exploring, knowing and planning (*op. cit.*, pp. 4 and 5). A further step for teachers is to plan Learning Units that, on the basis of the general educational objectives, transform individual skills into competences. The Learning Units effectively implemented with the differentiations that some children may require, form the Personalised Educational Plan, which is at the disposal of families and is an important document for the development of the Individual Competences Portfolio (*op. cit.*, p. 6). Throughout *scuola dell'infanzia*, each child records the competences acquired on a Portfolio composed of: a basic description of courses attended and progress made; a standard but significant documentation of his/her works information on learning resources, ways and timing, as well as on his/her personal interests, aptitudes and aspirations (*op. cit.*, p. 7).

Scuole dell'infanzia enjoy autonomous management and teaching methodology.[7] Much importance is given to setting up laboratories or investigation groups, to organise children's work, according to children's individual learning needs (by section/intersection, by level, by task or by choice).[8] The national government has demonstrated a high degree of flexibility allowing programmes to develop their own pedagogical orientations. The autonomy has led to highly-regarded innovative programmes in some settings (such as in Reggio Emilia, Pistoia and Milano) and much-less favourably perceived programmes in others. There is no set of national guidelines for *asili nido* services. Some municipal and regional projects give curriculum and pedagogical direction in particular localities.

Monitoring, evaluation and research: Because there are wide discretionary powers at the local government level, local districts apply their own criteria for admission to services, have their own recruitment examinations for teachers, in-service teacher training and pedagogical approaches. Innovations and research are similarly diverse in scale and size. Regions of Lombardia, Emilia Romagna, and Tuscany have contributed substantially to advanced ECEC programmes. *Nidi d'infanzia*, integrated services and private, confessional and municipal *scuole dell'infanzia* have always enjoyed a high degree of autonomy. With recent legislation,[9] state educational institutions – including state *scuole dell'infanzia* – enjoy autonomous management and are in charge of designing and carrying out their educational provision, within the framework of the tasks and functions transferred to regions and local authorities.[10] Each educational institution designs its Educational Plan. The Plan is the essential document for the definition of the cultural and planning identity of the school and/or nursery. It sets out the plan for curricular, extra-curricular, educational and organisational activities that each school adopts autonomously (*cf.* above, art. 3) Educational institutions enjoy autonomy in teaching methodology (*cf.* above, art. 4) organisation, (*cf.* above, art. 5) research, experimentation and development (*cf.* above, art. 6).

Besides enhancing the opportunities for autonomous management and teaching methodology, the reform of the school system introduces a new professional figure in *scuola dell'infanzia*: a teacher-co-ordinator of the pedagogical team, who works in one or more schools in the same area (if a school has less than three sections). This teacher has the task of promoting harmony and consistency in teaching and organisational planning in connection with families, local authorities and the head-teacher.[11] The co-ordinating teacher may also draw up agreements with local authorities to set up sections with children younger than 3 years, in association with *asili nido*, for the whole academic year or for shorter periods, according to the educational and teaching projects of the local schools (*ibid.*).

Parent and community involvement: In the *nidi d'infanzia* and in integrated services, parents' committees and councils guarantee the social management of the services. In the *scuole dell'infanzia* inter-section councils have been operating for years: they are composed of all teachers and one representative of parents, for each section. Parents of children enrolled in state *scuole dell'infanzia* can be elected in district councils (*consigli di circolo*).[12] *Scuole dell'infanzia paritare* must set up collective bodies based on democratic participation (Law No. 62 of 10 March 2000, art. 1, par. 4).

OECD policy issues

Among the issues for policy attention identified in 2001 by the OECD review team for Italy were:

- A *relative neglect of children from 0-3 years*: In terms of state intervention, the early childhood system in Italy has been focused most strongly on the 3- to 6-year-olds. There is an urgent need for the State to take on greater responsibility to meet the needs of children under 3 and their parents. The recent extension of paid parental leave has been a significant step forward. Further support to municipalities to extend their integrated programmes would help to address the learning and socialisation needs of infants and toddlers, even when being cared for by a parent. Besides the increase in number (+27.5%, from 2 180 to 3 008) and provision (from 5.8% to 7.4%) of *asili nido*, the provision of integrated services has also improved and is more diversified thanks to the setting up of "in-home" and "company" services. Moreover, the recent reform provides the possibility for centres to enrol children younger than 3 years in *scuole dell'infanzia*: for the time being, only those who will be 3 years old by 28 February of the academic year; and later on, children who will be 3 years old by 30 April (Law No. 53 of 28 March 2003, and Government decree No. 59 of 19 February 2004).

- *Co-ordination of administrations and services*: Fragmentation of responsibility has been a longstanding problem to be solved in order to facilitate the coherence of ECEC services in Italy. A need is perceived for increased co-ordination of policy formulation and planning both vertically (state, regional and municipal levels) and horizontally (across state, municipal and private providers). More collaborative projects between the different partners may be useful. Recent legislation on school autonomy provides for centres to set up or participate in school networks (Decree of the President of the Republic No. 275 of 8 March 1999, art. 7, par. 1). Educational institutions can also promote or participate in agreements for the co-ordination of joint activities within the framework of specific projects involving various schools, bodies, volunteer and private non-profit organisations (Decree of the President of the Republic No. 275 of 8 March 1999, art. 7, par. 9). Finally, schools can set up or participate in public and private consortia in order to carry out institutional tasks coherent with the Educational Plan and to acquire goods and services facilitating the educational tasks.

● *The effectiveness of policy formulation and its actual outreach to the municipalities and regions:* Basic texts governing ECEC services are not necessarily applicable in parts of the private system. More effective monitoring of the system is needed. Standards need to be developed enabling internal evaluation and communication to the public as to how resources and services are managed. Integrated in-service training for administrators and teachers from the different networks is recommended. The National Guidelines for Personalised Educational Plans in *scuole dell'Infanzia* provide for the possibility to draw up agreements with local authorities to set up sections with children younger than 3 years, in association with *asili nido*, for the whole academic year or for shorter periods, according to the schools' educational and teaching projects.

● *Dissemination of research and good practice:* Italian early childhood educators have a wealth of knowledge about young children, and many Italian programmes are recognised world-wide for their high quality. To date, however, much of what has been learned in the various cities and schools in Italy has remained in those settings, to the benefit of small numbers of children and their families. A number of in-service training activities for teachers of state *scuole dell'infanzia* have been carried out for the implementation of the current reform. In particular, the National Documentation Institute for Educational Innovation and Research (INDIRE) has developed on-line training activities.

Developments

The *nidi d'infanzia* for children up to three years, although still underdeveloped, have steadily increased in number (+27.5%, from 2 180 in 1992 to 3 008 in 2000) and provision (from 5.8% in 1992 to 7.4% in 2000).[13] In parallel, all ECEC services for the younger children – *nidi*, integrated services (play areas, centres for children and parents, in-home services) and recent innovative pilot schemes (in-home and company services) – have become more complex and diversified. Two elements may be noted:

● The diversification of the provision, with the development of new types of services, which is a result both of the lack of resources necessary to further develop the *nidi* (in a situation of unmet demand) and of the families' interest for alternative services.

● The diversification of ECEC providers, with the growing development of private services offered in most cases in connection with public authorities.[14]

In the *scuole dell'infanzia*, catering for the 3- to 6-year-olds, the most significant innovations introduced by the reform are: the possibility for parents to enrol children younger than 3 years; and the publication of National Guidelines for Personalised Educational Plans in *Scuole dell'Infanzia*.[15] These guidelines set out:

● The "general objectives of the educational process", and "specific learning objectives" in the following areas: the self and others; body, movement and health; receiving and producing messages; exploring, knowing and planning.

● The relation between educational objectives and personalised educational plans.

● A number of clarifications about the development of the individual competences portfolio.

Organisational rules and guidelines for school staff have also been published, dealing with:

● Opportunities for autonomy in management and teaching methodology.

● The appointment of a teacher to coordinate the pedagogical team.

- The definition of an annual timetable allowing centres to set up annual modules ranging from 875 to 1 700 hours that families can choose when they enrol children.

- Centre agreements with local authorities to set up sections with children younger than 3 years, in association with *asili nido*, for the whole academic year or for shorter periods, according to the schools' educational and teaching projects.

Notes

1. "I servizi educativi per la prima infanzia. Indagine sui nidi d'infanzia e sui servizi educativi 0-3 anni integrativi al nido al 30 settembre 2000", Florence, Istituto degli innocenti, 2002, p. 13.

2. "I servizi educativi per la prima infanzia. Indagine sui nidi d'infanzia e sui servizi educativi 0-3 anni integrativi al nido al 30 settembre 2000", Florence, Istituto degli innocenti, 2002, p. 14.

3. Data drawn from "Sedi, Alunni, classi, dotazioni organiche del personale docente della scuola statale, Anno scolastico 2004-2005", MIUR, September 2004, p. 29.

4. Data drawn from "Alunni con cittadina non italiana, Anno scolastico 2003-2004", MIUR, September 2004 p. 33.

5. Law No. 444 of 18 March 1968, art. 1: "Enrolment is optional, attendance is free."

6. The "Indicazioni Nazionali per i Piani Personalizzati delle Attività Educative nelle Scuole dell'Infanzia" are attached to the Government decree No. 59 of 19 February 2004, Annex A.

7. Decree of the President of the Republic No. 275 of 8 March 1999 – Regulation on school autonomy under law No. 59 of 15 March 1997, art. 21.

8. "Indicazioni Nazionali per i Piani Personalizzati delle Attività Educative nelle Scuole dell'Infanzia", p. 8.

9. Law No. 59 of 15 March 1997, art. 21, and Decree of the President of the Republic No. 275 of 8 March 1999.

10. Decree of the President of the Republic No. 275 of 8 March 1999, art. 1, item 1.

11. "Indicazioni Nazionali per i Piani Personalizzati delle Attività Educative nelle Scuole dell'Infanzia", p. 8.

12. The functioning of collective bodies is still regulated by the Decree of the President of the Republic No. 416 of 1974, contained in the Consolidation Act of 1994.

13. I servizi educativi per la prima infanzia. Indagine sui nidi d'infanzia e sui servizi educativi 0-3 anni integrativi al nido al 30 settembre 2000, Florence, Istituto degli innocenti, 2002.

14. Aldo Fortunati, "I servizi educativi per la prima infanzia come risorsa ed opportunità per bambini e genitori: tendenze e prospettive", in *Cittadini in Crescita*, 2004, pp. 18-19.

15. Indicazioni Nazionali per i Piani Personalizzati delle Attività Educative nelle Scuole dell'Infanzia.

Korea

Population: 45.9 m. **Fertility rate:** 1.3 X1.16 (2005). **GDP per capita:** USD 20 300. **Children under 6 years:** almost 4 million (2005).

Female labour force participation: 53.9% of women are employed, 11.9% of whom are in part-time employment (male part-time is 5.9%). A significant percentage of women in employment are in non-regular work, and do not benefit from parental leave rights, child benefits or pension rights. Labour participation rates of women with a child under age 6 are low by OECD standards, with national statistics indicating that a sharp drop in female employment until children are reared.

Remunerated maternity and parental leave: A system of limited-allowance and parental leave for birth and child-rearing (0-5 years) was incorporated into legislation with adjustments from 1987 to 2001. Three months of maternity leave is paid at approximately USD 400 monthly. The take-up has been extremely low among women and negligible among men.

Duration of compulsory school education: 6-15 years, that is, 9 years.

Social expenditure: 6.1% of GDP **Child poverty rate:** Not available.

Funding of kindergartens (ISCED Level 0): 0.16% of GDP (0.05% public and 0.11% private) (OECD, *Education at a Glance*, 2005). Expenditure on kindergartens corresponds to 2% of the education budget, but kindergartens cater for approximately 5% of educational enrolments.

Unit cost per child in kindergartens (in USD using PPP): USD 2 497 (OECD, *Education at a Glance*, 2005).

Funding of services for children under age 3: Percentage of GDP not available.

Average costs to parents: In kindergarten, 78% of enrolled children are in the private sector where parents pay 100% of the costs. In the formal child care sector, parents bear 66% of total child care costs.

Legal entitlement to a free service: Free child care and early education are offered in principle from the age of 5 years, but demand far outstrips supply. About 30% of 5-year-olds, mainly those from lower income families, receive this benefit.

Major service types and duration: Kindergartens for 3- to 6-year-olds operate traditionally on a half-day basis, but more recently, 51% offer extended services and 30% open full day for the academic year. 85.6% of child care centres for 0- to 6-year-olds offer 12 hours/day for the full year. *Hakwons* (private educational academies) offering various learning curricula normally open 8-10hours/day for the full-year, catering for children from age 3 to 12 years.

Rate of access to regulated services: Children 0-3 years: 19.6%; 3-6 years (including child care): 68.3%; 78.9% of children 5-6 years attended ECEC services in 2005. Out-of-school provision is being developed but figures are not available.

Designation and qualifications of lead staff: In public kindergartens, 66% of teachers hold a 4-year university degree; in private kindergartens, 88% of teachers hold a 2-year college diploma. In child care centres, about 15% of teachers have a 4-year degree; around 60% a 2-year college award; and about 25% have received a one-year child care training after high school or tertiary education.

Child-staff ratios: There are no required or recommended child-staff ratios for the kindergarten system, but cities and provinces recommend child-teacher ratios for kindergarten classes. The average in 2005 was 20:1. In child care, infants 3:1, 1 year 5:1, 2 years 7:1, 3 years 15:1, 4-6 years 20:1.

Maximum group size: Kindergarten: ages 4-5: 25-30; age 3: 15-25; mixed age: 20-30 children per group.

Auspices

Legislative responsibilities for government acts, decrees and resolutions on ECEC are vested mainly with two ministries: the Ministry of Gender Equality and Family (MOGEF), the Ministry of Education and Human Resource Development (MOE). In addition, the Ministries of Health and Welfare; Labour; Government Administration and Home Affairs; and Agriculture and Forestry are also involved in ECEC policy and legislation, mainly because their departments attend to the increased participation of women in the paid labour market and the subsequent expansion of child care provision. Research activity on ECEC in Korea is under the auspices of two government-funded institutes: the Korean Education Development Institute (KEDI); and the Korea Women's Development Institute (KWDI); respectively linked to the Ministry of Education and the Ministry of Gender Equality and Family. A new institute KICCE (Korea Institute of Child Care and Education) was established in 2005 to research early childhood education and care policy in a more unified way. Researchers specialised in ECEC policy in KEDI, KWDI and KIHASA (Korean Institute for Health and Social Affairs) have been assigned to work in the new institute.

In June 2004, the Ministry of Gender Equality took responsibility for services providing a child care focus, for children aged 0-6. This Ministry is charged with the establishment and mediation of plans for children's services, in particular the development of a public child care system. This is the result of a paradigm shift by government, from selective child care (which supports children from families with low income and with parents in the paid workforce), to general child care (providing equal opportunities to every young child). The Ministry's responsibility includes maintenance and revision of the Child Care Act and related laws; research on child care; establishment and delivery of various functions related to child care services, for example, subsidy standards and financial support; facilities standards; staff training and credentialing; child care curriculum; and support of child care information centres.

The MOE is responsible for kindergarten services with an educational focus for children aged 3-6 years, as well as for all other school services. The Ministry's major tasks include: the establishment and revision of the Early Education Act and related laws; the establishment and mediation of comprehensive plans for early childhood education; teacher training and qualifications management; the development and delivery of curriculum; the planning and delivery of free-education for 5-year-olds as well as children with special needs, and fee payment support for younger children targeting low-income families.

Within the remaining group of involved ministries, several departments are specifically engaged. These include the Office of Policy on Women within the Ministry of Government Administration and Home Affairs, the Office of Policy on Women within the Ministry of Agriculture and Forestry; and the Gender Equality Policy Division in the Ministry of Labour. These departments are engaged with child care policy and the new directions being led by the Ministry of Gender Equality and Family.

Private academic institutions for young children, called *Hakwon* (Learning Places), existed outside these administrative processes. In 2001 the National Assembly approved the educational functions of *Hakwons* although they are excluded from processes which allow the use of a government vouchers for free ECEC education, indicating that they are not official ECEC institutions in Korea and therefore not eligible for funding from government. In 2004, the Korean government offered voucher funding to the quality *hakwon* system (private learning academies), if providers accept the national kindergarten curriculum, kindergarten teacher certification, and the national supervisory and environmental regulations.

Context

Labour force rates: In 2004, the labour participation rate for women aged 15-64 was 53.9%, increasing from 49.9% in 1990. Of those, 11.9% work part-time, while 5.9% of men work part-time (OECD, *Employment Outlook*, 2005). In 2002, 68% of adults over 15 were in the workforce with 49.8% of women reported as taking part. Almost 78% of women in the workforce are married (Background Report, 2003), and carry the greatest burden of household work in addition to engagement in paid employment. This proportion has been increasing over time. Workplace culture and practice militate against the employment of women with young children. Just over 20% of Koreans live in double income environments, relatively small by OECD standards.

Parental leave: A system of parental leave was institutionalised in 2001 with the parental leave allowance and job protection. However, few working parents take up this leave as workplace culture does not encourage parental leave (not least for men), or family-friendly measures. In addition, large numbers of women are in casual employment and are therefore unable to access this leave. Furthermore, the allowance offered to parents taking leave is too low to sustain a family. Some commentators link the difficulties faced by young women seeking to raise a family with the low fertility rate (1.3) in Korea. The participation rate of women in the formal labour market continues to show an M shaped distribution for women in the period between age 25 and 34, the typical child-bearing age. Linked to the unsatisfactory nature of parental leave is the high demand for infant care services that appear inadequate both in environmental and pedagogical quality.

Access and provision

ECEC provision in Korea is predominantly private. In the child care sector covering children from birth to elementary school entrance, private services constitute 93.9% of provision. Approximately 21% of children 0-6 attend child care settings. These private services, both kindergarten and child care, are mainly run by not-for-profit or for-profit entities even if they legally appear as not-for-profit entities. In the kindergarten sector catering for children from 3-6 years, although there are more public (50.8%) than private (49.2%) kindergartens, "72% of the classes, 79% of the teachers and 78% of the enrolled children fall within the private kindergarten sector" (Background Report for Korea, 2003,

p. 30). In rural areas only, public kindergartens form over 50% of the enrolment. Although 59% of 3- to 6-year-olds and 10% of 0- to 2-year-olds in Korea make use of ECEC services, the total percentage of public child care provision and kindergarten is relatively low.

Rates of provision

0-3 years: Approximately 19.6% of infants and toddlers attend child care facilities. Of this group, 13% attend public child care facilities and 86.9% attend private centres. There is high, unmet demand for child care places for children between 0-3 years (see "parental leave" above).

3-5 years: Services are increasingly differentiated by age. Those children of age 3-4 who access services predominately receive child care programmes. Some 44.9% of 3-year-olds are in child care settings with a further 14.6% in kindergartens. Most of these children are in private facilities. At age 4, kindergarten participation increases to 29.7% of this age cohort and 36.7% in child care. A third of 4-year-olds do not obtain any place, although they may attend *hakwon* sports centres and other programmes.

5-6 years: At age 5, 78.9% of children are enrolled either in child care (31.7%), or kindergarten (47.2%).

Children with diverse needs

Children with disabilities: The Special Education Promotion Act accords free education to those with physical or mental handicaps. Older children with handicaps are screened and well catered for in special education schools although data on the overall number of such children are difficult to obtain. A relatively small number of ECEC facilities focus on the needs of very young children with special needs. About 1% (14 978 children) with special needs were enrolled in kindergartens and child care centres in 2005.

Children from low-income families: Although priority is given in cost-support structures to low-income families, this type of support does not alleviate the burden of parents who cannot find suitable places for their children. Approximately 18.8 % of families in 2005 received some support to purchase a place, having met strict criteria based on the number of family members, total income and total assets. Many kindergartens and child care facilities view government funding for a low-income family as insufficient to deter them from offering the place to the child of a family who can pay fees and extras.

Ethnic and bilingual children: Because immigration from other countries is not common, there is very little variation from the dominant primary culture.

Quality

Licensing and regulatory regimes: Kindergartens function under the Primary and Secondary Education Act (2002) and the Early Childhood Education Promotion Act (2001) and child care centres function under the Child Care Act (2001). However, since 1997 Korea has been under great pressure to rapidly expand its ECEC services. As a result, the system – with the exception of the public kindergartens – works on reported activity rather than through licensing and accreditation. The licensing of centres has become a simple process of notification whereby new child care services can start up by simply reporting their opening to the local child care office. Many private providers are said to have facilities that supply a smaller amount of space per child although public and private centres have the same legal requirements. With more focus being now given to high quality, there is some consideration at present to reverting to a more focused system of licensing. Systematic external evaluation of curriculum and pedagogy is limited in practice to kindergartens, which benefit from a school inspection system. Visits are made by local area superintendents twice per year.

Funding: Expenditure on pre-primary educational institutions (kindergartens only) as a percentage of GDP is 0.16%. 31.8% of this expenditure came from public sources and 68.2% from private sources including 65.1% from parental contributions. 2.2% of total expenditure on education is allocated to pre-primary whereas 4.8% of the children are enrolled at this level of education (OECD, *Education at a Glance*, 2005). The Background Report for Korea (2003) indicated that in 2002, government support of early childhood education and child care amounted to 44.6% of the total costs of ECEC, this allocation being 0.13% of GDP. Approximately 30% of this allocation derives from central government funds and the remainder from the sixteen local authorities. Local authorities have direct taxation powers, and obtain proportional augmentation of their funding from the national government.

Staffing: The staffing of ECEC varies according to the regulatory requirements. The main details are outlined in the overview above. Kindergarten teachers in public kindergartens, in addition to their early childhood qualification, must meet the requirements to be a public official. The level of adult support (teacher aide, assistant) available to teachers in ECEC programmes is unclear.

Training requirements: Fixed statutory requirements set the standards of qualification for early education in ECEC in Korea. Four levels of kindergarten qualification exist: principal, vice-principal, 1st grade teacher, and 2nd grade teacher. To be a 2nd grade teacher, one should have, at least, a two-year college diploma in early childhood education area. First grade teachers normally hold a four-year university degree in early childhood. 70% of kindergarten staff are 2-year college graduates and 30% are 4-year university graduates. In child care, staff may graduate with two- or four-year college diplomas, specialising in early childhood education or child welfare. Almost 60% of child care staff have two-year college diplomas, with a further 15% holding 4-year college awards. With one-year training in ECEC programmes, high school graduates or persons in tertiary education may also work in child care. Requirements are not set for assistants, who may be trained *in situ* as they work.

Work conditions: Although most staff work full-time, the exact percentage of part-time staff in ECEC settings is unknown. Statutory working hours are 44 hours, but many staff work longer hours. A statutory requirement exists to fund a minimum level of staff development and recommendations regarding annual hours of in-service training, for example, new kindergarten teachers must take 60 hours and child care teachers 40 hours of professional development every 3 years. In addition, a set number of days of further training are necessary when staff whish to be promoted, *e.g.* a level-2 teacher must take 30 days (180 hours) further training to gain level-1 status. The status of ECEC staff in non-school services is low. Compared with teachers in kindergartens, child care staff have longer contact hours (60 vs. approximately 40/week), greater responsibility, fewer holidays, less planning time and lower wages. Men are hardly represented in care services or pre-school. The Ministry of Gender Equality and Family wishes the participation of men in child care; to help nurture children in gender equality from the early stages and to support women and men in making home and work compatible.

Child-staff ratios: The Korean system focuses on space per child, facilities and equipment standards both for indoors and outdoors spaces, while cities and provinces recommend child-staff ratios for kindergartens. Nationally, group sizes for 4- to 6-year-olds, 3-year-olds and mixed-age groups are 25-30, 15-25 and 20-30 respectively. In child care facilities the child-staff ratios are: infants 3:1, 1 year 5:1, 2 years 7:1, 3 years 15:1, 4-6 years 20:1. Child care facilities including children with special needs must maintain a 5:1 ratio.

Curriculum and pedagogy: Korea has a National Kindergarten Curriculum that serves as a broad framework. It was first issued by the Ministry of Education in 1969 with new editions being developed about every five years. Specific guidelines for curricula vary according to the discretion of each city/provincial Office of Education. Local guidelines stipulate annual school-dates and hours, including the availability of extended- and full-day programmes, places in each district, special education provision, parent education and continuity arrangements with local elementary schools (Background Report, 2003). Although the curriculum clearly sets the scene for rich learning experiences, the OECD review team visiting in 2003 noted some centres using pre-set activities and colouring sheets downloaded from web-sites. In child care centres, a planning framework, based on nutrition, health, safety and community welfare, was issued by the Ministry of Health and Welfare in 1993. Again, the review team observed that thematic choice, activities and procedures in centres visited were generally based on teacher decisions, to the detriment of child agency and choice.

Monitoring, evaluation and research: National monitoring and reporting at population level is available in the education sector from two sources: the Annual Statistics on Education data-set; and Current State of Kindergarten. Workforce and child access details through these sources are publicly posted on the Web site of the Ministry of Education. Statistics on child care are available on a web-site through the Ministry of Gender Equality and Family. Hence, two separate sets of information are gathered. At the services level, there is no overall system to evaluate the quality of ECEC programmes.

Parent and community involvement: Families are encouraged to participate in services by becoming a volunteer assistant in some sessions or by taking part in parent education programmes. The Early Childhood Education Promotion Act allows volunteer assistants to receive 20 hours training and in turn, two assistants may work with classes having a child-adult ratio of 26:1 (Background Report for Korea, 2003, p. 90). Parent education programmes are encouraged in order to maximise the effects of ECEC, and enable kindergarten staff to share knowledge and skills on child development with parents. Na and Moon (*Integrating Policies and Systems for Early Childhood Education and Care: The Case of the Republic of Korea*, Paris, UNESCO, 2003) indicated that in 2002, 57% of parents reported participating in kindergartens. As most parent education is conducted during the day, many parents are not able to take part (Background Report for Korea, 2003).

OECD policy issues

Among the issues for policy attention identified in 2003 by the OECD review team for Korea were:

- *Place the best interests of children at the centre*: The perception of ECEC as a separate domain encourages Korean parents and providers to see this area as preparation for school. In this context, the review team encouraged emphasis on the participation rights and needs of young children.

● *Focus on a family-friendly society sustained by law and public policy*: The review team encourages the re-examination of this complex but critical area from a gender equity perspective, especially with regard to workplace culture, irregular *versus* formal employment, and flexibility in work practices for parents. It was thought that the public services, which are major employers of women, should take the lead.

● *Increase public funding and steering, and incorporate the quality private providers into the public system*: Although expenditure in this area is increasing steadily, the review team considered that low-cost solutions adopted to sustain a system of private service providers may not ensure a strong, high quality system in the long term. Certain high-quality, private forms of provision should be brought within the public network and funding system.

● *Rationalise the government management of early childhood services*: The team encouraged the Office of Government Policy Coordination to continue efforts to bring ministries together and work towards improving the integration of services at local level.

● *End the conceptual and training rift between education and care*: This conceptual division impacts strongly on the status and training of staff, especially child care professionals. Many practical issues are involved, including low public investment in young children, the presence of a large private sector which operates outside government financing and control, convenience and affordability for parents and the prevailing culture of education competition.

● *Further democratise the system through decentralisation and parent participation*: A proactive programme to engage parents in the life and organisation of centres could have a number of benefits, such as: promoting positive attitudes among parents to more active and creative learning contents and processes; fostering continuity between children's learning at home and in the early childhood centres; providing information and referrals to other support services; and supporting community involvement in early education and care matters.

● *Raise the quality of all programmes, including in the* hakwons: The review team encouraged staff development in team-work and quality improvement processes in all services, linking training, critical reflection and evaluation.

● *Establish a regular policy review/research cycle*: The team noted the research capacity already in place through government research institutes engaged in ECEC research. The establishment of a regular policy review cycle, linked to a planned research and evaluation agenda, was encouraged.

Developments

The transfer of child care administration from the Ministry of Health and Welfare to the Ministry of Gender Equality was enacted in June 2004. This change prompted positive responses from some sectors because it draws attention to the issue of equal opportunity for women in the labour market and in Korean society in general. However, others pointed out that the change does not make progress on the fundamental issue of cross-ministry collaboration and service integration at the field level, in the interests of children. In sum, direct collaboration between the education and care sectors needs to be encouraged.

Since the OECD review, significant progress has been made in the area of gender equality and parental leave – policies that are extremely important for the well-being of infants and families as a whole. Parental leave has been significantly extended and remuneration has increased.

In parallel, the past several years have shown rapid expansion of child care services. This is due to increased demand (increasing numbers of women do not wish to leave the workplace after the birth of children), but the growth in the percentage of children covered may also be explained by the significant decline in the total number of children.

Korea has also increased financial support for low-income families to access the services; extended opening hours to more than 12 hours of care every day; and loosened regulatory requirements. The latter has encouraged many private providers to enter the field, but has lowered quality. As a result, current policy has become more focused on quality assurance and improvement, although expansion still remains an imperative.

To address concerns over the quality of the child care centres, the Child Care Act of 2004 has been revised to introduce several mechanisms to ensure high-quality care. First, the government is moving away from a "report system" to a "licensing system" for running child care centres. Regulatory requirements for establishing and operating child care centres are to be more stringent. Each child care educator will take care of smaller number of children and working conditions will be strictly monitored by the government. A National Accreditation System for the child care centres is to be introduced from 2005 and a National Child Care Curriculum is now in development to be set in place by 2005. In early 2004, the Early Childhood Education Act (ECE Act) was established. Without an "independent" ECE Act in the past, the legal basis of early childhood education was totally bound to the Primary and Secondary Education Act. The new Act has brought into being a new system of Basic Education Law, consisting of 4 parts: Early Childhood Education, Elementary and Middle School Education, Higher Education, and Lifelong Education. The ECE Act also provides a legal foundation for spending public funds on private kindergartens and long-day programmes, and establishing Centres for ECE Promotion to conduct research, training, evaluation and other activities to develop programmes in ECE.

In Korea, investment in child care has been increasing by USD 100 million per year since 2002, and by USD 200 million in 2005, a 50% increase from 2004. The government also changed in 2005 its support system to child care from a direct subsidy system (payment of salaries and some capital costs) to support in the form of subsidies to parents to meet the costs of child care. In parallel, the budget subsidising kindergarten fees, including free education for 5-year-olds, was increased in 2005 by 150% compared to the budget of 2004. With this increase, 30% of 5-year-olds in kindergartens and child care centres will benefit.

A ground-breaking initiative has been taken by a Presidential advisory committee towards the integrated model of early childhood education and care – for example, in the form of the establishment of a joint research centre. In 2004, this committee made a president-addressed report on support for early childhood education and care and plans to provide a second report on how to combine child care and education in the second quarter of 2005. After the second report, government policy on Korean child care and education will comply better with the aim of raising healthy young children.

Mexico

Population: 101 m. **Fertility rate:** 2.27. **GDP per capita:** USD 9 370. **Children under 6 years:** 12.4 million, of whom about 1.5 million children come from indigenous language groups. The 3- to 6-year-olds number is 8.6 million.

Female labour force participation: 42.8% of women (15-64) participate, 27.6% of whom are in part-time employment (male part-time is 8.1%), but up to 50% of the eligible working population are reported to be engaged in the informal sector, often in conjunction with a formal job (Mexico Country Note, 2004).

Labour force participation rate of women with child(ren) under 6 years: The participation rate is calculated at about 50% in urban centres, but difficult to calculate because of the size of the informal sector.

Maternity and parental leave: Maternity leave only exists – fully paid 6 weeks leave before birth and 6 weeks after. Paid leave is available only to women working in the formal sector and enrolled in social security.

Average duration of parental leave: 12 weeks.

Compulsory school age: Compulsory primary schooling traditionally began at 6 years, but the Law of Obligatory Pre-schooling of November 2002 makes it obligatory for parents to send their children to a pre-school from the age of 3 years by 2009, and for each State to provide the necessary places.

Social expenditure: 11.8% of GDP. According to some estimates, 40%-60% of the population lives below the poverty line. 1 million families are reached by the *Opportunidades* anti-poverty programme. There are no educational subsidies for child care or pre-school programmes.

Child poverty rate: According to UNICEF figures, 27.7% after taxes and transfers (OECD average is 11.2%).

Funding of pre-primary educational services (ISCED Level 0): 0.61% of GDP (0.52% public and 0.08% private), that is, 9.7% of education budget but with 11.7% of education enrolments.

Unit cost per child (in USD converted using PPP): USD 1 643 (OECD, *Education at a Glance*, 2005).

Funding of services for children under 3: Missing. **Average ECEC costs to parents:** Missing.

Legal entitlement to a free service: 3 years from 2009, when obligatory pre-school for 3-year olds is scheduled.

Major service types and daily duration: Initial education (*educación inicial* or child care with an educational purpose) for children 0-3 years is divided into two approaches: centre-based, direct attention focused on the children themselves; and indirect attention programmes focused on parents and families. Pre-school education for children 3-6 years (*educación preescolar*): now becoming obligatory from age 3, operates 3-4 hours daily during the school year. Out-of-school provision (OSP) for children 6-12 years is rarely addressed as the emphasis is on expanding pre-school education.

Designation and professional qualifications of key staff: The multi-disciplinary nature and different auspices of initial education across Mexico, and its emphasis on protection, mean that workers come from diverse backgrounds in health, nutrition, psychology and other fields as well as from education. Centres frequently have certified doctors, nutritionists and psychologists. However, the great majority of people in charge of providing direct attention to children under 3 of age do not have professional training and their level of education varies from incomplete primary to university education and professional studies. Recently a specific course for training educators at this level has been set up in several States. This important initiative seems to have been welcomed as filling a gap but raises a question about the wisdom of separating training for educators in initial education and pre-school education.

In *educación preescolar*, the lead professionals are docents or teachers, who receive tertiary-level training in the 200 normal (teacher training) colleges across the country. This training delivers a university degree or *licentiatura* in child development and learning.

Rate of access to regulated services: Children 0-3 years: less then 3%; children 3-6 years: 69.3%.

Child-staff ratios: There is no official regulation governing child-staff ratios. For planning purposes, the Ministry of Education recommends a ratio of 25:1, and the overall ratio (dividing the number of children by the number of teachers) is 22:1. However, numbers well above 30 or even 40 children per educator can be observed in urban classrooms.

Auspices

For a country as large and diverse as Mexico, it is not possible to speak of one ECEC system. At present there are several sub-systems operating, with relatively loose coordination, under the auspices of different ministries, notably, Education (SEP) and Social Development (SEDESOL); under different social security institutes (IMSS and ISSSTE); and under other national auspices, *e.g.* the National System for Integral Family Development (DIF), the National Council for Educational Promotion (CONAFE), as well as private organisations. These sub-systems are distinguished by different historical origins and purposes, different target populations and age groups, as well as by their forms of organisation, norms and content. The situation is further diversified by the federal nature of the Mexican State with its 32 distinct administrative entities. A concentration of early childhood services is now being operated under the Law of Obligatory Pre-schooling (2002), which will make *educación preescolar* (pre-school education for 3- to 6-year-olds) obligatory by 2009, and place it under the auspices of the federal and state ministries of education.

Context

Governance: Mexico has a federal system of government. The country is divided into 32 "Federal Entities" or states, which in turn are divided into 2 443 municipalities incorporating a number of local governments (towns and agencies). The President of Mexico is elected every six years for one term only. The cabinet is made up of 20 heads of ministries (called Secretariats). Most Secretariats and programmes, including education and health, are decentralised. However, although administration is decentralised, power and policy is still concentrated at the centre and relationships tend to be hierarchical. The legal capacity accorded to States to raise their own revenues is very weak, limiting their independence. Most revenues accrue to the national government, which then redistributes funds to the States and municipalities according to a complex set of rules and processes of negotiation.

Cultural diversity: According to estimates by the *Instituto Nacional de Estadística Geografía y Informática* (INEGI), about 8% of the population (8 381 752 people) is classified as "indigenous" distributed among 64 ethnic groups. Of these, about 1.5 million are children under 6 years who live in families where an indigenous language is spoken. This extraordinarily rich cultural diversity sets a policy challenge for Mexico as the risks of dilution or even extinction of some indigenous cultures are real. The economic and educational circumstances in these families are very different from the national average, with literacy and income levels among indigenous groups much lower, while infant mortality rates are significantly higher.

Labour force rates: In 2004, the labour participation rate for women aged 15-64 was 42.8%, increasing from 35.7% in 1990. Of those, 27.6% work part-time, while 8.1% of men work part-time (OECD, *Employment Outlook*, 2005). However, some estimates place 50% of the labour force in the informal sector. In particular, women have to take part time, low paying jobs in the informal sector in order to balance their work and parenting roles, given the widespread scarcity of child care options. This means that many women do not enjoy the right to social protection and the child care benefits that accrue to workers in the formal sector. In Mexico, distribution of wealth is extremely uneven, and current estimates by the government indicate that 40% of the population (over 40 million people) live below the poverty line. The high levels of poverty mean that many families cannot afford the expenses for clothing and materials, let alone the fees and materials that are usually associated with participation in a child care or an early education programme.

Parental leave: Only maternity leave exists, and this leave is available only to women working in formal employment and enrolled in social security. Leave is fully paid 6 weeks leave before birth and 6 weeks after. The average duration of parental leave is 12 weeks but most Mexican mothers do not have the possibility of accessing remunerated leave.

Educational context

Education in Mexico, according to the Constitution (Article 3), is free and secular. Today, full responsibility for the organisation of basic education, adult education, rural community education, technical education and some other programmes has been decentralised to the States. Despite this decentralisation of administrative responsibility, the central government maintains normative, planning, evaluative and programming functions. Accordingly, although the federal system produces variation, as States and municipalities experiment with their own organisational and supervisory and training models or make adjustments to national programmes, the federal government retains control. The general guidelines for the system continue to be set out from the centre in a national programme created by each new government as it enters office for its six-year period. The educational programme of the present administration has placed increasing emphasis on improving the quality of education and on moderating inequities in the system.

Obligatory "basic education" in Mexico includes pre-school, primary school and lower secondary school, covering the period from age 3 to age 15. The Law of Obligatory Pre-schooling, November, 2002, backed strongly by the National Teacher's Union (SNTE), not only makes it obligatory for the State to provide pre-school education services for children 3 to 6 years of age when that is demanded, but also makes it obligatory for parents to see that their children attend a public or private pre-school. At the moment, private schooling accounts for about 10% of the basic education enrolment. The law sets a schedule for attaining universal enrolment: for children age 5 that should occur at the beginning of the 2004-05 school year, for age 4, in 2005-06, and for age 3, in the 2008-09 school year. It also states that pre-school teachers should have a professional preparation. Services for 0- to 3-year-olds are considered to be education but are not part of the basic education cycle.

Access and provision

Children from 0-3 years

Educación inicial, or child care with an educational purpose, caters for about 3% of children 0-3 years, mostly in the Federal District and other large administrative centres. Programmes are generally divided into programmes of *direct* (centre-based services for young children) or *indirect* attention (targeted at parents and families). Programmes of direct attention reach the fewest children (about 30% of the total), and then, in majority, the children of women holding a recognised job, often within the state sector. Small programmes organised by DIF and SEDESOL attempt to address the needs of children of working women without social security.

Most direct attention programmes are delivered by formal government CENDIs (Centres of Integrated Development), attached to the Mexican Institute for Social Security (IMSS), the Institute for the Social Security and Services of State Workers (ISSSTE), the Ministry of Education (SEP), universities, unions and other bodies. In CENDIs, care is provided for children from 45 days up to 4 years of age. CENDIs are generally well-regulated, with good resources and favourable child-staff ratios. In general, they use a curriculum elaborated by SEP, but as they are located predominantly within and staffed from the health and social security sectors, they tend to pursue a health/protective approach, although today with a growing emphasis on child development.

To a lesser degree, some smaller, more community-based centres for initial education (CEIs) have emerged, generally as activities of community-based organisations seeking community development. Such initiatives are essentially non-governmental and non-profit in origin and operation. Some are linked to political interest groups and in recent years, some few have grown out of the women's movement. It is not known how many children attend these centres, but a survey of the Federal District (Mexico Country Note, 2004) suggests that as many as a third of all services for children from 0-4 years in the District may be provided by social, community and private arrangements, *e.g.* more than 2 000 children are enrolled in community centres affiliated with COPOME, a network of community-based centres operated by *madres educadoras.* In principle, these centres are supervised by the local SEP district authority and receive some materials, but are expected to fund and manage themselves.

70% of enrolments in *educación inicial* occur in programmes of indirect attention, that is, programmes addressed to parents and families. Again, the largest of these programmes are governmental, *e.g.* the CONAFE-PRODEI programme (CONAFE is the National Council for Educational Promotion and PRODEI is the Programme of Non-formal Initial Education); the programme run by the National Institute for Adult Education (INEA); programmes embedded in the formal, direct attention programmes mentioned above, generally under the form of giving talks to parents; the publication of materials for parents by the Teachers' Union; and many others. There is little evidence of research on the impact of these different strategies.

Children 3-6 years

Educación preescolar or pre-school education for children 3-6 years is a governmental responsibility in Mexico. With the Law of Obligatory Pre-schooling of 2002, pre-school education is now part of obligatory basic education covering children from 3-15 years. Only about 10% of pre-schools are private. Responsibility for pre-schools resides in the Public Education Secretariat (SEP), and more particularly, between 1948 and 1992, was placed in the Office of Pre-school Education (*Dirección General de Educación Preescolar*). The sub-secretariat for basic education within SEP is responsible for pre-school education. It has charge of national currícula and programmes, as well as of the training and professional development of the teaching corps at all levels.

Three types of pre-school exist: general, indigenous and community pre-schools. Most children (88.1%) are enrolled in the general pre-school programme in both urban and rural areas. The indigenous pre-school programme, administered by a special division within the SEP, accounts for another 8.4% of children. Community pre-schools, offered by CONAFE to children in rural communities with less than 500 people, enrol the remaining 3.5%. As indicated in the previous section, children of pre-school age can also be found in initial education programmes administered by the National System for Integral Family Development (DIF), by the social security institutions (IMSS, ISSSTE), SEDESOL and others.

In general, pre-schools operate along age cohort lines, and open for 3 or 4 hours daily, five days a week. Some pre-schools offer a morning and an afternoon session. A special subset of pre-schools are labelled "mixed pre-schools" (*jardínes mixtos*) because they combine a regular pre-school session with care during a day-long programme. This pre-school model is not very extensive, limited mostly to the Federal District, with a few centres in other large cities.

A spurt of enrolments in pre-school took place during the period from 1975 to 1985, and then slowed from 1988 to the present growth rate of about 2% per year. The official statistics indicate:

* Although over 81% of children are enrolled at 5 years, only slightly over half the children (55%) of the total 3- to 6-year-old population is currently enrolled. Enrolment ratios are essentially the same for girls and boys.

* There is a relatively wide disparity among States in their enrolment ratios (65% to 113% for age 5; 2% to 53% for age 3). There is a tendency for the poorest States to have the lowest ratios although there are exceptions to this.

* Participation by the private sector in providing services is relatively low (10.2%), and has grown only slowly in recent years. It varies by State, reaching 30.4% in the Federal District and 24.5% in Nuevo Leon as contrasted with 2% in Oaxaca and 2.2% in Chiapas.

* The main responsibility for administering (but not funding) government-run pre-school programmes is at the state level (about 80%).

* The gap between present coverage and universal coverage of 3- to 6-year-olds, as required by the mandatory pre-school education law, is considerable. At present, 2 884 000 children are not enrolled. To include them would require the creation of new places for over 450 000 children per year for the next six years.

Rates of provision

0-3 years: In 2002-03, according to official statistics, a total of 682 996 children under 4 years of age were enrolled in direct and indirect initial education programmes, representing about 8% of the total. Programmes of direct attention enrolled 195 931 children or less than 3% of the age group with the remainder indirectly attended through non-formal parental education programmes.

3-6 years: Over 55% of 6.5 million children are currently enrolled (that is, 3.6 million children), with over 81% of children in pre-schools or primary school by the age of 5 years, predominantly in the general pre-school programme.

Children with diverse learning needs and disabilities: The General Education Law mandates the inclusion of children with special needs into regular classrooms. Data about the actual inclusion of these children is scarce. In present circumstances, the appropriate inclusion of these children is extremely challenged, as group sizes and child-staff ratios are high. As in all countries, far greater numbers of children are found in the category of children with additional learning needs, namely, children from low-income families, ethnic and bilingual children.

Children from low-income families: The growth rates in pre-school education over the last decade are generally higher for children in rural areas than in urban areas and for indigenous than for non-indigenous children. Although it is not possible to show with hard data, it is probable that growth rates in recent years are also higher for low-income than higher income populations. However, enrolments in rural areas and for indigenous groups are still considerably lower than for urban middle class and non-indigenous populations. The migration of low-income parents to agro-industrial areas, mainly in Northern States, has led to prolonged parental (usually paternal) absences and/or to uprooting of children, with attendant discontinuities in their participation in ECEC programmes. Special programmes for children of migrant workers have been established at migration destination.

Ethnic and bilingual children: About 8% of the population (8 381 752 people) is classified as "indigenous", distributed among 64 ethnic groups. Of these, 1 233 455 are children under 5 who live in families where an indigenous language is spoken. The economic and educational circumstances in these families are much poorer than the national average. The indigenous pre-school programme is administered by a special division within the SEP, and a new programme of inter-cultural education is also exploring ways to attend better to these groups. A variety of other programmes also exist for particular populations including indigenous children, those in small rural communities, children of migrant workers, children of women working in the informal sector, mothers in prisons, etc., but outreach is small compared to the number of children and families concerned. The National System for Integral Family Development (DIF), the social security institutions (IMSS, ISSSTE), SEDESOL and others administer these programmes.

Quality

Licensing and regulatory regimes: As noted above, diverse licensing and regulatory regimes exist in the different sub-systems of early childhood in Mexico, particularly in initial education (0-3 years). Under IMSS regulations, and given the multi-disciplinary nature of initial education, public formal centres employ staff from diverse backgrounds in health, nutrition, psychology and other fields as well as from education. These formal centres (generally catering for public employees), frequently have certified doctors, nutritionists and psychologists, which is not the case in the community services. Overall, "the great majority of people in charge of providing direct attention to children under 3 of age do not have professional training and their level of education varies from incomplete primary to university education and professional studies" (ISSSTE comment on the country report, p. 8). Some have attended a school for child care assistants but in many cases they begin without any formal qualification.

In pre-school education, although differences in licensing and standards exist between sub-systems and States, the situation is more standardised, given the strong role of the federal State in the public education system.

Funding: The Mexican economy follows a neo-liberal model in which the State increasingly sets norms, provides incentives for investment and ensures a minimal safety-net for the most indigent groups. Governmental expenditure is relatively low and priority given to the reduction of a large internal public debt. Where education is concerned, Mexico spends almost double on education (pre-primary, primary and lower secondary education) than OECD countries relative to total public expenditure, but in percentage terms of GDP, educational expenditure is just over average. Expenditure on pre-primary educational institutions as a percentage of GDP is more than 0.5%. Over 80% of this expenditure comes from public sources and almost 19% from parental contributions. Of the total expenditure on education, almost 10% is allocated to pre-primary whereas 11.7% of the children/students are enrolled at this level of education (OECD, *Education at a Glance*, 2005). With the Law of Obligatory Pre-schooling, enrolments in pre-primary are likely to grow exponentially, requiring much stronger investment from the State.

Training requirements: The 200 normal schools that provide training are evenly split between public and private institutions, and produce each year about 8 500 educators with a *licentiatura* in child development and learning. The new obligatory pre-school law calls for professional teachers in all pre-schools. This has reinforced a move to accredit teachers on the basis of experience as well as course work. A system of incorporation is being developed to certify teachers and caregivers on the basis of their experience (Agreement No. 286 of the SEP). Two proposals have been made, one emphasising examinations and one emphasising experience with observation of practice.

With regard to professional education, teachers who have been accepted into the *Carrera Magistral*, or teaching career, can take courses that are considered part of the career line and make them eligible for pay raises. Teachers also take courses that may or may not have a salary implication. In recent years, a general upgrading workshop (*Taller General de Actualización*) has been introduced in which all teachers are required to participate during three days prior to the beginning the school year.

Work conditions: Salaries for those involved in ECEC in Mexico are modest. In order to increase their earnings, some teachers work a double shift. Others take a second job outside education. Benefits are often limited unless staff are part of a union as is the case, for instance, with workers in the conventional centres of IMSS. Access to a professional career line is limited. It would appear that promotion in a teaching career line is not, at present, a competitive process related to merit. It is said that positions of director, supervisor or administrator in an educational authority are often influenced by political or union considerations.

Child-staff ratios: Ratios of 30 or more children per teacher are common, particularly in urban areas or in situations when a teacher is recognised as being effective. In some cases high ratios occur simply because there are too few teachers. The Teachers' Union does not accept child assistants in the classrooms.

Curriculum and pedagogy: The curriculum of reference for the last decade has been *Programa de Educación Preescolar* (PEP92). In the opinion of teachers, this programme lacked clear orientatons to allow the development of pedagogical work. In 2003, a new curriculum for pre-school was formulated – *Programa de Educación Preescolar 2004* – based on extensive consultation with teachers and directors of pre-schools. It was piloted during 2004-05 in a broad selection of pre-schools (general, indigenous and CONAFE). Six areas of development are chosen for pre-school children – Personal and social development; Language and communication; Mathematical thinking; Investigation and knowledge of the world; Artistic expression and appreciation; Health and physical development – with a series of competences to be achieved and their indicators defined in each area.

Monitoring, evaluation and research: The OECD PISA results show that learning achievement in the Mexican lower secondary education system is low. It may be inferred that this is also the case for pre-school education. Despite the significant investment in the field – which must be increased in coming years – outcomes for young children remain weak as numbers of children per trained teacher are high, and resources and materials seem scarce. Teacher education may also be in question as many teachers in pre-school classrooms still use an instructional approach. Greater attention to continuing teacher education, accompaniment and support may also be necessary. Until such issues are addressed, and full-day services become the norm, the system is unlikely to radically improve quality or meet the needs and aspirations of the upcoming generation of children.

Parent and community involvement: There are several governmental parental education programmes currently operating as well as some non-governmental initiatives. In general, however, parental involvement is restricted to helping with school maintenance, paying special assessments or providing information.

OECD policy issues

Among the issues for policy attention identified in 2003 by the OECD review team for Mexico were:

- *Purpose and concept of early childhood education and care*: The OECD review team recommended setting common goals for young children in both initial education and the pre-school, and defining clearly the basic competences thought to be necessary, for instance: to foster and maintain health; to relate well and empathetically to others; to learn how to learn; to participate socially in a democratic manner; to live in a plural society and celebrate differences; to understand and protect the environment; and to develop human potential through the mastery of diverse languages (linguistic, idiomatic, aesthetic, scientific, mathematic, physical, etc.). This work of definition should be based on broad consultation in which ministries, early childhood experts, teachers and parents are involved together.

- *Organisation and management*: Improve decentralisation processes while strengthening ECEC expertise both at central and state administrative levels. ECEC is a large and important sector in Mexican education, and pre-school administrative units, both at central and state levels, need reinforcement and stability. The organisation of regular ECEC consultations between SEP and the States could help to build greater coordination across the sub-systems.

- *Access and enrolment*: A number of challenges exist: to provide improved access for children under 3 of age, especially children of women working in the informal sector. Another major challenge will be to maintain the schedule set by the Law of Obligatory Pre-schooling, while improving quality. And thirdly, to moderate inequities in access across different social groups, and between states and regions.

- *Financing and funding*: To increase the level of financing and to streamline different funding channels, with particular attention to assisting low-income families.

- *Educational process and curricular reform*: Reduce the number of service types and establish common norms; safeguard the specificity of ECEC pedagogy (at present, the child-staff ratios incite an instructional model unsuitable for young children); provide training and support to teachers to move curricular innovations into action in the classrooms.

- *Training and working conditions of staff*: Strengthen initial and in-service training; integrate educators without formal qualifications who are representative of their communities, while maintaining quality standards; rethink supervision and accompaniment; establish a professional career line; promote early childhood professional associations and broaden choices of labour union affiliation.

- *Information – monitoring, evaluation and tesearch*: Strengthen information and monitoring systems; continue research initiatives linked to policy and programme priorities; support practitioner research; and increase the availability and use of information.

Netherlands

Population: 16.3 m. **Fertility rate:** 1.75. **GDP per capita:** USD 9 000. **Children under 6 years:** c. 1 000 000.

Female labour force participation: 69.2% of women (15-64) participate, 60.2% of whom are in part-time employment (male part-time is 15.1%).

Labour force participation rate of women with a child under 6 years: For mothers with children under 6: 71%, are employed and make up 79% of part-time employment (OECD, *Society at a Glance*, 2005); for mothers with children under 3: 66.4% work (EUROSTAT); 60% for two-parent families, 39% for single parent families.

Remunerated maternity and parental leave: 16 weeks of maternity leave paid at 100% of earnings, plus additional unpaid parental leave of 6 months for parents who work at least 20 hours.

Average duration of parental leave: 4 months.

Compulsory school age: 5 years.

Social expenditure: 21.8% of GDP (2001). **Child poverty rate:** 9.8% after taxes and transfers (UNICEF, 2005) (OECD average is 11.2%).

Funding of pre-primary educational services (ISCED Level 0): 0.38% of GDP (0.37% public and 0.01% private), 7.5% of education budget with 10.6% of enrolments.

Unit cost per child (in USD converted using PPP): USD 4 923 (OECD, *Education at a Glance*, 2005).

Type and funding of services for children under 4 years: Since 2004, child care has changed from a supply-side system funded by (local) government to a market system funded by government (tax credits), companies and parents. The level of funding is not available.

Average costs to parents: For child care services as a whole c. 44%. Depending on income, the range of contribution is 3.5% to 100%.

Legal entitlement to a free service: At 4 years. No entitlement to child care.

Major service types and duration: Day nurseries providing full day care for the work year for children from 3 months to 4 years; pre-school playgroups offering developmental activities to young children generally on a sessional basis, but sometimes full-day; pre-primary education for 4- to 6-year-olds on a half-day basis for the academic year; out-of-school care (OSP) for 4- to 12-year-olds during the work year; child minders (family day care), sometimes supervised by agencies, who provide care to children from 0-12 years either in their own home or in the child's home. Except for child-minding, all these services may be provided at one site in multi-functional community schools.

Rate of access to regulated services: Children 0-3 years: 22.5%; 2.5-4 years: 89%; 4-6 years: 100%. Most services are part-time or are used part-time.

Designation and qualifications of key staff: In child care, most directors of centres have an HBO (4-year tertiary award). Other staff have an SPW-3 (a 3-year vocational training in general social-pedagogic work) or an MBO (senior secondary level vocational qualification of 2-3 years). A further possibility is an SPH, vocational training specifically focused on developmental challenges and family dysfunction. Pre-primary staff are teachers with a 4-year tertiary diploma from primary teacher training colleges, specialised in teaching of 4- to 8-year-old children.

Child-staff ratios: Children 0 years: 4:1; 1-2 years: 5:1; 2-3 years: 6:1; 3-4years: 8:1; 4-12 years: 10:1.

Maximum group size: Average group size in registered child care 0-4 years:12:1; average group size in primary education 4-7 years: 20:1, 8-12 years: 27.7:1.

Auspices

ECEC policy and provision in the Netherlands has traditionally been a shared responsibility between national, provincial and local governments. The national government takes on those tasks that can be more efficiently organised at national level, *e.g.* legislation, rules and regulations, developing policy frameworks, formulating national standards and attainment targets, promoting innovations, national monitoring and evaluations of quality. It is not clear yet how these functions are affected in the new deregulated system of child care (see below).

At central government level, three ministries have had major responsibility for young children: the Ministry for Social Affairs and Employment; the Ministry of Health, Welfare and Sport (VWS); and the Ministry of Education, Culture and Science (OCW). The Ministry of Education, Culture and Science (OCW) is responsible for the whole educational system, including access, equity and quality for all young children from 4 years onwards. Since 2002, the Ministry for Social Affairs and Employment is responsible for child care policy, including the recent Child Care Act (2005). The Ministry of Health, Welfare and Sport (VWS) has responsibility for the Welfare Act which includes pre-school playgroups for 2- to 3-year-olds. Child care and out-of-school provision are located, however, at local authority level, with some collaboration – particularly in the case of child minder organisation – at regional level. 90% of local authorities organise these services. The Ministry of VWS is also responsible for youth health care.

Primary education, under the auspices of the Ministry of Education (OCW), includes children from 4-6 years (compulsory schooling begins at 5 years but children remain in the early years cycle up to 6 years). Freedom of education in the Netherlands means that school boards (public or private) are equally funded when they subscribe to the Primary Education Act. Choice of staff, teaching materials and pedagogy is a school level responsibility. In addition to the different levels of local government, other major bodies are expected to play a role in decision-making and implementing early childhood policy, viz. the employers, unions, parents, youth and professional organisations.

A fundamental change has taken in the child care sector under the present government which has placed child care firmly in the field of Social Affairs and Employment (SZW).

Context

Labour force rates: In 2004, the labour participation rate for women aged 15-64 was 69.2%, increasing from 52.4% in 1990. Of those, 60.2% work part-time, while 15.1% of men work part-time (OECD, *Employment Outlook*, 2005). In 2004, only 26.2% of women 15-64 years were in full-time paid employment, while 68.1% of men of the same cohort were in full-time, paid employment. Instead of the "two-times three-quarters" work share between men and women announced during the first OECD review in 1999, a "one-and-a-quarter" arrangement has emerged as the dominant pattern (OECD, *Babies and Bosses*, 2002). Mothers with a youngest child under 6 years had an employment rate of 71% in 2002, and constituted 79% of part-time employment (OECD, *Society at a Glance*). In 2004, mothers with children under 3 had an employment rate of 66.4%.

Parental leave: 16 weeks (4 months) parental leave at 100% earnings is available, plus additional unpaid, partial leave of six months (if parents work at least 20 hours per week), a regulation among the lowest in European Union countries. Family-friendly work policies have been introduced, with initiatives to bring flexibility into the length and timing of work hours.

Access and provision

Three "circles of provision" have been created around the child and family: *i)* general provision for young children aged 0-6 years; *ii)* interventions towards families and children who need special attention; and *iii)* specialised or intensive forms of help for children with special education needs (SEN). General provision includes child care in centre-based day nurseries for 0-4 years (generally full-day for the work year), family day care for children of 0-12 years old (full-day for the work year) and out-of-school care for the 4- to 12-year-olds (sessional services for the work year provided in 90% of municipalities). Kindergartens, pre-schools and pre-primary education services operate either half- or full-day for the academic (school) year. Two-thirds of schools are privately managed, but all are fully publicly funded. Each type of provision has its own aim, background, funding system and governing structure.

Rates of provision

0-4 years: Whereas in 2001 22.5% of these children were in services, in 2003 access and usage of the registered services had increased to 29%. Most children remain in the care of parents, assisted by close family[1] and partial use of different services. From 2.5 to 4 years, some 89% of children in this cohort are engaged in child care, playgroup or early learning services, a 9% increase since 2001. Playgroups are the most popular form of provision for 2.5- to 4-year-olds in the Netherlands. They are usually established by private bodies with the legal status of foundations. Many of these foundations are independent; others are part of a larger co-operative structure, frequently a child care organisation or general welfare foundation. Children usually visit the playgroups twice a week (2-3 hours per visit) to play with their peers or participate in an intervention programme.

4-6 years: Pre-primary education is an integrated phase of education within primary education or the basic school. Compulsory school age is 5 years, although from the day children turn 4 years they can be enrolled, free of charge, in a primary school. Dutch parents welcome early education and enrol 98% of all 4-year-olds in pre-primary classes where children are present 4 to 6 hours daily.

In 2003, out-of-school care services were accessed by 14% of pre-schoolers, double the proportion achieved in 2001.

Children with diverse needs

Children with disabilities: 5% of children 0-6 years are reported to have organic disabilities. With a growing awareness of the benefits of including children with light handicaps in ECEC, more children are being integrated into mainstream services (80%). 20% of this designated group are in special services. Subsequent special education is well funded, though often apart.

Children from low-income families: The child poverty rate is 9.8% after taxes and transfers (UNICEF, 2005). Low-income families are supported in various ways, for example through the scheme for subsidising child care costs for (single) parents on low income or welfare support. This enables the parent to train for re-entry to the labour market. Ethnic minority groups are over-represented in this category.

Ethnic and bilingual children: The immigrant population is significant in the Netherlands: 12% of children between 0-5 years are from ethnic or bilingual backgrounds, mainly concentrated in the large cities. 25% of children 0-6 years are considered to have particular educational needs originating primarily from socio-economic, cultural and/or linguistic factors. Youth Health Centres reach almost all families with an infant. Hence, they are given the task of identifying children and families with social risks and guiding them to services such as ECEC programmes for children at risk. Where schools manage a certain percentage of children from lower SES or from ethnic minority groups, additional funding is provided to recruit additional staff, either to lower the group size or ensure specialist assistance. Large investments have been made in both sectors to improve general quality and to integrate more effectively children at risk.

Current Netherlands policy aims at 50% participation of these children in ECEC programmes from 2.5- to 6-year-olds, additional funding being made available for this purpose since 2000 (EUR 110 million since 2002). This funding is not to support the basic provision. Rather, it is to increase the child-staff ratio (15:2 in pre-school, playgroup and the primary years 1 and 2), double the hours spent by at-risk children in pre-school playgroups, and ensure trained staff and professionally designed programmes in special pre-school classes for disadvantaged children 2.5-4 years old, such as *Kaleidoscope* (based on *High-Scope*), and *Pyramide* (based on *Success for All*). Government and local authorities make important investments in social integration and targeted educational programmes.

Quality

Within the context of the new Child Care Act, the quality control mechanisms employed previously in the Netherlands, especially by municipalities with regard to child care facilities, are no longer operational. According to SZW:

> *The new Act no longer prescribes specific quality requirements in relation to the child care centre. This allows the sector more room to determine its own regulations in order to ensure that child care facilities satisfy the legal requirement to provide responsible child care. Operators must make an inventory of safety and health risks themselves. They must also be able to demonstrate that they pay attention, among other things, to the number of children per supervisor, the size of the group and the educational background of staff members.*

Furthermore, the child care centre operator may only deviate from the advice of the Parents' Committee if he/she provides a written explanation for doing so.

With the Child Care Act, the minister wishes to stimulate the transformation of the child care sector into a sector with greater scope for market forces and to provide parents with more freedom of choice. By reducing the number of regulations, the administrative burden on operators will decrease, something which could also have a favourable effect on the costs of child care.

Licensing and regulatory regimes: In January 2005, local policies on child care quality were replaced by the general regulation in the new Child Care Act requiring basic standards on health and safety, information to parents, and attention by providers to certain fundamental quality indicators. In future, basic quality standards are formulated through self-regulation in the form of a covenant between providers organisations and the parents organisation. A parent board is required to support and monitor progress and the local municipality is responsible for regular health and safety inspections. In the education sector (provision for 4- to 6-year-olds), quality control is ensured by the school inspectorate, which undertakes systematic and holistic analyses of whole schools, noting in particular the ways in which schools give account of their pedagogical policy to parents.

Funding: Expenditure on pre-primary educational institutions as a percentage of GDP is 0.38. Some 96.7% of this expenditure came from public sources and 3.3% from private sources including 0.6% parental contributions (OECD, *Education at a Glance*, 2005). According to the latter report, 7.5% of total expenditure on educational institutions is allocated to pre-primary whereas 10.6% of the children/students are enrolled at this level of education. Fees for 0-3 services are primarily set by the market whereas services for 4- to 6-year-olds are within primary education and free of charge. The funding of child care is a mix of public and private. Private provision is primarily for-profit and public provision is provided predominately by other bodies subsidised by government.

Unlike most other countries, employers in the Netherlands are important stakeholders in child care, either setting up their own child care services or, more usually, purchasing or renting "company places" in child care centres. Under the new Child Care Act, public subventions are directed primarily to parents. Parents contribute 44% of overall costs to the child care system as a whole. Individual levels of contribution (between 3.5% and 100%) depend on household income under the new child care law of 2005. Government expenditure on ECEC has expanded from EUR 617 m in 2003 to EUR 800 m in 2005, the growth being related to the growing use of child care.

The new Child Care Act has reformed the funding system. "Demand-side funding" provided to parents by the central government and employers replaces the previous "supply-side, operational funding" provided by the municipal authorities to services. According to the SZW Web site:

The Child Care Act provides for a new method of financing child care. The bill assumes that parents, employers and government collectively bear the costs of child care. The expectation is that in 2005 68% of employees will be able to receive a contribution for child care from their employer. The target figure is 90% by 2008. The government will give partial compensation to parents who do not receive a contribution from their employer. From 2006, the compensation scheme will be gradually dismantled. From 2009, only parents with an income of up to EUR 45 000 will retain the right to partial compensation.

Through the Tax Department, parents will receive directly the amount that the government contributes to child care. The direct subsidising of facilities will cease as a result. Child care facilities will compete in terms of price and quality, since parents will be able to opt for a different care establishment if the price is too high or if the quality is found wanting. In sum, child care organisations will increasingly be subject to market forces.

Staffing and training requirements: Children in registered child care services for 0-4 years and out-of-school care services for 4+ years are cared for by a variety of providers and staff. ECEC workers in contact with children are required to have, in principle, a higher professional qualification, either an HBO for directors (four-year tertiary, non-university qualification) or an MBO for other staff (a senior secondary level, vocational education qualification of 2-3 years). For playgroups the quality regulations, including staff qualifications, are set by the municipalities. In the education sector, teaching staff are trained for four years in the PABOs or primary teaching training colleges as polyvalent teachers who can work in the entire 4-12-year age range. They take, however, a specialisation for either the age group 4-8 years or 5-12 years. Regardless of what class they teach, all teachers are now paid at equal rates.

Work conditions: The status of staff, almost wholly female, has traditionally been low, particularly in the day care and playgroup sector. There have been acute recruitment problems and staff shortages, but efforts are now being made to address the issue through raising wages and improving secondary labour conditions. More attention is being given to investment in multi-functional accommodation so that more integrated services might be achieved. This gives increased opportunity for staff to work across two types of provision, for example by working as a classroom assistant during school hours (appointed by the school board) and as an out-of-school carer after school hours (appointed by the local child care service). These combined jobs are stimulated by three policy interventions: *a)* co-financing incentive funds; *b)* harmonising labour conditions; and *c)* integrating training programmes.

Child-staff ratios: In the new Child Care Act, no child-staff ratios have been fixed. The Act speaks simply of "well-considered care". This implies that child care should contribute to a sound and balanced development of children in a safe and healthy environment. The Act stipulates some concrete quality regulations, such as risk assessment of child centres, the use of Dutch language and the establishing of a parent council, as well as global quality requirements, which include group size. Two national child care organisations and the lobby-organisation for parents in child care have made the criteria for quality more concrete through a quality covenant. In principle, these agreed quality criteria will become a basis for inspection and the monitoring of quality.

Curriculum and pedagogy: National curricula do not exist in the Netherlands at any level of education. However, a co-ordinated curriculum effort has been made over the past decade to improve the quality of early childhood education for 2.5- to 6-year-olds from low SES and ethnic minority backgrounds. Two curriculum programmes have been validated for use (*Pyramide* and *Kaleidoscope*) and a third programme is under evaluation. A group of expert advisors work with teachers across the Netherlands to determine effective pedagogies for children from these backgrounds. In addition, the expert centre for teaching the Dutch language, *Expertise Centrum Netherlands,* developed protocols in 2004-05 to improve mastery of the Dutch language within validated curriculum programmes. Many municipalities also have policies to raise the awareness of parents about the importance of ECEC for their children.

Monitoring, evaluation and research: Monitoring processes for family day care and crèche under the Child Care Act involve registration by the municipalities and annual health and safety checks. Public pre-primary education monitoring is more substantive, requiring in addition curriculum standards, in-service training and regular pedagogical supervision by an accredited supervisory body. Investment in information systems management is also progressing in education, and results are expected from the introduction of a "pupil number" in the education system. This identifier will enable tracking of the progress of each child through their school career, the resulting generalised data pool enabling review of achievement, disaggregated by particular categories – for example, gender, SES, special needs. This system records the child's antecedent experience of ECEC services and will be fully operational in 2007. Linkage of this data system to a targeted research and evaluation plan is being considered.

Parent and community involvement: Parent engagement is promoted both in policy and programming. A special campaign was launched in 2002 to inform and stimulate parents from ethnic minority groups to enrol their children in pre-school playgroups, especially in playgroups that offer intensified and quality programmes. Preventative health care programmes also guide parents towards the use of ECEC services. The new Child Care Act requires all provisions to have a parent board.

OECD policy issues

Among the issues for policy attention identified (in 1999) by the OECD review team were:

- *Coherence and co-ordination of services*: During the early years of decentralisation, the co-ordination and coherence of the system were often stretched in terms of management, training and categorisation of personnel, equitable access and quality control.

- *Understandings of childhood and early education*: During the early 90s, ECEC was mainly seen from a protection and care angle. Progress is being made, particularly in playgroup and early primary school provision, where a number of improved educational programmes have come on stream. However, the institutional division between care and education still remains, leading to quite separate treatment of infant/toddlers and "pre-primary" children.

- *Greater support to parents*: The funding of Dutch ECEC services relies heavily on parents in terms of fees, opportunity costs and daily time devoted to children, a contribution borne in particular by mothers. The review team recommends further attention to gender issues. A reduction of costs to parents may also be necessary, particularly to encourage greater use of services by low-income parents. The parental contribution to child-rearing could further be supported by expanded maternity and parental leave and the provision of more out-of-school care.

- *Staffing and training*: Imminent staff shortages may be explained by a combination of factors, but within the care sector, relatively low status, uncertainty about career paths, poorer work conditions and wages, are issues that merit attention.

Developments

The Child Care Act heralds a shift in direction for ECEC service provision in the Netherlands. This Act brings in a demand-driven system where parents buy child care in the market and the central government supports the demand by offering a means-tested subsidy. In addition, employers are expected to pay one third of the costs of child care for their employees. The supply of services will be at the discretion of market forces, but no doubt, targeted programming sustained by public funding will be continued. It is evident that this new experiment in the organisation of child care will be watched closely by other OECD countries.[2]

Another development in the Netherlands has been better collaboration between schools and youth care institutes. At the national level, marked division of responsibilities for child care, education, youth health care and pre-school playgroups remain. The appointment of a High Commissioner for Children and Youth Policy in late 2003, by the ministers who share responsibility for children and youth policy, has brought down some of the legislative and administrative barriers encountered by local policy makers in their efforts to offer children more cohesive services. In the coming years, the High Commissioner for Children and Youth Policy will advise the government on measures to be taken in order to offer families and children a smooth and high quality continuum of services in early care and education.

Another striking feature of Dutch early childhood policy has been the further development of research and the intensive trialling of new curricula and programmes. A number of such programmes, including intensive pre-primary early education programmes, have been mainstreamed to the advantage of children both in school and pre-school services.

Dutch attention to diversity and equity issues has also continued. The education sector, in particular, continues to do excellent work in providing educational programmes for ethnic and disadvantaged young children before they enter pre-primary education. The time may now be ripe to bring playgroups and pre-primary schools together. As suggested during the first OECD review, governments in the future may wish to consider bringing child care centres, playgroups and pre-primary together into one universal system that ensures, with equity, continuity of care and education for all children.

Notes

1. According to data for 2003, 35% of young children were in (partial) unpaid care by grandparents, 13% in unpaid care by non-family members, 3% in paid care by grandparents, 15% in paid care by non-family members and 5% in formal home care.

2. In Chapter 5 of this text, the analysis of funding modalities suggests that market systems in ECEC tend to generate inequalities of service provision, unremarkable quality, class and ethnic segregation, and the fragmentation of services. This may be due to the newness of the approach, and the inexperience of administrations in creating the necessary safeguards. Although much work has been undertaken in recent years in the United States in trying to control these effects in the marketised parts of the education system, no real solution to these drawbacks has yet been found, except more regulated partnerships between public authorities and providers.

Norway

Population: 4.57 m. **Fertility rate:** 1.83. **GDP per capita:** USD 35 000 in 2003. **Children under 6 years:** 358 563.

Female labour force participation: 75.7% of women (15-64) are employed, of whom 33.2% are in part-time employment, compared to 10.3% of men (OECD, *Employment Outlook*, 2005).

Labour force participation rate of women with children under 6 years: In 2003, 65% of employed women with children 0-6 years worked full-time and 35% worked part-time.

Maternity and parental leave: Since 2005, 43 weeks at 100% of earnings or 53 weeks of leave paid at 80% of earnings. 5 weeks leave for fathers are also available. In 2004, 89% of the fathers who were entitled to a father's quota (four weeks), made use of this right. 16.6% of the fathers made use of more than four weeks parental leave. Mothers took the rest of the parental benefit period, when families made use of all then 42/52 weeks.

Average duration of parental leave: Statistics are not available on the average duration of parental leave.

Compulsory school age: 6 years (for the first four grades, duration of schooling is 4 hours per day).

Social expenditure: 23.9% GDP. **Child poverty rate:** 3.4% after taxes and transfers (OECD average is 11.2%).

Total educational expenditure: 6.46% of GDP. **Legal entitlement to a free service:** From 6 years.

Funding of services for children 0-6 years: NOK 17.3 billion, or USD 2.768 billion dollars were expended by the State in 2003, that is 1.7% of GDP. This figure does not include the Child Benefit which remunerates parents who care for their child at home. For a child under 3, the annual unit cost for the State in the *barnehager* amounted to EUR 9 773 per annum; for a child between 3-6 years, EUR 5 355 per year.

Major service types and duration: *Familiebarnehager* or family day care (FDC) and *Barnehager* (kindergartens) offer either half-day or full-day, full year services for children 0-6 year. *Skolefritidsordningen* (SFOs) or out-of-school provision (OSP) or "day care facilities for school children" are available before and after school, during the academic year for class levels 1-4 (up to class level 7 for children with special needs).

Average costs to parents (ECEC): For children 0-6 years, parental fees are now capped at no more than 20% of costs. For out-of-school time provision (OSP) for children 6-10 years, municipalities decide the parental share of costs for this service.

Rate of access to regulated services (2003): Children 1-3 years: 48%; children 3-6 years: 88%; OSP for children 6-10 years: 68.2% of 6-year-olds, the figure declining after that age. The overall percentage access for 6- to 10-year-olds is 53%.

Designation and qualifications of key staff: In family day care (FDC), owner-managers are not required to be qualified pre-school teachers, but regulated FDC has to be supervised by a qualified pre-school teacher on a regular basis. *Barnehager* are staffed by *pedagogiske ledere* (pedagogues) with a 3-year tertiary college degree, and by assistants with a 2-year, post-16 apprenticeship. However, assistants do not necessarily need a diploma, and only one-third of staff are trained pedagogues. Qualifications of staff in SFOs are not regulated by national law, and municipal authorities or school owners decide which level of qualification is necessary, according to local needs, When the SFO is provided by a school, the school's head master/mistress should normally be the head of the SFO as well. The overall percentage of qualified staff in services comes to 32%.

Child-staff ratios: For children 0-3 years, the ratio is 7-9 children per trained pre-school pedagogue when children attend more than six hours per day. For children 3-6 years, the ratio is 14-18 children per trained educated pedagogue, but there can be several non-trained staff also present. In leisure-time facilities (SFOs) for children 6-10 years, there is no limit, but factual information shows an average of 8.6:1.

Maximum group size: Maximum group size is not regulated but decided at local level.

Auspices

In Norway, responsibility for development of ECEC legislation, and for funding and policy has been with the Ministry of Children and Family Affairs (BFD) up to the end of 2005. The Ministry of Education and Research will now have responsibility for early childhood education and care, as well as for schools, out-of-school care and the training of pedagogues. At regional level, the county governor now has responsibility for both schools and ECEC.

In recent years, greater administrative responsibility has been devolved to the 19 counties and 435 *kommuner* or municipalities in Norway, which for the most part, have unified school and early childhood services into one department resulting in closer cooperation and coordination. The county governor administers the state grants to *familiebarnehager* (family day care), *barnehager* (kindergarten), and *apen barnehager* (open kindergartens or drop-in centres for parent and child, led by a trained pre-school pedagogue). The county informs and supports the different municipalities in the region on ECEC questions and policy. This involves planning and building ECEC places according to local need, approving of new facilities, supervising and inspecting new services. The municipalities can choose either to own and administer the services themselves or to contract private owners to operate ECEC. There is a national regulatory framework for *barnehager*, the *Barnehager Act*, 1995. A revised *Barnehage Act* entered into force on 1st January 2006. A new Framework Plan was introduced by the Ministry on 1st March 2006 and enters into force on 1st August. The national *Framework Plan for Barnehager* provides guidelines to *barnehager* concerning values and objectives, curricular aims, and pedagogical approaches.

Context

Labour force rates: In 2004, the labour participation rate for women aged 15-64 was 75.7%, increasing from 70.7% in 1990. Of those, 33.2% worked part-time, while 10.3% of men worked part-time (OECD, *Employment Outlook*, 2005). Mothers with a youngest child under

6 years had an employment rate of 18% in 2003, of whom 65% were working full-time and 35% were working part-time.

Parental leave: Since 1993 Norway has offered a universal 42 weeks of parental leave at 100% of earnings, or 52 weeks at 80%. From 1st July 2005 the period was lengthened with one week to 43/53 weeks. Mothers must take three weeks prior to the birth-date and a further six weeks after birth. Where both mother and father qualify for the parental leave entitlement and the mother has been in paid employment of at least half-time, a one month use-it-or-lose-it paternity leave is included in the parental leave quota. From 1st July 2005 the paternity quota was increased by one week, to five weeks in total. In 2004, 89% of the fathers who were entitled to a father's quota (four weeks), made use of this right, and 16.6% of the fathers made use of more than four weeks parental leave. Mothers took the rest of the parental benefit period, when families made use of all the 42/52 weeks. Time accounts are also used to enable parents to combine partial parental leave with flexible work hours, enabling a parent working part-time to benefit from parental leave for two years or more. The parental benefit is calculated on the income of the parent who takes the leave. If the parent's income exceeds 6 times the National Insurance basic sum (in 2005, NOK 364 194 annual) parental benefit does not cover the additional amount. In 2002, 77.8% of women giving birth qualified for parental benefit. Women who do not qualify receive a lump sum grant (in 2005, NOK 33 584/EUR 3 981/USD 4 852).

Access and provision

The operating hours and annual duration of services vary according to service type. Some 47% of *barnehager* are public (municipal) and cater for 57% of children using the service. Private *barnehager* are more numerous but smaller, and cater for 43% of children, but provision in private kindergartens is growing, and by 2005 was the majority provider. Provision rates are as follows.

Rates of provision

0-1 years: Care is predominantly home care by parents. Only 3% of children are in centre-based care.

1-3 years: Based on Norwegian government survey data, 42% of this group are cared for full-time by parents and 48% are cared for in ECEC regulated services. Given the high participation of mothers in the workforce, it may be presumed that some parents are choosing to use family and informal child-minding. The goal of the Ministry is to have full coverage (meeting demand) for pre-school children by the year 2006.

3-6 years: 88% of all children in this age group are cared for in ECEC services.

Out-of-school time provision is generally available for children aged 6-12 years. The highest level of usage is made by children aged 6 years in the first year of school, 68.2% of whom access out-of-school care. The overall percentage access for 6- to 10-year-olds is 53%.

Children with diverse needs

Children with disabilities: Children with disabilities have a priority right to services provided it is deemed by an expert that the child will be able to benefit from attending the day care institution. In 2003, nearly 2.5% of children in *barnehager* had a disability, and 3.2% received additional support.

Children from low-income families: The child poverty rate in Norway is 3.4% after taxes and transfers, compared to the OECD average of 11.2%. Because of effective redistribution policies, targeting low-income groups is not a focus for ECEC policy although additional educators may be supplied to centres receiving more migrant or low-income children. The *barnehage* is considered to play an important role in terms of preventive child welfare. In cases of children living in at-risk circumstances, places are fully funded by municipalities. Supports are provided also to enable *barnehager* accommodate children with disabilities, children from low-income families and bilingual children.

Ethnic and bilingual children: An indigenous ethnic group, the Sami, constitute 1.7% of the Norwegian population. Sami language kindergartens are funded generously whenever there is a concentration of Sami families. New immigrant groups constitute 3% of the population, with 28 000 children in primary schools (just less than 6% of school population) registered as non-Norwegian-speaking children. In the 1- to 6-year-old population, 7.8% of children (not including children speaking Danish, English or Swedish as their first language) do not have Norwegian as their first language. Of this group, approximately 50% are in ECEC services (2003).

Quality

Licensing and regulatory regimes: Municipalities are responsible for the licensing regimes for family day care and ECEC services and must ensure that all services are registered and undergo annual health and safety checks. Ownership, purpose of the institution (*e.g.* the particular pedagogical or religious purpose), criteria for access, fees, opening hours and physical spaces are considered as part of licensing. Municipalities have responsibility for supervision and authorisations.

Funding: Total expenditure on ECEC, amounted in 2004 to 1.7% of GDP for children 0-6 years old. In 2004 Parliament set a parental fee of NOK 2 750/month (or EUR 326/ USD 397) for an ordinary place in ECEC comprising a full-day or 41 hours or more per week. Part-time places are charged in proportion. Since 2005, fees should not exceed 20% of the cost of services – at the moment a maximum of EUR 280 per month. The costs to the State are as follows: the unit cost for a child under 3 amounts to EUR 9 773 per annum; for a child between 3-6 years, EUR 5 355 per year (Moser, personal communication, 2005). These costs, in so far as we can judge, do not include the Cash Benefit home care allowance (see below) or the 20% or so of fees that parents contribute. In centres, a separate charge is levied for meals. Municipalities have the duty to provide funding to their own services and to private providers. They also provide subsidies for additional places for families where more than one child is in ECEC, even when the children participate in different ECEC services within the municipality. In addition to family allowances and lone parent (22% of families) allowances, all parents are allowed tax deductions to cover care and kindergarten costs. There is also a Cash Benefit scheme that provides a cash grant to a parent who cares for a child at home (the intention of the policy), or part-time home and part-time regulated ECEC, or who places a child in an ECEC context that does not receive state grants (*e.g.* with a child minder or relative). At the time of writing (2005), the amount of the full-time grant is about USD 545 per month.

Staffing: 35% of the contact staff in Norwegian *barnehager* are qualified ECEC pedagogues. This is according to the personnel norms stated in the law. There are regional shortages of trained personnel but at the national level, forecasts of student enrolment in the training colleges suggest that sufficient numbers of personnel will be trained to meet the demands of current regulations. The percentage of tertiary trained pedagogues is currently low compared to Denmark (60%) or Sweden (51%).

Training requirements: Heads and pedagogues in ECEC have 3-year tertiary level training at one of the state university colleges or private colleges. There is no formal qualification requirement for assistants, who make up the bulk of the staff in direct contact with children; although an increasing number holds either secondary vocational or tertiary diplomas.

Work conditions: Statutory working hours for ECEC staff are 37.5 hours per week. There are no statutory requirements for staff to receive either minimum or total hours of professional development. Working conditions are negotiated at local and at state regional levels. Based on a government survey of services (2002), 84% of staff conducted yearly reviews of performance (organised co-worker conversations), 72% participated in internal staff development programmes and 48% of services had separate budgets for this purpose. The status, pay and working condition of ECEC pedagogues compare unfavourably to those of primary school teachers. Men make up 8% of all ECEC staff in direct contact with children. A ministerial plan 1997-2000 aimed to bring the proportion of men up to 20% by the end of 2000. The aim was not reached, now the aim is 20% men by the end of 2007. Issues of status, pay, working conditions and programme content may need further consideration before the percentage can be achieved.

Child-staff ratios: For children 0-3 years, the ratio is 7-9 children per trained pre-school pedagogue when children attend more than six hours per day. For children 3-6 years, the ratio is 14-18 children per trained educated pedagogue. There is no fixed regulation for the number of assistants that can or should be employed. In regulated family day care homes, a maximum of five children over the age of 3 may be present at one time. A suitable home and staffing can be accredited for a double group of children (maximum 10 children) over 3. If the majority of children is under the age of 3, the number must be reduced to an unspecified level. In addition, for children in family day care, a trained pre-school pedagogue must be available for every 30 children. The 1995 and 2005 Acts also stipulate that the number and level of staff must be sufficient to carry out satisfactory educational activities based on the Framework Plan.

Curriculum and pedagogy: The first national curriculum plan – called a *Framework Plan* – came into force in 1996. The curriculum, which must be used by all *barnehager*, is based on the Nordic tradition of combining education and care. A Sami supplement is integrated in the plan. All *barnehager*, including *familiebarnehager* and *open barnehager*, must base their annual plans on this Framework, which is the National Curriculum. The *Framework Plan* emphasises that both local cultural values and the national cultural heritage, as reflected in the childhood environment, must be represented in the activity of the *barnehage* (Background Report for Norway, 1999). A revised *Framework Plan* enters into force on 1st August 2006. The main principles are the same, with the new Kindergarten Act giving children a legal right to participate in all questions concerning their daily lives in ECEC.

Monitoring, evaluation and research: In 2001, Norway introduced a three-year quality programme across ECEC to establish instruments and systems for maintaining and further developing the quality of services. Survey data (2002) indicated that there are quality improvement efforts underway in most services. There was no significant difference due to ownership (public or private), although in larger centres quality work is further advanced. The high level of staff stability was a strong feature. Observation is the most commonly used method for evaluating children's well-being and progress. In autumn 2006, the Ministry of Education and Research will introduce a plan to increase evaluation competence in the sector, and will allocate almost NOK 60 million for this purpose.

Parent and community involvement: To ensure opportunities for involvement and co-operation between *barnehage* staff and parents, the 1995 and 2005 *Barnehage* Acts state that every *barnehage* must have a parents' council and a parent-pedagogue-owner co-ordinating committee. According to the regulations, the parents` council should promote the parents' shared interests and contribute to ensuring good collaboration. It has the right to express an opinion on all matters of importance to parental relationships with the *barnehage*. The co-ordination committee should in particular participate in discussions of the *barnehage*'s underlying aims and practice and seek to promote contact between the *barnehage* and the local community. Parents are actively encouraged to take part in quality monitoring and in reviewing *barnehage* activity through meetings, conversations, committees and regular surveys.

Developments

In Norway, an integrated system of services for children from 0 to 6, with a well-established and extensive system of publicly-funded *barnehager,* has existed for many years. Underpinning the system is a clearly articulated vision of children, both individually and as a social group, of their place in society and their relationship with the environment. Since 2001 substantial adjustments to legislation and funding processes have been underway as Norway moves towards universal access to ECEC services for all children under 6 years. In 2003, an amendment to the Day Care Institution Act made ECEC services a legal duty of the municipalities, similar to health and social services. The amendment ensures that all municipalities must offer an ECEC place to all parents in the municipality who want to enrol their child. As yet, corresponding legislation has not been drafted to give a legal right to all parents to a place for their child, although this is anticipated once full coverage is attained in 2007. The aim is to give all parents, in the interim, a place for their child according to their needs and wishes. Children with special needs (physical and/or intellectual handicap) have had by law for many years a primary right of access.

In line with the strong progress towards universal access, the Norwegian government has committed itself to increased funding of *barnehager* in order to avoid excluding certain categories of children because of costs to parents. Parliament granted substantial additional investments to ECEC (from NOK 4.5 billion in 2000 to NOK 14.8 billion in 2006). The government aims that by 2006, state and municipality funding will cover at least 80% of ECEC services costs, leaving a maximum 20% to parents.

In addition, the Norwegian Parliament has passed a law requiring equal treatment of private and non-private ECEC where public financing is concerned. Until the passing of this law, municipalities were not legally obliged to fund the private sector services and hence, fees to parents using those services were higher. A maximum fee for a full-time place in all settings, whatever the age of the child, was set by the Parliament in May 2004. In the same legislation, siblings in a family are entitled to reduced fees (30% reduction for the second child, 50% reduction for third and subsequent children). Municipalities also must have subsidy schemes for low-income parents.

In parallel to this development towards universal service provision, the administration is also co-ordinating work to assess and evaluate the Day Care Institution Act, in order to make the law a tool for creating and ensuring good quality ECEC services. In mid-2004, an expert group made up of researchers, various partners in the field and ECEC field participants reported on revisions needed to the Act of Day Care Institutions and the *Framework Plan*. The group further articulated responsibilities and duties at various levels of authority, and assessed the need for documentation and information-sharing across the different levels. Another expert group was appointed by the Ministry to propose in July 2005, a revised *Framework Plan*. The new legislation entered into force in January 2006, and the revised framework plan is implemented in August 2006.

A striking development has been the transfer of ECEC policy and funding from the Ministry of Children and Family Affairs (BFD) to the Ministry of Education and Research. Several developments have been promised by the new government:

- Full coverage will be achieved by 2007.

- The maximum parental fees are to be reduced to NOK 2 250 from 1st January 2006, then further reductions to approximately NOK 1 800 (c. USD 279 or EUR 231) per month, per child.

- Government grants will be earmarked until full coverage is met, when a legal right to a place will be introduced.

- The number of pedagogues will be increased in the kindergartens (at present, 35%).

- Equal wage and working conditions will be enacted for both private and public ECEC.

- When full coverage is met, and not before 2008, the cash benefit scheme will be restructed. A limited scheme will be maintained throughout this parliamentary period.

Portugal

Population: 10.5 m. **Fertility rate:** 1.44. **GDP per capita:** USD 18 400. **Children under 6 years:** 666 762.

Female labour force participation: 67% of women (15-64) participated, with 14% in part-time (compared to 5.8% part-time for men – OECD, *Employment Outlook*, 2005); 79% of mothers with children under 6 were employed, accounting for 6% of part-time employment (OECD, *Society at a Glance*, 2005); 70.8% of mothers with children under 3 were also employed (OECD, *Babies and Bosses*, 2004).

Maternity and parental leave: 16 weeks at 100% of earnings or 20 weeks at 80%. Fathers can also benefit from this remunerated leave if the couple agrees.

Average duration of parental leave: Not available.

Compulsory school age: 6 years.

Social expenditure: 21.1% **Child poverty rate:** 15.6% after taxes and transfers (OECD average is 11.2%).

Funding of pre-primary educational services (ISCED Level 0): 0.44% of GDP and 6% of education budget for approximately 13% of educational enrolments.

Unit cost per child in early education: EUR 4 158 or USD 4 986 per child (public institutions only, *Education at a Glance*, 2005)

Funding to children under 3: Information not available.

Average costs to parents for a child in a crèche: 11% of average annual salary.

Legal entitlement to a free service: From age 3 years, children have a right to the educational component of the *jardim de infância* (kindergarten) programme. Places are not always available but the situation is improving.

Major service types and daily duration: Children 0-3 years: Centre-based crèches (11% coverage – 8-9 hours daily); crèche familiare (1.5% coverage). Children 3-6 years: *jardim de infância*, for 5 or 6 hours daily). Out-of-school time provision (OSP) for children 6-12 years: information on coverage is not available.

Rate and pattern of access to regulated services: Children 0-3 years: Almost 90% of children 0-3 years are cared for by their families or in informal care arrangements. Some 12% of children attend some form of regulated full-day crèche or family day care. Children 3-6 years: from age 3, about 60% of children attend *jardims de infância* rising to 90% by age 5-6 years (average coverage for children 3-6 years is 76.3%).

Designation and professional qualifications of key staff: Crèches are staffed by *educadores* (with a 4-year university or polytechnic training), nurses and social workers, all of whom have tertiary-level, professional qualifications. Kindergartens are staffed by *educadores de infância* with a 4-year university or polytechnic training. Secondary education alone is obligatory only for teaching assistants, but training is now being introduced for education assistants.

Child-staff ratios: 10 or 12:2 in crèches; in *jardims* the ratio is 25:1 or 25:2 depending on whether a full-time assistant is being employed; in out-of-school time provision (OSP) the ratio is normally 15:1 or 20:2.

Maximum group size: In crèches, maximum group sizes practised are 10-12 children; in *jardims*, 25 children.

Auspices

The 1997 National Framework Law provides the definitions, major policy aims, orientations and implementation strategies for pre-school (kindergarten) education. The law perceives pre-school as the first stage of lifelong learning. Co-operation with families is emphasised. The national early childhood network in Portugal is both public and private, and overall policy responsibility for the network is shared by the Ministry of Education and the Ministry of Social Security and Labour (MSTT). Different partners work with the ministries, each having defined statutory roles. The Ministry of Education defines the normative aspects of pre-school education (hours of operation; organisation; pedagogical directions; evaluation and monitoring), and funds kindergartens (*jardims de infância*) for the age group 3-6 years. The Ministry of Social Security and Labour has charge of the regulation and funding of ECEC services focused on 0- to 3-year-olds, and of providing support to low-income families to enable children to attend kindergarten education, *e.g.* through the provision of free meals, subsidies to low-income families, etc.

A move towards decentralisation has taken place over recent years, and several policy and organisation matters are now being decided by municipalities, *e.g.* concerning training, posts and remuneration for assistant workers in *jardims* and the organisation of the out-of-school time provision in the public network with parents associations. The Regional Directorates of Education and the Regional Social Security Centres have the responsibility of enabling the implementation of national ECEC policies in their regions. To ensure co-ordination, a Bureau for the Expansion and Development of Pre-school Education was established in 1996 (working until 1998), bringing together the major ECEC stakeholders, including the National Association of Municipalities and the larger non-profit or voluntary providers, such as the Private Institutions of Social Solidarity (IPSS).

Context

Labour force rates: In 2004, the labour participation rate for women aged 15-64 was 67%, increasing from 59.6% in 1990. Of those, 14.0% worked part-time, compared to 5.8% of men working part-time (OECD, *Employment Outlook*, 2005). About 70% of mothers with a child or children under 6 years are employed, mostly full-time with about 10% in part-time work (OECD, *Babies and Bosses*, 2004).

Parental leave: In Portugal, a 16 weeks maternity period is allocated at 100% of earnings, or 20 weeks at 80% of earnings. Fathers can benefit from this remunerated leave if the couple agrees: 5 days simultaneous with mother or up to 120 days instead of mother at 100%. A parental leave period without remuneration can also be taken for a period from 3 months up to 4 years, until children are 6 years old. There is also a grandparent leave, amounting to 30 days if parent is less than 16 years at time of birth.

Access and provision

The operating hours and annual duration of services vary according to service type. Children from 3 months to 3 years can attend full-day crèches or family day care. Children from 3-6 years generally attend kindergarten or *jardims de infância*. The *jardims* open from 5-6 hours daily (depending on auspices). Children can also attend socio-educational activities when pre-school activities are over, if working parents need this extra time.

Rates of provision

0-3 years: Almost 90% of children are cared for by their families or within informal care arrangements; some 12% of children attend some form of crèche or family day care.

3-6 years: For the age group 3-6 years, enrolment rates relative to child age cohort in *jardims de infância* are: 3-4 years: 60% enrolled; 4-5 years: 75% and from 5-6 years: almost 90% are enrolled. Community centres and itinerant provision are also available on a small scale in areas where it is difficult to maintain a *jardim de infância*. Access to the "learning period" (the educative component) of the public *jardims de infância* is free, and since 2000/01, has become free also for children of 3, 4 and 5 years in the non-profit institutions of the private network (IPSS).

Children with diverse needs

Children with disabilities: In Portugal, there is growing inclusion of children with disabilities in all branches of education. The place of children with special needs within the pre-school system is protected in law. The policy goal is inclusion within regular kindergartens whenever possible, and in many settings, children with special educational needs are well integrated. However, referral rates for children 6 to 10 years of age are significantly higher than for the 0 to 6 age group, which suggests that many children are having their special needs identified too late.

Children from low-income families, ethnic and bilingual children: The child poverty level in Portugal is high and affects 15.6% of children after taxes and transfers (UNICEF, 2005). For children at-risk, several social integration programmes with an educational component have been sponsored by the High Commission for Ethnic Minorities, government ministries and municipalities. Children at risk are given priority entrance in some services – after children already enrolled and after children who will begin compulsory school in the following year. However, it was suggested by the OECD review team that identification and health intervention strategies for these children often fall as access is not appropriate.

Quality

Licensing and regulatory regimes: The State is responsible for the definition of general norms concerning pre-school education in relation to its organisational, pedagogical and technical components. It seeks to ensure their application through follow-up, evaluation and inspection. For children aged 0-3 years, the Ministry of Social Welfare (*Ministério da Segurança Social, da Família e da Criança*) is responsible for quality. In practice, however, there exists significant decentralisation to the regions with regard to pedagogical action and the management of the human, material and financial resources. For example, the geographically decentralised District Centres of Social Security are the units responsible for guaranteeing, in the respective area where they act, the management of social security schemes, the recognition of rights and fulfilment of duties in social security schemes and the implementation of social measures. The crèches (0/3 years of age) and kindergartens or *jardims* (3/6 years) are under the control of these centres. The licensing process for family day care services involves formal registration and the implementation of annual health and safety checks. In crèche, kindergarten and accredited out-of-school care programmes, there is an additional requirement to follow a curriculum.

Funding: Expenditure on pre-primary educational institutions as a percentage of GDP is 0.44%. (OECD, *Education at a Glance*, 2005). Approximately 92% of this expenditure came from public sources and 7.7% from private sources. 6% of total expenditure on educational institutions is allocated to pre-primary, but this expenditure covers approximately 13% of total educational enrolments. OECD (*Education at a Glance*, 2005) provides a figure of EUR 4 158 as the unit cost per child in pre-primary education. Public provision is mainly indirect, serviced by accredited agencies (government independents) subsidised by government. The subsidies are supplied directly to the service providers. Private provision is mainly non-profit, as only non-profit providers can receive public funds.

Parental fees for 0- to 3-year-olds are predominately determined in the free market, but some public free provision is also available to certain groups. Parents accessing the public network may not have to pay any cost. In the private non-profit solidarity networks, parental fees hould cover about 38% of costs; and in private services, parental contributions may account for 95% of costs. Average costs to parents for child care amounts to about 11% of an average aggregate family income. For 3- to 6-year-olds, the educational component of pre-school education is free, except in for-profit institutions. In these, the State can support low-income families through "development contracts" with the institutions. In addition, the State, through the Ministry of Social Security and Labour, heavily subsidises "family support" components of ECEC programmes, that is, meals, medical supervision, socio-cultural activities. Low-income families received enhanced reductions. Families also receive tax exemption for various educational expenses.

Staffing: All settings should have a pedagogical director, and each class a qualified early childhood teacher (*educador*). Crèches are staffed by *educadores*, nurses and social workers, all of whom have tertiary-level, professional qualifications. They are assisted by auxiliary workers who are not required to have a particular qualification, but training is now being required and put into place. The proportion of trained staff in crèches is not available. In the *jardims de infância*, the *educadores* or early childhood teachers are the lead staff. *Educadores* have the same pay conditions as primary school teachers, but their pay levels and conditions of work may be considerably reduced when they work in the social child care sector.

Training requirements: The minimum qualification required for social workers and early childhood nurses working in creches is a four-year university degree. In the *jardims*, *educadores* are required to complete a four-year university degree as polyvalent educators. Normally, one of the early childhood teachers holds the post of pedagogical director.

Work conditions: There are few part-time staff in ECEC settings. The statutory working hours for trained staff and assistants are 30 hours per week. As noted above, *educadores* have the same pay conditions as primary school teachers, but their pay levels and conditions of work may be considerably reduced when they work in the social sector.

Professional development: On-going training for pre-school teachers and teachers is co-funded by the State and the European Social Fund. It is provided mainly in the Training Centres of the School Associations. Local municipal or inter-municipal training centres can also be set up and managed by teachers representing various levels of education and teaching. Training courses can either be the result of one single initiative or of an association between several schools. *Educadores* must be provided with 56 hours annual of professional development courses, but they are not obliged to use their training quota. However, without a minimum of in-service training hours per year, they may not move up in their teaching career. Despite the fact that access to on-going training is mainly for infant teachers on the public network, those teaching on the private network may also attend. On-going training is also being planned and provided for education assistants in the form of courses or unit modules that can be accumulated.

Child-staff ratios: The maximum group size for *jardims* (kindergarten classes) is 25 with staff/child ratio being in general 25:1, and in some cases 25:2. The legislation requires one assistant worker for every two classrooms, with 25 children in each. When a *jardim* or pre-school in the public network has only one classroom, it is assigned one early childhood teacher and one assistant worker. This situation occurs more frequently in rural areas. In regulated family day care services, the maximum group size is 4, and the child-staff ratio 4:1. In the crèches, group sizes are 12 (solidarity network centres) or 10 (private centres) with ratios of 12:2 or 10:2. Accredited out-of-school care provision operates with maximum group size of 20 and child-staff ratios of 20:2. For socio-educational activities outside the "learning component", requirements depend on the municipality. Generally, one social educator is present for each group of 15-25 children.

Curriculum and pedagogy: The Ministry of Education introduced *Curriculum Guidelines* in 1997 to improve pedagogical method and content. The guidelines (for kindergarten) indicate recognition of the importance of quality early childhood settings both for children's early development and learning, and as a support to working parents. The guidelines allow for local expression in different parts of the country. As yet, it is unknown what impact this development has had on children's daily experiences. Whether a play-based pedagogy has been retained is also unclear. Another development likely to influence the shape and direction of curriculum and pedagogy is the recent design of multi-media material to support pedagogy and help early childhood teachers. An assessment process has begun to evaluate the application of the guidelines for pre-school education, with the purpose of reformulation and bringing it up to date. Furthermore, an inquiry is being made among experts in pre-school education and curriculum development, about the pertinence of defining competences to be developed in pre-school education.

Monitoring, evaluation and research: Quality control in all parts of the system needs to be strengthened. Few inspectors specialised in ECEC are assigned to quality evaluation and support of the *jardims*. Although the State gives substantial grants to voluntary and charitable organisations, it does not always contractually require in return verifiable evidence of target achievement or outcome measures. In order to develop a culture of accountability, appraisal and inspection, the ministry is developing a system to monitor and supervise curriculum development in pre-school education. The monitoring system will cover kindergartens from both the public and private networks working in diverse situations. To accomplish this action partnerships have been established with the Regional Education Authorities and Institutions of Higher Education.

Parent and community involvement: The regime for the autonomy, administration and management of schools, approved by Decree-Law No. 115-A/98, includes the participation of parents in various bodies in schools and in the preparation and approval of the school's internal rules of procedure. Where *jardims* are concerned, participation in the activities of the pre-school is reinforced by the work of Parents Associations, legally established by Decree-Law No. 80/99. There are also Municipal Education Councils ("bodies for co-ordination and consultation that promote within the municipality the co-ordination of education policy, co-ordinating intervention within the education system of agents of education and the social partners involved", D.L No. 7/2003) where parents associations and those responsible for education are represented. How these legal requirements work out in practice is not clear.

Policy developments in the areas identified by the OECD

Among the policy developments that have been signalled to the OECD since the review, the following are noteworthy.

Progress towards universal access, with particular attention to children under 3 and to children in need of special support. Within the Private Solidarity Network, the State has been increasingly co-funding the quality improvement of the services provided. It also shares with institutions and families, depending on their income, the costs incurred by both the educational and family support components. To meet educational component costs, the State pays the salaries of the early childhood educators and of auxiliary staff members as well as a proportion of costs of didactic and pedagogical materials. The State also subsidises a family support component in ECEC, *e.g.* meals and social educational activities. The increase in the numbers of children enjoying special supports is outlined in the table below:

1997/98	1998/99	1999/00	2000/01	2001/02	2002/03
4 434	6 009	6 108	6 943	7 174	7 696

Curriculum reform: No changes have been made to the Curriculum Guidelines for pre-school education (3/6 years), introduced in 1997, and educators continue to develop their practice using these guidelines. Currently, the articulation of subject areas as the basic structure of the ECEC curriculum is under study, alongside intentions to define pre-school education competences. Pilot work in the 2004/05 school year was undertaken in preparation for implementation of the new curriculum at national level in 2005/06. The Ministry of Education is planning a project to define the skills and learning required by pre-school children to develop their skills. This work is part of a wider curriculum reform ranging from pre-school to secondary education, which has emerged in response to concerns for better linkages and smoother transitions between ECEC programmes and the first cycle of basic education (6/10 years). The project includes also attention to inter-cultural understanding as a cultural value in Portuguese society and in current policy coordination work.

Quality inspections: The General Inspectorate of Education (*Inspecção-Geral de Educação –* IGE) conducted an assessment programme of about 600 pre-schools or *jardims* between 1999 and 2002, with the aim of encouraging improvement in these centres. The fields of observation covered the following teaching and process indicators: planning learning, curricular guidelines, educational aids, learning resources, assessment of learning and progress made, inter-personal relationships, co-operation among teachers; forms of communication/information adopted, as well as the interaction of the centre with the surrounding community. Currently, the IGE has developed a project to assess the quality of teaching processes. This will cover pre-school education and the first cycle of basic education. The project will focus on small-scale units that have not been inspected for five years or more. Monitoring will focus on pedagogical achievement, the work of the educator and community integration.

Integration of jardims and play-schools into school clusters: The Ministry of Education is attempting to integrate play-schools and *jardims* into schools and promote better co-ordination between early childhood education (3/6 years) and basic education. There will be a focus on annual planning for the whole school, on common projects and on the process of transition from infant to primary school (6/10 years).

Improved educador and education assistant training: Under the Ministry of Education, the category of teaching assistant has been created and existing staff can now be promoted once they have attended adequate training lasting 80 hours (Decree-Law No. 184/2004). To begin the career of education assistant the minimum qualification is now the completion of Grade 12 of secondary education or equivalent, with a specific training course lasting for 180 hours. The Ministry of Social Welfare has also been investing in improving the qualifications of auxiliary staff and has decided to change the name of the profession to social and education assistant, social and education assistant for special education, direct action assistant or occupation assistant.

New foci for research: In the context of co-ordination between the Ministry of Education and the Colleges of Higher Education, a project has been developed with a view to promoting the use of new technologies among young children. In the context of the APROXIMAR project, research has been undertaken by the University of Évora into new technologies used in pre-school education (3/6 years old) and in the first cycle of basic education. This project began in the early 1990s in some pre-schools in Portugal (Alentejo) where isolation had become a challenge due to the exodus of the rural population to the towns. The project is now being extended to the majority of pre-schools and to first cycle primary schools.

Sweden

Population: 8.99 m. **Fertility rate:** 1.71. **GDP per capita:** USD 28 100 **Children under 7 years:** c. 420 000.

Female labour force participation: 76.6% of women (15-64) participate, 20.8% of whom are in part-time employment (male part-time is 8.5%) (OECD, *Employment Outlook*, 2005).

Labour force participation rate of women with children under 6 years: In 2004, the labour participation rate for women aged 15-64 was 76.6%, decreasing from 82.5% in 1990. Of those, 20.8% work part-time, compared to 8.5% of men (OECD, *Employment Outlook*, 2005).

Employment rate of women with children under 3: 44% full-time and 36.2% part-time.

Remunerated maternity and parental leave: 480 days of parental leave to be divided between the two parents. 390 days are paid at 80% of earnings, the remaining 90 days at a flat rate. 60 days are reserved exclusively for mothers, 60 days for fathers, and the remaining days divided between them as they choose. 35% of fathers take their 60 days, much the highest proportion in OECD countries.

Average duration of parental leave: About 87% of leave days are used, mothers used 82.8% of the total days and fathers 17.2%.

Social expenditure: 28.9% of GDP. **Child poverty rate:** 4.2% after taxes and transfers (UNICEF, 2005). Though still very low by OECD standards, the rate has risen by over 50% in the past five years.

Compulsory school age: 7 years.

Funding of pre-school services: Public investment in ECEC was reported as over 1.9% of GDP in 2004. Funding per child in centred-based ECEC is second highest among OECD countries (after Denmark), reaching on average in 2004, USD 12 097 per child (Martin-Korpi, 2005).*

Average costs to parents: Parental fees cover about 9% of costs in pre-school, amounting to about 2% of average income. Parents with one child pay maximum USD 135 monthly; with two children USD 107 monthly; and with 3 children USD 54 monthly.

Legal entitlement to a free service: From age 4 years (from 3 years if a child has additional needs, *e.g.* second-language children) for a free pre-school morning service of 3 hours.

Major service types and duration: Pre-school (*förskola*) offers full-time care for pre-school children aged from 1 to 6 years. Pre-schools are open throughout the year, with daily hours adjusted to meet the needs of working parents. Leisure-time centres (*fritidshem*) offer part-time activities for children from 6 to 12 years. Open pre-schools (*öppen förskola*) offer part-time activities for children. They are intended for use by parents caring for children at home and for family day care providers. Family day care homes

---

* Martin-Korpi, B. (2005), "Early Childhood Education and Care in Sweden – A Universal Welfare Model", *Learning with other Countries*, Policy Paper No. 4, Daycare Trust, London.

(*familjedaghem*) offer full-time care for pre-school aged children. The pre-school class (*förskoleklass*) for 6- to 7-year-old children is specially conceived to facilitate transition towards the primary school.

Rate of access to regulated services: 45% of 1- to 2-year-olds and 86% of 2- to 3-year olds; 91% of 3- to 4-year olds; 96% of 5- to 6-year-olds. In the age group 6-7 years, 91% of children attend the pre-school class, with another 7% already in compulsory school. OSP for children 6-12 years: X50%.

Designation and professional qualifications of lead staff: *Familjedajhem*: family day care parents employed by the local commune, by whom initial training levels are fixed. Many family day carers are former teachers (university level education) or child assistants (senior secondary vocational training). *Förskola* or pre-school centres for children aged 1-6 years are staffed to 50% by pre-school teachers (*Förskollärare* teacher/pedagogues – pre-school educators with a 3.5-year university degree) and 50% by trained child assistants with a 3-year upper secondary training certificate. *Fritidshem* is out-of-school provision (OSP), staffed by leisure-time pedagogues, with a 3.5-year- university degree.

Child-staff ratios and maximum group size: Specific national standards regarding adult-child ratios and group size do not exist. These are set by each municipality, and vary considerably from one municipality to another. In centre-based ECEC centres and in family day care, the ratio is typically 5 to 6 children per adult. Maximum group size in pre-school centres, based on national statistical averages data, is 17 children per group, with a ratio of 5.4 children per trained adult. Maximum group size in out-of-school provision (OSP) is 30 children, with an 18.4:1 child-staff ratio.

Auspices

Auspices for young children 1-6 are unified in Sweden. Responsibility for central policy, for the goals, guidelines and financial framework of ECEC lies solely with the Swedish Ministry of Education and Science. Distinctions between day care and kindergarten were removed by the 1998 School Act, which sees all services for young children from 1-6 as "pre-school" and from 6-7 years as "pre-school class". Compulsory schooling begins at 7 years. Like the shifting of responsibility for the sector towards the Ministry of Education some years earlier, this Act signals – and reinforces – a major shift of understanding in Sweden with regard to early childhood services, which are now seen as being concerned primarily with individual, and social development.

The School Act also devolves major responsibilities to the 290 municipalities, which have the full responsibility of providing ECEC. Municipalities have the duty to create sufficient numbers of pre-school and leisure-time places, to monitor the quality of ECEC services and to provide sufficient resources. The Ministry of Education and Science has the main responsibility for national policy-making, and the National Agency for Education is responsible for overall evaluation, data collection, development and supervision of ECEC at central and regional levels.

Context

Labour force rates: In 2004, the labour participation rate for women aged 15-64 was 76.6%, decreasing from 82.5% in 1990. Of those, 20.8% work part-time, compared to 8.5% of men (OECD, *Employment Outlook*, 2005). 44% of women with at least one child under 3 were in full-time paid employment and 36.2% in part-time paid employment (OECD Survey Data, 2004).

Parental leave: The duration of combined (covering both parents), remunerated parental leave is 480 days. 390 days are paid 80% of annual earnings and 90 days paid at a universally applicable flat rate of SEK 60/day (EUR 6.58/USD 8), which is doubled for indigent families. About 87% of leave days are used, mothers used 82.8% of the total days and fathers 17.2%. The 480 cash-benefit days can be divided equally between parents. A parent may transfer up to 180 of her or his days to the other parent. (60 days are reserved exclusively for fathers and 60 days exclusively for mothers on a use-it, lose-it basis). Around 95% of the 390 high-rate benefit days and some 80% of the flat-rate days are claimed. In addition, temporary parental benefit is payable to a parent who is caring for a sick child up to the age of 12 and in some cases, 16 years. For these purposes, 120 cash-benefit days are available at 80% of the qualifying income. An average of 7 days per child are drawn each year. A further pregnancy benefit of 80% of earnings is paid for expectant mothers in employment who are unable to go on working from 60 to 11 days before birth.

Access and provision

By law, all children 1-12 years have a right to pre-school education. Most pre-school provision is provided directly by municipalities in day care centres. Provision through municipal, family day care covers about 12% of children, especially in rural areas. Private day care provided by parental and personnel co-operatives, churches, corporations and other providers exists also for 13% of children. Except for parental fees, private provision is funded by the municipalities and contractually, is expected to meet the basic standards of public child care, although without the obligation to follow the Pre-school Curriculum. Currently, parental contributions to ECEC are capped at 11% of costs, and are waived for families in economic difficulties. For families with more than one child, fees are capped at 3.2 and 1% of the combined household income for the first, second and third child respectively.

Rates of provision

0-1 years: Few children under the age of 18 months are in ECEC, due to the parental leave system (see "Parental leave", above). Almost all children are cared for by a parent (generally, the mother) in the home. Children have a right to a place in an ECEC centre from their first birthday. In general, children begin in day care at from about 15-18 months.

1-6 years: 45% of 1- to 2-year-olds and 86% of 2- to 3-year-olds are in ECEC services. For 3- to 4-year-olds participation rises to 91% and for 5- to 6-year-olds about 96%. Family day care caters for about 7% of children 1-6 years. Like centre-based ECEC and accredited out-of-school (leisure time) care services, family day care is in operation full-time for the working year.

6-7 years: 91% of children attend the pre-school class, with another 7% already in compulsory school. Over 50% of children 3-12 years are enrolled in leisure-time centres, participation peaking to about 75% for children from 6-9 years. In addition, "open pre-schools" (drop-in centres) offer a service to children and families (often low-income, immigrant) for a few hours every day. In rural areas, some of these drop-in centres are being transformed into family resource centres. The National Agency for Education has formulated guidelines for the conduct of these centres, and family day care.

Children with diverse needs

Children with disabilities: Children with disabilities or psycho-social challenges have a priority right to services and are well integrated. In fact, there is no categorisation of these children, who are well represented in the Swedish pre-school.

Children from low-income families: The child poverty level, after taxes and transfers, is 4.2%; the lowest in OECD countries. Targeting low-income groups is therefore not a focus at this level, although additional educators are often supplied to centres receiving more low-income or immigrant children.

Ethnic and bilingual children: Sweden has a growing immigrant population. 14% of children in the early services have a mother tongue other than Swedish. Government has made funds available to provide daily, a free 3-hour session of day care for bilingual children from the age of 3 years. All children in need of specialist support are entitled to mainstream ECEC free of charge.

In a national evaluation of pre-schools in 2004, the National Agency for Education expressed concern about the lack of "equivalence" of pre-schools across municipalities (Skolverket, 2004/239[1]). The economic downturn of the 1990s – combined with rising enrolment rates –increased financial pressures on particular municipalities and affected the quality of provision through an increase of the average group size (to 14.6 in the age group 1-3, and 19.7 in age group 3-5). Further, while the number of children in need of special support had also increased (due to larger group size, more difficult living conditions, and immigration), the evaluation recorded unacceptable disparities in pre-school quality between municipalities – and even within the same municipality: "In a decentralised organisation, there is a risk that pre-schools facing worse conditions do not receive sufficient support to carry out their tasks. The evaluation shows that lack of support in terms of resources and management appears to affect primarily pre-schools in low-resource catchment areas" (Skolverket, 2004/239, p. 33). The report suggests that disparities in quality are due in some cases to a lack of targeting (to match differences in need) and, in other cases, to inadequate overall resources. This is a matter of concern, given the fact that child poverty in Sweden rose significantly during the late 1990s (UNICEF, 2005).

Quality

Regulation and monitoring of services: Regulation and monitoring of ECEC services are the responsibility of one central agency, the Nation Agency for Education or *Skolverket*. Family day care, centre-based care and out-of-school care services all are required to be registered, undergo annual reviews, follow national curriculum guidelines and incorporate in-service training. Pedagogical management and supervision is a normal part of quality monitoring processes. ECEC services (for children 1-5) have similar regulations to schools, including annual quality reporting. National indicators on ECEC are developed and monitored by the National Agency for Education, but rather than relying solely on regulation, *Skolverket* publishes yearly reports on ECEC services, including analyses of child-staff ratios and other quality indicators.

Funding: The funding of pre-school services in 2004 amounted to 1.9% of GDP. Funding per child in centred-based ECEC is second highest among OECD countries (after Denmark), reaching on average in 2004, USD 12 097 per child (Korpi, 2005).[2]

Staffing: Each centre has a director, educational pedagogues (pre-school teachers) and child minders (trained assistants). Pre-school teachers make up 50% of the personnel in the pre-schools. Like leisure-time pedagogues, they are assisted by child assistants (comprising 38% of personnel). Unlike most other countries, leisure-time staff in Sweden are also highly trained, and like pre-school pedagogues have a 3.5-year university level degree. About 2-3% of pre-school personnel are men.

Training requirements: Almost all (98%) staff in Swedish pre-school centres are trained to work with children. Centre directors must have a university teaching or pedagogue qualification. Pedagogues (both educational and leisure-time) require a three- to four-year tertiary degree from a higher level university college. Most child assistants, who work alongside pedagogues, have completed a post-secondary professional diploma of three years, focused on "Children and Leisure-time Activities". Some older staff have fewer formal qualifications, but the current career ladder has various points of entry for child minders to take up higher training leading to pedagogue status. Family day care providers are not required to have a qualification, but some 70% have either a child assistant certificate or have received 50-100 hours of mandatory training from their municipal employers. The National Agency for Education recommends that family day carers should receive a training and certification equivalent to the child assistants in the pre-schools.

Work conditions: Statutory weekly hours for all ECEC staff are 40 hours/week. There is no statutory requirement for a minimum level of staff development or for recommended staff development hours per year. However, in-service training (staff development) is well recognised by municipalities as necessary for centre-based day carers and leisure-time staff, but less well for family day carers.

Child-staff ratios: National statutory requirements for child-staff ratios do not exist, but monitoring of the actual ratios practised is compulsory and ongoing. In centre-based ECEC centres and in family day care, the ratio is typically 5 to 6 children per adult. Maximum group size in centres, based on national statistical averages data, is 17 children per group. In accredited out-of-school care/leisure centres the average group size is now around 30 children per group (with a pedagogue and assistant), but this ratio is considered by parents and professional as too high. The government bill on quality issues forwarded to Parliament (*Riksdag*) in September 2004 includes significant additional finance to provide about 6 000 new staff in order to improve adult-child ratios in ECEC services. This could mean a 10% increase in pre-school staff.

Curriculum and pedagogy: The Ministry of Education and Science published in 1998 a general curriculum (Lpfö, 1998) for all centre-based services, in order to ensure a high level of cohesion in curriculum and pedagogy across the country. At the same time, consistent with the devolution of operational authority to the municipalities, centres are free to evolve their own local curricula and pedagogical methods, from the principles outlined in the state curriculum. Lpfö (1998) specifies only broad goals and guidelines, leaving open the means by which these goals should be achieved. Philosophically, the curriculum builds on the idea of the child as competent learner, active thinker and involved doer. A strong orientation towards: democratic values; continuous learning and development; connecting to the child's experiences; development in groups; and the pedagogical importance of both care and play, underpin curriculum development and enactment in ECEC programmes. Co-operation between the pre-school class, the school, and the after-school care centre is emphasised. Municipalities have responsibility for programme implementation and evaluation.

Monitoring, evaluation and research: Substantial research and analysis of early childhood epistemology and pedagogy is a feature of Swedish ECEC. However, funding for this research, particularly for social research on children, is limited with much research being self-funded (Country Note for Sweden, 1999). Research that is publicly funded is supported by the government and funded through the Foundation for Social Research.

Parent and community involvement: The role of parents has been relatively weak in the Swedish pre-school. New regulations on parents' involvement and influence in ECEC are being prepared. These regulations will further enhance parent involvement and influence, a central element of quality monitoring and service responsiveness.

Developments

Several far-reaching developments have taken place in ECEC in Sweden since the OECD review. In addition to consolidating the transfer of ECEC into the sphere of education, the system has been significantly expanded and reformed. The right of every child to a place "within reasonable limit" (defined as not more than three months) is assured in almost all municipalities. A government bill to make pre-school universal and free for all 4- and 5-year olds was legislated in 2003. For children from bilingual backgrounds, a free 3-hour kindergarten programme is available every morning from the age of 3. Fee variability across municipalities, which hindered low-income parents from using services, has been countered in the legislation. In addition, the restrictions on access for children of unemployed parents, and for children of parents on parental leave, have been completely removed; the right is now attached to the child, irrespective of the situation of parents. Further legislation introduced a low flat, parental fee for services. The municipalities received increased state grants to implement the legislation. In 2001-2003, SEK 5.6 billion were added to budgets for this development.

Quality too has been greatly emphasised. In 2004 a grant of SEK 2 billion increased state grants to local authorities for the employment of 6 000 additional pre-school teachers and child assistants, primarily to reduce class sizes and improve adult-child ratios to 1:5 on average for this period of childhood (0-6 years). Much of this effort has been devoted to improving quality for the older children. A Government Bill on quality issues was presented in September 2004 setting out the regulations on extra staffing, pre-school (for ages 1-5) as part of the school system. Also included are regulations on ECEC during evenings and weekends as well as curricula development to reflect multicultural ECEC services. Like the rest of the education system, ECEC in Sweden will also receive in the future annual quality reports, and national indicators for quality are being developed by the National Agency for Education.

In 2002, a new teacher education programme for pre-school teachers, school teachers and leisure time workers was introduced. The development allows a common psycho-pedagogical training for teachers and leisure time pedagogues. A common core of training in general education is provided for the three categories followed then by optional "fields of study" and "specialisations" suited to the type of work – early childhood, compulsory school and leisure-time work – to be chosen. This new training entitles the three groups to work together in teams with children 1-10 years in pre-school, school and after-school centres. No evaluation of the reform has been undertaken to date, but evidence from the ground suggests that fewer candidates are selecting the pre-school option, possibly because of the longer working hours and slightly lower pay. A possible resolution of the issue may be one of equalising the working conditions (salaries, weekly and annual hours, etc.) of all teachers.

Notes

1. Skolverket (2004), *Preschool in Transition: A National Evaluation of the Swedish Preschool*, National Agency for Education, Stockholm.

2. OECD (*Education at a Glance*, 2005) provides a figure for Sweden of USD 4 107 per child in pre-primary education according to the ISCED Level 0 definition, but we have not been able to ascertain what Statistics Sweden understands by this term. The investment level of USD 12 097 corresponds well to realistic assessments of costs in high quality services, and to the structural features of Swedish pre-school, such as, the child-staff ratios practised and the education levels and salaries of staff.

United Kingdom (England)[1]
(most of the following profile applies to England only)

Population: 60.2 m (United Kingdom). **Fertility rate:** 1.7. **GDP per capita:** USD 28 000. **Children under 6 years:** c. 5 000 000.

Female labour force participation: 69.6% of women (15-64) participate in the labour market, 40.4% of whom are in part-time employment (male part-time is 10.0%) (OECD, *Employment Outlook*, 2005).

Labour force participation rate of women with children: 57% of mothers with children under 6 were employed, accounting for 58% of part-time employment in 2002; in 2003, 49.2% of mothers with children under 3 were employed.

Maternity and parental leave: 26 weeks of maternity leave paid at 90% of earnings for 6 weeks followed by a fixed rate for the remaining period (c. GBP 106/week from April 2005). 26 additional weeks unpaid leave are available plus a further 26 weeks unpaid leave if a mother has worked for an employer for more than 26 weeks. Paid paternity leave of 2 weeks at birth of child was introduced in 2003. The goal of a 12-month paid maternity leave has been set for 2010.

Average duration of parental leave: Missing.

Compulsory school age: School term after 5th birthday.

Social expenditure: 21.8% (2001) of GDP. **Child poverty rate:** 15.4% after taxes and transfers (UNICEF, 2005) (OECD average is 11.2%). Though still one of the highest rates in Europe, this figure represents a significant reduction of 25%, since a government commitment to reduce child poverty was made in 1998/99.

Funding of pre-primary educational services (ISCED Level 0): 0.47% of GDP (0.45% public and 0.02% private). The sum constitutes 8% of educational investment, covering 7% of education enrolments. In 2004, the United Kingdom committed substantial additional investment in this area.

Unit cost per child in pre-primary education: USD 8 452 (OECD, *Education at a Glance*, 2005). See note in text.

Funding of services for children under 3: Missing.

Average costs to parents: c. 45%. Costs to parents vary greatly according to service type and income category. According to estimates, costs for low-and medium income parent may be covered to 80%, but parents using private child care services (the majority) often pay full costs.

Legal entitlement to a free service: All children have currently 12.5 hours free early education provision from term after 3rd birthday to statutory school age (5 years), for the academic year (currently 33 weeks annually). This is to be extended to 20 hours by 2010 for 38 weeks. The entitlement will rise to 15 hours in 2007. Some Local Authorities are piloting free entitlement for disadvantaged 2-year-olds. A free out-of-school provision (OSP) place for all children 3-14 years is also planned by 2010 either in Children's Centres or through Extended Schools programmes.

Major service types: State maintained Nursery Schools currently provide an educational programme for 3- and 4-year-olds for 12.5 hours per week, flexibly delivered (may be in half- or full-day blocks) during the academic year. Some provide full-time places of 6 hours per day. Reception classes, located within primary schools, are usually full time, but generally without an extended day: Many schools are now developing breakfast and out-of-school clubs for these children. Pre-schools/playgroups are occasional, sessional or all-day programmes serving children 2 to years of age; Children's Centre are designated one-stop-centres for parents and children, providing on a single site early education and care, family support, health services, employment advice, etc., all year round and on an extended day basis: "dawn to dusk". All forms of provision are now transforming to become part of a Children's Centre or Extended School. Local Authorities are responsible for quality improvement and ensuring seamless cover of ECEC provision for all who want it. A subsidiarity principle is at work whereby Local Authorities will provide services only if no private, voluntary or community sector provision is available.

Rate of access to regulated services: Children 0-3 years: about 20% of children have access to licensed services; children 3-4 years: 96%; children 4-5 years: full enrolment; data on OSP for children 6-12 years are not available.

Designation and qualifications of key staff: In maintained (funded by the State) nursery and primary education, teachers with 3-year or 4-year university degrees lead the early years programmes for 3- to 5-year-olds. Teachers are supported by qualified (to Level 3 Diploma) nursery assistants. In childcare settings, staff qualifications vary across services. 50% of staff in day nurseries have a Level 3 qualification or above, with 20% having a university or tertiary qualification, but 30% of staff in day nurseries have no qualification. 16% childminders are qualified to Level 3 or above.

Child-staff ratios: Family day care: 6:1 with less than 3 children under 5 years; centre-based care programmes: 3:1 for under 2 years; 4:1 for 2-year-olds; 8:1 for 3- to 7-year-olds; nursery schools and classes: 13:1; reception classes: 30:2 (a teacher and a Level 3 assistant).

Auspices

Most of the following profile applies to England only. The United Kingdom decentralises responsibility for education to its constituent jurisdictions: Northern Ireland, Scotland and Wales, each of which have independent legislatures and ministries responsible for care and education. In the past decade, different ECEC profiles have emerged in the four jurisdictions.

Responsibility for ECEC policy in England is shared between national and local government. At central level, in an effort better to articulate ECEC policy and to overcome the division between education and care, the government has given responsibility for children's services and education to the Sure Start Unit within the Department for Education and Skills. The Sure Start Unit has the remit to work across government to achieve more integrated services for children and families. It functions as an interdepartmental unit accountable to both the Department for Education and Skills and the Department of Work and Pensions. It is responsible for enacting the government programme to deliver the best start for every child by bringing together early education, child care, health, and family support. Sure Start and the Local Authorities work closely on the delivery of early years and child care provision (the former Early Years Development and Child care Partnerships are now given a more advisory role). Starting from birth, the Sure Start strategy brings together health, early learning and parenting support in a way that is designed to meet the needs of local parents, their children and local communities.

Context

Labour force rates: In 2004, the labour participation rate for women aged 15-64 was 69.6%, increasing from 67.3% in 1990. Of those, 40.4% work part-time, compared to 10% of men (OECD, *Employment Outlook*, 2005). Mothers with a youngest child under 6 years had an employment rate of 57% in 2002 (increasing from 42% in 1990) while mothers with children under 3 had an employment rate of 49.2% (OECD, *Babies and Bosses*, 2005). Mothers of younger children are more likely to work part-time with the shift to full-time employment correlating with children's age. On average, mothers work 29 hours/week. The higher the number of children a mother has the greater likelihood she is not in paid employment. Flexible working arrangements are increasingly available with more than 25% of women having some form of flexible working arrangement.

Parental leave: In 2003, the government extended paid maternity leave from 18 to 26 weeks, augmented by capacity to take a further 26 weeks unpaid leave if the mother had worked for the employer for more than 26 weeks. The statutory maternity payment is 90% of full salary for the first 6 weeks followed by GBP 102.80/week for the remaining 20 weeks (or 90% of earnings if lower). In addition, since 2003, fathers who have worked for the same employer for 26 weeks have been entitled to 2 weeks paid paternity leave to be taken within 56 days of the birth. Since 1999, parents (both mothers and fathers) who have completed at least one year's service with their employer are entitled to up to 13 weeks' parental leave in the child's first 5 years (18 weeks up to age 18 if the child is disabled). Further changes have now been announced for implementation in April 2007: 9 months paid maternity leave (with a proportion able to be taken by the father) and a goal of 12-month paid maternity leave by end of next Parliament (please see the *10-Year Strategy* for more information on this topic).

Access and provision

Since 1998, ECEC provision in the United Kingdom has significantly developed, having begun from a low base relative to other European countries. In general, children 0-3 of working parents are cared for by private child minders, playgroups and day nurseries, constituting the highest proportion of private "child care" in Europe. Until the introduction of the Child Care Tax Credit in 1998 (now Working Tax Credit Child Care Element), children in these services were not eligible for public funding, unless they qualified for special services or were considered to be seriously at risk. From 3-4 years, almost all children enrol in nursery school and join playgroups, moving towards reception class at age 4. Four-year-olds are in either state-funded primary school reception classes (the majority) or in private nursery school provision. Compulsory school begins in England in the term after the 5th birthday has been reached, and most children of this age are in reception or primary classes, operated mostly by Local Authorities. However, the 2004 *Five Year Strategy for Children and Learners* heralds significant change including a plan to address the division between education and child care and to merge services into a single integrated offer. By 2010, all 3- and 4-year-old children will receive 20 hours per week of free education (from 15 hours per week at present) for 38 weeks annually (from 33 weeks at present), with in addition, a longer term goal of 20 hours per week of free, high quality out-of-school care. This extended offer will be more flexible: the aim is to make it possible for parents to use early education services flexibly across the week, including joining it up with care parents pay for – so parents can access a seamless package of care to suit them and their children. This is to be accompanied by a revised quality framework for the early years from birth to 6 years, and an integrated inspection of education and child care. The current provision patterns are as follows:

0-1 year: Most children in their first year of life are cared for by parents or, informally, by relatives. Approximately 20% of the age group are in formal care, predominantly private day nurseries and child minders (2001 figures).

1-3 years: Other than family and informal care (the majority mode of care for 1-year-olds), ECEC for this age group is mostly child care type provision. Few 1-year-olds attend playgroups or sessional care. Approximately 30% of the age group (556k in the 1-2 age cohort, and 570k in the year 2-3) attend child minders or private day nurseries (accounting for 86% of the provision), with a further 30% of 2-year-olds attending a playgroup or other sessional care, two-thirds of which are run by church or voluntary associations, and one-third by private persons or agencies. It is expected that "the (private day nursery) market is likely to consolidate into five or six major chains over the next five years, accounting for a larger percentage of market share" (*Nursery Market News*, 2003, cited in Cohen, Moss, Petrie and Wallace, 2004, *A New Deal for Children? Reforming Education and Care in England, Scotland and Sweden*, Policy Press, England).

3-5 years: Currently, a free early education place (2.5-hours, five days a week, 33 weeks a year) is now guaranteed for 3- and 4-year-olds. 96% of 3-year-olds are enrolled, of whom 54% are enrolled in the private and voluntary sector (DfES, Sure Start Unit, 2005). 98% of 4-year-olds are enrolled in a free nursery education place for at least two-and-a-half hours daily. Local education authorities currently provide 70% of early education places for 4-year-olds, mainly through nursery schools, nursery classes and reception classes. The private sector (generally companies or trusts) provides about 20% of school places in independent, fee-charging pre-schools, while community and voluntary (non-profit) agencies provide 9% of places.

5-6 years: Compulsory schooling begins in England at 5 years. All 5-year-olds have a full-day (normally 6.5 hours daily from 9:00-15:30), early education place for the academic year (normally 38 weeks). Again enrolments are divided between the public and private sectors.

Formal, public *out-of-school time provision* (OSP) is developing, much of the new provision being funded by the New Opportunities Fund of the National Lottery. The number of places has increased from 137 000 in 1997 to 490 000 in 2004. The *10-Year Strategy* (2004) sets a target for the year 2010 of an affordable out-of-school child care place, linked to schools, for all children aged 3-14 years. It is envisaged that this place should cater for children between the hours of 8 a.m. and 6 p.m. every weekday, all year round, and combine care with "enrichment activities", including art and sport. Data on current access to this type of provision is unavailable.

Children with diverse needs

Since 1998/99, the United Kingdom has invested significantly in services for children most at risk, primarily by targeting the Sure Start programme to disadvantaged areas, on the basis that this will reach a large proportion of children at-risk. This targeted approach is set within a policy of "progressive universalism" with services available for all, but with greater support for children and families who are most in need. In parallel, there has been a pledge by the present government to eradicate child poverty by 2020, with the current target being to ensure that there are fewer than 1m children in absolute low-income by 2010-11, compared with 3.4m in 1998. Within this objective, the aim is to halve the number of children experiencing a combination of relative low-income and material deprivation, from a 1998-99 baseline. A key element of the strategy for achieving this target is to provide affordable and accessible early years services so that parents from all backgrounds can work and ensure for their children equal educational opportunities to maximise their potential. According to UNICEF (2005), progress is on track to reach the reduction of child poverty goals.

Children with disabilities: The growing awareness of the benefits of mainstreaming children with special education needs led to the Education Act of 1993, which encouraged inclusion in schools, and the Special Educational Needs and Disability Act 2001, which provided a revised statutory framework and guidelines for inclusion. The situation on the ground is varied with some boroughs being able to include up to 25% of children with additional learning and social needs, and in contrast, evident lack of progress in other schools and education authorities (Ofsted, *Special needs and disability: towards inclusive schools,* 2004). A growing body of opinion favours both inclusion and the retention of special schools (over a 1 000 in the United Kingdom), especially from secondary level onwards. Teachers observe that schools are generally not equipped to cater appropriately for children with special needs, and parents are often concerned about bullying or they fear that mainstream schools are too large and uncaring for children with special needs. A challenge to inclusiveness in the early childhood sector is that it is largely voluntary or private, and without strong public financing and support, providers are unlikely to accept children with special needs. For this reason, considerable funding to ensure support to children with special educational needs in the private, voluntary and independent sector has also been allocated. At the time of writing, a further report from government is expected.

Children from low-income families: For the United Kingdom, the proportion of children (0-15) living in low-income households in 2002-03, after taxes and transfers and before housing costs, was 21%. About 22% of children under 5 years are being raised by a lone parent (Department for Work and Pensions, 2004). Substantial attention has been given in recent years to reducing child poverty through supporting low-income families. Lone parents, in particular, are encouraged into work through child tax credits, including support for up to 70% of child care costs.

Ethnic and bilingual children: 9% of the British population is composed of ethnic minorities (in some areas such as London and the West Midlands, this proportion rises to above 15%). As research indicates that children from some ethnic minorities are seriously underachieving in education, policies to prevent discrimination and racism have been strengthened.

Quality

Licensing and regulatory regimes: A licensing regime applies to services for children under 8 where care is provided for more than two hours per day. Funded pre-primary education places for 3- to 4-year-olds are subject to the curriculum requirements of the QCA (the governmental Qualifications and Curriculum Authority). Where private or voluntary sector settings provide nursery education, different registration requirements exist to those of schools offering pre-primary education. Monitoring of licensed and funded services varies also according to service type and their different regulatory frameworks (some child care, some education), although there is a commitment to integrate at some future date inspection processes for all care and education services. Licensed child-minding and day care, including family day care, crèche, day nursery and out-of-school provision, are inspected every two years. Funded pre-primary (nursery) education is inspected at least every 4 years (6 years in schools). The intention is to move from 2005 towards a common inspection frequency of 3 years for all care and education services for under eights, including schools. All inspection will be integrated under Ofsted.

Funding: Expenditure on pre-primary educational institutions as a percentage of GDP for pre-primary education is 0.47% (OECD, *Education at a Glance*, 2005). About 95.8% of this expenditure (0.45%) came from public sources and 4.2% from private (household) sources (OECD, *Education at a Glance*, 2005). 8% of all expenditure on educational institutions is directed to pre-primary whereas 7% of the children/students are enrolled at this level of education (OECD, *Education at a Glance*, 2005). According to the same source (Table B.1.1), the unit cost in early education services (3-6 years) is USD 8 452 per child – the highest of all the OECD countries. It is difficult to reconcile this figure with other figures provided in the same table, and with calculations of British expenditure provided by other OECD sources.[2]

According to 2002-03 National Audit Office figures based on DfES, Inland Revenue and other sources, the main contributors to funding ECEC are: families 45%, nursery education 38% (public), Sure Start general grant 10% (public), child care tax credit 5% (public), employers 2%. Based on a total investment of GBP 6.685 billion in 2002-03, government supply-side funding totalled GBP 3.6 billion in the same year; reached GBP 3.8 billion in 2004-05 and is due to rise to GBP 4.4 billion by 2007/08. This compares with an equivalent investment of GBP 1.1 billion in 1996/97. According to DfES sources, the increase in spending aligns with a major re-focus on ECEC services and provision in England, not least to address policy and quality issues. In the period 1998/99 to 2004/05, the government spent an additional GBP 14 billion supporting families and children with further substantial increases committed until 2008. A doubling of investment in early childhood services (excluding tax credits) is foreseen between 2004/05 and 2007/08, that is, an annual increase of 23% in real terms.

Most of the expansion of child care places has been a result of public subsidy both at provider and user levels. Providers receive start-up costs, and families (at low- and middle-income levels) receive tax credits through the Working Tax Credit Child care Element (formerly the Child care Tax Credit). This benefit pays up to 70% of child care costs, up to a limit of GBP 135 per week for 1 child and GBP 200 per week for 2 or more children and is available to parents who work at least 16 hours a week, including lone parents working at least 16 hours. (Note: benefit will increase from April 2006 to a maximum of GBP 300 per week, GBP 175 or one child, 80% of costs). Public subsidies through grants or fees can be paid to profit or non-profit providers, the latter being predominant in provision for children up to compulsory schooling, as the entitlement to a free education place is still only 15 hours per week for 33 weeks in the year. To be eligible for grants, providers must meet certain conditions, in particular, to be registered with and undergo inspection by Ofsted (the Office for Standards in Education), and to work towards government defined learning goals. Although tax and national insurance contribution exemptions for employer-supported child care have been introduced, few employers provide assistance, financial or otherwise, to child care.

A large part of the public sector subsidy (the Sure Start grant) is channelled to Children's Trusts in Local Authorities, which commission and plan local services. This grant is used to deliver new child care places; to improve the sustainability of existing child care provision; to develop and support Children's Centres and Neighbourhood Nurseries (these now being transformed to Children's Centres); to develop the workforce; and to develop nursery schools. The grant brings together six previously separate funding streams, thereby reducing administration and enabling service planning and delivery to be more coordinated. Further subsidy is also available through the Local Authorities to support families with additional needs and to ensure that all 3- and 4-year-olds in the area get an early education place.

Public provision is provided to families both in the form of free services and indirectly through tax credits and grants that parents may use in any area of the marketplace. Fees in the child care sector are largely set by the market. To improve equity of access, a new proposal has been made to cap charges in service that are in receipt of public funding. Education is free for 5-year-olds, as compulsory education in England begins at this age. For 3- and 4-year-olds, each child has an entitlement to 15 hours weekly for 33 weeks annually. This means that parents of children in this age group must also find "wrap-around" services in the voluntary or private child care and pre-school sectors. Costs to parents vary greatly according to service provider, service type and income category. The average contribution of parents to child care is estimated to be 45% of full costs. Costs for low-income and some middle-income parent may be covered to 80%, but parents using private child care and pre-school services (the majority) often pay full costs.

Training requirements: Levels and types of qualifications differ by service type and setting. The national standards for under eights day care and child-minding require service providers to ensure that persons-in-charge and supervisors in group-based programmes hold appropriate Level 3 (professional diploma) or higher qualifications. At least half the staff in each setting must hold at least Level 2 qualifications (capacity to work under supervision on the care/development of children). Child minders are required to complete a Local Authority approved pre-registration course within 6 months of service commencement. Where service providers do not meet the requirements of the qualification standards, an action plan must be lodged with the Ofsted child care inspector detailing how the standard will be met over time and setting out the training to be undertaken to update skills. Several strategies are employed to raise recruitment and qualification levels in all forms of provision: increased funding, the capping of certain charge on providers and the relaxation of stringent child-staff ratios against higher qualification levels.

Staffing: The 2002/2003 Childcare and Early Years Workforce Survey indicated that since 2001, the workforce has become more qualified. In state-funded nursery schools and reception classes, regulations require that the children be in the care of a qualified teacher (university degree), but this requirement is not always met. Support to children in the classroom is provided by nursery assistants with a Level 3 diploma, that is, a professional diploma showing competence to work with young children without supervision. In child care settings, staff qualifications vary across services. 50% of staff in day nurseries have a Level 3 qualification or above, with 20% having a university or tertiary qualification, but 30% of staff in day nurseries have no qualification. 16% child minders are qualified to Level 3 or above. 80% of playgroup and day nursery managers are qualified at Level 3 or over. Across all settings, the workforce is 98% female. Full-time or part-time appointments vary widely according to service type. The ratio of full-time to part-time workers in each service is as follows: primary school-site nursery/reception classes 66:33; primary school-site (reception class only) 50:50; nursery schools 63:27; full-day care 80:20; playgroup 10:90; holiday clubs 65:45; out-of-school clubs 23:77.

Work conditions: Statutory working hours, minimum levels of staff development and set requirements for annual staff development (in-service training) are not part of national reporting and may vary across the country. Wide ranging recruitment campaigns are in place. DfES recognises the importance of a clear progression structure for child care workers and this is being addressed in the pay and workforce strategy for children's services. The strategy will "review rewards, incentives and relativities across children's practice". It will contain action to make working with children a more attractive career option. Some of the issues covered in the strategy will be the development of flexible career and training pathways, the development of a Common core of skills and knowledge and the establishment of a Children, Young People and Families Workforce Council which will represent the interests of the sector. The Common Core will provide a foundation level of core skills and knowledge necessary for staff when working with children, young people and families; in different jobs in different services. It enables a shared understanding of key issues and the ability to move across professional boundaries. The Common Core also will provide the basic structure to steer the next more technical phase of revising national occupational standards, of creating a climbing frame of qualifications, and in particular, to guide the creation of a core early years professional profile in all settings.

Child-staff ratios: In regulated child-minding (family day care), maximum group size is 6 (or 12 children if the child minder has an assistant) of whom no more than 3 (with some exceptions allowed) may be under 5 years old. In crèches, centre-based ECEC, accredited playgroups and accredited out-of-school provision, the maximum group size is 26, with ratios of 3:1 for children under 2, 4:1 for children aged 2 and 8:1 for children 3-7 years old. In kindergartens or pre-schools, the maximum group size is 26 with ratios of 10:1 if the head-teacher combines teaching with administrative tasks, or 13:1 if the head teacher is not engaged in teaching. In public pre-primary education (reception classes), there is no set maximum group size, although this does not usually exceed 26 children per adult. For children 3-4 years, the ratio is 13:1. The possibility of linking ratios with staff qualifications is being studied.

Curriculum and pedagogy: Significant developments to improve quality in early childhood settings have been introduced since 2000. In 2001, National Standards for under age 8-day care and child-minding services were introduced, setting a national benchmark of quality below which no provider may fall. In late 2002 a curricular guideline *Birth to three matters: A framework to support children in their earliest years* was introduced offering information, guidance and support to those working with this age group. A Foundation Stage curriculum (for 3- to 5-year-olds) was introduced in 2000 and confirmed in legislation as the first stage of the National Curriculum in 2002. A centrally organised support programme for the Early Years Foundation Stage led by a National Director with a team of regional Foundation Stage Advisors aims to improve the quality of the Foundation Stage and provide guidance to practitioners to deliver high quality early education experiences for young children. All practitioners access 4 days of training per year (2004-06) with various projects underway to develop the curriculum, including: an early speech and communication project (to improve practice and practitioner knowledge); training materials to embed the practice of listening to children; a project to promote and support good quality outdoor play; and a project on the transition between the Foundation Stage and Key Stage 1. The Foundation Stage Profile is a continuous teacher-led assessment to accompany the Foundation Stage. It replaces the previous "Baseline Assessment" as the statutory assessment requirement for this age group. The Early Years Foundation Stage itself is being further developed to cover children from birth to 5 years, and will be accompanied by a new Quality Framework for the whole age group.

Monitoring and evaluation: The expansion in early years and child care services since 1998 has been accompanied by a greater emphasis on performance monitoring and evaluation as part of the overall government thrust to improve the performance of public services. A series of national level performance targets and outcome indicators for ECEC have been formulated, with an increased emphasis on evidence-based policy-making. To facilitate performance monitoring, use of central data collection systems has increased both to reduce the burden on Local Authorities and to achieve a coherent and consistent picture of national progress. Local Authorities have been made accountable for the quality of early years provision in their areas, while Ofsted (the Office for Standards in Education) has responsibility for the inspection both of child care (including family day care) and early education settings.

Research: The Sure Start Unit has in place a large research and evaluation programme (annual budget approx GBP 6 million/USD 10 748 400) to provide evidence related to developing early years policies. A longitudinal study of the Sure Start (local) programme has been established to track the development of children in Sure Start programme areas from infancy through childhood to examine the short, medium and long term impacts of the programme. There is also a large evaluation study of the neighbourhood nursery initiative underway. Another major research programme supporting quality improvement processes is the Effective Provision of Pre-School Education (EPPE), a study examining the effect of pre-school provision on children's outcomes from start-of-school to age 11. Findings from this study – that have shown the positive benefits of good quality pre-school education on subsequent child development – have been influential in shaping policy.

Parent and community involvement: Parental involvement is a strong plank of current ECEC policy in the United Kingdom. The Sure Start and Children's Centre programmes emphasise parental involvement, providing parenting support and facilitating access for parents to training and development. In Sure Start local programmes, parents play a major role in running the programmes (the partnerships contain some 50% parent/community members). Parents are extensively consulted on the types of services they want. A recent impact evaluation of the project (NESS Impact Study, 2005, *Early Impacts of Sure Start Local Programmes on Children and Families*, Birbeck, University of London) shows, however, that Sure Start local programmes have had only modest effects on parents, either positive or adverse. The curricula frameworks *Birth to three matters* and the present Foundation Stage emphasise the importance of parental involvement in their child's development and education. The new (draft) Early Years Foundation Stage document and new legislation (Childcare Act 2006) require that parents are involved in planning, development, delivery and evaluation of local services.

OECD policy issues

● In all areas reviewed by the OECD review team in 2000 – funding; policy coordination; expansion of access; staff recruitment and training; quality assurance and inspection regimes; work-family supports – significant progress has been made. The United Kingdom government published their *10-Year Strategy for Child Care – Choice for Parents, the Best Start for Children* (in December 2004) to reinforce this progress and call attention to the following challenges, which it will address over the coming years.

- Although free nursery education for 15 hours weekly is now available for 3- and 4-year old children, the session is insufficiently linked to other ECEC that parents need to arrange. Wrap-around services are not always available, and parents are often obliged to navigate a maze of different providers, professionals and agencies to obtain the services they need. Much of this fragmentation should be resolved through the new integrated Children's Centres.

- There are too few appropriately trained staff, especially in the child care sector. High turnover of staff (reaching 40% annually in some instances) is a threat to both quality and the attachment needs of young children. Plans are now underway to generate a new educator profile to cover the whole age group 1-6 years. The strategy sets out a radical reform of the early years and child care workforce that will work towards a better qualified, higher status workforce. More staff will be trained to degree-level, and all full day care settings will be led by graduate qualified early years professionals. In order to support expansion and meet standards, 80 500 new staff are expected to be recruited into the child care sector by 2006, and trained to Level 2 or 3. Targets, jointly set by Local Authorities and local Learning and Skills Councils, are in place to meet this challenge. Funding of GBP 129.9 million (USD 232 702 860) for the two financial years 2004-06 will be provided to Local Authorities for workforce development. In the recent reform of local government, a new "Transformation Fund" has been created part of which can be used to encourage the employment of graduates in early childhood services and pay better salaries in private and voluntary sector settings

- Affordability is still a real barrier to low-income (especially lone parents) and lower mid-income parents in accessing formal child care and school holiday care. Deprived families in affluent areas are likewise affected.

- The situation of children with disabilities and/or additional learning needs in early childhood services is not clear. Whatever about the validity of arguments to have more specialised environments for these children from late primary or secondary level, early childhood services would seem to be the most effective and protected level for the inclusion of all types of children. This seems to be the practice in Finland, Italy, Norway, Sweden, the United States and other countries. Early childhood is also a critical moment where mainstream children are concerned. Research on community conflict tends to show that the seeds of prejudice – or of positive attitudes towards diversity – are sown very early in children's minds. Obviously, inclusion at this level must also be appropriate with additional resources (including specialised staff) allocated to centres enrolling these children. The Children's Centres are specifically charged with meeting the needs of children with disabilities and special needs.

- An important new development is the new Child Care Act 2006, which gives all parents a statutory entitlement to child care, integrated with early education. In the future, Local Authorities are charged to be "champions of parents" ands managers of the "child care market", and not necessarily service providers.

Notes

1. The OECD review focused on England (50 million inhabitants), but the review team also visited Scotland, which has taken a different approach to ECEC policy. Please see the United Kingdom Country Note for more details on Northern Ireland, Scotland, and Wales.

2. In the table in question, unit costs per child for Denmark and Sweden are given as USD 4 673, and USD 4 107 respectively. Denmark and Sweden currently spend about 2% of GDP on early childhood services, adopt pay rates for lead staff equivalent to British rates, practise far lower child-staff ratios in services for children 3-6 years (Denmark averages 7.2 children and Sweden 5.6 children per trained adult) and provide considerably longer educational sessions for 3- and 4-year-olds. In our estimation, the amounts attributed to Denmark and Sweden refer to the preschool class only. A significant increase in investment towards children and families has occurred in the United Kingdom over the last decade (see for example, the improvement in child poverty figures), but the extent of public expenditure on ECEC services is not clear. A comparative analysis of ECEC expenditure, based on information supplied by national authorities, appears in *Babies and Bosses* (OECD, 2005), which provides the following figures for Sweden (2002 figures) and the United Kingdom (2003 figures): child care only: Sweden 1.4% of GDP; United Kingdom: 0.1%; pre-primary education only: Sweden: 0.2% of GDP (accounting for 1 year only); United Kingdom: 0.2% (accounting for 2 years); out-of-school care: Sweden: 0.4%; United Kingdom: data not available and probably minimal. The same volume provides a figure of USD 4 096 invested per child in the pre-school class (6-7 years) in Sweden, and a figure of USD 3 986 invested per child by the United Kingdom in pre-primary education (3-5 years). Roughly similar figures are provided in Cohen *et al.* (2004). A more recent figure for Sweden provided by Martin-Korpi (2005) gives an annual expenditure figure of USD 12 354 per child in Swedish preschool services for children 1-6 years.

United States

Population: 293 m. **Fertility rate:** 2.07. **GDP per capita:** USD 36 700.

Children under 5 years: US Census Bureau lists number of children under age 5 as 19.8 million, but does not provide a category for children under 6 years (*www.census.gov/popest/age.html*).

Female labour force participation: 69.8% of women participate in the labour market in 2004, 18.8% of whom are in part-time employment as against 8.1% male part-time employment (part-time employment is defined as less than 30 hours weekly in salaried employment. Many part-time, cash economy jobs are not included in these figures).

Labour force participation rate of women with children under 6 years: c. 58% (Current Population Survey for year 2000). Demand for ECEC places is almost as high among non-employed parents, and the level of family income and of maternal education remain prime indicators of participation.

Maternity and parental leave: Under the Family and Medical Leave Act, covered employers must grant an eligible employee up to a total of 12-work weeks of unpaid leave during any 12-month period in specified circumstances, including the birth and care of a newborn child of the employee. Five States pay temporary disability benefit for 10 weeks.

Average duration of parental leave: Data not available.

Compulsory school age: Generally 6 years.

Public social expenditure: 15.7% (OECD average is 22% – OECD, *Society at a Glance*, 2005). **Child poverty rate:** 21.9% after taxes and transfers – OECD average is 11.2% (UNICEF, 2005). Head Start and similar programmes serve about 3 out of 5 children in poverty, generally on a sessional or half-day basis, but increasingly full-day.

Funding of public pre-primary educational services (ISCED Level 0): About 0.4% of GDP is provided from public funds (OECD, *Society at a Glance*, 2005) for pre-kindergarten education, essentially from state and local government funds. The unit cost per child 3-6 years (public institutions only) amounts to USD 7 881 (this figure probably includes private contributions which, in the United States, amount to about two-thirds of cost). According to NIEER figures the average state investment in pre-kindergarten is less than USD 3 600 per child enrolled. Head Start invests just over USD 7 200 per child enrolled, but receives a further 20% cash or in-kind contribution from various sources, bringing investment per child to USD 8 626 (NIEER, 2005, *The State of Pre-School Yearbook*, Rutgers University, NJ, *nieer.org/yearbook/pdf/yearbook.pdf*).

Average costs to parents: Outside school services and Head Start, parents may assume all the costs of child care. Overall, the federal government underwrites 25% of costs, State and local government 15% and parents the remaining 60%. Low-income parents pay on average 18% of family income per child enrolled in child care.

Legal entitlement to a free service: c. 5 years, but increasingly children have access to state-funded pre-kindergarten programmes at age 4 years (see below).

Major service types: i) The purchase of services system, generally licensed and supervised by state child care agencies. It is composed of private family day care, child care and early education centres (under a wide variety of names) offering a range of full-day and part-day programmes for children 0-6 years; ii) the public school system under the responsibility of each State offering pre-school (publicly funded pre-kindergarten programmes for 3- and 4-year old children) and kindergarten programmes (mainly serving 5-year-olds); and iii) Head Start programmes for low-income families primarily serve 3- and 4-year-olds.

Rate of access to regulated services: In 2002, c. 38% of children in the age group 0-3 years had access to licensed services; 56.4% of 3- to 5-year-olds had access (NCCIC, 2005, *www.nccic.org/*, figures for 2002). Over 90% of children are enrolled in state kindergarten 5-6 years. According to Barnett ("Testimony to the House Subcommittee on Education Reform: Hearing on 'Early Childhood Education: Improvement Through Integration'", 2005), more recent attendance figures are: "7 of 10 children now attend a pre-school programme at age 4; 4 of 10 children attend a pre-school programme at age 3 (House Subcommittee Hearing, April 2005)". Head Start covers 11% of all 3- and 4-year-olds; state pre-kindergarten covers about 2.5% of 3-year-olds and 16% of 4-year-olds. Georgia and Oklahoma make pre-kindergarten available to all 4-year-olds.

Designation and professional qualifications of key staff: Teachers with 4-year degrees lead the kindergarten/pre-kindergarten programmes in public schools. 75% of staff leading Head Start programmes have at least a 1-year Child Development Course and approximately 57% of these have an Associates Degree or higher. In the private sector (c. 90% of child care provision), the proportion of qualified staff is not known.

Child-staff ratios: Different standards apply across the United States. In general, a ratio of 4-6:1 exists for infants; 10-to 20:1 for pre-school. NIEER (*2005 State Preschool Yearbook*, 2006) sets the maximum ratio of 10:1 as a benchmark in classrooms for both 3- and 4-year-old children and 37 States have reached this benchmark or have done better.

Maximum group size: Wide variation exists across States. In regulated centre-based settings, the maximum group size generally ranges from 8 to 24 for 0- to 3-year-olds and 14 to 40 for 3- to 5-year-olds.

Auspices

American attitudes towards early childhood and family policy have traditionally been underpinned by a high value placed on individual responsibility; consideration of the family as a private unit; and volunteerism rather than statutory enactment of social welfare policies (public social welfare expenditure in the United States is well below the OECD average). In accordance with a philosophy of limiting government intervention in matters related to family, there is no overall national child or family policy, nor is there any one federal state department in charge of children's services. However, the Federal Government, through Congress and the Administration, attends to broad ECEC goals and the funding of services to children considered "at risk" (Clearinghouse on International Developments, Columbia University, 2004). Head Start is the most important targeted federal programme, and in 2003-04 covered 7% of 3-year-olds and 11% of 4-year-olds (about 21% of American children under 5 years live in poverty, UNICEF, 2005). Market-based businesses, funded mostly by parents, provide the greater part of early care and education programmes for 0- to 4-year-olds. Employer-sponsored child care and employer contributions to child care remain weak.

The US Department of Health and Human Services (DHHS) manages most of the funding for social services (including the Head Start programme), but policy and provision of child care are matters for each State. Public education is primarily a state responsibility, and may include compensatory and special education for 3- to 5-year-olds deemed to be disadvantaged, funded mainly by the United States Department of Education. According to the United States General Accounting Office (2000), 69 different federal programmes were providing or supporting education and care for children under 5 years; and nine different federal agencies and departments administered these programmes. The United States Department of Health and Human Services and the United States Department of Education also provide technical assistance and research support to assist States in implementing their programmes and to encourage the replication of best practices. In 2002, the Bush Administration launched the *Good Start, Grow Smart* early literacy initiative to improve children's school readiness. The initiative focuses on four areas: clear expectations for young children; professional development for teachers; research support and dissemination of good practice; and the stimulation of partnerships (see Box 6.2 in Chapter 6).

In recent times, States increasingly take a leadership role in developing and implementing pre-kindergarten services and early intervention services for young children at risk. Policy decisions are made with regard to eligibility, the extent of the supply and availability of services, the allocation of services and benefits, and the scope and quality of services, including health and safety standards. States use legislation, supplemental funding and regulation to implement policy decisions. However, the policies in place and the allocation of resources vary greatly across and within States, and 10 States provided no state funding for pre-kindergarten in 2004. Local government and community participation in the development of early childhood policies is encouraged in some States through the formation of local planning groups, who must raise matched funding and develop local plans. Other States assume nearly complete fiscal, regulatory and policy-making responsibilities for early childhood education and care.

Context

Labour force rates: In 2004, 69.8% of women participated in the United States labour force, of whom 18.8% worked part-time compared to 8.1% of men (part-time work figures do not take into account casual or cash economy labour). Of families with children under 6 years, 10.5% have no parent employed. 56.6% of mothers with a child under 3 are employed, and 60% of mothers with a child between 3-6 years – a rate slightly under the OECD average (OECD, *Society at a Glance*, 2005).

Parental leave: Unpaid family leave is the normal solution adopted by mothers in the United States at the time of birth. Five States (California, Hawaii, New Jersey, New York and Rhode Island) have a paid temporary disability benefit that includes pregnancy and maternity, typically for 10-12 weeks. Numerous employers offer maternity leave under temporary disability plans. The 1993 Family and Medical Leave Act (FMLA) provides for a 12-week job-protected but unpaid leave (for employees in firms with 50 or more workers) at the time of pregnancy, childbirth, or illness. Employers can require that employees use their vacation and sick leave before claiming the family leave. Despite initiatives in some

States to provide more flexible leave-taking, the situation is essentially unchanged since 1993 (Clearinghouse on International Developments, Columbia University, 2004).

Access and provision

ECEC programmes in the United States include a wide range of part-day and full-day programmes having an education and/or social welfare focus. Across the country, private family day care and centre-based ECEC constitute 90% of provision for the 0-3 age group. About two-thirds of this provision is non-profit and one-third for-profit but most is licensed. The most usual forms of provision outside the home for children up to the age of 3 years are private, giving way gradually to publicly-funded pre-kindergarten and kindergarten provision by the school districts as children mature. Pre-kindergarten and kindergarten programmes are normally made available to children from the age of 4 or 5, and increasingly from 3 years. Overall, there are three broad types of provision:

* *The purchase of services system:* The large purchase of services system is composed of private centres and family day care homes providing programmes for the general population. These services are subject to licensing and funding standards proposed by state social service agencies, but pedagogical and pre-service staff requirements can be very low or non-existent. Most States, however, now require a certain number of annual hours of further training from all staff. Families may also purchase care in unregulated or informal settings, such as the homes of family, friends, or neighbours.

* *The public school system:* The public school system is under the responsibility of each State. In general, all States offer free, half-day kindergarten for 5-year-olds, and have reached a coverage level of about 90%. Most States offer pre-school, that is, publicly funded pre-kindergarten programmes for some 4- and 3-year-old children (see access rates below).

* *Head Start:* Head Start and Early Head Start are comprehensive child development programmes that serve children from 0 to age 5, pregnant women, and their families, but primarily enrol 3- and 4-year-olds. They are child- and family focused programmes and have the overall goal of increasing the school readiness of young children in low-income families.

Rates of provision

0-2 years: By 9 months, about 50% of infants are in a regular child care arrangement, such as a centre-based care arrangement or care provided by a non-relative or relative in a private home (NCES, 2004, *http://nces.ed.gov/*). The share of relative care is 26%.

2-3 years: Provision is characterised by decreasing at-home or relative care (39%) and increasing use of family day care, centre-based settings and pre-school education programmes, *e.g.* 48% of 3-year-old children are enrolled, mostly in private, part-day, nursery school programmes. Only Kentucky, Massachusetts and New Jersey have more than 10% of their 3-year-olds enrolled in public pre-kindergarten programmes (NIEER, 2004, *Pre-School Policy Matters*, Issue 6, Rutgers University, NJ).

3-6 years: Overall, approximately 56% of United States children aged 3-6 years are enrolled in state pre-primary programmes (Clearinghouse on International Developments, Columbia University, 2004). Most school districts offer free half- or full-day kindergarten to all 5-year-olds as part of formal primary schooling, 90% of whom are now enrolled (kindergarten is the first year of formal schooling in the United States). 16.1% of 4-year-olds are enrolled in state pre-kindergarten programmes and 3% of 3-year-olds have similar access. Wide variations exist, however, across States: 22 States enrol less than 10% of pre-kindergarten children and 10 States do not fund these programmes. In contrast, a few States are moving towards universal access for 4-year-olds. In 2001-02, Georgia expanded funding to allow places for the children of all parents who wish their child to attend. Oklahoma has succeeded in enrolling 60% of its 4-year-olds. New York established a "universal" programme some years ago, but the necessary financial resources were not found. In general, free places are provided only for children said to be "at risk".

Children with diverse needs

Children with disabilities: Federal law requires that public early childhood programmes should accommodate children with disabilities in "the least restrictive environment". In most States, there is growing inclusion of children with disabilities. 10% of available places in Head Start are intended for these children (the actual percentage of children with disabilities in Head Start programmes is 12%). Special education programmes reach 5% of all 3- and 4-year-olds.

Children from low-income families: The child poverty rate in the United States is 21.9% after taxes and transfers (OECD average is 11.2%). Rapid economic growth and expanded labour markets during the 1990s brought many families out of poverty, but according to the UNICEF analysis, government support to families still on welfare has fallen to an annual USD 2 779 per child. Of families who received Child Care and Development Fund subsidies in 2003, approximately half were below the Federal Poverty Level (USD 15 260 annual for a family of three).

Ethnic and bilingual children: Of the children receiving Child Care and Development Fund subsidies in 2003, 41% were African American; 35% white; 16% Hispanic and 3% multi-racial; 1% Asian; and 1% Native American or Native Alaskan. Both federal agencies and state governments provide multiple outreach efforts to reach these and other populations, such as providing application forms and consumer education materials in multiple languages. For example, in 2004, the Child Care Bureau released a brochure on "What Providers Should Know About Care Assistance for Families" as a targeted effort to reach Hispanic families and providers.

Quality

Licensing and accreditation: Licensing standards and programme accreditation are strongly co-related with higher quality in early childhood education and care (CQCO Study Team, 1995). Licensing makes requirements with regard to space per child, health and hygiene; maximum group size, child-staff ratios; staff qualifications and other structural features of programming. Across the United States, there are large variations in state regulations and different standards in licensing requirements. According to Helburn and Bergmann (*America's Child Care Problem: The Way Out*, New York, St. Martin's Press, 2002) licensing standards are so low in nearly one-third of States as to threaten children's physical safety and health. In yet others, the enforcement of licensing and programme standards is weak. However, States increasingly use funds to provide grants and loans to providers for specific quality improvements; for training and technical assistance; and for monitoring compliance with regulatory requirements. According to the United States Child Care Bureau (2005), both the federal and state governments are investing significant resources in a variety of efforts to improve the quality of child care. The Child Care Bureau funds a network of technical assistance resources to provide information, guidance and support to States in implementing policies and practices that promote child care quality and access. States also increasingly promote programme accreditation by providing incentives and rewards, such as quality rating systems and tiered subsidy reimbursement, that encourage providers to go beyond the minimum licensing standards.

Funding: Although child care funding has tripled over the last ten years and is now at a historically high level,[1] the total public expenditure of USD 20.4 billion dollars on children 0-5 years amounts to 0.2% of GDP. According to OECD (*Education at a Glance*, 2005), public expenditure on educational institutions as a percentage of GDP for pre-primary amounts to nearly 0.4% of GDP (this figure presumably includes expenditure on kindergarten for children, 5-6 years). Approximately 34% of expenditure on pre-school from 3-6 years came from public sources and 66% from private sources, half of this being from household expenditure. Federal funding is largely targeted on children with disabilities and children from low-income families. The NIEER *State of Pre-school 2005* indicates state spending per pre-school child in 2004 to be USD 3 551 for children in pre-kindergarten (less than in 2001-02); USD 7 222 (federal contribution only) for children in a Head Start programme,[2] compared to an average of USD 9 173 (figure from 2003) spent per child in K-12 classrooms from state, federal and local sources. The same author indicates that in most States "spending per child appears to be too low to support a high-quality pre-school programme" (p. 17, 2003 edition).

Parental contributions: Where child care is concerned, families in many instances pay all costs, but on average contribute about 60%, with the federal government contributing 25%, and States and local government about 15%. Depending on the State, parents pay on average more than USD 3 000 annually per child for child care, with low-income families paying on average 18% of income, and families earning less than USD 1 200 per month paying 25% of income. Some costs can be recuperated through federal tax benefits for parents. Low-income families can benefit from fee subsidies through the Child Care and Development Fund (CCDF) block grant, but many low-income families tend to use informal, unregulated arrangements. (For further information on the cost of child care in the United States, please see: *www.nccic.org/poptopics/averagecost.html*).

Staffing and training: No national system exists to set the qualifications of early childhood workers; each State is free to establish its own standards in order to meet its particular needs and circumstances.

Head Start has created its own professional profile and relies primarily on Child Development Associates (CDA)[3] to lead the programmes. This training is equivalent (depending on the State) to half a two-year, tertiary-level, professional diploma or associate degree. It is widely recognised across the United States and provides some credits for a university degree in several States. 75% of Head Start programme leaders have taken at least a one-year child development course qualifying them for CDA status, and approximately 57% have earned an Associates Degree or higher. The proportion of CDAs to staff in the programmes is not available.

In the early education sector (pre-kindergarten and kindergarten), a two-tiered system exists, with teacher degree requirements being more stringent in the public school settings than in non-public settings (NIEER, 2004, *Pre-School Policy Matters*, Issue 6, Rutgers University, NJ). In 23 of the 44 States that fund pre-school initiatives all lead teachers are required to have a bachelor's degree, but fewer than half the States make this requirement of lead teachers in private settings, although most require a CDA qualification (NIEER, 2004). In the public school system, lead kindergarten staff are certified teachers (98%) with at least a 4-year degree, but certification (specialised training) in early childhood education is required in only 29 States. The proportion of lead teachers in the various sectors is not available. A small number of assistant teachers work in pre-schools, but only 12 States require assistants to have at least a CDA qualification.

Child care services employ a wide range of adults, many untrained. A report, *Counting the Child Care Workforce: A Catalogue of State Data Sources to Quantify and Describe Child Caregivers in the Fifty States and the District of Columbia* (Stahr-Breunig et al., 2003) found that approximately half of the States lack the current child care workforce data necessary to estimate the size and characteristics of the child care workforce. According to Kagan and Rigby (2003) (see note 1 above), 37 States require no or minimal training for child care providers in the private sector who supply the majority of services for children under 3. The educational levels and working conditions of the majority of staff in this sector are low, and annual staff turnover rates of 35% are not uncommon.

Professional development: Again, similar diversity exists in the area of professional development, with again weak regulation of the purchase-of-services sector. In public pre-kindergarten and kindergarten, 27 States require teachers to participate in at least 15 hours annually of in-service training. Alabama sets the highest annual in-service requirement in the United States: 40 clock hours per year.

Work conditions: In the United States, the status of early childhood staff outside the public school system is low, and annual staff turnover rates of over 30% are frequent. Professional status appears to be aligned to education and salaries, with staff in programmes that offer more training or require more competence generally commanding higher salaries and benefits. The Bureau of Labor Statistics indicates that only 15 of 764 occupations have lower median wages than child care workers.[4] Teachers who work in the public school system in K-12 receive better pay (in many localities twice the pay) than Head Start or purchase-of-service staff. Outside the school system, there are no uniform statutory requirements regarding working hours or employer provision of training.

Child-staff ratios: Wide variations in state regulations, different standards in licensing requirements, different funding standards, voluntary accreditation standards and voluntary goals standards make it difficult to describe child-staff ratios for the United States as a whole. In general, ratios of 4-6:1 are required for infants; ratios of between 10 to 20 children per teacher in pre-school settings, with 2- and 3-year-old children having ratios somewhere in the middle. However, according to Helburn and Bergmann (2002), standards in about one-third of the States are low and the enforcement of licensing regulations weak. Many programmes are exempted from regulation and licensing agencies are often under-staffed and cannot adequately monitor providers (National Survey of Early Childhood Health, 2000). At the same time, NCCIC research indicates that child-staff ratios became more stringent in the United States between 1986 and 2002, and that fewer States leave ECEC unregulated (LeMoine et al., 2004, *Child Care Center Licensing Regulations: Child:Staff Ratios and Maximum Group Size Requirements*, NCCIC, Washington). In addition, although state regulations concerning child-staff ratios may not always be observed, the overall picture is better that in the traditional pre-primary education sector in Europe where ratios of 20+ children to 1 teacher are not uncommon. According to NIEER (2005), child-staff ratios of 10:1 or better are achieved in pre-school settings in 37 of the 50 States in the United States.

Curriculum and pedagogy: Broad curriculum typologies exist across school districts, church providers, commercial chains or networks providing child care and pre-school services. In this tradition of independence, many eclectic curricula and practices continue to exist. In state programmes, programme content and pedagogical approach were traditionally left open for each centre to decide, unless a curriculum had been adopted by an entire school district. In 2002, the *Good Start, Grow Smart* (GSGS) early learning initiative was launched to promote literacy and school readiness (see Box 6.2, Chapter 6). GSGS encourages States to develop early learning guidelines that include expectations for what children should know and be able to do when they enter kindergarten, in the areas of early reading and early math skills, aligned with State K-12 standards. These standards now tend to govern the choice of curricula by programmes and school districts. Almost all States have drafted early learning guidelines and at least 27 States have begun implementation. Over 90% of States have gone beyond the original requirement, and have offered guidelines in most areas of child development. The GSGS initiative works with States to develop plans for offering education and training activities to child care and pre-school teachers that support early learning guidelines.

Monitoring, evaluation and research: National monitoring and reporting at population level is limited because the focus and direction of ECEC policy and provision is largely within States. The federal government has set challenging operating standards for Head Start, which are sometimes aspired to by other bodies and centres. Voluntary guidelines at national level have also been developed in the United States by the National Association for the Education of Young Children (NAEYC), the National Early Childhood Programme Accreditation (NECPA) and the National Association for Family Child Care (NAFCC), which impact positively on a wide range of service types. States also provide their own licensing and accreditation guidelines, such as the Arkansas Department of Education *Rules Governing the Arkansas Better Chance Programme*. State monitoring and oversight often include inspections of licensed centres and homes, although as mentioned, licensing agencies are often overstretched. In the private sector, it is expected that licensing standards, self-regulation, competition, information, and client supervision will be sufficient to maintain quality.

Research: As in the formal education field, the United States is pre-eminent in research on child development and early education. Evaluation studies tend to predominate, but substantial longitudinal and policy studies are also funded (please see Chapter 9 of this report). Research activity is generally linked to universities, several of which have significant ECEC research centres. The United States Child Care Bureau annually provides USD 10 million for child care research, demonstration and evaluation activities that increase the capacity for child care research at the national, state, and local levels while addressing critical questions with implications for children and families.

Parent and community involvement: In the United States, parent involvement figures prominently in early childhood programming, and state and national agency regulations in this regard are more demanding than in most other countries. The requirement to consult and involve parents in their children's learning is understood and practised in most early childhood settings. Public opinion rates parental choice as a major consideration in setting public policy, although research indicates that parental choice of child care is often limited by availability and affordability (Fuller, Livas and Bridges, 2005, "How to Expand and Improve Preschool in California: Ideals, Evidence, and Policy Options", PACE Working Paper, UC-Berkeley). Although subsidies made available through the Child Care and Development Fund help many low-income working families to access a wider range of child care options, high costs and insufficient numbers of reliable caregivers restrict the choice of many families (Bainbridge, Marcia, Meyers, Tanaka' and Waldfogel, 2005, "Who Gets an Early Education? Family Income and the Enrollment of Three- to Five-Year-Olds from 1968 to 2000", *Social Science Quarterly*, Volume 86). The Child Care Bureau also funds public information and outreach activities to help parents to make well-informed choices.

OECD policy issues

Among the issues for policy attention identified by the OECD review team for the United States were (OECD, 1999)

- *The need to create a co-ordinated and comprehensive ECEC system*: The present (at that time) patchwork of services, regulations and funding sources leads to confusion, uneven quality and inequality of access. The responsibility to provide political leadership, funding, clear policy goals and frameworks rests with government, both at federal and state level. An effective first step might be the nomination of a national commission to propose how government roles in ECEC could be strengthened. Stronger implication by Education Departments may be vital for creating a more equitable system with broad public support. Stable networks of inter-agency partnerships at the state level could also be effective.

- *The urgent need to address access issues*: The access of children 3-5 years from ethnic and low-income backgrounds is a serious concern. Only 45% of children from 3-5 years from low-income families are enrolled in pre-school, compared to 75% among high-income families. These inequalities are often linked to contextual issues, such as housing policy, which tends to support segregation of families by income and ethnic origin. A more proactive stance towards child poverty and diversity is recommended.

- *The need for quality improvement*: Quality in child care can be very weak, especially for the 0-3 age group, and regulations in many States may set standards far too low, even for health and safety issues. In addition, families of 4-year-old children often have access only to narrowly focused, instructional type programmes. Voluntary accreditation of centres as proposed by the NAEYC can dramatically improve standards and the use of well-known methods (*e.g.* the Project Approach) or guidelines (*e.g.* the revised *Developmentally Appropriate Practice in Early Childhood Programmes*) can contribute significantly to the effectiveness of programmes.

- *Creating an effective staff training and professional development system*: Serious weaknesses occur in the initial and continued training of staff at all levels. In addition, concerns were expressed about recruitment, remuneration, status, retention and career development. Projects such as T.E.A.C.H. address many of these issues. The articulation of qualifications and staff licensing within and across States is also a challenge.

Developments

Both the Education Commission of the States (2006) and NIEER (2005 *State Preschool Yearbook*, 2006) provide an insight into the rapid development of ECEC in the United States in recent years, in particular in state public education services:

Access

● 41 States provide funding today for pre-school programmes, spending an estimated USD 3.5 billion dollars compared with just under USD 200 million dollars in 1999.

● A move towards universal provision for pre-kindergarten, beyond the traditional targeted approach adopted previously. Some six States have now achieved over 60% enrolment of children of 4-5 years in public programmes.

● A move towards full-day rather than half-day kindergarten.

Improving programme quality

● In 2005, governors in 10 States identified efforts they will make to strengthen the delivery and quality of early learning programmes, including the use of quality rating systems. Connecticut, for example, will increase subsidies to stabilise the finances of struggling programmes, to improve the credentials of child care workers and to create a kindergarten readiness assessment tool. Rating systems typically address standards, accountability, professional development, finance and parent outreach. Currently, 10 States are using such systems.

● Favoured means of improving quality in the American States are:

❖ *The development of quality standards, e.g.* Florida's Voluntary Pre-Kindergarten Education Programme requires the development of performance standards for the children enrolled.

❖ *Upgrading or improving the qualifications and training of teachers, e.g.* in Delaware, Florida, Illinois, Massachussetts…

❖ *Licensing and accreditation* to ensure more uniform quality across programmes.

❖ *A focus on school readiness:* for example, the Texas Early Start initiative, focused on improving language and pre-literacy skills, must ensure that teachers concentrate on the goal of preparing children for school. Both Florida and Massachussetts have voted funds to develop kindergarten readiness assessment tools.

● A concern about quality remains, however, as though funding increased in 27 States in 2005 and numbers enrolled continue to rise, overall expenditure remains modest (about 1% of K-12 spending). In fact, expenditure per pre-kindergarten child enrolled has fallen in value since 2001 (NIEER, 2005).

Consolidating governance structure

● In addition to the States mentioned in Chapter 2 (Georgia, Maryland, Massachusetts), Connecticut, Washington State, Mississippi, and other States are moving towards consolidating ECEC governance structures through creating early learning agencies or through the use of state education plans (South Dakota, South Carolina). Currently, six approaches to renewing governance have been adopted, including the creation of (ECS, March 2006, *www.ecs.org/*):

❖ A new ECEC agency in state government.

❖ A new unit of office within the executive branch.

❖ An early childhood cabinet, *e.g.* Connectitut.

❖ A management team or office, *e.g.* North Carolina's Office of School Readiness.

❖ A public-private organisation, *e.g.* the Ohio Partnership for Continued Learning.

❖ A collaborative task force or council.

P-3 alignment

● In an effort to maintain the advances made by children in their kindergarten years, some States wish to align standards, curriculum, instructional practice and assessment within and across grade levels to P-3 levels. The advantages and risks of such an approach are discussed in Chapter 3 of the present text.

Notes

1. Combined federal and state funding for child care totals (in 2003-4) about USD 11.5 billion, the Head Start investment stands at USD 6.5 billion, and state investment in pre-kindergarten is about USD 2.4 billion (Kagan and Rigby, 2003, "Policy Matters: Setting and Measuring Benchmarks for State Policies. Improving the Readiness of Children for School. A Discussion Paper", Center for the Study of Social Policy, Washington, DC; NIEER, 2004, *Pre-School Policy Matters*, Issue 6, Rutgers University, NJ; Gilliam and Zigler, 2004, "A Critical Meta-analysis of All Evaluations of State-funded Preschool from 1977 to 2004", Rutgers University, NIEER Working Paper).

2. Although Head Start programmes use many untrained personnel and salaries are typically low, the unit cost per child is high as programmes provide not only education and care for young children, but also intensive family support and community outreach. Head Start programmes generally obtain an addditional funding of about 20%, which brings up the unit cost to USD 8 626 per year per child.

3. A CDA is a state-awarded certificate, to someone who is 18 years or older, holds a high school diploma or GED, and has completed 480 hours or more of work experience with young children within the past five years. Individuals must also have completed 120 clock hours or more of instruction in the 8 subject areas of: planning a safe, healthy learning environment; steps to advance children's physical, intellectual development; positive ways to support children's social and emotional development; strategies to establish productive relationships with families; strategies to manage an effective programme operation; maintaining a commitment to professionalism; observing and recording children's behavior; and principles of child growth and development. Requirements must also include performance-based assessment of their skills in working with young children and their families.

4. In a communication during 2005, the United States National Child Care Bureau indicated that there might be a definitional problem with how this data related to child care.

ANNEX F

Members of Review Teams

Australia

National Co-ordinator
Tony Greer

Members of the Review Team
John Bennett (OECD)
Wolfgang Dichans (Germany)
Helen May (Rapporteur) (New Zealand)
Michelle Neuman (OECD)
Mikko Ojala (Finland)

Austria

National Co-ordinator
Marisa Krenn-Wache

Members of the Review Team
John Bennett (OECD)
Martha Friendly (Canada)
Wassilios Fthenakis (Germany)
Collette Tayler (Australia)

Belgium, Flemish Community

National Co-ordinator
Sonja Van Craeymeersch

Members of the Review Team
Boudewijn Bekkers (Netherlands)
John Bennett (OECD)
Tarja Kahiluoto (Finland)
Michelle Neuman (OECD)
Helen Penn (Rapporteur) (United Kingdom)

Belgium, French Community

National Co-ordinator
Dominique Barthélémy

Members of the Review Team

John Bennett (OECD)

Sylvie Rayna (Rapporteur) (France)

Isabel Lopes da Silva (Portugal)

Michelle Neuman (OECD)

Canada

National Co-ordinators

Ross Ezzedin

Kathryn McDade

Lindy VanAmburg

Members of the Review Team

John Bennett (OECD)

Bea Buysse (Belgium)

Païvi Lindberg (Finland)

Helen Penn (Rapporteur) (United Kingdom)

The Czech Republic

National Co-ordinators

Petr Roupec

Jaroslav Sekot

Members of the Review Team

Josette Combes (France)

Lars Gunnarsson (Rapporteur) (Sweden)

Márta Korintus (Hungary)

Michelle Neuman (OECD)

Denmark

National Co-ordinators

Helle Beknes

Lisbeth Denkov

Members of the Review Team

John Bennett (OECD)

Patrizia Orsola Ghedini (Italy)

Perrine Humblet (Belgium)

Michelle Neuman (OECD)

Bridie Raban (Rapporteur) (Australia)

Finland

National Co-ordinators

Sirkku Grierson (until June 2000)

Barbro Högström (from June 2000)

Members of the Review Team

John Bennett (OECD)

Philip Gammage (Rapporteur) (Australia)

Michelle Neuman (OECD)

Ulla Nordenstam (Sweden)

Milada Rabušicová (Czech Republic)

France

National Co-ordinators

Viviane Bouysse

Nadine Prost

Members of the Review Team

John Bennett (OECD)

Fred Deven (Belgium)

Ferre Laevers (Belgium)

Michelle Neuman (Rapporteur) (United States)

Tullia Musatti (Italy)

Germany

National Co-ordinator

Wolfgang Dichans

Members of the Review Team

John Bennett (OECD)

Marisa Krenn-Wache (Austria)

Peter Moss (Rapporteur) (United Kingdom)

Jung Na (Korea)

Hungary

National Co-ordinator

Márta Korintus

Members of the Review Team

John Bennett (OECD)

Richard M. Clifford (Rapporteur) (United States)

Milada Rabušicová (Czech Republic)

Heino Schonfeld (Ireland)

Peter Jorna (Netherlands)

Ireland

National Co-ordinator

John Fanning

Members of the Review Team

John Bennett (OECD)

Colette Kelleher (United Kingdom)

Pamela Oberhuemer (Rapporteur) (Germany)

Anke Vedder (Netherlands)

Italy

National Co-ordinator

Mario Giacomo Dutto

Members of the Review Team

Abrar Hasan (OECD)

Barbara Martin Korpi (Sweden)

Michelle Neuman (OECD)

Rebecca New (Rapporteur) (United States)

Martin Woodhead (United Kingdom)

Korea

National Co-ordinator

Jung Na

Members of the Review Team

John Bennett (OECD)

Kathleen Flanagan-Rochon (Canada)

Marta Korintus (Hungary)

Collette Tayler (Rapporteur) (Australia)

Mark Weekenborg (Netherlands)

Mexico

National Co-ordinator

Dulce Maria Nieto

Members of the Review Team

Irene Balaguer (Spain)

John Bennett (OECD)

Robert Myers (Rapporteur) (Mexico)

Ofelia Reveco Vergara (Chile)

The Netherlands

National Co-ordinators

Mark Weekenborg

Anke Vedder

Members of the Review Team

John Bennett (OECD)

Tricia David (Rapporteur) (United Kingdom)

Abrar Hasan (OECD)

Pino Kosiander (Norway)

Michelle Neuman (OECD)

Teresa Vasconcelos (Portugal)

Norway

National Co-ordinators

Kristin Bruusgaard Arneberg (until September 2000)

Eli Sundby (from September 2000)

Kari Jacobsen

Members of the Review Team

Peter Moss (Rapporteur) (United Kingdom)

Michelle Neuman (OECD)

Rosemary Renwick (New Zealand)

Albert Tuijnman (Sweden)

Anke Vedder (Netherlands)

Portugal

National Co-ordinator

Teresa Vasconcelos

Members of the Review Team

Anthony Bertram (Rapporteur) (United Kingdom)

Jo Hermanns (Netherlands)

Kari Jacobsen (Norway)

Michelle Neuman (OECD)

Patrick Werquin (OECD)

Sweden

National Co-ordinator

Barbara Martin Korpi

Members of the Review Team

John Bennett (OECD)

Sharon Lynn Kagan (Rapporteur) (United States)

Susanna Mantovani (Italy)

Michelle Neuman (OECD)

Tine Rostgaard (Denmark)

The United Kingdom

National Co-ordinators

Nick Blake (from March 2000)

Patrick Curran (until March 2000)

Members of the Review Team

Kristin Bruusgaard Arneberg (Norway)

Ferre Laevers (Belgium)

Sally Lubeck (Rapporteur) (United States)

Michelle Neuman (OECD)

The United States

National Co-ordinator

Naomi Karp

Members of the Review Team

Jytte Juul Jensen (Denmark)

Michelle Neuman (OECD)

Pamela Oberhuemer (Rapporteur) (Germany)

Mark Weekenborg (Netherlands)

OECD PUBLICATIONS, 2, rue André-Pascal, 75775 PARIS CEDEX 16
PRINTED IN FRANCE
(91 2006 03 1 P) ISBN 92-64-03545-1 – No. 55213 2006